Peterson's Competitive Colleges® 1992-93

Eleventh Edition

Peterson's Guides

Princeton, New Jersey

Copyright © 1992 by Peterson's Guides, Inc.

Previous editions © 1981, 1982, 1983, 1984, 1985, 1986, 1987, 1988, 1989, 1990, 1991

Competitive Colleges is a registered trademark of Peterson's Guides, Inc.

All rights reserved. No part of this book may be reproduced, stored in a retrieval system, or transmitted, in any form or by any means—electronic, mechanical, photocopying, recording, or otherwise—except for citations of data for scholarly or reference purposes with full acknowledgment of title, edition, and publisher and written notification to Peterson's Guides prior to such use.

ISSN 0887-0152
ISBN 1-56079-142-X

Composition and design by Peterson's Guides

Printed in the United States of America

10 9 8 7 6 5 4 3 2 1

Contents

What Is a Competitive College?   v

Planning, Choosing, and Applying   1

The Campus Visit   3

Paying for College   5

Representative Profile   12

Comparative Profiles of the Competitive Colleges   14

Competitive Colleges Directories   345
    Colleges Costing $7000 or Less   346
    Colleges with the Most Financial Aid Recipients   346
    Ten Largest Colleges   347
    Ten Smallest Colleges   347
    Colleges Accepting Fewer than Half of Their Applicants   347
    Colleges Requiring All Students to Take a Computer Course   348
    Single-Sex Colleges   348
    Predominantly African-American Colleges   349
    Colleges with Religious Affiliation   349
    Public Colleges   350
    Colleges with the Most Students Completing a Degree   351

Profiles of Competitive Arts Colleges and Conservatories   352

Geographical Index of Colleges   358

What Is a Competitive College?

The eleventh edition of *Peterson's Competitive Colleges* is intended to widen the horizons of those of you who are considering applying to challenging colleges. We hope that by identifying a wide range of colleges with competitive admissions and by presenting easy-to-read data profiles of each one, we will broaden your college choice possibilities.

The main section of this book contains profiles of more than 300 colleges. The primary parameters used to identify colleges for inclusion are the percentage of freshmen scoring in *each centile* on the SAT verbal and math portions or in particular ranges on the ACT and the percentages coming from the top half, top quarter, and the top tenth of their high school class. By looking for certain percentages in each of these categories, we can realistically and carefully identify colleges at which the entering class has performed, as a group, in a superior fashion. While this information is not used to rank colleges in any way, it does indicate that high-achieving students are present in a significant proportion on these campuses. The data enable students to find colleges with the characteristics they are looking for and to easily identify those colleges that are alike in important respects—size, majors offered, location, student achievements, and postgraduation patterns. The asterisk at the top of the profile page indicates that that institution has sponsored a special distribution of this book.

As before, we have retained in this edition several colleges whose statistics have fallen outside our criteria, perhaps only temporarily. We do this because we feel that students will not be best served if we allow annual fluctuations to dictate the group included. Rather we believe that once a college has been identified for inclusion in *Competitive Colleges*, it should be kept in the group until a downward statistical trend is reported for more than two consecutive years.

Data variance allowances are made for a few distinct types of institutions. For example, for colleges that emphasize business or technology programs, unusually high math scores are judged to offset lower verbal scores. Allowances are also made for large minority enrollments, permitting a number of colleges to be seen in relation to others in a relevant subgroup.

It will be noted that a handful of colleges are included despite deficiencies in reported data. In a few cases, we simply used our judgment that a college should be included by every rational measurement, and we hope that the missing information will be given in the future. Several colleges that do not require entrance tests have nevertheless been included because we believe that, based on their history and other data, they belong in this group. Generally speaking, however, colleges that did not report a majority of the needed data, or any data at all, could not be considered for inclusion.

Because independent art and music schools require, for the most part, entirely different capabilities of their applicants, have different types of facilities, and are not easily comparable to traditional colleges or universities, we have listed the statistically most competitive of those schools in a separate section.

Planning, Choosing, and Applying

PLANNING

- Even before you think of college, think about what you want to do after college. College can help you get where you want to go, but only if you have some idea of where that is. It will help to think about your abilities (what you are good at doing), your interests (what you enjoy doing), and your values (what's important to you). It's hard to do this by yourself. Be sure to talk with your parents, your friends, your teachers, and your guidance counselor.
- Identify colleges that will allow you to keep as many of your career—or other—options open as possible. This means finding colleges that offer all of the majors in which you might be interested.
- Look closely at the entrance requirements for the colleges in which you are interested. Be sure that you are studying the right things in high school.
- Think about other college characteristics that are important to you. Then make a list. It might include such things as the size of the college, location, sports programs, and other extracurricular activities. Try your list out on your parents, friends, and counselor. Decide which items are most important to you and put them in order.
- Learn the special terms that you will encounter in the admission process. Talk with an admission person or your counselor, or read a good book on the subject. You should understand early decision, Candidates Reply Date, advanced placement, early action, rolling admission, deferred admission, and other terms routinely used in the admission process.
- Learn how you can pay for your college education. You and your parents need to become well-informed about financial planning as well as financial aid. (See Paying for College, beginning on page 5.)

CHOOSING

- Make a list of fifteen to twenty-five colleges that have all the academic and nonacademic features that you are seeking. You can make this list with the help of a college guide or a software package that helps locate colleges that meet your needs.
- Research all the colleges on your list. Gather complete information by writing for college literature, visiting the colleges, and speaking with their staff and students. Also ask for the names of alumni in your area and arrange to meet with them.
- Make a final choice of about four to six colleges. You should feel good about each of these. Talk over your reasons for these choices with your parents and your guidance counselor, and be sure the reasons are good ones.
- Take the standard admission test required by the colleges you are considering. You will probably have to take the SAT (Scholastic Aptitude Test) or the ACT (American College Testing Program) Assessment. You may want to take these tests more than once. Prep courses and study books are available to familiarize you with test procedures and contents.

APPLYING

- Apply on time—early in your senior year is best but in any case before the stated deadline.
- Fill out applications to reflect the best in yourself. Make photocopies of the forms when you receive them, and practice

filling them out before you do each one in final form. Be sure to keep copies of what you send to each college.
- After you receive admission offers, make sure that you and your parents understand the financial aid package you have been offered if you applied for aid.

- It is important that you accept or turn down your admission offers by the stated dates. This ensures that your place will be held and also allows another student to fill the place you turn down.

The Campus Visit
by Donald G. Dickason
Excerpted from *Making the Most of Your Campus Visit*

INTRODUCTION

A campus visit is an essential part of your college search process. At its simplest level, the purpose of the college visit is to gain information so that a proper and informed decision can be made about whether you and the college are a good match. The responsibility for this information exchange rests with both you and the college. You should never forget that you are basically in a buyer/seller relationship and you want to be able to evaluate the purchase of an education.

WHEN TO VISIT

Students usually begin visiting campuses in the junior year, perhaps even the sophomore year. While the visiting process can be divided into the two phases described below, your own circumstances will dictate when and where to visit. The following are meant to be helpful guidelines.

In the first phase of visiting colleges, you should take the opportunity to visit any college that you have the chance to be near. Visit a college in your own town or a nearby town. Take the opportunity to visit colleges when you and your family travel on vacation or your parents are on business trips. You will begin to "feel" the differences in types of colleges. The purpose of visiting at this time is strictly to explore. Do not feel that you have to have an individual interview, but take the opportunity to participate in group tours and general open houses that colleges offer.

The second phase of campus visits would typically occur in the spring of your junior year, in the summer between your junior and senior years, and in the fall of your senior year. These are visits with the explicit purpose of deciding whether or not a particular college is one to which you would like to apply. It is appropriate during these visits to seek not only group interviews or tours but also individual appointments. Admissions officers are busy through most of the spring with students who are at that time in their senior year, so juniors should not anticipate personalized campus visits until about May. At that time, the admissions officers' schedules begin to loosen up, and they have the time to spend with students who are in the exploration process. However, it is also important to schedule your visit for a time that will allow you to "see what goes on." Don't go during exam time or for very special events, such as Homecoming Weekend. Neither time allows you to see the campus as it is on a day-to-day basis. You should also visit, if possible, when there are a representative number of students on campus.

SCHEDULING A VISIT

The first step is very straightforward and simple: AT&T, MCI, Sprint, or your local telephone company. Always use the telephone. Mail takes too long!

Make arrangements to have a guided tour of the campus, if possible, and ask if the admissions counselor can arrange a class visit and a visit with a professor. This is the best way to investigate the academic side of college life. On the social side, find out if there is a campuswide event you can attend so that you can check out the social atmosphere. An overnight visit is an excellent way to accomplish all your goals; most colleges are happy to make arrangements for you to stay in a dorm with a current student. Schedule your interview, if you are having one, for a time *after* your tour and after you have had a chance to look at the campus on your own. This may be just the opposite of the way most colleges arrange their schedules, but this is the most efficient order of events.

WHAT TO DO WHEN YOU GET THERE

Make sure you build in an adequate amount of time for your visit. A practical *minimum* for a campus visit is a half day. (Phase one visits could certainly be shorter, as you are just beginning the process.) Of course, the first place you would go on campus would be the Admissions Office. This is probably where your tour would start. A guided tour is the best way to become acquainted with the campus. Seeing the facilities firsthand will also form the basis for additional questions. Make use of the time with your tour guide, usually a student. Ask intelligent questions that are geared to your interests. Ask the tour guide questions about your particular academic area. Is there a professor that you should see? Ask about extracurricular activities. The best question might be "What attracted you to this school?" You might also ask the guide for advice on what to see and do while you tour the campus on your own. Be sure you take notes; writing information down helps keep facts straight and also can help form other questions.

WHAT *NOT* TO DO

- Don't visit without adequate preparation. Read the catalog and any other material so that you:
- Don't ask questions that are already answered in the school's material. This is a waste of the college representative's time—and it reflects poorly on you.
- Don't let the size of the student population, whether large or small, keep you from exploring all possibilities. For example, "bigness" is not automatically bad and "smallness" is not automatically stifling. You will end up knowing just about the same number of students at either size college. How you interact with the people and the place is more important than its size.
- Don't go looking for the "ideal" college. Every one will have some flaw. Use each visit to gain perspective, experience, and insight into the kind of college in which you can be happy and successful.
- Don't pretend to be someone you are not. This admonition speaks for itself and is probably the best advice in any situation.
- Don't let your parents run the visit. Parents should stay well in the background. Part of the impression you make results from how maturely and independently you handle this experience. It is your future you are exploring; you deserve the chance to make your own way. This is *not* to say that college visits are off-limits to your parents. This *is* a good opportunity for parents to share this decision with you and to have financial aid and other questions answered.

EVALUATION

As you leave the campus, take a few moments to think about your experience and your overall impressions. Put your general reactions in writing, if possible. This should be a deliberate evaluation, but do not try to rate the college on a numerical scale. You need to review the facts you learned during your visit, but you should also allow your feelings and subjective evaluation to surface. Don't worry about the number of volumes in the library but how accessible they seem to be. Don't worry about the size of the dormitory rooms but how energetic the students living in them are. Don't think about the size of the classroom but how interested the students and faculty are in what goes on in the classroom. Evaluate all of your experiences during your visit. Don't let one unusually good or unusually bad experience make your decision for you. Look at your overall impression of the college, its students, and faculty.

Paying for College
by Don Betterton, Director of Financial Aid at Princeton University
Excerpted from *How to Pay for College*

Regardless of which college a student chooses, higher education requires a major investment of time, energy, and money. By taking advantage of a variety of available resources, most students can bring the education that is right for them within reach.

A NOTE OF ENCOURAGEMENT

While there is no denying that the cost of education at a competitive college can be high, it is important to recognize that, although the rate of increase in costs since 1980 has outpaced gains in family income, there are more options available to pay for college than ever before.

Many families find it is economically wise to spread costs out over a number of years by borrowing money for college. Although increases in federal student aid funding have fallen short of college cost increases, there remains a significant amount of government money, both federal and state, available to students. Moreover, colleges themselves have expanded their own student aid efforts considerably. In spite of rapidly increasing costs, most competitive colleges have been able to provide financial aid to all admitted students with demonstrated need.

In addition, many colleges have developed ways to assist families who are not eligible for need-based assistance. There also are a number of organizations that give merit awards based on a student's academic record, talent, or special characteristics. Thus, regardless of your family's income, if you are academically qualified and knowledgeable about the many different sources of aid, you should be able to attend the college of your choice.

ESTIMATING COSTS

The first step is to make a realistic estimate of the total costs of attending the colleges you are interested in. Most colleges publish annual tuition and room and board charges in their catalogs and often include an estimate of how much a student can expect to spend for books and incidentals. You should add to this total the cost of two round trips home each year. If you have not yet settled on specific colleges and you would like to begin *early* financial planning, an estimated budget can be used. Based on actual 1991–92 charges, we can estimate 1992–93 expenses at a typical competitive college as follows: tuition and fees (covering instructional costs, matriculation and graduation fees, medical insurance, and use of the library, infirmary, and laboratories)—about $13,800; room and board—about $5500; and an allowance for books and miscellaneous expenses—about $1500. Thus, a rough budget (excluding travel expenses) for the year is $20,800. With an estimate of college expenses in mind, each family can begin to explore ways to meet these costs.

IDENTIFYING RESOURCES

There are essentially four sources of funds you can use to pay for college: (1) money from your parents; (2) need-based scholarships or grants from a college or outside organization; (3) your own contribution from savings, loans, and jobs; and (4) assistance unrelated to demonstrated financial need. All of these are considered by the financial aid office, and the aid "package" given to a student after the parental contribution has been determined usually consists of a combination of scholarships, loans, and campus work.

The Parental Contribution

The financial aid policies of most colleges are based on the assumption that parents should contribute as much as they reasonably can to the educational expenses of their children. Thus, the parental contribution is considered a primary resource for meeting college costs. The amount of this contribution varies greatly, but almost every family can be expected to pay something.

Often families with relatively high incomes will be eligible for financial aid from a competitive college. Since it is generally true that applying for financial aid does not affect a student's chances of being admitted, any candidate for admission should apply for aid if his or her family feels they will be unable to pay the entire cost of attendance. (NOTE: Although the vast majority of competitive colleges practice need-blind admissions, you may want to ask the college you are interested in if it considers whether or not a student is an aid applicant in making its admission decisions.)

Because there is no limit on aid eligibility based solely on income, the best rule of thumb is *apply for financial aid if there is any reasonable doubt about your ability to meet college costs.*

Application for aid is normally made by completing the Financial Aid Form (FAF) of the College Scholarship Service or the Family Financial Statement (FFS) of the American College Testing Program. (Some states, like California and Pennsylvania, have their own version of the aid form.) The financial aid section of a college's admission information booklet will tell you which financial aid application is required, when it should be filed, and whether a separate aid form of the college's own design is also necessary.

Colleges use the same national system to determine the parental contribution. This process, called "need analysis," examines income, assets, the number of family members, the number attending college, unusual expenses, and other variables that affect a family's financial strength. In addition, the need analysis system makes allowances for federal and state taxes, the basic living expenses of the family, and an asset reserve for retirement needs. This procedure results in an "adjusted available income" to which a graduated taxing rate is applied to determine the expected parental contribution. The chart below, developed from actual experience at a competitive college, shows the average eligibility of families in various income ranges as determined by the financial aid office.

NEED ANALYSIS RESULTS CHART
AVERAGE AID ELIGIBILITY AT A TYPICAL HIGH-COST COLLEGE IN 1991–92

Family Income of Aid Applicants	No. Applying for Aid	% with Financial Need	Average Need of Those Eligible
To $29,999	162	98	$17,850
$30,000–$34,999	50	100	$15,300
$35,000–$39,999	37	100	$15,400
$40,000–$44,999	55	96	$13,800
$45,000–$54,999	131	93	$12,900
$55,000–$64,999	126	96	$10,700
$65,000–$74,999	97	88	$ 9,700
$75,000–$84,999	99	77	$ 6,700
$85,000–$94,999	98	60	$ 6,200
$95,000–$104,999	73	48	$ 6,000
$105,000 and over	196	26	$ 5,000

For an early estimate of how much your parents might be asked to contribute for college, consult the chart on page 10. (Keep in mind that the actual parental contribution is determined on campus by a financial aid officer, using the national system as a guideline.) A more detailed analysis is furnished as part of Peterson's Financial Aid Service, a comprehensive software program that provides a personalized method of judging parental ability to pay for college expenses and gives details on college, government, and private student aid sources. It can be found in many high school guidance offices.

Parental Borrowing

Some families who are judged to have sufficient resources to be able to finance their children's college costs find that cash-flow problems prevent them from doing so without difficulty. Other families prefer to use less current income by extending their payments over more than four years. In both instances, these types of families rely on borrowing to assist with college payments. Each year parental loans become a more important form of college financing.

There is a federal parent loan program called PLUS to help both aid and non-aid families. These 9–10 percent loans are available primarily from banks that offer Stafford Student Loans. Repayment of the $4000 yearly maximum begins sixty days after the student enrolls and continues for ten years after graduation. By placing restrictions on the Stafford Student Loan Program, Congress has shifted some of the responsibility for financing a college education from the student to the parents. The PLUS program is part of this effort. It allows parents to pay a greater share of educational costs by borrowing at a reasonable interest rate, with the backing of the federal government.

Many competitive colleges, state governments, and commercial lenders also have their own parental loan programs patterned along the lines of PLUS. Eligible families may borrow the amount of tuition, room, and board charges that remains after student aid has been subtracted. Repayment terms vary from ten to eighteen years, and interest rates range from 9 to 13 percent. For more information about parental loans, contact a college financial aid office or your state higher education department.

Need-Based Scholarship or Grant Assistance

Scholarship funds for eligible students are available from colleges themselves as well as from external sources. Although competitive colleges often have a number of separate scholarship funds with varying restrictions, it is not necessary for a student to apply directly for a particular scholarship at a college; the financial aid office will match an eligible applicant with the appropriate fund.

The primary sources of external grants are awards made by federal and state governments. The Pell Grant is by far the largest single form of federal student assistance, totaling about $4.9-billion in 1991–92. Families with incomes of up to $25,000 (possibly higher in some cases) may be eligible for grants ranging from $350 to $2400.

An excellent source for more information on the major federal aid programs is the pamphlet *The Student Guide: Five Federal Financial Aid Programs*. The Federal Student Aid Information Center toll-free hotline number is 800-333-INFO. All states also have grant and financial assistance programs. Your school guidance counselor can help you find out about these programs, or you can write a letter to your state department of higher education for the necessary details. Specific addresses can be obtained from your school or public library.

There are also a wide variety of awards sponsored by civic organizations, schools, corporations, unions, and the National Merit Scholarship Program. High school guidance offices are good sources of information about local grants, and publications that list state, regional, and national scholarships can be found in public libraries or purchased at bookstores.

Aid applicants are expected to apply directly to outside organizations for any scholarships for which they may be eligible. It is particularly important to apply for a federal Pell Grant and a state scholarship. Application for both Pell and state scholarships is normally made by checking the appropriate box on either the Financial Aid Form or the Family Financial Statement mentioned above. (Aid recipients are required to notify the college financial aid office about outside awards, as colleges take into consideration grants from all sources before assigning scholarships from their own funds.)

Student Self-Help

All undergraduates, not only those who apply for financial aid, can assume responsibility for meeting a portion of their college expenses by borrowing, working during the academic year and the summer, and contributing a portion of their savings. Colleges require aid recipients to provide a "self-help" contribution before awarding scholarship money because they believe students should cover a reasonable portion of their own educational costs.

Student Loans

Many students will be able to borrow to help pay for college. Loans are offered on the assumption that students should be willing to invest in their own future. Colleges normally administer two loans (both backed by the federal government), the Stafford Student Loan and the Perkins Loan. Students must demonstrate financial need to be eligible for either. A third loan, Supplemental Loans for Students (SLS), is available for *independent* undergraduate students.

Stafford Student Loans. These are available at an 8 percent interest rate from local lenders—banks and credit unions—as well as from some colleges. While the student is in school, the government pays the yearly interest. The annual borrowing limit is $2625 for freshmen and sophomores and $4000 for juniors and seniors. Total undergraduate borrowing may not exceed $17,250. Repayment of the loan principal and interest begins six months after student status ends. The repayment term is normally ten years, and the interest rate rises from 8 percent to 10 percent in the fifth year. The monthly amount to be repaid (based on 8 percent) is $12.70 per $1000 borrowed. Each time you apply for a loan, you also pay a 5 percent fee, which is subtracted from your loan check.

Perkins Loans. Perkins Loans are financed by the federal government and are given to colleges to distribute to eligible students. These loans carry a 5 percent interest rate. The borrowing limit for four undergraduate years is $9000, but there is a maximum of $4500 for the first two years. While the student is enrolled in college, interest is not charged. Repayment of the principal and interest commences nine months after graduation, and there is a ten-year repayment period. The monthly amount to be repaid is $10.61 per $1000 borrowed.

Supplemental Loans for Students (SLS). These loans, for *independent* undergraduate students, are made on the same basis as PLUS loans for parents. The borrowing amounts, limits, and terms of repayment are the same as PLUS. These loans, like Stafford Student Loans, come from banks in your community.

Summer Employment

All students, whether or not they are receiving financial aid, should plan to work during the summer months. Students can be expected to save from $700 to $1500 before their freshman year and $1300 to $2000 each summer while enrolled in college. It is often worthwhile for a student to begin working while in high school to increase the chances of finding summer employment during college vacations.

Term-Time Employment

Colleges have student employment offices that find jobs for students during the school year. Aid recipients on work-study receive priority in placement, but once they have been assisted, non-aid students are helped as well. Some jobs relate closely to academic interests; others should be viewed as a source of income rather than intellectual stimulation. A standard 8- to 10-hour-per-week job does not normally interfere with academic work or extracurricular activities and results in approximately $1200 to $1800 in earnings during the year.

Student Savings

Student savings should be divided by four and a set amount earmarked for college each year. This source can often be quite substantial, particularly when families have accumulated large sums in the student's name (or in a trust fund with the student as the beneficiary) to gain a tax advantage. Federal tax codes are now more restrictive in this area, and parents should be aware of the current rules before deciding how to set aside money for college.

Aid Not Requiring Need as an Eligibility Criterion

There are scholarships available to students whether or not they receive financial aid. Awards based on merit rather than need are given by certain state scholarship programs, and National Merit Scholarship winners usually receive a $2000 stipend regardless of family financial circumstances. Scholarships and prizes are also awarded by community organizations and other local groups. In addition, some parents receive tuition payments for their children as employment benefits. Most colleges offer merit scholarships to a limited group of highly qualified applicants. The selection of recipients for such awards depends on unusual talent in a specific area or on overall academic excellence. (See *Peterson's Paying Less for College* for a list of these awards.)

The Reserve Officers' Training Corps sponsors an extensive scholarship program

Paying for College

that pays for tuition and books and provides $100 per month. The Army, Air Force, and Navy/Marine Corps have ROTC units at many colleges. High school guidance offices have brochures describing ROTC application procedures. For comprehensive information about financial aid programs sponsored by the military, see Peterson's *How the Military Will Help You Pay for College* (second edition).

A Simple Method for Determining How Much Families Will Be Asked to Contribute Toward College Expenses in 1992–93

The chart that follows will enable parents to make an approximation of the yearly amount the national financial aid need analysis system would expect them to pay for college in academic year 1992–93.

To use the chart, you need to work with your income, assets, and size of your family. Read the instructions below and enter the proper amounts in the spaces provided.

1. Parents' total 1991 income before taxes
    A. Adjusted gross income (equivalent to tax return entry; use actual or estimated) _____ A

    B. Nontaxable income (Social Security benefits, child support, welfare, etc.) _____ B

    Total Income: A + B _____ ①

2. Parents' total assets
    C. Home residence equity (estimated value of home less unpaid balance on mortgage) _____ C

    D. Total of cash, savings, and checking accounts _____ D

    E. Total value of investments (stocks, bonds, real estate other than home, etc.) _____ E

    Total Assets: C + D + E _____ ②

3. Family size (include student, parents, other dependent children, and other dependents) _____ ③

Now find the figures on the chart that correspond to your entries in ①, ②, and ③ to determine your approximate expected parental contribution, interpolating as necessary. (If there will be more than one family member in college half-time or more during 1992–93, divide the result by the number in college. This figure represents an approximate expected parental contribution for each person in college.)

Paying for College

APPROXIMATE EXPECTED FOR THE ACADEMIC

ASSETS ▼	FAMILY SIZE	INCOME BEFORE TAXES							
		$ 5,000	10,000	15,000	20,000	25,000	30,000	35,000	40,000
$ 10,000	3	$ 0	0	0	300	1,100	2,000	3,000	4,200
	4	0	0	0	0	500	1,400	2,200	3,200
	5	0	0	0	0	0	700	1,600	2,400
	6	0	0	0	0	0	0	900	1,700
$ 20,000	3	$ 0	0	0	400	1,200	2,100	3,000	4,200
	4	0	0	0	0	600	1,400	2,200	3,200
	5	0	0	0	0	0	800	1,600	2,500
	6	0	0	0	0	0	100	900	1,800
$ 30,000	3	$ 0	0	0	500	1,300	2,100	3,100	4,200
	4	0	0	0	0	700	1,500	2,300	3,300
	5	0	0	0	0	100	900	1,700	2,500
	6	0	0	0	0	0	300	1,000	1,800
$ 40,000	3	$ 0	0	0	700	1,400	2,200	3,100	4,300
	4	0	0	0	100	800	1,600	2,400	3,400
	5	0	0	0	0	300	1,000	1,800	2,600
	6	0	0	0	0	0	400	1,200	1,900
$ 50,000	3	$ 0	0	200	900	1,700	2,500	3,500	4,800
	4	0	0	0	300	1,000	1,900	2,700	3,800
	5	0	0	0	0	500	1,300	2,100	3,000
	6	0	0	0	0	0	700	1,400	2,200
$ 60,000	3	$ 0	0	700	1,200	1,900	2,800	3,900	5,300
	4	0	0	0	600	1,400	2,100	3,100	4,200
	5	0	0	0	0	800	1,600	2,400	3,300
	6	0	0	0	0	200	900	1,700	2,500
$ 80,000	3	$ 0	100	1,000	1,700	2,500	3,600	4,900	6,400
	4	0	0	400	1,100	1,900	2,700	3,800	5,200
	5	0	0	100	600	1,300	2,100	3,000	4,100
	6	0	0	0	0	700	1,400	2,200	3,200
$100,000	3	$ 0	600	1,500	2,300	3,200	4,400	5,900	7,600
	4	0	0	900	1,600	2,500	3,500	4,700	6,300
	5	0	0	300	1,100	1,800	2,700	3,800	5,100
	6	0	0	0	500	1,200	2,000	2,900	4,000
$120,000	3	$ 200	1,200	2,000	2,900	4,000	5,400	7,100	8,700
	4	0	500	1,400	2,200	3,100	4,300	5,800	7,400
	5	0	0	800	1,600	2,400	3,400	4,700	6,200
	6	0	0	100	1,000	1,700	2,600	3,100	4,900
$140,000	3	$ 800	1,700	2,600	3,700	5,000	6,600	8,200	9,800
	4	100	1,000	1,900	2,800	3,900	5,300	6,900	8,600
	5	0	400	1,300	2,200	3,100	4,200	5,700	7,400
	6	0	0	600	1,500	2,300	3,300	4,500	6,000

NOTE: The expected parental contribution that you determined with the help of this chart is intended to give you a rough idea of how need analysis works. While the figure should be useful as you make financial plans for college, you should realize that your family's financial situation is likely to be more complicated than the simple model used here. For example, the table is based on the assumptions that there are two parents (of whom only one works), state and local taxes average 8 percent of income, there are standard deductions,

PARENTAL CONTRIBUTION YEAR 1992–93

ASSETS ▼ / FAMILY SIZE	INCOME BEFORE TAXES							
	$45,000	50,000	55,000	60,000	70,000	80,000	90,000	100,000
$ 10,000								
3	$ 5,700	7,100	8,500	10,000	12,900	15,800	18,800	21,600
4	4,500	6,000	7,400	8,800	11,800	14,700	17,700	20,500
5	3,600	4,900	6,300	7,800	10,700	13,600	16,600	19,500
6	2,600	3,800	5,100	6,500	9,500	12,400	15,400	18,300
$ 20,000								
3	$ 5,700	7,100	8,500	10,000	12,900	15,800	18,800	21,600
4	4,500	6,000	7,400	8,800	11,800	14,700	17,700	20,500
5	3,600	4,900	6,300	7,800	10,700	13,600	16,600	19,500
6	2,600	3,800	5,100	6,500	9,500	12,400	15,400	18,300
$ 30,000								
3	$ 5,700	7,100	8,500	10,000	12,900	15,800	18,800	21,600
4	4,500	6,000	7,400	8,800	11,800	14,700	17,700	20,500
5	3,600	4,900	6,300	7,800	10,700	13,600	16,600	19,500
6	2,700	3,800	5,100	6,500	9,500	12,400	15,400	18,300
$ 40,000								
3	$ 5,800	7,200	8,600	10,100	13,000	15,900	18,900	21,700
4	4,600	6,100	7,400	8,900	11,900	14,800	17,700	20,600
5	3,700	5,000	6,400	7,800	10,800	13,700	16,700	19,600
6	2,800	3,900	5,200	6,600	9,600	12,500	15,400	18,400
$ 50,000								
3	$ 6,400	7,800	9,200	10,600	13,600	16,500	19,400	22,300
4	5,100	6,600	8,000	9,500	12,400	15,400	18,300	21,200
5	4,100	5,500	6,900	8,400	11,400	14,300	17,200	20,200
6	3,100	4,300	5,700	7,200	10,100	13,100	16,000	19,000
$ 60,000								
3	$ 7,000	8,300	9,700	11,200	14,100	17,100	20,000	22,900
4	5,700	7,200	8,600	10,000	13,000	15,900	18,900	21,800
5	4,600	6,100	7,500	9,000	11,900	14,900	17,800	20,700
6	3,500	4,800	6,300	7,800	10,700	13,600	16,600	19,500
$ 80,000								
3	$ 8,100	9,500	10,800	12,300	15,300	18,200	21,100	24,000
4	6,800	8,300	9,700	11,200	14,100	17,100	20,000	22,900
5	5,600	9,200	8,600	10,100	13,000	16,000	18,900	21,800
6	4,400	5,900	7,400	8,900	11,800	14,800	17,700	20,600
$100,000								
3	$ 9,200	10,600	12,000	13,400	16,400	19,300	22,300	25,100
4	7,900	9,500	10,800	12,300	15,200	18,200	21,100	24,000
5	6,700	8,400	9,800	11,200	14,200	17,100	20,100	23,000
6	5,400	7,000	8,500	10,000	13,000	15,900	18,800	21,800
$120,000								
3	$10,300	11,700	13,100	14,600	17,500	20,400	23,400	26,200
4	9,100	10,600	12,000	13,400	16,400	19,300	22,200	25,100
5	7,900	9,500	10,900	12,400	15,300	18,200	21,200	24,100
6	6,500	8,100	9,700	11,100	14,100	17,000	20,000	22,900
$140,000								
3	$11,500	12,900	14,200	15,700	18,600	21,600	24,500	27,400
4	10,200	11,700	13,100	14,600	17,500	20,400	23,400	26,300
5	9,000	10,600	12,000	13,500	16,400	19,400	22,300	25,200
6	7,600	9,300	10,800	12,300	15,200	18,100	21,100	24,000

and there are no unusual expenses. Factors such as high medical expenses, two working parents, private secondary school tuition payments, and ownership of a business or farm will all affect the eventual calculation of the expected parental contribution by the financial aid office at the colleges you apply to. A more detailed analysis is available as part of Peterson's Financial Aid Service.

Representative Profile with Some Typical Student Questions

In the college profiles that follow, items of interest to students, families, guidance counselors, and educators are given in a consistent format for quick comparison and ease of review.

This representative profile illustrates the various components that comprise a typical entry.

Indicates college has sponsored a special distribution of this book

What proportion of students are undergraduates?

What is the student-faculty ratio?

How extensive are the computer facilities?

Is a computer course required?

Are the sports I am interested in available?

What will it cost to attend this college?

What is the student body like?

What is the freshman attrition rate?

How many graduates go on to further study?

Does it offer the degree program I want?

When do I have to have my application in?

Where is the Admissions Office located?

Representative Profile

✳ Oglethorpe University

Atlanta, Georgia

Founded 1835
Urban setting
Independent
Coed
Awards B, M

Enrollment	1,147 total; 1,061 undergraduates (200 freshmen)
Faculty	99 total; 41 full-time (95% have doctorate/terminal degree); student-faculty ratio is 11:1; grad assistants teach no undergraduate courses.
Libraries	88,469 bound volumes, 1 title on microform, 809 periodical subscriptions
Computing	*Terminals/PCs available for student use:* 24, located in computer center; PC not required.
Of Special Interest	*Core academic program:* yes. Computer course required for business administration, economics, accounting majors. Academic exchange with University Center in Georgia. Sponsors and participates in study-abroad programs. Cooperative Army ROTC, cooperative Naval ROTC, cooperative Air Force ROTC.
On Campus	Drama/theater group; student-run newspaper. *Social organizations:* 4 national fraternities, 2 national sororities; 33% of eligible undergraduate men and 25% of eligible undergraduate women are members.
Athletics	Member NCAA (Division III). *Intercollegiate sports:* baseball (M), basketball (M, W), cross-country running (M, W), soccer (M, W), tennis (M, W), track and field (M, W), volleyball (W).

Costs (1991–92) & Aid				
	Comprehensive fee	$13,950	Need-based scholarships (average)	$2112
	Tuition	$10,250	Non-need scholarships (average)	$3885
	Mandatory fees	N/App	Short-term loans (average)	$248
	Room and board	$3700	Long-term loans—college funds (average)	$1145
	Financial aid recipients	83%	Long-term loans—external funds (average)	$2953

Undergraduate Facts				
	Part-time	30%	*Freshman Data:* 752 applied, 84% were accepted, 32% (200) of those entered	
	State residents	62%		
	Transfers	7%	From top tenth of high school class	47%
	African-Americans	7%	SAT-takers scoring 600 or over on verbal	24%
	Native Americans	1%	SAT-takers scoring 700 or over on verbal	5%
	Hispanics	1%	SAT-takers scoring 600 or over on math	50%
	Asian-Americans	4%	SAT-takers scoring 700 or over on math	9%
	International students	4%	ACT-takers scoring 26 or over	63%
	Freshmen returning for sophomore year	73%	ACT-takers scoring 30 or over	12%
	Students completing degree within 5 years	59%	*Majors with most degrees conferred:* business, accounting, psychology.	
	Grads pursuing further study	32%		

Majors	Accounting, American studies, art/fine arts, behavioral sciences, biology/biological sciences, business, business economics, chemistry, commercial art, communication, computer management, computer science, creative writing, (pre)dentistry sequence, early childhood education, economics, education, elementary education, English, French, history, interdisciplinary studies, international studies, (pre)law sequence, liberal arts/general studies, mathematics, medical technology, (pre)medicine sequence, music, philosophy, physics, political science/government, psychology, science, secondary education, social work, sociology, studio art, (pre)veterinary medicine sequence.
Applying	*Required:* high school transcript, 3 years of high school math, 1 recommendation, SAT or ACT. *Recommended:* 3 years of high school science, some high school foreign language, interview, minimum 2.5 GPA. Interview required for some. *Application deadlines:* 8/1, 12/1 for early decision, 5/1 priority date for financial aid. *Contact:* Mr. Dennis T. Matthews, Director of Admissions, 4484 Peachtree Road, Atlanta, GA 30319, 404-364-8307.

- What is the campus setting?
- Is this school coed?
- What is the highest degree awarded?
- Are personal computers required?
- Can I study abroad?
- Is ROTC available?
- What extracurricular activities are available on campus?
- What types of aid are available?
- What are my chances of being accepted?
- What is the high school background of the freshmen?
- How do my test scores stack up?
- What are the most popular majors?
- What tests do I have to take before I apply?
- What are the high school course requirements?
- Whom do I contact for more information?

Agnes Scott College

Decatur, Georgia

Founded 1889
Urban setting
Independent/affiliated with Presbyterian Church
Women
Awards B

Enrollment 612 total—all undergraduates (153 freshmen)

Faculty 80 total; 63 full-time (97% have doctorate/terminal degree); student-faculty ratio is 8:1.

Libraries 189,781 bound volumes, 22,682 titles on microform, 818 periodical subscriptions

Computing *Terminals/PCs available for student use:* 59, located in library, dormitories Collaborative Learning Center, writing lab; PC not required but available for purchase.

Of Special Interest *Core academic program:* yes. Phi Beta Kappa chapter. Academic exchange with Mills College, American University, University Center in Georgia. Sponsors and participates in study-abroad programs. Cooperative Naval ROTC, cooperative Air Force ROTC.

On Campus Drama/theater group; student-run newspaper. No national or local sororities on campus.

Athletics Member NAIA. *Intercollegiate sports:* basketball, cross-country running, soccer, tennis, volleyball.

Costs (1991–92) & Aid				
	Comprehensive fee	$15,585	Need-based scholarships (average)	$5448
	Tuition	$10,945	Non-need scholarships (average)	$3896
	Mandatory fees	$125	Short-term loans	N/Avail
	Room and board	$4515	Long-term loans—college funds (average)	$2589
	Financial aid recipients	60%	Long-term loans—external funds (average)	$3513

Undergraduate Facts				
	Part-time	11%	*Freshman Data:* 530 applied, 80% were accepted, 36% (153) of those entered	
	State residents	63%		
	Transfers	7%	From top tenth of high school class	46%
	African-Americans	12%	SAT-takers scoring 600 or over on verbal	N/R
	Native Americans	1%	SAT-takers scoring 700 or over on verbal	N/R
	Hispanics	2%	SAT-takers scoring 600 or over on math	N/R
	Asian-Americans	3%	SAT-takers scoring 700 or over on math	N/R
	International students	4%	ACT-takers scoring 26 or over	N/R
	Freshmen returning for sophomore year	78%	ACT-takers scoring 30 or over	N/R
	Students completing degree within 5 years	47%	*Majors with most degrees conferred:* psychology, international studies, English.	
	Grads pursuing further study	N/R		

Majors Anthropology, art/fine arts, art history, astrophysics, biblical studies, biology/biological sciences, chemistry, classics, creative writing, economics, English, French, German, Greek, history, international studies, Latin, Latin American studies, literature, mathematics, music, philosophy, physics, political science/government, psychobiology, psychology, religious studies, sociology, Spanish, theater arts/drama.

Applying *Required:* essay, high school transcript, 1 recommendation, SAT or ACT. *Recommended:* 3 years of high school math and science, 2 years of high school foreign language, interview, 3 Achievements. *Application deadlines:* 3/1, 11/15 for early decision, 3/1 priority date for financial aid. *Contact:* Ms. Jennifer D. Cooper, Acting Director of Admissions, 141 East College Avenue, Decatur, GA 30030, 404-371-6285.

Albert A. List College, Jewish Theological Seminary of America
New York, New York

Founded 1886
Urban setting
Independent, Jewish
Coed

Awards B, M, D (double B with Barnard or Columbia)

Enrollment	490 total; 118 undergraduates (27 freshmen)
Faculty	105 total; 55 full-time (98% have doctorate/terminal degree); student-faculty ratio is 5:1; grad assistants teach a few undergraduate courses.
Libraries	271,000 bound volumes, 9,100 titles on microform, 720 periodical subscriptions
Computing	*Terminals/PCs available for student use:* 20, located in library; PC not required. Campus network links student PCs.
Of Special Interest	*Core academic program:* yes. Academic exchange with Barnard College, Columbia University. Sponsors and participates in study-abroad programs.
On Campus	Drama/theater group. No national or local fraternities or sororities on campus.
Athletics	None

Costs (1992–93) & Aid				
	Comprehensive fee	N/App	Need-based scholarships	Avail
	Tuition	$6040	Non-need scholarships (average)	$4000
	Mandatory fees	$190	Short-term loans	N/Avail
	Room only	$3410	Long-term loans—college funds (average)	$1000
	Financial aid recipients	50%	Long-term loans—external funds (average)	$2500

Undergraduate Facts				
	Part-time	0%	*Freshman Data:* 80 applied, 71% were accepted, 47% (27) of those entered	
	State residents	15%		
	Transfers	1%	From top tenth of high school class	25%
	African-Americans	0%	SAT-takers scoring 600 or over on verbal	50%
	Native Americans	N/R	SAT-takers scoring 700 or over on verbal	4%
	Hispanics	N/R	SAT-takers scoring 600 or over on math	50%
	Asian-Americans	N/R	SAT-takers scoring 700 or over on math	4%
	International students	3%	ACT-takers scoring 26 or over	50%
	Freshmen returning for sophomore year	99%	ACT-takers scoring 30 or over	0%
	Students completing degree within 5 years	98%		
	Grads pursuing further study	80%		

Majors Biblical studies, history, Judaic studies, literature, philosophy, religious studies.

Applying *Required:* essay, high school transcript, 3 years of high school math and science, some high school foreign language, 2 recommendations, SAT or ACT, 1 Achievement, English Composition Test. *Recommended:* interview. *Application deadlines:* 2/1, 11/15 for early decision, continuous to 3/16 for financial aid. *Contact:* Ms. Barbara Millman, Director of Admissions, Suite 100 Brush, 3080 Broadway, New York, NY 10027, 212-678-8832.

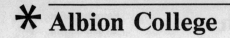
Albion College

Founded 1835
Small-town setting
Independent, Methodist
Coed
Awards B

Albion, Michigan

Enrollment	1,655 total—all undergraduates (548 freshmen)
Faculty	131 total; 110 full-time (84% have doctorate/terminal degree); student-faculty ratio is 13:1.
Libraries	380,000 bound volumes, 1,200 periodical subscriptions
Computing	*Terminals/PCs available for student use:* 75, located in library, academic buildings; PC not required. Campus network links student PCs.
Of Special Interest	*Core academic program:* yes. Computer course required for economics, management majors. Phi Beta Kappa, Sigma Xi chapters. Academic exchange with 11 members of the Great Lakes Colleges Association. Sponsors and participates in study-abroad programs.
On Campus	Drama/theater group; student-run newspaper and radio station. *Social organizations:* 6 national fraternities, 5 national sororities; 52% of eligible undergraduate men and 48% of eligible undergraduate women are members.
Athletics	Member NCAA (Division III). *Intercollegiate sports:* baseball (M), basketball (M, W), cross-country running (M, W), football (M), golf (M), soccer (M), softball (W), swimming and diving (M, W), tennis (M, W), track and field (M, W), volleyball (W).

Costs (1991–92) & Aid				
	Comprehensive fee	$15,128	Need-based scholarships (average)	$5547
	Tuition	$10,300	Non-need scholarships (average)	$4700
	Mandatory fees	$764	Short-term loans	N/Avail
	Room and board	$4064	Long-term loans	N/Avail
	Financial aid recipients	50%		

Undergraduate Facts				
	Part-time	0%	*Freshman Data:* 1,720 applied, 89% were accepted, 36% (548) of those entered	
	State residents	88%		
	Transfers	1%	From top tenth of high school class	39%
	African-Americans	2%	SAT-takers scoring 600 or over on verbal	N/R
	Native Americans	N/R	SAT-takers scoring 700 or over on verbal	N/R
	Hispanics	1%	SAT-takers scoring 600 or over on math	N/R
	Asian-Americans	3%	SAT-takers scoring 700 or over on math	N/R
	International students	2%	ACT-takers scoring 26 or over	N/R
	Freshmen returning for sophomore year	86%	ACT-takers scoring 30 or over	N/R
	Students completing degree within 5 years	66%	*Majors with most degrees conferred:* economics, English, biology/biological sciences.	
	Grads pursuing further study	35%		

Majors American studies, anthropology, art/fine arts, biology/biological sciences, business, chemistry, communication, (pre)dentistry sequence, economics, English, French, geology, German, history, (pre)law sequence, mathematics, (pre)medicine sequence, modern languages, music, philosophy, physical education, physics, political science/government, psychology, religious studies, sociology, Spanish, theater arts/drama, (pre)veterinary medicine sequence.

Applying *Required:* high school transcript, 1 recommendation, SAT or ACT. *Application deadlines:* rolling, 3/1 priority date for financial aid. *Contact:* Dr. Frank Bonta, Dean of Admissions, 616 East Michigan, Albion, MI 49224, 517-629-0321.

Albright College

Reading, Pennsylvania

Founded 1856
Suburban setting
Independent/affiliated with United Methodist Church
Coed
Awards B

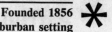

Enrollment 1,090 total—all undergraduates (263 freshmen)

Faculty 129 total; 92 full-time (85% have doctorate/terminal degree); student-faculty ratio is 10:1.

Libraries 175,000 bound volumes, 9,000 titles on microform, 1,020 periodical subscriptions

Computing *Terminals/PCs available for student use:* 225, located in computer center, library, dormitories, labs in classroom buildings; PC not required. Campus network links student PCs.

Of Special Interest *Core academic program:* yes. Computer course required for business, political science, math, physics, accounting majors. Academic exchange with Philadelphia College of Textiles and Science, Fashion Institute of Technology, American University. Sponsors and participates in study-abroad programs. Cooperative Army ROTC, cooperative Air Force ROTC.

On Campus Drama/theater group; student-run newspaper and radio station. *Social organizations:* 6 national fraternities, 4 national sororities; 25% of eligible undergraduate men and 27% of eligible undergraduate women are members.

Athletics Member NCAA (Division III). *Intercollegiate sports:* badminton (W), baseball (M), basketball (M, W), cross-country running (M, W), field hockey (W), football (M), golf (M), soccer (M), softball (W), tennis (M, W), track and field (M, W), volleyball (W), wrestling (M).

Costs (1991–92) & Aid				
	Comprehensive fee	$17,575	Need-based scholarships (average)	$5378
	Tuition	$13,400	Non-need scholarships (average)	$2250
	Mandatory fees	$160	Short-term loans	N/Avail
	Room and board	$4015	Long-term loans—college funds	N/Avail
	Financial aid recipients	75%	Long-term loans—external funds (average)	$2623

Undergraduate Facts				
	Part-time	6%	*Freshman Data:* 1,158 applied, 71% were accepted, 32% (263) of those entered	
	State residents	42%		
	Transfers	5%	From top tenth of high school class	27%
	African-Americans	4%	SAT-takers scoring 600 or over on verbal	14%
	Native Americans	1%	SAT-takers scoring 700 or over on verbal	1%
	Hispanics	2%	SAT-takers scoring 600 or over on math	38%
	Asian-Americans	4%	SAT-takers scoring 700 or over on math	6%
	International students	9%	ACT-takers scoring 26 or over	36%
	Freshmen returning for sophomore year	95%	ACT-takers scoring 30 or over	6%
	Students completing degree within 5 years	N/R	*Majors with most degrees conferred:* business, biology/biological sciences, psychology.	
	Grads pursuing further study	N/R		

Majors Accounting, American studies, art/fine arts, biochemistry, biology/biological sciences, business, business economics, chemistry, child care/child and family studies, child psychology/child development, computer information systems, computer science, (pre)dentistry sequence, dietetics, early childhood education, economics, education, elementary education, English, environmental sciences, fashion design and technology, fashion merchandising, finance/banking, French, German, history, home economics, home economics education, human ecology, interdisciplinary studies, international business, international studies, (pre)law sequence, marketing/retailing/merchandising, mathematics, medical technology, (pre)medicine sequence, nutrition, philosophy, physics, political science/government, psychobiology, psychology, public administration, religious studies, secondary education, social work, sociology, Spanish, textiles and clothing, (pre)veterinary medicine sequence.

Applying *Required:* essay, high school transcript, 2 years of high school foreign language, 2 recommendations, SAT or ACT. *Recommended:* 3 years of high school math and science, interview, 3 Achievements, English Composition Test. *Application deadlines:* 3/15, 12/15 for early decision, 4/1 priority date for financial aid. *Contact:* Ms. S. Elizabeth VanVelsor, Director of Admissions, 13th and Exets, Reading, PA 19612, 215-921-7512.

✱ Alfred University

Alfred, New York

Founded 1836
Rural setting
Independent
Coed
Awards B, M, D

Enrollment 2,258 total; 1,936 undergraduates (461 freshmen)

Faculty 208 total; 172 full-time (83% have doctorate/terminal degree); student-faculty ratio is 12:1; grad assistants teach no undergraduate courses.

Libraries 323,234 bound volumes, 92,643 titles on microform, 2,527 periodical subscriptions

Computing *Terminals/PCs available for student use:* 400, located in computer center, library, dormitories, academic departments; PC not required.

Of Special Interest *Core academic program:* yes. Computer course required for liberal arts, science, business, engineering majors. Sigma Xi chapter. Academic exchange with State University of New York College of Technology at Alfred. Sponsors and participates in study-abroad programs. Cooperative Army ROTC.

On Campus Drama/theater group; student-run newspaper and radio station. *Social organizations:* 5 national fraternities, 1 national sorority, 2 local fraternities, 3 local sororities; 30% of eligible undergraduate men and 15% of eligible undergraduate women are members.

Athletics Member NCAA (Division III). *Intercollegiate sports:* basketball (M, W), equestrian sports (M, W), football (M), golf (M, W), lacrosse (M), skiing (downhill) (M, W), soccer (M, W), softball (W), swimming and diving (M, W), tennis (M, W), track and field (M), volleyball (W).

Costs (1991–92) & Aid				
	Comprehensive fee	$18,580	Need-based scholarships (average)	$5000
	Tuition*	$13,960	Non-need scholarships (average)	$4790
	Mandatory fees	$150	Short-term loans (average)	$50
	Room and board	$4470	Long-term loans—college funds (average)	$4000
	Financial aid recipients	65%	Long-term loans—external funds (average)	$2767

Undergraduate Facts				
	Part-time	15%	*Freshman Data:* 1,890 applied, 80% were accepted, 31% (461) of those entered	
	State residents	69%		
	Transfers	24%	From top tenth of high school class	27%
	African-Americans	6%	SAT-takers scoring 600 or over on verbal	15%
	Native Americans	1%	SAT-takers scoring 700 or over on verbal	2%
	Hispanics	2%	SAT-takers scoring 600 or over on math	47%
	Asian-Americans	2%	SAT-takers scoring 700 or over on math	10%
	International students	1%	ACT-takers scoring 26 or over	56%
	Freshmen returning for sophomore year	92%	ACT-takers scoring 30 or over	8%
	Students completing degree within 5 years	73%	*Majors with most degrees conferred:* ceramic engineering, business, psychology.	
	Grads pursuing further study	27%		

Majors Accounting, applied art, art education, art/fine arts, art therapy, bilingual/bicultural education, biology/biological sciences, biomedical technologies, business, business economics, business education, ceramic art and design, ceramic engineering, ceramic sciences, chemistry, clinical psychology, commercial art, communication, computer information systems, computer science, criminal justice, dance, (pre)dentistry sequence, earth science, ecology/environmental studies, economics, education, electrical engineering, elementary education, English, environmental sciences, experimental psychology, finance/banking, forestry, French, geology, gerontology, graphic arts, health services administration, history, industrial engineering, interdisciplinary studies, international business, (pre)law sequence, liberal arts/general studies, literature, marketing/retailing/merchandising, mathematics, mechanical engineering, medical laboratory technology, (pre)medicine sequence, modern languages, painting/drawing, philosophy, photography, physics, political science/government, psychology, public administration, science, science education, sculpture, secondary education, sociology, Spanish, special education, studio art, theater arts/drama, (pre)veterinary medicine sequence.

Applying *Required:* essay, high school transcript, 1 recommendation, SAT or ACT. *Recommended:* 3 years of high school math and science, some high school foreign language, interview. 3 years of high school math and science, interview required for some. *Application deadlines:* 2/1, 12/1 for early decision, continuous processing for financial aid. *Contact:* Mr. Daniel L. Meyer, Dean of Admissions, Alumni Hill, Alfred, NY 14802, 607-871-2115 or toll-free 800-541-9229.

* For state-supported units, tuition is $5050 for state residents and $7200 for nonresidents.

Allegheny College

Meadville, Pennsylvania

Founded 1815
Small-town setting
Independent/affiliated with United Methodist Church
Coed
Awards B

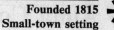

Enrollment 1,858 total—all undergraduates (619 freshmen)

Faculty 198 total; 160 full-time (88% have doctorate/terminal degree); student-faculty ratio is 11:1.

Libraries 376,696 bound volumes, 134,334 titles on microform, 1,211 periodical subscriptions

Computing *Terminals/PCs available for student use:* 324, located in computer center, student center, library, academic buildings; PC not required. Campus network links student PCs.

Of Special Interest *Core academic program:* yes. Phi Beta Kappa, Sigma Xi chapters. Academic exchange with American University, Union College (KY), Chatham College, University of Chicago, Duke University. Sponsors and participates in study-abroad programs. Cooperative Army ROTC.

On Campus Drama/theater group; student-run newspaper and radio station. *Social organizations:* 6 national fraternities, 5 national sororities, 1 eating club; 40% of eligible undergraduate men and 45% of eligible undergraduate women are members.

Athletics Member NCAA (Division III). *Intercollegiate sports:* baseball (M), basketball (M, W), cross-country running (M, W), fencing (M, W), football (M), golf (M), ice hockey (M), lacrosse (M, W), rugby (M), soccer (M, W), softball (W), swimming and diving (M, W), tennis (M, W), track and field (M, W), volleyball (M, W), wrestling (M).

Costs (1992–93) & Aid				
	Comprehensive fee	$18,270	Need-based scholarships (average)	$4736
	Tuition	$13,800	Non-need scholarships (average)	$3580
	Mandatory fees	$260	Short-term loans	N/Avail
	Room and board	$4210	Long-term loans—college funds (average)	$2902
	Financial aid recipients	83%	Long-term loans—external funds (average)	$3173

Undergraduate Facts				
	Part-time	2%	*Freshman Data:* 2,419 applied, 82% were accepted, 31% (619) of those entered	
	State residents	48%		
	Transfers	4%	From top tenth of high school class	28%
	African-Americans	4%	SAT-takers scoring 600 or over on verbal	13%
	Native Americans	1%	SAT-takers scoring 700 or over on verbal	2%
	Hispanics	1%	SAT-takers scoring 600 or over on math	33%
	Asian-Americans	2%	SAT-takers scoring 700 or over on math	4%
	International students	4%	ACT-takers scoring 26 or over	35%
	Freshmen returning for sophomore year	83%	ACT-takers scoring 30 or over	6%
	Students completing degree within 5 years	72%	*Majors with most degrees conferred:* political science/government, psychology, English.	
	Grads pursuing further study	25%		

Majors Anthropology, art/fine arts, art history, biology/biological sciences, chemistry, classics, communication, computer science, (pre)dentistry sequence, ecology/environmental studies, economics, education, elementary education, English, environmental sciences, French, geology, German, Greek, history, international studies, Latin, (pre)law sequence, mathematics, (pre)medicine sequence, modern languages, music, philosophy, physics, political science/government, psychology, religious studies, Russian, secondary education, sociology, Spanish, speech/rhetoric/public address/debate, studio art, theater arts/drama, (pre)veterinary medicine sequence.

Applying *Required:* essay, high school transcript, 2 recommendations, SAT or ACT. *Recommended:* 3 years of high school math and science, 2 years of high school foreign language, interview, 2 Achievements, English Composition Test (with essay). *Application deadlines:* 2/15, 1/15 for early decision, 2/15 priority date for financial aid. *Contact:* Ms. Gayle W. Pollock, Director of Admissions, Park Avenue, Meadville, PA 16335, 814-332-4351 or toll-free 800-521-5293.

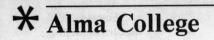

Alma College

Alma, Michigan

Founded 1886
Small-town setting
Independent, Presbyterian
Coed
Awards B

Enrollment 1,224 total—all undergraduates (297 freshmen)

Faculty 112 total; 72 full-time (78% have doctorate/terminal degree); student-faculty ratio is 15:1.

Libraries 190,000 bound volumes, 24,800 titles on microform, 1,150 periodical subscriptions

Computing *Terminals/PCs available for student use:* 350, located in computer center, library, dormitories, faculty offices; PC not required. Campus network links student PCs.

Of Special Interest *Core academic program:* yes. Computer course required for physics, chemistry, math majors. Phi Beta Kappa chapter. Academic exchange with the May Term Consortium, Midwest Consortium for Study Abroad. Sponsors and participates in study-abroad programs. Cooperative Army ROTC.

On Campus Drama/theater group; student-run newspaper and radio station. *Social organizations:* 4 national fraternities, 3 national sororities, 1 local fraternity, 1 local sorority; 40% of eligible undergraduate men and 40% of eligible undergraduate women are members.

Athletics Member NCAA (Division III). *Intercollegiate sports:* baseball (M), basketball (M, W), cross-country running (M, W), football (M), golf (M, W), soccer (M, W), softball (W), swimming and diving (M, W), tennis (M, W), track and field (M, W), volleyball (W).

Costs (1991–92) & Aid				
	Comprehensive fee	$14,513	Need-based scholarships (average)	$4516
	Tuition	$10,532	Non-need scholarships (average)	$4580
	Mandatory fees	$103	Short-term loans (average)	$1000
	Room and board	$3878	Long-term loans—college funds (average)	$1100
	Financial aid recipients	90%	Long-term loans—external funds (average)	$2860

Undergraduate Facts				
	Part-time	3%	*Freshman Data:* 920 applied, 84% were accepted, 38% (297) of those entered	
	State residents	92%		
	Transfers	3%	From top tenth of high school class	43%
	African-Americans	2%	SAT-takers scoring 600 or over on verbal	23%
	Native Americans	1%	SAT-takers scoring 700 or over on verbal	2%
	Hispanics	1%	SAT-takers scoring 600 or over on math	38%
	Asian-Americans	1%	SAT-takers scoring 700 or over on math	14%
	International students	1%	ACT-takers scoring 26 or over	42%
	Freshmen returning for sophomore year	85%	ACT-takers scoring 30 or over	8%
	Students completing degree within 5 years	70%	*Majors with most degrees conferred:* business, biology/biological sciences, history.	
	Grads pursuing further study	31%		

Majors Accounting, art education, art/fine arts, biochemistry, biology/biological sciences, business, business economics, chemistry, communication, computer information systems, computer science, dance, (pre)dentistry sequence, ecology/environmental studies, economics, education, elementary education, English, finance/banking, forestry, French, German, health science, history, humanities, international business, journalism, (pre)law sequence, liberal arts/general studies, literature, marketing/retailing/merchandising, mathematics, medical technology, (pre)medicine sequence, modern languages, music, music education, occupational therapy, painting/drawing, philosophy, physical fitness/human movement, physics, political science/government, psychology, recreation and leisure services, religious studies, retail management, science, secondary education, social science, sociology, Spanish, speech/rhetoric/public address/debate, sports medicine, stringed instruments, teaching English as a second language, theater arts/drama, (pre)veterinary medicine sequence, voice, wind and percussion instruments.

Applying *Required:* high school transcript, 2 recommendations, SAT or ACT. *Recommended:* essay, 3 years of high school math and science, 2 years of high school foreign language. Campus interview required for some. *Application deadlines:* rolling, 11/1 for early decision, 3/1 priority date for financial aid. *Contact:* Mr. John Seveland, Vice President for Enrollment and Student Affairs, 614 West Superior Street, Alma, MI 48801-1599, 517-463-7139 or toll-free 800-321-ALMA.

American University

Washington, District of Columbia

Founded 1893
Suburban setting
Independent, Methodist
Coed
Awards A, B, M, D

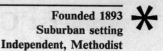

Enrollment	10,153 total; 5,120 undergraduates (1,043 freshmen)
Faculty	1,060 total; 385 full-time (92% have doctorate/terminal degree); student-faculty ratio is 15:1; grad assistants teach no undergraduate courses.
Libraries	440,881 bound volumes, 425,409 titles on microform, 2,576 periodical subscriptions
Computing	*Terminals/PCs available for student use:* 500, located in computer center, student center, labs; PC not required.
Of Special Interest	*Core academic program:* yes. Computer course required for anthropology, business, chemistry, physics, statistics, international service majors. Sigma Xi chapter. Academic exchange with Consortium of Universities of the Washington Metropolitan Area. Sponsors and participates in study-abroad programs. Cooperative Army ROTC, cooperative Naval ROTC, cooperative Air Force ROTC.
On Campus	Drama/theater group; student-run newspaper and radio station. *Social organizations:* 5 national fraternities, 6 national sororities; 20% of eligible undergraduate men and 20% of eligible undergraduate women are members.
Athletics	Member NCAA (Division I). *Intercollegiate sports:* basketball (M, W), cross-country running (M, W), field hockey (W), golf (M), soccer (M, W), swimming and diving (M, W), tennis (M, W), volleyball (W), wrestling (M). *Scholarships:* M, W.

Costs (1992–93) & Aid				
	Comprehensive fee	$20,566	Need-based scholarships (average)	$3748
	Tuition	$14,384	Non-need scholarships	Avail
	Mandatory fees	$210	Short-term loans (average)	$100
	Room and board	$5972	Long-term loans—college funds (average)	$1100
	Financial aid recipients	70%	Long-term loans—external funds (average)	$2800

Under-graduate Facts				
	Part-time	12%	*Freshman Data:* 4,302 applied, 78% were accepted, 31% (1,043) of those entered	
	State residents	6%		
	Transfers	20%	From top tenth of high school class	35%
	African-Americans	6%	SAT-takers scoring 600 or over on verbal	32%
	Native Americans	0%	SAT-takers scoring 700 or over on verbal	3%
	Hispanics	3%	SAT-takers scoring 600 or over on math	28%
	Asian-Americans	5%	SAT-takers scoring 700 or over on math	3%
	International students	10%	ACT-takers scoring 26 or over	N/R
	Freshmen returning for sophomore year	86%	ACT-takers scoring 30 or over	N/R
	Students completing degree within 5 years	64%	*Majors with most degrees conferred:* international studies, communication, political science/government.	
	Grads pursuing further study	N/R		

Majors Accounting, American studies, anthropology, applied art, applied mathematics, art/fine arts, art history, audio engineering, biology/biological sciences, broadcasting, business, chemistry, communication, computer management, computer science, early childhood education, ecology/environmental studies, economics, education, elementary education, environmental sciences, European studies, film studies, finance/banking, French, German, Germanic languages and literature, graphic arts, history, interdisciplinary studies, international business, international studies, journalism, Judaic studies, labor and industrial relations, Latin American studies, legal studies, liberal arts/general studies, literature, management information systems, marketing/retailing/merchandising, mathematics, modern languages, music, philosophy, physics, political science/government, psychology, public administration, public affairs and policy studies, public relations, radio and television studies, real estate, religious studies, Russian, Russian and Slavic studies, science, secondary education, social science, sociology, Spanish, special education, statistics, studio art, theater arts/drama, urban studies.

Applying *Required:* essay, high school transcript, 3 years of high school math, 1 recommendation, SAT or ACT. *Recommended:* 3 years of high school science, 2 years of high school foreign language, 1 Achievement, English Composition Test. *Application deadlines:* 2/1, 11/15 for early decision, 3/1 priority date for financial aid. *Contact:* Ms. Marcelle D. Heerschap, Director of Admissions, 4400 Massachusetts Avenue, NW, Washington, DC 20016, 202-885-6000.

✷ Amherst College

Amherst, Massachusetts

Founded 1821
Small-town setting
Independent
Coed
Awards B

Enrollment 1,581 total—all undergraduates (439 freshmen)

Faculty 180 total; 165 full-time (86% have doctorate/terminal degree); student-faculty ratio is 9:1.

Libraries 735,000 bound volumes, 348,000 titles on microform, 2,430 periodical subscriptions

Computing *Terminals/PCs available for student use:* 75, located in computer center, library, academic departments; PC not required.

Of Special Interest *Core academic program:* no. Phi Beta Kappa, Sigma Xi chapters. Academic exchange with Twelve College Exchange Program, Five Colleges, Inc. Participates in study-abroad programs.

On Campus Drama/theater group; student-run newspaper and radio station. No national or local fraternities or sororities on campus.

Athletics Member NCAA (Division III). *Intercollegiate sports:* basketball (M, W), crew (M, W), cross-country running (M, W), field hockey (W), football (M), golf (M, W), ice hockey (M, W), lacrosse (M, W), rugby (M, W), sailing (M, W), skiing (downhill) (M, W), soccer (M, W), softball (W), squash (M, W), swimming and diving (M, W), tennis (M, W), track and field (M, W), volleyball (M, W), water polo (M, W).

Costs (1991–92) & Aid				
	Comprehensive fee	$21,555	Need-based scholarships (average)	$11,929
	Tuition	$16,690	Non-need scholarships	N/Avail
	Mandatory fees	$265	Short-term loans (average)	$300
	Room and board	$4600	Long-term loans—college funds (average)	$2044
	Financial aid recipients	44%	Long-term loans—external funds (average)	$2460

Undergraduate Facts				
	Part-time	0%	*Freshman Data:* 4,408 applied, 25% were accepted, 41% (439) of those entered	
	State residents	12%		
	Transfers	5%	From top tenth of high school class	84%
	African-Americans	7%	SAT-takers scoring 600 or over on verbal	72%
	Native Americans	1%	SAT-takers scoring 700 or over on verbal	28%
	Hispanics	8%	SAT-takers scoring 600 or over on math	85%
	Asian-Americans	11%	SAT-takers scoring 700 or over on math	51%
	International students	3%	ACT-takers scoring 26 or over	N/R
	Freshmen returning for sophomore year	98%	ACT-takers scoring 30 or over	N/R
	Students completing degree within 5 years	97%	*Majors with most degrees conferred:* English, political science/government, economics.	
	Grads pursuing further study	28%		

Majors American studies, anthropology, art/fine arts, Asian/Oriental studies, astronomy, biology/biological sciences, black/African-American studies, chemistry, classics, computer science, dance, economics, English, European studies, French, geology, German, Greek, history, interdisciplinary studies, Latin, mathematics, music, neurosciences, philosophy, physics, political science/government, psychology, religious studies, Romance languages, Russian, sociology, Spanish, theater arts/drama, women's studies.

Applying *Required:* essay, high school transcript, 3 years of high school math, 3 recommendations, SAT or ACT, 3 Achievements. *Recommended:* 4 years of high school math, 3 years of high school science, 3 years of high school foreign language, English Composition Test. *Application deadlines:* 1/1, 11/15 for early decision, 2/1 priority date for financial aid. *Contact:* Ms. Jane E. Reynolds, Dean of Admission, Route 116, South Pleasant Street, Amherst, MA 01002, 413-542-2328.

Auburn University

Auburn, Alabama

Founded 1856
Small-town setting
State-supported
Coed
Awards B, M, D

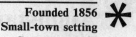

Enrollment 21,836 total; 18,985 undergraduates (3,012 freshmen)

Faculty 1,188 total; 1,128 full-time (89% have doctorate/terminal degree); student-faculty ratio is 16:1; grad assistants teach a few undergraduate courses.

Libraries 1.7 million bound volumes, 1.9 million titles on microform, 21,237 periodical subscriptions

Computing *Terminals/PCs available for student use:* 600, located in computer center, library, dormitories, computer labs; PC not required.

Of Special Interest *Core academic program:* yes. Computer course required for engineering, business, forest products, building science, industrial design majors. Sigma Xi chapter. Academic exchange program: no. Sponsors and participates in study-abroad programs. Army ROTC, Naval ROTC, Air Force ROTC.

On Campus Drama/theater group; student-run newspaper and radio station. *Social organizations:* 32 national fraternities, 18 national sororities; 20% of eligible undergraduate men and 30% of eligible undergraduate women are members.

Athletics Member NCAA (Division I). *Intercollegiate sports:* baseball (M), basketball (M, W), cross-country running (M, W), football (M), golf (M, W), gymnastics (W), swimming and diving (M, W), tennis (M, W), track and field (M, W), volleyball (W). *Scholarships:* M, W.

Costs (1991–92) & Aid				
State resident tuition	$1596	537 Need-based scholarships (average)	$1000
Nonresident tuition	$4788	733 Non-need scholarships (average)	$1039
Mandatory fees	N/App	Short-term loans (average)	$100
Room only	$1350	Long-term loans—college funds (average)	$1500
Financial aid recipients	35%	Long-term loans—external funds (average)	$2736

Undergraduate Facts			
Part-time	10%	*Freshman Data:* 8,428 applied, 89% were accepted, 40% (3,012) of those entered	
State residents	61%		
Transfers	35%	From top tenth of high school class	19%
African-Americans	5%	SAT-takers scoring 600 or over on verbal	12%
Native Americans	1%	SAT-takers scoring 700 or over on verbal	1%
Hispanics	1%	SAT-takers scoring 600 or over on math	40%
Asian-Americans	1%	SAT-takers scoring 700 or over on math	6%
International students	1%	ACT-takers scoring 26 or over	32%
Freshmen returning for sophomore year	85%	ACT-takers scoring 30 or over	7%
Students completing degree within 5 years	55%	*Majors with most degrees conferred:* business, engineering (general), education.	
Grads pursuing further study	25%		

Majors Accounting, adult and continuing education, aerospace engineering, agricultural business, agricultural economics, agricultural education, agricultural engineering, agricultural sciences, agronomy/soil and crop sciences, animal sciences, anthropology, applied art, applied mathematics, architecture, art/fine arts, aviation administration, biochemistry, biology/biological sciences, botany/plant sciences, broadcasting, business, business economics, business education, chemical engineering, chemistry, child care/child and family studies, child psychology/child development, civil engineering, commercial art, communication, computer engineering, computer science, construction management, corrections, criminal justice, dairy sciences, (pre)dentistry sequence, dietetics, early childhood education, earth science, East European and Soviet studies, economics, education, electrical engineering, elementary education, engineering (general), English, entomology, environmental design, environmental sciences, family and consumer studies, fashion merchandising, finance/banking, fish and game management, food sciences, forest engineering, forestry, forest technology, French, geography, geological engineering, geology, German, graphic arts, health education, health services administration, history, home economics, home economics education, horticulture, hotel and restaurant management, human resources, illustration, industrial arts, industrial design, industrial engineering, interior design, international business, journalism, laboratory technologies, landscape architecture/design, Latin American studies, law enforcement/police sciences, (pre)law sequence, management information systems, marine biology, marketing/retailing/merchandising, materials engineering, mathematics, mechanical engineering, medical laboratory technology, medical technology, (pre)medicine sequence, microbiology, middle school education, molecular biology, music, music education, nursing, nutrition, ornamental horticulture, painting/drawing, pest control technology, pharmacy/pharmaceutical sciences, philosophy, physical education, physical fitness/human movement, physics, piano/organ, political science/government, poultry sciences, psychology, public administration, public relations, radio and television studies, recreation and leisure services, rehabilitation therapy, religious studies, science education, sculpture, secondary education, social work, sociology, Spanish, special education, speech pathology and audiology, speech/rhetoric/public address/debate, speech therapy, studio art, textile arts, textile engineering, textiles and clothing, theater arts/drama, transportation technologies, (pre)veterinary medicine sequence, vocational education, voice, wildlife management, wood sciences, zoology.

Applying *Required:* high school transcript, 3 years of high school math, SAT or ACT. *Recommended:* 3 years of high school science, 1 year of high school foreign language. *Application deadlines:* 9/1, 1/15 for nonresidents, 4/15 priority date for financial aid. *Contact:* Dr. Charles F. Reeder, Director of Admissions, 202 Mary Martin Hall, Auburn University, AL 36849, 205-844-4080 or toll-free 800-392-8051 (in-state).

Augustana College

Rock Island, Illinois

Founded 1860
Urban setting
Independent/affiliated with Evangelical Lutheran Church in America
Coed
Awards B

Enrollment	2,182 total—all undergraduates (527 freshmen)
Faculty	185 total; 142 full-time (80% have doctorate/terminal degree); student-faculty ratio is 13:1.
Libraries	225,834 bound volumes, 7,080 titles on microform, 1,535 periodical subscriptions
Computing	*Terminals/PCs available for student use:* 150, located in computer center, student center, library, dormitories, all classroom buildings; PC not required. Campus network links student PCs.
Of Special Interest	*Core academic program:* yes. Computer course required for accounting, business, physics, sociology, social work, geography majors. Phi Beta Kappa chapter. Academic exchange program: no. Sponsors study-abroad programs.
On Campus	Drama/theater group; student-run newspaper and radio station. *Social organizations:* 7 local fraternities, 7 local sororities; 30% of eligible undergraduate men and 30% of eligible undergraduate women are members.
Athletics	Member NCAA (Division III). *Intercollegiate sports:* baseball (M), basketball (M, W), cross-country running (M, W), football (M), golf (M), soccer (M), softball (W), swimming and diving (M, W), tennis (M, W), track and field (M, W), volleyball (W), wrestling (M).

Costs (1992–93) & Aid	Comprehensive fee	$15,858	Need-based scholarships (average)	$2365
	Tuition	$11,952	Non-need scholarships (average)	$2289
	Mandatory fees	$57	Short-term loans	N/Avail
	Room and board	$3849	Long-term loans—college funds	N/Avail
	Financial aid recipients	80%	Long-term loans—external funds (average)	$2945
Undergraduate Facts	Part-time	1%	*Freshman Data:* 1,832 applied, 90% were accepted, 32% (527) of those entered	
	State residents	80%		
	Transfers	4%	From top tenth of high school class	34%
	African-Americans	3%	SAT-takers scoring 600 or over on verbal	8%
	Native Americans	0%	SAT-takers scoring 700 or over on verbal	1%
	Hispanics	2%	SAT-takers scoring 600 or over on math	41%
	Asian-Americans	2%	SAT-takers scoring 700 or over on math	5%
	International students	2%	ACT-takers scoring 26 or over	34%
	Freshmen returning for sophomore year	86%	ACT-takers scoring 30 or over	8%
	Students completing degree within 5 years	70%	*Majors with most degrees conferred:* business, biology/biological sciences, English.	
	Grads pursuing further study	33%		

Majors Accounting, anthropology, art education, art/fine arts, art history, Asian/Oriental studies, athletic training, biology/biological sciences, business, chemistry, classics, communication, computer science, creative writing, cytotechnology, (pre)dentistry sequence, earth science, East Asian studies, ecology/environmental studies, economics, education, elementary education, engineering physics, English, environmental sciences, finance/banking, French, geography, geology, German, Greek, health education, history, international business, jazz, journalism, Latin, Latin American studies, (pre)law sequence, liberal arts/general studies, literature, marketing/retailing/merchandising, mathematics, medical technology, (pre)medicine sequence, music, music education, occupational therapy, philosophy, physical education, physical therapy, physics, piano/organ, political science/government, psychology, public administration, religious studies, sacred music, Scandinavian languages/studies, secondary education, social work, sociology, Spanish, speech pathology and audiology, speech/rhetoric/public address/debate, speech therapy, stringed instruments, studio art, theater arts/drama, urban studies, (pre)veterinary medicine sequence, voice, wind and percussion instruments, women's studies.

Applying *Required:* high school transcript, SAT or ACT. *Recommended:* 3 years of high school math and science, 1 year of high school foreign language. Essay, 2 recommendations, interview required for some. *Application deadlines:* rolling, 4/1 priority date for financial aid. *Contact:* Mr. Harold R. Velline, Director of Admissions, 820 38th Street, Rock Island, IL 61201, 309-794-7341 or toll-free 800-798-8100.

Augustana College

Sioux Falls, South Dakota

Founded 1860
Urban setting
Independent/affiliated with Evangelical Lutheran Church in America
Coed
Awards A, B, M

Enrollment 1,925 total; 1,881 undergraduates (380 freshmen)

Faculty 142 total; 106 full-time (65% have doctorate/terminal degree); student-faculty ratio is 15:1; grad assistants teach no undergraduate courses.

Libraries 243,705 bound volumes, 152,411 titles on microform, 1,069 periodical subscriptions

Computing *Terminals/PCs available for student use:* 140, located in computer center, student center, library, dormitories, academic departments; PC not required.

Of Special Interest *Core academic program:* yes. Computer course required. Academic exchange with 10 other colleges in the upper Midwest. Sponsors and participates in study-abroad programs.

On Campus Drama/theater group; student-run newspaper and radio station. *Social organizations:* 7 local fraternities, 7 local sororities; 20% of eligible undergraduate men and 20% of eligible undergraduate women are members.

Athletics Member NCAA (Division II). *Intercollegiate sports:* baseball (M), basketball (M, W), cross-country running (M, W), football (M), golf (M), racquetball (M, W), softball (W), tennis (M, W), track and field (M, W), volleyball (W), wrestling (M). *Scholarships:* M, W.

Costs (1991–92) & Aid				
	Comprehensive fee	$12,800	Need-based scholarships	Avail
	Tuition	$9800	Non-need scholarships	Avail
	Mandatory fees	N/App	Short-term loans	N/Avail
	Room and board	$3000	Long-term loans—college funds	N/Avail
	Financial aid recipients	85%	Long-term loans—external funds (average)	$2720

Undergraduate Facts				
	Part-time	21%	*Freshman Data:* 765 applied, 99% were accepted, 50% (380) of those entered	
	State residents	50%		
	Transfers	6%	From top tenth of high school class	21%
	African-Americans	1%	SAT-takers scoring 600 or over on verbal	14%
	Native Americans	1%	SAT-takers scoring 700 or over on verbal	1%
	Hispanics	N/R	SAT-takers scoring 600 or over on math	30%
	Asian-Americans	N/R	SAT-takers scoring 700 or over on math	5%
	International students	3%	ACT-takers scoring 26 or over	23%
	Freshmen returning for sophomore year	68%	ACT-takers scoring 30 or over	4%
	Students completing degree within 5 years	53%	*Majors with most degrees conferred:* business, education, biology/biological sciences.	
	Grads pursuing further study	22%		

Majors Accounting, art education, aviation administration, biochemistry, biology/biological sciences, biophysics, business, chemistry, classics, communication, comparative literature, computer science, early childhood education, earth science, ecology/environmental studies, economics, education, elementary education, English, French, geography, German, Greek, health services administration, history, international studies, journalism, (pre)law sequence, liberal arts/general studies, management information systems, mathematics, medical technology, (pre)medicine sequence, music, music education, nursing, philosophy, physical education, physics, political science/government, psychology, religious studies, Romance languages, secondary education, social work, sociology, special education, speech pathology and audiology, theater arts/drama.

Applying *Required:* high school transcript, 2 recommendations, ACT. *Recommended:* essay, 3 years of high school math and science, some high school foreign language, interview. SAT required for some. *Application deadlines:* rolling, 4/15 priority date for financial aid. *Contact:* Mr. Brad Heegel, Director of Admissions, 29th and Summit, Sioux Falls, SD 57197, 605-336-5516 or toll-free 800-727-2844.

From the College A new-student seminar, Augustana Conversations, is preparation for beginning the liberal arts college experience in a Christian context. This seminar initiates students into conversations, discourse, and dialogue about ideas—a process that continues throughout the students' college career, culminating in a Capstone Course in the senior year.

Austin College

Sherman, Texas

Founded 1849
Suburban setting
Independent, Presbyterian
Coed
Awards B, M

Enrollment 1,178 total; 1,155 undergraduates (307 freshmen)

Faculty 95 total; 85 full-time (86% have doctorate/terminal degree); student-faculty ratio is 14:1; grad assistants teach no undergraduate courses.

Libraries 212,982 bound volumes, 116,601 titles on microform, 933 periodical subscriptions

Computing *Terminals/PCs available for student use:* 70, located in computer center, library, psychology department, social science lab; PC not required but available for purchase.

Of Special Interest *Core academic program:* yes. Academic exchange with American University, The Washington Center. Sponsors and participates in study-abroad programs.

On Campus Drama/theater group; student-run newspaper. *Social organizations:* 9 local fraternities, 9 local sororities; 28% of eligible undergraduate men and 30% of eligible undergraduate women are members.

Athletics Member NAIA. *Intercollegiate sports:* baseball (M), basketball (M, W), football (M), golf (M), soccer (M), swimming and diving (M, W), tennis (M, W), track and field (M, W), volleyball (W).

Costs (1991–92) & Aid				
	Comprehensive fee	$13,210	Need-based scholarships (average)	$1804
	Tuition	$9365	Non-need scholarships (average)	$2054
	Mandatory fees	$100	Short-term loans (average)	$300
	Room and board	$3745	Long-term loans—college funds (average)	$1751
	Financial aid recipients	82%	Long-term loans—external funds (average)	$2836

Undergraduate Facts				
	Part-time	2%	*Freshman Data:* 883 applied, 83% were accepted, 42% (307) of those entered	
	State residents	90%		
	Transfers	15%	From top tenth of high school class	45%
	African-Americans	4%	SAT-takers scoring 600 or over on verbal	11%
	Native Americans	1%	SAT-takers scoring 700 or over on verbal	1%
	Hispanics	5%	SAT-takers scoring 600 or over on math	30%
	Asian-Americans	4%	SAT-takers scoring 700 or over on math	5%
	International students	1%	ACT-takers scoring 26 or over	41%
	Freshmen returning for sophomore year	81%	ACT-takers scoring 30 or over	8%
	Students completing degree within 5 years	62%	*Majors with most degrees conferred:* psychology, business, biology/biological sciences.	
	Grads pursuing further study	34%		

Majors American studies, art/fine arts, biology/biological sciences, business, chemistry, classics, communication, (pre)dentistry sequence, economics, English, French, German, history, interdisciplinary studies, international studies, Latin American studies, (pre)law sequence, mathematics, (pre)medicine sequence, music, philosophy, physical education, physics, political science/government, psychology, religious studies, sociology, Spanish, speech/rhetoric/public address/debate.

Applying *Required:* essay, high school transcript, 2 recommendations, SAT or ACT. *Recommended:* 3 years of high school math and science, 2 years of high school foreign language, interview. Interview required for some. *Application deadlines:* 3/15, 12/1 for early action, continuous to 7/1 for financial aid. *Contact:* Mr. Rodney Oto, Dean of Admission and Financial Aid, 900 North Grand Avenue, Sherman, TX 75091, 903-813-2387 or toll-free 800-442-5363.

Babson College

Wellesley, Massachusetts

Founded 1919
Suburban setting
Independent
Coed
Awards B, M

Enrollment 3,031 total; 1,596 undergraduates (368 freshmen)

Faculty 160 total; 117 full-time (92% have doctorate/terminal degree); student-faculty ratio is 16:1; grad assistants teach no undergraduate courses.

Libraries 120,000 bound volumes, 348,224 titles on microform, 1,482 periodical subscriptions

Computing *Terminals/PCs available for student use:* 120, located in computer center; PC not required.

Of Special Interest *Core academic program:* yes. Computer course required. Academic exchange with Pine Manor College, Regis College (MA), Brandeis University, Wellesley College. Sponsors and participates in study-abroad programs. Cooperative Army ROTC, cooperative Naval ROTC, cooperative Air Force ROTC.

On Campus Drama/theater group; student-run newspaper. *Social organizations:* 4 national fraternities, 2 national sororities; 12% of eligible undergraduate men and 8% of eligible undergraduate women are members.

Athletics Member NCAA (Division III). *Intercollegiate sports:* baseball (M), basketball (M, W), cross-country running (M, W), field hockey (W), golf (M, W), ice hockey (M), lacrosse (M, W), rugby (M), sailing (M, W), skiing (downhill) (M, W), soccer (M, W), softball (W), swimming and diving (M, W), tennis (M, W), volleyball (M, W).

Costs (1991–92) & Aid		
Comprehensive fee	$20,988	
Tuition	$14,272	
Mandatory fees	$566	
Room and board	$6150	
Financial aid recipients	42%	
Need-based scholarships (average)		$7844
Non-need scholarships		N/Avail
Short-term loans (average)		$200
Long-term loans—college funds		Avail
Long-term loans—external funds (average)		$2836

Undergraduate Facts

Part-time	0%			
State residents	45%			
Transfers	14%			
African-Americans	2%			
Native Americans	0%			
Hispanics	2%			
Asian-Americans	4%			
International students	14%			
Freshmen returning for sophomore year	94%			
Students completing degree within 5 years	87%			
Grads pursuing further study	5%			

Freshman Data: 1,507 applied, 69% were accepted, 35% (368) of those entered
From top tenth of high school class — 27%
SAT-takers scoring 600 or over on verbal — 7%
SAT-takers scoring 700 or over on verbal — 0%
SAT-takers scoring 600 or over on math — 39%
SAT-takers scoring 700 or over on math — 6%
ACT-takers scoring 26 or over — N/R
ACT-takers scoring 30 or over — N/R
Majors with most degrees conferred: finance/banking, marketing/retailing/merchandising, accounting.

Majors Accounting, American studies, business, communication, economics, finance/banking, international business, management information systems, marketing/retailing/merchandising.

Applying *Required:* essay, high school transcript, 3 years of high school math, 1 recommendation, SAT or ACT, 2 Achievements. *Recommended:* 4 years of high school math, 3 years of high school science, some high school foreign language, campus interview, English Composition Test (with essay). *Application deadlines:* 2/1, 12/1 for early decision, 2/1 for financial aid. *Contact:* Dr. Charles Nolan, Dean of Undergraduate Admission, Mustard Hall, Babson Park, MA 02157, 617-239-5522 or toll-free 800-488-3696.

✻ Bard College

Annandale-on-Hudson, New York

Founded 1860
Rural setting
Independent
Coed
Awards B, M

Enrollment 1,160 total; 1,025 undergraduates (318 freshmen)

Faculty 135 total; 92 full-time (90% have doctorate/terminal degree); student-faculty ratio is 10:1; grad assistants teach no undergraduate courses.

Libraries 195,000 bound volumes, 5,250 titles on microform, 650 periodical subscriptions

Computing *Terminals/PCs available for student use:* 75, located in computer center, library, academic departments; PC not required. Campus network links student PCs.

Of Special Interest *Core academic program:* yes. Academic exchange with Vassar College, State University of New York College at New Paltz. Sponsors and participates in study-abroad programs.

On Campus Drama/theater group; student-run newspaper and radio station. No national or local fraternities or sororities on campus.

Athletics Member NCAA (Division III), NAIA. *Intercollegiate sports:* basketball (M), cross-country running (M, W), fencing (M, W), soccer (M, W), squash (M), tennis (M, W), volleyball (M, W).

Costs (1991–92) & Aid				
	Comprehensive fee	$22,675	Need-based scholarships (average)	$8139
	Tuition	$16,650	Non-need scholarships (average)	$16,887
	Mandatory fees	$460	Short-term loans	N/Avail
	Room and board	$5565	Long-term loans—college funds (average)	$1000
	Financial aid recipients	65%	Long-term loans—external funds (average)	$3000

Undergraduate Facts				
	Part-time	3%	*Freshman Data:* 1,500 applied, 53% were accepted, 40% (318) of those entered	
	State residents	25%		
	Transfers	12%	From top tenth of high school class	N/R
	African-Americans	8%	SAT-takers scoring 600 or over on verbal	N/R
	Native Americans	1%	SAT-takers scoring 700 or over on verbal	N/R
	Hispanics	4%	SAT-takers scoring 600 or over on math	N/R
	Asian-Americans	4%	SAT-takers scoring 700 or over on math	N/R
	International students	12%	ACT-takers scoring 26 or over	N/R
	Freshmen returning for sophomore year	89%	ACT-takers scoring 30 or over	N/R
	Students completing degree within 5 years	77%	*Majors with most degrees conferred:* social science, art/fine arts, literature.	
	Grads pursuing further study	50%		

Majors American studies, anthropology, art/fine arts, art history, Asian/Oriental studies, biology/biological sciences, chemistry, Chinese, city/community/regional planning, classics, comparative literature, creative writing, dance, (pre)dentistry sequence, East European and Soviet studies, ecology/environmental studies, economics, English, environmental sciences, ethnic studies, European studies, film and video, film studies, French, German, Germanic languages and literature, Greek, history, history of science, humanities, interdisciplinary studies, international economics, international studies, jazz, Latin, (pre)law sequence, literature, mathematics, (pre)medicine sequence, medieval studies, modern languages, music, music history, natural sciences, painting/drawing, philosophy, photography, physical sciences, physics, political science/government, psychology, religious studies, Romance languages, Russian, Russian and Slavic studies, science, sculpture, social science, sociology, Spanish, studio art, theater arts/drama, (pre)veterinary medicine sequence, women's studies.

Applying *Required:* essay, high school transcript, 3 recommendations. *Recommended:* 4 years of high school math and science, 3 years of high school foreign language, interview, SAT or ACT, Achievements, English Composition Test. Interview required for some. *Application deadlines:* 2/15, 12/1 for early decision, 2/15 priority date for financial aid. *Contact:* Ms. Mary Inga Backland, Director of Admissions, Annandale Road, Annandale-on-Hudson, NY 12504, 914-758-7472.

Barnard College
Part of Columbia University
New York, New York

Founded 1889
Urban setting
Independent
Women
Awards B

Enrollment	2,130 undergraduates (487 freshmen)
Faculty	264 total; 160 full-time (98% have doctorate/terminal degree); student-faculty ratio is 12:1; grad assistants teach no undergraduate courses.
Libraries	162,991 bound volumes, 13,751 titles on microform, 722 periodical subscriptions
Computing	*Terminals/PCs available for student use:* 108, located in computer center, student center, library, dormitories; PC not required.
Of Special Interest	*Core academic program:* yes. Computer course required for some majors. Phi Beta Kappa, Sigma Xi chapters. Academic exchange with Manhattan School of Music, Albert A. List College of the Jewish Theological Seminary of America, Juilliard School. Sponsors and participates in study-abroad programs.
On Campus	Drama/theater group; student-run newspaper and radio station. *Social organizations:* 1 local sorority; 1% of eligible undergraduates are members.
Athletics	Member NCAA (Division I). *Intercollegiate sports:* archery, basketball, crew, cross-country running, fencing, soccer, softball, swimming and diving, tennis, track and field, volleyball.

Costs (1991–92) & Aid				
	Comprehensive fee	$22,774	Need-based scholarships (average)	$10,400
	Tuition	$15,280	Non-need scholarships	N/Avail
	Mandatory fees	$594	Short-term loans (average)	$120
	Room and board	$6900	Long-term loans—college funds (average)	$2000
	Financial aid recipients	53%	Long-term loans—external funds (average)	$2600

Undergraduate Facts				
	Part-time	0%	*Freshman Data:* 1,753 applied, 57% were accepted, 49% (487) of those entered	
	State residents	42%		
	Transfers	14%	From top tenth of high school class	56%
	African-Americans	4%	SAT-takers scoring 600 or over on verbal	51%
	Native Americans	0%	SAT-takers scoring 700 or over on verbal	7%
	Hispanics	5%	SAT-takers scoring 600 or over on math	63%
	Asian-Americans	23%	SAT-takers scoring 700 or over on math	9%
	International students	4%	ACT-takers scoring 26 or over	N/R
	Freshmen returning for sophomore year	95%	ACT-takers scoring 30 or over	N/R
	Students completing degree within 5 years	82%	*Majors with most degrees conferred:* English, political science/government, psychology.	
	Grads pursuing further study	21%		

Majors American studies, anthropology, architecture, art history, Asian/Oriental studies, astronomy, biochemistry, biology/biological sciences, chemistry, classics, computer science, dance, East Asian studies, ecology/environmental studies, economics, education, English, European studies, French, German, history, interdisciplinary studies, Italian, Latin American studies, mathematics, medieval studies, music, philosophy, physics, political science/government, psychobiology, psychology, religious studies, Russian, Russian and Slavic studies, sociology, Spanish, statistics, theater arts/drama, urban studies, Western civilization and culture, women's studies.

Applying *Required:* essay, high school transcript, 3 years of high school math, 3 recommendations, SAT or ACT, 3 Achievements, English Composition Test. *Recommended:* 3 years of high school science, 3 years of high school foreign language, interview. *Application deadlines:* 2/1, 11/15 for early decision, 2/1 for financial aid. *Contact:* Ms. Doris Davis, Director of Admissions, 11 Millbank Hall, New York, NY 10027-6598, 212-854-2014.

From the College Barnard, a select, women's liberal arts college, has its own campus across the street from Columbia University. Its top-flight faculty is committed to undergraduate education, and affiliation with Columbia provides access to a coed life-style and additional academic riches. New York City provides extraordinary internship opportunities as well as unparalleled cultural and social offerings.

Bates College

Lewiston, Maine

Founded 1855
Suburban setting
Independent
Coed
Awards B

Enrollment	1,500 total—all undergraduates (373 freshmen)
Faculty	165 total; 130 full-time (91% have doctorate/terminal degree); student-faculty ratio is 11:1.
Libraries	531,043 bound volumes, 232,917 titles on microform, 1,722 periodical subscriptions
Computing	*Terminals/PCs available for student use:* 225, located in computer center, classroom buildings; PC not required.
Of Special Interest	*Core academic program:* yes. Computer course required for math, economics, psychology, sociology, chemistry, physics majors. Phi Beta Kappa, Sigma Xi chapters. Academic exchange with American University, Williams College (Mystic Seaport Program), McGill University, Washington and Lee University. Sponsors and participates in study-abroad programs.
On Campus	Drama/theater group; student-run newspaper and radio station. No national or local fraternities or sororities on campus.
Athletics	Member NCAA (Division III). *Intercollegiate sports:* baseball (M), basketball (M, W), crew (M, W), cross-country running (M, W), equestrian sports (M, W), fencing (M, W), field hockey (W), football (M), golf (M, W), ice hockey (M, W), lacrosse (M, W), rugby (M, W), sailing (M, W), skiing (cross-country) (M, W), skiing (downhill) (M, W), soccer (M, W), softball (W), squash (M, W), swimming and diving (M, W), tennis (M, W), track and field (M, W), volleyball (M, W), water polo (M, W).

Costs (1991–92) & Aid				
	Comprehensive fee	$21,400	Need-based scholarships (average)	$11,200
	Tuition	N/App	Non-need scholarships	N/Avail
	Mandatory fees	N/App	Short-term loans	N/Avail
	Room and board	N/App	Long-term loans—college funds (average)	$1500
	Financial aid recipients	40%	Long-term loans—external funds (average)	$1900

Undergraduate Facts				
	Part-time	1%	*Freshman Data:* 3,491 applied, 32% were accepted, 33% (373) of those entered	
	State residents	13%		
	Transfers	8%	From top tenth of high school class	51%
	African-Americans	2%	SAT-takers scoring 600 or over on verbal	50%
	Native Americans	0%	SAT-takers scoring 700 or over on verbal	7%
	Hispanics	1%	SAT-takers scoring 600 or over on math	82%
	Asian-Americans	4%	SAT-takers scoring 700 or over on math	23%
	International students	3%	ACT-takers scoring 26 or over	N/R
	Freshmen returning for sophomore year	98%	ACT-takers scoring 30 or over	N/R
	Students completing degree within 5 years	90%		
	Grads pursuing further study	N/R		

Majors Anthropology, art/fine arts, biology/biological sciences, chemistry, classics, economics, English, French, geology, German, history, interdisciplinary studies, mathematics, medieval studies, music, philosophy, physics, political science/government, psychology, religious studies, Russian, sociology, Spanish, speech/rhetoric/public address/debate, theater arts/drama, women's studies.

Applying *Required:* essay, high school transcript, 3 recommendations. *Recommended:* 3 years of high school math and science, some high school foreign language, interview. *Application deadlines:* 2/1, 1/1 for early decision, 2/1 for financial aid. *Contact:* Dr. William C. Hiss, Vice President for Administrative Services/Dean of Admission, Lindholm House, 23 Campus Avenue, Lewiston, ME 04240, 207-786-6000.

Baylor University

Waco, Texas

Founded 1845
Urban setting
Independent, Baptist
Coed
Awards B, M, D

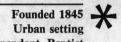

Enrollment	11,810 total; 10,180 undergraduates (2,156 freshmen)
Faculty	635 total; 598 full-time; student-faculty ratio is 16:1; grad assistants teach a few undergraduate courses.
Libraries	1.4 million bound volumes, 15,030 titles on microform, 7,275 periodical subscriptions
Computing	*Terminals/PCs available for student use:* 451, located in computer center, library, dormitories, all major academic buildings; PC not required. Campus network links student PCs.
Of Special Interest	*Core academic program:* yes. Computer course required for business, engineering, interior design, math, physics, education, communications, dietetics, museum studies, home economics, fashion design, fashion merchandising, child and family studies majors. Phi Beta Kappa, Sigma Xi chapters. Academic exchange program: no. Sponsors and participates in study-abroad programs. Air Force ROTC.
On Campus	Drama/theater group; student-run newspaper and radio station. *Social organizations:* 15 national fraternities, 12 national sororities, 3 local fraternities, 1 local sorority; 25% of eligible undergraduate men and 29% of eligible undergraduate women are members.
Athletics	Member NCAA (Division I). *Intercollegiate sports:* badminton (M, W), baseball (M), basketball (M, W), cross-country running (M, W), football (M), golf (M), lacrosse (M, W), riflery (M, W), sailing (M, W), soccer (M, W), tennis (M, W), track and field (M, W), volleyball (M, W). *Scholarships:* M, W.

Costs (1992–93) & Aid				
	Comprehensive fee	$10,345	Need-based scholarships	Avail
	Tuition	$6000	Non-need scholarships	Avail
	Mandatory fees	$540	Short-term loans	N/Avail
	Room and board	$3805	Long-term loans—college funds	N/Avail
	Financial aid recipients	60%	Long-term loans—external funds	Avail

Undergraduate Facts				
	Part-time	4%	*Freshman Data:*	
	State residents	78%	From top tenth of high school class	N/R
	Transfers	5%	SAT-takers scoring 600 or over on verbal	12%
	African-Americans	4%	SAT-takers scoring 700 or over on verbal	2%
	Native Americans	0%	SAT-takers scoring 600 or over on math	35%
	Hispanics	5%	SAT-takers scoring 700 or over on math	7%
	Asian-Americans	5%	ACT-takers scoring 26 or over	23%
	International students	3%	ACT-takers scoring 30 or over	3%
	Freshmen returning for sophomore year	85%	*Majors with most degrees conferred:* education, marketing/retailing/merchandising, accounting.	
	Students completing degree within 5 years	N/R		
	Grads pursuing further study	N/R		

Majors Accounting, American studies, anthropology, applied art, archaeology, art education, art/fine arts, Asian/Oriental studies, aviation technology, biblical languages, biology/biological sciences, broadcasting, business, business economics, business education, chemistry, child care/child and family studies, child psychology/child development, commercial art, communication, computer engineering, computer information systems, computer programming, computer science, (pre)dentistry sequence, dietetics, early childhood education, earth science, ecology/environmental studies, economics, education, electrical engineering, elementary education, engineering (general), English, environmental sciences, fashion design and technology, fashion merchandising, finance/banking, forestry, French, geology, geophysics, German, Greek, health education, history, home economics, home economics education, human resources, insurance, interdisciplinary studies, interior design, international business, international studies, journalism, Latin, Latin American studies, (pre)law sequence, management information systems, marketing/retailing/merchandising, mathematics, mechanical engineering, medical technology, (pre)medicine sequence, museum studies, music, music education, music history, nursing, operations research, optometry, philosophy, physical education, physical sciences, physics, piano/organ, political science/government, psychology, public administration, real estate, recreation and leisure services, religious studies, Russian, Russian and Slavic studies, sacred music, science, science education, secondary education, social work, sociology, Spanish, speech pathology and audiology, speech/rhetoric/public address/debate, speech therapy, stringed instruments, studio art, technical writing, telecommunications, theater arts/drama, urban studies, voice, wind and percussion instruments.

Applying *Required:* essay, high school transcript, SAT or ACT. *Recommended:* 3 years of high school math and science, some high school foreign language, recommendations, campus interview. *Application deadlines:* rolling, 5/15 priority date for financial aid. *Contact:* Office of School Relations, PO Box 97056, Waco, TX 76798, 817-755-3435; *Office location:* Pat Neff Hall.

Bellarmine College

Louisville, Kentucky

Founded 1950
Suburban setting
Independent, Roman Catholic
Coed
Awards B, M

Enrollment 2,294 total; 1,758 undergraduates (265 freshmen)

Faculty 126 total; 85 full-time (80% have doctorate/terminal degree); student-faculty ratio is 15:1; grad assistants teach no undergraduate courses.

Libraries 113,166 bound volumes, 481,771 titles on microform, 630 periodical subscriptions

Computing *Terminals/PCs available for student use:* N/R; PC not required. Campus network links student PCs.

Of Special Interest *Core academic program:* yes. Computer course required for accounting, science, business, education, nursing majors. Academic exchange with University of Louisville, Spalding University, Indiana University Southeast, Southern Baptist Theological Seminary, Presbyterian Seminary, Jefferson Community College. Sponsors and participates in study-abroad programs. Cooperative Army ROTC, cooperative Air Force ROTC.

On Campus Drama/theater group; student-run newspaper. *Social organizations:* 2 local fraternities, 1 local sorority; 20% of eligible undergraduate men and 20% of eligible undergraduate women are members.

Athletics Member NCAA (Division II). *Intercollegiate sports:* baseball (M), basketball (M, W), cross-country running (M, W), field hockey (W), golf (M), soccer (M, W), softball (W), tennis (M, W), track and field (M, W), volleyball (W). *Scholarships:* M, W.

Costs (1991–92) & Aid				
	Comprehensive fee	$9710	Need-based scholarships	Avail
	Tuition	$7160	Non-need scholarships	Avail
	Mandatory fees	$100	Short-term loans	N/Avail
	Room and board	$2450	Long-term loans—college funds	Avail
	Financial aid recipients	90%	Long-term loans—external funds	Avail

Undergraduate Facts				
	Part-time	38%	*Freshman Data:* 610 applied, 91% were accepted, 47% (265) of those entered	
	State residents	80%		
	Transfers	9%	From top tenth of high school class	36%
	African-Americans	2%	SAT-takers scoring 600 or over on verbal	N/R
	Native Americans	0%	SAT-takers scoring 700 or over on verbal	N/R
	Hispanics	1%	SAT-takers scoring 600 or over on math	N/R
	Asian-Americans	1%	SAT-takers scoring 700 or over on math	N/R
	International students	1%	ACT-takers scoring 26 or over	34%
	Freshmen returning for sophomore year	80%	ACT-takers scoring 30 or over	6%
	Students completing degree within 5 years	62%	*Majors with most degrees conferred:* business, accounting, nursing.	
	Grads pursuing further study	20%		

Majors Accounting, actuarial science, art education, art/fine arts, biology/biological sciences, business, chemistry, communication, computer engineering, computer science, data processing, (pre)dentistry sequence, economics, education, elementary education, English, health services administration, history, jazz, (pre)law sequence, liberal arts/general studies, mathematics, (pre)medicine sequence, middle school education, music, music education, nursing, philosophy, political science/government, psychology, science education, secondary education, sociology, special education, studio art, theater arts/drama, theology, (pre)veterinary medicine sequence.

Applying *Required:* essay, high school transcript, 3 years of high school math, SAT or ACT. *Recommended:* 3 years of high school science, 2 years of high school foreign language, interview. Recommendations required for some. *Application deadlines:* 8/1, 4/1 priority date for financial aid. *Contact:* Mr. Tim Sturgeon, Assistant Dean of Admissions, 2001 Newburg Road, Louisville, KY 40205, 800-928-4723 or toll-free 800-928-4723.

Beloit College

Beloit, Wisconsin

Founded 1846
Small-town setting
Independent
Coed
Awards B, M

Enrollment	1,176 total; 1,172 undergraduates (267 freshmen)
Faculty	127 total; 86 full-time (94% have doctorate/terminal degree); student-faculty ratio is 12:1; grad assistants teach no undergraduate courses.
Libraries	222,501 bound volumes, 4,826 titles on microform, 847 periodical subscriptions
Computing	*Terminals/PCs available for student use:* 110, located in computer center, student center, library, dormitories; PC not required. Campus network links student PCs.
Of Special Interest	*Core academic program:* yes. Computer course required for math majors. Phi Beta Kappa chapter. Academic exchange with University of Wisconsin-Madison. Sponsors and participates in study-abroad programs.
On Campus	Drama/theater group; student-run newspaper and radio station. *Social organizations:* 4 national fraternities, 2 local sororities; 25% of eligible undergraduate men and 11% of eligible undergraduate women are members.
Athletics	Member NCAA (Division III). *Intercollegiate sports:* baseball (M), basketball (M, W), cross-country running (M, W), fencing (M, W), football (M), golf (M), ice hockey (M), lacrosse (M, W), soccer (M, W), softball (W), swimming and diving (M, W), tennis (M, W), track and field (M, W), volleyball (W).

Costs (1992–93) & Aid				
	Comprehensive fee	$17,670	Need-based scholarships (average)	$2906
	Tuition	$14,080	Non-need scholarships (average)	$2371
	Mandatory fees	$170	Short-term loans (average)	$100
	Room and board	$3420	Long-term loans—college funds (average)	$1010
	Financial aid recipients	83%	Long-term loans—external funds (average)	$1961

Undergraduate Facts				
	Part-time	8%	*Freshman Data:* 978 applied, 85% were accepted, 32% (267) of those entered	
	State residents	22%		
	Transfers	8%	From top tenth of high school class	27%
	African-Americans	3%	SAT-takers scoring 600 or over on verbal	32%
	Native Americans	0%	SAT-takers scoring 700 or over on verbal	3%
	Hispanics	1%	SAT-takers scoring 600 or over on math	39%
	Asian-Americans	4%	SAT-takers scoring 700 or over on math	8%
	International students	10%	ACT-takers scoring 26 or over	47%
	Freshmen returning for sophomore year	92%	ACT-takers scoring 30 or over	12%
	Students completing degree within 5 years	69%	*Majors with most degrees conferred:* psychology, creative writing, economics.	
	Grads pursuing further study	N/R		

Majors Anthropology, art education, art/fine arts, art history, bilingual/bicultural education, biochemistry, biology/biological sciences, business, cell biology, chemistry, classics, communication, comparative literature, computer science, creative writing, (pre)dentistry sequence, economics, education, elementary education, English, environmental biology, environmental sciences, French, geology, German, history, interdisciplinary studies, international business, international studies, Latin American studies, (pre)law sequence, liberal arts/general studies, literature, mathematics, (pre)medicine sequence, modern languages, molecular biology, museum studies, music, music education, philosophy, physics, political science/government, psychology, religious studies, Romance languages, Russian, Russian and Slavic studies, science education, secondary education, sociology, Spanish, studio art, theater arts/drama, women's studies.

Applying *Required:* essay, high school transcript, SAT or ACT. *Recommended:* 3 years of high school math and science, 2 years of high school foreign language, interview. 1 recommendation, campus interview required for some. *Application deadlines:* rolling, 12/15 for early decision, 4/15 priority date for financial aid. *Contact:* Mr. Thomas Martin, Dean of Admissions, 700 College Street, Beloit, WI 53511, 608-363-2500 or toll-free 800-356-0751 (out-of-state).

✳ **Bennington College**

Bennington, Vermont

Founded 1932
Small-town setting
Independent
Coed
Awards B, M

Enrollment 544 total; 514 undergraduates (174 freshmen)

Faculty 79 total; 55 full-time (38% have doctorate/terminal degree); student-faculty ratio is 7:1; grad assistants teach a few undergraduate courses.

Libraries 100,000 bound volumes, 5,252 titles on microform, 630 periodical subscriptions

Computing *Terminals/PCs available for student use:* 18, located in computer center; PC not required.

Of Special Interest *Core academic program:* yes. Computer course required for some majors. Academic exchange with Brown University. Sponsors and participates in study-abroad programs.

On Campus Drama/theater group; student-run newspaper. No national or local fraternities or sororities on campus.

Athletics *Intercollegiate sports:* soccer (M, W), volleyball (M, W).

Costs (1991–92) & Aid
Comprehensive fee	$23,200	
Tuition	$19,400	
Mandatory fees	N/App	
Room and board	$3800	
Financial aid recipients	56%	
Need-based scholarships (average)		$11,190
Non-need scholarships		N/Avail
Short-term loans		N/Avail
Long-term loans—college funds (average)		$2500
Long-term loans—external funds (average)		$2850

Undergraduate Facts
Part-time	1%
State residents	6%
Transfers	18%
African-Americans	3%
Native Americans	0%
Hispanics	2%
Asian-Americans	3%
International students	5%
Freshmen returning for sophomore year	79%
Students completing degree within 5 years	58%
Grads pursuing further study	N/R

Freshman Data: 552 applied, 75% were accepted, 42% (174) of those entered
From top tenth of high school class	20%
SAT-takers scoring 600 or over on verbal	30%
SAT-takers scoring 700 or over on verbal	4%
SAT-takers scoring 600 or over on math	30%
SAT-takers scoring 700 or over on math	4%
ACT-takers scoring 26 or over	N/R
ACT-takers scoring 30 or over	N/R

Majors with most degrees conferred: literature, interdisciplinary studies, theater arts/drama.

Majors Anthropology, architecture, art/fine arts, biology/biological sciences, ceramic art and design, chemistry, child psychology/child development, Chinese, computer science, creative writing, dance, early childhood education, ecology/environmental studies, economics, English, environmental biology, environmental sciences, French, German, graphic arts, history, interdisciplinary studies, international studies, jazz, (pre)law sequence, literature, mathematics, (pre)medicine sequence, modern languages, music, natural sciences, painting/drawing, philosophy, photography, physics, piano/organ, political science/government, psychology, sculpture, Spanish, stringed instruments, studio art, theater arts/drama, (pre)veterinary medicine sequence, voice.

Applying *Required:* essay, high school transcript, some high school foreign language, 2 recommendations, interview, SAT or ACT. *Recommended:* 3 years of high school math and science. *Application deadlines:* 3/1, 12/1 for early decision, 3/1 priority date for financial aid. *Contact:* Ms. Karen S. Parker, Acting Director of Admissions, The Barn, Bennington, VT 05201, 802-442-6349.

Berry College

Rome, Georgia

Founded 1902
Small-town setting
Independent
Coed
Awards B, M

Enrollment	1,740 total; 1,609 undergraduates (430 freshmen)
Faculty	138 total; 95 full-time (84% have doctorate/terminal degree); student-faculty ratio is 15:1; grad assistants teach no undergraduate courses.
Libraries	137,125 bound volumes, 329,600 titles on microform, 1,390 periodical subscriptions
Computing	*Terminals/PCs available for student use:* 96, located in computer center, library, classroom labs; PC not required.
Of Special Interest	*Core academic program:* yes. Computer course required for some majors. Academic exchange program: no. Sponsors and participates in study-abroad programs.
On Campus	Drama/theater group; student-run newspaper. No national or local fraternities or sororities on campus.
Athletics	Member NAIA. *Intercollegiate sports:* baseball (M), basketball (M, W), cross-country running (M, W), equestrian sports (W), golf (M), soccer (M, W), tennis (M, W), track and field (M, W). *Scholarships:* M, W.

Costs (1991–92) & Aid				
	Comprehensive fee	$10,570	Need-based scholarships (average)	$2252
	Tuition	$6990	Non-need scholarships (average)	$1959
	Mandatory fees	N/App	Short-term loans (average)	$100
	Room and board	$3580	Long-term loans—college funds (average)	$1854
	Financial aid recipients	90%	Long-term loans—external funds (average)	$2346

Undergraduate Facts				
	Part-time	3%	*Freshman Data:* 1,666 applied, 73% were accepted, 36% (430) of those entered	
	State residents	83%		
	Transfers	15%	From top tenth of high school class	N/R
	African-Americans	2%	SAT-takers scoring 600 or over on verbal	14%
	Native Americans	0%	SAT-takers scoring 700 or over on verbal	2%
	Hispanics	1%	SAT-takers scoring 600 or over on math	26%
	Asian-Americans	1%	SAT-takers scoring 700 or over on math	2%
	International students	1%	ACT-takers scoring 26 or over	35%
	Freshmen returning for sophomore year	78%	ACT-takers scoring 30 or over	5%
	Students completing degree within 5 years	53%	*Majors with most degrees conferred:* business, education, psychology.	
	Grads pursuing further study	25%		

Majors Accounting, animal sciences, applied art, art education, art/fine arts, behavioral sciences, biochemistry, biology/biological sciences, business, business economics, chemistry, communication, computer science, (pre)dentistry sequence, early childhood education, economics, education, elementary education, engineering technology, English, family and consumer studies, fashion merchandising, finance/banking, food sciences, French, German, health education, history, home economics, home economics education, hotel and restaurant management, interdisciplinary studies, international studies, (pre)law sequence, manufacturing technology, marketing/retailing/merchandising, mathematics, (pre)medicine sequence, music, music business, music education, ornamental horticulture, philosophy, physical education, physics, piano/organ, political science/government, psychology, religious studies, science education, secondary education, social science, sociology, Spanish, speech/rhetoric/public address/debate, studio art, theater arts/drama, (pre)veterinary medicine sequence, voice.

Applying *Required:* high school transcript, 3 years of high school math and science, 2 years of high school foreign language, SAT or ACT. *Application deadlines:* rolling, 7/15 priority date for financial aid. *Contact:* Mr. George Gaddie, Dean of Admissions, Hermann Hall, Rome, GA 30149-0159, 404-236-2215 or toll-free 800-682-3779 (in-state), 800-237-7942 (out-of-state).

Bethel College

St. Paul, Minnesota

Founded 1871
Suburban setting
Independent/affiliated with Baptist General Conference
Coed
Awards A, B, M

Enrollment 2,001 total; 1,783 undergraduates (393 freshmen)

Faculty 181 total; 110 full-time (68% have doctorate/terminal degree); student-faculty ratio is 15:1; grad assistants teach no undergraduate courses.

Libraries 129,000 bound volumes, 640 periodical subscriptions

Computing *Terminals/PCs available for student use:* 74, located in computer center, dormitories; PC not required. Campus network links student PCs.

Of Special Interest *Core academic program:* yes. Computer course required for engineering, math, business majors. Academic exchange with members of the Christian College Consortium, Au Sable Trails Institute of Environmental Studies. Sponsors and participates in study-abroad programs. Cooperative Army ROTC, cooperative Naval ROTC, cooperative Air Force ROTC.

On Campus Drama/theater group; student-run newspaper and radio station. No national or local fraternities or sororities on campus.

Athletics Member NCAA (Division III). *Intercollegiate sports:* baseball (M), basketball (M, W), cross-country running (M, W), football (M), golf (M), ice hockey (M), soccer (M), tennis (M, W), track and field (M, W), volleyball (W).

Costs (1991–92) & Aid				
Comprehensive fee	$13,540	Need-based scholarships (average)	$2000
Tuition	$9950	Non-need scholarships (average)	$800
Mandatory fees	N/App	Short-term loans (average)	$330
Room and board	$3590	Long-term loans—college funds	N/Avail
Financial aid recipients	91%	Long-term loans—external funds (average)	$2750

Undergraduate Facts			
Part-time	6%	*Freshman Data:* 882 applied, 78% were accepted, 57% (393) of those entered	
State residents	65%		
Transfers	9%	From top tenth of high school class	29%
African-Americans	1%	SAT-takers scoring 600 or over on verbal	9%
Native Americans	1%	SAT-takers scoring 700 or over on verbal	2%
Hispanics	1%	SAT-takers scoring 600 or over on math	26%
Asian-Americans	2%	SAT-takers scoring 700 or over on math	8%
International students	1%	ACT-takers scoring 26 or over	24%
Freshmen returning for sophomore year	74%	ACT-takers scoring 30 or over	2%
Students completing degree within 5 years	52%	*Majors with most degrees conferred:* business, education, nursing.	
Grads pursuing further study	N/R		

Majors Accounting, adult and continuing education, anthropology, art education, art/fine arts, art history, biblical studies, biology/biological sciences, business, chemistry, child care/child and family studies, child psychology/child development, communication, computer science, creative writing, (pre)dentistry sequence, early childhood education, economics, education, elementary education, English, finance/banking, health education, history, international studies, (pre)law sequence, literature, management information systems, mathematics, (pre)medicine sequence, ministries, molecular biology, music, music education, natural sciences, nursing, philosophy, physical education, physics, political science/government, psychology, sacred music, science education, secondary education, social science, social work, sociology, Spanish, speech/rhetoric/public address/debate, studio art, theater arts/drama, theology, (pre)veterinary medicine sequence.

Applying *Required:* essay, high school transcript, 3 recommendations, SAT or ACT, PSAT. *Recommended:* 3 years of high school math and science, interview. *Application deadlines:* rolling, 4/15 priority date for financial aid. *Contact:* Mr. John C. Lassen, Director of Admissions, 3900 Bethel Drive, St. Paul, MN 55112, 612-638-6242 or toll-free 800-255-8706.

From the College Because Bethel's academic program is so strong, students are well prepared for a career or grad school when they leave Bethel. In fact, 98 percent of the students who work with the Office of Career Counseling find positions—many before graduation. And 90 percent of Bethel premed students are accepted into medical school.

Birmingham-Southern College

Birmingham, Alabama

Founded 1856
Urban setting
Independent, Methodist
Coed
Awards B, M

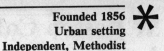

Enrollment	1,825 total; 1,726 undergraduates (287 freshmen)
Faculty	141 total; 99 full-time (75% have doctorate/terminal degree); student-faculty ratio is 15:1; grad assistants teach no undergraduate courses.
Libraries	167,391 bound volumes, 33,184 titles on microform, 819 periodical subscriptions
Computing	*Terminals/PCs available for student use:* 112, located in computer center, dormitories, classroom buildings; PC not required.
Of Special Interest	*Core academic program:* yes. Computer course required for business administration, math, economics majors. Phi Beta Kappa chapter. Academic exchange with University of Alabama at Birmingham, Samford University. Sponsors and participates in study-abroad programs. Cooperative Army ROTC, cooperative Air Force ROTC.
On Campus	Drama/theater group; student-run newspaper. *Social organizations:* 6 national fraternities, 6 national sororities; 60% of eligible undergraduate men and 60% of eligible undergraduate women are members.
Athletics	Member NAIA. *Intercollegiate sports:* basketball (M), soccer (M), tennis (M, W). *Scholarships:* M, W.

Costs (1991–92) & Aid				
	Comprehensive fee	$13,509	Need-based scholarships (average)	$1800
	Tuition	$9550	Non-need scholarships (average)	$3100
	Mandatory fees	$99	Short-term loans	N/Avail
	Room and board	$3860	Long-term loans—college funds	N/Avail
	Financial aid recipients	80%	Long-term loans—external funds (average)	$1200

Undergraduate Facts				
	Part-time	3%	*Freshman Data:* 801 applied, 72% were accepted, 50% (287) of those entered	
	State residents	70%	From top tenth of high school class	39%
	Transfers	10%	SAT-takers scoring 600 or over on verbal	24%
	African-Americans	13%	SAT-takers scoring 700 or over on verbal	8%
	Native Americans	0%	SAT-takers scoring 600 or over on math	35%
	Hispanics	0%	SAT-takers scoring 700 or over on math	5%
	Asian-Americans	2%	ACT-takers scoring 26 or over	51%
	International students	1%	ACT-takers scoring 30 or over	20%
	Freshmen returning for sophomore year	91%	*Majors with most degrees conferred:* business, biology/biological sciences, English.	
	Students completing degree within 5 years	73%		
	Grads pursuing further study	42%		

Majors Accounting, art education, art/fine arts, art history, biology/biological sciences, business, chemistry, computer science, dance, early childhood education, economics, education, elementary education, English, French, German, history, human resources, interdisciplinary studies, (pre)law sequence, mathematics, (pre)medicine sequence, music, music education, music history, philosophy, physics, piano/organ, political science/government, psychology, religious studies, sculpture, secondary education, sociology, Spanish, studio art, theater arts/drama, voice.

Applying *Required:* essay, high school transcript, 3 years of high school math and science, recommendations, SAT or ACT. *Recommended:* some high school foreign language. Interview required for some. *Application deadlines:* 3/1, 12/1 for early action, 3/15 priority date for financial aid. *Contact:* Mr. Bobby Johnson, Director of Admissions, 900 Arkadelphia Road, Birmingham, AL 35254, 205-226-4696 or toll-free 800-523-5793.

Peterson's Competitive Colleges 1992–93

✱ Boston College

Chestnut Hill, Massachusetts

Founded 1863
Suburban setting
Independent, Roman Catholic (Jesuit)
Coed
Awards B, M, D

Enrollment 14,557 total; 8,806 undergraduates (2,578 freshmen)

Faculty 936 total; 579 full-time (91% have doctorate/terminal degree); student-faculty ratio is 15:1; grad assistants teach about a quarter of the undergraduate courses.

Libraries 1.2 million bound volumes, 2 million titles on microform, 13,905 periodical subscriptions

Computing *Terminals/PCs available for student use:* 175, located in computer center; PC not required but available for purchase. Campus network links student PCs.

Of Special Interest *Core academic program:* yes. Computer course required for business, math majors. Phi Beta Kappa, Sigma Xi chapters. Academic exchange with Boston University, Brandeis University, Hebrew College, Pine Manor College, Regis College (MA), Tufts University. Sponsors and participates in study-abroad programs. Cooperative Army ROTC, cooperative Naval ROTC, cooperative Air Force ROTC.

On Campus Drama/theater group; student-run newspaper and radio station. No national or local fraternities or sororities on campus.

Athletics Member NCAA (Division I). *Intercollegiate sports:* baseball (M), basketball (M, W), cross-country running (M, W), fencing (W), field hockey (W), football (M), golf (M, W), ice hockey (M), lacrosse (M, W), sailing (M, W), skiing (downhill) (M, W), soccer (M, W), softball (W), swimming and diving (M, W), tennis (M, W), track and field (M, W), volleyball (W), water polo (M), wrestling (M). *Scholarships:* M, W.

Costs (1991–92) & Aid				
	Comprehensive fee	$20,244	Need-based scholarships (average)	$6197
	Tuition	$13,690	Non-need scholarships (average)	$6845
	Mandatory fees	$404	Short-term loans	N/Avail
	Room and board	$6150	Long-term loans—college funds (average)	$1317
	Financial aid recipients	67%	Long-term loans—external funds (average)	$3123

Undergraduate Facts				
	Part-time	1%	*Freshman Data:* 11,516 applied, 56% were accepted, 40% (2,578) of those entered	
	State residents	35%		
	Transfers	10%	From top tenth of high school class	79%
	African-Americans	3%	SAT-takers scoring 600 or over on verbal	33%
	Native Americans	1%	SAT-takers scoring 700 or over on verbal	3%
	Hispanics	5%	SAT-takers scoring 600 or over on math	71%
	Asian-Americans	6%	SAT-takers scoring 700 or over on math	18%
	International students	3%	ACT-takers scoring 26 or over	N/R
	Freshmen returning for sophomore year	93%	ACT-takers scoring 30 or over	N/R
	Students completing degree within 5 years	84%		
	Grads pursuing further study	28%		

Majors Accounting, art history, biochemistry, biology/biological sciences, business, chemistry, classics, communication, computer information systems, computer science, (pre)dentistry sequence, early childhood education, economics, education, elementary education, English, environmental sciences, finance/banking, French, geology, geophysics, German, Germanic languages and literature, Greek, history, human development, human resources, interdisciplinary studies, Italian, Latin, (pre)law sequence, linguistics, management information systems, marketing/retailing/merchandising, mathematics, (pre)medicine sequence, music, nursing, operations research, philosophy, physics, political science/government, psychology, Romance languages, Russian, secondary education, Slavic languages, sociology, Spanish, special education, studio art, theater arts/drama, theology.

Applying *Required:* essay, high school transcript, 4 years of high school math, 3 years of high school science, 2 recommendations, SAT or ACT, 3 Achievements, English Composition Test. *Recommended:* 4 years of high school foreign language, interview, English Composition Test (with essay). *Application deadlines:* 1/10, 11/1 for early action, 2/1 priority date for financial aid. *Contact:* Mr. John L. Mahoney Jr., Director of Admissions, 140 Commonwealth Avenue, Lyons Hall 120, Chestnut Hill, MA 02167, 617-552-3100.

From the College Boston College students enjoy the quiet, suburban atmosphere of Chestnut Hill, with easy access to the cultural and historical richness of Boston. Ten Presidential Scholars in each freshman class receive a half-tuition scholarship irrespective of need, with funding available to meet full demonstrated need. These students, selected from the top 1 percent of the early notification applicant pool, participate in the most rewarding intellectual experience offered at the College.

Boston University

Boston, Massachusetts

Founded 1839
Urban setting
Independent
Coed
Awards A, B, M, D

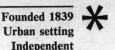

Enrollment 24,348 total; 14,230 undergraduates (3,487 freshmen)

Faculty 2,141 total; 1,169 full-time (81% have doctorate/terminal degree); student-faculty ratio is 15:1; grad assistants teach a few undergraduate courses.

Libraries 1.8 million bound volumes, 3.0 million titles on microform, 29,500 periodical subscriptions

Computing *Terminals/PCs available for student use:* 400, located in computer center, student center, library, dormitories, academic departments; PC not required but available for purchase. Campus network links student PCs.

Of Special Interest *Core academic program:* yes. Computer course required for engineering, management, math, science majors. Phi Beta Kappa, Sigma Xi chapters. Academic exchange with Boston College, Brandeis University, Tufts University, Hebrew College. Sponsors and participates in study-abroad programs. Army ROTC, Naval ROTC, Air Force ROTC.

On Campus Drama/theater group; student-run newspaper and radio station. *Social organizations:* 14 national fraternities, 10 national sororities, local fraternities, local sororities; 9% of eligible undergraduate men and 9% of eligible undergraduate women are members.

Athletics Member NCAA (Division I). *Intercollegiate sports:* archery (M, W), badminton (M, W), baseball (M), basketball (M, W), bowling (M, W), crew (M, W), cross-country running (M, W), equestrian sports (M, W), fencing (M, W), field hockey (W), football (M), golf (M, W), gymnastics (M, W), ice hockey (M, W), lacrosse (M, W), rugby (M, W), sailing (M, W), skiing (cross-country) (W), soccer (M, W), softball (M, W), swimming and diving (M, W), tennis (M, W), track and field (M, W), volleyball (M, W), water polo (M, W), wrestling (M). *Scholarships:* M, W.

Costs (1992–93) & Aid
Comprehensive fee	$23,157
Tuition	$16,590
Mandatory fees	$247
Room and board	$6320
Financial aid recipients	61%
Need-based scholarships (average)	$8616
Non-need scholarships (average)	$10,561
Short-term loans (average)	$300
Long-term loans—college funds (average)	$931
Long-term loans—external funds (average)	$3008

Undergraduate Facts
Part-time	5%
State residents	21%
Transfers	5%
African-Americans	4%
Native Americans	0%
Hispanics	5%
Asian-Americans	13%
International students	11%
Freshmen returning for sophomore year	85%
Students completing degree within 5 years	69%
Grads pursuing further study	N/R

Freshman Data: 17,000 applied, 71% were accepted, 29% (3,487) of those entered
From top tenth of high school class	42%
SAT-takers scoring 600 or over on verbal	23%
SAT-takers scoring 700 or over on verbal	3%
SAT-takers scoring 600 or over on math	49%
SAT-takers scoring 700 or over on math	11%
ACT-takers scoring 26 or over	56%
ACT-takers scoring 30 or over	19%

Majors with most degrees conferred: social science, business, communication.

Majors Accounting, advertising, aerospace engineering, African studies, American studies, anthropology, archaeology, art education, art/fine arts, art history, astronomy, astrophysics, athletic training, bilingual/bicultural education, biology/biological sciences, biomedical engineering, biotechnology, broadcasting, business, chemistry, classics, communication, computer engineering, computer information systems, computer science, (pre)dentistry sequence, early childhood education, earth science, East Asian studies, East European and Soviet studies, economics, education, electrical engineering, elementary education, engineering (general), engineering management, English, environmental sciences, film studies, finance/banking, food services management, French, geography, geology, German, Germanic languages and literature, graphic arts, Greek, health science, Hispanic studies, history, hotel and restaurant management, interdisciplinary studies, international business, international studies, Italian, journalism, Latin, Latin American studies, (pre)law sequence, liberal arts/general studies, linguistics, management information systems, manufacturing engineering, marine biology, marine sciences, marketing/retailing/merchandising, mathematics, mechanical engineering, medical assistant technologies, medical technology, (pre)medicine sequence, mental health/rehabilitation counseling, modern languages, music, music education, music history, occupational therapy, opera, operations research, painting/drawing, paralegal studies, philosophy, photography, physical education, physical fitness/human movement, physics, piano/organ, political science/government, psychology, public relations, recreation and leisure services, rehabilitation therapy, religious studies, Russian, Russian and Slavic studies, science education, sculpture, secondary education, social science, social work, sociology, Spanish, special education, speech pathology and audiology, speech therapy, sports medicine, statistics, stringed instruments, studio art, systems engineering, teaching English as a second language, theater arts/drama, urban studies, voice, wind and percussion instruments.

Applying *Required:* essay, high school transcript, 4 years of high school math, 1 recommendation, SAT or ACT. *Recommended:* 3 years of high school science, 3 years of high school foreign language. Campus interview, Achievements, English Composition Test (with essay) required for some. *Application deadlines:* 1/15, 11/15 for early decision, 3/1 priority date for financial aid. *Contact:* Ms. Debra Kocar, Associate Director, Admissions Reception Center, 121 Bay State Road, Boston, MA 02215, 617-353-2300.

✻ Bowdoin College

Brunswick, Maine

Founded 1794
Small-town setting
Independent
Coed
Awards B

Enrollment 1,400 total—all undergraduates (420 freshmen)

Faculty 135 total; 124 full-time (99% have doctorate/terminal degree); student-faculty ratio is 10:1.

Libraries 760,000 bound volumes, 120,000 titles on microform, 2,100 periodical subscriptions

Computing *Terminals/PCs available for student use:* 90, located in computer center, library, academic departments; PC not required. Campus network links student PCs.

Of Special Interest *Core academic program:* yes. Phi Beta Kappa chapter. Academic exchange with Twelve College Exchange Program, National Theater Institute, American University (Washington Semester), Boston University, Williams College (Mystic Seaport Program), Tougaloo College, Woods Hole Oceanographic Institute. Sponsors and participates in study-abroad programs. Cooperative Army ROTC.

On Campus Drama/theater group; student-run newspaper and radio station. *Social organizations:* 2 national fraternities, 6 local fraternities, 8 coed fraternities; 20% of eligible undergraduate men and 14% of eligible undergraduate women are members.

Athletics Member NCAA (Division III). *Intercollegiate sports:* baseball (M), basketball (M, W), cross-country running (M, W), field hockey (W), football (M), golf (M, W), ice hockey (M, W), lacrosse (M, W), sailing (M, W), skiing (cross-country) (M, W), skiing (downhill) (M, W), soccer (M, W), softball (W), squash (M, W), swimming and diving (M, W), tennis (M, W), track and field (M, W), volleyball (W).

Costs (1991–92) & Aid				
	Comprehensive fee	$21,970	Need-based scholarships (average)	$10,660
	Tuition	$16,070	Non-need scholarships	N/Avail
	Mandatory fees	$310	Short-term loans	N/Avail
	Room and board	$5590	Long-term loans—college funds (average)	$1435
	Financial aid recipients	60%	Long-term loans—external funds (average)	$1182

Undergraduate Facts				
	Part-time	0%	*Freshman Data:* 3,143 applied, 32% were accepted, 41% (420) of those entered	
	State residents	17%		
	Transfers	1%	From top tenth of high school class	78%
	African-Americans	4%	SAT-takers scoring 600 or over on verbal	64%
	Native Americans	N/R	SAT-takers scoring 700 or over on verbal	6%
	Hispanics	3%	SAT-takers scoring 600 or over on math	85%
	Asian-Americans	4%	SAT-takers scoring 700 or over on math	35%
	International students	3%	ACT-takers scoring 26 or over	N/R
	Freshmen returning for sophomore year	96%	ACT-takers scoring 30 or over	N/R
	Students completing degree within 5 years	90%	*Majors with most degrees conferred:* political science/government, history, economics.	
	Grads pursuing further study	18%		

Majors Anthropology, art history, Asian/Oriental studies, biochemistry, biology/biological sciences, black/African-American studies, chemistry, classics, computer science, ecology/environmental studies, economics, English, French, geology, German, history, interdisciplinary studies, mathematics, music, neurosciences, philosophy, physics, political science/government, psychology, religious studies, Romance languages, Russian, sociology, Spanish, studio art.

Applying *Required:* essay, high school transcript, 3 recommendations. *Recommended:* 4 years of high school math, 3 years of high school science, 4 years of high school foreign language, interview, SAT or ACT, Achievements, English Composition Test. *Application deadlines:* 1/15, 11/15 for early decision, 3/1 priority date for financial aid. *Contact:* Dr. Richard E. Steele, Dean of Admissions, College Street, Bunswick, ME 04011, 207-725-3190.

From the College Bowdoin College has achieved nearly 200 years of distinguished teaching. Small classes, first-year seminars, independent study, and new curricula in calculus, chemistry, and computer science contribute to an excellent academic program. Bowdoin's scenic mid-coastal Maine location and beautiful campus provide a first-rate setting for a residential, liberal arts education.

Bradley University

Peoria, Illinois

Founded 1897
Urban setting
Independent
Coed
Awards B, M

Enrollment 6,233 total; 5,287 undergraduates (1,010 freshmen)

Faculty 433 total; 294 full-time (94% have doctorate/terminal degree); student-faculty ratio is 18:1; grad assistants teach a few undergraduate courses.

Libraries 510,537 bound volumes, 670,900 titles on microform, 2,407 periodical subscriptions

Computing *Terminals/PCs available for student use:* 993, located in computer center, student center, library, dormitories, lab; PC not required.

Of Special Interest *Core academic program:* yes. Computer course required. Sigma Xi chapter. Academic exchange program: no. Sponsors and participates in study-abroad programs. Army ROTC.

On Campus Drama/theater group; student-run newspaper and radio station. *Social organizations:* 20 national fraternities, 10 national sororities, 1 local sorority; 49% of eligible undergraduate men and 33% of eligible undergraduate women are members.

Athletics Member NCAA (Division I). *Intercollegiate sports:* baseball (M), basketball (M, W), cross-country running (M, W), golf (M, W), ice hockey (M), soccer (M), softball (W), swimming and diving (M), tennis (M, W), track and field (M, W), volleyball (W). *Scholarships:* M, W.

Costs (1991–92) & Aid				
	Comprehensive fee	$13,058	Need-based scholarships (average)	$1876
	Tuition	$9050	Non-need scholarships (average)	$2290
	Mandatory fees	$48	Short-term loans	N/Avail
	Room and board	$3960	Long-term loans—college funds	N/Avail
	Financial aid recipients	90%	Long-term loans—external funds (average)	$2400

Undergraduate Facts				
	Part-time	11%	*Freshman Data:* 3,354 applied, 95% were accepted, 32% (1,010) of those entered	
	State residents	78%		
	Transfers	27%	From top tenth of high school class	31%
	African-Americans	7%	SAT-takers scoring 600 or over on verbal	18%
	Native Americans	0%	SAT-takers scoring 700 or over on verbal	3%
	Hispanics	1%	SAT-takers scoring 600 or over on math	44%
	Asian-Americans	2%	SAT-takers scoring 700 or over on math	11%
	International students	2%	ACT-takers scoring 26 or over	36%
	Freshmen returning for sophomore year	88%	ACT-takers scoring 30 or over	6%
	Students completing degree within 5 years	58%		
	Grads pursuing further study	13%		

Majors Accounting, advertising, applied art, art education, art/fine arts, art history, biochemistry, biology/biological sciences, biotechnology, broadcasting, business, business economics, ceramic art and design, chemistry, civil engineering, communication, computer engineering, computer information systems, computer programming, computer science, construction engineering, construction management, criminal justice, (pre)dentistry sequence, dietetics, early childhood education, ecology/environmental studies, economics, education, electrical engineering, electrical engineering technology, elementary education, engineering physics, English, environmental biology, environmental sciences, fashion merchandising, film studies, finance/banking, French, geology, German, graphic arts, history, home economics, industrial engineering, interior design, international business, international studies, jewelry and metalsmithing, journalism, law enforcement/police sciences, (pre)law sequence, liberal arts/general studies, management information systems, manufacturing engineering, manufacturing technology, marketing/retailing/merchandising, mathematics, mechanical engineering, mechanical engineering technology, medical technology, (pre)medicine sequence, music, music education, nursing, nutrition, painting/drawing, philosophy, photography, physical therapy, physics, piano/organ, political science/government, psychology, radio and television studies, religious studies, sculpture, secondary education, social work, sociology, Spanish, special education, stringed instruments, studio art, theater arts/drama, (pre)veterinary medicine sequence, voice, wind and percussion instruments.

Applying *Required:* high school transcript, SAT or ACT. *Recommended:* essay, some high school foreign language, 2 recommendations, interview. 3 years of high school math and science required for some. *Application deadlines:* rolling, 3/1 priority date for financial aid. *Contact:* Mr. Gary Bergman, Executive Director of Enrollment Management, 100 Swords Hall, Peoria, IL 61625, 309-677-1000 or toll-free 800-447-6460.

✷ Brandeis University

Waltham, Massachusetts

Founded 1948
Suburban setting
Independent
Coed
Awards B, M, D

Enrollment 3,772 total; 2,898 undergraduates (751 freshmen)

Faculty 464 total; 355 full-time (93% have doctorate/terminal degree); student-faculty ratio is 6:1; grad assistants teach a few undergraduate courses.

Libraries 900,000 bound volumes, 785,000 titles on microform, 7,300 periodical subscriptions

Computing *Terminals/PCs available for student use:* 100, located in computer center, library, 4 computer rooms; PC not required. Campus network links student PCs.

Of Special Interest *Core academic program:* yes. Phi Beta Kappa chapter. Academic exchange with Tufts University, Boston University, Boston College, Wellesley College. Participates in study-abroad programs. Cooperative Army ROTC, cooperative Air Force ROTC.

On Campus Drama/theater group; student-run newspaper and radio station. No national or local fraternities or sororities on campus.

Athletics Member NCAA (Division III), NAIA. *Intercollegiate sports:* baseball (M), basketball (M, W), crew (M, W), cross-country running (M, W), equestrian sports (M, W), fencing (M, W), field hockey (W), golf (M), ice hockey (M), lacrosse (M), rugby (M), sailing (M, W), soccer (M, W), softball (W), swimming and diving (M, W), tennis (M, W), track and field (M, W), volleyball (W).

Costs (1991–92) & Aid
Comprehensive fee	$22,695	
Tuition	$16,085	
Mandatory fees	$390	
Room and board	$6220	
Financial aid recipients	51%	
Need-based scholarships (average)		$11,400
Non-need scholarships (average)		$7500
Short-term loans		N/Avail
Long-term loans—college funds (average)		$2000
Long-term loans—external funds (average)		$3300

Undergraduate Facts
Part-time	2%
State residents	35%
Transfers	2%
African-Americans	4%
Native Americans	0%
Hispanics	3%
Asian-Americans	8%
International students	4%
Freshmen returning for sophomore year	90%
Students completing degree within 5 years	79%
Grads pursuing further study	40%

Freshman Data: 3,773 applied, 73% were accepted, 27% (751) of those entered
From top tenth of high school class	50%
SAT-takers scoring 600 or over on verbal	N/R
SAT-takers scoring 700 or over on verbal	N/R
SAT-takers scoring 600 or over on math	N/R
SAT-takers scoring 700 or over on math	N/R
ACT-takers scoring 26 or over	N/R
ACT-takers scoring 30 or over	N/R

Majors with most degrees conferred: psychology, political science/government, economics.

Majors American studies, anthropology, archaeology, art/fine arts, art history, biochemistry, biology/biological sciences, biophysics, black/African-American studies, chemistry, classics, comparative literature, computer science, creative writing, economics, engineering physics, English, European studies, French, German, Germanic languages and literature, Greek, history, international economics, Italian, Judaic studies, Latin, Latin American studies, linguistics, literature, mathematics, music, music history, Near and Middle Eastern studies, neurosciences, philosophy, physics, political science/government, psychology, Russian, science, sociology, Spanish, theater arts/drama, Western civilization and culture.

Applying *Required:* essay, high school transcript, 3 years of high school foreign language, 2 recommendations, ACT or SAT and 3 College Board Achievement Tests. *Recommended:* 3 years of high school math and science, interview, English Composition Test (with essay). *Application deadlines:* 2/1, 1/1 for early decision, 2/15 priority date for financial aid. *Contact:* Mr. David L. Gould, Dean of Admissions, 415 South Street, Waltham, MA 02254, 617-736-3500 or toll-free 800-622-0622 (out-of-state).

Brigham Young University

Independent/affiliated with Church of Jesus Christ of Latter-day Saints

Provo, Utah

Founded 1875
Urban setting
Coed
Awards A, B, M, D

Enrollment 30,898 total; 28,134 undergraduates (4,634 freshmen)

Faculty 1,605 total; 1,295 full-time (77% have doctorate/terminal degree); student-faculty ratio is 32:1; grad assistants teach a few undergraduate courses.

Libraries 2.2 million bound volumes, 1.2 million titles on microform, 18,582 periodical subscriptions

Computing *Terminals/PCs available for student use:* N/R; PC not required.

Of Special Interest *Core academic program:* yes. Computer course required for engineering, business majors. Sigma Xi chapter. Academic exchange program: no. Sponsors study-abroad programs. Army ROTC, Air Force ROTC.

On Campus Dress code; drama/theater group; student-run newspaper and radio station. No national or local fraternities or sororities on campus.

Athletics Member NCAA (Division I). *Intercollegiate sports:* baseball (M), basketball (M, W), cross-country running (M, W), football (M), golf (M, W), gymnastics (M, W), swimming and diving (M, W), tennis (M, W), track and field (M, W), volleyball (M, W), wrestling (M). *Scholarships:* M, W.

Costs (1992–93) & Aid			
Comprehensive fee	$5280	Need-based scholarships	Avail
Tuition	$2120	Non-need scholarships (average)	$1220
Mandatory fees	N/App	Short-term loans (average)	$879
Room and board	$3160	Long-term loans—college funds	Avail
Financial aid recipients	56%	Long-term loans—external funds (average)	$2451

Undergraduate Facts			
Part-time	5%	*Freshman Data:* 7,238 applied, 77% were accepted, 83% (4,634) of those entered	
State residents	31%		
Transfers	34%	From top tenth of high school class	48%
African-Americans	N/R	SAT-takers scoring 600 or over on verbal	N/App
Native Americans	1%	SAT-takers scoring 700 or over on verbal	N/App
Hispanics	1%	SAT-takers scoring 600 or over on math	N/App
Asian-Americans	1%	SAT-takers scoring 700 or over on math	N/App
International students	5%	ACT-takers scoring 26 or over	44%
Freshmen returning for sophomore year	N/R	ACT-takers scoring 30 or over	11%
Students completing degree within 5 years	N/R	*Majors with most degrees conferred:* business, elementary education, communication.	
Grads pursuing further study	N/R		

Majors Accounting, actuarial science, advertising, agricultural business, agricultural economics, agronomy/soil and crop sciences, American studies, animal sciences, anthropology, applied art, art education, art/fine arts, art history, Asian/Oriental studies, astronomy, athletic training, biblical languages, biochemistry, biology/biological sciences, biotechnology, botany/plant sciences, broadcasting, business, business economics, business education, Canadian studies, cartography, ceramic art and design, chemical engineering, chemistry, child care/child and family studies, child psychology/child development, Chinese, civil engineering, classics, communication, community services, comparative literature, computer engineering, computer information systems, computer science, conservation, construction management, dance, (pre)dentistry sequence, dietetics, drafting and design, early childhood education, earth science, East Asian studies, economics, education, electrical and electronics technologies, electrical engineering, electrical engineering technology, electronics engineering technology, elementary education, engineering (general), engineering and applied sciences, engineering technology, English, entomology, European studies, family and consumer studies, family services, farm and ranch management, fashion design and technology, fashion merchandising, film studies, finance/banking, food sciences, food services management, French, geological engineering, geology, German, graphic arts, Greek, health education, health science, history, home economics, home economics education, horticulture, humanities, human resources, illustration, industrial administration, industrial arts, industrial design, information science, interior design, international business, international studies, Italian, Japanese, journalism, Latin, Latin American studies, (pre)law sequence, linguistics, literature, management information systems, manufacturing engineering, manufacturing technology, marketing/retailing/merchandising, mathematics, mechanical engineering, (pre)medicine sequence, Mexican-American/Chicano studies, microbiology, molecular biology, music, music education, Near and Middle Eastern studies, nursing, nutrition, ornamental horticulture, painting/drawing, parks management, philosophy, photography, physical education, physical fitness/human movement, physical sciences, physical therapy, physics, piano/organ, political science/government, Portuguese, printing technologies, printmaking, psychology, public affairs and policy studies, public relations, radio and television studies, range management, real estate, recreational facilities management, recreation and leisure services, recreation therapy, retail management, Russian, science education, sculpture, secondary education, social science, social work, sociology, Spanish, special education, speech pathology and audiology, sports administration, statistics, studio art, textiles and clothing, theater arts/drama, tourism and travel, (pre)veterinary medicine sequence, vocational education, voice, wildlife biology, wildlife management, zoology.

Applying *Required:* essay, high school transcript, 1 recommendation, interview, ACT. *Recommended:* 3 years of high school math and science, 2 years of high school foreign language. *Application deadlines:* 2/15, 3/1 priority date for financial aid. *Contact:* Mr. Erlend D. Peterson, Dean of Admissions and Records, A-183 Abraham Smoot Building, Provo, UT 84602, 801-378-2539.

✱ Brown University

Providence, Rhode Island

Founded 1764
Urban setting
Independent
Coed
Awards B, M, D

Enrollment	7,532 total; 5,906 undergraduates (1,407 freshmen)
Faculty	665 total; 535 full-time (98% have doctorate/terminal degree); student-faculty ratio is 9:1; grad assistants teach a few undergraduate courses.
Libraries	2.3 million bound volumes, 15,090 periodical subscriptions
Computing	*Terminals/PCs available for student use:* 300, located in computer center, student center, library, dormitories; PC not required. Campus network links student PCs.
Of Special Interest	*Core academic program:* no. Computer course required for applied math majors. Phi Beta Kappa, Sigma Xi chapters. Academic exchange with Rhode Island School of Design, Tougaloo College. Sponsors and participates in study-abroad programs. Cooperative Army ROTC.
On Campus	Drama/theater group; student-run newspaper and radio station. *Social organizations:* 11 national fraternities, 2 national sororities, 1 coed fraternity; 10% of eligible undergraduate men and 2% of eligible undergraduate women are members.
Athletics	Member NCAA (Division I). *Intercollegiate sports:* baseball (M), basketball (M, W), crew (M, W), cross-country running (M, W), fencing (M, W), field hockey (W), football (M), golf (M, W), gymnastics (M, W), ice hockey (M, W), lacrosse (M, W), rugby (M, W), sailing (M, W), skiing (cross-country) (M, W), skiing (downhill) (M, W), soccer (M, W), softball (W), squash (M, W), swimming and diving (M, W), tennis (M, W), track and field (M, W), volleyball (M, W), water polo (M, W), wrestling (M).

Costs (1991–92) & Aid				
	Comprehensive fee	$21,946	Need-based scholarships (average)	$9821
	Tuition	$16,256	Non-need scholarships	N/Avail
	Mandatory fees	$471	Short-term loans (average)	$200
	Room and board	$5219	Long-term loans—college funds (average)	$2057
	Financial aid recipients	33%	Long-term loans—external funds (average)	$2852

Undergraduate Facts				
	Part-time	6%	*Freshman Data:* 11,793 applied, 23% were accepted, 51% (1,407) of those entered	
	State residents	3%		
	Transfers	2%	From top tenth of high school class	80%
	African-Americans	7%	SAT-takers scoring 600 or over on verbal	69%
	Native Americans	1%	SAT-takers scoring 700 or over on verbal	21%
	Hispanics	5%	SAT-takers scoring 600 or over on math	85%
	Asian-Americans	12%	SAT-takers scoring 700 or over on math	40%
	International students	10%	ACT-takers scoring 26 or over	75%
	Freshmen returning for sophomore year	96%	ACT-takers scoring 30 or over	25%
	Students completing degree within 5 years	91%	*Majors with most degrees conferred:* history, international studies, political science/government.	
	Grads pursuing further study	30%		

Majors American studies, anthropology, applied mathematics, art/fine arts, art history, Asian/Oriental studies, behavioral sciences, biochemistry, biology/biological sciences, biomedical engineering, biomedical sciences, biophysics, black/African-American studies, chemical engineering, chemistry, Chinese, civil engineering, classics, cognitive science, comparative literature, computer engineering, computer science, creative writing, dance, East Asian studies, ecology/environmental studies, economics, education, electrical engineering, engineering (general), engineering sciences, English, environmental sciences, film and video, French, geochemistry, geology, geophysics, German, Germanic languages and literature, Greek, Hispanic studies, history, international studies, Italian, Judaic studies, Latin, Latin American studies, linguistics, literature, marine biology, materials engineering, mathematics, mechanical engineering, medieval studies, modern languages, molecular biology, music, Near and Middle Eastern studies, neurosciences, philosophy, physics, political science/government, Portuguese, psychology, religious studies, Russian, Russian and Slavic studies, Slavic languages, sociology, South Asian studies, Spanish, studio art, theater arts/drama, urban studies, women's studies.

Applying *Required:* essay, high school transcript, 3 years of high school math and science, 3 years of high school foreign language, 2 recommendations, SAT or ACT, 3 Achievements. *Application deadlines:* 1/1, 11/1 for early action, 1/1 for financial aid. *Contact:* Eric Widmer, Dean of Admissions and Financial Aid, 45 Prospect Street, Providence, RI 02912, 401-863-2378.

Bryn Mawr College

Bryn Mawr, Pennsylvania

Founded 1885
Suburban setting
Independent
Primarily women
Awards B, M, D

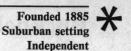

Enrollment	1,881 total; 1,243 undergraduates (320 freshmen)	
Faculty	209 total; 150 full-time (99% have doctorate/terminal degree); student-faculty ratio is 9:1; grad assistants teach a few undergraduate courses.	
Libraries	890,000 bound volumes, 1,980 periodical subscriptions	
Computing	*Terminals/PCs available for student use:* 150, located in computer center, student center, library, dormitories; PC not required but available for purchase.	
Of Special Interest	*Core academic program:* yes. Sigma Xi chapter. Academic exchange with Haverford College, Swarthmore College, University of Pennsylvania, Spelman College. Sponsors and participates in study-abroad programs. Cooperative Army ROTC, cooperative Naval ROTC, cooperative Air Force ROTC.	
On Campus	Drama/theater group; student-run newspaper and radio station. No national or local fraternities or sororities on campus.	
Athletics	Member NCAA (Division III). *Intercollegiate sports:* badminton (W), basketball (W), cross-country running (W), fencing (W), field hockey (W), gymnastics (W), ice hockey (W), lacrosse (W), rugby (W), sailing (W), soccer (W), swimming and diving (W), tennis (W), volleyball (W).	

Costs (1991–92) & Aid	Comprehensive fee	$21,450	Need-based scholarships (average)	$9262
	Tuition	$15,250	Non-need scholarships	N/Avail
	Mandatory fees	$350	Short-term loans (average)	$100
	Room and board	$5850	Long-term loans—college funds (average)	$700
	Financial aid recipients	50%	Long-term loans—external funds (average)	$2400

Undergraduate Facts	Part-time	1%	*Freshman Data:* 1,400 applied, 61% were accepted, 37% (320) of those entered	
	State residents	11%		
	Transfers	3%	From top tenth of high school class	70%
	African-Americans	5%	SAT-takers scoring 600 or over on verbal	71%
	Native Americans	1%	SAT-takers scoring 700 or over on verbal	19%
	Hispanics	3%	SAT-takers scoring 600 or over on math	67%
	Asian-Americans	14%	SAT-takers scoring 700 or over on math	16%
	International students	10%	ACT-takers scoring 26 or over	N/App
	Freshmen returning for sophomore year	96%	ACT-takers scoring 30 or over	N/App
	Students completing degree within 5 years	85%	*Majors with most degrees conferred:* English, political science/government, biology/biological sciences.	
	Grads pursuing further study	45%		

Majors African studies, American studies, anthropology, archaeology, art/fine arts, art history, Asian/Oriental studies, astronomy, behavioral sciences, biochemistry, biology/biological sciences, black/African-American studies, chemistry, classics, comparative literature, computer science, East Asian studies, economics, English, French, geology, German, Greek, Hispanic studies, history, Italian, Latin, Latin American studies, mathematics, music, neurosciences, philosophy, physics, political science/government, psychology, religious studies, Romance languages, Russian, Russian and Slavic studies, sociology, Spanish, urban studies.

Applying *Required:* essay, high school transcript, 3 years of high school math, some high school foreign language, 3 recommendations, interview, SAT, 3 Achievements, English Composition Test. *Recommended:* 3 years of high school science. *Application deadlines:* 1/15, 11/15 for early decision, 1/15 for financial aid. *Contact:* Ms. Elizabeth G. Vermey, Director of Admissions, Ely House, Bryn Mawr, PA 19010, 215-526-5152.

✱ Bucknell University

Lewisburg, Pennsylvania

Founded 1846
Small-town setting
Independent
Coed
Awards B, M

Enrollment 3,578 total; 3,307 undergraduates (904 freshmen)

Faculty 261 total; 234 full-time (95% have doctorate/terminal degree); student-faculty ratio is 13:1; grad assistants teach no undergraduate courses.

Libraries 512,000 bound volumes, 2,609 periodical subscriptions

Computing *Terminals/PCs available for student use:* 320, located in computer center, library, classrooms; PC not required.

Of Special Interest *Core academic program:* no. Computer course required for all majors except humanities. Phi Beta Kappa, Sigma Xi chapters. Academic exchange with American University, Drew University. Sponsors and participates in study-abroad programs. Army ROTC.

On Campus Drama/theater group; student-run newspaper and radio station. *Social organizations:* 12 national fraternities, 8 national sororities, 2 local fraternities, 2 local sororities; 52% of eligible undergraduate men and 54% of eligible undergraduate women are members.

Athletics Member NCAA (Division I). *Intercollegiate sports:* baseball (M), basketball (M, W), crew (M, W), cross-country running (M, W), field hockey (W), football (M), golf (M), ice hockey (M), lacrosse (M, W), riflery (M, W), rugby (M, W), sailing (M, W), skiing (cross-country) (M, W), soccer (M, W), softball (W), swimming and diving (M, W), tennis (M, W), track and field (M, W), volleyball (M, W), water polo (M), wrestling (M).

Costs (1992–93) & Aid
Comprehensive fee	$20,780	
Tuition	$16,560	
Mandatory fees	$110	
Room and board	$4110	
Financial aid recipients	47%	
Need-based scholarships (average)	$9200	
Non-need scholarships	N/Avail	
Short-term loans	N/Avail	
Long-term loans—college funds (average)	$900	
Long-term loans—external funds (average)	$1945	

Undergraduate Facts
Part-time	2%
State residents	31%
Transfers	2%
African-Americans	3%
Native Americans	1%
Hispanics	2%
Asian-Americans	4%
International students	3%
Freshmen returning for sophomore year	95%
Students completing degree within 5 years	88%
Grads pursuing further study	28%

Freshman Data: 5,868 applied, 57% were accepted, 27% (904) of those entered

From top tenth of high school class	59%
SAT-takers scoring 600 or over on verbal	21%
SAT-takers scoring 700 or over on verbal	1%
SAT-takers scoring 600 or over on math	67%
SAT-takers scoring 700 or over on math	16%
ACT-takers scoring 26 or over	N/R
ACT-takers scoring 30 or over	N/R

Majors with most degrees conferred: business, political science/government, economics.

Majors Accounting, animal sciences, anthropology, art/fine arts, art history, biochemistry, biology/biological sciences, business, cell biology, chemical engineering, chemistry, child psychology/child development, civil engineering, classics, computer engineering, computer science, (pre)dentistry sequence, early childhood education, economics, education, electrical engineering, elementary education, engineering management, English, environmental sciences, experimental psychology, French, geography, geology, German, history, international studies, Japanese, Latin American studies, mathematics, mechanical engineering, (pre)medicine sequence, modern languages, music, music education, music history, philosophy, physics, piano/organ, political science/government, psychology, religious studies, Russian, secondary education, sociology, Spanish, statistics, studio art, theater arts/drama, (pre)veterinary medicine sequence, voice.

Applying *Required:* essay, high school transcript, 3 years of high school math, some high school foreign language, recommendations, SAT, Achievements, English Composition Test. *Recommended:* 3 years of high school science, interview, English Composition Test (with essay). *Application deadlines:* 1/1, 12/1 for early decision, 2/15 priority date for financial aid. *Contact:* Mr. Mark D. Davies, Dean of Admissions, Freas Hall, Lewisburg, PA 17837, 717-524-1101.

From the College Bucknell, located in central Pennsylvania, offers a distinctive balance of quality in fine and performing arts, humanities, social sciences, science, education, business administration, and engineering on a scenic, 300-acre campus with a distinguished, accessible teaching faculty and modern residence, research, and study facilities.

Buena Vista College

Storm Lake, Iowa

Founded 1891
Small-town setting
Independent, Presbyterian
Coed
Awards B

Enrollment 1,032 total—all undergraduates (275 freshmen)

Faculty 96 total; 75 full-time (60% have doctorate/terminal degree); student-faculty ratio is 14:1.

Libraries 125,000 bound volumes, 13,132 titles on microform, 650 periodical subscriptions

Computing *Terminals/PCs available for student use:* 100, located in computer center, student center, library, dormitories mass communication building, media center; PC not required.

Of Special Interest *Core academic program:* yes. Computer course required for business, math, education majors. Academic exchange with 8 members of the Colleges of Mid-America. Sponsors and participates in study-abroad programs.

On Campus Drama/theater group; student-run newspaper and radio station. *Social organizations:* 1 national fraternity, 32 separate floor organizations; 40% of eligible undergraduate men and 40% of eligible undergraduate women are members.

Athletics Member NCAA (Division III). *Intercollegiate sports:* baseball (M), basketball (M, W), cross-country running (M, W), football (M), golf (M, W), softball (W), swimming and diving (M, W), tennis (M, W), track and field (M, W), volleyball (W), wrestling (M).

Costs (1991–92) & Aid				
	Comprehensive fee	$14,010	Need-based scholarships (average)	$3957
	Tuition	$10,900	Non-need scholarships (average)	$1247
	Mandatory fees	N/App	Short-term loans	Avail
	Room and board	$3110	Long-term loans—college funds (average)	$62
	Financial aid recipients	96%	Long-term loans—external funds (average)	$2963

Undergraduate Facts				
	Part-time	5%	*Freshman Data:* 878 applied, 91% were accepted, 34% (275) of those entered	
	State residents	75%		
	Transfers	25%	From top tenth of high school class	33%
	African-Americans	1%	SAT-takers scoring 600 or over on verbal	N/R
	Native Americans	N/R	SAT-takers scoring 700 or over on verbal	N/R
	Hispanics	N/R	SAT-takers scoring 600 or over on math	N/R
	Asian-Americans	2%	SAT-takers scoring 700 or over on math	N/R
	International students	5%	ACT-takers scoring 26 or over	31%
	Freshmen returning for sophomore year	82%	ACT-takers scoring 30 or over	5%
	Students completing degree within 5 years	60%	*Majors with most degrees conferred:* business, communication, education.	
	Grads pursuing further study	16%		

Majors Accounting, art education, art/fine arts, biology/biological sciences, business, business economics, business education, chemistry, communication, computer science, criminal justice, (pre)dentistry sequence, economics, education, elementary education, English, finance/banking, history, (pre)law sequence, liberal arts/general studies, management information systems, mathematics, (pre)medicine sequence, modern languages, music, music education, natural sciences, philosophy, physical education, physics, political science/government, psychology, radio and television studies, science, science education, secondary education, social science, social work, sociology, Spanish, special education, theater arts/drama, (pre)veterinary medicine sequence.

Applying *Required:* high school transcript, 1 recommendation, SAT or ACT. *Recommended:* 3 years of high school math and science, some high school foreign language. Interview required for some. *Application deadlines:* 5/1, 3/1 priority date for financial aid. *Contact:* Ms. Joanne Loonan, Director of Admissions, 610 West Fourth Street, Storm Lake, IA 50588, 712-749-2235 or toll-free 800-383-9600.

* Butler University

Indianapolis, Indiana

Founded 1855
Urban setting
Independent
Coed
Awards A, B, M

Enrollment	3,887 total; 2,792 undergraduates (631 freshmen)
Faculty	384 total; 214 full-time (78% have doctorate/terminal degree); student-faculty ratio is 13:1; grad assistants teach no undergraduate courses.
Libraries	280,074 bound volumes, 132,000 titles on microform, 2,203 periodical subscriptions
Computing	*Terminals/PCs available for student use:* 150, located in computer center, library, dormitories, classrooms, labs; PC not required.
Of Special Interest	*Core academic program:* yes. Computer course required. Sigma Xi chapter. Academic exchange with 6 members of the Consortium for Urban Education. Sponsors and participates in study-abroad programs. Cooperative Army ROTC, cooperative Air Force ROTC.
On Campus	Drama/theater group; student-run newspaper and radio station. *Social organizations:* 7 national fraternities, 7 national sororities, minority chapters; 43% of eligible undergraduate men and 38% of eligible undergraduate women are members.
Athletics	Member NCAA (Division I). *Intercollegiate sports:* baseball (M), basketball (M, W), crew (M, W), cross-country running (M, W), football (M), golf (M), lacrosse (M), soccer (M), softball (W), swimming and diving (M, W), tennis (M, W), track and field (M, W), volleyball (W). *Scholarships:* M, W.

Costs (1991–92) & Aid				
	Comprehensive fee	$14,410	Need-based scholarships (average)	$3429
	Tuition	$10,500	Non-need scholarships (average)	$3251
	Mandatory fees	$70	Short-term loans	N/Avail
	Room and board	$3840	Long-term loans—college funds (average)	$725
	Financial aid recipients	84%	Long-term loans—external funds (average)	$2611

Undergraduate Facts				
	Part-time	9%	*Freshman Data:* 2,059 applied, 87% were accepted, 35% (631) of those entered	
	State residents	73%		
	Transfers	10%	From top tenth of high school class	39%
	African-Americans	5%	SAT-takers scoring 600 or over on verbal	15%
	Native Americans	1%	SAT-takers scoring 700 or over on verbal	2%
	Hispanics	1%	SAT-takers scoring 600 or over on math	25%
	Asian-Americans	1%	SAT-takers scoring 700 or over on math	4%
	International students	1%	ACT-takers scoring 26 or over	N/R
	Freshmen returning for sophomore year	84%	ACT-takers scoring 30 or over	N/R
	Students completing degree within 5 years	60%	*Majors with most degrees conferred:* pharmacy/pharmaceutical sciences, elementary education, marketing/retailing/merchandising.	
	Grads pursuing further study	10%		

Majors Accounting, actuarial science, American studies, arts administration, biology/biological sciences, broadcasting, business, business economics, chemistry, communication, computer science, dance, early childhood education, ecology/environmental studies, economics, education, elementary education, English, environmental sciences, finance/banking, French, German, history, international studies, journalism, Latin, (pre)law sequence, marketing/retailing/merchandising, mathematics, medical technology, (pre)medicine sequence, modern languages, music, music business, music education, pharmacy/pharmaceutical sciences, philosophy, physical education, physics, piano/organ, political science/government, psychology, radio and television studies, religious studies, Romance languages, science education, secondary education, social science, sociology, Spanish, special education, speech pathology and audiology, speech/rhetoric/public address/debate, stringed instruments, telecommunications, theater arts/drama, voice, wind and percussion instruments.

Applying *Required:* essay, high school transcript, 3 years of high school math, 2 years of high school foreign language, SAT or ACT. 3 years of high school science, campus interview, audition required for some. *Application deadlines:* rolling, 9/15 for early action, continuous to 3/1 for financial aid. *Contact:* Mr. Richard Boyden, Dean of Admissions, 4600 Sunset Avenue, Indianapolis, IN 46208, 317-283-9255 or toll-free 800-348-5358 (in-state), 800-368-6852 (out-of-state).

From the College The Institute for Study Abroad, which also serves other students across the nation, is headquartered on the Butler University campus. Through the institute, students may take advantage of study-abroad opportunities in Australia, England, Ireland, New Zealand, and Scotland as well as fifty other countries throughout the world.

California Institute of Technology

Pasadena, California

Founded 1891
Suburban setting
Independent
Coed
Awards B, M, D

Enrollment	1,934 total; 853 undergraduates (225 freshmen)
Faculty	270 total; student-faculty ratio is 3:1; grad assistants teach no undergraduate courses.
Libraries	455,500 bound volumes, 6,370 periodical subscriptions
Computing	*Terminals/PCs available for student use:* N/R; PC not required. Campus network links student PCs.
Of Special Interest	*Core academic program:* yes. Computer course required. Sigma Xi chapter. Academic exchange with Occidental College, Scripps College, Art Center College of Design. Study-abroad programs: no. Cooperative Army ROTC, cooperative Air Force ROTC.
On Campus	Drama/theater group; student-run newspaper. No national or local fraternities or sororities on campus.
Athletics	Member NCAA (Division III). *Intercollegiate sports:* basketball (M), cross-country running (M, W), fencing (M, W), football (M), golf (M, W), ice hockey (M), sailing (M, W), soccer (M, W), swimming and diving (M, W), tennis (M, W), track and field (M, W), volleyball (W), water polo (M, W), wrestling (M).

Costs (1991–92) & Aid				
	Comprehensive fee	$18,643	Need-based scholarships (average)	$9000
	Tuition	$14,100	Non-need scholarships (average)	$9800
	Mandatory fees	$210	Short-term loans (average)	$600
	Room and board	$4333	Long-term loans—college funds (average)	$2500
	Financial aid recipients	70%	Long-term loans—external funds (average)	$2112

Undergraduate Facts				
	Part-time	0%	*Freshman Data:* 1,800 applied, 30% were accepted, 42% (225) of those entered	
	State residents	30%		
	Transfers	9%	From top tenth of high school class	100%
	African-Americans	2%	SAT-takers scoring 600 or over on verbal	84%
	Native Americans	0%	SAT-takers scoring 700 or over on verbal	21%
	Hispanics	4%	SAT-takers scoring 600 or over on math	100%
	Asian-Americans	23%	SAT-takers scoring 700 or over on math	93%
	International students	10%	ACT-takers scoring 26 or over	N/App
	Freshmen returning for sophomore year	94%	ACT-takers scoring 30 or over	N/App
	Students completing degree within 5 years	74%	*Majors with most degrees conferred:* engineering and applied sciences, physical sciences, biochemistry.	
	Grads pursuing further study	50%		

Majors Aerospace engineering, applied mathematics, astronomy, astrophysics, biochemistry, biology/biological sciences, cell biology, chemical engineering, chemistry, civil engineering, computer science, economics, electrical engineering, engineering and applied sciences, engineering physics, environmental engineering, geology, geophysics, history, literature, materials sciences, mathematics, mechanical engineering, molecular biology, nuclear physics, physical sciences, physics, planetary and space sciences, social science.

Applying *Required:* essay, high school transcript, 4 years of high school math, 3 recommendations, SAT, 3 Achievements, English Composition Test. *Recommended:* 3 years of high school science. *Application deadlines:* 1/1, 10/15 for early decision, 2/1 priority date for financial aid. *Contact:* Dr. Carole Snow, Director of Admissions, 1201 East California Boulevard, Pasadena, CA 91125, 818-356-6341 or toll-free 800-568-8324.

Calvin College

Grand Rapids, Michigan

Founded 1876
Suburban setting
Independent/affiliated with Christian Reformed Church
Coed
Awards B, M

Enrollment 4,025 total; 3,841 undergraduates (862 freshmen)

Faculty 281 total; 242 full-time (83% have doctorate/terminal degree); student-faculty ratio is 16:1; grad assistants teach no undergraduate courses.

Libraries 550,798 bound volumes, 476,090 titles on microform, 2,830 periodical subscriptions

Computing *Terminals/PCs available for student use:* 220, located in computer center, student center, library, dormitories; PC not required. Campus network links student PCs.

Of Special Interest *Core academic program:* yes. Computer course required for business, math, sociology, psychology, engineering majors. Academic exchange with Christian College Coalition, Central College, Trinity Christian College, Au Sable Institute for Environmental Studies, Dordt College Oregon Extension. Sponsors and participates in study-abroad programs.

On Campus Drama/theater group; student-run newspaper and radio station. No national or local fraternities or sororities on campus.

Athletics Member NCAA (Division III). *Intercollegiate sports:* baseball (M), basketball (M, W), cross-country running (M, W), golf (M, W), ice hockey (M), soccer (M, W), softball (W), swimming and diving (M, W), tennis (M, W), track and field (M, W), volleyball (W).

Costs (1991–92) & Aid			
Comprehensive fee	$11,475	Need-based scholarships (average)	$1730
Tuition	$8100	Non-need scholarships (average)	$660
Mandatory fees	$25	Short-term loans (average)	$100
Room and board	$3350	Long-term loans—college funds (average)	$2220
Financial aid recipients	88%	Long-term loans—external funds (average)	$2580

Undergraduate Facts			
Part-time	5%	*Freshman Data:* 1,440 applied, 95% were accepted, 63% (862) of those entered	
State residents	55%		
Transfers	4%	From top tenth of high school class	31%
African-Americans	1%	SAT-takers scoring 600 or over on verbal	19%
Native Americans	1%	SAT-takers scoring 700 or over on verbal	2%
Hispanics	1%	SAT-takers scoring 600 or over on math	39%
Asian-Americans	2%	SAT-takers scoring 700 or over on math	14%
International students	8%	ACT-takers scoring 26 or over	38%
Freshmen returning for sophomore year	81%	ACT-takers scoring 30 or over	11%
Students completing degree within 5 years	60%	*Majors with most degrees conferred:* education, business, engineering (general).	
Grads pursuing further study	22%		

Majors Accounting, art education, art/fine arts, art history, biblical studies, biochemistry, biology/biological sciences, business, business economics, chemistry, civil engineering, classics, communication, computer science, criminal justice, (pre)dentistry sequence, economics, education, electrical engineering, elementary education, engineering (general), English, European studies, French, geography, geology, German, Germanic languages and literature, Greek, history, humanities, interdisciplinary studies, Latin, (pre)law sequence, liberal arts/general studies, literature, mathematics, mechanical engineering, medical technology, (pre)medicine sequence, music, music education, nursing, philosophy, physical education, physical sciences, physics, political science/government, psychology, recreation and leisure services, religious education, religious studies, sacred music, science, science education, secondary education, social science, social work, sociology, Spanish, special education, speech/rhetoric/public address/debate, telecommunications, theology, voice.

Applying *Required:* high school transcript, 1 recommendation, ACT. *Recommended:* 3 years of high school math and science, 2 years of high school foreign language. SAT required for some. *Application deadlines:* rolling, 2/15 priority date for financial aid. *Contact:* Mr. Thomas E. McWhertor, Director of Admissions, 3201 Burton Street, SE, Grand Rapids, MI 49546, 616-957-6106 or toll-free 800-748-0122.

Carleton College

Northfield, Minnesota

Founded 1866
Small-town setting
Independent
Coed
Awards B

Enrollment	1,700 total—all undergraduates (472 freshmen)
Faculty	166 total; 151 full-time (93% have doctorate/terminal degree); student-faculty ratio is 11:1.
Libraries	460,609 bound volumes, 17,328 titles on microform, 1,425 periodical subscriptions
Computing	*Terminals/PCs available for student use:* 143, located in computer center, library, labs, academic buildings; PC not required.
Of Special Interest	*Core academic program:* yes. Computer course required for chemistry, math majors. Phi Beta Kappa, Sigma Xi chapters. Academic exchange with St. Olaf College. Sponsors and participates in study-abroad programs.
On Campus	Drama/theater group; student-run newspaper and radio station. No national or local fraternities or sororities on campus.
Athletics	Member NCAA (Division III). *Intercollegiate sports:* baseball (M), basketball (M, W), cross-country running (M, W), fencing (M, W), field hockey (W), football (M), golf (M), gymnastics (W), ice hockey (M), lacrosse (M), rugby (M, W), skiing (cross-country) (M, W), skiing (downhill) (M, W), soccer (M, W), softball (W), swimming and diving (M, W), tennis (M, W), track and field (M, W), volleyball (M, W), water polo (M), wrestling (M).

Costs (1992–93 estimated) & Aid	Comprehensive fee	$20,895	Need-based scholarships (average)	$7048
	Tuition	$17,223	Non-need scholarships (average)	$908
	Mandatory fees	$132	Short-term loans	N/Avail
	Room and board	$3540	Long-term loans—college funds (average)	$2231
	Financial aid recipients	58%	Long-term loans—external funds (average)	$2497

Undergraduate Facts	Part-time	0%	*Freshman Data:* 2,507 applied, 57% were accepted, 33% (472) of those entered	
	State residents	25%		
	Transfers	2%	From top tenth of high school class	74%
	African-Americans	3%	SAT-takers scoring 600 or over on verbal	63%
	Native Americans	1%	SAT-takers scoring 700 or over on verbal	20%
	Hispanics	3%	SAT-takers scoring 600 or over on math	77%
	Asian-Americans	8%	SAT-takers scoring 700 or over on math	34%
	International students	1%	ACT-takers scoring 26 or over	84%
	Freshmen returning for sophomore year	96%	ACT-takers scoring 30 or over	38%
	Students completing degree within 5 years	88%	*Majors with most degrees conferred:* English, political science/government, history.	
	Grads pursuing further study	N/R		

Majors Anthropology, art history, Asian/Oriental studies, biology/biological sciences, chemistry, classics, computer science, ecology/environmental studies, economics, English, French, geology, German, Greek, history, Latin, Latin American studies, (pre)law sequence, mathematics, (pre)medicine sequence, music, philosophy, physics, political science/government, psychology, religious studies, Romance languages, Russian, Russian and Slavic studies, sociology, Spanish, studio art, women's studies.

Applying *Required:* essay, high school transcript, 3 years of high school math, 3 recommendations, SAT or ACT. *Recommended:* 3 years of high school science, 2 years of high school foreign language, interview, 3 Achievements, English Composition Test. *Application deadlines:* 2/1, 11/15 for early decision, 3/1 priority date for financial aid. *Contact:* Mr. Paul Thiboutot, Dean of Admissions, 100 South College Street, Northfield, MN 55057, 507-663-4190 or toll-free 800-533-0466 (out-of-state).

Carnegie Mellon University

Pittsburgh, Pennsylvania

Founded 1900
Suburban setting
Independent
Coed
Awards B, M, D

Enrollment 7,150 total; 4,286 undergraduates (1,177 freshmen)

Faculty 797 total; 540 full-time (86% have doctorate/terminal degree); student-faculty ratio is 9:1; grad assistants teach a few undergraduate courses.

Libraries 767,307 bound volumes, 591,699 titles on microform, 4,276 periodical subscriptions

Computing *Terminals/PCs available for student use:* 350, located in computer center, student center, library, dormitories; PC not required. Campus network links student PCs.

Of Special Interest *Core academic program:* yes. Computer course required for engineering, science, business, humanities, social science majors. Sigma Xi chapter. Academic exchange with members of the Pittsburgh Council on Higher Education. Sponsors and participates in study-abroad programs. Army ROTC, Naval ROTC, Air Force ROTC.

On Campus Drama/theater group; student-run newspaper and radio station. *Social organizations:* 14 national fraternities, 5 national sororities; 30% of eligible undergraduate men and 30% of eligible undergraduate women are members.

Athletics Member NCAA (Division III). *Intercollegiate sports:* baseball (M), basketball (M, W), crew (M, W), cross-country running (M, W), fencing (M, W), football (M), golf (M, W), ice hockey (M), lacrosse (M), rugby (M), soccer (M, W), softball (W), swimming and diving (M, W), tennis (M, W), track and field (M, W), volleyball (W).

Costs (1992–93 estimated) & Aid

Comprehensive fee	$21,210	
Tuition	$16,000	
Mandatory fees	$100	
Room and board	$5110	
Financial aid recipients	64%	
Need-based scholarships (average)	$9000	
Non-need scholarships (average)	$3000	
Short-term loans	N/Avail	
Long-term loans—college funds	N/Avail	
Long-term loans—external funds (average)	$3400	

Undergraduate Facts

Part-time	3%
State residents	30%
Transfers	8%
African-Americans	5%
Native Americans	1%
Hispanics	3%
Asian-Americans	23%
International students	6%
Freshmen returning for sophomore year	93%
Students completing degree within 5 years	68%
Grads pursuing further study	30%

Freshman Data: 6,995 applied, 65% were accepted, 26% (1,177) of those entered

From top tenth of high school class	58%
SAT-takers scoring 600 or over on verbal	29%
SAT-takers scoring 700 or over on verbal	3%
SAT-takers scoring 600 or over on math	75%
SAT-takers scoring 700 or over on math	32%
ACT-takers scoring 26 or over	N/R
ACT-takers scoring 30 or over	N/R

Majors with most degrees conferred: electrical engineering, mechanical engineering, mathematics.

Majors Accounting, applied art, applied mathematics, architecture, art/fine arts, behavioral sciences, biochemistry, bioengineering, biology/biological sciences, biomedical engineering, biomedical sciences, biophysics, business, business economics, cell biology, ceramic art and design, chemical engineering, chemistry, child psychology/child development, city/community/regional planning, civil engineering, clinical psychology, commercial art, communication, comparative literature, computer engineering, computer information systems, computer management, computer programming, computer science, creative writing, (pre)dentistry sequence, economics, electrical engineering, electronics engineering, engineering (general), engineering and applied sciences, engineering design, engineering management, engineering mechanics, engineering sciences, English, environmental engineering, environmental sciences, European studies, experimental psychology, finance/banking, French, genetics, German, Germanic languages and literature, graphic arts, Hispanic studies, history, humanities, illustration, industrial administration, industrial design, information science, jewelry and metalsmithing, journalism, labor and industrial relations, (pre)law sequence, liberal arts/general studies, linguistics, literature, management information systems, manufacturing engineering, marketing/retailing/merchandising, materials engineering, materials sciences, mathematics, mechanical engineering, (pre)medicine sequence, metallurgical engineering, metallurgy, microbiology, modern languages, molecular biology, music, music education, opera, operations research, painting/drawing, philosophy, physics, piano/organ, political science/government, polymer science, printing technologies, psychology, public administration, public affairs and policy studies, publishing, robotics, sculpture, social science, sociology, Spanish, speech/rhetoric/public address/debate, statistics, stringed instruments, studio art, systems engineering, systems science, technical writing, technology and public affairs, textile arts, theater arts/drama, toxicology, urban studies, (pre)veterinary medicine sequence, voice, Western civilization and culture, wind and percussion instruments.

Applying *Required:* essay, high school transcript, 1 recommendation, SAT or ACT, 3 Achievements, English Composition Test (with essay). *Recommended:* 2 years of high school foreign language, interview. 4 years of high school math and science, portfolio, audition required for some. *Application deadlines:* 2/1, 12/1 for early decision, 2/15 for financial aid. *Contact:* Mr. Michael Steidel, Director of Admissions, Warner Hall, Room 101. Pittsburgh, PA 15213, 412-268-2082.

Carroll College

Waukesha, Wisconsin

Founded 1846
Suburban setting
Independent, Presbyterian
Coed
Awards B, M (M offered only in education)

Enrollment 1,443 total; 1,365 undergraduates (241 freshmen)

Faculty 129 total; 87 full-time (80% have doctorate/terminal degree); student-faculty ratio is 15:1; grad assistants teach no undergraduate courses.

Libraries 184,590 bound volumes, 15,650 titles on microform, 574 periodical subscriptions

Computing *Terminals/PCs available for student use:* 125, located in computer center, student center, library, dormitories, classrooms; PC not required. Campus network links student PCs.

Of Special Interest *Core academic program:* yes. Computer course required for physics, business, accounting, math, economics majors. Academic exchange with American University (Washington Semester), Drew University (United Nations Semester). Sponsors and participates in study-abroad programs.

On Campus Drama/theater group; student-run newspaper and radio station. *Social organizations:* 3 national fraternities, 4 national sororities, 2 local fraternities; 30% of eligible undergraduate men and 25% of eligible undergraduate women are members.

Athletics Member NCAA (Division III). *Intercollegiate sports:* baseball (M), basketball (M, W), cross-country running (M, W), football (M), golf (M), soccer (M, W), swimming and diving (M, W), tennis (M, W), track and field (M, W), volleyball (W), weight lifting (M, W), wrestling (M).

Costs (1991–92) & Aid				
	Comprehensive fee	$14,628	Need-based scholarships (average)	$3381
	Tuition	$10,960	Non-need scholarships (average)	$2839
	Mandatory fees	$108	Short-term loans (average)	$100
	Room and board	$3560	Long-term loans—college funds	N/Avail
	Financial aid recipients	90%	Long-term loans—external funds (average)	$2569

Undergraduate Facts				
	Part-time	0%	*Freshman Data:* 727 applied, 89% were accepted, 37% (241) of those entered	
	State residents	88%		
	Transfers	7%	From top tenth of high school class	26%
	African-Americans	3%	SAT-takers scoring 600 or over on verbal	N/R
	Native Americans	0%	SAT-takers scoring 700 or over on verbal	N/R
	Hispanics	3%	SAT-takers scoring 600 or over on math	N/R
	Asian-Americans	2%	SAT-takers scoring 700 or over on math	N/R
	International students	1%	ACT-takers scoring 26 or over	27%
	Freshmen returning for sophomore year	76%	ACT-takers scoring 30 or over	9%
	Students completing degree within 5 years	58%	*Majors with most degrees conferred:* nursing, business, communication.	
	Grads pursuing further study	7%		

Majors Accounting, applied art, art education, art/fine arts, biology/biological sciences, business, chemistry, clinical psychology, commercial art, communication, computer information systems, computer science, creative writing, criminal justice, (pre)dentistry sequence, early childhood education, ecology/environmental studies, economics, education, elementary education, English, environmental biology, environmental sciences, finance/banking, French, geography, German, health education, history, human resources, interdisciplinary studies, international studies, journalism, land use management and reclamation, (pre)law sequence, liberal arts/general studies, literature, management information systems, marketing/retailing/merchandising, mathematics, medical technology, (pre)medicine sequence, museum studies, music, music business, music education, natural sciences, nursing, pharmacy/pharmaceutical sciences, philosophy, physical education, physical fitness/human movement, physics, piano/organ, political science/government, psychology, religious studies, robotics, science education, secondary education, social work, sociology, Spanish, studio art, theater arts/drama, theology, (pre)veterinary medicine sequence, veterinary sciences, voice.

Applying *Required:* high school transcript, 1 recommendation, SAT or ACT. *Recommended:* 3 years of high school math and science, some high school foreign language, interview. Essay required for some. *Application deadlines:* rolling, 3/15 priority date for financial aid. *Contact:* Mr. Ken Moyer, Director of Admissions, 100 North East Avenue, Waukesha, WI 53186, 414-524-7223 or toll-free 800-CARROLL (in-state), 800-547-1233 (out-of-state).

Case Western Reserve University

Cleveland, Ohio

Founded 1826
Urban setting
Independent
Coed
Awards B, M, D

Enrollment 8,758 total; 3,227 undergraduates (646 freshmen)

Faculty 1,725 total; 1,678 full-time (97% have doctorate/terminal degree); student-faculty ratio is 8:1; grad assistants teach a few undergraduate courses.

Libraries 1.7 million bound volumes, 15,311 periodical subscriptions

Computing *Terminals/PCs available for student use:* 200, located in computer center, library, dormitories; PC not required but available for purchase. Campus network links student PCs.

Of Special Interest *Core academic program:* yes. Computer course required for engineering, math, science, accounting, management, some liberal arts majors. Phi Beta Kappa, Sigma Xi chapters. Academic exchange with Cleveland Institute of Art, Cleveland Institute of Music, 11 other Ohio institutions. Sponsors and participates in study-abroad programs. Cooperative Army ROTC, cooperative Air Force ROTC.

On Campus Drama/theater group; student-run newspaper and radio station. *Social organizations:* 18 national fraternities, 3 national sororities, 1 local sorority; 40% of eligible undergraduate men and 20% of eligible undergraduate women are members.

Athletics Member NCAA (Division III). *Intercollegiate sports:* archery (M, W), baseball (M), basketball (M, W), cross-country running (M, W), fencing (M, W), football (M), golf (M), ice hockey (M), lacrosse (M), soccer (M, W), swimming and diving (M, W), tennis (M, W), track and field (M, W), volleyball (M, W), water polo (M), wrestling (M).

Costs (1992–93) & Aid				
	Comprehensive fee	$19,725	Need-based scholarships (average)	$7522
	Tuition	$14,500	Non-need scholarships (average)	$6130
	Mandatory fees	$115	Short-term loans (average)	$150
	Room and board	$5110	Long-term loans—college funds (average)	$1589
	Financial aid recipients	71%	Long-term loans—external funds	Avail

Undergraduate Facts				
	Part-time	17%	*Freshman Data:* 2,992 applied, 77% were accepted, 28% (646) of those entered	
	State residents	60%		
	Transfers	17%	From top tenth of high school class	68%
	African-Americans	8%	SAT-takers scoring 600 or over on verbal	37%
	Native Americans	1%	SAT-takers scoring 700 or over on verbal	7%
	Hispanics	1%	SAT-takers scoring 600 or over on math	75%
	Asian-Americans	14%	SAT-takers scoring 700 or over on math	36%
	International students	9%	ACT-takers scoring 26 or over	73%
	Freshmen returning for sophomore year	93%	ACT-takers scoring 30 or over	32%
	Students completing degree within 5 years	67%	*Majors with most degrees conferred:* electrical engineering, mechanical engineering, psychology.	
	Grads pursuing further study	33%		

Majors Accounting, aerospace engineering, American studies, anthropology, applied mathematics, art education, art history, Asian/Oriental studies, astronomy, audio engineering, biochemistry, biology/biological sciences, biomedical engineering, business, chemical engineering, chemistry, civil engineering, classics, communication, comparative literature, computer engineering, computer science, (pre)dentistry sequence, dietetics, earth science, economics, electrical engineering, engineering (general), English, environmental sciences, finance/banking, fluid and thermal sciences, French, geology, gerontology, Greek, history, history of science, industrial engineering, Latin, (pre)law sequence, literature, management information systems, materials engineering, materials sciences, mathematics, mechanical engineering, medical technology, (pre)medicine sequence, metallurgy, music, music education, music therapy, natural sciences, nursing, nutrition, operations research, philosophy, physics, political science/government, polymer science, psychology, religious studies, secondary education, sociology, speech pathology and audiology, statistics, systems engineering, theater arts/drama, (pre)veterinary medicine sequence.

Applying *Required:* essay, high school transcript, 3 years of high school math, 1 recommendation, SAT or ACT. *Recommended:* 3 years of high school science, 2 years of high school foreign language, interview, 3 Achievements, English Composition Test (with essay). 3 Achievements, English Composition Test required for some. *Application deadlines:* 2/15, 1/15 for early decision, 2/1 priority date for financial aid. *Contact:* Mr. William T. Conley, Dean of Undergraduate Admissions, Tomlinson Hall, 10900 Euclid Avenue, Cleveland, OH 44106, 216-368-4450 or toll-free 800-967-8898.

Catholic University of America

Washington, District of Columbia

Founded 1887
Urban setting
Independent/affiliated with Roman Catholic Church
Coed
Awards B, M, D

Enrollment	6,632 total; 2,876 undergraduates (569 freshmen)
Faculty	706 total; 410 full-time (90% have doctorate/terminal degree); student-faculty ratio is 12:1; grad assistants teach a few undergraduate courses.
Libraries	1.2 million bound volumes, 730,000 titles on microform, 8,100 periodical subscriptions
Computing	*Terminals/PCs available for student use:* 109, located in computer center, dormitories; PC not required. Campus network links student PCs.
Of Special Interest	*Core academic program:* yes. Phi Beta Kappa, Sigma Xi chapters. Academic exchange with members of the Consortium of Universities of the Washington Metropolitan Area. Sponsors and participates in study-abroad programs. Cooperative Army ROTC, cooperative Naval ROTC, cooperative Air Force ROTC.
On Campus	Drama/theater group; student-run newspaper and radio station. *Social organizations:* 1 local fraternity, 1 local sorority; 1% of eligible undergraduate men and 1% of eligible undergraduate women are members.
Athletics	Member NCAA (Division III). *Intercollegiate sports:* basketball (M, W), cross-country running (M, W), field hockey (W), football (M), lacrosse (M), soccer (M, W), swimming and diving (M, W), tennis (M, W), track and field (M, W), volleyball (W).

Costs (1991–92) & Aid				
	Comprehensive fee	$17,772	Need-based scholarships (average)	$5350
	Tuition	$11,626	Non-need scholarships (average)	$11,626
	Mandatory fees	$310	Short-term loans (average)	$400
	Room and board	$5836	Long-term loans—college funds (average)	$2500
	Financial aid recipients	65%	Long-term loans—external funds (average)	$2480

Undergraduate Facts				
	Part-time	7%	*Freshman Data:* 1,835 applied, 91% were accepted, 34% (569) of those entered	
	State residents	4%		
	Transfers	23%	From top tenth of high school class	25%
	African-Americans	5%	SAT-takers scoring 600 or over on verbal	15%
	Native Americans	0%	SAT-takers scoring 700 or over on verbal	1%
	Hispanics	5%	SAT-takers scoring 600 or over on math	22%
	Asian-Americans	3%	SAT-takers scoring 700 or over on math	1%
	International students	8%	ACT-takers scoring 26 or over	N/R
	Freshmen returning for sophomore year	81%	ACT-takers scoring 30 or over	N/R
	Students completing degree within 5 years	63%		
	Grads pursuing further study	75%		

Majors Accounting, anthropology, architectural engineering, architecture, art education, art/fine arts, art history, biochemistry, biology/biological sciences, biomedical engineering, biophysics, business, chemistry, civil engineering, classics, computer engineering, computer science, construction engineering, construction management, economics, education, electrical engineering, elementary education, engineering (general), English, finance/banking, French, German, Greek, history, international economics, international studies, Latin, mathematics, mechanical engineering, medical technology, (pre)medicine sequence, modern languages, music, music education, nursing, philosophy, physics, piano/organ, political science/government, psychology, religious studies, secondary education, social work, sociology, Spanish, studio art, theater arts/drama, theology, voice, wind and percussion instruments.

Applying *Required:* essay, high school transcript, 3 years of high school math, 2 years of high school foreign language, 1 recommendation, SAT or ACT, 3 Achievements. *Recommended:* 3 years of high school science, interview, English Composition Test (with essay). *Application deadlines:* 2/15, 11/15 for early action, 2/15 for financial aid. *Contact:* Mr. Robert J. Talbot, Dean, Admissions and Financial Aid, 620 Michigan Avenue, NE, Washington, DC 20064, 202-319-5305.

From the College CUA's emphasis on the liberal arts helps students become conceptual, critical thinkers. Therefore, employers look to CUA students when filling top internships. CUA students work in Washington, D.C., congressional offices, executive agencies, professional organizations, research institutes, lobbying groups, and media. Overseas programs include internships with the British and Irish parliaments.

Centenary College of Louisiana

Shreveport, Louisiana

Founded 1825
Suburban setting
Independent, Methodist
Coed
Awards B, M

Enrollment 948 total; 794 undergraduates (195 freshmen)

Faculty 102 total; 72 full-time (86% have doctorate/terminal degree); student-faculty ratio is 11:1; grad assistants teach no undergraduate courses.

Libraries 165,000 bound volumes, 963 periodical subscriptions

Computing *Terminals/PCs available for student use:* 30, located in computer center, library, biology, chemistry labs, business center; PC not required.

Of Special Interest *Core academic program:* yes. Computer course required for business, math majors. Sigma Xi chapter. Academic exchange with Associated Colleges of the South. Sponsors and participates in study-abroad programs. Army ROTC.

On Campus Drama/theater group; student-run newspaper and radio station. *Social organizations:* 5 national fraternities, 2 national sororities; 30% of eligible undergraduate men and 30% of eligible undergraduate women are members.

Athletics Member NCAA (Division I). *Intercollegiate sports:* baseball (M), basketball (M), cross-country running (M, W), golf (M), gymnastics (W), riflery (M, W), soccer (M), softball (W), tennis (M, W), volleyball (W). *Scholarships:* M, W.

Costs (1991–92) & Aid				
	Comprehensive fee	$10,270	Need-based scholarships (average)	$962
	Tuition	$7000	Non-need scholarships (average)	$2070
	Mandatory fees	$210	Short-term loans	N/Avail
	Room and board	$3060	Long-term loans—college funds (average)	$1665
	Financial aid recipients	76%	Long-term loans—external funds (average)	$2875

Undergraduate Facts				
	Part-time	6%	*Freshman Data:* 421 applied, 83% were accepted, 56% (195) of those entered	
	State residents	60%		
	Transfers	9%	From top tenth of high school class	12%
	African-Americans	5%	SAT-takers scoring 600 or over on verbal	15%
	Native Americans	1%	SAT-takers scoring 700 or over on verbal	1%
	Hispanics	1%	SAT-takers scoring 600 or over on math	23%
	Asian-Americans	1%	SAT-takers scoring 700 or over on math	3%
	International students	2%	ACT-takers scoring 26 or over	42%
	Freshmen returning for sophomore year	87%	ACT-takers scoring 30 or over	9%
	Students completing degree within 5 years	66%		
	Grads pursuing further study	30%		

Majors Accounting, art/fine arts, arts administration, biochemistry, biology/biological sciences, business, business economics, chemistry, communication, computer science, (pre)dentistry sequence, early childhood education, economics, education, elementary education, English, French, geology, health science, history, (pre)law sequence, liberal arts/general studies, mathematics, (pre)medicine sequence, military science, music, music education, painting/drawing, philosophy, physical education, physical sciences, physical therapy, physics, piano/organ, political science/government, psychology, religious education, religious studies, sacred music, science education, secondary education, sociology, Spanish, speech/rhetoric/public address/debate, stringed instruments, studio art, theater arts/drama, (pre)veterinary medicine sequence, voice, wind and percussion instruments.

Applying *Required:* essay, high school transcript, recommendations, interview, SAT or ACT. *Recommended:* 3 years of high school math and science, some high school foreign language, 3 Achievements. *Application deadlines:* rolling, 3/15 priority date for financial aid. *Contact:* Ms. Caroline Kelsey, Director of Admissions, 2911 Centenary Boulevard, Shreveport, LA 71134, 318-869-5131.

From the College The Centenary Plan is a unique program that must be completed in order to receive a Centenary degree. It is composed of career explorations and internships; an intercultural experience, such as study in Europe; and a community service project, such as Habitat for Humanity.

Central University of Iowa

Pella, Iowa

Founded 1853
Small-town setting
Independent/affiliated with Reformed Church in America
Coed
Awards B

Enrollment	1,571 total—all undergraduates (417 freshmen)
Faculty	126 total; 82 full-time (86% have doctorate/terminal degree); student-faculty ratio is 15:1.
Libraries	164,827 bound volumes, 30,359 titles on microform, 925 periodical subscriptions
Computing	*Terminals/PCs available for student use:* 222, located in computer center, student center, library, dormitories, academic buildings; PC not required.
Of Special Interest	*Core academic program:* yes. Computer course required for math, systems management, business, biology, psychology majors. Academic exchange with Chicago Metro Program, The Washington Center. Sponsors and participates in study-abroad programs.
On Campus	Drama/theater group; student-run newspaper and radio station. *Social organizations:* 4 local fraternities, 2 local sororities; 7% of eligible undergraduate men and 4% of eligible undergraduate women are members.
Athletics	Member NCAA (Division III). *Intercollegiate sports:* baseball (M), basketball (M, W), cross-country running (M, W), football (M), golf (M, W), softball (W), tennis (M, W), track and field (M, W), volleyball (W), wrestling (M).

Costs (1992–93 estimated) & Aid				
	Comprehensive fee	$13,605	Need-based scholarships (average)	$4025
	Tuition	$9930	Non-need scholarships (average)	$3739
	Mandatory fees	$125	Short-term loans	N/Avail
	Room and board	$3550	Long-term loans—college funds	N/Avail
	Financial aid recipients	98%	Long-term loans—external funds (average)	$2228

Undergraduate Facts				
	Part-time	3%	*Freshman Data:* 1,239 applied, 88% were accepted, 38% (417) of those entered	
	State residents	77%		
	Transfers	12%	From top tenth of high school class	33%
	African-Americans	1%	SAT-takers scoring 600 or over on verbal	N/R
	Native Americans	0%	SAT-takers scoring 700 or over on verbal	N/R
	Hispanics	1%	SAT-takers scoring 600 or over on math	N/R
	Asian-Americans	2%	SAT-takers scoring 700 or over on math	N/R
	International students	3%	ACT-takers scoring 26 or over	N/R
	Freshmen returning for sophomore year	83%	ACT-takers scoring 30 or over	N/R
	Students completing degree within 5 years	70%	*Majors with most degrees conferred:* business, elementary education, liberal arts/general studies.	
	Grads pursuing further study	16%		

Majors Accounting, art education, art/fine arts, biology/biological sciences, business, chemistry, communication, computer science, (pre)dentistry sequence, economics, education, elementary education, English, environmental sciences, European studies, French, German, history, international business, international studies, Latin American studies, (pre)law sequence, liberal arts/general studies, linguistics, mathematics, (pre)medicine sequence, music, music education, philosophy, physical education, physics, political science/government, psychology, recreation and leisure services, religious studies, secondary education, sociology, Spanish, systems science, theater arts/drama, urban studies, (pre)veterinary medicine sequence.

Applying *Required:* high school transcript, SAT or ACT. *Recommended:* 3 years of high school math and science, 2 years of high school foreign language, interview. Essay, 3 recommendations required for some. *Application deadlines:* rolling, 4/1 priority date for financial aid. *Contact:* Mr. Eric Sickler, Director of Admission, 812 University Street, Pella, IA 50219, 515-628-5285 or toll-free 800-458-5503.

✱ Centre College

Danville, Kentucky

Founded 1819
Small-town setting
Independent/affiliated with Presbyterian Church
Coed
Awards B

Enrollment	880 total—all undergraduates (253 freshmen)
Faculty	89 total; 72 full-time (88% have doctorate/terminal degree); student-faculty ratio is 11:1.
Libraries	190,000 bound volumes, 30,000 titles on microform, 750 periodical subscriptions
Computing	*Terminals/PCs available for student use:* 80, located in computer center, student center, library, dormitories, classroom buildings; PC not required. Campus network links student PCs.
Of Special Interest	*Core academic program:* yes. Phi Beta Kappa chapter. Academic exchange with Associated Colleges of the South. Sponsors and participates in study-abroad programs. Cooperative Army ROTC.
On Campus	Drama/theater group; student-run newspaper. *Social organizations:* 6 national fraternities, 4 national sororities; 71% of eligible undergraduate men and 70% of eligible undergraduate women are members.
Athletics	Member NCAA (Division III). *Intercollegiate sports:* basketball (M, W), cross-country running (M, W), field hockey (W), football (M), golf (M), soccer (M, W), swimming and diving (M, W), tennis (M, W), track and field (M, W), volleyball (W).

Costs (1992–93) & Aid				
	Comprehensive fee	$14,955	Need-based scholarships (average)	$4515
	Tuition	$10,700	Non-need scholarships (average)	$3391
	Mandatory fees	$225	Short-term loans	N/Avail
	Room and board	$4030	Long-term loans—college funds (average)	$1770
	Financial aid recipients	52%	Long-term loans—external funds (average)	$2220

Undergraduate Facts				
	Part-time	1%	*Freshman Data:* 954 applied, 90% were accepted, 30% (253) of those entered	
	State residents	69%		
	Transfers	1%	From top tenth of high school class	65%
	African-Americans	2%	SAT-takers scoring 600 or over on verbal	N/R
	Native Americans	0%	SAT-takers scoring 700 or over on verbal	N/R
	Hispanics	1%	SAT-takers scoring 600 or over on math	N/R
	Asian-Americans	2%	SAT-takers scoring 700 or over on math	N/R
	International students	1%	ACT-takers scoring 26 or over	61%
	Freshmen returning for sophomore year	89%	ACT-takers scoring 30 or over	18%
	Students completing degree within 5 years	70%	*Majors with most degrees conferred:* English, economics, political science/government.	
	Grads pursuing further study	35%		

Majors Anthropology, art/fine arts, biochemistry, biology/biological sciences, chemistry, (pre)dentistry sequence, economics, elementary education, English, French, German, history, (pre)law sequence, mathematics, (pre)medicine sequence, molecular biology, music, philosophy, physics, political science/government, psychobiology, psychology, religious studies, sociology, Spanish, theater arts/drama.

Applying *Required:* essay, high school transcript, 4 years of high school math, 3 years of high school science, 1 recommendation, 2 years of high school social studies, SAT or ACT. *Recommended:* 2 years of high school foreign language, campus interview. *Application deadlines:* 3/1, 11/1 for early decision, 11/15 for early action, continuous to 3/15 for financial aid. *Contact:* Mr. John Rogers, Director of Admissions, 600 West Walnut Street, Danville, KY 40422, 606-238-5200.

Christian Brothers University

Memphis, Tennessee

Founded 1871
Urban setting
Independent, Roman Catholic
Coed
Awards B, M

Enrollment	1,736 total; 1,123 undergraduates (373 freshmen)
Faculty	149 total; 106 full-time (75% have doctorate/terminal degree); student-faculty ratio is 12:1; grad assistants teach no undergraduate courses.
Libraries	91,830 bound volumes, 4,000 titles on microform, 582 periodical subscriptions
Computing	*Terminals/PCs available for student use:* 127, located in computer center, classrooms, labs; PC not required. Campus network links student PCs.
Of Special Interest	*Core academic program:* yes. Computer course required for engineering, business, chemistry, math, physics, communications, performing arts, telecommunications majors. Academic exchange with Greater Memphis Consortium. Participates in study-abroad programs. Cooperative Army ROTC, cooperative Naval ROTC, cooperative Air Force ROTC.
On Campus	Drama/theater group; student-run newspaper. *Social organizations:* 4 national fraternities, 3 national sororities, 1 local fraternity, 2 local sororities, 25 social clubs; 60% of eligible undergraduate men and 60% of eligible undergraduate women are members.
Athletics	Member NAIA. *Intercollegiate sports:* baseball (M), basketball (M, W), soccer (M), softball (W), tennis (M, W), volleyball (W). *Scholarships:* M, W.

Costs (1991–92) & Aid				
	Comprehensive fee	$10,600	Need-based scholarships (average)	$2766
	Tuition	$7540	Non-need scholarships (average)	$2500
	Mandatory fees	$100	Short-term loans (average)	$2000
	Room and board	$2960	Long-term loans—college funds (average)	$1000
	Financial aid recipients	73%	Long-term loans—external funds (average)	$2625

Undergraduate Facts				
	Part-time	17%	*Freshman Data:* 855 applied, 77% were accepted, 56% (373) of those entered	
	State residents	77%		
	Transfers	7%	From top tenth of high school class	18%
	African-Americans	17%	SAT-takers scoring 600 or over on verbal	N/R
	Native Americans	1%	SAT-takers scoring 700 or over on verbal	N/R
	Hispanics	1%	SAT-takers scoring 600 or over on math	N/R
	Asian-Americans	3%	SAT-takers scoring 700 or over on math	N/R
	International students	4%	ACT-takers scoring 26 or over	31%
	Freshmen returning for sophomore year	73%	ACT-takers scoring 30 or over	8%
	Students completing degree within 5 years	46%	*Majors with most degrees conferred:* accounting, electrical engineering, business.	
	Grads pursuing further study	21%		

Majors Accounting, art/fine arts, biology/biological sciences, biomedical engineering, business, business economics, chemical engineering, chemistry, civil engineering, communication, computer information systems, computer science, construction engineering, (pre)dentistry sequence, economics, education, electrical engineering, elementary education, engineering physics, English, finance/banking, history, human development, humanities, journalism, (pre)law sequence, marketing/retailing/merchandising, mathematics, mechanical engineering, medical technology, (pre)medicine sequence, natural sciences, physics, psychology, secondary education, telecommunications, theater arts/drama.

Applying *Required:* high school transcript, SAT or ACT. *Recommended:* 3 years of high school math and science, some high school foreign language, interview. Essay, 2 recommendations required for some. *Application deadlines:* 7/1, 4/1 priority date for financial aid. *Contact:* Mr. Steven Pochard, Dean of Admissions, 650 East Parkway South, Memphis, TN 38104, 901-722-0210 or toll-free 800-288-7576.

Claremont McKenna College

Claremont, California

Founded 1946
Suburban setting
Independent
Coed
Awards B

Enrollment	852 total—all undergraduates (232 freshmen)
Faculty	107 total; 92 full-time (100% have doctorate/terminal degree); student-faculty ratio is 8:1.
Libraries	1.8 million bound volumes, 1 million titles on microform, 6,500 periodical subscriptions
Computing	*Terminals/PCs available for student use:* 75, located in computer center, research institutes; PC not required. Campus network links student PCs.
Of Special Interest	*Core academic program:* yes. Computer course required for government, information systems, physics, economics majors. Phi Beta Kappa, Sigma Xi chapters. Academic exchange with 5 members of The Claremont Colleges, Haverford College, Colby College, Spelman College. Sponsors and participates in study-abroad programs. Army ROTC, cooperative Naval ROTC, cooperative Air Force ROTC.
On Campus	Drama/theater group; student-run newspaper and radio station. No national or local fraternities or sororities on campus.
Athletics	Member NCAA (Division III). *Intercollegiate sports:* badminton (M, W), baseball (M), basketball (M, W), cross-country running (M, W), football (M), golf (M, W), lacrosse (M, W), rugby (M, W), skiing (downhill) (M, W), soccer (M, W), softball (W), swimming and diving (M, W), tennis (M, W), track and field (M, W), volleyball (M, W), water polo (M, W), wrestling (M).

Costs (1991–92) & Aid				
	Comprehensive fee	$19,990	Need-based scholarships (average)	$7498
	Tuition	$14,710	Non-need scholarships (average)	$2272
	Mandatory fees	$100	Short-term loans (average)	$350
	Room and board	$5180	Long-term loans—college funds (average)	$3563
	Financial aid recipients	75%	Long-term loans—external funds (average)	$2837

Undergraduate Facts				
	Part-time	0%	*Freshman Data:* 1,643 applied, 41% were accepted, 34% (232) of those entered	
	State residents	57%		
	Transfers	7%	From top tenth of high school class	63%
	African-Americans	5%	SAT-takers scoring 600 or over on verbal	55%
	Native Americans	1%	SAT-takers scoring 700 or over on verbal	8%
	Hispanics	10%	SAT-takers scoring 600 or over on math	78%
	Asian-Americans	13%	SAT-takers scoring 700 or over on math	26%
	International students	4%	ACT-takers scoring 26 or over	83%
	Freshmen returning for sophomore year	92%	ACT-takers scoring 30 or over	39%
	Students completing degree within 5 years	82%	*Majors with most degrees conferred:* economics, political science/government, international studies.	
	Grads pursuing further study	38%		

Majors Accounting, American studies, art/fine arts, Asian/Oriental studies, biochemistry, biology/biological sciences, black/African-American studies, chemistry, Chinese, classics, computer information systems, computer science, (pre)dentistry sequence, economics, English, environmental sciences, European studies, film studies, French, German, Greek, history, international studies, Italian, Japanese, Latin, Latin American studies, (pre)law sequence, legal studies, literature, management engineering, mathematics, (pre)medicine sequence, Mexican-American/Chicano studies, modern languages, music, philosophy, physics, political science/government, psychobiology, psychology, religious studies, Russian, Spanish, theater arts/drama, women's studies.

Applying *Required:* essay, high school transcript, 3 years of high school math, 2 years of high school foreign language, 2 recommendations, SAT or ACT. *Recommended:* 3 years of high school science, campus interview, 3 Achievements. *Application deadlines:* 2/1, 12/1 for early decision, 2/1 priority date for financial aid. *Contact:* Mr. Richard Vos, Vice-President/Dean of Admission and Financial Aid, 890 Columbia Avenue, Claremont, CA 91711, 714-621-8000.

From the College With a commitment to preparing students for responsible leadership in business, government, and the professions, CMC recognizes that environmental concerns are among the most important issues facing leaders today. The introduction of a new CMC major, the Environment, Economics and Politics, coincided with the opening of the $16.5-million Keck Science Center in December 1991.

Clarkson University

Potsdam, New York

Founded 1896
Small-town setting
Independent
Coed
Awards B, M, D

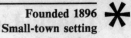

Enrollment 3,146 total; 2,776 undergraduates (637 freshmen)

Faculty 209 total; 188 full-time (92% have doctorate/terminal degree); student-faculty ratio is 16:1; grad assistants teach a few undergraduate courses.

Libraries 200,737 bound volumes, 243,602 titles on microform, 1,731 periodical subscriptions

Computing *Terminals/PCs available for student use:* 3,400, located in computer center, library, dormitories, classrooms; IBM PS 2 required for freshmen. All students participate in Clarkson's personal computer program.

Of Special Interest *Core academic program:* yes. Computer course required. Sigma Xi chapter. Academic exchange with Associated Colleges of the St. Lawrence Valley. Sponsors and participates in study-abroad programs. Army ROTC, Air Force ROTC.

On Campus Drama/theater group; student-run newspaper and radio station. *Social organizations:* 9 national fraternities, 3 national sororities, 5 local fraternities; 24% of eligible undergraduate men and 20% of eligible undergraduate women are members.

Athletics Member NCAA (Division III). *Intercollegiate sports:* baseball (M), basketball (M, W), cross-country running (M, W), golf (M), ice hockey (M), lacrosse (M, W), skiing (cross-country) (M), skiing (downhill) (M, W), soccer (M, W), swimming and diving (M, W), tennis (M, W), volleyball (W). *Scholarships:* M.

Costs (1991–92) & Aid				
	Comprehensive fee	$18,839	Need-based scholarships (average)	$3900
	Tuition	$13,380	Non-need scholarships (average)	$1250
	Mandatory fees	$295	Short-term loans	N/Avail
	Room and board	$5164	Long-term loans—college funds (average)	$1400
	Financial aid recipients	87%	Long-term loans—external funds (average)	$3100

Undergraduate Facts				
	Part-time	1%	*Freshman Data:* 2,545 applied, 88% were accepted, 28% (637) of those entered	
	State residents	75%		
	Transfers	15%	From top tenth of high school class	46%
	African-Americans	2%	SAT-takers scoring 600 or over on verbal	13%
	Native Americans	1%	SAT-takers scoring 700 or over on verbal	3%
	Hispanics	2%	SAT-takers scoring 600 or over on math	59%
	Asian-Americans	3%	SAT-takers scoring 700 or over on math	11%
	International students	3%	ACT-takers scoring 26 or over	N/R
	Freshmen returning for sophomore year	82%	ACT-takers scoring 30 or over	N/R
	Students completing degree within 5 years	76%	*Majors with most degrees conferred:* electrical engineering, mechanical engineering, civil engineering.	
	Grads pursuing further study	10%		

Majors Accounting, aerospace engineering, applied mathematics, biochemistry, biology/biological sciences, business, business economics, cell biology, chemical engineering, chemistry, civil engineering, computer engineering, computer information systems, computer management, computer science, economics, electrical engineering, engineering (general), engineering management, engineering sciences, environmental engineering, environmental health sciences, finance/banking, history, humanities, industrial engineering, interdisciplinary studies, (pre)law sequence, liberal arts/general studies, management engineering, management information systems, manufacturing engineering, marketing/retailing/merchandising, materials engineering, mathematics, mechanical engineering, (pre)medicine sequence, microbiology, occupational safety and health, operations research, physics, political science/government, psychology, social science, surveying engineering, technical writing, toxicology.

Applying *Required:* high school transcript, 3 years of high school math, 1 recommendation, SAT or ACT. *Recommended:* campus interview, Achievements, English Composition Test. 3 years of high school science required for some. *Application deadlines:* 3/15, 12/1 for early decision, 2/15 for financial aid. *Contact:* Mr. Dale Montague, Dean of Admissions and Financial Aid, Holcroft House, Potsdam, NY 13699, 315-268-6463 or toll-free 800-527-6577 (in-state), 800-527-6578 (out-of-state).

✱ Clark University

Worcester, Massachusetts

Founded 1887
Urban setting
Independent
Coed
Awards B, M, D

Enrollment 2,885 total; 2,151 undergraduates (564 freshmen)

Faculty 172 full-time (97% have doctorate/terminal degree); student-faculty ratio is 12:1; grad assistants teach a few undergraduate courses.

Libraries 507,000 bound volumes, 60,000 titles on microform, 2,166 periodical subscriptions

Computing *Terminals/PCs available for student use:* 100, located in computer center, library, academic buildings; PC not required but available for purchase. Campus network links student PCs.

Of Special Interest *Core academic program:* yes. Computer course required for some majors. Phi Beta Kappa chapter. Academic exchange with Worcester Consortium for Higher Education. Sponsors and participates in study-abroad programs. Cooperative Army ROTC, cooperative Air Force ROTC.

On Campus Drama/theater group; student-run newspaper. No national or local fraternities or sororities on campus.

Athletics Member NCAA (Division III). *Intercollegiate sports:* baseball (M), basketball (M, W), crew (M, W), cross-country running (M, W), field hockey (W), golf (M), lacrosse (M), soccer (M, W), softball (W), swimming and diving (M, W), tennis (M, W), track and field (M, W), volleyball (W).

Costs (1991–92) & Aid				
	Comprehensive fee	$19,880	Need-based scholarships (average)	$8082
	Tuition	$15,000	Non-need scholarships (average)	$5000
	Mandatory fees	$380	Short-term loans	N/Avail
	Room and board	$4500	Long-term loans—college funds (average)	$5069
	Financial aid recipients	43%	Long-term loans—external funds (average)	$2953

Undergraduate Facts				
	Part-time	1%	*Freshman Data:* 2,731 applied, 75% were accepted, 28% (564) of those entered	
	State residents	30%		
	Transfers	11%	From top tenth of high school class	32%
	African-Americans	2%	SAT-takers scoring 600 or over on verbal	N/R
	Native Americans	N/R	SAT-takers scoring 700 or over on verbal	N/R
	Hispanics	2%	SAT-takers scoring 600 or over on math	N/R
	Asian-Americans	5%	SAT-takers scoring 700 or over on math	N/R
	International students	12%	ACT-takers scoring 26 or over	N/R
	Freshmen returning for sophomore year	87%	ACT-takers scoring 30 or over	N/R
	Students completing degree within 5 years	N/R	*Majors with most degrees conferred:* psychology, international studies, economics.	
	Grads pursuing further study	28%		

Majors Art/fine arts, art history, biochemistry, biology/biological sciences, business, chemistry, classics, comparative literature, computer science, (pre)dentistry sequence, ecology/environmental studies, economics, English, environmental sciences, film studies, French, geography, German, history, interdisciplinary studies, international studies, (pre)law sequence, literature, mathematics, (pre)medicine sequence, molecular biology, music, philosophy, physics, political science/government, psychology, Romance languages, sociology, Spanish, studio art, theater arts/drama, (pre)veterinary medicine sequence.

Applying *Required:* essay, high school transcript, SAT or ACT, English Composition Test. *Recommended:* 3 years of high school math and science, 2 years of high school foreign language, 2 recommendations, interview, 3 Achievements, English Composition Test (with essay). *Application deadlines:* 2/15, 12/1 for early decision, continuous to 2/1 for financial aid. *Contact:* Mr. Richard W. Pierson, Dean of Admissions, Admissions House, 950 Main Street, Worcester, MA 01610-1477, 508-793-7431.

Coe College

Cedar Rapids, Iowa

Founded 1851
Urban setting
Independent/affiliated with Presbyterian Church
Coed
Awards B

Enrollment	1,248 total—all undergraduates (220 freshmen)
Faculty	113 total; 82 full-time (85% have doctorate/terminal degree); student-faculty ratio is 12:1.
Libraries	176,000 bound volumes, 34,941 titles on microform, 837 periodical subscriptions
Computing	*Terminals/PCs available for student use:* 80, located in computer center, library, personal computer lab; PC not required. Campus network links student PCs.
Of Special Interest	*Core academic program:* yes. Computer course required for physics majors. Phi Beta Kappa chapter. Academic exchange with University of Iowa, Mount Mercy College, Associated Colleges of the Midwest. Sponsors and participates in study-abroad programs. Cooperative Army ROTC.
On Campus	Drama/theater group; student-run newspaper. *Social organizations:* 4 national fraternities, 3 national sororities; 30% of eligible undergraduate men and 30% of eligible undergraduate women are members.
Athletics	Member NCAA (Division III). *Intercollegiate sports:* baseball (M), basketball (M, W), cross-country running (M, W), football (M), golf (M), soccer (M, W), softball (W), swimming and diving (M, W), tennis (M, W), track and field (M, W), volleyball (W), wrestling (M).

Costs (1992–93 estimated) & Aid				
	Comprehensive fee	$15,510	Need-based scholarships (average)	$3955
	Tuition	$11,200	Non-need scholarships (average)	$2820
	Mandatory fees	$125	Short-term loans	N/Avail
	Room and board	$4185	Long-term loans—college funds (average)	$2010
	Financial aid recipients	85%	Long-term loans—external funds (average)	$2875

Undergraduate Facts				
	Part-time	21%	*Freshman Data:* 820 applied, 78% were accepted, 34% (220) of those entered	
	State residents	58%		
	Transfers	9%	From top tenth of high school class	28%
	African-Americans	3%	SAT-takers scoring 600 or over on verbal	16%
	Native Americans	1%	SAT-takers scoring 700 or over on verbal	3%
	Hispanics	1%	SAT-takers scoring 600 or over on math	31%
	Asian-Americans	1%	SAT-takers scoring 700 or over on math	3%
	International students	8%	ACT-takers scoring 26 or over	36%
	Freshmen returning for sophomore year	83%	ACT-takers scoring 30 or over	10%
	Students completing degree within 5 years	65%		
	Grads pursuing further study	25%		

Majors Accounting, American studies, applied art, art education, art/fine arts, art history, Asian/Oriental studies, biology/biological sciences, black/African-American studies, business, chemistry, classics, computer science, (pre)dentistry sequence, economics, education, elementary education, English, French, German, history, interdisciplinary studies, (pre)law sequence, liberal arts/general studies, literature, mathematics, medical technology, (pre)medicine sequence, music, music education, nursing, philosophy, physical education, physical sciences, physics, political science/government, psychology, religious studies, science, science education, secondary education, sociology, Spanish, studio art, theater arts/drama.

Applying *Required:* essay, high school transcript, 1 recommendation, SAT or ACT. *Recommended:* 3 years of high school math and science, some high school foreign language, interview, 2 Achievements. *Application deadlines:* rolling, 12/1 for early decision, 3/1 priority date for financial aid. *Contact:* Mr. Michael White, Dean of Admissions and Financial Aid, 1220 1st Avenue, NE, Cedar Rapids, IA 52402, 319-399-8500 or toll-free 800-332-8404.

Colby College

Waterville, Maine

Founded 1813
Small-town setting
Independent
Coed
Awards B

Enrollment 1,716 total—all undergraduates (459 freshmen)

Faculty 173 total; 140 full-time (93% have doctorate/terminal degree); student-faculty ratio is 10:1.

Libraries 435,650 bound volumes, 214,350 titles on microform, 2,114 periodical subscriptions

Computing *Terminals/PCs available for student use:* 90, located in computer center, student center, library, science complex; PC not required. Campus network links student PCs.

Of Special Interest *Core academic program:* yes. Computer course required for some majors. Phi Beta Kappa chapter. Academic exchange with Pomona College, Pitzer College, Howard University, Claremont McKenna College, Scripps College, Boston University (Sea Semester), American University (Washington Semester), Williams College (Mystic Seaport Program). Sponsors and participates in study-abroad programs. Cooperative Army ROTC, cooperative Air Force ROTC.

On Campus Drama/theater group; student-run newspaper and radio station. No national or local fraternities or sororities on campus.

Athletics Member NCAA (Division III). *Intercollegiate sports:* baseball (M), basketball (M, W), crew (M, W), cross-country running (M, W), field hockey (W), football (M), golf (M, W), ice hockey (M, W), lacrosse (M, W), rugby (M, W), sailing (M, W), skiing (cross-country) (M, W), skiing (downhill) (M, W), soccer (M, W), softball (W), squash (M, W), swimming and diving (M, W), tennis (M, W), track and field (M, W), volleyball (M, W), water polo (M, W).

Costs (1991–92) & Aid				
	Comprehensive fee	$21,810	Need-based scholarships (average)	$10,320
	Tuition	$15,710	Non-need scholarships	N/Avail
	Mandatory fees	$750	Short-term loans (average)	$200
	Room and board	$5350	Long-term loans—college funds (average)	$910
	Financial aid recipients	70%	Long-term loans—external funds (average)	$2195

Undergraduate Facts				
	Part-time	2%	*Freshman Data:* 3,033 applied, 47% were accepted, 32% (459) of those entered	
	State residents	13%		
	Transfers	3%	From top tenth of high school class	50%
	African-Americans	2%	SAT-takers scoring 600 or over on verbal	N/R
	Native Americans	1%	SAT-takers scoring 700 or over on verbal	N/R
	Hispanics	2%	SAT-takers scoring 600 or over on math	N/R
	Asian-Americans	4%	SAT-takers scoring 700 or over on math	N/R
	International students	4%	ACT-takers scoring 26 or over	N/R
	Freshmen returning for sophomore year	94%	ACT-takers scoring 30 or over	N/R
	Students completing degree within 5 years	87%	*Majors with most degrees conferred:* political science/government, English, economics.	
	Grads pursuing further study	19%		

Majors American studies, anthropology, art/fine arts, art history, Asian/Oriental studies, biochemistry, biology/biological sciences, business, chemistry, classics, computer science, East Asian studies, economics, English, environmental sciences, French, geology, German, history, international studies, mathematics, music, philosophy, physics, political science/government, psychology, religious studies, Russian and Slavic studies, sociology, Spanish, theater arts/drama.

Applying *Required:* essay, high school transcript, 2 recommendations, SAT or ACT, 3 Achievements, English Composition Test. *Recommended:* 3 years of high school math and science, 3 years of high school foreign language, interview. *Application deadlines:* 1/15, 11/15 for early decision, 2/1 priority date for financial aid. *Contact:* Mr. Parker J. Beverage, Dean of Admissions and Financial Aid, 150 Mayflower Hill Drive, Waterville, ME 04901, 207-872-3168 or toll-free 800-723-3032.

Colgate University

Hamilton, New York

Founded 1819
Rural setting
Independent
Coed
Awards B, M

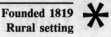

Enrollment	2,720 total; 2,705 undergraduates (695 freshmen)
Faculty	273 total; 197 full-time (94% have doctorate/terminal degree); student-faculty ratio is 11:1; grad assistants teach no undergraduate courses.
Libraries	489,266 bound volumes, 318,507 titles on microform, 2,583 periodical subscriptions
Computing	*Terminals/PCs available for student use:* 250, located in computer center, student center, library, various academic departments; PC not required. Campus network links student PCs.
Of Special Interest	*Core academic program:* yes. Computer course required for math majors. Phi Beta Kappa chapter. Academic exchange with New York State Visiting Student Program. Sponsors and participates in study-abroad programs.
On Campus	Drama/theater group; student-run newspaper and radio station. *Social organizations:* 8 national fraternities, 5 national sororities, 1 local fraternity; 37% of eligible undergraduate men and 32% of eligible undergraduate women are members.
Athletics	Member NCAA (Division I). *Intercollegiate sports:* baseball (M), basketball (M, W), crew (M, W), cross-country running (M, W), field hockey (W), football (M), golf (M), ice hockey (M, W), lacrosse (M, W), rugby (M, W), sailing (M, W), skiing (downhill) (M, W), soccer (M, W), softball (W), squash (M, W), swimming and diving (M, W), table tennis (M, W), tennis (M, W), track and field (M, W), volleyball (M, W), water polo (M).

Costs (1991–92) & Aid				
	Comprehensive fee	$21,220	Need-based scholarships (average)	$10,890
	Tuition	$16,012	Non-need scholarships	N/Avail
	Mandatory fees	$138	Short-term loans (average)	$275
	Room and board	$5070	Long-term loans—college funds	N/Avail
	Financial aid recipients	69%	Long-term loans—external funds (average)	$2500

Undergraduate Facts				
	Part-time	1%	*Freshman Data:* 5,193 applied, 44% were accepted, 30% (695) of those entered	
	State residents	36%		
	Transfers	1%	From top tenth of high school class	44%
	African-Americans	5%	SAT-takers scoring 600 or over on verbal	34%
	Native Americans	0%	SAT-takers scoring 700 or over on verbal	3%
	Hispanics	2%	SAT-takers scoring 600 or over on math	73%
	Asian-Americans	6%	SAT-takers scoring 700 or over on math	17%
	International students	4%	ACT-takers scoring 26 or over	99%
	Freshmen returning for sophomore year	96%	ACT-takers scoring 30 or over	32%
	Students completing degree within 5 years	87%		
	Grads pursuing further study	36%		

Majors Anthropology, art/fine arts, art history, Asian/Oriental studies, astronomy, astrophysics, biochemistry, biology/biological sciences, black/African-American studies, chemistry, Chinese, classics, cognitive science, computer science, (pre)dentistry sequence, earth science, East Asian studies, ecology/environmental studies, economics, education, English, experimental psychology, French, geography, geology, geophysics, German, Greek, Hispanic studies, history, humanities, interdisciplinary studies, international economics, international studies, Japanese, Latin, (pre)law sequence, liberal arts/general studies, literature, marine sciences, mathematics, (pre)medicine sequence, modern languages, molecular biology, music, Native American studies, natural sciences, neurosciences, peace studies, philosophy, physics, political science/government, psychology, religious studies, Romance languages, Russian, social science, sociology, South Asian studies, Spanish, (pre)veterinary medicine sequence, women's studies.

Applying *Required:* essay, high school transcript, 3 years of high school math, 3 years of high school foreign language, 3 recommendations, SAT or ACT, 3 Achievements, English Composition Test. *Recommended:* 4 years of high school science, English Composition Test (with essay). *Application deadlines:* 1/15, same for early decision, 2/1 priority date for financial aid. *Contact:* Mr. Thomas S. Anthony, Dean of Admission, 13 Oak Drive, Hamilton, NY 13346, 315-824-7401.

From the College Each year more than 200 Colgate students study away from campus in one of the twelve to fifteen study groups taught by members of the faculty. Students live among the customs and traditions of another society while studying subjects that range from language and culture to natural sciences, political science, economics, and history.

College of Insurance

New York, New York

Founded 1962
Urban setting
Independent
Coed
Awards A, B, M

Enrollment 1,676 total; 1,506 undergraduates (74 freshmen)

Faculty 93 total; 22 full-time (25% have doctorate/terminal degree); student-faculty ratio is 12:1; grad assistants teach no undergraduate courses.

Libraries 97,672 bound volumes, 427 periodical subscriptions

Computing *Terminals/PCs available for student use:* 15, located in computer lab; PC not required.

Of Special Interest *Core academic program:* yes. Computer course required. Academic exchange program: no. Participates in study-abroad programs.

On Campus Drama/theater group; student-run newspaper. *Social organizations:* 1 national fraternity; 5% of eligible undergraduate men are members.

Athletics *Intercollegiate sport:* bowling (M, W).

Costs (1991–92) & Aid				
	Comprehensive fee	$14,842	Need-based scholarships (average)	$2044
	Tuition	$8550	Non-need scholarships (average)	$5705
	Mandatory fees	$12	Short-term loans (average)	$941
	Room and board	$6280	Long-term loans—college funds (average)	$2267
	Financial aid recipients	95%	Long-term loans—external funds (average)	$2875

Undergraduate Facts				
	Part-time	32%	*Freshman Data:* 177 applied, 55% were accepted, 76% (74) of those entered	
	State residents	80%		
	Transfers	40%	From top tenth of high school class	35%
	African-Americans	10%	SAT-takers scoring 600 or over on verbal	4%
	Native Americans	N/R	SAT-takers scoring 700 or over on verbal	0%
	Hispanics	5%	SAT-takers scoring 600 or over on math	37%
	Asian-Americans	6%	SAT-takers scoring 700 or over on math	9%
	International students	4%	ACT-takers scoring 26 or over	N/R
	Freshmen returning for sophomore year	97%	ACT-takers scoring 30 or over	N/R
	Students completing degree within 5 years	N/R	*Majors with most degrees conferred:* insurance, actuarial science.	
	Grads pursuing further study	N/R		

Majors Actuarial science, business, finance/banking, insurance.

Applying *Required:* high school transcript, 3 years of high school math, interview, SAT or ACT. *Recommended:* essay, recommendations. *Application deadlines:* 3/1, 12/1 for early decision, 7/15 priority date for financial aid. *Contact:* Ms. Theresa C. Marro, Director of Admissions, 101 Murray Street, New York, NY 10007, 212-815-9232 or toll-free 800-356-5146.

From the College The College of Insurance is a fully accredited institution that is sponsored by over 300 companies in the insurance and financial services industry. Housed in an award-winning, self-contained building with dormitories on the top four floors, the College of Insurance offers qualified students the opportunity to participate in a unique Cooperative Work Study Program.

College of the Holy Cross

Worcester, Massachusetts

Founded 1843
Suburban setting
Independent, Roman Catholic (Jesuit)
Coed
Awards B

Enrollment 2,641 total—all undergraduates (728 freshmen)

Faculty 246 total; 204 full-time (94% have doctorate/terminal degree); student-faculty ratio is 14:1.

Libraries 459,000 bound volumes, 20,000 titles on microform, 2,543 periodical subscriptions

Computing *Terminals/PCs available for student use:* 100, located in computer center, library, science center; PC not required.

Of Special Interest *Core academic program:* yes. Phi Beta Kappa, Sigma Xi chapters. Academic exchange with members of the Worcester Consortium for Higher Education. Participates in study-abroad programs. Naval ROTC, cooperative Army ROTC, cooperative Air Force ROTC.

On Campus Drama/theater group; student-run newspaper and radio station. No national or local fraternities or sororities on campus.

Athletics Member NCAA (Division I). *Intercollegiate sports:* baseball (M), basketball (M, W), crew (M, W), cross-country running (M, W), fencing (M, W), field hockey (W), football (M), golf (M), ice hockey (M), lacrosse (M, W), soccer (M, W), softball (W), swimming and diving (M, W), tennis (M, W), track and field (M, W), volleyball (W).

Costs (1991–92) & Aid				
	Comprehensive fee	$21,230	Need-based scholarships (average)	$7868
	Tuition	$15,200	Non-need scholarships (average)	$15,200
	Mandatory fees	$330	Short-term loans (average)	$100
	Room and board	$5700	Long-term loans—college funds	N/Avail
	Financial aid recipients	60%	Long-term loans—external funds (average)	$3271

Undergraduate Facts				
	Part-time	0%	*Freshman Data:* 3,463 applied, 51% were accepted, 41% (728) of those entered	
	State residents	35%		
	Transfers	1%	From top tenth of high school class	60%
	African-Americans	4%	SAT-takers scoring 600 or over on verbal	N/R
	Native Americans	0%	SAT-takers scoring 700 or over on verbal	N/R
	Hispanics	3%	SAT-takers scoring 600 or over on math	N/R
	Asian-Americans	2%	SAT-takers scoring 700 or over on math	N/R
	International students	1%	ACT-takers scoring 26 or over	N/R
	Freshmen returning for sophomore year	96%	ACT-takers scoring 30 or over	N/R
	Students completing degree within 5 years	92%	*Majors with most degrees conferred:* English, political science/government, psychology.	
	Grads pursuing further study	23%		

Majors Accounting, anthropology, art/fine arts, art history, Asian/Oriental studies, biology/biological sciences, black/African-American studies, chemistry, classics, (pre)dentistry sequence, economics, English, French, German, history, international studies, mathematics, (pre)medicine sequence, modern languages, music, philosophy, physics, political science/government, psychobiology, psychology, religious studies, Russian, sociology, Spanish, studio art, theater arts/drama, (pre)veterinary medicine sequence, women's studies.

Applying *Required:* essay, high school transcript, 2 recommendations, SAT, 3 Achievements. *Recommended:* 3 years of high school math and science, some high school foreign language, interview, English Composition Test (with essay). *Application deadlines:* 2/1, 11/1 for early decision, 2/1 priority date for financial aid. *Contact:* Mr. William R. Mason, Director of Admissions, 1 College Street, Worcester, MA 01610, 508-793-2443.

College of William and Mary

Williamsburg, Virginia

Founded 1693
Small-town setting
State-supported
Coed
Awards B, M, D

Enrollment 7,710 total; 5,376 undergraduates (1,221 freshmen)

Faculty 596 total; 489 full-time (94% have doctorate/terminal degree); student-faculty ratio is 14:1; grad assistants teach no undergraduate courses.

Libraries 2 million bound volumes, 1.5 million titles on microform, 9,739 periodical subscriptions

Computing *Terminals/PCs available for student use:* 320, located in computer center, library, dormitories, classroom buildings; PC not required but available for purchase. Campus network links student PCs.

Of Special Interest *Core academic program:* yes. Computer course required for math majors. Phi Beta Kappa, Sigma Xi chapters. Academic exchange program: no. Sponsors and participates in study-abroad programs. Army ROTC.

On Campus Drama/theater group; student-run newspaper and radio station. *Social organizations:* 13 national fraternities, 12 national sororities; 40% of eligible undergraduate men and 36% of eligible undergraduate women are members.

Athletics Member NCAA (Division I). *Intercollegiate sports:* baseball (M), basketball (M, W), cross-country running (M, W), fencing (M, W), field hockey (W), football (M), golf (M, W), gymnastics (M, W), lacrosse (W), soccer (M, W), swimming and diving (M, W), tennis (M, W), track and field (M, W), volleyball (W), wrestling (M). *Scholarships:* M, W.

Costs (1991–92) & Aid				
	State resident tuition	$2240	Need-based scholarships (average)	$3300
	Nonresident tuition	$8960	66 Non-need scholarships (average)	$3195
	Mandatory fees	$1490	Short-term loans (average)	$100
	Room and board	$3752	Long-term loans—college funds	N/Avail
	Financial aid recipients	46%	Long-term loans—external funds (average)	$2716

Undergraduate Facts				
	Part-time	3%	*Freshman Data:* 7,161 applied, 40% were accepted, 42% (1,221) of those entered	
	State residents	68%		
	Transfers	1%	From top tenth of high school class	70%
	African-Americans	6%	SAT-takers scoring 600 or over on verbal	52%
	Native Americans	0%	SAT-takers scoring 700 or over on verbal	9%
	Hispanics	1%	SAT-takers scoring 600 or over on math	77%
	Asian-Americans	4%	SAT-takers scoring 700 or over on math	27%
	International students	4%	ACT-takers scoring 26 or over	N/R
	Freshmen returning for sophomore year	96%	ACT-takers scoring 30 or over	N/R
	Students completing degree within 5 years	84%	*Majors with most degrees conferred:* political science/government, English, economics.	
	Grads pursuing further study	30%		

Majors American studies, anthropology, art/fine arts, biology/biological sciences, business, chemistry, classics, comparative literature, computer science, East Asian studies, economics, English, environmental sciences, European studies, French, geology, German, Greek, history, interdisciplinary studies, international studies, Latin, Latin American studies, linguistics, mathematics, modern languages, music, philosophy, physical education, physics, political science/government, psychology, public affairs and policy studies, religious studies, Russian and Slavic studies, sociology, Spanish, speech/rhetoric/public address/debate, theater arts/drama, urban studies.

Applying *Required:* essay, high school transcript, SAT or ACT. *Recommended:* 4 years of high school math and science, 4 years of high school foreign language, 1 recommendation, 3 Achievements, English Composition Test (with essay). Campus interview required for some. *Application deadlines:* 1/15, 11/1 for early decision, 2/15 priority date for financial aid. *Contact:* Dr. Jean A. Scott, Dean of Admission, Richmond Road, Williamsburg, VA 23185, 804-221-3999.

The College of Wooster

Wooster, Ohio

Founded 1866
Small-town setting
Independent/affiliated with Presbyterian Church
Coed
Awards B

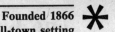

Enrollment	1,779 total—all undergraduates (468 freshmen)
Faculty	155 total; 145 full-time (95% have doctorate/terminal degree); student-faculty ratio is 12:1.
Libraries	663,387 bound volumes, 1,510 periodical subscriptions
Computing	*Terminals/PCs available for student use:* 150, located in computer center, library, dormitories, academic departments; PC not required. Campus network links student PCs.
Of Special Interest	*Core academic program:* yes. Computer course required for mathematical science majors. Phi Beta Kappa, Sigma Xi chapters. Academic exchange program: no. Sponsors and participates in study-abroad programs.
On Campus	Drama/theater group; student-run newspaper and radio station. *Social organizations:* 7 local fraternities, 5 local sororities, eating clubs, coed fraternity; 24% of eligible undergraduate men and 17% of eligible undergraduate women are members.
Athletics	Member NCAA (Division III). *Intercollegiate sports:* baseball (M), basketball (M, W), cross-country running (M, W), field hockey (W), football (M), golf (M), ice hockey (M), lacrosse (M, W), rugby (M), soccer (M, W), swimming and diving (M, W), tennis (M, W), track and field (M, W), volleyball (M, W), wrestling (M).

Costs (1991–92) & Aid				
	Comprehensive fee	$17,650	Need-based scholarships (average)	$7099
	Tuition	$13,410	Non-need scholarships (average)	$2708
	Mandatory fees	N/App	Short-term loans	N/Avail
	Room and board	$4240	Long-term loans—college funds (average)	$2530
	Financial aid recipients	62%	Long-term loans—external funds (average)	$2332

Undergraduate Facts				
	Part-time	0%	*Freshman Data:* 1,997 applied, 86% were accepted, 27% (468) of those entered	
	State residents	38%		
	Transfers	1%	From top tenth of high school class	34%
	African-Americans	6%	SAT-takers scoring 600 or over on verbal	13%
	Native Americans	1%	SAT-takers scoring 700 or over on verbal	2%
	Hispanics	1%	SAT-takers scoring 600 or over on math	30%
	Asian-Americans	1%	SAT-takers scoring 700 or over on math	4%
	International students	10%	ACT-takers scoring 26 or over	37%
	Freshmen returning for sophomore year	83%	ACT-takers scoring 30 or over	11%
	Students completing degree within 5 years	N/R	*Majors with most degrees conferred:* history, English, sociology.	
	Grads pursuing further study	N/R		

Majors African studies, art/fine arts, art history, Asian/Oriental studies, biology/biological sciences, black/African-American studies, business economics, chemistry, classics, communication, comparative literature, computer science, (pre)dentistry sequence, economics, English, European studies, French, geology, German, Greek, history, international studies, Latin, Latin American studies, (pre)law sequence, mathematics, (pre)medicine sequence, music, music education, music history, music therapy, Near and Middle Eastern studies, philosophy, physics, political science/government, psychology, religious studies, Russian, sociology, South Asian studies, Spanish, speech pathology and audiology, speech/rhetoric/public address/debate, studio art, theater arts/drama, urban studies, (pre)veterinary medicine sequence, voice.

Applying *Required:* essay, high school transcript, 2 recommendations, SAT or ACT. *Recommended:* 3 years of high school math and science, some high school foreign language, interview. *Application deadlines:* 2/15, 12/15 for early decision, 2/15 priority date for financial aid. *Contact:* Dr. W. A. Hayden Schilling, Dean of Admissions, 1101 North Bever Street, Wooster, OH 44691, 216-263-2270 or toll-free 800-877-9905.

The Colorado College

Colorado Springs, Colorado

Founded 1874
Suburban setting
Independent
Coed
Awards B, M (M offered only in education)

Enrollment 1,952 total; 1,917 undergraduates (463 freshmen)

Faculty 260 total; 152 full-time (94% have doctorate/terminal degree); student-faculty ratio is 13:1; grad assistants teach no undergraduate courses.

Libraries 675,000 bound volumes, 37,000 titles on microform, 1,540 periodical subscriptions

Computing *Terminals/PCs available for student use:* 120, located in computer center, student center, library, dormitories, academic buildings; PC not required.

Of Special Interest *Core academic program:* yes. Computer course required for economics majors. Phi Beta Kappa chapter. Academic exchange program: no. Sponsors and participates in study-abroad programs. Cooperative Army ROTC.

On Campus Drama/theater group; student-run newspaper and radio station. *Social organizations:* 4 national fraternities, 4 national sororities; 25% of eligible undergraduate men and 25% of eligible undergraduate women are members.

Athletics Member NCAA (Division III). *Intercollegiate sports:* baseball (M), basketball (M, W), cross-country running (M, W), field hockey (M, W), football (M), golf (M), ice hockey (M, W), lacrosse (M), soccer (M, W), squash (M, W), swimming and diving (M, W), tennis (M, W), track and field (M, W), volleyball (W). *Scholarships:* M, W.

Costs (1991–92) & Aid				
	Comprehensive fee	$17,310	Need-based scholarships (average)	$7600
	Tuition	$13,665	Non-need scholarships (average)	$11,000
	Mandatory fees	N/App	Short-term loans (average)	$200
	Room and board	$3645	Long-term loans—college funds (average)	$1000
	Financial aid recipients	55%	Long-term loans—external funds (average)	$2450

Undergraduate Facts				
	Part-time	0%	*Freshman Data:* 2,847 applied, 48% were accepted, 34% (463) of those entered	
	State residents	33%		
	Transfers	10%	From top tenth of high school class	52%
	African-Americans	2%	SAT-takers scoring 600 or over on verbal	30%
	Native Americans	2%	SAT-takers scoring 700 or over on verbal	4%
	Hispanics	5%	SAT-takers scoring 600 or over on math	52%
	Asian-Americans	3%	SAT-takers scoring 700 or over on math	11%
	International students	2%	ACT-takers scoring 26 or over	67%
	Freshmen returning for sophomore year	91%	ACT-takers scoring 30 or over	20%
	Students completing degree within 5 years	78%	*Majors with most degrees conferred:* English, political science/government, biology/biological sciences.	
	Grads pursuing further study	30%		

Majors Anthropology, art/fine arts, art history, biology/biological sciences, chemistry, classics, comparative literature, dance, (pre)dentistry sequence, economics, English, French, geology, German, history, interdisciplinary studies, (pre)law sequence, liberal arts/general studies, mathematics, medical technology, (pre)medicine sequence, music, peace studies, philosophy, physics, political science/government, psychology, religious studies, Romance languages, Russian and Slavic studies, sociology, Spanish, theater arts/drama, (pre)veterinary medicine sequence, women's studies.

Applying *Required:* essay, high school transcript, 3 recommendations, SAT or ACT. *Recommended:* 3 years of high school math and science, some high school foreign language. *Application deadlines:* 2/1, 12/1 for early action, 2/15 priority date for financial aid. *Contact:* Mr. Terrance K. Swenson, Director of Admissions, 14 East Cache La Poudre, Colorado Springs, CO 80903, 719-389-6344 or toll-free 800-542-7214.

Colorado School of Mines

Golden, Colorado

Founded 1874
Small-town setting
State-supported
Coed
Awards B, M, D

Enrollment	2,663 total; 1,764 undergraduates (424 freshmen)
Faculty	215 total; 190 full-time (90% have doctorate/terminal degree); student-faculty ratio is 13:1; grad assistants teach a few undergraduate courses.
Libraries	300,000 bound volumes, 2,000 titles on microform, 2,150 periodical subscriptions
Computing	*Terminals/PCs available for student use:* 200, located in computer center, dormitories, classroom buildings; PC not required.
Of Special Interest	*Core academic program:* no. Computer course required. Sigma Xi chapter. Academic exchange program: no. Participates in study-abroad programs. Army ROTC, cooperative Naval ROTC, cooperative Air Force ROTC.
On Campus	Drama/theater group; student-run newspaper. *Social organizations:* 7 national fraternities, 2 national sororities; 15% of eligible undergraduate men and 15% of eligible undergraduate women are members.
Athletics	Member NCAA (Division II), NAIA. *Intercollegiate sports:* baseball (M), basketball (M, W), cross-country running (M, W), football (M), golf (M, W), gymnastics (M, W), lacrosse (M), rugby (M), skiing (cross-country) (M, W), skiing (downhill) (M, W), soccer (M), softball (W), swimming and diving (M, W), tennis (M, W), track and field (M, W), volleyball (W), wrestling (M). *Scholarships:* M, W.

Costs (1991–92) & Aid	State resident tuition	$3718	870 Need-based scholarships (average)	$6600
	Nonresident tuition	$10,304	400 Non-need scholarships (average)	$3500
	Mandatory fees	$374	Short-term loans (average)	$310
	Room and board	$3770	Long-term loans—college funds (average)	$1800
	Financial aid recipients	75%	Long-term loans—external funds (average)	$3000

Undergraduate Facts				
Part-time	3%	*Freshman Data:* 1,278 applied, 84% were accepted, 39% (424) of those entered		
State residents	72%	From top tenth of high school class	56%
Transfers	20%	SAT-takers scoring 600 or over on verbal	20%
African-Americans	3%	SAT-takers scoring 700 or over on verbal	2%
Native Americans	1%	SAT-takers scoring 600 or over on math	75%
Hispanics	4%	SAT-takers scoring 700 or over on math	20%
Asian-Americans	4%	ACT-takers scoring 26 or over	75%
International students	9%	ACT-takers scoring 30 or over	10%
Freshmen returning for sophomore year	85%	*Majors with most degrees conferred:* engineering (general), chemical engineering, petroleum/natural gas engineering.	
Students completing degree within 5 years	65%		
Grads pursuing further study	15%		

Majors Chemical engineering, chemistry, civil engineering, computer science, electrical engineering, engineering (general), engineering and applied sciences, engineering physics, engineering sciences, geological engineering, geophysical engineering, materials sciences, mathematics, mechanical engineering, metallurgical engineering, mining and mineral engineering, petroleum/natural gas engineering, physics.

Applying *Required:* high school transcript, 4 years of high school math, 3 years of high school science, SAT or ACT. *Recommended:* some high school foreign language. Recommendations, interview required for some. *Application deadlines:* 8/15, 3/1 priority date for financial aid. *Contact:* Mr. A. William Young, Director of Enrollment Management, Twin Towers, 1811 Elm Street, Golden, CO 80401, 303-273-3220 or toll-free 800-245-1060 (in-state), 800-446-9488 (out-of-state).

Colorado State University

Fort Collins, Colorado

Founded 1862
Urban setting
State-supported
Coed
Awards B, M, D

Enrollment 20,967 total; 17,460 undergraduates (2,195 freshmen)

Faculty 1,019 total—all full-time (87% have doctorate/terminal degree); student-faculty ratio is 20:1; grad assistants teach a few undergraduate courses.

Libraries 1.5 million bound volumes, 1.6 million titles on microform, 20,000 periodical subscriptions

Computing *Terminals/PCs available for student use:* 750, located in computer center, student center, dormitories, classrooms; PC not required but available for purchase. Campus network links student PCs.

Of Special Interest *Core academic program:* yes. Computer course required for some business and engineering majors. Phi Beta Kappa, Sigma Xi chapters. Academic exchange with National Student Exchange. Participates in study-abroad programs. Army ROTC, Air Force ROTC.

On Campus Drama/theater group; student-run newspaper and radio station. *Social organizations:* 22 national fraternities, 14 national sororities, local fraternities, local sororities; 13% of eligible undergraduate men and 13% of eligible undergraduate women are members.

Athletics Member NCAA (Division I). *Intercollegiate sports:* baseball (M), basketball (M, W), cross-country running (M, W), football (M), golf (W), softball (W), swimming and diving (W), tennis (M, W), track and field (M, W), volleyball (W). *Scholarships:* M, W.

Costs (1991–92) & Aid				
	State resident tuition	$1855	Need-based scholarships	Avail
	Nonresident tuition	$6558	2228 Non-need scholarships (average)	$1154
	Mandatory fees	$507	Short-term loans (average)	$300
	Room and board	$3624	Long-term loans—college funds	N/Avail
	Financial aid recipients	48%	Long-term loans—external funds (average)	$3113

Undergraduate Facts				
	Part-time	11%	*Freshman Data:* 8,508 applied, 65% were accepted, 39% (2,195) of those entered	
	State residents	78%		
	Transfers	12%	From top tenth of high school class	24%
	African-Americans	2%	SAT-takers scoring 600 or over on verbal	8%
	Native Americans	1%	SAT-takers scoring 700 or over on verbal	1%
	Hispanics	5%	SAT-takers scoring 600 or over on math	25%
	Asian-Americans	2%	SAT-takers scoring 700 or over on math	3%
	International students	1%	ACT-takers scoring 26 or over	33%
	Freshmen returning for sophomore year	79%	ACT-takers scoring 30 or over	5%
	Students completing degree within 5 years	50%	*Majors with most degrees conferred:* business, psychology, human development.	
	Grads pursuing further study	N/R		

Majors Accounting, agricultural business, agricultural economics, agricultural education, agricultural engineering, agricultural sciences, agronomy/soil and crop sciences, animal sciences, anthropology, applied mathematics, art education, art/fine arts, art history, biochemistry, biology/biological sciences, botany/plant sciences, business, ceramic art and design, chemical engineering, chemistry, child care/child and family studies, civil engineering, computer information systems, computer science, construction management, consumer services, creative writing, dance, (pre)dentistry sequence, dietetics, economics, electrical engineering, engineering (general), engineering sciences, English, entomology, environmental health sciences, equestrian studies, family and consumer studies, farm and ranch management, fashion merchandising, finance/banking, fish and game management, food sciences, forestry, French, geology, German, graphic arts, history, home economics, home economics education, horticulture, hotel and restaurant management, human development, humanities, industrial arts, interior design, jewelry and metalsmithing, journalism, landscape architecture/design, (pre)law sequence, liberal arts/general studies, manufacturing technology, marketing/retailing/merchandising, mathematics, mechanical engineering, (pre)medicine sequence, microbiology, music, music education, music therapy, natural resource management, nutrition, occupational therapy, painting/drawing, parks management, philosophy, physical education, physical sciences, physics, political science/government, psychology, range management, real estate, sculpture, secondary education, social science, social work, sociology, Spanish, speech pathology and audiology, speech/rhetoric/public address/debate, statistics, studio art, textiles and clothing, theater arts/drama, (pre)veterinary medicine sequence, vocational education, wildlife biology, wood sciences, zoology.

Applying *Required:* high school transcript, 3 years of high school math, 4 years of high school English, SAT or ACT. *Recommended:* 2 years of high school foreign language, recommendations. Essay required for some. *Application deadlines:* 7/1, continuous processing for financial aid. *Contact:* Ms. Mary Ontiveros, Director of Admissions, Administration Building, Fort Collins, CO 80523, 303-491-6909.

From the College Colorado State University offers an education that has been described as comparable to that of Ivy League schools. The spectacular location, at the base of the Rocky Mountain foothills, provides the perfect background for intellectual and personal growth. And the friendly campus atmosphere and award-winning residence halls help students feel right at home.

Columbia College
Part of Columbia University

New York, New York

Founded 1754 *
Urban setting
Independent
Coed
Awards B

Enrollment	18,617 university total; 3,325 undergraduates (872 freshmen)
Faculty	475 total; student-faculty ratio is 7:1; grad assistants teach a few undergraduate courses.
Libraries	6 million bound volumes, 4 million titles on microform, 59,000 periodical subscriptions
Computing	*Terminals/PCs available for student use:* 200, located in computer center, library, dormitories; PC not required. Campus network links student PCs.
Of Special Interest	*Core academic program:* yes. Computer course required for economics majors. Phi Beta Kappa, Sigma Xi chapters. Academic exchange with Howard University. Sponsors and participates in study-abroad programs. Cooperative Army ROTC, cooperative Air Force ROTC.
On Campus	Drama/theater group; student-run newspaper and radio station. *Social organizations:* 19 national fraternities, 5 national sororities; 13% of eligible undergraduate men and 6% of eligible undergraduate women are members.
Athletics	Member NCAA (Division I). *Intercollegiate sports:* archery (M, W), badminton (M, W), baseball (M), basketball (M, W), crew (M, W), cross-country running (M, W), fencing (M, W), field hockey (W), football (M), golf (M), ice hockey (M), lacrosse (M, W), riflery (M, W), rugby (M), sailing (M, W), skiing (cross-country) (M, W), soccer (M, W), softball (W), squash (M), swimming and diving (M, W), table tennis (M, W), tennis (M, W), track and field (M, W), volleyball (M, W), water polo (M), wrestling (M).

Costs (1991–92) & Aid				
	Comprehensive fee	$21,980	Need-based scholarships (average)	$9800
	Tuition	$15,520	Non-need scholarships	N/Avail
	Mandatory fees	$338	Short-term loans (average)	$100
	Room and board	$6122	Long-term loans—college funds (average)	$1500
	Financial aid recipients	48%	Long-term loans—external funds (average)	$3300

Undergraduate Facts				
	Part-time	0%	*Freshman Data:* 6,079 applied, 32% were accepted, 44% (872) of those entered	
	State residents	19%		
	Transfers	5%	From top tenth of high school class	80%
	African-Americans	9%	SAT-takers scoring 600 or over on verbal	65%
	Native Americans	1%	SAT-takers scoring 700 or over on verbal	16%
	Hispanics	9%	SAT-takers scoring 600 or over on math	77%
	Asian-Americans	16%	SAT-takers scoring 700 or over on math	35%
	International students	2%	ACT-takers scoring 26 or over	N/R
	Freshmen returning for sophomore year	96%	ACT-takers scoring 30 or over	N/R
	Students completing degree within 5 years	90%		
	Grads pursuing further study	70%		

Majors African studies, anthropology, archaeology, architecture, art/fine arts, art history, Asian/Oriental studies, astronomy, astrophysics, biochemistry, biology/biological sciences, biophysics, black/African-American studies, chemistry, Chinese, classics, comparative literature, computer science, East Asian studies, East European and Soviet studies, ecology/environmental studies, economics, English, environmental sciences, film studies, French, geochemistry, geology, geophysics, German, Germanic languages and literature, Greek, Hebrew, history, interdisciplinary studies, Italian, Japanese, Latin, Latin American studies, mathematics, medieval studies, music, Near and Middle Eastern studies, philosophy, physics, political science/government, psychology, religious studies, Russian, Russian and Slavic studies, sociology, Spanish, statistics, theater arts/drama, urban studies, women's studies.

Applying *Required:* essay, high school transcript, 2 recommendations, SAT or ACT, 3 Achievements, English Composition Test. *Recommended:* 3 years of high school math and science, 3 years of high school foreign language, interview. *Application deadlines:* 1/10, 11/15 for early decision, 2/1 for financial aid. *Contact:* Lawrence J. Momo, Director of Admissions, 212 Hamilton Hall, New York, NY 10027, 212-854-2521.

From the College Columbia, in response to the needs and interests of its students, has added new undergraduate majors in film studies, theater arts, and visual arts. Columbia students have New York City's offerings in these areas as a backdrop to their campus work.

Columbia University, School of Engineering and Applied Science
New York, New York

Founded 1864
Urban setting
Independent
Coed
Awards B, M, D

Enrollment	18,617 university total; 1,811 school total; 972 undergraduates (232 freshmen)
Faculty	112 total—all full-time (100% have doctorate/terminal degree); student-faculty ratio is 6:1.
Libraries	5.6 million bound volumes, 3.5 million titles on microform, 59,196 periodical subscriptions
Computing	*Terminals/PCs available for student use:* 400, located in computer center, dormitories, engineering departments; PC not required but available for purchase. Campus network links student PCs.
Of Special Interest	*Core academic program:* yes. Computer course required. Sigma Xi chapter. Sponsors and participates in study-abroad programs. Cooperative Army ROTC, cooperative Naval ROTC, cooperative Air Force ROTC.
On Campus	Drama/theater group; student-run newspaper and radio station. *Social organizations:* 14 national fraternities, 3 national sororities, 2 local sororities, 6 coed social clubs; 7% of eligible undergraduate men and 2% of eligible undergraduate women are members.
Athletics	Member NCAA (Division I). *Intercollegiate sports:* archery (M, W), baseball (M), basketball (M, W), crew (M, W), cross-country running (M, W), fencing (M, W), field hockey (W), football (M), golf (M), soccer (M, W), swimming and diving (M, W), tennis (M, W), track and field (M, W), volleyball (W), wrestling (M).

Costs (1991–92) & Aid				
	Comprehensive fee	$21,582	Need-based scholarships	Avail
	Tuition	$15,520	Non-need scholarships	N/Avail
	Mandatory fees	$306	Short-term loans	N/Avail
	Room and board	$5756	Long-term loans—college funds	Avail
	Financial aid recipients	72%	Long-term loans—external funds	Avail

Undergraduate Facts				
	Part-time	0%	*Freshman Data:* 1,116 applied,	
	State residents	42%	From top tenth of high school class	72%
	Transfers	8%	SAT-takers scoring 600 or over on verbal	24%
	African-Americans	3%	SAT-takers scoring 700 or over on verbal	2%
	Native Americans	0%	SAT-takers scoring 600 or over on math	97%
	Hispanics	5%	SAT-takers scoring 700 or over on math	75%
	Asian-Americans	38%	ACT-takers scoring 26 or over	N/R
	International students	13%	ACT-takers scoring 30 or over	N/R
	Freshmen returning for sophomore year	94%	*Majors with most degrees conferred:* mechanical engineering, electrical engineering, computer science.	
	Students completing degree within 5 years	4%		
	Grads pursuing further study	41%		

Majors Applied mathematics, bioengineering, chemical engineering, civil engineering, computer science, electrical engineering, engineering mechanics, geophysics, industrial engineering, materials sciences, mechanical engineering, metallurgical engineering, metallurgy, mining and mineral engineering, operations research, physics.

Applying *Required:* essay, high school transcript, 4 years of high school math, 3 years of high school science, 2 recommendations, SAT or ACT, 3 Achievements, English Composition Test. *Recommended:* 2 years of high school foreign language, interview, English Composition Test (with essay). *Application deadlines:* 1/10, 11/15 for early decision, 2/1 for financial aid. *Contact:* Ms. Linda Meehan, Assistant Director of Admissions, 530 Seeley W. Mudd Building, New York, NY 10027, 212-854-2931.

Concordia College

Moorhead, Minnesota

Founded 1891
Suburban setting
Independent/affiliated with Lutheran Church
Coed
Awards B

Enrollment	2,933 total—all undergraduates (754 freshmen)
Faculty	253 total; 188 full-time (62% have doctorate/terminal degree); student-faculty ratio is 15:1.
Libraries	238,300 bound volumes, 28,600 titles on microform, 1,500 periodical subscriptions
Computing	*Terminals/PCs available for student use:* 75, located in computer center, library, classrooms; PC not required but available for purchase. Campus network links student PCs.
Of Special Interest	*Core academic program:* yes. Computer course required for business majors. Academic exchange with Moorhead State University, North Dakota State University, Tri-College University. Sponsors and participates in study-abroad programs. Air Force ROTC, cooperative Army ROTC.
On Campus	Drama/theater group; student-run newspaper and radio station. *Social organizations:* 3 local fraternities, 3 local sororities; 15% of eligible undergraduate men and 10% of eligible undergraduate women are members.
Athletics	Member NCAA (Division III). *Intercollegiate sports:* baseball (M), basketball (M, W), cross-country running (M, W), football (M), golf (M, W), ice hockey (M), soccer (M, W), softball (W), tennis (M, W), track and field (M, W), volleyball (W), wrestling (M).

Costs (1992–93) & Aid				
	Comprehensive fee	$12,100	Need-based scholarships	Avail
	Tuition	$9105	Non-need scholarships	Avail
	Mandatory fees	$95	Short-term loans (average)	$50
	Room and board	$2900	Long-term loans—college funds (average)	$2058
	Financial aid recipients	80%	Long-term loans—external funds (average)	$1850

Undergraduate Facts				
	Part-time	3%	*Freshman Data:* 1,772 applied, 92% were accepted, 46% (754) of those entered	
	State residents	64%		
	Transfers	4%	From top tenth of high school class	26%
	African-Americans	1%	SAT-takers scoring 600 or over on verbal	20%
	Native Americans	1%	SAT-takers scoring 700 or over on verbal	2%
	Hispanics	1%	SAT-takers scoring 600 or over on math	29%
	Asian-Americans	1%	SAT-takers scoring 700 or over on math	7%
	International students	4%	ACT-takers scoring 26 or over	29%
	Freshmen returning for sophomore year	83%	ACT-takers scoring 30 or over	8%
	Students completing degree within 5 years	68%	*Majors with most degrees conferred:* business, communication, elementary education.	
	Grads pursuing further study	20%		

Majors Accounting, advertising, art education, art/fine arts, art history, biology/biological sciences, broadcasting, business, business economics, business education, chemistry, classics, communication, computer science, creative writing, criminal justice, (pre)dentistry sequence, dietetics, economics, education, elementary education, English, environmental sciences, family and consumer studies, food sciences, French, German, health education, health services administration, history, home economics, home economics education, humanities, international business, international studies, journalism, Latin, (pre)law sequence, mathematics, medical technology, (pre)medicine sequence, music, music education, nursing, nutrition, philosophy, physical education, physics, piano/organ, political science/government, psychology, recreation and leisure services, religious studies, Scandinavian languages/studies, science education, secondary education, secretarial studies/office management, social work, sociology, Spanish, speech/rhetoric/public address/debate, studio art, theater arts/drama, (pre)veterinary medicine sequence, voice, wind and percussion instruments.

Applying *Required:* high school transcript, 2 recommendations, SAT or ACT. *Recommended:* interview. Application deadlines: rolling, 4/1 priority date for financial aid. *Contact:* Mr. James L. Hausmann, Vice-President for Admissions and Financial Aid, 901 South 8th Street, Moorhead, MN 56562, 218-299-3004.

From the College One of the largest private colleges in the Midwest, Concordia may also be the most affordable. The comprehensive fee is several thousand dollars less than comparable colleges. Financial assistance is also available to 80 percent of the students. High academic quality is made possible through gifts from numerous donors.

✱ Connecticut College

New London, Connecticut

Founded 1911
Small-town setting
Independent
Coed
Awards B, M

Enrollment	1,846 total; 1,777 undergraduates (461 freshmen)
Faculty	190 total; 143 full-time (94% have doctorate/terminal degree); grad assistants teach no undergraduate courses.
Libraries	440,500 bound volumes, 90,000 titles on microform, 1,698 periodical subscriptions
Computing	*Terminals/PCs available for student use:* 115, located in computer center, library, science building, dance and music studio, Winthrop Annex; PC not required but available for purchase. Campus network links student PCs.
Of Special Interest	*Core academic program:* yes. Computer course required for mathematical science majors. Phi Beta Kappa chapter. Academic exchange with members of the Twelve College Exchange Program, United States Coast Guard Academy, American University, Trinity College, Wesleyan University, National Theater Institute, Williams College. Sponsors and participates in study-abroad programs.
On Campus	Drama/theater group; student-run newspaper and radio station. No national or local fraternities or sororities on campus.
Athletics	Member NCAA (Division III). *Intercollegiate sports:* basketball (M, W), crew (M, W), cross-country running (M, W), equestrian sports (M, W), fencing (M, W), field hockey (W), golf (M, W), ice hockey (M, W), lacrosse (M, W), rugby (M, W), sailing (M, W), skiing (downhill) (M, W), soccer (M, W), squash (M, W), swimming and diving (M, W), tennis (M, W), track and field (M, W), volleyball (W).

Costs (1991–92) & Aid				
	Comprehensive fee	$21,640	Need-based scholarships (average)	$10,490
	Tuition	$16,080	Non-need scholarships	N/Avail
	Mandatory fees	$190	Short-term loans (average)	$100
	Room and board	$5370	Long-term loans—college funds (average)	$1800
	Financial aid recipients	41%	Long-term loans—external funds (average)	$2600

Undergraduate Facts				
	Part-time	4%	*Freshman Data:* 3,058 applied, 52% were accepted, 29% (461) of those entered	
	State residents	19%		
	Transfers	3%	From top tenth of high school class	54%
	African-Americans	4%	SAT-takers scoring 600 or over on verbal	52%
	Native Americans	1%	SAT-takers scoring 700 or over on verbal	6%
	Hispanics	3%	SAT-takers scoring 600 or over on math	67%
	Asian-Americans	3%	SAT-takers scoring 700 or over on math	15%
	International students	6%	ACT-takers scoring 26 or over	N/R
	Freshmen returning for sophomore year	94%	ACT-takers scoring 30 or over	N/R
	Students completing degree within 5 years	91%	*Majors with most degrees conferred:* political science/government, history, English.	
	Grads pursuing further study	20%		

Majors Anthropology, art/fine arts, art history, Asian/Oriental studies, biochemistry, biology/biological sciences, botany/plant sciences, chemistry, child psychology/child development, Chinese, classics, dance, economics, English, European studies, French, German, Hispanic studies, history, human ecology, interdisciplinary studies, international studies, Italian, Japanese, marine biology, mathematics, medieval studies, music, musical instrument technology, philosophy, physics, political science/government, psychology, religious studies, Russian, Russian and Slavic studies, sociology, studio art, theater arts/drama, urban studies, zoology.

Applying *Required:* essay, high school transcript, 3 recommendations, SAT or ACT, 3 Achievements, English Composition Test. *Recommended:* 3 years of high school math and science, 3 years of high school foreign language, interview, English Composition Test (with essay). *Application deadlines:* 1/15, 11/15 for early decision, 2/15 priority date for financial aid. *Contact:* Mrs. Claire K. Matthews, Dean of Admissions and Planning, 270 Mohegan Avenue, New London, CT 06320, 203-439-2200.

From the College The Center for International Studies in the Liberal Arts provides powerful preparation for global leadership. The College's strong honor code contributes to heightened focus on the development of new civic virtues. Paid science internships and the Center for Arts and Technology are among additional innovations of a faculty committed to preparing students for a new world order.

Cooper Union for the Advancement of Science and Art
New York, New York

Founded 1859
Urban setting
Independent
Coed
Awards B, M

Enrollment 1,085 total; 1,027 undergraduates (237 freshmen)

Faculty 167 total; 59 full-time (80% have doctorate/terminal degree); student-faculty ratio is 7:1; grad assistants teach no undergraduate courses.

Libraries 97,000 bound volumes, 4,700 titles on microform, 370 periodical subscriptions

Computing *Terminals/PCs available for student use:* 95, located in computer center; PC not required.

Of Special Interest *Core academic program:* yes. Computer course required for engineering majors. Academic exchange with East Coast members of the National Association of Schools of Art and Design, New York University, Eugene Lang College, New School for Social Research. Participates in study-abroad programs.

On Campus Drama/theater group; student-run newspaper. *Social organizations:* 3 national fraternities, 2 national sororities; 30% of eligible undergraduate men and 20% of eligible undergraduate women are members.

Athletics None

Costs (1992–93) & Aid				
Comprehensive fee	N/App	Need-based scholarships (average)	$2470
Tuition	$0	Non-need scholarships	N/Avail
Mandatory fees	$300	Short-term loans	N/Avail
Room only	$4000	Long-term loans—college funds	N/Avail
Financial aid recipients	40%	Long-term loans—external funds (average)	$2997

Undergraduate Facts			
Part-time	4%	*Freshman Data:* 2,330 applied, 15% were accepted, 66% (237) of those entered	
State residents	70%		
Transfers	14%	From top tenth of high school class	80%
African-Americans	7%	SAT-takers scoring 600 or over on verbal	N/R
Native Americans	1%	SAT-takers scoring 700 or over on verbal	N/R
Hispanics	7%	SAT-takers scoring 600 or over on math	N/R
Asian-Americans	28%	SAT-takers scoring 700 or over on math	N/R
International students	4%	ACT-takers scoring 26 or over	N/R
Freshmen returning for sophomore year	93%	ACT-takers scoring 30 or over	N/R
Students completing degree within 5 years	80%	*Majors with most degrees conferred:* art/fine arts, architecture, electrical engineering.	
Grads pursuing further study	60%		

Majors Architecture, art/fine arts, chemical engineering, civil engineering, electrical engineering, engineering (general), graphic arts, mechanical engineering.

Applying *Required:* high school transcript, SAT or ACT. 3 years of high school math and science, portfolio, minimum 3.5 GPA, 2 Achievements required for some. *Application deadlines:* 1/10, 12/1 for early decision, 4/15 for financial aid. *Contact:* Mr. Richard Bory, Dean of Admissions and Records, 41 Cooper Square, New York, NY 10003, 212-353-4121.

From the College Each of Cooper Union's schools—Art, Architecture, Engineering—adheres strongly to preparation for its profession within a design-centered, problem-solving philosophy of education in a tuition-free environment. A rigorous curriculum and group projects reinforce this unique atmosphere in higher education and are factors in *Money* magazine's decision to name Cooper Union "In a Class by Itself."

Cornell College

Mount Vernon, Iowa

Founded 1853
Small-town setting
Independent, Methodist
Coed
Awards B

Enrollment 1,111 total—all undergraduates (301 freshmen)

Faculty 127 total; 74 full-time (80% have doctorate/terminal degree); student-faculty ratio is 14:1.

Libraries 180,000 bound volumes, 615 titles on microform, 573 periodical subscriptions

Computing *Terminals/PCs available for student use:* 120, located in computer center, student center, library, classroom buildings.

Of Special Interest *Core academic program:* no. Computer course required for math, education majors. Phi Beta Kappa chapter. Academic exchange with Associated Colleges of the Midwest. Sponsors and participates in study-abroad programs.

On Campus Drama/theater group; student-run newspaper and radio station. *Social organizations:* 7 local fraternities, 6 local sororities, 1 coed fraternity; 35% of eligible undergraduate men and 35% of eligible undergraduate women are members.

Athletics Member NCAA (Division III). *Intercollegiate sports:* baseball (M), basketball (M, W), cross-country running (M, W), football (M), golf (M), ice hockey (M), soccer (M, W), softball (W), swimming and diving (M, W), tennis (M, W), track and field (M, W), volleyball (W), wrestling (M).

Costs (1991–92) & Aid				
	Comprehensive fee	$16,320	Need-based scholarships (average)	$4835
	Tuition	$12,240	Non-need scholarships (average)	$1796
	Mandatory fees	$110	Short-term loans	N/Avail
	Room and board	$3970	Long-term loans—college funds (average)	$1056
	Financial aid recipients	80%	Long-term loans—external funds (average)	$3303

Undergraduate Facts				
	Part-time	1%	*Freshman Data:* 1,209 applied, 86% were accepted, 29% (301) of those entered	
	State residents	29%		
	Transfers	1%	From top tenth of high school class	28%
	African-Americans	2%	SAT-takers scoring 600 or over on verbal	20%
	Native Americans	1%	SAT-takers scoring 700 or over on verbal	4%
	Hispanics	2%	SAT-takers scoring 600 or over on math	36%
	Asian-Americans	1%	SAT-takers scoring 700 or over on math	6%
	International students	2%	ACT-takers scoring 26 or over	44%
	Freshmen returning for sophomore year	71%	ACT-takers scoring 30 or over	10%
	Students completing degree within 5 years	56%	*Majors with most degrees conferred:* business, economics, English, history.	
	Grads pursuing further study	30%		

Majors Anthropology, architecture, art education, art/fine arts, art history, behavioral sciences, biology/biological sciences, business, business economics, business education, chemistry, classics, computer science, (pre)dentistry sequence, ecology/environmental studies, economics, education, elementary education, engineering sciences, English, environmental sciences, French, geology, German, history, interdisciplinary studies, international business, international studies, Latin American studies, (pre)law sequence, liberal arts/general studies, mathematics, medical technology, (pre)medicine sequence, medieval studies, modern languages, music, music education, philosophy, physical education, physics, political science/government, psychology, religious studies, Russian, Russian and Slavic studies, secondary education, sociology, Spanish, speech/rhetoric/public address/debate, studio art, theater arts/drama, (pre)veterinary medicine sequence, women's studies.

Applying *Required:* essay, high school transcript, 1 recommendation, SAT or ACT. *Recommended:* 3 years of high school math and science, some high school foreign language, interview. *Application deadlines:* 3/1, 12/1 for early decision, 3/1 priority date for financial aid. *Contact:* Mr. Peter S. Bryant, Vice President for Enrollment Services, 600 1st Street, West, Mount Vernon, IA 52314, 319-895-4290 or toll-free 800-747-1112 (out-of-state).

Cornell University

Ithaca, New York

Founded 1865
Small-town setting
Independent
Coed
Awards B, M, D

Enrollment	18,627 total; 12,915 undergraduates (3,042 freshmen)
Faculty	1,617 total; 1,562 full-time; grad assistants teach a few undergraduate courses.
Libraries	5 million bound volumes, 5 million titles on microform, 60,000 periodical subscriptions
Computing	*Terminals/PCs available for student use:* 750, located in various locations on campus; PC not required. Campus network links student PCs.
Of Special Interest	*Core academic program:* no. Computer course required for engineering majors. Phi Beta Kappa, Sigma Xi chapters. Academic exchange with Ithaca College. Sponsors and participates in study-abroad programs. Army ROTC, Naval ROTC, Air Force ROTC.
On Campus	Drama/theater group; student-run newspaper and radio station. *Social organizations:* 35 national fraternities, 17 national sororities, 13 local fraternities, 1 local sorority; 36% of eligible undergraduate men and 32% of eligible undergraduate women are members.
Athletics	Member NCAA (Division I). *Intercollegiate sports:* baseball (M), basketball (M, W), bowling (M, W), cross-country running (M, W), equestrian sports (M, W), fencing (M, W), field hockey (W), football (M), golf (M), gymnastics (M, W), ice hockey (M, W), lacrosse (M, W), riflery (M, W), sailing (M, W), skiing (cross-country) (M, W), skiing (downhill) (M, W), soccer (M, W), squash (M, W), swimming and diving (M, W), table tennis (M, W), tennis (M, W), track and field (M, W), volleyball (M, W), water polo (M, W), wrestling (M).

Costs (1991–92) & Aid				
	Comprehensive fee	$22,214	Need-based scholarships (average)	$7200
	Tuition*	$16,170	Non-need scholarships	N/Avail
	Mandatory fees	$44	Short-term loans (average)	$750
	Room and board	$6000	Long-term loans—college funds (average)	$1260
	Financial aid recipients	73%	Long-term loans—external funds (average)	$2800

Undergraduate Facts				
	Part-time	0%	*Freshman Data:* 20,328 applied, 31% were accepted, 49% (3,042) of those entered	
	State residents	46%		
	Transfers	2%	From top tenth of high school class	84%
	African-Americans	5%	SAT-takers scoring 600 or over on verbal	51%
	Native Americans	1%	SAT-takers scoring 700 or over on verbal	9%
	Hispanics	5%	SAT-takers scoring 600 or over on math	86%
	Asian-Americans	13%	SAT-takers scoring 700 or over on math	45%
	International students	4%	ACT-takers scoring 26 or over	N/R
	Freshmen returning for sophomore year	96%	ACT-takers scoring 30 or over	N/R
	Students completing degree within 5 years	88%	*Majors with most degrees conferred:* biology/biological sciences, political science/government, agricultural business.	
	Grads pursuing further study	N/R		

Majors African studies, agricultural business, agricultural economics, agricultural education, agricultural engineering, agricultural sciences, agricultural technologies, agronomy/soil and crop sciences, American studies, anatomy, animal sciences, anthropology, applied art, archaeology, architectural technologies, architecture, art/fine arts, art history, Asian/Oriental studies, astronomy, atmospheric sciences, behavioral sciences, biochemistry, bioengineering, biology/biological sciences, biometrics, black/African-American studies, botany/plant sciences, business, cell biology, chemical engineering, chemistry, child care/child and family studies, child psychology/child development, Chinese, city/community/regional planning, civil engineering, classics, communication, community services, comparative literature, computer information systems, computer science, consumer services, creative writing, dairy sciences, dance, dietetics, East Asian studies, East European and Soviet studies, ecology/environmental studies, economics, education, electrical engineering, engineering (general), engineering physics, engineering sciences, English, entomology, environmental design, environmental engineering, environmental sciences, European studies, family and consumer studies, family services, farm and ranch management, food sciences, food services management, French, genetics, geology, German, Germanic languages and literature, Greek, Hebrew, Hispanic studies, history, home economics education, horticulture, hotel and restaurant management, human development, human ecology, human services, industrial engineering, interdisciplinary studies, international studies, Italian, Japanese, Judaic studies, labor and industrial relations, labor studies, landscape architecture/design, Latin, Latin American studies, (pre)law sequence, liberal arts/general studies, linguistics, marine sciences, materials engineering, materials sciences, mathematics, mechanical engineering, (pre)medicine sequence, medieval studies, meteorology, microbiology, modern languages, molecular biology, music, Native American studies, natural resource management, Near and Middle Eastern studies, neurosciences, nutrition, operations research, ornamental horticulture, painting/drawing, pest control technology, philosophy, photography, physics, physiology, political science/government, poultry sciences, psychology, public affairs and policy studies, religious studies, Romance languages, Russian, Russian and Slavic studies, sculpture, Slavic languages, social work, sociobiology, sociology, Southeast Asian studies, Spanish, statistics, textile arts, textiles and clothing, theater arts/drama, urban studies, (pre)veterinary medicine sequence, women's studies, zoology.

Applying *Required:* essay, high school transcript, 3 years of high school math, 1 recommendation, SAT or ACT. 3 years of high school science, 3 years of high school foreign language, campus interview, 3 Achievements, English Composition Test required for some. *Application deadlines:* 1/1, 11/1 for early decision, 2/15 priority date for financial aid. *Contact:* Susan H. Murphy, Dean, Admissions and Financial Aid, 410 Thurston Avenue, Ithaca, NY 14850, 607-255-5241.

From the College Ezra Cornell created a university that offered instruction to all who were qualified, regardless of race or gender; welcomed rich and poor; and encouraged students to choose their own programs. Cornell is still a place where a wide variety of students engage in discovery in a curriculum that is unequaled in interdisciplinary breadth.

* For state-supported units, tuition is $6450 for state residents and $11,950 for nonresidents.

✱ Creighton University

Omaha, Nebraska

Founded 1878
Urban setting
Independent, Roman Catholic
Coed
Awards A, B, M, D

Enrollment	6,140 total; 4,113 undergraduates (773 freshmen)
Faculty	1,252 total; 559 full-time (85% have doctorate/terminal degree); student-faculty ratio is 14:1; grad assistants teach a few undergraduate courses.
Libraries	630,775 bound volumes, 874,836 titles on microform, 4,002 periodical subscriptions
Computing	*Terminals/PCs available for student use:* 175, located in computer center, College of Business Administration computer center, English composition lab; PC not required.
Of Special Interest	*Core academic program:* yes. Computer course required for business, nursing majors. Sigma Xi chapter. Academic exchange program: no. Sponsors and participates in study-abroad programs. Army ROTC, cooperative Air Force ROTC.
On Campus	Drama/theater group; student-run newspaper. *Social organizations:* 7 national fraternities, 5 national sororities; 30% of eligible undergraduate men and 30% of eligible undergraduate women are members.
Athletics	Member NCAA (Division I). *Intercollegiate sports:* baseball (M), basketball (M, W), crew (M, W), cross-country running (M, W), fencing (M, W), golf (M, W), ice hockey (M), lacrosse (M), rugby (M), sailing (M, W), soccer (M, W), softball (W), swimming and diving (M, W), tennis (M, W), volleyball (W). *Scholarships:* M, W.

Costs (1991–92) & Aid				
	Comprehensive fee	$12,794	Need-based scholarships	Avail
	Tuition	$8716	Non-need scholarships	Avail
	Mandatory fees	$280	Short-term loans (average)	$200
	Room and board	$3798	Long-term loans—college funds (average)	$1800
	Financial aid recipients	75%	Long-term loans—external funds (average)	$2775

Undergraduate Facts				
	Part-time	14%	*Freshman Data:* 2,561 applied, 89% were accepted, 34% (773) of those entered	
	State residents	47%		
	Transfers	5%	From top tenth of high school class	27%
	African-Americans	3%	SAT-takers scoring 600 or over on verbal	N/R
	Native Americans	1%	SAT-takers scoring 700 or over on verbal	N/R
	Hispanics	3%	SAT-takers scoring 600 or over on math	N/R
	Asian-Americans	5%	SAT-takers scoring 700 or over on math	N/R
	International students	3%	ACT-takers scoring 26 or over	36%
	Freshmen returning for sophomore year	82%	ACT-takers scoring 30 or over	8%
	Students completing degree within 5 years	55%	*Majors with most degrees conferred:* nursing, biology/biological sciences, psychology.	
	Grads pursuing further study	35%		

Majors Accounting, advertising, American studies, applied mathematics, art education, art/fine arts, art history, atmospheric sciences, biology/biological sciences, broadcasting, business, business economics, chemistry, classics, communication, comparative literature, computer science, creative writing, dance, (pre)dentistry sequence, economics, education, elementary education, English, environmental sciences, finance/banking, French, German, Greek, history, international studies, journalism, Latin, (pre)law sequence, literature, management information systems, marketing/retailing/merchandising, mathematics, (pre)medicine sequence, ministries, modern languages, nursing, occupational therapy, pharmacy/pharmaceutical sciences, philosophy, physical education, physical fitness/human movement, physics, political science/government, psychology, public relations, science education, secondary education, social work, sociology, Spanish, special education, speech/rhetoric/public address/debate, statistics, studio art, theater arts/drama, theology.

Applying *Required:* high school transcript, 1 recommendation, SAT or ACT. *Recommended:* 3 years of high school math and science, some high school foreign language. *Application deadlines:* rolling, 4/1 priority date for financial aid. *Contact:* Mr. Howard J. Bachman, Assistant Vice-President for Enrollment Management, California Street at 24th, Omaha, NE 68178, 402-280-2703.

Dartmouth College

Hanover, New Hampshire

Founded 1769
Rural setting
Independent
Coed
Awards B, M, D

Enrollment 5,475 total; 4,275 undergraduates (1,036 freshmen)

Faculty 468 total; 314 full-time (92% have doctorate/terminal degree); student-faculty ratio is 12:1; grad assistants teach no undergraduate courses.

Libraries 1.9 million bound volumes, 2.2 million titles on microform, 19,000 periodical subscriptions

Computing *Terminals/PCs available for student use:* 1,000, located in computer center, student center, library, dormitories, classrooms, academic departments; PC required for freshmen and available for purchase. Campus network links student PCs.

Of Special Interest *Core academic program:* yes. Computer course required for engineering science, math majors. Phi Beta Kappa, Sigma Xi chapters. Academic exchange with members of the Twelve College Exchange Program, University of California, San Diego. Sponsors and participates in study-abroad programs. Cooperative Army ROTC.

On Campus Drama/theater group; student-run newspaper and radio station. *Social organizations:* 9 national fraternities, 8 national sororities, 8 local fraternities, 1 local sorority, 5 coed fraternities; 52% of eligible undergraduate men and 58% of eligible undergraduate women are members.

Athletics Member NCAA (Division I). *Intercollegiate sports:* basketball (M, W), crew (M, W), cross-country running (M, W), equestrian sports (M, W), fencing (M, W), field hockey (W), football (M), golf (M, W), gymnastics (M), ice hockey (M, W), lacrosse (M, W), rugby (M, W), sailing (M, W), skiing (cross-country) (M, W), skiing (downhill) (M, W), soccer (M, W), squash (M, W), swimming and diving (M, W), tennis (M, W), track and field (M, W), volleyball (M, W), water polo (M, W), wrestling (M).

Costs (1991–92) & Aid				
	Comprehensive fee	$21,495	Need-based scholarships	Avail
	Tuition	$16,230	Non-need scholarships	N/Avail
	Mandatory fees	$105	Short-term loans	N/Avail
	Room and board	$5160	Long-term loans—college funds	Avail
	Financial aid recipients	41%	Long-term loans—external funds	Avail

Undergraduate Facts				
	Part-time	0%	*Freshman Data:* 8,071 applied, 25% were accepted, 51% (1,036) of those entered	
	State residents	4%		
	Transfers	2%	From top tenth of high school class	84%
	African-Americans	7%	SAT-takers scoring 600 or over on verbal	67%
	Native Americans	3%	SAT-takers scoring 700 or over on verbal	16%
	Hispanics	4%	SAT-takers scoring 600 or over on math	88%
	Asian-Americans	7%	SAT-takers scoring 700 or over on math	50%
	International students	5%	ACT-takers scoring 26 or over	N/R
	Freshmen returning for sophomore year	98%	ACT-takers scoring 30 or over	N/R
	Students completing degree within 5 years	94%		
	Grads pursuing further study	24%		

Majors Anthropology, applied art, archaeology, art history, Asian/Oriental studies, biochemistry, biology/biological sciences, black/African-American studies, chemistry, classics, cognitive science, comparative literature, computer science, earth science, economics, education, engineering sciences, English, environmental sciences, film studies, French, geography, German, history, Italian, linguistics, mathematics, music, Native American studies, philosophy, physics, political science/government, psychology, religious studies, Romance languages, Russian, sociology, Spanish, studio art, theater arts/drama, women's studies.

Applying *Required:* essay, high school transcript, SAT or ACT, 3 Achievements. *Recommended:* 3 years of high school math and science, some high school foreign language, interview, English Composition Test. *Application deadlines:* 1/1, 11/15 for early decision, 2/1 for financial aid. *Contact:* Mr. Alfred T. Quirk, Dean of Admissions and Financial Aid, McNutt Hall, Hanover, NH 03755, 603-646-2875.

From the College One of Dartmouth's great strengths lies in its size: large enough to be a research university with professional schools in business, engineering, and medicine and yet small enough to provide a very favorable faculty-student ratio for undergraduates. All of this is in a small community almost completely dedicated to education.

Davidson College

Davidson, North Carolina

Founded 1837
Small-town setting
Independent, Presbyterian
Coed
Awards B

Enrollment	1,555 total—all undergraduates (397 freshmen)
Faculty	127 total; 126 full-time (98% have doctorate/terminal degree); student-faculty ratio is 12:1.
Libraries	375,000 bound volumes, 83,000 titles on microform, 1,800 periodical subscriptions
Computing	*Terminals/PCs available for student use:* 60, located in computer center, library, academic buildings; PC not required.
Of Special Interest	*Core academic program:* yes. Computer course required for math majors. Phi Beta Kappa chapter. Academic exchange with 11 members of the Charlotte Area Educational Consortium. Sponsors and participates in study-abroad programs. Army ROTC, cooperative Air Force ROTC.
On Campus	Drama/theater group; student-run newspaper and radio station. *Social organizations:* 7 national fraternities, 3 local sororities; 55% of eligible undergraduate men and 65% of eligible undergraduate women are members.
Athletics	Member NCAA (Division I). *Intercollegiate sports:* baseball (M), basketball (M, W), crew (M, W), cross-country running (M, W), field hockey (W), football (M), golf (M), lacrosse (M, W), rugby (M), sailing (M, W), soccer (M, W), swimming and diving (M, W), tennis (M, W), track and field (M, W), volleyball (W), wrestling (M). *Scholarships:* M, W.

Costs (1992–93) & Aid				
	Comprehensive fee	$19,420	Need-based scholarships (average)	$7310
	Tuition	$14,400	Non-need scholarships (average)	$1210
	Mandatory fees	$550	Short-term loans	N/Avail
	Room and board	$4470	Long-term loans—college funds (average)	$1200
	Financial aid recipients	34%	Long-term loans—external funds (average)	$2100

Undergraduate Facts				
	Part-time	0%	*Freshman Data:* 2,258 applied, 37% were accepted, 48% (397) of those entered	
	State residents	29%		
	Transfers	1%	From top tenth of high school class	71%
	African-Americans	4%	SAT-takers scoring 600 or over on verbal	45%
	Native Americans	0%	SAT-takers scoring 700 or over on verbal	5%
	Hispanics	1%	SAT-takers scoring 600 or over on math	74%
	Asian-Americans	3%	SAT-takers scoring 700 or over on math	21%
	International students	5%	ACT-takers scoring 26 or over	86%
	Freshmen returning for sophomore year	98%	ACT-takers scoring 30 or over	48%
	Students completing degree within 5 years	90%	*Majors with most degrees conferred:* history, English, economics.	
	Grads pursuing further study	49%		

Majors Anthropology, art/fine arts, art history, biology/biological sciences, chemistry, classics, economics, English, French, German, history, mathematics, music, philosophy, physics, political science/government, psychology, religious studies, sociology, Spanish, studio art, theater arts/drama.

Applying *Required:* essay, high school transcript, 3 years of high school math, 2 years of high school foreign language, 4 recommendations, SAT or ACT. *Recommended:* 3 years of high school science, interview, 3 Achievements, English Composition Test (with essay). *Application deadlines:* 2/1, 12/1 for early decision, 2/15 for financial aid. *Contact:* Dr. Nancy Cable Wells, Dean of Admissions and Financial Aid, 405 North Main Street, Davidson, NC 28036, 704-892-2231 or toll-free 800-768-0380.

Deep Springs College

Deep Springs, California

Founded 1917
Rural setting
Independent
Men
Awards A

Enrollment 26 total—all undergraduates (13 freshmen)

Faculty 11 total; 7 full-time; student-faculty ratio is 5:1.

Libraries 25,000 bound volumes, 50 periodical subscriptions

Computing *Terminals/PCs available for student use:* 5, located in computer center, dormitories; PC not required. Campus network links student PCs.

Of Special Interest Core academic program: no. Academic exchange program: no. Study-abroad programs: no.

On Campus Drama/theater group; student-run radio station. No national or local fraternities on campus.

Athletics None

Costs	Comprehensive fee	$0	Financial aid	N/App
Undergraduate Facts	Part-time	0%	*Freshman Data:* 185 applied, 7% were accepted, 100% (13) of those entered	
	State residents	25%		
	Transfers	0%	From top tenth of high school class	100%
	African-Americans	0%	SAT-takers scoring 600 or over on verbal	100%
	Native Americans	0%	SAT-takers scoring 700 or over on verbal	83%
	Hispanics	7%	SAT-takers scoring 600 or over on math	100%
	Asian-Americans	7%	SAT-takers scoring 700 or over on math	85%
	International students	7%	ACT-takers scoring 26 or over	N/R
	Freshmen returning for sophomore year	100%	ACT-takers scoring 30 or over	N/R
	Students completing degree within 5 years	N/R		
	Grads pursuing further study	100%		

Major Liberal arts/general studies.

Applying *Required:* essay, high school transcript, interview, SAT, 2 Achievements. *Application deadline:* 11/15. *Contact:* Mr. Edward H. Hoenicke, President, HC 72, Box 45001, Dyer, NV 89010-9803, 619-872-2000.

From the College Deep Springs offers 26 students a rigorous two-year liberal arts education. It is located on a cattle ranch in eastern California and combines practical work with studies. Tuition, room, and board are free. Combined SAT scores average 1400.

✱ Denison University

Granville, Ohio

Founded 1831
Small-town setting
Independent
Coed
Awards B

Enrollment 2,022 total—all undergraduates (503 freshmen)

Faculty 171 total; 161 full-time (95% have doctorate/terminal degree); student-faculty ratio is 13:1.

Libraries 289,069 bound volumes, 23,461 titles on microform, 1,035 periodical subscriptions

Computing *Terminals/PCs available for student use:* 175, located in computer center, library, dormitories, all academic departments; PC not required.

Of Special Interest *Core academic program:* yes. Computer course required for math majors. Phi Beta Kappa, Sigma Xi chapters. Academic exchange with 3 members of the Black College Student Exchange, American University. Sponsors and participates in study-abroad programs.

On Campus Drama/theater group; student-run newspaper and radio station. *Social organizations:* 9 national fraternities, 7 national sororities; 59% of eligible undergraduate men and 67% of eligible undergraduate women are members.

Athletics Member NCAA (Division III). *Intercollegiate sports:* basketball (M, W), cross-country running (M, W), field hockey (W), football (M), golf (M), ice hockey (M), lacrosse (M, W), rugby (M, W), soccer (M, W), swimming and diving (M, W), tennis (M, W), track and field (M, W), volleyball (W), water polo (M, W).

Costs (1991–92) & Aid				
	Comprehensive fee	$18,710	Need-based scholarships (average)	$7960
	Tuition	$14,050	Non-need scholarships	Avail
	Mandatory fees	$650	Short-term loans (average)	$200
	Room and board	$4010	Long-term loans—college funds (average)	$1905
	Financial aid recipients	37%	Long-term loans—external funds (average)	$2973

Undergraduate Facts				
	Part-time	1%	*Freshman Data:* 2,870 applied, 76% were accepted, 23% (503) of those entered	
	State residents	30%		
	Transfers	4%	From top tenth of high school class	35%
	African-Americans	5%	SAT-takers scoring 600 or over on verbal	12%
	Native Americans	0%	SAT-takers scoring 700 or over on verbal	1%
	Hispanics	1%	SAT-takers scoring 600 or over on math	30%
	Asian-Americans	3%	SAT-takers scoring 700 or over on math	6%
	International students	3%	ACT-takers scoring 26 or over	39%
	Freshmen returning for sophomore year	90%	ACT-takers scoring 30 or over	10%
	Students completing degree within 5 years	N/R	*Majors with most degrees conferred:* economics, psychology.	
	Grads pursuing further study	N/R		

Majors Anthropology, art history, astronomy, biology/biological sciences, black/African-American studies, chemistry, classics, communication, computer science, creative writing, dance, (pre)dentistry sequence, East Asian studies, economics, education, English, environmental biology, environmental sciences, European studies, film studies, French, geology, German, history, international studies, Latin American studies, (pre)law sequence, mathematics, (pre)medicine sequence, music, music education, philosophy, physical education, physics, political science/government, psychology, religious studies, secondary education, sociology, Spanish, speech/rhetoric/public address/debate, studio art, theater arts/drama, (pre)veterinary medicine sequence, women's studies.

Applying *Required:* essay, high school transcript, 2 recommendations, SAT or ACT. *Recommended:* 3 years of high school math and science, 3 years of high school foreign language, interview, Achievements, English Composition Test (with essay). *Application deadlines:* 2/1, 1/1 for early decision, 2/15 priority date for financial aid. *Contact:* Mr. William W. Dennett, Dean of Admissions and Financial Aid, Box H, Granville, OH 43023, 614-587-6627 or toll-free 800-DENISON; *Office location:* Beth Eden Hall.

From the College Denison remains a traditional liberal arts college whose curriculum is based on general education requirements, close working relationships with faculty, and opportunities to engage in significant research in a variety of disciplines.

DePaul University

Chicago, Illinois

Founded 1898
Urban setting
Independent, Roman Catholic
Coed
Awards B, M, D

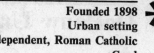

Enrollment	16,414 total; 9,757 undergraduates (1,103 freshmen)
Faculty	1,146 total; 470 full-time (88% have doctorate/terminal degree); student-faculty ratio is 17:1; grad assistants teach no undergraduate courses.
Libraries	597,481 bound volumes, 265,458 titles on microform, 16,316 periodical subscriptions
Computing	*Terminals/PCs available for student use:* 550, located in labs throughout the four campuses; PC not required but available for purchase. Campus network links student PCs.
Of Special Interest	*Core academic program:* yes. Computer course required for math, geography, science, business-related majors. Academic exchange program: no. Sponsors and participates in study-abroad programs. Army ROTC.
On Campus	Drama/theater group; student-run newspaper and radio station. *Social organizations:* 4 national fraternities, 4 national sororities, 1 local fraternity; 6% of eligible undergraduate men and 4% of eligible undergraduate women are members.
Athletics	Member NCAA (Division I). *Intercollegiate sports:* basketball (M, W), cross-country running (M, W), golf (M), riflery (M, W), soccer (M), softball (W), tennis (M, W), track and field (M, W), volleyball (W). *Scholarships:* M, W.

Costs (1991–92) & Aid				
	Comprehensive fee	$13,928	Need-based scholarships (average)	$1902
	Tuition	$9342	Non-need scholarships (average)	$2628
	Mandatory fees	$10	Short-term loans	N/Avail
	Room and board	$4576	Long-term loans—college funds (average)	$1454
	Financial aid recipients	65%	Long-term loans—external funds (average)	$2606

Undergraduate Facts				
	Part-time	36%	*Freshman Data:* 3,827 applied, 69% were accepted, 42% (1,103) of those entered	
	State residents	82%		
	Transfers	N/R	From top tenth of high school class	32%
	African-Americans	12%	SAT-takers scoring 600 or over on verbal	12%
	Native Americans	1%	SAT-takers scoring 700 or over on verbal	1%
	Hispanics	8%	SAT-takers scoring 600 or over on math	26%
	Asian-Americans	6%	SAT-takers scoring 700 or over on math	5%
	International students	1%	ACT-takers scoring 26 or over	30%
	Freshmen returning for sophomore year	82%	ACT-takers scoring 30 or over	6%
	Students completing degree within 5 years	N/R	*Majors with most degrees conferred:* accounting, marketing/retailing/merchandising, communication.	
	Grads pursuing further study	N/R		

Majors Accounting, actuarial science, adult and continuing education, advertising, American studies, anthropology, applied art, applied mathematics, art history, audio engineering, biology/biological sciences, black/African-American studies, business, business economics, chemistry, city/community/regional planning, commercial art, communication, computer information systems, computer programming, computer science, creative writing, criminal justice, (pre)dentistry sequence, early childhood education, ecology/environmental studies, economics, education, electrical and electronics technologies, elementary education, English, environmental sciences, finance/banking, French, geography, German, history, human development, human services, international business, international studies, Italian, jazz, Judaic studies, Latin American studies, (pre)law sequence, legal studies, linguistics, literature, marketing/retailing/merchandising, mathematics, medical technology, (pre)medicine sequence, modern languages, music, music business, music education, nursing, operations research, painting/drawing, philosophy, physical education, physics, piano/organ, political science/government, psychology, religious education, religious studies, sculpture, secondary education, social science, sociology, Spanish, statistics, stringed instruments, studio art, theater arts/drama, tourism and travel, urban studies, (pre)veterinary medicine sequence, voice, wind and percussion instruments, women's studies.

Applying *Required:* high school transcript, SAT or ACT. *Recommended:* 3 years of high school math and science, 2 years of high school foreign language, Achievements. Recommendations, interview, audition required for some. *Application deadlines:* 8/15, 11/15 for early action, 4/1 priority date for financial aid. *Contact:* Ms. Lucy Leusch, Director of Undergraduate Admissions, 25 East Jackson Boulevard, Chicago, IL 60604, 312-362-8300 or toll-free 800-4DE-PAUL (out-of-state).

From the College DePaul University is a growing, urban, Catholic institution, the second largest in the United States. At the Lincoln Park campus, three new residence halls have opened in the past four years, the new library is slated to open next fall, and the University recently acquired the 1,400-seat Blackstone Theatre. DePaul continues to emphasize teaching ability as a priority for faculty selection.

DePauw University

Greencastle, Indiana

Founded 1837
Small-town setting
Independent/affiliated with United Methodist Church
Coed
Awards B

Enrollment 2,171 total—all undergraduates (530 freshmen)

Faculty 230 total; 166 full-time (93% have doctorate/terminal degree); student-faculty ratio is 12:1.

Libraries 264,000 bound volumes, 1,380 periodical subscriptions

Computing *Terminals/PCs available for student use:* 111, located in computer center, library, dormitories; PC not required.

Of Special Interest *Core academic program:* yes. Phi Beta Kappa, Sigma Xi chapters. Academic exchange with Great Lakes Colleges Association, Associated Colleges of the Midwest, American University, Drew University. Sponsors and participates in study-abroad programs. Cooperative Army ROTC, cooperative Air Force ROTC.

On Campus Drama/theater group; student-run newspaper and radio station. *Social organizations:* 14 national fraternities, 10 national sororities; 80% of eligible undergraduate men and 80% of eligible undergraduate women are members.

Athletics Member NCAA (Division III). *Intercollegiate sports:* archery (M, W), baseball (M), basketball (M, W), crew (M, W), cross-country running (M, W), equestrian sports (M, W), fencing (M, W), field hockey (W), football (M), golf (M, W), lacrosse (M), sailing (M, W), soccer (M, W), swimming and diving (M, W), tennis (M, W), track and field (M, W), volleyball (W), wrestling (M).

Costs (1991–92) & Aid				
	Comprehensive fee	$16,748	Need-based scholarships (average)	$5965
	Tuition	$12,288	Non-need scholarships (average)	$4250
	Mandatory fees	$40	Short-term loans	N/Avail
	Room and board	$4420	Long-term loans—college funds (average)	$1126
	Financial aid recipients	50%	Long-term loans—external funds (average)	$2231

Undergraduate Facts				
	Part-time	2%	*Freshman Data:* 1,908 applied, 85% were accepted, 33% (530) of those entered	
	State residents	40%		
	Transfers	2%	From top tenth of high school class	44%
	African-Americans	7%	SAT-takers scoring 600 or over on verbal	30%
	Native Americans	1%	SAT-takers scoring 700 or over on verbal	5%
	Hispanics	1%	SAT-takers scoring 600 or over on math	51%
	Asian-Americans	2%	SAT-takers scoring 700 or over on math	15%
	International students	2%	ACT-takers scoring 26 or over	N/R
	Freshmen returning for sophomore year	89%	ACT-takers scoring 30 or over	N/R
	Students completing degree within 5 years	78%	*Majors with most degrees conferred:* economics, communication, political science/government.	
	Grads pursuing further study	N/R		

Majors Anthropology, art history, biology/biological sciences, chemistry, classics, communication, computer science, earth science, economics, elementary education, English, French, geography, geology, German, Greek, history, interdisciplinary studies, Latin, literature, mathematics, medical technology, music, music business, music education, philosophy, physical education, physics, piano/organ, political science/government, psychology, recreation and leisure services, religious studies, Romance languages, Russian and Slavic studies, sociology, Spanish, studio art, voice.

Applying *Required:* essay, high school transcript, 3 years of high school math and science, 1 recommendation, SAT or ACT. *Recommended:* 2 years of high school foreign language, campus interview. *Application deadlines:* 2/15, 12/1 for early action, 2/15 priority date for financial aid. *Contact:* Mr. David Murray, Dean of Admissions, Associate Provost, 313 South Locust Street, Greencastle, IN 46135, 317-658-4006 or toll-free 800-447-2495.

Dickinson College

Carlisle, Pennsylvania

Founded 1773
Small-town setting
Independent
Coed
Awards B

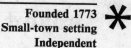

Enrollment	2,029 total—all undergraduates (559 freshmen)
Faculty	186 total; student-faculty ratio is 12:1.
Libraries	503,540 bound volumes, 155,580 titles on microform, 1,689 periodical subscriptions
Computing	*Terminals/PCs available for student use:* 450, located in computer center, student center, library, dormitories, computer rooms in classroom buildings; PC not required. Campus network links student PCs.
Of Special Interest	*Core academic program:* yes. Computer course required for math majors. Phi Beta Kappa chapter. Academic exchange with members of the Central Pennsylvania Consortium, Franklin and Marshall College, Gettysburg College. Sponsors and participates in study-abroad programs. Army ROTC.
On Campus	Drama/theater group; student-run newspaper and radio station. *Social organizations:* 7 national fraternities, 4 national sororities, 1 local fraternity, 1 local sorority; 47% of eligible undergraduate men and 56% of eligible undergraduate women are members.
Athletics	Member NCAA (Division III). *Intercollegiate sports:* baseball (M), basketball (M, W), cross-country running (M, W), equestrian sports (M, W), fencing (M, W), field hockey (W), football (M), golf (M), ice hockey (M), lacrosse (M, W), rugby (M), skiing (downhill) (M, W), soccer (M, W), softball (W), swimming and diving (M, W), tennis (M, W), track and field (M, W), volleyball (M, W).

Costs (1991–92) & Aid				
	Comprehensive fee	$20,095	Need-based scholarships (average)	$8368
	Tuition	$15,450	Non-need scholarships (average)	$215
	Mandatory fees	$115	Short-term loans	N/Avail
	Room and board	$4530	Long-term loans—college funds (average)	$2090
	Financial aid recipients	62%	Long-term loans—external funds (average)	$3253

Undergraduate Facts				
	Part-time	0%	*Freshman Data:* 3,346 applied, 75% were accepted, 22% (559) of those entered	
	State residents	40%		
	Transfers	10%	From top tenth of high school class	39%
	African-Americans	1%	SAT-takers scoring 600 or over on verbal	20%
	Native Americans	1%	SAT-takers scoring 700 or over on verbal	1%
	Hispanics	2%	SAT-takers scoring 600 or over on math	36%
	Asian-Americans	3%	SAT-takers scoring 700 or over on math	4%
	International students	3%	ACT-takers scoring 26 or over	N/R
	Freshmen returning for sophomore year	94%	ACT-takers scoring 30 or over	N/R
	Students completing degree within 5 years	84%	*Majors with most degrees conferred:* political science/government, English, history.	
	Grads pursuing further study	10%		

Majors American studies, anthropology, art/fine arts, biology/biological sciences, chemistry, computer science, East Asian studies, economics, English, French, geology, German, Greek, history, international studies, Italian, Judaic studies, Latin, mathematics, music, philosophy, physics, political science/government, psychology, public affairs and policy studies, religious studies, Russian, Russian and Slavic studies, sociology, Spanish, theater arts/drama.

Applying *Required:* essay, high school transcript, 2 years of high school foreign language, 1 recommendation, SAT or ACT. *Recommended:* 3 years of high school math and science, interview, Achievements. *Application deadlines:* 3/1, 12/15 for early decision, 2/15 priority date for financial aid. *Contact:* Mr. J. Larry Mench, Dean of Admissions and Enrollment, 272 West High Street, Carlisle, PA 17013, 717-245-1231.

From the College Dickinson's Freshman Seminar Program offers a distinctive vehicle of transition: There are over thirty-five seminars from which to choose; participants in each seminar are housed together; in most cases, seminar instructors are also faculty advisers to the students; and the seminar is the first class, starting during orientation.

*Drake University

Des Moines, Iowa

Founded 1881
Suburban setting
Independent
Coed
Awards B, M, D

Enrollment 8,096 total; 4,273 undergraduates (756 freshmen)

Faculty 275 total—all full-time (93% have doctorate/terminal degree); student-faculty ratio is 17:1; grad assistants teach a few undergraduate courses.

Libraries 505,000 bound volumes, 550,000 titles on microform, 2,600 periodical subscriptions

Computing *Terminals/PCs available for student use:* 750, located in computer center, student center, library, dormitories, academic buildings; PC not required. Campus network links student PCs.

Of Special Interest *Core academic program:* no. Computer course required for business, journalism, mass communication, biology, chemistry, economics, math, pharmacy majors. Phi Beta Kappa, Sigma Xi chapters. Academic exchange with 2 members of the Des Moines Consortium. Sponsors and participates in study-abroad programs. Army ROTC, cooperative Air Force ROTC.

On Campus Drama/theater group; student-run newspaper and radio station. *Social organizations:* 11 national fraternities, 10 national sororities; 29% of eligible undergraduate men and 31% of eligible undergraduate women are members.

Athletics Member NCAA (Division I). *Intercollegiate sports:* baseball (M), basketball (M, W), crew (M, W), cross-country running (M, W), football (M), golf (M), ice hockey (M), lacrosse (M), rugby (M), soccer (M), softball (W), swimming and diving (M, W), tennis (M, W), track and field (M, W), volleyball (M, W), wrestling (M). *Scholarships:* M, W.

Costs (1991–92) & Aid				
	Comprehensive fee	$15,255	Need-based scholarships (average)	$2500
	Tuition	$11,040	Non-need scholarships (average)	$3250
	Mandatory fees	N/App	Short-term loans (average)	$75
	Room and board	$4215	Long-term loans—college funds (average)	$500
	Financial aid recipients	75%	Long-term loans—external funds (average)	$3000

Undergraduate Facts				
	Part-time	21%	*Freshman Data:* 2,357 applied, 91% were accepted, 35% (756) of those entered	
	State residents	35%		
	Transfers	20%	From top tenth of high school class	31%
	African-Americans	5%	SAT-takers scoring 600 or over on verbal	13%
	Native Americans	1%	SAT-takers scoring 700 or over on verbal	1%
	Hispanics	1%	SAT-takers scoring 600 or over on math	34%
	Asian-Americans	3%	SAT-takers scoring 700 or over on math	5%
	International students	4%	ACT-takers scoring 26 or over	46%
	Freshmen returning for sophomore year	86%	ACT-takers scoring 30 or over	15%
	Students completing degree within 5 years	67%	*Majors with most degrees conferred:* pharmacy/ pharmaceutical sciences, advertising, marketing/ retailing/merchandising.	
	Grads pursuing further study	17%		

Majors Accounting, actuarial science, advertising, applied art, art education, art/fine arts, art history, Asian/Oriental studies, astronomy, biology/biological sciences, broadcasting, business, business education, chemistry, clinical psychology, commercial art, communication, computer information systems, computer science, (pre)dentistry sequence, early childhood education, earth science, economics, education, educational administration, elementary education, English, environmental sciences, experimental psychology, finance/banking, French, geography, German, gerontology, graphic arts, history, insurance, interior design, international business, international studies, journalism, Latin American studies, (pre)law sequence, literature, marine sciences, marketing/retailing/merchandising, mathematics, medical technology, (pre)medicine sequence, military science, music, music business, music education, nursing, painting/drawing, pharmacy/pharmaceutical sciences, philosophy, physical sciences, physics, piano/organ, political science/government, psychology, public administration, public relations, radio and television studies, religious studies, sacred music, science, science education, sculpture, secondary education, social science, sociology, Spanish, speech/rhetoric/public address/debate, stringed instruments, studio art, theater arts/drama, (pre)veterinary medicine sequence, voice, wind and percussion instruments, women's studies.

Applying *Required:* high school transcript, recommendations, SAT or ACT. *Recommended:* essay, 2 years of high school foreign language, interview. 3 years of high school math and science required for some. *Application deadlines:* rolling, 3/1 priority date for financial aid. *Contact:* Mr. Thomas F. Willoughby, Director of Admission, 2507 University Avenue, Des Moines, IA 50311, 515-271-3181 or toll-free 800-44 DRAKE.

From the College The success of its students is Drake University's top priority. Drake offers more than sixty undergraduate majors, outstanding faculty, a computer and printer in every freshman residence hall room, more than 140 student organizations, and excellent financial aid—all designed to enhance the education, career, and life of each Drake student. A campus visit is encouraged.

Drew University

Madison, New Jersey

Founded 1867
Suburban setting
Independent/affiliated with United Methodist Church
Coed
Awards B, M, D

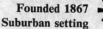

Enrollment 2,089 total; 1,331 undergraduates (278 freshmen)

Faculty 175 total; 96 full-time (89% have doctorate/terminal degree); student-faculty ratio is 12:1; grad assistants teach a few undergraduate courses.

Libraries 414,985 bound volumes, 180,300 titles on microform, 2,031 periodical subscriptions

Computing *Terminals/PCs available for student use:* 2,100, located in computer center, library, dormitories. Campus network links student PCs. Every student in the College of Liberal Arts is given a personal computer, printer, and software.

Of Special Interest *Core academic program:* yes. Computer course required for applied math majors. Phi Beta Kappa chapter. Academic exchange with College of Saint Elizabeth. Sponsors and participates in study-abroad programs. Cooperative Army ROTC.

On Campus Drama/theater group; student-run newspaper and radio station. No national or local fraternities or sororities on campus.

Athletics Member NCAA (Division III). *Intercollegiate sports:* baseball (M), basketball (M, W), cross-country running (M, W), equestrian sports (M, W), fencing (M, W), field hockey (W), lacrosse (M, W), rugby (M), soccer (M, W), softball (W), swimming and diving (M, W), tennis (M, W).

Costs (1991–92) & Aid

Comprehensive fee	$21,274	
Tuition	$16,104	
Mandatory fees	$320	
Room and board	$4850	
Financial aid recipients	61%	
Need-based scholarships (average)		$8573
Non-need scholarships (average)		$4309
Short-term loans		N/Avail
Long-term loans—college funds		N/Avail
Long-term loans—external funds (average)		$2852

Undergraduate Facts

Part-time	7%
State residents	54%
Transfers	6%
African-Americans	4%
Native Americans	0%
Hispanics	4%
Asian-Americans	4%
International students	3%
Freshmen returning for sophomore year	85%
Students completing degree within 5 years	77%
Grads pursuing further study	30%

Freshman Data: 1,613 applied, 79% were accepted, 22% (278) of those entered

From top tenth of high school class	50%
SAT-takers scoring 600 or over on verbal	37%
SAT-takers scoring 700 or over on verbal	7%
SAT-takers scoring 600 or over on math	49%
SAT-takers scoring 700 or over on math	13%
ACT-takers scoring 26 or over	N/R
ACT-takers scoring 30 or over	N/R

Majors with most degrees conferred: political science/government, psychology, English.

Majors American studies, anthropology, applied mathematics, art/fine arts, art history, behavioral sciences, biochemistry, biology/biological sciences, chemistry, classics, computer science, economics, English, French, German, history, liberal arts/general studies, mathematics, music, philosophy, physics, political science/government, psychobiology, psychology, religious studies, Russian, Russian and Slavic studies, sociology, Spanish, studio art, theater arts/drama.

Applying *Required:* essay, high school transcript, 3 years of high school math, 2 years of high school foreign language, 2 recommendations, SAT or ACT. *Recommended:* 3 years of high school science, interview, Achievements, English Composition Test. *Application deadlines:* 2/15, 1/15 for early decision, 3/1 priority date for financial aid. *Contact:* Mr. Roberto Noya, Director of Admissions for the College of Liberal Arts, Madison Avenue, Madison, NJ 07940, 201-408-3739.

✱ **Drury College**

Springfield, Missouri

Founded 1873
Urban setting
Independent-Religious
Coed
Awards B, M

Enrollment	1,579 total; 1,161 undergraduates (307 freshmen)
Faculty	113 total; 86 full-time (90% have doctorate/terminal degree); student-faculty ratio is 13:1; grad assistants teach no undergraduate courses.
Libraries	170,000 bound volumes, 900 periodical subscriptions
Computing	*Terminals/PCs available for student use:* 56, located in computer center, student center, academic departments.
Of Special Interest	*Core academic program:* yes. Computer course required for business majors. Academic exchange with American University. Sponsors and participates in study-abroad programs. Cooperative Army ROTC.
On Campus	Drama/theater group; student-run newspaper and radio station. *Social organizations:* 4 national fraternities, 4 national sororities; 40% of eligible undergraduate men and 40% of eligible undergraduate women are members.
Athletics	Member NAIA. *Intercollegiate sports:* basketball (M), golf (M), soccer (M), swimming and diving (M, W), tennis (M, W), volleyball (W). *Scholarships:* M, W.

Costs (1992–93) & Aid	Comprehensive fee	$11,870	Need-based scholarships (average)	$3200
	Tuition	$8200	Non-need scholarships (average)	$2350
	Mandatory fees	$250	Short-term loans	N/Avail
	Room and board	$3420	Long-term loans—college funds (average)	$1500
	Financial aid recipients	78%	Long-term loans—external funds (average)	$2000

Undergraduate Facts	Part-time	5%	*Freshman Data:* 651 applied, 90% were accepted, 52% (307) of those entered	
	State residents	85%		
	Transfers	15%	From top tenth of high school class	37%
	African-Americans	2%	SAT-takers scoring 600 or over on verbal	N/R
	Native Americans	1%	SAT-takers scoring 700 or over on verbal	N/R
	Hispanics	1%	SAT-takers scoring 600 or over on math	N/R
	Asian-Americans	1%	SAT-takers scoring 700 or over on math	N/R
	International students	1%	ACT-takers scoring 26 or over	39%
	Freshmen returning for sophomore year	77%	ACT-takers scoring 30 or over	11%
	Students completing degree within 5 years	52%	*Majors with most degrees conferred:* business, communication, behavioral sciences.	
	Grads pursuing further study	24%		

Majors Accounting, architecture, art education, art/fine arts, art history, behavioral sciences, biology/biological sciences, business, chemistry, communication, criminal justice, (pre)dentistry sequence, economics, education, elementary education, English, French, German, history, (pre)law sequence, mathematics, medical technology, (pre)medicine sequence, music, music education, nursing, philosophy, physical education, physics, political science/government, psychology, religious studies, secondary education, sociology, Spanish, special education, studio art, theater arts/drama, (pre)veterinary medicine sequence.

Applying *Required:* essay, high school transcript, 1 recommendation, SAT or ACT. *Recommended:* 3 years of high school math and science, 1 year of high school foreign language, campus interview. *Application deadlines:* rolling, 2/15 priority date for financial aid. *Contact:* Mr. Michael Thomas, Director of Admissions, Burnham Hall, Springfield, MO 65802, 417-865-8731 Ext. 205.

Duke University

Durham, North Carolina

Founded 1838
Suburban setting
Independent/affiliated with United Methodist Church
Coed
Awards B, M, D

Enrollment	10,736 total; 6,043 undergraduates (1,556 freshmen)
Faculty	1,530 total; student-faculty ratio is 12:1; grad assistants teach a few undergraduate courses.
Libraries	4 million bound volumes, 1.6 million titles on microform, 35,554 periodical subscriptions
Computing	*Terminals/PCs available for student use:* 450, located in computer center, library, dormitories, academic buildings; PC not required but available for purchase. Campus network links student PCs.
Of Special Interest	*Core academic program:* yes. Computer course required for engineering majors. Phi Beta Kappa, Sigma Xi chapters. Academic exchange with University of North Carolina at Chapel Hill, North Carolina Central University, North Carolina State University. Sponsors and participates in study-abroad programs. Army ROTC, Naval ROTC, Air Force ROTC.
On Campus	Drama/theater group; student-run newspaper and radio station. *Social organizations:* 21 national fraternities, 13 national sororities; 35% of eligible undergraduate men and 40% of eligible undergraduate women are members.
Athletics	Member NCAA (Division I). *Intercollegiate sports:* badminton (M, W), baseball (M), basketball (M, W), crew (M, W), cross-country running (M, W), equestrian sports (M, W), fencing (M, W), field hockey (M, W), football (M, W), golf (M, W), ice hockey (M, W), lacrosse (M, W), racquetball (M, W), rugby (M, W), sailing (M, W), skiing (cross-country) (M, W), skiing (downhill) (M, W), soccer (M, W), softball (M, W), swimming and diving (M, W), tennis (M, W), track and field (M, W), volleyball (M, W), water polo (M, W), wrestling (M). *Scholarships:* M, W.

Costs (1992–93 estimated) & Aid				
	Comprehensive fee	$21,001	Need-based scholarships (average)	$9683
	Tuition	$15,430	Non-need scholarships (average)	$10,888
	Mandatory fees	$421	Short-term loans	N/Avail
	Room and board	$5150	Long-term loans—college funds (average)	$1500
	Financial aid recipients	38%	Long-term loans—external funds (average)	$1898

Undergraduate Facts				
	Part-time	1%	*Freshman Data:* 12,199 applied, 29% were accepted, 43% (1,556) of those entered	
	State residents	12%		
	Transfers	1%	From top tenth of high school class	88%
	African-Americans	8%	SAT-takers scoring 600 or over on verbal	67%
	Native Americans	1%	SAT-takers scoring 700 or over on verbal	14%
	Hispanics	4%	SAT-takers scoring 600 or over on math	89%
	Asian-Americans	8%	SAT-takers scoring 700 or over on math	52%
	International students	1%	ACT-takers scoring 26 or over	N/R
	Freshmen returning for sophomore year	99%	ACT-takers scoring 30 or over	N/R
	Students completing degree within 5 years	94%	*Majors with most degrees conferred:* political science/government, history, English.	
	Grads pursuing further study	38%		

Majors African studies, anatomy, anthropology, art/fine arts, art history, biology/biological sciences, biomedical engineering, black/African-American studies, Canadian studies, chemistry, civil engineering, classics, computer science, East Asian studies, East European and Soviet studies, economics, electrical engineering, English, environmental engineering, European studies, French, geology, Germanic languages and literature, Greek, history, Italian, Latin, Latin American studies, literature, materials sciences, mathematics, mechanical engineering, medieval studies, music, philosophy, physics, political science/government, psychology, public affairs and policy studies, religious studies, Slavic languages, sociology, South Asian studies, Spanish, theater arts/drama.

Applying *Required:* essay, high school transcript, 3 recommendations, SAT or ACT, English Composition Test. *Recommended:* 3 years of high school math and science, 3 years of high school foreign language, interview, audition tape for applicants with outstanding dance, dramatic, or musical talent; slides of artwork. 3 Achievements required for some. *Application deadlines:* 1/2, 11/1 for early decision, 2/1 priority date for financial aid. *Contact:* Mr. Harold M. Wingood, Director of Undergraduate Admissions, 2138 Campus Drive, Durham, NC 27706, 919-684-3214.

Earlham College

Richmond, Indiana

Founded 1847
Small-town setting
Independent/affiliated with Society of Friends
Coed
Awards B, M

Enrollment 1,213 total; 1,151 undergraduates (260 freshmen)

Faculty 114 total; 96 full-time (87% have doctorate/terminal degree); student-faculty ratio is 12:1; grad assistants teach no undergraduate courses.

Libraries 348,000 bound volumes, 152,000 titles on microform, 1,398 periodical subscriptions

Computing *Terminals/PCs available for student use:* 115, located in computer center, library, classroom buildings; PC not required.

Of Special Interest *Core academic program:* yes. Computer course required for some majors. Phi Beta Kappa chapter. Academic exchange with members of the Great Lakes Colleges Association. Sponsors and participates in study-abroad programs.

On Campus Drama/theater group; student-run newspaper and radio station. No national or local fraternities or sororities on campus.

Athletics Member NCAA (Division III), NAIA. *Intercollegiate sports:* baseball (M), basketball (M, W), cross-country running (M, W), field hockey (W), football (M), golf (M), lacrosse (W), soccer (M, W), softball (W), tennis (M, W), track and field (M, W), volleyball (M, W).

Costs (1991–92) & Aid				
	Comprehensive fee	$17,205	Need-based scholarships (average)	$6307
	Tuition	$13,218	Non-need scholarships (average)	$2413
	Mandatory fees	$261	Short-term loans (average)	$50
	Room and board	$3726	Long-term loans—college funds (average)	$1259
	Financial aid recipients	62%	Long-term loans—external funds (average)	$2660

Undergraduate Facts				
	Part-time	1%	*Freshman Data:* 1,213 applied, 67% were accepted, 32% (260) of those entered	
	State residents	22%		
	Transfers	3%	From top tenth of high school class	33%
	African-Americans	6%	SAT-takers scoring 600 or over on verbal	32%
	Native Americans	0%	SAT-takers scoring 700 or over on verbal	9%
	Hispanics	1%	SAT-takers scoring 600 or over on math	42%
	Asian-Americans	3%	SAT-takers scoring 700 or over on math	8%
	International students	2%	ACT-takers scoring 26 or over	55%
	Freshmen returning for sophomore year	90%	ACT-takers scoring 30 or over	21%
	Students completing degree within 5 years	75%		
	Grads pursuing further study	48%		

Majors African studies, anthropology, art/fine arts, astronomy, biology/biological sciences, black/African-American studies, chemistry, classics, computer science, East Asian studies, ecology/environmental studies, economics, education, elementary education, English, environmental sciences, French, geology, German, history, human development, international studies, Japanese, (pre)law sequence, literature, mathematics, (pre)medicine sequence, museum studies, music, peace studies, philosophy, physics, political science/government, psychology, religious studies, secondary education, sociology, Spanish, theater arts/drama, (pre)veterinary medicine sequence, women's studies.

Applying *Required:* essay, high school transcript, 3 years of high school math, 2 years of high school foreign language, 2 recommendations, SAT or ACT. *Recommended:* 3 years of high school science, campus interview. *Application deadlines:* 2/15, 12/1 for early decision, 1/15 for early action, 3/1 priority date for financial aid. *Contact:* Mr. Robert L. deVeer, Dean of Admissions, National Road West, Richmond, IN 47374, 317-983-1600 or toll-free 800-382-6906 (in-state), 800-428-6958 (out-of-state).

Eckerd College

St. Petersburg, Florida

Founded 1958
Suburban setting
Independent, Presbyterian
Coed
Awards B ★

Enrollment 1,368 total—all undergraduates (340 freshmen)

Faculty 113 total; 84 full-time (95% have doctorate/terminal degree); student-faculty ratio is 12:1.

Libraries 110,000 bound volumes, 13,000 titles on microform, 1,000 periodical subscriptions

Computing *Terminals/PCs available for student use:* 162, located in computer center, library, computer lab; PC not required.

Of Special Interest *Core academic program:* yes. Computer course required for math, management majors. Sigma Xi chapter. Academic exchange with other colleges having a 4-1-4 calendar. Sponsors and participates in study-abroad programs. Army ROTC.

On Campus Drama/theater group; student-run newspaper and radio station. No national or local fraternities or sororities on campus.

Athletics Member NCAA (Division II). *Intercollegiate sports:* baseball (M), basketball (M, W), cross-country running (M, W), golf (M), sailing (M, W), soccer (M, W), softball (W), tennis (M, W), volleyball (M, W). *Scholarships:* M, W.

Costs (1991–92) & Aid				
	Comprehensive fee	$16,250	Need-based scholarships (average)	$4500
	Tuition	$12,900	Non-need scholarships (average)	$5500
	Mandatory fees	$140	Short-term loans (average)	$250
	Room and board	$3210	Long-term loans—college funds (average)	$750
	Financial aid recipients	80%	Long-term loans—external funds (average)	$3250

Undergraduate Facts				
	Part-time	2%	*Freshman Data:* 1,508 applied, 69% were accepted, 33% (340) of those entered	
	State residents	30%		
	Transfers	15%	From top tenth of high school class	28%
	African-Americans	4%	SAT-takers scoring 600 or over on verbal	21%
	Native Americans	1%	SAT-takers scoring 700 or over on verbal	4%
	Hispanics	3%	SAT-takers scoring 600 or over on math	32%
	Asian-Americans	2%	SAT-takers scoring 700 or over on math	5%
	International students	11%	ACT-takers scoring 26 or over	42%
	Freshmen returning for sophomore year	80%	ACT-takers scoring 30 or over	10%
	Students completing degree within 5 years	60%	*Majors with most degrees conferred:* business, international business, human development.	
	Grads pursuing further study	45%		

Majors American studies, anthropology, art/fine arts, biology/biological sciences, business, chemistry, comparative literature, computer science, creative writing, (pre)dentistry sequence, ecology/environmental studies, economics, education, elementary education, English, environmental sciences, French, German, history, human development, humanities, interdisciplinary studies, international business, international studies, (pre)law sequence, literature, marine sciences, mathematics, medical technology, (pre)medicine sequence, modern languages, music, philosophy, physics, political science/government, psychology, religious studies, Russian and Slavic studies, secondary education, sociology, Spanish, theater arts/drama, (pre)veterinary medicine sequence, women's studies.

Applying *Required:* essay, high school transcript, 3 years of high school math and science, 2 years of high school foreign language, 1 recommendation, SAT or ACT. *Recommended:* interview, Achievements, English Composition Test (with essay). *Application deadlines:* rolling, 3/1 priority date for financial aid. *Contact:* Dr. Richard R. Hallin, Dean of Admissions, 4200 54th Avenue, South, St. Petersburg, FL 33733, 813-864-8331 or toll-free 800-456-9009.

From the College A new marine science laboratory on the waterfront will open in October 1992. Eckerd is also constructing a necropsy laboratory on campus in which students can assist with autopsy research on marine mammals. The chairman of Eckerd's marine science program has been appointed by President Bush to chair the U.S. Marine Mammal Commission.

Elizabethtown College

Elizabethtown, Pennsylvania

Founded 1899
Small-town setting
Independent/affiliated with Church of the Brethren
Coed
Awards B

Enrollment	1,809 total—all undergraduates (467 freshmen)
Faculty	147 total; 110 full-time (70% have doctorate/terminal degree); student-faculty ratio is 14:1.
Libraries	149,530 bound volumes, 800 titles on microform, 1,100 periodical subscriptions
Computing	*Terminals/PCs available for student use:* 90, located in classroom buildings; PC not required. Campus network links student PCs.
Of Special Interest	*Core academic program:* yes. Computer course required for business, communications, engineering, English, math, science majors. Academic exchange program: no. Sponsors and participates in study-abroad programs.
On Campus	Drama/theater group; student-run newspaper and radio station. No national or local fraternities or sororities on campus.
Athletics	Member NCAA (Division III). *Intercollegiate sports:* baseball (M), basketball (M, W), cross-country running (M, W), field hockey (W), golf (M), soccer (M, W), softball (W), swimming and diving (M, W), tennis (M, W), volleyball (M, W), wrestling (M).

Costs (1991–92) & Aid	Comprehensive fee	$15,600	Need-based scholarships (average)	$4282
	Tuition	$11,325	Non-need scholarships (average)	$2400
	Mandatory fees	$325	Short-term loans (average)	$1000
	Room and board	$3950	Long-term loans—college funds	N/Avail
	Financial aid recipients	81%	Long-term loans—external funds (average)	$2875
Undergraduate Facts	Part-time	3%	*Freshman Data:* 2,210 applied, 78% were accepted, 27% (467) of those entered	
	State residents	62%		
	Transfers	9%	From top tenth of high school class	33%
	African-Americans	2%	SAT-takers scoring 600 or over on verbal	8%
	Native Americans	0%	SAT-takers scoring 700 or over on verbal	1%
	Hispanics	1%	SAT-takers scoring 600 or over on math	20%
	Asian-Americans	2%	SAT-takers scoring 700 or over on math	2%
	International students	2%	ACT-takers scoring 26 or over	N/R
	Freshmen returning for sophomore year	80%	ACT-takers scoring 30 or over	N/R
	Students completing degree within 5 years	62%		
	Grads pursuing further study	10%		

Majors Accounting, actuarial science, anthropology, applied mathematics, art/fine arts, biochemistry, biology/biological sciences, broadcasting, business, chemistry, communication, computer engineering, computer information systems, computer science, cytotechnology, dental services, (pre)dentistry sequence, early childhood education, ecology/environmental studies, economics, education, elementary education, engineering physics, engineering sciences, English, environmental biology, finance/banking, forestry, French, German, history, industrial engineering, international business, international studies, journalism, (pre)law sequence, literature, marketing/retailing/merchandising, mathematics, medical technology, (pre)medicine sequence, modern languages, music, music education, music therapy, nursing, occupational therapy, peace studies, philosophy, physical therapy, physics, political science/government, psychology, public administration, public relations, radio and television studies, religious studies, science, science education, secondary education, social science, social work, sociology, Spanish, statistics, technical writing, (pre)veterinary medicine sequence.

Applying *Required:* high school transcript, 3 years of high school math and science, 2 years of high school foreign language, 2 recommendations, SAT or ACT. *Recommended:* interview. Campus interview required for some. *Application deadlines:* rolling, 4/1 priority date for financial aid. *Contact:* Mr. Ronald D. Potier, Director of Admissions, 1 Alpha Drive, Elizabethtown, PA 17022, 717-361-1400.

Emory University

Atlanta, Georgia

Founded 1836
Suburban setting
Independent, Methodist
Coed
Awards B, M, D

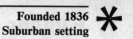

Enrollment 9,483 total; 4,974 undergraduates (1,180 freshmen)

Faculty 621 total; 512 full-time (96% have doctorate/terminal degree); student-faculty ratio is 10:1; grad assistants teach a few undergraduate courses.

Libraries 2.2 million bound volumes, 17,000 periodical subscriptions

Computing *Terminals/PCs available for student use:* 400, located in computer center, library, dormitories law school, theological school buildings, 5 computer labs; PC not required but available for purchase. Campus network links student PCs.

Of Special Interest *Core academic program:* yes. Computer course required for math, business majors. Phi Beta Kappa, Sigma Xi chapters. Academic exchange with University Center in Georgia, George Washington University (Washington semester). Sponsors and participates in study-abroad programs.

On Campus Drama/theater group; student-run newspaper and radio station. *Social organizations:* 15 national fraternities, 10 national sororities; 40% of eligible undergraduate men and 45% of eligible undergraduate women are members.

Athletics Member NCAA (Division III). *Intercollegiate sports:* badminton (M, W), basketball (M, W), bowling (M, W), crew (M, W), cross-country running (M, W), fencing (M, W), field hockey (W), golf (M), ice hockey (M), lacrosse (M), racquetball (M, W), rugby (M), sailing (M, W), soccer (M, W), swimming and diving (M, W), tennis (M, W), track and field (M, W), volleyball (M, W), wrestling (M).

Costs (1991–92) & Aid				
	Comprehensive fee	$18,242	Need-based scholarships (average)	$8000
	Tuition	$14,580	Non-need scholarships (average)	$10,000
	Mandatory fees	$200	Short-term loans	N/Avail
	Room and board	$3462	Long-term loans—college funds (average)	$10,000
	Financial aid recipients	52%	Long-term loans—external funds (average)	$2600

Undergraduate Facts				
	Part-time	3%	*Freshman Data:* 6,750 applied, 64% were accepted, 27% (1,180) of those entered	
	State residents	20%		
	Transfers	2%	From top tenth of high school class	N/R
	African-Americans	7%	SAT-takers scoring 600 or over on verbal	33%
	Native Americans	0%	SAT-takers scoring 700 or over on verbal	4%
	Hispanics	2%	SAT-takers scoring 600 or over on math	69%
	Asian-Americans	6%	SAT-takers scoring 700 or over on math	16%
	International students	4%	ACT-takers scoring 26 or over	58%
	Freshmen returning for sophomore year	92%	ACT-takers scoring 30 or over	12%
	Students completing degree within 5 years	80%	*Majors with most degrees conferred:* psychology, biology/biological sciences, business.	
	Grads pursuing further study	66%		

Majors Accounting, African studies, anthropology, art history, biology/biological sciences, biomedical sciences, black/African-American studies, business, business economics, chemistry, classics, comparative literature, computer science, creative writing, East European and Soviet studies, economics, education, elementary education, English, film studies, finance/banking, French, German, Germanic languages and literature, Greek, history, human ecology, humanities, international studies, Judaic studies, Latin, Latin American studies, liberal arts/general studies, literature, marketing/retailing/merchandising, mathematics, medieval studies, music, nursing, philosophy, physics, political science/government, psychology, radiological technology, religious studies, respiratory therapy, Russian, secondary education, sociology, Spanish, theater arts/drama, women's studies.

Applying *Required:* essay, high school transcript, 3 years of high school math and science, some high school foreign language, 1 recommendation, SAT or ACT. *Recommended:* Achievements. Campus interview required for some. *Application deadlines:* 2/1, 11/15 for early decision, 2/15 priority date for financial aid. *Contact:* Mr. Daniel C. Walls, Dean of Admissions, Boisfeuillet Jones Center–Office of Admissions, Atlanta, GA 30322, 404-727-6036 or toll-free 800-727-6036.

From the College Some typical Emory scenes: a small psychology seminar meets outside on the grass of the quad, taking advantage of a warm fall afternoon; a lecture hall is filled to capacity with students intently focusing on the comments of University Distinguished Professor Jimmy Carter; volunteer Emory participants spend the morning preparing sandwiches to be taken to Atlanta's inner-city homeless for dinner.

Eugene Lang College, New School for Social Research
New York, New York

Founded 1985
Urban setting
Independent
Coed
Awards B

Enrollment 6,250 university total; 360 undergraduates (100 freshmen)

Faculty 60 total; 12 full-time (95% have doctorate/terminal degree); student-faculty ratio is 6:1; grad assistants teach a few undergraduate courses.

Libraries 155,000 bound volumes, 65,000 titles on microform, 700 periodical subscriptions

Computing *Terminals/PCs available for student use:* 75, located in computer center; PC not required.

Of Special Interest *Core academic program:* no. Academic exchange with Polytechnic University, Cooper Union for the Advancement of Science and Art. Sponsors and participates in study-abroad programs.

On Campus Drama/theater group; student-run newspaper. No national or local fraternities or sororities on campus.

Athletics None

Costs (1991–92) & Aid				
	Comprehensive fee	$18,794	Need-based scholarships (average)	$4600
	Tuition	$11,794	Non-need scholarships	N/Avail
	Mandatory fees	$150	Short-term loans	N/Avail
	Room and board	$6850	Long-term loans—college funds	N/Avail
	Financial aid recipients	81%	Long-term loans—external funds (average)	$2750

Undergraduate Facts				
	Part-time	5%	*Freshman Data:* 319 applied, 85% were accepted, 37% (100) of those entered	
	State residents	29%		
	Transfers	22%	From top tenth of high school class	21%
	African-Americans	5%	SAT-takers scoring 600 or over on verbal	25%
	Native Americans	1%	SAT-takers scoring 700 or over on verbal	6%
	Hispanics	5%	SAT-takers scoring 600 or over on math	22%
	Asian-Americans	4%	SAT-takers scoring 700 or over on math	1%
	International students	5%	ACT-takers scoring 26 or over	N/R
	Freshmen returning for sophomore year	85%	ACT-takers scoring 30 or over	N/R
	Students completing degree within 5 years	70%	*Majors with most degrees conferred:* creative writing, theater arts/drama, women's studies.	
	Grads pursuing further study	50%		

Majors Anthropology, communication, creative writing, economics, English, history, history of science, humanities, interdisciplinary studies, international economics, international studies, journalism, liberal arts/general studies, literature, music, philosophy, political science/government, psychology, science, social science, sociology, theater arts/drama, urban studies, Western civilization and culture, women's studies.

Applying *Required:* essay, high school transcript, 2 recommendations, interview, SAT or ACT. *Recommended:* 3 years of high school math and science, 2 years of high school foreign language. *Application deadlines:* 2/1, 11/15 for early decision, 2/1 for financial aid. *Contact:* Ms. Laura Bruno, Director of Admissions, 65 West 11th Street, New York, NY 10011, 212-229-5665.

Fairfield University

Fairfield, Connecticut

Founded 1942
Suburban setting
Independent, Roman Catholic (Jesuit)
Coed
Awards B, M

Enrollment	4,804 total; 2,911 undergraduates (749 freshmen)
Faculty	274 total; 173 full-time (87% have doctorate/terminal degree); student-faculty ratio is 16:1; grad assistants teach no undergraduate courses.
Libraries	276,025 bound volumes, 373,642 titles on microform, 1,804 periodical subscriptions
Computing	*Terminals/PCs available for student use:* 127, located in computer center, library, classroom buildings; PC not required.
Of Special Interest	*Core academic program:* yes. Computer course required for business majors. Academic exchange with University of Bridgeport, Sacred Heart University. Participates in study-abroad programs.
On Campus	Drama/theater group; student-run newspaper and radio station. No national or local fraternities or sororities on campus.
Athletics	Member NCAA (Division I). *Intercollegiate sports:* baseball (M), basketball (M, W), cross-country running (M, W), field hockey (W), golf (M), ice hockey (M), lacrosse (M), soccer (M, W), softball (W), swimming and diving (M, W), tennis (M, W), volleyball (W). *Scholarships:* M, W.

Costs (1991–92) & Aid				
	Comprehensive fee	$18,270	Need-based scholarships (average)	$5670
	Tuition	$12,650	Non-need scholarships (average)	$2050
	Mandatory fees	$270	Short-term loans	N/Avail
	Room and board	$5350	Long-term loans—college funds	N/Avail
	Financial aid recipients	65%	Long-term loans—external funds (average)	$2900

Undergraduate Facts				
	Part-time	0%	*Freshman Data:* 4,764 applied, 64% were accepted, 25% (749) of those entered	
	State residents	32%		
	Transfers	2%	From top tenth of high school class	29%
	African-Americans	2%	SAT-takers scoring 600 or over on verbal	11%
	Native Americans	0%	SAT-takers scoring 700 or over on verbal	1%
	Hispanics	3%	SAT-takers scoring 600 or over on math	36%
	Asian-Americans	3%	SAT-takers scoring 700 or over on math	5%
	International students	1%	ACT-takers scoring 26 or over	N/R
	Freshmen returning for sophomore year	91%	ACT-takers scoring 30 or over	N/R
	Students completing degree within 5 years	85%	*Majors with most degrees conferred:* English, marketing/retailing/merchandising, political science/government.	
	Grads pursuing further study	12%		

Majors Accounting, American studies, art/fine arts, biology/biological sciences, business, chemistry, clinical psychology, communication, computer information systems, computer science, economics, English, finance/banking, French, German, history, management information systems, marketing/retailing/merchandising, mathematics, modern languages, music history, nursing, philosophy, physics, political science/government, psychology, religious studies, secondary education, sociology, Spanish.

Applying *Required:* high school transcript, 3 years of high school math and science, 2 years of high school foreign language, rank in upper 40% of high school class, minimum 2.5 GPA for transfers from two-year colleges, SAT or ACT. *Recommended:* recommendations, interview, Achievements. 4 years of high school math and science required for some. *Application deadlines:* 3/1, 12/1 for early decision, 2/1 for financial aid. *Contact:* Mr. David Flynn, Dean of Admissions, North Benson Road, Fairfield, CT 06430, 203-254-4000 Ext. 4100.

* **Fisk University**

Nashville, Tennessee

Founded 1866
Urban setting
Independent/affiliated with United Church of Christ
Coed
Awards B, M

Enrollment 875 total; 847 undergraduates (215 freshmen)

Faculty 81 total; 71 full-time (63% have doctorate/terminal degree); student-faculty ratio is 10:1; grad assistants teach a few undergraduate courses.

Libraries 197,000 bound volumes, 5,670 titles on microform, 330 periodical subscriptions

Computing *Terminals/PCs available for student use:* N/R; PC not required. Campus network links student PCs.

Of Special Interest *Core academic program:* yes. Computer course required for management majors. Phi Beta Kappa, Sigma Xi chapters. Academic exchange with 4 members of the Nashville University Center, 17 other institutions. Participates in study-abroad programs. Cooperative Army ROTC, cooperative Naval ROTC, cooperative Air Force ROTC.

On Campus Drama/theater group; student-run newspaper and radio station. *Social organizations:* 4 national fraternities, 4 national sororities; 25% of eligible undergraduate men and 35% of eligible undergraduate women are members.

Athletics Member NCAA (Division III). *Intercollegiate sports:* basketball (M, W), cross-country running (M, W), golf (M), tennis (M, W), track and field (M, W), volleyball (W).

Costs (1991–92) & Aid				
	Comprehensive fee	$8065	Need-based scholarships (average)	$1049
	Tuition	$4950	Non-need scholarships (average)	$4286
	Mandatory fees	$65	Short-term loans	N/Avail
	Room and board	$3050	Long-term loans—college funds	N/Avail
	Financial aid recipients	68%	Long-term loans—external funds (average)	$2000

Undergraduate Facts				
	Part-time	0%	*Freshman Data:* 938 applied, 66% were accepted, 35% (215) of those entered	
	State residents	10%		
	Transfers	6%	From top tenth of high school class	18%
	African-Americans	98%	SAT-takers scoring 600 or over on verbal	N/R
	Native Americans	1%	SAT-takers scoring 700 or over on verbal	N/R
	Hispanics	1%	SAT-takers scoring 600 or over on math	N/R
	Asian-Americans	0%	SAT-takers scoring 700 or over on math	N/R
	International students	11%	ACT-takers scoring 26 or over	N/R
	Freshmen returning for sophomore year	67%	ACT-takers scoring 30 or over	N/R
	Students completing degree within 5 years	61%	*Majors with most degrees conferred:* business, chemistry, psychology.	
	Grads pursuing further study	45%		

Majors Accounting, art/fine arts, biology/biological sciences, business, chemistry, economics, English, finance/banking, French, health services administration, history, mathematics, music, music education, philosophy, physics, political science/government, psychology, public administration, religious studies, sociology, Spanish, speech/rhetoric/public address/debate, theater arts/drama.

Applying *Required:* essay, high school transcript, 2 recommendations, medical history. *Recommended:* 3 years of high school math, some high school foreign language, SAT or ACT, Achievements. *Application deadlines:* 6/15, 4/1 priority date for financial aid. *Contact:* Mr. Harrison F. DeShields Jr., Director of Admissions and Records/Foreign Student Adviser, 1000 17th Avenue, North, Nashville, TN 37208, 615-329-8665.

Florida Institute of Technology

Founded 1958
Small-town setting
Independent
Coed

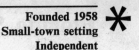

Melbourne, Florida

Awards B, M, D

Enrollment	5,947 total; 3,865 undergraduates (500 freshmen)
Faculty	446 total; 191 full-time (85% have doctorate/terminal degree); student-faculty ratio is 15:1; grad assistants teach a few undergraduate courses.
Libraries	168,589 bound volumes, 486,000 titles on microform, 1,369 periodical subscriptions
Computing	*Terminals/PCs available for student use:* N/R; PC not required.
Of Special Interest	*Core academic program:* yes. Computer course required. Sigma Xi chapter. Academic exchange with High Point College. Study-abroad programs: no. Army ROTC.
On Campus	Drama/theater group; student-run newspaper and radio station. *Social organizations:* 7 national fraternities, 2 national sororities, 1 local fraternity; 8% of eligible undergraduate men and 10% of eligible undergraduate women are members.
Athletics	Member NCAA (Division II). *Intercollegiate sports:* basketball (M, W), crew (M, W), cross-country running (M, W), fencing (M, W), riflery (M, W), sailing (M, W), soccer (M), tennis (M), volleyball (W). *Scholarships:* M, W.

Costs (1992–93) & Aid				
	Comprehensive fee	$15,177	Need-based scholarships	Avail
	Tuition	$11,577	Non-need scholarships	Avail
	Mandatory fees	$135	Short-term loans	N/Avail
	Room and board	$3465	Long-term loans—college funds (average)	$1500
	Financial aid recipients	60%	Long-term loans—external funds (average)	$3000

Undergraduate Facts				
	Part-time	17%	*Freshman Data:* 2,800 applied, 64% were accepted, 28% (500) of those entered	
	State residents	40%		
	Transfers	25%	From top tenth of high school class	22%
	African-Americans	5%	SAT-takers scoring 600 or over on verbal	12%
	Native Americans	1%	SAT-takers scoring 700 or over on verbal	0%
	Hispanics	5%	SAT-takers scoring 600 or over on math	37%
	Asian-Americans	1%	SAT-takers scoring 700 or over on math	4%
	International students	13%	ACT-takers scoring 26 or over	N/R
	Freshmen returning for sophomore year	80%	ACT-takers scoring 30 or over	N/R
	Students completing degree within 5 years	60%	*Majors with most degrees conferred:* biology/biological sciences, aerospace sciences, mechanical engineering.	
	Grads pursuing further study	N/R		

Majors Accounting, aerospace engineering, aerospace sciences, applied mathematics, aviation administration, biochemistry, biology/biological sciences, business, chemical engineering, chemistry, civil engineering, computer engineering, computer science, data processing, (pre)dentistry sequence, economics, education, electrical engineering, environmental sciences, finance/banking, flight training, humanities, liberal arts/general studies, marine biology, marketing/retailing/merchandising, mathematics, mechanical engineering, (pre)medicine sequence, molecular biology, ocean engineering, oceanography, physics, planetary and space sciences, psychology, science education, technical writing, (pre)veterinary medicine sequence.

Applying *Required:* essay, high school transcript, 4 years of high school math, SAT or ACT. *Recommended:* recommendations, interview. 3 years of high school science required for some. *Application deadlines:* 6/1, 2/15 priority date for financial aid. *Contact:* Ms. Jacklyn S. Wilson, Director, Undergraduate Admissions, 150 West University Boulevard, Melbourne, FL 32901, 407-768-8000 Ext. 8030 or toll-free 800-348-4636 (in-state), 800-352-8324 (out-of-state).

From the College Located on the Space Coast of Florida, Florida Tech is the ideal environment for a co-op at the Kennedy Space Center or a day of surfing at the beach. Florida Tech's competitive nature carries over to its nationally recognized varsity sports: the soccer team has won the NCAA Division II championship for the second time in five years.

Florida State University

Tallahassee, Florida

Founded 1857
Suburban setting
State-supported
Coed
Awards A, B, M, D

Enrollment 28,607 total; 21,300 undergraduates (2,587 freshmen)

Faculty 1,577 total; 1,384 full-time (80% have doctorate/terminal degree); grad assistants teach about a quarter of the undergraduate courses.

Libraries 1.9 million bound volumes, 4.4 million titles on microform, 25,807 periodical subscriptions

Computing *Terminals/PCs available for student use:* N/R; PC not required. Campus network links student PCs.

Of Special Interest *Core academic program:* yes. Computer course required for business, chemistry, engineering, math, math education, meteorology, science education, statistics majors. Phi Beta Kappa, Sigma Xi chapters. Academic exchange with Florida Agricultural and Mechanical University, Tallahassee Community College. Sponsors and participates in study-abroad programs. Army ROTC, Air Force ROTC, cooperative Naval ROTC.

On Campus Drama/theater group; student-run newspaper and radio station. *Social organizations:* 25 national fraternities, 20 national sororities, local fraternities, local sororities; 20% of eligible undergraduate men and 20% of eligible undergraduate women are members.

Athletics Member NCAA (Division I). *Intercollegiate sports:* baseball (M), basketball (M, W), cross-country running (M, W), football (M), golf (M, W), softball (W), swimming and diving (M, W), tennis (M, W), track and field (M, W), volleyball (W). *Scholarships:* M, W.

Costs (1991–92) & Aid

State resident tuition	$1492	5120 Need-based scholarships (average)	$1100
Nonresident tuition	$5631	3214 Non-need scholarships (average)	$2500
Mandatory fees	N/App	Short-term loans (average)	$500
Room and board	$3679	Long-term loans—college funds	N/Avail
Financial aid recipients	47%	Long-term loans—external funds (average)	$3500

Undergraduate Facts

Part-time	12%	*Freshman Data:* 11,977 applied, 64% were accepted, 34% (2,587) of those entered	
State residents	80%		
Transfers	12%	From top tenth of high school class	N/R
African-Americans	8%	SAT-takers scoring 600 or over on verbal	21%
Native Americans	1%	SAT-takers scoring 700 or over on verbal	5%
Hispanics	4%	SAT-takers scoring 600 or over on math	30%
Asian-Americans	2%	SAT-takers scoring 700 or over on math	6%
International students	3%	ACT-takers scoring 26 or over	40%
Freshmen returning for sophomore year	85%	ACT-takers scoring 30 or over	11%
Students completing degree within 5 years	46%	*Majors with most degrees conferred:*	
Grads pursuing further study	N/R	communication, criminal justice, finance/banking.	

Majors Accounting, advertising, American studies, anthropology, applied mathematics, archaeology, art education, art/fine arts, art history, art therapy, Asian/Oriental studies, bilingual/bicultural education, biochemistry, biology/biological sciences, botany/plant sciences, broadcasting, business, cell biology, chemical engineering, chemistry, child psychology/child development, civil engineering, classics, clinical psychology, communication, comparative literature, computer engineering, computer science, corrections, creative writing, criminal justice, dance, (pre)dentistry sequence, dietetics, early childhood education, East Asian studies, East European and Soviet studies, ecology/environmental studies, economics, education, electrical engineering, electronics engineering, elementary education, English, environmental sciences, evolutionary biology, experimental psychology, family and consumer studies, family services, fashion design and technology, fashion merchandising, film studies, finance/banking, food services management, French, genetics, geography, geology, German, graphic arts, Greek, health education, history, home economics, home economics education, hospitality services, humanities, human resources, industrial engineering, insurance, interdisciplinary studies, interior design, international business, international studies, Italian, Latin, Latin American studies, law enforcement/police sciences, (pre)law sequence, linguistics, literature, management information systems, marine biology, marketing/retailing/merchandising, mathematics, mechanical engineering, medical technology, (pre)medicine sequence, meteorology, molecular biology, music, music education, music history, music therapy, neurosciences, nursing, nutrition, painting/drawing, philosophy, photography, physical education, physics, physiology, piano/organ, political science/government, printmaking, psychology, public relations, purchasing/inventory management, radio and television studies, reading education, real estate, recreation and leisure services, rehabilitation therapy, religious studies, Russian, Russian and Slavic studies, science education, sculpture, secondary education, Slavic languages, social science, social work, sociology, Spanish, special education, speech pathology and audiology, statistics, stringed instruments, studio art, systems engineering, textiles and clothing, theater arts/drama, urban studies, (pre)veterinary medicine sequence, voice, wind and percussion instruments, zoology.

Applying *Required:* high school transcript, 3 years of high school math and science, 2 years of high school foreign language, SAT or ACT. Audition required for some. *Application deadlines:* 3/2, 4/1 priority date for financial aid. *Contact:* Dr. Peter F. Metarko, Director of Admissions, 216B William Johnston Building, Tallahassee, FL 32306, 904-644-6200.

Fordham University

New York, New York

Founded 1841
Urban setting
Independent, Roman Catholic (Jesuit)
Coed
Awards B, M, D

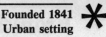

Enrollment	14,243 total; 7,089 undergraduates (956 freshmen)
Faculty	594 total; 413 full-time (96% have doctorate/terminal degree); student-faculty ratio is 17:1; grad assistants teach a few undergraduate courses.
Libraries	1.1 million bound volumes, 1.2 million titles on microform, 5,000 periodical subscriptions
Computing	*Terminals/PCs available for student use:* 160, located in computer center, classrooms; PC not required but available for purchase.
Of Special Interest	*Core academic program:* yes. Computer course required for business, math majors. Phi Beta Kappa, Sigma Xi chapters. Academic exchange with University of San Francisco, Talladega College, New York State Visiting Student Program. Sponsors and participates in study-abroad programs. Army ROTC, cooperative Naval ROTC, cooperative Air Force ROTC.
On Campus	Drama/theater group; student-run newspaper and radio station. No national or local fraternities or sororities on campus.
Athletics	Member NCAA (Division I). *Intercollegiate sports:* baseball (M), basketball (M, W), crew (M, W), cross-country running (M, W), equestrian sports (M, W), football (M), golf (M), ice hockey (M), lacrosse (M, W), rugby (M), soccer (M, W), softball (W), squash (M), swimming and diving (M, W), tennis (M, W), track and field (M, W), volleyball (W), water polo (M), wrestling (M). *Scholarships:* M, W.

Costs (1991–92) & Aid				
	Comprehensive fee	$17,625	Need-based scholarships (average)	$5350
	Tuition	$10,950	Non-need scholarships (average)	$5350
	Mandatory fees	$150	Short-term loans	N/Avail
	Room and board	$6525	Long-term loans—college funds (average)	$1575
	Financial aid recipients	85%	Long-term loans—external funds (average)	$700

Undergraduate Facts				
	Part-time	27%	*Freshman Data:* 3,763 applied, 76% were accepted, 33% (956) of those entered	
	State residents	67%	From top tenth of high school class	35%
	Transfers	5%	SAT-takers scoring 600 or over on verbal	17%
	African-Americans	6%	SAT-takers scoring 700 or over on verbal	3%
	Native Americans	1%	SAT-takers scoring 600 or over on math	22%
	Hispanics	6%	SAT-takers scoring 700 or over on math	3%
	Asian-Americans	3%	ACT-takers scoring 26 or over	N/R
	International students	3%	ACT-takers scoring 30 or over	N/R
	Freshmen returning for sophomore year	93%	*Majors with most degrees conferred:* communication, political science/government, economics.	
	Students completing degree within 5 years	84%		
	Grads pursuing further study	26%		

Majors Accounting, African studies, American studies, anthropology, art/fine arts, art history, bilingual/bicultural education, biology/biological sciences, black/African-American studies, broadcasting, business, business economics, chemistry, classics, communication, comparative literature, computer information systems, computer management, computer science, creative writing, criminal justice, (pre)dentistry sequence, East European and Soviet studies, economics, education, elementary education, English, ethnic studies, film studies, finance/banking, French, German, Germanic languages and literature, gerontology, Greek, Hispanic studies, history, information science, interdisciplinary studies, international business, international studies, Italian, journalism, Latin, Latin American studies, (pre)law sequence, liberal arts/general studies, literature, management information systems, marketing/retailing/merchandising, mathematics, medical technology, (pre)medicine sequence, medieval studies, modern languages, music history, natural sciences, Near and Middle Eastern studies, peace studies, philosophy, physical sciences, physics, political science/government, psychology, public administration, radio and television studies, religious studies, Romance languages, Russian, Russian and Slavic studies, science, science education, secondary education, social science, sociology, Spanish, studio art, theater arts/drama, theology, urban studies, (pre)veterinary medicine sequence, women's studies.

Applying *Required:* essay, high school transcript, 1 recommendation, SAT or ACT. *Recommended:* 3 years of high school math and science, 2 years of high school foreign language, interview, Achievements, English Composition Test (with essay). Campus interview required for some. *Application deadlines:* 2/1, 11/1 for early action, 2/15 for financial aid. *Contact:* Mr. William DiBrienza, Director of Admissions, Dealy Hall, Room 115, New York, NY 10458, 212-579-2133.

From the College A Fordham education is characterized by excellent, personalized teaching with an average class size of 25 and a low student-faculty ratio. The internship program offers students the opportunity to work with more than 2,000 organizations in the New York metropolitan area. Special academic options include an honors program and study abroad.

Franklin and Marshall College

Lancaster, Pennsylvania

Founded 1787
Suburban setting
Independent
Coed
Awards B

Enrollment	1,793 total—all undergraduates (500 freshmen)
Faculty	170 total; 148 full-time (95% have doctorate/terminal degree); student-faculty ratio is 12:1.
Libraries	303,000 bound volumes, 241,000 titles on microform, 1,775 periodical subscriptions
Computing	*Terminals/PCs available for student use:* 100, located in computer center, library, classroom buildings; PC not required but available for purchase. Campus network links student PCs.
Of Special Interest	*Core academic program:* yes. Phi Beta Kappa, Sigma Xi chapters. Academic exchange with Gettysburg College, Dickinson College, Columbia University, National Theatre Institute, School of Visual Arts, Boston University, American University. Participates in study-abroad programs.
On Campus	Drama/theater group; student-run newspaper and radio station. *Social organizations:* 8 national fraternities, 3 national sororities, 1 local fraternity; 50% of eligible undergraduate men and 30% of eligible undergraduate women are members.
Athletics	Member NCAA (Division III). *Intercollegiate sports:* badminton (M, W), baseball (M), basketball (M, W), crew (M, W), cross-country running (M, W), fencing (M, W), field hockey (W), football (M), golf (M, W), ice hockey (M), lacrosse (M, W), rugby (M, W), sailing (M, W), soccer (M, W), softball (W), squash (M, W), swimming and diving (M, W), tennis (M, W), track and field (M, W), volleyball (M, W), water polo (M, W), wrestling (M).

Costs (1992–93) & Aid				
	Comprehensive fee	$22,330	Need-based scholarships (average)	$8144
	Tuition	N/App	Non-need scholarships	N/Avail
	Mandatory fees	N/App	Short-term loans	N/Avail
	Room and board	N/App	Long-term loans—college funds (average)	$1500
	Financial aid recipients	43%	Long-term loans—external funds (average)	$2625

Undergraduate Facts				
	Part-time	3%	*Freshman Data:* 3,220 applied, 60% were accepted, 26% (500) of those entered	
	State residents	35%		
	Transfers	1%	From top tenth of high school class	42%
	African-Americans	3%	SAT-takers scoring 600 or over on verbal	24%
	Native Americans	0%	SAT-takers scoring 700 or over on verbal	4%
	Hispanics	3%	SAT-takers scoring 600 or over on math	58%
	Asian-Americans	8%	SAT-takers scoring 700 or over on math	12%
	International students	6%	ACT-takers scoring 26 or over	55%
	Freshmen returning for sophomore year	93%	ACT-takers scoring 30 or over	5%
	Students completing degree within 5 years	85%	*Majors with most degrees conferred:* political science/government, business, English.	
	Grads pursuing further study	32%		

Majors Accounting, American studies, anthropology, art/fine arts, biology/biological sciences, business, chemistry, classics, economics, English, French, geology, German, Greek, history, interdisciplinary studies, Latin, mathematics, music, philosophy, physics, political science/government, psychology, religious studies, sociology, Spanish, theater arts/drama.

Applying *Required:* essay, high school transcript, 2 recommendations. *Recommended:* 4 years of high school math, 3 years of high school science, 3 years of high school foreign language, interview. SAT or ACT, 1 Achievement, English Composition Test (with essay) required for some. *Application deadlines:* 2/10, 2/1 for early decision, 3/1 priority date for financial aid. *Contact:* Mr. Peter W. VanBuskirk, Director of Admissions, College Avenue, Lancaster, PA 17604-3003, 717-291-3953.

Furman University

Greenville, South Carolina

Founded 1826　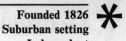
Suburban setting
Independent
Coed
Awards B, M

Enrollment 2,703 total; 2,496 undergraduates (718 freshmen)

Faculty 213 total; 203 full-time (89% have doctorate/terminal degree); student-faculty ratio is 12:1; grad assistants teach no undergraduate courses.

Libraries 350,000 bound volumes, 2,465 periodical subscriptions

Computing *Terminals/PCs available for student use:* 160, located in computer center, library, academic buildings; PC not required.

Of Special Interest *Core academic program:* yes. Computer course required for some majors. Phi Beta Kappa chapter. Academic exchange program: no. Sponsors and participates in study-abroad programs. Army ROTC.

On Campus Drama/theater group; student-run newspaper and radio station. *Social organizations:* 7 local fraternities, 7 local sororities; 35% of eligible undergraduate men and 25% of eligible undergraduate women are members.

Athletics Member NCAA (Division I). *Intercollegiate sports:* baseball (M), basketball (M, W), crew (M, W), cross-country running (M), field hockey (W), football (M), golf (M, W), lacrosse (M), soccer (M, W), softball (W), tennis (M, W), track and field (M), volleyball (W), wrestling (M). *Scholarships:* M, W.

Costs (1991–92) & Aid				
	Comprehensive fee	$14,555	Need-based scholarships (average)	$2500
	Tuition	$10,720	Non-need scholarships (average)	$3500
	Mandatory fees	$107	Short-term loans (average)	$1000
	Room and board	$3728	Long-term loans—college funds	N/Avail
	Financial aid recipients	72%	Long-term loans—external funds (average)	$2500

Undergraduate Facts				
	Part-time	6%	*Freshman Data:* 2,259 applied, 82% were accepted, 39% (718) of those entered	
	State residents	47%		
	Transfers	6%	From top tenth of high school class	53%
	African-Americans	3%	SAT-takers scoring 600 or over on verbal	22%
	Native Americans	0%	SAT-takers scoring 700 or over on verbal	3%
	Hispanics	1%	SAT-takers scoring 600 or over on math	45%
	Asian-Americans	1%	SAT-takers scoring 700 or over on math	9%
	International students	1%	ACT-takers scoring 26 or over	N/R
	Freshmen returning for sophomore year	93%	ACT-takers scoring 30 or over	N/R
	Students completing degree within 5 years	80%		
	Grads pursuing further study	43%		

Majors Accounting, art education, art/fine arts, art history, Asian/Oriental studies, biology/biological sciences, business, chemistry, classics, computer science, economics, education, English, French, geology, German, Greek, health education, history, Latin, (pre)law sequence, liberal arts/general studies, mathematics, (pre)medicine sequence, modern languages, music, music education, philosophy, physical education, physics, piano/organ, political science/government, psychology, religious studies, sacred music, sociology, Spanish, special education, sports administration, sports medicine, theater arts/drama, urban studies, (pre)veterinary medicine sequence, voice.

Applying *Required:* essay, high school transcript, 3 years of high school math and science, some high school foreign language, SAT or ACT. *Recommended:* recommendations. *Application deadlines:* 2/1, 12/1 for early decision, 2/15 priority date for financial aid. *Contact:* Mr. J. Carey Thompson, Director of Admissions, 3300 Pointsett Highway, Greenville, SC 29613, 803-294-2034.

Georgetown University

Washington, District of Columbia

Founded 1789
Urban setting
Independent, Roman Catholic (Jesuit)
Coed
Awards B, M, D

Enrollment 11,861 total; 5,775 undergraduates (1,375 freshmen)

Faculty 729 total; 481 full-time (89% have doctorate/terminal degree); student-faculty ratio is 13:1; grad assistants teach no undergraduate courses.

Libraries 1.3 million bound volumes, 12,488 periodical subscriptions

Computing *Terminals/PCs available for student use:* 152, located in computer center, library; PC not required. Campus network links student PCs.

Of Special Interest *Core academic program:* yes. Computer course required for business administration, math majors. Phi Beta Kappa, Sigma Xi chapters. Academic exchange with Consortium of Universities of the Washington Metropolitan Area. Sponsors and participates in study-abroad programs. Army ROTC, cooperative Naval ROTC, cooperative Air Force ROTC.

On Campus Drama/theater group; student-run newspaper and radio station. No national or local fraternities or sororities on campus.

Athletics Member NCAA (Division I). *Intercollegiate sports:* baseball (M), basketball (M, W), crew (M, W), cross-country running (M, W), field hockey (W), football (M), golf (M), ice hockey (M), lacrosse (M, W), rugby (M), sailing (M, W), soccer (M, W), swimming and diving (M, W), tennis (M, W), track and field (M, W), volleyball (W). *Scholarships:* M, W.

Costs (1991–92) & Aid				
	Comprehensive fee	$21,736	Need-based scholarships (average)	$10,200
	Tuition	$15,510	Non-need scholarships	N/Avail
	Mandatory fees	$142	Short-term loans (average)	$250
	Room and board	$6084	Long-term loans—college funds (average)	$1500
	Financial aid recipients	45%	Long-term loans—external funds (average)	$2900

Undergraduate Facts				
	Part-time	5%	*Freshman Data:* 8,729 applied, 32% were accepted, 50% (1,375) of those entered	
	State residents	3%		
	Transfers	11%	From top tenth of high school class	71%
	African-Americans	8%	SAT-takers scoring 600 or over on verbal	54%
	Native Americans	1%	SAT-takers scoring 700 or over on verbal	9%
	Hispanics	4%	SAT-takers scoring 600 or over on math	75%
	Asian-Americans	6%	SAT-takers scoring 700 or over on math	25%
	International students	10%	ACT-takers scoring 26 or over	80%
	Freshmen returning for sophomore year	96%	ACT-takers scoring 30 or over	44%
	Students completing degree within 5 years	89%	*Majors with most degrees conferred:* international studies, political science/government, English.	
	Grads pursuing further study	25%		

Majors Accounting, American studies, Arabic, art/fine arts, biology/biological sciences, business, chemistry, Chinese, classics, computer science, (pre)dentistry sequence, economics, English, finance/banking, French, German, history, interdisciplinary studies, international business, international economics, international studies, Italian, Japanese, liberal arts/general studies, linguistics, marketing/retailing/merchandising, mathematics, (pre)medicine sequence, nursing, philosophy, physics, political science/government, Portuguese, psychology, religious studies, Russian, sociology, Spanish.

Applying *Required:* essay, high school transcript, 2 recommendations, interview, SAT or ACT. *Recommended:* 3 years of high school math and science, some high school foreign language, 3 Achievements, English Composition Test (with essay). *Application deadlines:* 1/10, 11/1 for early action, 1/15 priority date for financial aid. *Contact:* Mr. Charles A. Deacon, Dean of Undergraduate Admissions, 57th and O Streets, NW, Washington, DC 20057, 202-687-3600.

George Washington University

Washington, District of Columbia

Founded 1821
Urban setting
Independent
Coed
Awards A, B, M, D

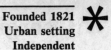

Enrollment	16,712 total; 6,285 undergraduates (1,174 freshmen)
Faculty	1,221 total; 671 full-time (91% have doctorate/terminal degree); student-faculty ratio is 8:1; grad assistants teach no undergraduate courses.
Libraries	1.6 million bound volumes, 1.7 million titles on microform, 17,235 periodical subscriptions
Computing	*Terminals/PCs available for student use:* 500, located in computer center, student center, library, dormitories, word processing center; PC not required. Campus network links student PCs.
Of Special Interest	*Core academic program:* yes. Computer course required for business, engineering, some liberal arts majors. Phi Beta Kappa, Sigma Xi chapters. Academic exchange with Consortium of Universities of the Washington Metropolitan Area. Sponsors and participates in study-abroad programs. Naval ROTC, cooperative Army ROTC, cooperative Air Force ROTC.
On Campus	Drama/theater group; student-run newspaper and radio station. *Social organizations:* 16 national fraternities, 11 national sororities; 25% of eligible undergraduate men and 17% of eligible undergraduate women are members.
Athletics	Member NCAA (Division I). *Intercollegiate sports:* baseball (M), basketball (M, W), crew (M, W), cross-country running (M, W), golf (M), gymnastics (W), soccer (M, W), swimming and diving (M, W), tennis (M, W), volleyball (W), water polo (M). *Scholarships:* M, W.

Costs (1991–92) & Aid				
	Comprehensive fee	$21,258	Need-based scholarships (average)	$8924
	Tuition	$14,600	Non-need scholarships (average)	$8105
	Mandatory fees	$302	Short-term loans (average)	$200
	Room and board	$6356	Long-term loans—college funds (average)	$2000
	Financial aid recipients	53%	Long-term loans—external funds (average)	$2861

Undergraduate Facts				
	Part-time	11%	*Freshman Data:* 6,025 applied, 74% were accepted, 26% (1,174) of those entered	
	State residents	6%		
	Transfers	22%	From top tenth of high school class	42%
	African-Americans	6%	SAT-takers scoring 600 or over on verbal	33%
	Native Americans	1%	SAT-takers scoring 700 or over on verbal	6%
	Hispanics	4%	SAT-takers scoring 600 or over on math	51%
	Asian-Americans	8%	SAT-takers scoring 700 or over on math	12%
	International students	11%	ACT-takers scoring 26 or over	65%
	Freshmen returning for sophomore year	85%	ACT-takers scoring 30 or over	29%
	Students completing degree within 5 years	69%	*Majors with most degrees conferred:* international studies, political science/government, psychology.	
	Grads pursuing further study	N/R		

Majors Accounting, anthropology, applied mathematics, archaeology, art/fine arts, art history, Asian/Oriental studies, biology/biological sciences, business, business economics, chemistry, Chinese, civil engineering, classics, communication, computer engineering, computer information systems, computer science, criminal justice, dance, (pre)dentistry sequence, East Asian studies, ecology/environmental studies, economics, electrical engineering, emergency medical technology, English, environmental engineering, environmental sciences, European studies, finance/banking, French, geography, geology, Germanic languages and literature, history, human resources, human services, information science, interdisciplinary studies, international business, international economics, international studies, journalism, Judaic studies, Latin American studies, (pre)law sequence, liberal arts/general studies, management information systems, marketing/retailing/merchandising, mathematics, mechanical engineering, medical records services, medical technology, (pre)medicine sequence, music, operations research, philosophy, physical fitness/human movement, physician's assistant studies, physics, political science/government, psychology, public affairs and policy studies, radio and television studies, radiological sciences, recreation and leisure services, religious studies, Russian and Slavic studies, sociology, Spanish, speech pathology and audiology, speech/rhetoric/public address/debate, statistics, studio art, systems engineering, theater arts/drama.

Applying *Required:* essay, high school transcript, 2 years of high school foreign language, 2 recommendations, SAT or ACT. *Recommended:* 2 Achievements, English Composition Test. 4 years of high school math, 3 years of high school science required for some. *Application deadlines:* 2/1, 11/15 for early decision, continuous to 2/1 for financial aid. *Contact:* Mr. George W. G. Stoner, Director of Undergraduate Admissions, Office of Undergraduate Admissions, Washington, DC 20052, 202-994-6051 or toll-free 800-447-3765; *Office location:* Rice Hall, 2121 I Street, NW.

From the College All applicants are automatically considered for Presidential Honor, Alumni State, and Valedictorian scholarships, which range from $2500 to $15,000 annually. GW offers awards for finalists and semifinalists of National Merit, National Achievement, and National Hispanic Award programs. Those selected for the University Honors Program or the Performing Arts Award (auditions required) receive a $7500 award.

Georgia Institute of Technology

Atlanta, Georgia

Founded 1885
Urban setting
State-supported
Coed
Awards B, M, D

Enrollment	12,814 total; 9,487 undergraduates (1,742 freshmen)
Faculty	615 total; 607 full-time (90% have doctorate/terminal degree); student-faculty ratio is 21:1; grad assistants teach a few undergraduate courses.
Libraries	1.7 million bound volumes, 22,200 periodical subscriptions
Computing	*Terminals/PCs available for student use:* 500, located in computer center, student center, library, dormitories, academic buildings; PC not required. Campus network links student PCs.
Of Special Interest	*Core academic program:* yes. Computer course required for engineering, math, psychology majors. Sigma Xi chapter. Academic exchange with University Center in Georgia. Sponsors and participates in study-abroad programs. Army ROTC, Naval ROTC, Air Force ROTC.
On Campus	Drama/theater group; student-run newspaper and radio station. *Social organizations:* 32 national fraternities, 8 national sororities; 30% of eligible undergraduate men and 24% of eligible undergraduate women are members.
Athletics	Member NCAA (Division I). *Intercollegiate sports:* baseball (M), basketball (M, W), cross-country running (M, W), football (M), golf (M), ice hockey (M), lacrosse (M), rugby (M), swimming and diving (M, W), tennis (M, W), track and field (M, W), volleyball (W), wrestling (M). *Scholarships:* M, W.

Costs (1991–92) & Aid				
	State resident tuition	$1722	Need-based scholarships	Avail
	Nonresident tuition	$5883	Non-need scholarships	Avail
	Mandatory fees	$396	Short-term loans	Avail
	Room and board	$3965	Long-term loans—college funds	Avail
	Financial aid recipients	39%	Long-term loans—external funds	Avail

Undergraduate Facts				
	Part-time	7%	*Freshman Data:* 6,932 applied, 62% were accepted, 41% (1,742) of those entered	
	State residents	61%		
	Transfers	19%	From top tenth of high school class	72%
	African-Americans	8%	SAT-takers scoring 600 or over on verbal	25%
	Native Americans	0%	SAT-takers scoring 700 or over on verbal	3%
	Hispanics	3%	SAT-takers scoring 600 or over on math	78%
	Asian-Americans	6%	SAT-takers scoring 700 or over on math	27%
	International students	3%	ACT-takers scoring 26 or over	N/R
	Freshmen returning for sophomore year	87%	ACT-takers scoring 30 or over	N/R
	Students completing degree within 5 years	51%		
	Grads pursuing further study	N/R		

Majors Aerospace engineering, applied mathematics, architecture, atmospheric sciences, biochemistry, biology/biological sciences, business, ceramic engineering, chemical engineering, chemistry, civil engineering, computer engineering, computer information systems, computer science, construction management, construction technologies, earth science, economics, electrical engineering, engineering mechanics, engineering sciences, health science, history of science, industrial design, industrial engineering, international studies, literature, materials engineering, mathematics, mechanical engineering, nuclear engineering, operations research, physics, polymer science, psychology, systems engineering, technology and public affairs, textile engineering, textiles and clothing.

Applying *Required:* high school transcript, 4 years of high school math, 3 years of high school science, 2 years of high school foreign language, SAT. ACT required for some. *Application deadlines:* 2/1, 3/1 priority date for financial aid. *Contact:* Ms. Deborah Smith, Assistant Department Manager, Admissions, 225 North Avenue, Atlanta, GA 30332-0320, 404-894-4154.

From the College In addition to excellent engineering and science degree programs, Georgia Tech now offers a bachelor's degree in international affairs; one in science, technology, and culture; and a degree program in history, technology, and society. Tech will be the site of the Olympic Village and several Olympic events when Atlanta hosts the 1996 Olympic Games.

Gettysburg College

Gettysburg, Pennsylvania

Founded 1832
Small-town setting
Independent/affiliated with Evangelical Lutheran Church in America
Coed
Awards B

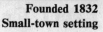

Enrollment 1,950 total—all undergraduates (583 freshmen)

Faculty 150 total; 140 full-time (90% have doctorate/terminal degree); student-faculty ratio is 13:1.

Libraries 321,000 bound volumes, 35,000 titles on microform, 1,350 periodical subscriptions

Computing *Terminals/PCs available for student use:* 100, located in computer center, student center, library, dormitories; PC not required. Campus network links student PCs.

Of Special Interest *Core academic program:* yes. Computer course required for some majors. Phi Beta Kappa chapter. Academic exchange with 2 members of the Central Pennsylvania Consortium. Sponsors and participates in study-abroad programs.

On Campus Drama/theater group; student-run newspaper and radio station. *Social organizations:* 11 national fraternities, 7 national sororities; 55% of eligible undergraduate men and 45% of eligible undergraduate women are members.

Athletics Member NCAA (Division III). *Intercollegiate sports:* baseball (M), basketball (M, W), cross-country running (M, W), field hockey (W), football (M), golf (M, W), lacrosse (M, W), rugby (M), soccer (M, W), softball (W), swimming and diving (M, W), tennis (M, W), track and field (M, W), volleyball (W), wrestling (M).

Costs (1991–92) & Aid				
	Comprehensive fee	$19,970	Need-based scholarships (average)	$8700
	Tuition	$16,500	Non-need scholarships	N/Avail
	Mandatory fees	N/App	Short-term loans	N/Avail
	Room and board	$3470	Long-term loans—college funds (average)	$2200
	Financial aid recipients	40%	Long-term loans—external funds (average)	$2650

Undergraduate Facts				
	Part-time	1%	*Freshman Data:* 3,466 applied, 70% were accepted, 24% (583) of those entered	
	State residents	25%		
	Transfers	3%	From top tenth of high school class	40%
	African-Americans	3%	SAT-takers scoring 600 or over on verbal	17%
	Native Americans	1%	SAT-takers scoring 700 or over on verbal	2%
	Hispanics	2%	SAT-takers scoring 600 or over on math	40%
	Asian-Americans	3%	SAT-takers scoring 700 or over on math	6%
	International students	2%	ACT-takers scoring 26 or over	55%
	Freshmen returning for sophomore year	90%	ACT-takers scoring 30 or over	10%
	Students completing degree within 5 years	80%	*Majors with most degrees conferred:* business, political science/government, psychology.	
	Grads pursuing further study	33%		

Majors Accounting, anthropology, art/fine arts, art history, biology/biological sciences, business, chemistry, classics, computer science, (pre)dentistry sequence, economics, education, elementary education, English, French, German, Greek, history, Latin, (pre)law sequence, liberal arts/general studies, literature, mathematics, (pre)medicine sequence, modern languages, music, music education, philosophy, physical education, physics, political science/government, psychology, religious studies, secondary education, sociology, South Asian studies, Spanish, studio art, theater arts/drama, (pre)veterinary medicine sequence.

Applying *Required:* essay, high school transcript, 1 recommendation, SAT or ACT. *Recommended:* 3 years of high school math and science, some high school foreign language, campus interview, 3 Achievements, English Composition Test (with essay). *Application deadlines:* 2/15, 2/1 for early decision, 2/1 priority date for financial aid. *Contact:* Mr. Delwin K. Gustafson, Dean of Admissions, Eisenhower House, Gettysburg, PA 17325, 717-337-6100 or toll-free 800-431-0803.

GMI Engineering & Management Institute
Flint, Michigan

Founded 1919
Suburban setting
Independent
Coed
Awards B, M

Enrollment 3,104 total; 2,382 undergraduates (580 freshmen)

Faculty 130 total—all full-time (65% have doctorate/terminal degree); student-faculty ratio is 13:1; grad assistants teach no undergraduate courses.

Libraries 80,000 bound volumes, 31,000 titles on microform, 770 periodical subscriptions

Computing *Terminals/PCs available for student use:* 300, located in computer center, classrooms, labs; PC not required. Campus network links student PCs.

Of Special Interest *Core academic program:* yes. Computer course required. Academic exchange program: no. Sponsors study-abroad programs.

On Campus Drama/theater group; student-run newspaper and radio station. *Social organizations:* 14 national fraternities, 6 national sororities; 65% of eligible undergraduate men and 60% of eligible undergraduate women are members.

Athletics *Intercollegiate sports:* ice hockey (M), soccer (M), volleyball (M).

Costs (1991–92) & Aid				
	Comprehensive fee	$12,330	Need-based scholarships (average)	$974
	Tuition	$9400	Non-need scholarships (average)	$2303
	Mandatory fees	$90	Short-term loans	Avail
	Room and board	$2840	Long-term loans—college funds	Avail
	Financial aid recipients	50%	Long-term loans—external funds (average)	$2946

Undergraduate Facts				
	Part-time	0%	*Freshman Data:* 2,072 applied, 69% were accepted, 41% (580) of those entered	
	State residents	48%		
	Transfers	10%	From top tenth of high school class	50%
	African-Americans	6%	SAT-takers scoring 600 or over on verbal	10%
	Native Americans	1%	SAT-takers scoring 700 or over on verbal	1%
	Hispanics	2%	SAT-takers scoring 600 or over on math	74%
	Asian-Americans	8%	SAT-takers scoring 700 or over on math	17%
	International students	6%	ACT-takers scoring 26 or over	56%
	Freshmen returning for sophomore year	95%	ACT-takers scoring 30 or over	12%
	Students completing degree within 5 years	75%	*Majors with most degrees conferred:* mechanical engineering, electrical engineering, manufacturing engineering.	
	Grads pursuing further study	6%		

Majors Accounting, applied mathematics, business, computer engineering, computer information systems, computer science, electrical engineering, industrial administration, industrial engineering, management information systems, manufacturing engineering, marketing/retailing/merchandising, mechanical engineering, statistics, systems engineering.

Applying *Required:* essay, high school transcript, 3 years of high school math and science, 1 recommendation, interview, SAT or ACT. *Recommended:* some high school foreign language, 2 Achievements. *Application deadlines:* rolling, 3/30 priority date for financial aid. *Contact:* Mr. Thomas Cerny, Director of Admissions,1700 West Third Avenue, Flint, MI 48504, 313-762-7865 or toll-free 800-955-4464.

From the College GMI Engineering & Management Institute is an independent college established in 1919 that operates on a unique five-year, fully cooperative plan of education. Students alternate twelve-week academic terms on campus with twelve-week terms of paid work experience with their co-op employer. Affiliated employers are located in forty-three states and several countries; 70 percent of students are able to live at home during work sessions.

Goshen College

Goshen, Indiana

Founded 1894
Small-town setting
Independent, Mennonite
Coed
Awards B

Enrollment	1,039 total—all undergraduates (199 freshmen)
Faculty	125 total; 85 full-time (62% have doctorate/terminal degree); student-faculty ratio is 14:1.
Libraries	120,000 bound volumes, 100 titles on microform, 800 periodical subscriptions
Computing	*Terminals/PCs available for student use:* 75, located in computer center, dormitories; PC not required.
Of Special Interest	*Core academic program:* yes. Computer course required for accounting, business, math, economics majors. Academic exchange with Northern Indiana Consortium for Education. Sponsors and participates in study-abroad programs.
On Campus	Mandatory chapel; drama/theater group; student-run newspaper and radio station. No national or local fraternities or sororities on campus.
Athletics	Member NAIA. *Intercollegiate sports:* basketball (M, W), cross-country running (M, W), golf (M), soccer (M, W), softball (W), tennis (M, W), track and field (M, W), volleyball (W).

Costs (1992–93) & Aid				
Comprehensive fee	$11,810	Need-based scholarships (average)		$770
Tuition	$8310	Non-need scholarships (average)		$911
Mandatory fees	N/App	Short-term loans		N/Avail
Room and board	$3500	Long-term loans—college funds (average)		$1518
Financial aid recipients	86%	Long-term loans—external funds (average)		$2020

Undergraduate Facts			
Part-time	10%	*Freshman Data:* 442 applied, 88% were accepted, 51% (199) of those entered	
State residents	41%		
Transfers	9%	From top tenth of high school class	25%
African-Americans	5%	SAT-takers scoring 600 or over on verbal	17%
Native Americans	0%	SAT-takers scoring 700 or over on verbal	3%
Hispanics	3%	SAT-takers scoring 600 or over on math	18%
Asian-Americans	1%	SAT-takers scoring 700 or over on math	5%
International students	7%	ACT-takers scoring 26 or over	N/R
Freshmen returning for sophomore year	81%	ACT-takers scoring 30 or over	N/R
Students completing degree within 5 years	N/R	*Majors with most degrees conferred:* business, nursing, elementary education.	
Grads pursuing further study	N/R		

Majors Accounting, art education, art/fine arts, art therapy, biblical studies, bilingual/bicultural education, biology/biological sciences, broadcasting, business, business education, chemistry, child care/child and family studies, communication, computer information systems, computer science, (pre)dentistry sequence, dietetics, early childhood education, economics, education, elementary education, English, family services, German, Hispanic studies, history, journalism, (pre)law sequence, liberal arts/general studies, mathematics, (pre)medicine sequence, music, music education, natural sciences, nursing, nutrition, physical education, physical sciences, physics, political science/government, psychology, religious studies, science education, secondary education, social work, sociology, Spanish, teaching English as a second language, theater arts/drama, (pre)veterinary medicine sequence.

Applying *Required:* high school transcript, 1 recommendation, SAT or ACT. *Recommended:* 3 years of high school math and science, some high school foreign language, interview. *Application deadlines:* rolling, 3/1 priority date for financial aid. *Contact:* Ms. Martha Hooley, Director of Admissions, 1700 South Main Street, Goshen, IN 46526, 219-535-7535 or toll-free 800-348-7422 (out-of-state).

From the College Nearly all students complete graduation requirements by spending thirteen weeks in another country in Goshen's internationally acclaimed Study-Service Term (SST). In most cases, SST costs the same as a term on campus. While on SST, students develop the communication skills and personal maturity that translate into a rewarding personal and professional life after college.

Grinnell College

Grinnell, Iowa

Founded 1846
Small-town setting
Independent
Coed
Awards B

Enrollment 1,291 total—all undergraduates (328 freshmen)

Faculty 150 total; 131 full-time (92% have doctorate/terminal degree); student-faculty ratio is 10:1.

Libraries 329,561 bound volumes, 6,838 titles on microform, 2,210 periodical subscriptions

Computing *Terminals/PCs available for student use:* 220, located in computer center, library, dormitories science building, Carnegie Hall, classroom buildings; PC not required.

Of Special Interest *Core academic program:* no. Phi Beta Kappa chapter. Academic exchange with 13 members of the Associated Colleges of the Midwest. Sponsors and participates in study-abroad programs.

On Campus Drama/theater group; student-run newspaper and radio station. No national or local fraternities or sororities on campus.

Athletics Member NCAA (Division III). *Intercollegiate sports:* baseball (M), basketball (M, W), cross-country running (M, W), football (M), golf (M), soccer (M, W), softball (W), swimming and diving (M, W), tennis (M, W), track and field (M, W), volleyball (W).

Costs (1991–92) & Aid				
	Comprehensive fee	$17,610	Need-based scholarships (average)	$6138
	Tuition	$13,424	Non-need scholarships (average)	$2797
	Mandatory fees	$318	Short-term loans (average)	$100
	Room and board	$3868	Long-term loans—college funds (average)	$2216
	Financial aid recipients	70%	Long-term loans—external funds (average)	$2113

Undergraduate Facts				
	Part-time	0%	*Freshman Data:* 1,566 applied, 63% were accepted, 33% (328) of those entered	
	State residents	17%		
	Transfers	8%	From top tenth of high school class	58%
	African-Americans	5%	SAT-takers scoring 600 or over on verbal	54%
	Native Americans	1%	SAT-takers scoring 700 or over on verbal	10%
	Hispanics	2%	SAT-takers scoring 600 or over on math	68%
	Asian-Americans	4%	SAT-takers scoring 700 or over on math	23%
	International students	10%	ACT-takers scoring 26 or over	83%
	Freshmen returning for sophomore year	94%	ACT-takers scoring 30 or over	43%
	Students completing degree within 5 years	83%	*Majors with most degrees conferred:* biology/biological sciences, economics, English.	
	Grads pursuing further study	N/R		

Majors American studies, anthropology, art/fine arts, biology/biological sciences, black/African-American studies, chemistry, Chinese, classics, computer science, (pre)dentistry sequence, East Asian studies, East European and Soviet studies, ecology/environmental studies, economics, education, elementary education, English, European studies, French, German, history, interdisciplinary studies, Latin American studies, (pre)law sequence, liberal arts/general studies, mathematics, (pre)medicine sequence, music, philosophy, physical sciences, physics, political science/government, psychology, religious studies, Russian, science, secondary education, sociology, Spanish, theater arts/drama, (pre)veterinary medicine sequence, women's studies.

Applying *Required:* essay, high school transcript, 2 recommendations, SAT or ACT. *Recommended:* 3 years of high school math and science, 3 years of high school foreign language, interview. *Application deadlines:* 2/1, 12/1 for early decision, continuous to 3/1 for financial aid. *Contact:* Mr. John R. Hopkins, Director of Admission, Grinnell, IA 50112, 515-269-3600.

Grove City College

Grove City, Pennsylvania

Founded 1876
Small-town setting
Independent, Presbyterian
Coed
Awards B

Enrollment 2,173 total—all undergraduates (617 freshmen)

Faculty 133 total; 104 full-time (61% have doctorate/terminal degree); student-faculty ratio is 20:1.

Libraries 156,650 bound volumes, 208,419 titles on microform, 1,200 periodical subscriptions

Computing *Terminals/PCs available for student use:* 135, located in computer center; PC not required. Campus network links student PCs.

Of Special Interest *Core academic program:* yes. Computer course required for math, engineering majors. Academic exchange program: no. Participates in study-abroad programs.

On Campus Mandatory chapel; drama/theater group; student-run newspaper and radio station. *Social organizations:* 9 local fraternities, 9 local sororities; 29% of eligible undergraduate men and 51% of eligible undergraduate women are members.

Athletics Member NCAA (Division III). *Intercollegiate sports:* baseball (M), basketball (M, W), cross-country running (M, W), football (M), golf (M), soccer (M), softball (W), swimming and diving (M, W), tennis (M, W), track and field (M, W), volleyball (W).

Costs (1991–92) & Aid				
	Comprehensive fee	$7400	Need-based scholarships (average)	$1255
	Tuition	$4630	Non-need scholarships (average)	$3355
	Mandatory fees	$100	Short-term loans (average)	$50
	Room and board	$2670	Long-term loans—college funds (average)	$1023
	Financial aid recipients	50%	Long-term loans—external funds (average)	$3183

Undergraduate Facts				
	Part-time	1%	*Freshman Data:* 2,253 applied, 46% were accepted, 59% (617) of those entered	
	State residents	68%		
	Transfers	2%	From top tenth of high school class	48%
	African-Americans	1%	SAT-takers scoring 600 or over on verbal	11%
	Native Americans	1%	SAT-takers scoring 700 or over on verbal	1%
	Hispanics	1%	SAT-takers scoring 600 or over on math	45%
	Asian-Americans	1%	SAT-takers scoring 700 or over on math	8%
	International students	3%	ACT-takers scoring 26 or over	48%
	Freshmen returning for sophomore year	85%	ACT-takers scoring 30 or over	10%
	Students completing degree within 5 years	77%	*Majors with most degrees conferred:* business, engineering (general), elementary education.	
	Grads pursuing further study	12%		

Majors Accounting, biochemistry, biology/biological sciences, business, chemistry, communication, computer science, (pre)dentistry sequence, economics, electrical engineering, elementary education, engineering (general), finance/banking, French, history, international studies, (pre)law sequence, literature, mathematics, mechanical engineering, (pre)medicine sequence, ministries, modern languages, molecular biology, music education, physics, political science/government, psychology, religious studies, secondary education, Spanish, (pre)veterinary medicine sequence.

Applying *Required:* essay, high school transcript, 1 recommendation, SAT or ACT. *Recommended:* 3 years of high school math and science, some high school foreign language, campus interview. *Application deadlines:* 2/15, 11/15 for early decision, 5/1 priority date for financial aid. *Contact:* Mr. Jeffrey C. Mincey, Director of Admissions, 100 Campus Drive, Grove City, PA 16127-2104, 412-458-2100.

From the College Outstanding scholars and leaders in education, science, and international affairs visit Grove City College each year. The magnificent Pew Fine Arts Center houses facilities for theater, music, dance, photography, and the visual arts. An NCAA Division III sports program, with excellent facilities, provides great intercollegiate competition in sixteen sports for men and women. At Grove City, students get a high-quality education in a Christian environment at an affordable price.

Guilford College

Greensboro, North Carolina

Founded 1837
Suburban setting
Independent/affiliated with Society of Friends
Coed
Awards B

Enrollment 1,177 total—all undergraduates (324 freshmen)

Faculty 111 total; 91 full-time (90% have doctorate/terminal degree); student-faculty ratio is 14:1.

Libraries 220,000 bound volumes, 1,050 periodical subscriptions

Computing *Terminals/PCs available for student use:* 120, located in computer center, student center, library, dormitories, classroom buildings; PC not required. Campus network links student PCs.

Of Special Interest *Core academic program:* yes. Computer course required for management, math, all science majors. Sigma Xi chapter. Academic exchange with 7 members of the Piedmont Independent Colleges Association of North Carolina. Sponsors and participates in study-abroad programs. Cooperative Army ROTC, cooperative Air Force ROTC.

On Campus Drama/theater group; student-run newspaper and radio station. No national or local fraternities or sororities on campus.

Athletics Member NCAA (Division III). *Intercollegiate sports:* baseball (M), basketball (M, W), football (M), golf (M), lacrosse (M, W), rugby (M), soccer (M, W), tennis (M, W), volleyball (W).

Costs (1991–92) & Aid				
Comprehensive fee	$14,984	Need-based scholarships (average)	$3341
Tuition	$10,270	Non-need scholarships (average)	$3475
Mandatory fees	$200	Short-term loans (average)	$2250
Room and board	$4514	Long-term loans—college funds (average)	$2500
Financial aid recipients	67%	Long-term loans—external funds (average)	$2795

Undergraduate Facts			
Part-time	2%	*Freshman Data:* 1,212 applied, 75% were accepted, 36% (324) of those entered	
State residents	37%		
Transfers	10%	From top tenth of high school class	18%
African-Americans	6%	SAT-takers scoring 600 or over on verbal	20%
Native Americans	1%	SAT-takers scoring 700 or over on verbal	3%
Hispanics	1%	SAT-takers scoring 600 or over on math	28%
Asian-Americans	1%	SAT-takers scoring 700 or over on math	4%
International students	5%	ACT-takers scoring 26 or over	44%
Freshmen returning for sophomore year	80%	ACT-takers scoring 30 or over	14%
Students completing degree within 5 years	63%		
Grads pursuing further study	15%		

Majors Accounting, anthropology, art/fine arts, biology/biological sciences, business, chemistry, criminal justice, (pre)dentistry sequence, early childhood education, earth science, economics, education, elementary education, English, French, geology, German, history, humanities, (pre)law sequence, liberal arts/general studies, mathematics, music, philosophy, physical education, physician's assistant studies, physics, political science/government, psychology, religious studies, secondary education, sociology, sports administration, sports medicine, theater arts/drama, (pre)veterinary medicine sequence.

Applying *Required:* essay, high school transcript, 3 years of high school math, 2 years of high school foreign language, 1 recommendation, SAT or ACT. *Recommended:* 3 years of high school science, interview. *Application deadlines:* 3/1, 12/1 for early decision, 3/1 for financial aid. *Contact:* Mr. Larry West, Director of Admission, 5800 West Friendly Avenue, Greensboro, NC 27410, 919-316-2000 Ext. 124 or toll-free 800-992-7759.

From the College With the opening of the new and renovated Hege Library, which contains seven art galleries, Guilford is able to display one of the finest teaching collections of art on any college campus. The collection changes periodically to display modern as well as medieval works of art.

Gustavus Adolphus College

St. Peter, Minnesota

Founded 1862
Small-town setting
Independent/affiliated with Evangelical Lutheran Church in America
Coed
Awards B

Enrollment	2,305 total—all undergraduates (628 freshmen)
Faculty	206 total; 156 full-time (81% have doctorate/terminal degree); student-faculty ratio is 14:1.
Libraries	223,000 bound volumes, 29,014 titles on microform, 1,192 periodical subscriptions
Computing	*Terminals/PCs available for student use:* 132, located in computer center, library, classroom buildings; PC not required.
Of Special Interest	*Core academic program:* yes. Phi Beta Kappa, Sigma Xi chapters. Academic exchange program: no. Sponsors and participates in study-abroad programs. Cooperative Army ROTC.
On Campus	Drama/theater group; student-run newspaper and radio station. No national or local fraternities or sororities on campus.
Athletics	Member NCAA (Division III). *Intercollegiate sports:* baseball (M), basketball (M, W), cross-country running (M, W), football (M), golf (M, W), gymnastics (W), ice hockey (M), soccer (M, W), softball (W), swimming and diving (M, W), tennis (M, W), track and field (M, W), volleyball (W).

Costs (1992–93 estimated) & Aid	Comprehensive fee	$12,835	Need-based scholarships (average)	$2950
	Tuition	$10,100	Non-need scholarships (average)	$3000
	Mandatory fees	$35	Short-term loans (average)	$100
	Room and board	$2700	Long-term loans—college funds	N/Avail
	Financial aid recipients	62%	Long-term loans—external funds (average)	$2200

Undergraduate Facts	Part-time	2%	*Freshman Data:* 1,482 applied, 83% were accepted, 51% (628) of those entered	
	State residents	74%		
	Transfers	3%	From top tenth of high school class	38%
	African-Americans	2%	SAT-takers scoring 600 or over on verbal	20%
	Native Americans	0%	SAT-takers scoring 700 or over on verbal	3%
	Hispanics	1%	SAT-takers scoring 600 or over on math	44%
	Asian-Americans	2%	SAT-takers scoring 700 or over on math	13%
	International students	2%	ACT-takers scoring 26 or over	37%
	Freshmen returning for sophomore year	92%	ACT-takers scoring 30 or over	10%
	Students completing degree within 5 years	76%		
	Grads pursuing further study	30%		

Majors Accounting, American studies, anthropology, art education, art/fine arts, arts administration, biology/biological sciences, business, business economics, chemistry, classics, communication, computer science, criminal justice, dance, (pre)dentistry sequence, economics, education, elementary education, English, French, geography, geology, German, health education, history, interdisciplinary studies, international business, Latin American studies, (pre)law sequence, mathematics, (pre)medicine sequence, music, music education, nursing, philosophy, physical education, physical therapy, physics, political science/government, psychology, religious studies, Russian, Russian and Slavic studies, sacred music, Scandinavian languages/studies, secondary education, social science, sociology, Spanish, speech/rhetoric/public address/debate, theater arts/drama, (pre)veterinary medicine sequence.

Applying *Required:* essay, high school transcript, 2 recommendations, SAT or ACT. *Recommended:* 3 years of high school math and science, some high school foreign language, interview. *Application deadlines:* 4/1, 11/15 for early decision, 4/1 priority date for financial aid. *Contact:* Mr. Mark Anderson, Director of Admissions, 800 College Avenue, St. Peter, MN 56082, 507-933-7676.

✱ Hamilton College

Clinton, New York

Founded 1812
Rural setting
Independent
Coed
Awards B

Enrollment 1,698 total—all undergraduates (462 freshmen)

Faculty 189 total; 163 full-time (98% have doctorate/terminal degree); student-faculty ratio is 11:1.

Libraries 465,000 bound volumes, 337,000 titles on microform, 1,900 periodical subscriptions

Computing *Terminals/PCs available for student use:* 300, located in computer center, student center, library, reading/writing center; PC not required. Campus network links student PCs.

Of Special Interest *Core academic program:* yes. Phi Beta Kappa, Sigma Xi chapters. Academic exchange with Colgate University, Syracuse University, Utica College of Syracuse University. Sponsors and participates in study-abroad programs. Cooperative Army ROTC.

On Campus Drama/theater group; student-run newspaper and radio station. *Social organizations:* 8 national fraternities, 1 national sorority, 1 local sorority, 1 private society; 45% of eligible undergraduate men and 12% of eligible undergraduate women are members.

Athletics Member NCAA (Division III). *Intercollegiate sports:* baseball (M), basketball (M, W), crew (M, W), cross-country running (M, W), fencing (M, W), field hockey (W), football (M), golf (M, W), ice hockey (M, W), lacrosse (M, W), rugby (M, W), sailing (M, W), skiing (downhill) (M, W), soccer (M, W), softball (W), squash (M, W), swimming and diving (M, W), tennis (M, W), track and field (M, W), volleyball (M, W).

Costs (1991–92) & Aid

Comprehensive fee	$21,200	
Tuition	$16,650	
Mandatory fees	N/App	
Room and board	$4550	
Financial aid recipients	65%	
Need-based scholarships (average)		$8569
Non-need scholarships		N/Avail
Short-term loans		N/Avail
Long-term loans—college funds (average)		$2625
Long-term loans—external funds (average)		$3086

Undergraduate Facts

Part-time	1%	
State residents	46%	
Transfers	2%	
African-Americans	4%	
Native Americans	0%	
Hispanics	3%	
Asian-Americans	3%	
International students	5%	
Freshmen returning for sophomore year	95%	
Students completing degree within 5 years	90%	
Grads pursuing further study	20%	

Freshman Data: 3,568 applied, 49% were accepted, 27% (462) of those entered

From top tenth of high school class	41%
SAT-takers scoring 600 or over on verbal	28%
SAT-takers scoring 700 or over on verbal	3%
SAT-takers scoring 600 or over on math	58%
SAT-takers scoring 700 or over on math	12%
ACT-takers scoring 26 or over	N/R
ACT-takers scoring 30 or over	N/R

Majors with most degrees conferred: history, English, political science/government.

Majors American studies, anthropology, art/fine arts, art history, Asian/Oriental studies, biochemistry, biology/biological sciences, chemistry, classics, comparative literature, computer science, creative writing, dance, economics, English, French, geology, German, Greek, history, international studies, Latin, linguistics, literature, mathematics, modern languages, molecular biology, music, Near and Middle Eastern studies, philosophy, physics, political science/government, psychobiology, psychology, public affairs and policy studies, religious studies, Russian and Slavic studies, sociology, Spanish, studio art, theater arts/drama, Western civilization and culture, women's studies.

Applying *Required:* essay, high school transcript, 1 recommendation, sample of expository prose, SAT or ACT. *Recommended:* 3 years of high school math and science, 3 years of high school foreign language, interview, 3 Achievements. *Application deadlines:* 1/15, 11/15 for early decision, 2/1 for financial aid. *Contact:* Mr. Douglas C. Thompson, Dean of Admission, 198 College Hill Road, Clinton, NY 13323, 315-859-4421 or toll-free 800-843-2655.

Hamline University

St. Paul, Minnesota

Founded 1854
Urban setting
Independent/affiliated with United Methodist Church
Coed
Awards B, M, D

Enrollment 2,443 total; 1,448 undergraduates (256 freshmen)

Faculty 129 total; 93 full-time (91% have doctorate/terminal degree); student-faculty ratio is 14:1; grad assistants teach no undergraduate courses.

Libraries 180,000 bound volumes, 1,000 titles on microform, 800 periodical subscriptions

Computing *Terminals/PCs available for student use:* 100, located in computer center, library, dormitories, science building; PC not required. Campus network links student PCs.

Of Special Interest *Core academic program:* yes. Computer course required. Phi Beta Kappa chapter. Academic exchange with members of the Associated Colleges of the Twin Cities, American University (Washington Semester). Sponsors and participates in study-abroad programs. Cooperative Air Force ROTC.

On Campus Drama/theater group; student-run newspaper. *Social organizations:* 2 national fraternities, 2 local sororities; 9% of eligible undergraduate men and 7% of eligible undergraduate women are members.

Athletics Member NCAA (Division III). *Intercollegiate sports:* baseball (M), basketball (M, W), cross-country running (M, W), football (M), golf (M), gymnastics (W), ice hockey (M), soccer (M, W), softball (W), swimming and diving (M, W), tennis (M, W), track and field (M, W), volleyball (W), wrestling (M).

Costs (1991-92) & Aid				
	Comprehensive fee	$15,356	Need-based scholarships (average)	$3279
	Tuition	$11,550	Non-need scholarships (average)	$3736
	Mandatory fees	$175	Short-term loans	N/Avail
	Room and board	$3631	Long-term loans—college funds	N/Avail
	Financial aid recipients	82%	Long-term loans—external funds (average)	$2600

Undergraduate Facts				
	Part-time	5%	*Freshman Data:* 796 applied, 84% were accepted, 38% (256) of those entered	
	State residents	82%		
	Transfers	11%	From top tenth of high school class	37%
	African-Americans	3%	SAT-takers scoring 600 or over on verbal	25%
	Native Americans	1%	SAT-takers scoring 700 or over on verbal	2%
	Hispanics	1%	SAT-takers scoring 600 or over on math	45%
	Asian-Americans	3%	SAT-takers scoring 700 or over on math	3%
	International students	3%	ACT-takers scoring 26 or over	64%
	Freshmen returning for sophomore year	82%	ACT-takers scoring 30 or over	4%
	Students completing degree within 5 years	62%	*Majors with most degrees conferred:* psychology, English, business.	
	Grads pursuing further study	25%		

Majors American studies, anthropology, art education, art/fine arts, art history, Asian/Oriental studies, biology/biological sciences, business, chemistry, communication, (pre)dentistry sequence, East Asian studies, ecology/environmental studies, economics, education, elementary education, English, environmental sciences, French, German, health education, history, international business, international studies, Judaic studies, Latin American studies, (pre)law sequence, legal studies, mathematics, medical technology, (pre)medicine sequence, music, music education, paralegal studies, philosophy, physical education, physics, political science/government, psychology, public administration, religious studies, Russian and Slavic studies, science education, secondary education, social science, sociology, Spanish, studio art, theater arts/drama, urban studies, (pre)veterinary medicine sequence, women's studies.

Applying *Required:* essay, high school transcript, 1 recommendation, SAT or ACT. *Recommended:* 3 years of high school math and science, 2 years of high school foreign language, interview. *Application deadlines:* rolling, 12/1 for early action, 4/15 priority date for financial aid. *Contact:* Dr. W. Scott Friedhoff, Dean of Undergraduate Admissions, 833 Snelling Avenue, St. Paul, MN 55104, 612-641-2207 or toll-free 800-753-9753.

✷ Hampden-Sydney College

Hampden-Sydney, Virginia

Founded 1776
Rural setting
Independent, Presbyterian
Men
Awards B

Enrollment 972 total—all undergraduates (296 freshmen)

Faculty 91 total; 62 full-time (87% have doctorate/terminal degree); student-faculty ratio is 13:1.

Libraries 175,000 bound volumes, 22,000 titles on microform, 804 periodical subscriptions

Computing *Terminals/PCs available for student use:* 120, located in computer center, library, dormitories, classroom buildings; PC not required.

Of Special Interest *Core academic program:* yes. Computer course required for math, some economics majors. Phi Beta Kappa, Sigma Xi chapters. Academic exchange with Seven-College Exchange Program, Longwood College Cooperative Program. Sponsors and participates in study-abroad programs. Cooperative Army ROTC.

On Campus Drama/theater group; student-run newspaper and radio station. *Social organizations:* 12 national fraternities; 52% of eligible undergraduates are members.

Athletics Member NCAA (Division III). *Intercollegiate sports:* baseball, basketball, cross-country running, fencing, football, golf, lacrosse, rugby, soccer, tennis, volleyball, water polo.

Costs (1991–92) & Aid				
	Comprehensive fee	$15,656	Need-based scholarships (average)	$5279
	Tuition	$11,316	Non-need scholarships (average)	$7534
	Mandatory fees	$360	Short-term loans (average)	$150
	Room and board	$3980	Long-term loans—college funds (average)	$2071
	Financial aid recipients	38%	Long-term loans—external funds (average)	$2732

Undergraduate Facts				
	Part-time	0%	*Freshman Data:* 772 applied, 80% were accepted, 48% (296) of those entered	
	State residents	50%		
	Transfers	2%	From top tenth of high school class	15%
	African-Americans	3%	SAT-takers scoring 600 or over on verbal	9%
	Native Americans	0%	SAT-takers scoring 700 or over on verbal	1%
	Hispanics	1%	SAT-takers scoring 600 or over on math	30%
	Asian-Americans	1%	SAT-takers scoring 700 or over on math	3%
	International students	1%	ACT-takers scoring 26 or over	N/R
	Freshmen returning for sophomore year	87%	ACT-takers scoring 30 or over	N/R
	Students completing degree within 5 years	65%	*Majors with most degrees conferred:* economics, history, political science/government.	
	Grads pursuing further study	11%		

Majors Biochemistry, biology/biological sciences, biophysics, business economics, chemistry, classics, computer science, economics, English, French, German, Greek, history, humanities, Latin, mathematics, philosophy, physics, political science/government, psychology, religious studies, Spanish.

Applying *Required:* essay, high school transcript, 3 years of high school math, 2 years of high school foreign language, 2 recommendations, SAT or ACT. *Recommended:* 3 years of high school science, campus interview, Achievements, English Composition Test. *Application deadlines:* 3/1, 11/15 for early decision, 3/1 priority date for financial aid. *Contact:* Mr. Robert H. Jones, Senior Vice-President/Dean of Admissions, College Road, Hampden-Sydney, VA 23943, 804-223-6120 or toll-free 800-755-0733 (in-state).

From the College The spirit of Hampden-Sydney lies in its sense of community. Students are in small classes and find it easy to get extra help from professors. A big bonus of small-college life is that everybody is involved. Athletics, debating, publications, fraternity life—all are part of the process that produces a well-rounded Hampden-Sydney graduate.

Hampshire College

Amherst, Massachusetts

Founded 1965
Rural setting
Independent
Coed
Awards B

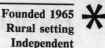

Enrollment	1,235 total—all undergraduates (286 freshmen)
Faculty	97 total; 89 full-time (80% have doctorate/terminal degree); student-faculty ratio is 13:1.
Libraries	111,000 bound volumes, 400 titles on microform, 800 periodical subscriptions
Computing	*Terminals/PCs available for student use:* 71, located in computer center, library, communications, natural and cognitive science buildings; PC not required.
Of Special Interest	*Core academic program:* yes. Academic exchange with members of Five Colleges, Inc. Participates in study-abroad programs.
On Campus	Drama/theater group; student-run newspaper. No national or local fraternities or sororities on campus.
Athletics	*Intercollegiate sports:* badminton (M, W), baseball (M), basketball (M, W), equestrian sports (M, W), soccer (M, W), volleyball (M, W).

Costs (1991–92) & Aid				
	Comprehensive fee	$22,020	Need-based scholarships (average)	$11,195
	Tuition	$17,200	Non-need scholarships (average)	$2575
	Mandatory fees	$260	Short-term loans	N/Avail
	Room and board	$4560	Long-term loans—college funds (average)	$2500
	Financial aid recipients	50%	Long-term loans—external funds (average)	$3000

Undergraduate Facts				
	Part-time	0%	*Freshman Data:* 1,241 applied, 69% were accepted, 33% (286) of those entered	
	State residents	14%		
	Transfers	16%	From top tenth of high school class	24%
	African-Americans	3%	SAT-takers scoring 600 or over on verbal	N/R
	Native Americans	1%	SAT-takers scoring 700 or over on verbal	N/R
	Hispanics	3%	SAT-takers scoring 600 or over on math	N/R
	Asian-Americans	3%	SAT-takers scoring 700 or over on math	N/R
	International students	2%	ACT-takers scoring 26 or over	N/R
	Freshmen returning for sophomore year	87%	ACT-takers scoring 30 or over	N/R
	Students completing degree within 5 years	46%	*Majors with most degrees conferred:* psychology, history, creative writing.	
	Grads pursuing further study	N/R		

Majors African studies, agricultural sciences, American studies, animal sciences, anthropology, archaeology, architecture, art education, art/fine arts, art history, art therapy, Asian/Oriental studies, astronomy, behavioral sciences, biochemistry, biology/biological sciences, black/African-American studies, botany/plant sciences, Canadian studies, cell biology, chemistry, child care/child and family studies, child psychology/child development, cognitive science, communication, community services, comparative literature, computer graphics, computer science, conservation, creative writing, dance, early childhood education, earth science, East Asian studies, East European and Soviet studies, ecology/environmental studies, economics, education, elementary education, English, environmental biology, environmental design, environmental education, environmental health sciences, environmental sciences, ethnic studies, European studies, family and consumer studies, film and video, film studies, genetics, geography, geology, health science, Hispanic studies, history, history of philosophy, history of science, human development, humanities, information science, interdisciplinary studies, international business, international economics, international studies, Islamic studies, jazz, journalism, Judaic studies, labor and industrial relations, labor studies, Latin American studies, legal studies, liberal arts/general studies, linguistics, literature, marine biology, marine sciences, mathematics, (pre)medicine sequence, medieval studies, Mexican-American/Chicano studies, microbiology, molecular biology, music, music history, Native American studies, natural sciences, Near and Middle Eastern studies, neurosciences, nutrition, painting/drawing, peace studies, philosophy, photography, physical fitness/human movement, physical sciences, physics, physiology, political science/government, psychobiology, psychology, public affairs and policy studies, public health, radio and television studies, religious studies, science, sculpture, secondary education, social science, sociology, solar technologies, South Asian studies, Southeast Asian studies, statistics, studio art, telecommunications, theater arts/drama, urban studies, (pre)veterinary medicine sequence, wildlife biology, women's studies.

Applying *Required:* essay, high school transcript, 2 recommendations. *Recommended:* interview. *Application deadlines:* 2/1, 11/15 for early decision, 1/1 for early action, 2/15 priority date for financial aid. *Contact:* Ms. Audrey Smith, Director of Admissions, West Street, Amherst, MA 01002, 413-549-4600 Ext. 728.

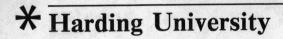

✱ Harding University

Searcy, Arkansas

Founded 1924
Small-town setting
Independent/affiliated with Church of Christ
Coed
Awards A, B, M

Enrollment	3,386 total; 3,122 undergraduates (736 freshmen)
Faculty	190 total; 165 full-time (70% have doctorate/terminal degree); student-faculty ratio is 16:1; grad assistants teach no undergraduate courses.
Libraries	347,000 bound volumes, 72,720 titles on microform, 1,337 periodical subscriptions
Computing	*Terminals/PCs available for student use:* 250, located in computer center, library, classroom buildings; PC not required.
Of Special Interest	*Core academic program:* yes. Computer course required. Academic exchange program: no. Sponsors and participates in study-abroad programs.
On Campus	Dress code; mandatory chapel; drama/theater group; student-run newspaper and radio station. *Social organizations:* local fraternities, local sororities, social clubs; 90% of eligible undergraduate men and 79% of eligible undergraduate women are members.
Athletics	Member NAIA. *Intercollegiate sports:* baseball (M), basketball (M, W), cross-country running (M, W), football (M), golf (M), tennis (M, W), track and field (M, W), volleyball (W). *Scholarships:* M, W.

Costs (1992–93 estimated) & Aid				
	Comprehensive fee	$9250	Need-based scholarships (average)	$500
	Tuition	$5200	Non-need scholarships (average)	$1000
	Mandatory fees	$750	Short-term loans (average)	$500
	Room and board	$3300	Long-term loans—college funds	N/Avail
	Financial aid recipients	70%	Long-term loans—external funds (average)	$1200

Undergraduate Facts				
	Part-time	10%	*Freshman Data:* 1,408 applied, 64% were accepted, 81% (736) of those entered	
	State residents	29%		
	Transfers	4%	From top tenth of high school class	30%
	African-Americans	5%	SAT-takers scoring 600 or over on verbal	N/R
	Native Americans	N/R	SAT-takers scoring 700 or over on verbal	N/R
	Hispanics	2%	SAT-takers scoring 600 or over on math	N/R
	Asian-Americans	N/R	SAT-takers scoring 700 or over on math	N/R
	International students	5%	ACT-takers scoring 26 or over	50%
	Freshmen returning for sophomore year	78%	ACT-takers scoring 30 or over	10%
	Students completing degree within 5 years	N/R		
	Grads pursuing further study	N/R		

Majors Accounting, advertising, American studies, art education, art/fine arts, art history, biblical languages, biblical studies, biochemistry, biology/biological sciences, business, business education, chemistry, communication, computer information systems, computer programming, computer science, data processing, (pre)dentistry sequence, dietetics, early childhood education, economics, education, elementary education, English, fashion merchandising, finance/banking, food marketing, food services management, French, history, home economics, home economics education, interior design, international studies, journalism, (pre)law sequence, marketing/retailing/merchandising, mathematics, (pre)medicine sequence, modern languages, music, music education, nursing, painting/drawing, physical education, physics, piano/organ, political science/government, psychology, public administration, public relations, radio and television studies, religious education, religious studies, science, science education, secondary education, secretarial studies/office management, social science, social work, sociology, Spanish, special education, speech pathology and audiology, speech/rhetoric/public address/debate, sports administration, stringed instruments, systems science, theater arts/drama, theology, (pre)veterinary medicine sequence, voice.

Applying *Required:* high school transcript, 3 years of high school math and science, 2 recommendations, interview, SAT or ACT. *Recommended:* 2 years of high school foreign language. *Application deadlines:* 7/1, 1/1 for early action, 3/1 priority date for financial aid. *Contact:* Mr. Mike Williams, Director of Admissions, Administration Building, Searcy, AR 72143, 501-279-4407 or toll-free 800-477-4407.

Harvard University

Cambridge, Massachusetts

Founded 1636
Urban setting
Independent
Coed
Awards B, M, D

Enrollment	18,179 total; 6,622 undergraduates (1,609 freshmen)
Faculty	800 total—all full-time (100% have doctorate/terminal degree); student-faculty ratio is 8:1; grad assistants teach a few undergraduate courses.
Libraries	13 million bound volumes, 3 million titles on microform, 100,000 periodical subscriptions
Computing	*Terminals/PCs available for student use:* 200, located in computer center, "Houses"; PC not required but available for purchase.
Of Special Interest	*Core academic program:* yes. Computer course required. Phi Beta Kappa, Sigma Xi chapters. Academic exchange with Massachusetts Institute of Technology. Participates in study-abroad programs. Cooperative Army ROTC, cooperative Naval ROTC, cooperative Air Force ROTC.
On Campus	Drama/theater group; student-run newspaper and radio station. *Social organizations:* "House" system; 99% of eligible undergraduate men and 99% of eligible undergraduate women are members.
Athletics	Member NCAA (Division I). *Intercollegiate sports:* baseball (M), basketball (M, W), crew (M, W), cross-country running (M, W), fencing (M, W), field hockey (W), football (M), golf (M, W), ice hockey (M, W), lacrosse (M, W), sailing (M, W), skiing (cross-country) (M, W), skiing (downhill) (M, W), soccer (M, W), softball (W), squash (M, W), swimming and diving (M, W), tennis (M, W), track and field (M, W), volleyball (M, W), water polo (M, W), wrestling (M).

Costs (1991–92) & Aid	Comprehensive fee	$22,080	Need-based scholarships (average)	$10,891
	Tuition	$15,410	Non-need scholarships	N/Avail
	Mandatory fees	$1150	Short-term loans	N/Avail
	Room and board	$5520	Long-term loans—college funds (average)	$2300
	Financial aid recipients	74%	Long-term loans—external funds (average)	$2500

Undergraduate Facts	Part-time	0%	*Freshman Data:* 12,589 applied, 17% were accepted, 74% (1,609) of those entered	
	State residents	16%		
	Transfers	4%	From top tenth of high school class	95%
	African-Americans	8%	SAT-takers scoring 600 or over on verbal	N/R
	Native Americans	1%	SAT-takers scoring 700 or over on verbal	N/R
	Hispanics	7%	SAT-takers scoring 600 or over on math	N/R
	Asian-Americans	19%	SAT-takers scoring 700 or over on math	N/R
	International students	8%	ACT-takers scoring 26 or over	N/R
	Freshmen returning for sophomore year	97%	ACT-takers scoring 30 or over	N/R
	Students completing degree within 5 years	96%	*Majors with most degrees conferred:* political science/government, literature, history.	
	Grads pursuing further study	N/R		

Majors African languages, African studies, anthropology, applied mathematics, Arabic, archaeology, art/fine arts, art history, Asian/Oriental studies, astronomy, astrophysics, biblical languages, biochemistry, bioengineering, biology/biological sciences, biomedical engineering, biophysics, black/African-American studies, chemistry, Chinese, classics, comparative literature, computer science, creative writing, East Asian studies, East European and Soviet studies, ecology/environmental studies, economics, electronics engineering, engineering (general), engineering and applied sciences, engineering physics, engineering sciences, English, environmental design, environmental engineering, environmental sciences, European studies, folklore, French, geology, German, Germanic languages and literature, Greek, Hebrew, Hispanic studies, history, history of science, humanities, Italian, Japanese, Judaic studies, Latin, linguistics, literature, materials engineering, mathematics, mechanical engineering, music, music history, Near and Middle Eastern studies, philosophy, physical sciences, physics, political science/government, Portuguese, psychology, religious studies, Romance languages, Russian, Russian and Slavic studies, Scandinavian languages/studies, Slavic languages, social science, sociology, South Asian studies, Southeast Asian studies, Spanish, statistics, systems engineering, Western civilization and culture, women's studies.

Applying *Required:* essay, high school transcript, 2 recommendations, interview, SAT or ACT, 3 Achievements. *Recommended:* 4 years of high school math, 3 years of high school science, 3 years of high school foreign language. *Application deadlines:* 1/1, 11/1 for early action, 2/15 priority date for financial aid. *Contact:* Dr. William R. Fitzsimmons, Dean of Admissions and Financial Aid, 8 Garden Street, Cambridge, MA 02138, 617-495-1551.

Harvey Mudd College

Claremont, California

Founded 1955
Small-town setting
Independent
Coed
Awards B, M

Enrollment 624 total; 618 undergraduates (179 freshmen)

Faculty 77 total; 68 full-time (100% have doctorate/terminal degree); student-faculty ratio is 8:1; grad assistants teach no undergraduate courses.

Libraries 1.7 million bound volumes, 6,800 periodical subscriptions

Computing *Terminals/PCs available for student use:* 80, located in dormitories, computer labs; PC not required.

Of Special Interest *Core academic program:* yes. Computer course required. Sigma Xi chapter. Academic exchange with other members of The Claremont Colleges, Swarthmore College, Rensselaer Polytechnic Institute. Sponsors and participates in study-abroad programs. Air Force ROTC, cooperative Army ROTC.

On Campus Drama/theater group; student-run newspaper and radio station. No national or local fraternities or sororities on campus.

Athletics Member NCAA (Division III). *Intercollegiate sports:* baseball (M), basketball (M, W), cross-country running (M, W), football (M), golf (M), soccer (M, W), softball (W), swimming and diving (M, W), tennis (M, W), track and field (M, W), volleyball (W), water polo (M).

Costs (1991–92) & Aid
Comprehensive fee	$20,800
Tuition	$14,470
Mandatory fees	$440
Room and board	$5890
Financial aid recipients	80%
Need-based scholarships (average)	$8430
Non-need scholarships	Avail
Short-term loans (average)	$100
Long-term loans—college funds (average)	$2500
Long-term loans—external funds (average)	$2401

Undergraduate Facts
Part-time	1%
State residents	51%
Transfers	2%
African-Americans	2%
Native Americans	0%
Hispanics	5%
Asian-Americans	20%
International students	3%
Freshmen returning for sophomore year	90%
Students completing degree within 5 years	76%
Grads pursuing further study	50%

Freshman Data: 1,124 applied, 44% were accepted, 36% (179) of those entered
From top tenth of high school class	100%
SAT-takers scoring 600 or over on verbal	65%
SAT-takers scoring 700 or over on verbal	18%
SAT-takers scoring 600 or over on math	99%
SAT-takers scoring 700 or over on math	75%
ACT-takers scoring 26 or over	N/App
ACT-takers scoring 30 or over	N/App

Majors Biology/biological sciences, chemistry, computer science, engineering (general), mathematics, physics.

Applying *Required:* essay, high school transcript, 4 years of high school math, 3 years of high school science, 2 recommendations, SAT, 3 Achievements, English Composition Test. *Recommended:* 2 years of high school foreign language, interview. Application deadlines: 2/1, 12/1 for early decision, 2/15 priority date for financial aid. *Contact:* Ms. Patricia Coleman, Dean of Admission, 301 East 12th Street, Kingston Hall, Claremont, CA 91711, 714-621-8011.

Haverford College

Haverford, Pennsylvania

Founded 1833
Suburban setting
Independent
Coed
Awards B

Enrollment	1,113 total—all undergraduates (296 freshmen)
Faculty	107 total; 91 full-time (92% have doctorate/terminal degree); student-faculty ratio is 11:1.
Libraries	400,000 bound volumes, 50,992 titles on microform, 1,257 periodical subscriptions
Computing	*Terminals/PCs available for student use:* 110, located in computer center, library, dormitories, clusters throughout campus; PC not required. Campus network links student PCs.
Of Special Interest	*Core academic program:* yes. Phi Beta Kappa chapter. Academic exchange with University of Pennsylvania, Swarthmore College, Bryn Mawr College. Participates in study-abroad programs.
On Campus	Drama/theater group; student-run newspaper and radio station. No national or local fraternities or sororities on campus.
Athletics	Member NCAA (Division III). *Intercollegiate sports:* baseball (M), basketball (M, W), cross-country running (M, W), fencing (M, W), field hockey (W), lacrosse (M, W), soccer (M, W), softball (W), squash (M, W), swimming and diving (M, W), tennis (M, W), track and field (M, W), volleyball (W).

Costs (1991–92) & Aid				
	Comprehensive fee	$21,550	Need-based scholarships (average)	$10,820
	Tuition	$15,992	Non-need scholarships	N/Avail
	Mandatory fees	$158	Short-term loans	N/Avail
	Room and board	$5400	Long-term loans—college funds	N/Avail
	Financial aid recipients	35%	Long-term loans—external funds (average)	$2698

Undergraduate Facts				
	Part-time	0%	*Freshman Data:* 2,017 applied, 43% were accepted, 34% (296) of those entered	
	State residents	16%		
	Transfers	1%	From top tenth of high school class	71%
	African-Americans	5%	SAT-takers scoring 600 or over on verbal	66%
	Native Americans	0%	SAT-takers scoring 700 or over on verbal	16%
	Hispanics	4%	SAT-takers scoring 600 or over on math	81%
	Asian-Americans	9%	SAT-takers scoring 700 or over on math	38%
	International students	2%	ACT-takers scoring 26 or over	N/App
	Freshmen returning for sophomore year	99%	ACT-takers scoring 30 or over	N/App
	Students completing degree within 5 years	90%	*Majors with most degrees conferred:* English, history, biology/biological sciences.	
	Grads pursuing further study	28%		

Majors African studies, anthropology, archaeology, art/fine arts, art history, astronomy, biology/biological sciences, chemistry, classics, comparative literature, computer science, East Asian studies, economics, English, French, geology, German, Greek, history, international studies, Italian, Latin, Latin American studies, (pre)law sequence, mathematics, (pre)medicine sequence, music, peace studies, philosophy, physics, political science/government, psychology, religious studies, Russian, sociology, Spanish, urban studies, (pre)veterinary medicine sequence, women's studies.

Applying *Required:* essay, high school transcript, 3 years of high school math, 3 years of high school foreign language, 2 recommendations, SAT, 2 Achievements. *Recommended:* 3 years of high school science, interview, English Composition Test (with essay). *Application deadlines:* 1/15, 11/15 for early decision, 1/31 for financial aid. *Contact:* Ms. Delsie Phillips, Director of Admissions, 370 Lancaster Avenue, Haverford, PA 19041, 215-896-1350.

Hendrix College

Conway, Arkansas

Founded 1876
Small-town setting
Independent, United Methodist
Coed
Awards B

Enrollment 980 total—all undergraduates (285 freshmen)

Faculty 76 total; 64 full-time (90% have doctorate/terminal degree); student-faculty ratio is 14:1.

Libraries 189,299 bound volumes, 106,324 titles on microform, 598 periodical subscriptions

Computing *Terminals/PCs available for student use:* 45, located in computer center, terminal room, labs; PC not required. Campus network links student PCs.

Of Special Interest *Core academic program:* yes. Computer course required for economics, math, physics majors. Academic exchange program: no. Sponsors and participates in study-abroad programs. Cooperative Army ROTC.

On Campus Drama/theater group; student-run newspaper and radio station. No national or local fraternities or sororities on campus.

Athletics Member NCAA (Division III). *Intercollegiate sports:* baseball (M), basketball (M, W), cross-country running (M, W), golf (M, W), rugby (M), soccer (M, W), swimming and diving (M, W), tennis (M, W), track and field (M, W), volleyball (W).

Costs (1991–92) & Aid

Comprehensive fee	$9928	Need-based scholarships (average)	$1717
Tuition	$7050	Non-need scholarships (average)	$2358
Mandatory fees	$103	Short-term loans	N/Avail
Room and board	$2775	Long-term loans—college funds (average)	$1942
Financial aid recipients	71%	Long-term loans—external funds (average)	$2840

Undergraduate Facts

Part-time	N/R	*Freshman Data:* 750 applied, 81% were accepted, 47% (285) of those entered	
State residents	75%		
Transfers	3%	From top tenth of high school class	49%
African-Americans	6%	SAT-takers scoring 600 or over on verbal	17%
Native Americans	0%	SAT-takers scoring 700 or over on verbal	0%
Hispanics	1%	SAT-takers scoring 600 or over on math	38%
Asian-Americans	2%	SAT-takers scoring 700 or over on math	5%
International students	3%	ACT-takers scoring 26 or over	51%
Freshmen returning for sophomore year	84%	ACT-takers scoring 30 or over	14%
Students completing degree within 5 years	60%	*Majors with most degrees conferred:* biology/biological sciences, psychology, economics.	
Grads pursuing further study	50%		

Majors Accounting, American studies, art/fine arts, biology/biological sciences, chemistry, (pre)dentistry sequence, economics, education, elementary education, English, French, German, history, humanities, international business, international studies, (pre)law sequence, mathematics, (pre)medicine sequence, music, philosophy, physical education, physics, political science/government, psychology, religious studies, sociology, Spanish, theater arts/drama, (pre)veterinary medicine sequence.

Applying *Required:* essay, high school transcript, SAT or ACT. *Recommended:* 3 years of high school math and science, 1 year of high school foreign language. 1 recommendation, campus interview required for some. *Application deadlines:* rolling, 4/1 priority date for financial aid. *Contact:* Mr. Rudy R. Pollan, Vice-President of Enrollment, 1601 Harkrider Street, Conway, AR 72032-3080, 501-450-1362.

Hillsdale College

Hillsdale, Michigan

Founded 1844
Small-town setting
Independent
Coed
Awards B

Enrollment 1,140 total—all undergraduates (361 freshmen)

Faculty 103 total; 78 full-time (78% have doctorate/terminal degree); student-faculty ratio is 12:1.

Libraries 175,000 bound volumes, 16,000 titles on microform, 1,500 periodical subscriptions

Computing *Terminals/PCs available for student use:* 170, located in computer center, library, dormitories; PC not required.

Of Special Interest *Core academic program:* yes. Computer course required for physics, math majors. Academic exchange program: no. Sponsors and participates in study-abroad programs. Cooperative Army ROTC, cooperative Naval ROTC, cooperative Air Force ROTC.

On Campus Drama/theater group; student-run newspaper. *Social organizations:* 5 national fraternities, 4 national sororities; 50% of eligible undergraduate men and 50% of eligible undergraduate women are members.

Athletics Member NCAA (Division II), NAIA. *Intercollegiate sports:* baseball (M), basketball (M, W), cross-country running (M, W), football (M), golf (M), softball (W), swimming and diving (W), tennis (M, W), track and field (M, W), volleyball (W). *Scholarships:* M, W.

Costs (1991–92) & Aid				
	Comprehensive fee	$13,610	Need-based scholarships (average)	$3200
	Tuition	$9400	Non-need scholarships (average)	$4200
	Mandatory fees	$210	Short-term loans (average)	$500
	Room and board	$4000	Long-term loans—college funds (average)	$2900
	Financial aid recipients	75%	Long-term loans—external funds (average)	$2910

Undergraduate Facts				
	Part-time	5%	*Freshman Data:* 950 applied, 82% were accepted, 47% (361) of those entered	
	State residents	56%		
	Transfers	12%	From top tenth of high school class	27%
	African-Americans	2%	SAT-takers scoring 600 or over on verbal	14%
	Native Americans	N/R	SAT-takers scoring 700 or over on verbal	2%
	Hispanics	N/R	SAT-takers scoring 600 or over on math	23%
	Asian-Americans	N/R	SAT-takers scoring 700 or over on math	5%
	International students	2%	ACT-takers scoring 26 or over	35%
	Freshmen returning for sophomore year	84%	ACT-takers scoring 30 or over	13%
	Students completing degree within 5 years	75%	*Majors with most degrees conferred:* business, English, education.	
	Grads pursuing further study	22%		

Majors Accounting, American studies, art/fine arts, biology/biological sciences, business, chemistry, classics, comparative literature, early childhood education, economics, education, elementary education, English, environmental sciences, European studies, French, German, history, interdisciplinary studies, international business, mathematics, music, philosophy, physical education, physics, political science/government, psychology, religious studies, secondary education, sociology, Spanish, speech/rhetoric/public address/debate, theater arts/drama.

Applying *Required:* essay, high school transcript, SAT or ACT. *Recommended:* 3 years of high school math and science, 3 years of high school foreign language, recommendations, Achievements, English Composition Test. Campus interview required for some. *Application deadlines:* rolling, 3/15 priority date for financial aid. *Contact:* Mr. Jeffrey S. Lantis, Director of Admissions, 33 College Street, Hillsdale, MI 49242, 517-437-7341 Ext. 2327.

From the College Located in south-central Michigan, Hillsdale College provides a value-based liberal arts education grounded in the Judeo-Christian heritage and the traditions of the Western world. The refusal of government funding is what makes Hillsdale unique. The College's fierce independence is critical to the level and type of educational excellence Hillsdale is able to provide.

✻ Hiram College

Hiram, Ohio

Founded 1850
Rural setting
Independent/affiliated with Christian Church (Disciples of Christ)
Coed
Awards B

Enrollment 883 total—all undergraduates (262 freshmen)

Faculty 90 total; 78 full-time (88% have doctorate/terminal degree); student-faculty ratio is 12:1.

Libraries 163,546 bound volumes, 67,606 titles on microform, 865 periodical subscriptions

Computing *Terminals/PCs available for student use:* 104, located in computer center, student center, library, academic buildings.

Of Special Interest *Core academic program:* yes. Computer course required for physics, management, economics majors. Phi Beta Kappa chapter. Academic exchange with members of the East Central College Consortium. Sponsors and participates in study-abroad programs.

On Campus Drama/theater group; student-run newspaper and radio station. *Social organizations:* 3 men's social clubs, 3 women's social clubs; 20% of eligible undergraduate men and 20% of eligible undergraduate women are members.

Athletics Member NCAA (Division III). *Intercollegiate sports:* basketball (M, W), cross-country running (M, W), equestrian sports (M, W), football (M), golf (M), rugby (M, W), sailing (M, W), skiing (cross-country) (M, W), skiing (downhill) (M, W), soccer (M, W), swimming and diving (M, W), tennis (M, W), track and field (M, W), volleyball (W).

Costs (1991–92) & Aid				
	Comprehensive fee	$15,822	Need-based scholarships	Avail
	Tuition	$11,802	Non-need scholarships	Avail
	Mandatory fees	$240	Short-term loans	N/Avail
	Room and board	$3780	Long-term loans—college funds	N/Avail
	Financial aid recipients	80%	Long-term loans—external funds (average)	$2500

Undergraduate Facts				
	Part-time	N/R	*Freshman Data:* 808 applied, 83% were accepted, 39% (262) of those entered	
	State residents	75%		
	Transfers	9%	From top tenth of high school class	35%
	African-Americans	8%	SAT-takers scoring 600 or over on verbal	18%
	Native Americans	0%	SAT-takers scoring 700 or over on verbal	4%
	Hispanics	1%	SAT-takers scoring 600 or over on math	25%
	Asian-Americans	2%	SAT-takers scoring 700 or over on math	6%
	International students	1%	ACT-takers scoring 26 or over	37%
	Freshmen returning for sophomore year	84%	ACT-takers scoring 30 or over	11%
	Students completing degree within 5 years	N/R	*Majors with most degrees conferred:* biology/ biological sciences, psychology, business.	
	Grads pursuing further study	N/R		

Majors Art history, biology/biological sciences, business, chemistry, classics, communication, computer science, (pre)dentistry sequence, economics, education, elementary education, English, French, German, history, international business, international economics, (pre)law sequence, mathematics, (pre)medicine sequence, music, philosophy, physical education, physics, political science/government, psychobiology, psychology, religious studies, science, secondary education, sociology, Spanish, special education, studio art, theater arts/drama, (pre)veterinary medicine sequence.

Applying *Required:* high school transcript, SAT or ACT or 3 College Board Achievement Tests. *Recommended:* essay, 3 years of high school math and science, some high school foreign language, 1 recommendation, campus interview. *Application deadlines:* 4/15, 3/1 priority date for financial aid. *Contact:* Mr. Gary G. Craig, Dean of Admissions, Rodefar House, Hiram, OH 44234, 216-569-5173 or toll-free 800-362-5280 (in-state).

Hobart College
Coordinate with William Smith College
Geneva, New York

Founded 1822
Small-town setting
Independent, Episcopal
Men
Awards B

Enrollment 1,015 total—all undergraduates (296 freshmen)

Faculty 180 total; 146 full-time (97% have doctorate/terminal degree); student-faculty ratio is 13:1.

Libraries 300,000 bound volumes, 40,000 titles on microform, 1,809 periodical subscriptions

Computing *Terminals/PCs available for student use:* 180, located in computer center, library, honors room; PC not required but available for purchase. Campus network links student PCs.

Of Special Interest *Core academic program:* yes. Computer course required for math majors. Phi Beta Kappa, Sigma Xi chapters. Academic exchange with Rochester Area Colleges. Sponsors and participates in study-abroad programs.

On Campus Drama/theater group; student-run newspaper and radio station. *Social organizations:* 8 national fraternities; 30% of eligible undergraduates are members.

Athletics Member NCAA (Division III). *Intercollegiate sports:* baseball, basketball, crew, cross-country running, football, golf, ice hockey, lacrosse, rugby, sailing, skiing (cross-country), skiing (downhill), soccer, squash, swimming and diving, tennis, track and field.

Costs (1991–92) & Aid				
	Comprehensive fee	$21,542	Need-based scholarships (average)	$8695
	Tuition	$16,077	Non-need scholarships	N/Avail
	Mandatory fees	$299	Short-term loans	N/Avail
	Room and board	$5166	Long-term loans—college funds	N/Avail
	Financial aid recipients	43%	Long-term loans—external funds (average)	$2840

Undergraduate Facts				
	Part-time	0%	*Freshman Data:* 1,593 applied, 69% were accepted, 27% (296) of those entered	
	State residents	36%		
	Transfers	1%	From top tenth of high school class	20%
	African-Americans	4%	SAT-takers scoring 600 or over on verbal	9%
	Native Americans	1%	SAT-takers scoring 700 or over on verbal	1%
	Hispanics	3%	SAT-takers scoring 600 or over on math	40%
	Asian-Americans	2%	SAT-takers scoring 700 or over on math	4%
	International students	4%	ACT-takers scoring 26 or over	55%
	Freshmen returning for sophomore year	95%	ACT-takers scoring 30 or over	2%
	Students completing degree within 5 years	80%	*Majors with most degrees conferred:* economics, English, political science/government.	
	Grads pursuing further study	35%		

Majors American studies, anthropology, art/fine arts, art history, Asian/Oriental studies, biology/biological sciences, black/African-American studies, chemistry, classics, communication, comparative literature, computer science, dance, (pre)dentistry sequence, economics, education, English, environmental sciences, French, geology, German, Greek, history, journalism, Latin, (pre)law sequence, mathematics, (pre)medicine sequence, modern languages, music, philosophy, physics, political science/government, psychology, religious studies, Russian, sociology, Spanish, studio art, urban studies, (pre)veterinary medicine sequence, women's studies.

Applying *Required:* essay, high school transcript, 3 years of high school math, 2 years of high school foreign language, 2 recommendations, SAT or ACT, 3 Achievements, English Composition Test. *Recommended:* 3 years of high school science, interview. *Application deadlines:* 2/15, 1/1 for early decision, 2/15 priority date for financial aid. *Contact:* Mr. Leonard Wood Jr., Director of Admission, 639 South Main Street, Geneva, NY 14456, 315-781-3623 or toll-free 800-852-2256.

Note: Hobart and William Smith students share a central administration, faculty, and campus and attend all classes together. At the same time, they have separate deans, admission offices, physical education programs, student governments, and alumni and alumnae associations.

Hope College

Holland, Michigan

Founded 1862
Small-town setting
Independent/affiliated with Reformed Church in America
Coed
Awards B

Enrollment   2,746 total—all undergraduates (520 freshmen)

Faculty   237 total; 175 full-time (76% have doctorate/terminal degree); student-faculty ratio is 12:1.

Libraries   270,764 bound volumes, 112,609 titles on microform, 1,622 periodical subscriptions

Computing   *Terminals/PCs available for student use:* 260, located in student center, library, dormitories, academic buildings; PC not required. Campus network links student PCs.

Of Special Interest   *Core academic program:* yes. Computer course required for physics, math, psychology, business majors. Phi Beta Kappa, Sigma Xi chapters. Academic exchange with members of the Great Lakes Colleges Association, Associated Colleges of the Midwest, Institute of European Studies. Sponsors and participates in study-abroad programs.

On Campus   Drama/theater group; student-run newspaper and radio station. *Social organizations:* 5 local fraternities, 6 local sororities; 9% of eligible undergraduate men and 10% of eligible undergraduate women are members.

Athletics   Member NCAA (Division III). *Intercollegiate sports:* baseball (M), basketball (M, W), cross-country running (M, W), field hockey (W), football (M), golf (M, W), lacrosse (M), soccer (M, W), softball (W), swimming and diving (M, W), tennis (M, W), track and field (M, W), volleyball (M, W).

Costs (1991–92) & Aid

Comprehensive fee	$13,774	
Tuition	$10,022	
Mandatory fees	$64	
Room and board	$3688	
Financial aid recipients	57%	
Need-based scholarships (average)		$3033
Non-need scholarships (average)		$1470
Short-term loans		N/Avail
Long-term loans—college funds (average)		$858
Long-term loans—external funds (average)		$2500

Undergraduate Facts

Part-time	11%
State residents	73%
Transfers	4%
African-Americans	1%
Native Americans	0%
Hispanics	1%
Asian-Americans	1%
International students	3%
Freshmen returning for sophomore year	85%
Students completing degree within 5 years	72%
Grads pursuing further study	28%

Freshman Data: 1,339 applied, 88% were accepted, 44% (520) of those entered

From top tenth of high school class	31%
SAT-takers scoring 600 or over on verbal	14%
SAT-takers scoring 700 or over on verbal	2%
SAT-takers scoring 600 or over on math	37%
SAT-takers scoring 700 or over on math	7%
ACT-takers scoring 26 or over	31%
ACT-takers scoring 30 or over	7%

Majors with most degrees conferred: business, biology/biological sciences, psychology.

Majors   Accounting, applied art, art education, art/fine arts, art history, biochemistry, biology/biological sciences, business, chemistry, classics, communication, computer science, dance, dance therapy, (pre)dentistry sequence, economics, education, elementary education, engineering physics, English, environmental sciences, French, geochemistry, geology, geophysics, German, history, humanities, interdisciplinary studies, international studies, Latin, (pre)law sequence, mathematics, medical technology, (pre)medicine sequence, music, music education, nursing, philosophy, physical education, physics, political science/government, psychology, religious education, religious studies, science education, secondary education, social work, sociology, Spanish, special education, sports medicine, theater arts/drama, (pre)veterinary medicine sequence.

Applying   *Required:* essay, high school transcript, 3 years of high school math, SAT or ACT. *Recommended:* 3 years of high school science, 2 years of high school foreign language, interview. 1 recommendation required for some. *Application deadlines:* rolling, 3/1 priority date for financial aid. *Contact:* Dr. James R. Bekkering, Vice President for Admissions and Student Life, 69 East 10th Street, Holland, MI 49423, 616-394-7800 or toll-free 800-822-HOPE (in-state), 800-654-HOPE (out-of-state).

Houghton College

Houghton, New York

Founded 1883
Rural setting
Independent, Wesleyan
Coed
Awards A, B

Enrollment 1,146 total—all undergraduates (247 freshmen)

Faculty 100 total; 64 full-time (69% have doctorate/terminal degree); student-faculty ratio is 14:1.

Libraries 206,731 bound volumes, 398 titles on microform, 624 periodical subscriptions

Computing *Terminals/PCs available for student use:* 130, located in computer center, library, dormitories, computer lab, divisional offices; PC not required.

Of Special Interest *Core academic program:* yes. Computer course required for business administration majors. Academic exchange with members of the Western New York Consortium and the Christian College Consortium. Participates in study-abroad programs. Cooperative Army ROTC.

On Campus Mandatory chapel; drama/theater group; student-run newspaper and radio station. No national or local fraternities or sororities on campus.

Athletics Member NAIA. *Intercollegiate sports:* basketball (M, W), cross-country running (M, W), field hockey (W), soccer (M, W), track and field (M, W), volleyball (W). *Scholarships:* M, W.

Costs (1992–93 estimated) & Aid				
	Comprehensive fee	$11,810	Need-based scholarships (average)	$1292
	Tuition	$8330	Non-need scholarships (average)	$1313
	Mandatory fees	$346	Short-term loans (average)	$500
	Room and board	$3134	Long-term loans—college funds	N/Avail
	Financial aid recipients	91%	Long-term loans—external funds (average)	$2749

Undergraduate Facts				
	Part-time	4%	*Freshman Data:* 638 applied, 91% were accepted, 42% (247) of those entered	
	State residents	64%		
	Transfers	5%	From top tenth of high school class	29%
	African-Americans	2%	SAT-takers scoring 600 or over on verbal	20%
	Native Americans	1%	SAT-takers scoring 700 or over on verbal	2%
	Hispanics	1%	SAT-takers scoring 600 or over on math	21%
	Asian-Americans	1%	SAT-takers scoring 700 or over on math	3%
	International students	5%	ACT-takers scoring 26 or over	28%
	Freshmen returning for sophomore year	88%	ACT-takers scoring 30 or over	4%
	Students completing degree within 5 years	62%	*Majors with most degrees conferred:* elementary education, psychology, biblical studies.	
	Grads pursuing further study	18%		

Majors Accounting, art education, art/fine arts, biblical studies, biology/biological sciences, business, chemistry, communication, creative writing, (pre)dentistry sequence, early childhood education, education, elementary education, English, French, history, humanities, international studies, (pre)law sequence, literature, mathematics, medical laboratory technology, medical technology, (pre)medicine sequence, ministries, music, music education, natural sciences, pastoral studies, philosophy, physical education, physical sciences, physics, piano/organ, political science/government, psychology, recreation and leisure services, religious education, religious studies, sacred music, science, science education, secondary education, social science, sociology, Spanish, stringed instruments, (pre)veterinary medicine sequence, voice, wind and percussion instruments.

Applying *Required:* essay, high school transcript, 1 recommendation, pastoral recommendation, SAT or ACT. *Recommended:* 3 years of high school math, some high school foreign language, interview. *Application deadlines:* 8/1, 3/15 priority date for financial aid. *Contact:* Mr. Timothy R. Fuller, Executive Director of Admissions and Alumni, PO Box 128, Houghton, NY 14744, 716-567-9353 or toll-free 800-777-2556; *Office location:* 1 Willard Avenue.

Howard University

Washington, District of Columbia

Founded 1867
Urban setting
Independent
Coed
Awards B, M, D

Enrollment 10,871 total; 8,100 undergraduates (1,250 freshmen)

Faculty 2,000 total; student-faculty ratio is 6:1; grad assistants teach a few undergraduate courses.

Libraries 1.7 million bound volumes, 1.5 million titles on microform, 24,966 periodical subscriptions

Computing *Terminals/PCs available for student use:* 140, located in computer center, library, dormitories, academic buildings; PC not required.

Of Special Interest *Core academic program:* yes. Computer course required for business, economics, math, engineering majors. Phi Beta Kappa, Sigma Xi chapters. Academic exchange with 9 members of the Consortium of Universities of the Washington Metropolitan Area, over 15 colleges and universities, including Duke University, University of California at Berkeley, Smith College, Vassar College, Williams College. Participates in study-abroad programs. Army ROTC, Air Force ROTC, cooperative Naval ROTC.

On Campus Drama/theater group; student-run newspaper and radio station. *Social organizations:* 5 national fraternities, 4 national sororities, 3 local fraternities; 1% of eligible undergraduate men and 1% of eligible undergraduate women are members.

Athletics Member NCAA (Division I). *Intercollegiate sports:* basketball (M, W), cross-country running (M, W), football (M), soccer (M), swimming and diving (M, W), tennis (M, W), track and field (M, W), volleyball (W), wrestling (M). *Scholarships:* M, W.

Costs (1991–92) & Aid				
	Comprehensive fee	$9985	Need-based scholarships (average)	$2000
	Tuition	$5825	Non-need scholarships	Avail
	Mandatory fees	$580	Short-term loans	Avail
	Room and board	$3580	Long-term loans—college funds	N/Avail
	Financial aid recipients	84%	Long-term loans—external funds (average)	$2200

Undergraduate Facts				
	Part-time	13%	*Freshman Data:* 5,270 applied, 51% were accepted, 47% (1,250) of those entered	
	State residents	13%		
	Transfers	8%	From top tenth of high school class	N/R
	African-Americans	80%	SAT-takers scoring 600 or over on verbal	N/R
	Native Americans	N/R	SAT-takers scoring 700 or over on verbal	N/R
	Hispanics	1%	SAT-takers scoring 600 or over on math	N/R
	Asian-Americans	1%	SAT-takers scoring 700 or over on math	N/R
	International students	16%	ACT-takers scoring 26 or over	N/R
	Freshmen returning for sophomore year	75%	ACT-takers scoring 30 or over	N/R
	Students completing degree within 5 years	N/R		
	Grads pursuing further study	N/R		

Majors Accounting, anatomy, anthropology, applied art, architecture, art education, art/fine arts, art history, art therapy, astronomy, astrophysics, biology/biological sciences, biomedical sciences, biophysics, black/African-American studies, botany/plant sciences, broadcasting, business, ceramic art and design, chemical engineering, chemistry, child care/child and family studies, civil engineering, classics, commercial art, communication, computer information systems, dental services, dietetics, drama therapy, early childhood education, ecology/environmental studies, economics, education, electrical engineering, elementary education, English, environmental design, family and consumer studies, fashion design and technology, film studies, finance/banking, food services management, French, geology, German, graphic arts, guidance and counseling, history, home economics, home economics education, hotel and restaurant management, human development, human ecology, insurance, interior design, international business, international economics, journalism, laboratory technologies, law enforcement/police sciences, marketing/retailing/merchandising, mathematics, mechanical engineering, medical technology, microbiology, music, music education, music history, nursing, nutrition, occupational therapy, pharmacy/pharmaceutical sciences, philosophy, photography, physical education, physical therapy, physician's assistant studies, physics, political science/government, psychology, radio and television studies, radiological technology, Russian, social work, sociology, Spanish, textiles and clothing, theater arts/drama, zoology.

Applying *Required:* high school transcript, SAT or ACT. 3 years of high school math and science, some high school foreign language, 2 recommendations, Achievements required for some. *Application deadlines:* 4/1, 4/1 priority date for financial aid. *Contact:* Mr. Emmett R. Griffin Jr., Director of Admissions, Washington, DC 20059, 202-806-2750 or toll-free 800-822-6363 (out-of-state).

Illinois Institute of Technology

Chicago, Illinois

Founded 1892
Urban setting
Independent
Coed
Awards B, M, D

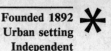

Enrollment 6,504 total; 2,457 undergraduates (290 freshmen)

Faculty 498 total; 315 full-time (91% have doctorate/terminal degree); student-faculty ratio is 9:1; grad assistants teach a few undergraduate courses.

Libraries 800,000 bound volumes, 50,000 titles on microform, 7,000 periodical subscriptions

Computing *Terminals/PCs available for student use:* 250, located in computer center, library, dormitories, academic buildings; PC not required.

Of Special Interest *Core academic program:* yes. Computer course required. Sigma Xi chapter. Academic exchange program: no. Sponsors and participates in study-abroad programs. Naval ROTC, Air Force ROTC, cooperative Army ROTC.

On Campus Student-run newspaper and radio station. *Social organizations:* 9 national fraternities, 1 national sorority, 1 local sorority; 26% of eligible undergraduate men and 14% of eligible undergraduate women are members.

Athletics Member NCAA (Division II), NAIA. *Intercollegiate sports:* baseball (M), basketball (M), bowling (M, W), cross-country running (M, W), golf (M, W), ice hockey (M), swimming and diving (M, W), tennis (M, W), volleyball (W). *Scholarships:* M, W.

Costs (1992–93 estimated) & Aid				
	Comprehensive fee	$17,080	Need-based scholarships	Avail
	Tuition	$12,690	Non-need scholarships	Avail
	Mandatory fees	$40	Short-term loans	N/Avail
	Room and board	$4350	Long-term loans—college funds	Avail
	Financial aid recipients	80%	Long-term loans—external funds	Avail

Undergraduate Facts				
	Part-time	29%	*Freshman Data:* 1,054 applied, 85% were accepted, 32% (290) of those entered	
	State residents	58%		
	Transfers	32%	From top tenth of high school class	41%
	African-Americans	14%	SAT-takers scoring 600 or over on verbal	11%
	Native Americans	0%	SAT-takers scoring 700 or over on verbal	1%
	Hispanics	8%	SAT-takers scoring 600 or over on math	39%
	Asian-Americans	22%	SAT-takers scoring 700 or over on math	10%
	International students	8%	ACT-takers scoring 26 or over	40%
	Freshmen returning for sophomore year	80%	ACT-takers scoring 30 or over	8%
	Students completing degree within 5 years	57%	*Majors with most degrees conferred:* electrical engineering, mechanical engineering, architecture.	
	Grads pursuing further study	10%		

Majors Accounting, aerospace engineering, aerospace sciences, applied mathematics, architecture, art/fine arts, biology/biological sciences, business, chemical engineering, chemistry, civil engineering, computer engineering, computer information systems, computer programming, computer science, construction engineering, (pre)dentistry sequence, economics, electrical engineering, engineering (general), engineering design, engineering management, engineering physics, engineering sciences, English, finance/banking, graphic arts, humanities, industrial administration, industrial design, (pre)law sequence, marketing/retailing/merchandising, materials engineering, mathematics, mechanical engineering, medical technology, (pre)medicine sequence, metallurgical engineering, military science, naval sciences, photography, physics, physiology, plastics engineering, political science/government, psychology, public administration, technical writing, technology and public affairs.

Applying *Required:* essay, high school transcript, 3 years of high school math, 1 recommendation, SAT or ACT. *Recommended:* 3 years of high school science, interview, Achievements. *Application deadlines:* 2/15, 12/1 for early action, 5/1 priority date for financial aid. *Contact:* Mr. Steve Gutknecht, Director of Admissions, 10 West 33rd Street, Room 101, Chicago, IL 60616, 312-567-3025 or toll-free 800-572-1587 (in-state), 800-448-2329 (out-of-state).

✳ Illinois Wesleyan University

Bloomington, Illinois

Founded 1850
Suburban setting
Independent, United Methodist
Coed
Awards B

Enrollment	1,770 total—all undergraduates (504 freshmen)
Faculty	167 total; 137 full-time (85% have doctorate/terminal degree); student-faculty ratio is 13:1.
Libraries	177,557 bound volumes, 108,000 titles on microform, 1,267 periodical subscriptions
Computing	*Terminals/PCs available for student use:* 151, located in computer center, library, dormitories, special labs; PC not required.
Of Special Interest	*Core academic program:* yes. Computer course required for business, psychology, physics, math majors. Academic exchange with Case Western Reserve University, Northwestern University, Washington University, Dartmouth College. Sponsors and participates in study-abroad programs. Cooperative Army ROTC.
On Campus	Drama/theater group; student-run newspaper and radio station. *Social organizations:* 6 national fraternities, 5 national sororities; 25% of eligible undergraduate men and 25% of eligible undergraduate women are members.
Athletics	Member NCAA (Division III). *Intercollegiate sports:* baseball (M), basketball (M, W), cross-country running (M, W), football (M), golf (M), sailing (M, W), soccer (M), swimming and diving (M, W), tennis (M, W), track and field (M, W), volleyball (W).

Costs (1992-93 estimated) & Aid				
	Comprehensive fee	$16,135	Need-based scholarships (average)	$2743
	Tuition	$12,120	Non-need scholarships (average)	$2977
	Mandatory fees	$100	Short-term loans (average)	$155
	Room and board	$3915	Long-term loans—college funds (average)	$2160
	Financial aid recipients	80%	Long-term loans—external funds (average)	$2641

Undergraduate Facts				
	Part-time	1%	*Freshman Data:* 2,915 applied, 45% were accepted, 38% (504) of those entered	
	State residents	82%		
	Transfers	2%	From top tenth of high school class	52%
	African-Americans	3%	SAT-takers scoring 600 or over on verbal	27%
	Native Americans	1%	SAT-takers scoring 700 or over on verbal	9%
	Hispanics	1%	SAT-takers scoring 600 or over on math	53%
	Asian-Americans	4%	SAT-takers scoring 700 or over on math	18%
	International students	5%	ACT-takers scoring 26 or over	63%
	Freshmen returning for sophomore year	96%	ACT-takers scoring 30 or over	13%
	Students completing degree within 5 years	82%	*Majors with most degrees conferred:* business, biology/biological sciences, music.	
	Grads pursuing further study	30%		

Majors Accounting, applied art, art education, art/fine arts, art history, arts administration, biology/biological sciences, business, chemistry, computer science, (pre)dentistry sequence, economics, education, elementary education, English, European studies, French, German, graphic arts, history, insurance, interdisciplinary studies, Latin American studies, (pre)law sequence, liberal arts/general studies, mathematics, medical technology, (pre)medicine sequence, music, music business, music education, nursing, painting/drawing, philosophy, physics, piano/organ, political science/government, psychology, religious studies, sacred music, science education, secondary education, sociology, Spanish, stringed instruments, studio art, theater arts/drama, (pre)veterinary medicine sequence, voice, wind and percussion instruments.

Applying *Required:* essay, high school transcript, SAT or ACT. *Recommended:* 3 years of high school math and science, some high school foreign language, 3 recommendations, campus interview. *Application deadlines:* rolling, 3/1 priority date for financial aid. *Contact:* Mr. James R. Ruoti, Dean of Admissions, 1312 North Park Street, Bloomington, IL 61702, 309-556-3031.

Iowa State University of Science and Technology
Ames, Iowa

Founded 1858
Suburban setting
State-supported
Coed
Awards B, M, D

Enrollment 25,250 total; 20,855 undergraduates (3,255 freshmen)

Faculty 1,907 total; 1,701 full-time (81% have doctorate/terminal degree); student-faculty ratio is 19:1; grad assistants teach a few undergraduate courses.

Libraries 1.9 million bound volumes, 2.3 million titles on microform, 21,503 periodical subscriptions

Computing *Terminals/PCs available for student use:* 1,000, located in computer center, library, dormitories, classrooms, labs; PC not required. Campus network links student PCs.

Of Special Interest *Core academic program:* no. Computer course required for engineering, business, most science majors. Phi Beta Kappa, Sigma Xi chapters. Academic exchange with Iowa Regents' Universities Student Exchange. Sponsors and participates in study-abroad programs. Army ROTC, Naval ROTC, Air Force ROTC.

On Campus Drama/theater group; student-run newspaper and radio station. *Social organizations:* 36 national fraternities, 19 national sororities; 17% of eligible undergraduate men and 16% of eligible undergraduate women are members.

Athletics Member NCAA (Division I). *Intercollegiate sports:* baseball (M), basketball (M, W), cross-country running (M, W), football (M), golf (M, W), gymnastics (M, W), softball (W), swimming and diving (M, W), tennis (M, W), track and field (M, W), volleyball (W), wrestling (M). *Scholarships:* M, W.

Costs (1992–93 estimated) & Aid

State resident tuition	$2088	3414 Need-based scholarships (average)	$2875
Nonresident tuition	$6856	5398 Non-need scholarships (average)	$1383
Mandatory fees	N/App	Short-term loans (average)	$600
Room and board	$2850	Long-term loans—college funds (average)	$1800
Financial aid recipients	68%	Long-term loans—external funds (average)	$4410

Undergraduate Facts

Part-time	8%
State residents	79%
Transfers	34%
African-Americans	2%
Native Americans	0%
Hispanics	1%
Asian-Americans	2%
International students	4%
Freshmen returning for sophomore year	81%
Students completing degree within 5 years	56%
Grads pursuing further study	11%

Freshman Data: 6,855 applied, 89% were accepted, 53% (3,255) of those entered

From top tenth of high school class	27%
SAT-takers scoring 600 or over on verbal	10%
SAT-takers scoring 700 or over on verbal	1%
SAT-takers scoring 600 or over on math	34%
SAT-takers scoring 700 or over on math	10%
ACT-takers scoring 26 or over	36%
ACT-takers scoring 30 or over	10%

Majors with most degrees conferred: elementary education, finance/banking, marketing/retailing/merchandising.

Majors Accounting, advertising, aerospace engineering, agricultural business, agricultural education, agricultural engineering, agricultural sciences, agricultural technologies, agronomy/soil and crop sciences, animal sciences, anthropology, applied art, architecture, art education, art/fine arts, biochemistry, biology/biological sciences, biophysics, botany/plant sciences, broadcasting, business, ceramic engineering, chemical engineering, chemistry, child psychology/child development, city/community/regional planning, civil engineering, communication, community services, computer engineering, computer science, construction engineering, consumer services, dairy sciences, (pre)dentistry sequence, dietetics, early childhood education, earth science, ecology/environmental studies, economics, education, electrical engineering, elementary education, engineering (general), engineering sciences, English, entomology, family and consumer studies, family services, farm and ranch management, fashion design and technology, fashion merchandising, finance/banking, fish and game management, food sciences, food services management, food services technology, forestry, French, genetics, geology, German, graphic arts, health education, history, home economics, home economics education, horticulture, hotel and restaurant management, industrial engineering, interdisciplinary studies, interior design, international studies, journalism, landscape architecture/design, (pre)law sequence, liberal arts/general studies, linguistics, management information systems, marketing/retailing/merchandising, mathematics, mechanical engineering, medical illustration, (pre)medicine sequence, metallurgical engineering, metallurgy, meteorology, microbiology, music, music education, natural sciences, naval sciences, nutrition, ornamental horticulture, philosophy, physical education, physics, political science/government, psychology, public administration, radio and television studies, recreation and leisure services, religious studies, Russian, secondary education, social work, sociology, Spanish, speech/rhetoric/public address/debate, statistics, textiles and clothing, theater arts/drama, transportation technologies, (pre)veterinary medicine sequence, vocational education, wildlife biology, zoology.

Applying *Required:* high school transcript, 3 years of high school math and science, rank in upper half of high school class or achieve a satisfactory combination of high school rank and ACT/SAT scores, SAT or ACT. *Recommended:* 2 years of high school foreign language. 2 years of high school foreign language required for some. *Application deadlines:* rolling, 3/1 priority date for financial aid. *Contact:* Mr. Phil Caffrey, Assistant Director for Freshman Admissions, 100 Alumni Hall, Ames, IA 50011, 515-294-5836 or toll-free 800-262-3810.

From the College Iowa State is nationally recognized for the high quality of its academic, campus life, and out-of-class experiences. New classroom and research facilities include the Durham Computation Center and the molecular biology building. Iowa State provides the advantages of a major university and a friendly and warm campus environment.

James Madison University

Harrisonburg, Virginia

Founded 1908
Small-town setting
State-supported
Coed
Awards B, M

Enrollment 11,264 total; 9,946 undergraduates (2,123 freshmen)

Faculty 679 total; 482 full-time (80% have doctorate/terminal degree); student-faculty ratio is 19:1; grad assistants teach a few undergraduate courses.

Libraries 387,451 bound volumes, 1.2 million titles on microform, 2,986 periodical subscriptions

Computing *Terminals/PCs available for student use:* 379, located in computer center, dormitories, academic buildings; PC not required.

Of Special Interest *Core academic program:* yes. Computer course required. Academic exchange program: no. Sponsors and participates in study-abroad programs. Army ROTC.

On Campus Drama/theater group; student-run newspaper and radio station. *Social organizations:* 17 national fraternities, 12 national sororities; 23% of eligible undergraduate men and 18% of eligible undergraduate women are members.

Athletics Member NCAA (Division I). *Intercollegiate sports:* archery (M, W), baseball (M), basketball (M, W), cross-country running (M, W), fencing (W), field hockey (W), football (M), golf (M, W), gymnastics (M, W), lacrosse (W), soccer (M, W), swimming and diving (M, W), tennis (M, W), track and field (M, W), volleyball (W), wrestling (M). *Scholarships:* M, W.

Costs (1991–92) & Aid				
	State resident tuition	$3298	1200 Need-based scholarships (average)	$1914
	Nonresident tuition	$6650	1287 Non-need scholarships (average)	$2054
	Mandatory fees	N/App	Short-term loans (average)	$100
	Room and board	$4102	Long-term loans—college funds (average)	$500
	Financial aid recipients	47%	Long-term loans—external funds (average)	$2414

Undergraduate Facts				
	Part-time	4%	*Freshman Data:* 11,726 applied, 45% were accepted, 41% (2,123) of those entered	
	State residents	76%		
	Transfers	5%	From top tenth of high school class	29%
	African-Americans	9%	SAT-takers scoring 600 or over on verbal	12%
	Native Americans	1%	SAT-takers scoring 700 or over on verbal	1%
	Hispanics	1%	SAT-takers scoring 600 or over on math	39%
	Asian-Americans	2%	SAT-takers scoring 700 or over on math	4%
	International students	1%	ACT-takers scoring 26 or over	N/App
	Freshmen returning for sophomore year	93%	ACT-takers scoring 30 or over	N/App
	Students completing degree within 5 years	79%	*Majors with most degrees conferred:* psychology, political science/government, communication.	
	Grads pursuing further study	16%		

Majors Accounting, anthropology, art/fine arts, art history, biology/biological sciences, business, business economics, business education, chemistry, communication, computer information systems, computer science, dance, (pre)dentistry sequence, dietetics, early childhood education, economics, elementary education, English, finance/banking, French, geography, geology, German, health education, health science, history, home economics, hotel and restaurant management, industrial administration, international business, international studies, (pre)law sequence, liberal arts/general studies, library science, marketing/retailing/merchandising, mathematics, medical technology, (pre)medicine sequence, modern languages, music, nursing, philosophy, physical education, physics, political science/government, psychology, public administration, religious studies, Russian, secretarial studies/office management, social science, social work, sociology, Spanish, special education, speech pathology and audiology, theater arts/drama, (pre)veterinary medicine sequence.

Applying *Required:* essay, high school transcript, English proficiency for foreign students, SAT. Some high school foreign language required for some. *Application deadlines:* 2/1, 2/15 priority date for financial aid. *Contact:* Mr. Alan Cerveny, Director of Admissions, Varner House, Harrisonburg, VA 22807, 703-568-6147.

From the College James Madison University has been called the Ultimate University. Its diverse, close-knit community possesses a unique atmosphere that current students call the JMU Way. The JMU Way emphasizes excellence in all aspects of a student's life. Students are challenged both inside and outside the classroom by talented, caring faculty and staff and by other JMU students who are friendly and actively involved in their own education.

John Carroll University

University Heights, Ohio

Founded 1886
Suburban setting
Independent, Roman Catholic (Jesuit)
Coed
Awards B, M

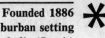

Enrollment	4,666 total; 3,715 undergraduates (766 freshmen)
Faculty	316 total; 206 full-time (85% have doctorate/terminal degree); student-faculty ratio is 14:1; grad assistants teach a few undergraduate courses.
Libraries	506,441 bound volumes, 158,001 titles on microform, 1,605 periodical subscriptions
Computing	*Terminals/PCs available for student use:* 100, located in computer center, student center, library, dormitories, personal computer labs; PC not required.
Of Special Interest	*Core academic program:* yes. Computer course required for business, math majors. Academic exchange with Cleveland Commission on Higher Education. Sponsors and participates in study-abroad programs. Army ROTC.
On Campus	Drama/theater group; student-run newspaper and radio station. *Social organizations:* 10 local fraternities, 6 local sororities; 32% of eligible undergraduate men and 35% of eligible undergraduate women are members.
Athletics	Member NCAA (Division III). *Intercollegiate sports:* baseball (M), basketball (M, W), cross-country running (M, W), football (M), golf (M), ice hockey (M), lacrosse (M, W), rugby (M), sailing (M), skiing (cross-country) (M, W), skiing (downhill) (M, W), soccer (M, W), softball (W), swimming and diving (M, W), tennis (M, W), track and field (M, W), volleyball (M, W), wrestling (M).

Costs (1992–93) & Aid				
	Comprehensive fee	$15,530	Need-based scholarships (average)	$2639
	Tuition	$10,080	Non-need scholarships (average)	$2435
	Mandatory fees	N/App	Short-term loans	N/Avail
	Room and board	$5450	Long-term loans—college funds (average)	$2114
	Financial aid recipients	85%	Long-term loans—external funds (average)	$3083

Undergraduate Facts				
	Part-time	13%	*Freshman Data:* 2,311 applied, 82% were accepted, 41% (766) of those entered	
	State residents	60%		
	Transfers	5%	From top tenth of high school class	25%
	African-Americans	4%	SAT-takers scoring 600 or over on verbal	12%
	Native Americans	0%	SAT-takers scoring 700 or over on verbal	2%
	Hispanics	1%	SAT-takers scoring 600 or over on math	34%
	Asian-Americans	2%	SAT-takers scoring 700 or over on math	5%
	International students	1%	ACT-takers scoring 26 or over	25%
	Freshmen returning for sophomore year	92%	ACT-takers scoring 30 or over	4%
	Students completing degree within 5 years	70%	*Majors with most degrees conferred:* communication, English, marketing/retailing/merchandising.	
	Grads pursuing further study	30%		

Majors Accounting, art history, biology/biological sciences, business, chemistry, child psychology/child development, classics, communication, computer science, (pre)dentistry sequence, early childhood education, East Asian studies, economics, education, elementary education, engineering physics, English, finance/banking, French, German, gerontology, Greek, history, humanities, international business, international economics, international studies, Latin, (pre)law sequence, literature, marketing/retailing/merchandising, mathematics, (pre)medicine sequence, neurosciences, philosophy, physical education, physics, political science/government, psychology, public administration, religious education, religious studies, science, secondary education, sociology, Spanish, special education, sports medicine, (pre)veterinary medicine sequence.

Applying *Required:* high school transcript, 3 years of high school math, 2 years of high school foreign language, 1 recommendation, SAT or ACT. *Recommended:* essay, 3 years of high school science, campus interview, Achievements, English Composition Test. *Application deadlines:* rolling, 3/1 priority date for financial aid. *Contact:* Ms. Laryn Runco, Director of Admission, 20700 North Park Boulevard, University Heights, OH 44118, 216-397-4294.

✱ Johns Hopkins University

Baltimore, Maryland

Founded 1876
Urban setting
Independent
Coed
Awards B, M, D

Enrollment 4,578 total; 3,125 undergraduates (846 freshmen)

Faculty 472 total; 346 full-time (99% have doctorate/terminal degree); student-faculty ratio is 11:1; grad assistants teach a few undergraduate courses.

Libraries 2.9 million bound volumes, 1.6 million titles on microform, 20,000 periodical subscriptions

Computing *Terminals/PCs available for student use:* 75, located in computer center, library, dormitories, academic buildings; PC not required. Campus network links student PCs.

Of Special Interest *Core academic program:* yes. Computer course required for all engineering majors. Phi Beta Kappa, Sigma Xi chapters. Academic exchange with Loyola College, Towson State University, Morgan State University, College of Notre Dame of Maryland, Maryland Institute, College of Art, Goucher College, Baltimore Hebrew Academy. Sponsors and participates in study-abroad programs. Army ROTC, cooperative Air Force ROTC.

On Campus Drama/theater group; student-run newspaper and radio station. *Social organizations:* 13 national fraternities, 5 national sororities; 30% of eligible undergraduate men and 25% of eligible undergraduate women are members.

Athletics Member NCAA (Division III). *Intercollegiate sports:* basketball (M, W), crew (M, W), cross-country running (M, W), fencing (M, W), field hockey (W), football (M), golf (M), ice hockey (M), lacrosse (M, W), riflery (M, W), rugby (M), soccer (M, W), squash (W), swimming and diving (M, W), tennis (M, W), track and field (M, W), volleyball (W), water polo (M, W), wrestling (M). *Scholarships:* M.

Costs (1991–92) & Aid				
	Comprehensive fee	$22,120	Need-based scholarships (average)	$8300
	Tuition	$16,000	Non-need scholarships (average)	$10,800
	Mandatory fees	N/App	Short-term loans (average)	$300
	Room and board	$6120	Long-term loans—college funds (average)	$2200
	Financial aid recipients	58%	Long-term loans—external funds (average)	$2600

Undergraduate Facts				
	Part-time	0%	*Freshman Data:* 6,179 applied, 49% were accepted, 28% (846) of those entered	
	State residents	15%		
	Transfers	4%	From top tenth of high school class	70%
	African-Americans	6%	SAT-takers scoring 600 or over on verbal	62%
	Native Americans	1%	SAT-takers scoring 700 or over on verbal	9%
	Hispanics	3%	SAT-takers scoring 600 or over on math	89%
	Asian-Americans	17%	SAT-takers scoring 700 or over on math	44%
	International students	3%	ACT-takers scoring 26 or over	91%
	Freshmen returning for sophomore year	95%	ACT-takers scoring 30 or over	48%
	Students completing degree within 5 years	86%	*Majors with most degrees conferred:* biology/biological sciences, international studies, biomedical engineering.	
	Grads pursuing further study	62%		

Majors Anthropology, art history, astronomy, astrophysics, behavioral sciences, biology/biological sciences, biomedical engineering, biophysics, chemical engineering, chemistry, civil engineering, classics, cognitive science, computer engineering, computer science, creative writing, earth science, economics, electrical engineering, engineering (general), engineering mechanics, English, environmental engineering, environmental sciences, French, geography, German, Hispanic studies, history, history of science, humanities, international studies, Italian, Latin American studies, liberal arts/general studies, materials engineering, materials sciences, mathematics, mechanical engineering, music, natural sciences, Near and Middle Eastern studies, philosophy, physics, planetary and space sciences, political science/government, psychology, social science, sociology, Spanish.

Applying *Required:* essay, high school transcript, 1 recommendation, SAT or ACT, 3 Achievements, English Composition Test. *Recommended:* 3 years of high school math and science, 3 years of high school foreign language, interview. *Application deadlines:* 1/1, 11/15 for early decision, 1/15 for financial aid. *Contact:* Mr Richard M. Fuller, Director of Admissions, 3400 North Charles Street, Baltimore, MD 21218, 410-516-8171.

Juniata College

Huntingdon, Pennsylvania

Founded 1876
Small-town setting
Independent
Coed
Awards B

Enrollment	1,118 total—all undergraduates (255 freshmen)
Faculty	104 total; 75 full-time (90% have doctorate/terminal degree); student-faculty ratio is 14:1.
Libraries	129,809 bound volumes, 9,435 titles on microform, 895 periodical subscriptions
Computing	*Terminals/PCs available for student use:* 90, located in computer center, library, academic buildings; PC not required.
Of Special Interest	*Core academic program:* yes. Computer course required. Academic exchange with Duke University. Sponsors and participates in study-abroad programs.
On Campus	Drama/theater group; student-run newspaper and radio station. No national or local fraternities or sororities on campus.
Athletics	Member NCAA (Division III). *Intercollegiate sports:* baseball (M), basketball (M, W), cross-country running (M, W), field hockey (W), football (M), golf (M, W), lacrosse (M), rugby (M), skiing (downhill) (M), soccer (M), softball (W), swimming and diving (M, W), tennis (M, W), track and field (M, W), volleyball (M, W), wrestling (M).

Costs (1992–93) & Aid				
	Comprehensive fee	$17,260	Need-based scholarships (average)	$4500
	Tuition	$13,250	Non-need scholarships (average)	$3000
	Mandatory fees	N/App	Short-term loans (average)	$1500
	Room and board	$4010	Long-term loans—college funds (average)	$2400
	Financial aid recipients	70%	Long-term loans—external funds (average)	$2737

Undergraduate Facts			
Part-time	4%	*Freshman Data:* 909 applied, 81% were accepted, 35% (255) of those entered	
State residents	70%		
Transfers	6%	From top tenth of high school class	36%
African-Americans	1%	SAT-takers scoring 600 or over on verbal	10%
Native Americans	0%	SAT-takers scoring 700 or over on verbal	0%
Hispanics	1%	SAT-takers scoring 600 or over on math	28%
Asian-Americans	1%	SAT-takers scoring 700 or over on math	2%
International students	2%	ACT-takers scoring 26 or over	23%
Freshmen returning for sophomore year	94%	ACT-takers scoring 30 or over	3%
Students completing degree within 5 years	72%	*Majors with most degrees conferred:* business, education, natural sciences.	
Grads pursuing further study	34%		

Majors Accounting, American studies, anthropology, applied mathematics, art/fine arts, art history, behavioral sciences, biochemistry, biology/biological sciences, botany/plant sciences, business, business economics, chemistry, communication, computer science, cytotechnology, (pre)dentistry sequence, early childhood education, ecology/environmental studies, economics, education, elementary education, engineering sciences, English, environmental biology, environmental sciences, European studies, experimental psychology, finance/banking, French, geology, German, health science, history, humanities, human resources, interdisciplinary studies, international studies, (pre)law sequence, liberal arts/general studies, literature, management information systems, marine biology, marketing/retailing/merchandising, mathematics, medical technology, (pre)medicine sequence, microbiology, molecular biology, music, natural sciences, peace studies, philosophy, physics, political science/government, psychology, public administration, public relations, radiological technology, religious studies, Russian, science education, secondary education, social science, social work, sociology, Spanish, studio art, (pre)veterinary medicine sequence.

Applying *Required:* essay, high school transcript, 2 years of high school foreign language, 1 recommendation, SAT or ACT. *Recommended:* 3 years of high school math and science, campus interview, Achievements. Interview required for some. *Application deadlines:* 3/1, 11/15 for early decision, 3/1 priority date for financial aid. *Contact:* Mr. Carlton E. Surbeck III, Director of Admissions, 1700 Moore Street, Huntingdon, PA 16652, 814-643-4310 Ext. 420 or toll-free 800-526-1970.

Kalamazoo College

Kalamazoo, Michigan

Founded 1833
Suburban setting
Independent
Coed
Awards B

Enrollment	1,271 total—all undergraduates (337 freshmen)
Faculty	109 total; 89 full-time (85% have doctorate/terminal degree); student-faculty ratio is 12:1.
Libraries	286,219 bound volumes, 153 titles on microform, 1,100 periodical subscriptions
Computing	*Terminals/PCs available for student use:* 42, located in computer center, classroom buildings; PC not required but available for purchase.
Of Special Interest	*Core academic program:* yes. Computer course required for natural science, math, some social science majors. Phi Beta Kappa chapter. Academic exchange with Kalamazoo Consortium. Sponsors and participates in study-abroad programs. Cooperative Army ROTC.
On Campus	Drama/theater group; student-run newspaper and radio station. No national or local fraternities or sororities on campus.
Athletics	Member NCAA (Division III). *Intercollegiate sports:* baseball (M), basketball (M, W), cross-country running (M, W), football (M), golf (M, W), soccer (M, W), softball (W), swimming and diving (M, W), tennis (M, W), volleyball (W).

Costs (1991–92) & Aid				
	Comprehensive fee	$16,722	Need-based scholarships (average)	$2690
	Tuition	$12,669	Non-need scholarships (average)	$2142
	Mandatory fees	N/App	Short-term loans	N/Avail
	Room and board	$4053	Long-term loans—college funds	N/Avail
	Financial aid recipients	55%	Long-term loans—external funds (average)	$1590

Undergraduate Facts				
	Part-time	0%	*Freshman Data:* 1,174 applied, 86% were accepted, 33% (337) of those entered	
	State residents	77%		
	Transfers	10%	From top tenth of high school class	42%
	African-Americans	3%	SAT-takers scoring 600 or over on verbal	20%
	Native Americans	1%	SAT-takers scoring 700 or over on verbal	4%
	Hispanics	1%	SAT-takers scoring 600 or over on math	46%
	Asian-Americans	5%	SAT-takers scoring 700 or over on math	11%
	International students	4%	ACT-takers scoring 26 or over	54%
	Freshmen returning for sophomore year	86%	ACT-takers scoring 30 or over	18%
	Students completing degree within 5 years	70%	*Majors with most degrees conferred:* business economics, English, political science/government.	
	Grads pursuing further study	30%		

Majors African studies, American studies, anthropology, art/fine arts, art history, biology/biological sciences, business, business economics, chemistry, Chinese, classics, computer science, (pre)dentistry sequence, economics, English, environmental sciences, European studies, French, German, Greek, health science, history, human resources, human services, international business, international economics, international studies, Italian, Japanese, Latin, (pre)law sequence, literature, mathematics, (pre)medicine sequence, modern languages, music, philosophy, physics, political science/government, psychology, public affairs and policy studies, religious studies, Romance languages, Russian, secondary education, sociology, Spanish, studio art, theater arts/drama, women's studies.

Applying *Required:* essay, high school transcript, 2 recommendations, SAT or ACT. *Recommended:* 3 years of high school math and science, some high school foreign language, interview. *Application deadlines:* rolling, 2/15 priority date for financial aid. *Contact:* Ms. Teresa M. Lahti, Dean of Admission, Mandelle Hall, Kalamazoo, MI 49007, 616-383-8408 or toll-free 800-253-3602.

Kentucky Wesleyan College

Owensboro, Kentucky

Founded 1858
Suburban setting
Independent, Methodist
Coed
Awards A, B

Enrollment 747 total—all undergraduates (203 freshmen)

Faculty 80 total; 54 full-time (70% have doctorate/terminal degree); student-faculty ratio is 11:1.

Libraries 82,175 bound volumes, 19,000 titles on microform, 588 periodical subscriptions

Computing *Terminals/PCs available for student use:* 40, located in computer center, library, dormitories, classrooms; PC not required. Campus network links student PCs.

Of Special Interest *Core academic program:* yes. Computer course required for business, math, accounting, criminal justice, history, political science, all science majors. Academic exchange program. Sponsors and participates in study-abroad programs.

On Campus Drama/theater group; student-run newspaper and radio station. *Social organizations:* 3 national fraternities, 2 national sororities; 31% of eligible undergraduate men and 35% of eligible undergraduate women are members.

Athletics Member NCAA (Division II). *Intercollegiate sports:* baseball (M), basketball (M, W), cross-country running (M), football (M), golf (M), soccer (M), tennis (W), volleyball (W). *Scholarships:* M, W.

Costs (1991–92) & Aid				
	Comprehensive fee	$10,450	Need-based scholarships	Avail
	Tuition	$6500	Non-need scholarships (average)	$3700
	Mandatory fees	$190	Short-term loans	N/Avail
	Room and board	$3760	Long-term loans—college funds	N/Avail
	Financial aid recipients	85%	Long-term loans—external funds (average)	$3000

Undergraduate Facts

Part-time	8%	*Freshman Data:* 652 applied, 81% were accepted, 38% (203) of those entered		
State residents	70%			
Transfers	20%	From top tenth of high school class	30%	
African-Americans	7%	SAT-takers scoring 600 or over on verbal	N/R	
Native Americans	0%	SAT-takers scoring 700 or over on verbal	N/R	
Hispanics	0%	SAT-takers scoring 600 or over on math	N/R	
Asian-Americans	2%	SAT-takers scoring 700 or over on math	N/R	
International students	6%	ACT-takers scoring 26 or over	17%	
Freshmen returning for sophomore year	60%	ACT-takers scoring 30 or over	1%	
Students completing degree within 5 years	45%	*Majors with most degrees conferred:* nursing, business, communication.		
Grads pursuing further study	26%			

Majors Accounting, art education, art/fine arts, biology/biological sciences, business, chemistry, communication, computer science, criminal justice, (pre)dentistry sequence, elementary education, English, history, human resources, (pre)law sequence, mathematics, medical technology, (pre)medicine sequence, middle school education, modern languages, music, music education, nursing, philosophy, physical education, physics, political science/government, psychology, radio and television studies, religious studies, secondary education, social science, sociology, speech/rhetoric/public address/debate, telecommunications, theater arts/drama, (pre)veterinary medicine sequence.

Applying *Required:* high school transcript, SAT or ACT. *Recommended:* essay, 3 years of high school math and science, 2 years of high school foreign language. Recommendations, interview required for some. *Application deadlines:* 9/4, 4/1 priority date for financial aid. *Contact:* Mr. Richard G. Ernst, Director of Enrollment Services, 3000 Frederica Street. Owensboro, KY 42302-1039, 502-926-3111 Ext. 145 or toll-free 800-999-0592.

✱ Kenyon College

Gambier, Ohio

Founded 1824
Rural setting
Independent
Coed
Awards B

Enrollment 1,507 total—all undergraduates (420 freshmen)

Faculty 138 total; 112 full-time (11% have doctorate/terminal degree); student-faculty ratio is 11:1.

Libraries 368,090 bound volumes, 254,231 titles on microform, 1,360 periodical subscriptions

Computing *Terminals/PCs available for student use:* 195, located in computer center, library, dormitories, classroom buildings; PC not required. Campus network links student PCs.

Of Special Interest *Core academic program:* yes. Computer course required for physics, math, economics, chemistry, biology, psychology majors. Phi Beta Kappa chapter. Academic exchange program: no. Sponsors and participates in study-abroad programs.

On Campus Drama/theater group; student-run newspaper and radio station. *Social organizations:* 7 national fraternities, 1 local sorority; 41% of eligible undergraduate men and 4% of eligible undergraduate women are members.

Athletics Member NCAA (Division III). *Intercollegiate sports:* baseball (M), basketball (M, W), cross-country running (M, W), field hockey (W), football (M), golf (M, W), lacrosse (M, W), soccer (M, W), swimming and diving (M, W), tennis (M, W), track and field (M, W), volleyball (W).

Costs (1991–92) & Aid		
Comprehensive fee	$19,425	
Tuition	$15,525	
Mandatory fees	$525	
Room and board	$3375	
Financial aid recipients	37%	
Need-based scholarships (average)		$8335
Non-need scholarships (average)		$10,200
Short-term loans (average)		$500
Long-term loans—college funds (average)		$1100
Long-term loans—external funds (average)		$1615

Undergraduate Facts

Part-time	0%
State residents	23%
Transfers	3%
African-Americans	3%
Native Americans	N/R
Hispanics	2%
Asian-Americans	4%
International students	2%
Freshmen returning for sophomore year	95%
Students completing degree within 5 years	86%
Grads pursuing further study	25%

Freshman Data: 2,221 applied, 70% were accepted, 27% (420) of those entered

From top tenth of high school class	44%
SAT-takers scoring 600 or over on verbal	37%
SAT-takers scoring 700 or over on verbal	8%
SAT-takers scoring 600 or over on math	53%
SAT-takers scoring 700 or over on math	12%
ACT-takers scoring 26 or over	77%
ACT-takers scoring 30 or over	20%

Majors with most degrees conferred: English, political science/government, psychology.

Majors American studies, anthropology, art/fine arts, art history, Asian/Oriental studies, biology/biological sciences, black/African-American studies, chemistry, classics, computer science, creative writing, dance, (pre)dentistry sequence, economics, English, French, German, Greek, history, interdisciplinary studies, international studies, Latin, (pre)law sequence, literature, mathematics, (pre)medicine sequence, modern languages, music, philosophy, physics, political science/government, psychology, religious studies, Romance languages, Russian, sociology, Spanish, studio art, theater arts/drama, (pre)veterinary medicine sequence, women's studies.

Applying *Required:* essay, high school transcript, 3 years of high school math, 2 years of high school foreign language, 1 recommendation, SAT or ACT. *Recommended:* 3 years of high school science, interview. *Application deadlines:* 2/15, 12/1 for early decision, 2/15 for financial aid. *Contact:* Mr. John W. Anderson, Dean of Admissions, Ransom Hall, Gambier, OH 43022, 614-427-5778 or toll-free 800-282-2459 (in-state), 800-848-2468 (out-of-state).

Knox College

Galesburg, Illinois

Founded 1837
Small-town setting
Independent
Coed
Awards B

Enrollment 943 total—all undergraduates (241 freshmen)

Faculty 84 total; 79 full-time (92% have doctorate/terminal degree); student-faculty ratio is 11:1.

Libraries 253,577 bound volumes, 85,000 titles on microform, 720 periodical subscriptions

Computing *Terminals/PCs available for student use:* 80, located in computer center, all academic buildings; PC not required.

Of Special Interest *Core academic program:* yes. Computer course required for economics majors. Phi Beta Kappa, Sigma Xi chapters. Academic exchange with 14 members of the Associated Colleges of the Midwest, Great Lakes Colleges Association. Sponsors and participates in study-abroad programs. Cooperative Army ROTC.

On Campus Drama/theater group; student-run newspaper and radio station. *Social organizations:* 5 national fraternities, 2 national sororities; 35% of eligible undergraduate men and 20% of eligible undergraduate women are members.

Athletics Member NCAA (Division III). *Intercollegiate sports:* baseball (M), basketball (M, W), cross-country running (M, W), football (M), golf (M), soccer (M, W), softball (W), swimming and diving (M, W), tennis (M, W), track and field (M, W), volleyball (W), wrestling (M).

Costs & Aid				
	Comprehensive fee	$17,700	Need-based scholarships (average)	$5937
	Tuition	$13,677	Non-need scholarships (average)	$3231
	Mandatory fees	$165	Short-term loans	N/Avail
	Room and board	$3858	Long-term loans—college funds (average)	$1155
	Financial aid recipients	82%	Long-term loans—external funds (average)	$2545

Undergraduate Facts				
	Part-time	4%	*Freshman Data:* 881 applied, 80% were accepted, 34% (241) of those entered	
	State residents	59%		
	Transfers	12%	From top tenth of high school class	36%
	African-Americans	6%	SAT-takers scoring 600 or over on verbal	21%
	Native Americans	1%	SAT-takers scoring 700 or over on verbal	6%
	Hispanics	3%	SAT-takers scoring 600 or over on math	33%
	Asian-Americans	5%	SAT-takers scoring 700 or over on math	12%
	International students	6%	ACT-takers scoring 26 or over	47%
	Freshmen returning for sophomore year	86%	ACT-takers scoring 30 or over	14%
	Students completing degree within 5 years	75%	*Majors with most degrees conferred:* economics, political science/government, psychology.	
	Grads pursuing further study	42%		

Majors American studies, anthropology, art/fine arts, art history, biochemistry, biology/biological sciences, chemistry, classics, computer science, creative writing, (pre)dentistry sequence, economics, education, elementary education, English, French, German, history, literature, mathematics, (pre)medicine sequence, modern languages, music, philosophy, physics, political science/government, psychology, religious studies, Russian, Russian and Slavic studies, secondary education, sociology, Spanish, studio art, theater arts/drama, (pre)veterinary medicine sequence, women's studies.

Applying *Required:* essay, high school transcript, 3 years of high school math and science, 2 recommendations, SAT or ACT. *Recommended:* some high school foreign language, interview. *Application deadlines:* 2/15, 12/1 for early action, 3/1 priority date for financial aid. *Contact:* Mr. Charles Richardson, Director of Admissions, Center for Fine Arts, Galesburg, IL 61401, 309-343-0112 Ext. 123 or toll-free 800-678-KNOX.

✱ **Lafayette College**

Founded 1826
Small-town setting
Independent/affiliated with Presbyterian Church (U.S.A.)
Coed

Easton, Pennsylvania

Awards B

Enrollment	2,225 total—all undergraduates (538 freshmen)
Faculty	224 total; 169 full-time (92% have doctorate/terminal degree); student-faculty ratio is 10:1.
Libraries	390,000 bound volumes, 70,358 titles on microform, 1,750 periodical subscriptions
Computing	*Terminals/PCs available for student use:* 225, located in computer center, library, dormitories, classroom buildings; PC not required. Campus network links student PCs.
Of Special Interest	*Core academic program:* yes. Computer course required for engineering majors. Phi Beta Kappa, Sigma Xi chapters. Academic exchange with 5 members of the Lehigh Valley Association of Independent Colleges, American University (Washington Semester). Sponsors and participates in study-abroad programs. Army ROTC, cooperative Air Force ROTC.
On Campus	Drama/theater group; student-run newspaper and radio station. *Social organizations:* 11 national fraternities, 5 national sororities, 2 social dorms; 53% of eligible undergraduate men and 46% of eligible undergraduate women are members.
Athletics	Member NCAA (Division I). *Intercollegiate sports:* basketball (M, W), crew (M, W), cross-country running (M, W), equestrian sports (M, W), fencing (M, W), field hockey (W), football (M), golf (M), lacrosse (M, W), rugby (M), skiing (downhill) (M, W), soccer (M, W), swimming and diving (M, W), tennis (M, W), track and field (M, W), volleyball (W), weight lifting (M, W), wrestling (M).

Costs (1991–92) & Aid				
	Comprehensive fee	$20,375	Need-based scholarships (average)	$9468
	Tuition	$15,475	Non-need scholarships	N/Avail
	Mandatory fees	N/App	Short-term loans (average)	$200
	Room and board	$4900	Long-term loans—college funds (average)	$1682
	Financial aid recipients	58%	Long-term loans—external funds (average)	$2623

Undergraduate Facts				
	Part-time	13%	*Freshman Data:* 4,164 applied, 49% were accepted, 26% (538) of those entered	
	State residents	25%		
	Transfers	5%	From top tenth of high school class	48%
	African-Americans	4%	SAT-takers scoring 600 or over on verbal	21%
	Native Americans	1%	SAT-takers scoring 700 or over on verbal	1%
	Hispanics	2%	SAT-takers scoring 600 or over on math	65%
	Asian-Americans	3%	SAT-takers scoring 700 or over on math	16%
	International students	7%	ACT-takers scoring 26 or over	N/App
	Freshmen returning for sophomore year	94%	ACT-takers scoring 30 or over	N/App
	Students completing degree within 5 years	89%	*Majors with most degrees conferred:* business economics, English, political science/government.	
	Grads pursuing further study	28%		

Majors American studies, anthropology, art/fine arts, art history, biochemistry, biology/biological sciences, business economics, chemical engineering, chemistry, civil engineering, computer science, economics, electrical engineering, engineering (general), English, French, geology, German, history, international studies, mathematics, mechanical engineering, music, music history, philosophy, physics, political science/government, psychobiology, psychology, religious studies, Russian, sociology, Spanish, studio art.

Applying *Required:* essay, high school transcript, 3 years of high school math, 2 years of high school foreign language, 2 recommendations, SAT, 3 Achievements, English Composition Test. *Recommended:* 3 years of high school science, interview, English Composition Test (with essay). *Application deadlines:* 2/1, 11/1 for early decision, 2/15 priority date for financial aid. *Contact:* Ms. Carol A. Rowlands, Acting Director of Admissions, Markle Hall, Easton, PA 18042, 215-250-5110.

Lake Forest College

Lake Forest, Illinois

Founded 1857
Suburban setting
Independent
Coed
Awards B, M

Enrollment	1,059 total; 1,037 undergraduates (237 freshmen)
Faculty	107 total; 83 full-time (95% have doctorate/terminal degree); student-faculty ratio is 11:1; grad assistants teach no undergraduate courses.
Libraries	270,000 bound volumes, 79,000 titles on microform, 1,300 periodical subscriptions
Computing	*Terminals/PCs available for student use:* 154, located in computer center, student center, library, dormitories, classroom buildings; PC not required but available for purchase.
Of Special Interest	*Core academic program:* no. Computer course required for economics, psychology, sociology, math, science majors. Phi Beta Kappa, Sigma Xi chapters. Academic exchange with Rush University. Sponsors and participates in study-abroad programs.
On Campus	Drama/theater group; student-run newspaper and radio station. *Social organizations:* 3 local fraternities, 2 local sororities; 9% of eligible undergraduate men and 7% of eligible undergraduate women are members.
Athletics	Member NCAA (Division III). *Intercollegiate sports:* baseball (M), basketball (M, W), football (M), ice hockey (M), lacrosse (M), sailing (M, W), soccer (M, W), softball (W), swimming and diving (M, W), tennis (M, W), volleyball (W), water polo (M).

Costs (1991–92) & Aid				
	Comprehensive fee	$17,050	Need-based scholarships (average)	$9950
	Tuition	$13,710	Non-need scholarships	N/Avail
	Mandatory fees	$185	Short-term loans	N/Avail
	Room and board	$3155	Long-term loans—college funds	N/Avail
	Financial aid recipients	57%	Long-term loans—external funds (average)	$1500

Undergraduate Facts				
	Part-time	1%	*Freshman Data:* 959 applied, 64% were accepted, 38% (237) of those entered	
	State residents	34%		
	Transfers	21%	From top tenth of high school class	27%
	African-Americans	6%	SAT-takers scoring 600 or over on verbal	11%
	Native Americans	1%	SAT-takers scoring 700 or over on verbal	1%
	Hispanics	1%	SAT-takers scoring 600 or over on math	18%
	Asian-Americans	3%	SAT-takers scoring 700 or over on math	4%
	International students	2%	ACT-takers scoring 26 or over	43%
	Freshmen returning for sophomore year	89%	ACT-takers scoring 30 or over	5%
	Students completing degree within 5 years	74%	*Majors with most degrees conferred:* psychology, English, business economics.	
	Grads pursuing further study	19%		

Majors American studies, anthropology, art history, Asian/Oriental studies, biology/biological sciences, business economics, chemistry, city/community/regional planning, comparative literature, computer science, economics, education, English, environmental sciences, finance/banking, French, German, history, international studies, mathematics, music, philosophy, physics, political science/government, psychology, public administration, sociology, Spanish, studio art, urban studies.

Applying *Required:* essay, high school transcript, 2 recommendations, SAT or ACT. *Recommended:* 3 years of high school math, 2 years of high school foreign language, interview. *Application deadlines:* 2/15, 2/15 for early decision, 3/1 for financial aid. *Contact:* Mr. Francis B. Gummere Jr., Dean of Admissions, 555 North Sheridan Road, Lake Forest, IL 60045, 708-234-3100 Ext. 200.

✷ La Salle University

Philadelphia, Pennsylvania

Founded 1863
Suburban setting
Independent, Roman Catholic
Coed
Awards B, M

Enrollment 6,029 total; 4,820 undergraduates (690 freshmen)

Faculty 326 total; 228 full-time (86% have doctorate/terminal degree); student-faculty ratio is 15:1; grad assistants teach no undergraduate courses.

Libraries 345,000 bound volumes, 19,101 titles on microform, 1,650 periodical subscriptions

Computing *Terminals/PCs available for student use:* 310, located in computer center, student center, library; PC not required. Campus network links student PCs.

Of Special Interest *Core academic program:* yes. Computer course required. Academic exchange with Chestnut Hill College. Sponsors and participates in study-abroad programs. Cooperative Army ROTC, cooperative Naval ROTC, cooperative Air Force ROTC.

On Campus Drama/theater group; student-run newspaper and radio station. *Social organizations:* 7 national fraternities, 4 national sororities, 1 local fraternity, 1 local sorority; 12% of eligible undergraduate men and 12% of eligible undergraduate women are members.

Athletics Member NCAA (Division I), NAIA. *Intercollegiate sports:* baseball (M), basketball (M, W), crew (M, W), cross-country running (M, W), field hockey (W), golf (M, W), soccer (M, W), softball (W), swimming and diving (M, W), tennis (M, W), track and field (M, W), volleyball (W), wrestling (M). *Scholarships:* M, W.

Costs (1991–92) & Aid				
	Comprehensive fee	$14,800	Need-based scholarships	Avail
	Tuition	$10,250	Non-need scholarships (average)	$6000
	Mandatory fees	$50	Short-term loans	N/Avail
	Room and board	$4500	Long-term loans—college funds	N/Avail
	Financial aid recipients	85%	Long-term loans—external funds (average)	$3200

Undergraduate Facts				
	Part-time	36%	*Freshman Data:* 2,860 applied, 60% were accepted, 40% (690) of those entered	
	State residents	80%		
	Transfers	8%	From top tenth of high school class	25%
	African-Americans	10%	SAT-takers scoring 600 or over on verbal	24%
	Native Americans	0%	SAT-takers scoring 700 or over on verbal	10%
	Hispanics	3%	SAT-takers scoring 600 or over on math	35%
	Asian-Americans	3%	SAT-takers scoring 700 or over on math	15%
	International students	2%	ACT-takers scoring 26 or over	N/R
	Freshmen returning for sophomore year	91%	ACT-takers scoring 30 or over	N/R
	Students completing degree within 5 years	89%	*Majors with most degrees conferred:* accounting, (pre)medicine sequence, communication.	
	Grads pursuing further study	20%		

Majors Accounting, applied mathematics, art education, art/fine arts, art history, biology/biological sciences, business, business economics, business education, business machine technologies, chemistry, classics, communication, computer information systems, computer programming, computer science, creative writing, criminal justice, (pre)dentistry sequence, early childhood education, earth science, economics, education, elementary education, English, film studies, finance/banking, French, geology, German, Germanic languages and literature, Greek, health services administration, history, human resources, information science, international business, international studies, Italian, journalism, labor and industrial relations, labor studies, Latin, (pre)law sequence, liberal arts/general studies, literature, management information systems, marketing/retailing/merchandising, mathematics, (pre)medicine sequence, modern languages, music, music history, nursing, philosophy, physics, political science/government, psychology, public administration, radio and television studies, religious education, religious studies, retail management, Russian, Russian and Slavic studies, science education, secondary education, social science, social work, sociology, Spanish, special education, speech/rhetoric/public address/debate, theology, (pre)veterinary medicine sequence, women's studies.

Applying *Required:* essay, high school transcript, 3 years of high school math, 2 years of high school foreign language, SAT or ACT. *Recommended:* recommendations, campus interview, Achievements, English Composition Test. *Application deadlines:* 8/15, 2/15 priority date for financial aid. *Contact:* Br. Gerald Fitzgerald, Director of Admissions, 20th and Olney Avenue, Philadelphia, PA 19141, 215-951-1500.

From the College La Salle University has been ranked among the nation's leading colleges by *U.S. News & World Report, Money* magazine, Barron's, and the *New York Times.* The La Salle Honors Program serves as a national model and has been praised for its extraordinary record in terms of garnering Fulbright, Danforth, and Marshall fellowships, according to the National Collegiate Honors Council.

Lawrence University

Appleton, Wisconsin

Founded 1847
Small-town setting
Independent
Coed
Awards B

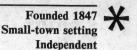

Enrollment 1,194 total—all undergraduates (291 freshmen)

Faculty 118 total; 110 full-time (93% have doctorate/terminal degree); student-faculty ratio is 11:1.

Libraries 310,000 bound volumes, 100,000 titles on microform, 1,252 periodical subscriptions

Computing *Terminals/PCs available for student use:* 120, located in computer center, library, dormitories, academic buildings; PC not required.

Of Special Interest *Core academic program:* yes. Computer course required for math, physics majors. Phi Beta Kappa chapter. Academic exchange program: no. Sponsors and participates in study-abroad programs.

On Campus Drama/theater group; student-run newspaper. *Social organizations:* 5 national fraternities, 3 national sororities; 42% of eligible undergraduate men and 35% of eligible undergraduate women are members.

Athletics Member NCAA (Division III). *Intercollegiate sports:* baseball (M), basketball (M, W), crew (M, W), cross-country running (M, W), fencing (M, W), football (M), golf (M), ice hockey (M), lacrosse (M, W), rugby (W), soccer (M, W), softball (W), swimming and diving (M, W), tennis (M, W), track and field (M, W), volleyball (W), wrestling (M).

Costs (1992–93) & Aid
Comprehensive fee	$18,771	
Tuition	$15,342	
Mandatory fees	N/App	
Room and board	$3429	
Financial aid recipients	66%	
Need-based scholarships (average)		$9109
Non-need scholarships (average)		$1863
Short-term loans (average)		$50
Long-term loans—college funds (average)		$2350
Long-term loans—external funds (average)		$2462

Undergraduate Facts
Part-time	3%
State residents	40%
Transfers	8%
African-Americans	4%
Native Americans	1%
Hispanics	2%
Asian-Americans	2%
International students	9%
Freshmen returning for sophomore year	85%
Students completing degree within 5 years	75%
Grads pursuing further study	22%

Freshman Data: 1,067 applied, 78% were accepted, 35% (291) of those entered
From top tenth of high school class	40%
SAT-takers scoring 600 or over on verbal	37%
SAT-takers scoring 700 or over on verbal	4%
SAT-takers scoring 600 or over on math	56%
SAT-takers scoring 700 or over on math	17%
ACT-takers scoring 26 or over	56%
ACT-takers scoring 30 or over	16%

Majors with most degrees conferred: English, biology/biological sciences, psychology.

Majors Anthropology, art/fine arts, art history, biology/biological sciences, chemistry, classics, computer science, (pre)dentistry sequence, East Asian studies, ecology/environmental studies, economics, English, environmental sciences, French, geology, German, Greek, history, international economics, international studies, Latin, (pre)law sequence, linguistics, mathematics, (pre)medicine sequence, music, music education, neurosciences, philosophy, physics, piano/organ, political science/government, psychology, public affairs and policy studies, religious studies, Russian, Russian and Slavic studies, secondary education, Slavic languages, Spanish, stringed instruments, studio art, theater arts/drama, (pre)veterinary medicine sequence, voice, wind and percussion instruments, women's studies.

Applying *Required:* essay, high school transcript, 2 recommendations, audition for music majors, SAT or ACT. *Recommended:* 3 years of high school math and science, 2 years of high school foreign language, interview. *Application deadlines:* 2/15, 12/1 for early decision, 3/1 priority date for financial aid. *Contact:* Mr. Kim Straus, Director of Admissions, 706 East College Avenue, Appleton, WI 54912, 414-832-6500 or toll-free 800-227-0982.

From the College Freshman Studies, a distinctive core program of great intellectual and artistic works taught in classes of 16 students, introduces new Lawrentians to rigorous curricular expections and opportunities for close interaction with faculty. Over 90 percent of all Lawrentians engage in independent study and nearly half study abroad. The Honor Code nurtures an atmosphere of trust and collaboration rather than competition.

Lehigh University

Bethlehem, Pennsylvania

Founded 1865
Suburban setting
Independent
Coed
Awards B, M, D

Enrollment 6,556 total; 4,489 undergraduates (1,118 freshmen)

Faculty 484 total; 411 full-time (98% have doctorate/terminal degree); student-faculty ratio is 11:1; grad assistants teach no undergraduate courses.

Libraries 1 million bound volumes, 1.75 million titles on microform, 9,700 periodical subscriptions

Computing *Terminals/PCs available for student use:* 430, located in computer center, library, academic buildings; PC not required. Campus network links student PCs.

Of Special Interest *Core academic program:* yes. Computer course required for engineering, business, science, math majors. Phi Beta Kappa, Sigma Xi chapters. Academic exchange with members of the Lehigh Valley Association of Independent Colleges, Great Lakes Colleges Association, American University. Sponsors and participates in study-abroad programs. Army ROTC, Air Force ROTC.

On Campus Drama/theater group; student-run newspaper and radio station. *Social organizations:* 28 national fraternities, 8 national sororities; 38% of eligible undergraduate men and 31% of eligible undergraduate women are members.

Athletics Member NCAA (Division I). *Intercollegiate sports:* baseball (M), basketball (M, W), crew (M, W), cross-country running (M, W), equestrian sports (M, W), field hockey (W), football (M, W), golf (M), gymnastics (W), ice hockey (M), lacrosse (M, W), riflery (M, W), rugby (M), sailing (M, W), skiing (downhill) (M, W), soccer (M, W), softball (W), squash (M), swimming and diving (M, W), tennis (M, W), track and field (M, W), volleyball (M, W), water polo (M), wrestling (M).

Costs (1992–93) & Aid					
	Comprehensive fee	$21,940	Need-based scholarships (average)		$8601
	Tuition	$16,700	Non-need scholarships (average)		$15,650
	Mandatory fees	N/App	Short-term loans (average)		$300
	Room and board	$5240	Long-term loans—college funds (average)		$1200
	Financial aid recipients	47%	Long-term loans—external funds (average)		$2625

Undergraduate Facts				
	Part-time	1%	*Freshman Data:* 5,707 applied, 66% were accepted, 30% (1,118) of those entered	
	State residents	29%		
	Transfers	2%	From top tenth of high school class	40%
	African-Americans	2%	SAT-takers scoring 600 or over on verbal	14%
	Native Americans	0%	SAT-takers scoring 700 or over on verbal	1%
	Hispanics	2%	SAT-takers scoring 600 or over on math	68%
	Asian-Americans	5%	SAT-takers scoring 700 or over on math	18%
	International students	2%	ACT-takers scoring 26 or over	N/R
	Freshmen returning for sophomore year	92%	ACT-takers scoring 30 or over	N/R
	Students completing degree within 5 years	88%	*Majors with most degrees conferred:* mechanical engineering, accounting, finance/banking.	
	Grads pursuing further study	21%		

Majors Accounting, American studies, anthropology, applied mathematics, architecture, art/fine arts, behavioral sciences, biochemistry, bioengineering, biology/biological sciences, biomedical engineering, biophysics, black/African-American studies, business, business economics, chemical engineering, chemistry, civil engineering, classics, cognitive science, computer engineering, computer science, (pre)dentistry sequence, earth science, East Asian studies, East European and Soviet studies, ecology/environmental studies, economics, electrical engineering, engineering and applied sciences, engineering mechanics, engineering physics, English, environmental sciences, finance/banking, French, geochemistry, geological engineering, geology, geophysics, German, history, industrial engineering, information science, international business, international studies, journalism, Latin American studies, (pre)law sequence, marketing/retailing/merchandising, materials engineering, materials sciences, mathematics, mechanical engineering, (pre)medicine sequence, metallurgical engineering, modern languages, molecular biology, music, natural sciences, neurosciences, philosophy, physics, political science/government, psychology, religious studies, Romance languages, Russian and Slavic studies, social science, sociology, Spanish, statistics, technical writing, theater arts/drama, urban studies, (pre)veterinary medicine sequence.

Applying *Required:* essay, high school transcript, 3 years of high school math, 2 years of high school foreign language, 1 recommendation, SAT or ACT, 3 Achievements, English Composition Test. *Recommended:* campus interview. 3 years of high school science required for some. *Application deadlines:* 2/15, 12/1 for early decision, 2/7 priority date for financial aid. *Contact:* Mrs. Patricia G. Boig, Director of Admissions, Alumni Memorial Building, Bethlehem, PA 18015, 215-758-3100.

Le Moyne College

Syracuse, New York

Founded 1946
Suburban setting
Independent, Roman Catholic (Jesuit)
Coed
Awards B

Enrollment 2,049 total—all undergraduates (406 freshmen)

Faculty 201 total; 122 full-time (94% have doctorate/terminal degree); student-faculty ratio is 10:1.

Libraries 195,121 bound volumes, 242 titles on microform, 1,619 periodical subscriptions

Computing *Terminals/PCs available for student use:* 105, located in computer center, library, dormitories, science center; PC not required.

Of Special Interest *Core academic program:* yes. Computer course required for accounting, business, economics, math, management majors. Academic exchange with Syracuse Consortium for the Cultural Foundations of Medicine. Participates in study-abroad programs. Cooperative Army ROTC, cooperative Air Force ROTC.

On Campus Drama/theater group; student-run newspaper and radio station. No national or local fraternities or sororities on campus.

Athletics Member NCAA (Division II). *Intercollegiate sports:* baseball (M), basketball (M, W), cross-country running (M, W), golf (M), lacrosse (M), soccer (M, W), softball (W), swimming and diving (M, W), tennis (M, W), volleyball (W). *Scholarships:* M, W.

Costs (1991–92) & Aid				
	Comprehensive fee	$13,210	Need-based scholarships (average)	$4200
	Tuition	$8990	Non-need scholarships (average)	$1750
	Mandatory fees	$200	Short-term loans	N/Avail
	Room and board	$4020	Long-term loans—college funds (average)	$1050
	Financial aid recipients	75%	Long-term loans—external funds (average)	$2600

Undergraduate Facts				
	Part-time	8%	*Freshman Data:* 1,468 applied, 81% were accepted, 34% (406) of those entered	
	State residents	85%		
	Transfers	8%	From top tenth of high school class	20%
	African-Americans	3%	SAT-takers scoring 600 or over on verbal	5%
	Native Americans	1%	SAT-takers scoring 700 or over on verbal	1%
	Hispanics	2%	SAT-takers scoring 600 or over on math	21%
	Asian-Americans	2%	SAT-takers scoring 700 or over on math	3%
	International students	1%	ACT-takers scoring 26 or over	19%
	Freshmen returning for sophomore year	92%	ACT-takers scoring 30 or over	1%
	Students completing degree within 5 years	73%	*Majors with most degrees conferred:* business, accounting, English.	
	Grads pursuing further study	23%		

Majors Accounting, biology/biological sciences, business, business education, chemistry, communication, computer science, criminal justice, (pre)dentistry sequence, economics, education, elementary education, English, finance/banking, French, history, human resources, international business, international studies, labor and industrial relations, (pre)law sequence, marketing/retailing/merchandising, mathematics, (pre)medicine sequence, modern languages, philosophy, physics, political science/government, psychology, religious education, religious studies, science, science education, secondary education, sociology, Spanish, special education, teaching English as a second language, urban studies, (pre)veterinary medicine sequence.

Applying *Required:* essay, high school transcript, 3 years of high school math, 1 recommendation, SAT or ACT. *Recommended:* 2 years of high school foreign language, campus interview. 3 years of high school science required for some. *Application deadlines:* 3/15, 12/1 for early action, 2/15 priority date for financial aid. *Contact:* Dr. Edwin B. Harris, Director of Admissions, Le Moyne Heights, Syracuse, NY 13214, 315-445-4300 or toll-free 800-333-4733.

LeTourneau University

Longview, Texas

Founded 1946
Small-town setting
Independent, nondenominational
Coed
Awards A, B

Enrollment 858 total—all undergraduates (210 freshmen)

Faculty 64 total; 49 full-time (63% have doctorate/terminal degree); student-faculty ratio is 16:1.

Libraries 98,641 bound volumes, 38,520 titles on microform, 435 periodical subscriptions

Computing *Terminals/PCs available for student use:* 300, located in computer center, library; PC not required.

Of Special Interest *Core academic program:* yes. Computer course required. Academic exchange program: no. Participates in study-abroad programs.

On Campus Dress code; mandatory chapel; drama/theater group; student-run newspaper. *Social organizations:* 5 local fraternities; 13% of eligible undergraduate men are members.

Athletics Member NAIA. *Intercollegiate sports:* baseball (M), basketball (M), cross-country running (M, W), soccer (M), track and field (M, W), volleyball (W).

Costs (1992–93) & Aid

Comprehensive fee	$11,800	
Tuition	$7830	
Mandatory fees	$110	
Room and board	$3860	
Financial aid recipients	80%	
Need-based scholarships (average)		$1070
Non-need scholarships (average)		$1066
Short-term loans		N/Avail
Long-term loans—college funds (average)		$1350
Long-term loans—external funds (average)		$2530

Undergraduate Facts

Part-time	10%
State residents	31%
Transfers	30%
African-Americans	4%
Native Americans	1%
Hispanics	2%
Asian-Americans	1%
International students	6%
Freshmen returning for sophomore year	64%
Students completing degree within 5 years	N/R
Grads pursuing further study	N/R

Freshman Data: 411 applied, 95% were accepted, 54% (210) of those entered

From top tenth of high school class	26%
SAT-takers scoring 600 or over on verbal	15%
SAT-takers scoring 700 or over on verbal	2%
SAT-takers scoring 600 or over on math	39%
SAT-takers scoring 700 or over on math	11%
ACT-takers scoring 26 or over	28%
ACT-takers scoring 30 or over	5%

Majors with most degrees conferred: aviation technology, electrical engineering, mechanical engineering.

Majors Accounting, aviation technology, biblical studies, biology/biological sciences, business, chemistry, computer engineering, computer science, computer technologies, (pre)dentistry sequence, electrical engineering, electrical engineering technology, engineering (general), engineering technology, English, flight training, history, industrial administration, (pre)law sequence, marketing/retailing/merchandising, mathematics, mechanical engineering, mechanical engineering technology, medical technology, (pre)medicine sequence, natural sciences, physical education, public administration, sports administration, (pre)veterinary medicine sequence, welding engineering, welding technology.

Applying *Required:* essay, high school transcript, 2 recommendations, SAT or ACT. *Recommended:* 3 years of high school science. 3 years of high school math, campus interview required for some. *Application deadlines:* 8/15, 2/15 priority date for financial aid. *Contact:* Mr. Roger Kieffer, Dean of Enrollment Management, 2100 South Mobberly, Longview, TX 75607, 903-753-0231 Ext. 240 or toll-free 800-759-8811.

Lewis and Clark College

Portland, Oregon

Founded 1867
Suburban setting
Independent
Coed
Awards B, M, D

Enrollment	3,112 total; 1,880 undergraduates (382 freshmen)
Faculty	141 total; 106 full-time (96% have doctorate/terminal degree); student-faculty ratio is 14:1; grad assistants teach no undergraduate courses.
Libraries	343,000 bound volumes, 48,000 titles on microform, 3,244 periodical subscriptions
Computing	*Terminals/PCs available for student use:* 250, located in computer center, library, dormitories, computer terminal rooms; PC not required. Campus network links student PCs.
Of Special Interest	*Core academic program:* yes. Computer course required for math majors. Academic exchange program: no. Sponsors and participates in study-abroad programs.
On Campus	Drama/theater group; student-run newspaper and radio station. *Social organizations:* 2 national fraternities; 1% of eligible undergraduate men are members.
Athletics	Member NAIA. *Intercollegiate sports:* baseball (M), basketball (M, W), crew (M, W), cross-country running (M, W), fencing (M, W), football (M), golf (M), lacrosse (M, W), rugby (M), sailing (M, W), skiing (cross-country) (M, W), skiing (downhill) (M, W), soccer (M, W), softball (W), swimming and diving (M, W), tennis (M, W), track and field (M, W), volleyball (M, W).

Costs (1991–92) & Aid				
	Comprehensive fee	$18,123	Need-based scholarships (average)	$6200
	Tuition	$12,969	Non-need scholarships (average)	$1680
	Mandatory fees	$501	Short-term loans (average)	$150
	Room and board	$4653	Long-term loans—college funds	N/Avail
	Financial aid recipients	75%	Long-term loans—external funds (average)	$3584

Undergraduate Facts				
	Part-time	3%	*Freshman Data:* 2,195 applied, 76% were accepted, 23% (382) of those entered	
	State residents	29%		
	Transfers	18%	From top tenth of high school class	37%
	African-Americans	2%	SAT-takers scoring 600 or over on verbal	17%
	Native Americans	1%	SAT-takers scoring 700 or over on verbal	4%
	Hispanics	2%	SAT-takers scoring 600 or over on math	33%
	Asian-Americans	9%	SAT-takers scoring 700 or over on math	6%
	International students	6%	ACT-takers scoring 26 or over	45%
	Freshmen returning for sophomore year	74%	ACT-takers scoring 30 or over	7%
	Students completing degree within 5 years	68%		
	Grads pursuing further study	22%		

Majors Anthropology, art/fine arts, art history, biochemistry, biology/biological sciences, business, chemistry, communication, computer science, (pre)dentistry sequence, economics, education, English, French, German, history, international studies, (pre)law sequence, mathematics, (pre)medicine sequence, modern languages, music, music education, natural sciences, philosophy, physics, political science/government, psychology, religious studies, science, science education, sociology, Spanish, theater arts/drama, (pre)veterinary medicine sequence.

Applying *Required:* essay, high school transcript, 2 recommendations. *Recommended:* 3 years of high school math and science, 2 years of high school foreign language, interview. Individualized portfolio, SAT or ACT required for some. *Application deadlines:* 2/1, 11/15 for early decision, 12/1 for early action, 2/15 priority date for financial aid. *Contact:* Mr. Michael Sexton, Dean of Admissions, 615 Southwest Palatine Hill Road, Portland, OR 97219, 503-768-7040 or toll-free 800-444-4111 (out-of-state).

✳ Linfield College

McMinnville, Oregon

Founded 1849
Small-town setting
Independent, American Baptist
Coed
Awards B, M

Enrollment 1,476 total; 1,418 undergraduates (422 freshmen)

Faculty 126 total; 116 full-time (84% have doctorate/terminal degree); student-faculty ratio is 13:1; grad assistants teach no undergraduate courses.

Libraries 128,705 bound volumes, 116,363 titles on microform, 1,029 periodical subscriptions

Computing *Terminals/PCs available for student use:* 160, located in computer center, dormitories; PC not required but available for purchase.

Of Special Interest *Core academic program:* yes. Computer course required for business-related majors. Academic exchange with American Baptist Colleges and Universities. Sponsors and participates in study-abroad programs. Cooperative Air Force ROTC.

On Campus Drama/theater group; student-run newspaper and radio station. *Social organizations:* 3 national fraternities, 2 national sororities, 1 local fraternity, 1 local sorority; 30% of eligible undergraduate men and 30% of eligible undergraduate women are members.

Athletics Member NAIA. *Intercollegiate sports:* baseball (M), basketball (M, W), cross-country running (M, W), football (M), golf (M), lacrosse (M), soccer (M, W), softball (W), swimming and diving (M, W), tennis (M, W), track and field (M, W), volleyball (W). *Scholarships:* M, W.

Costs (1991–92) & Aid				
	Comprehensive fee	$14,550	Need-based scholarships (average)	$3003
	Tuition	$10,930	Non-need scholarships (average)	$3050
	Mandatory fees	$120	Short-term loans (average)	$600
	Room and board	$3500	Long-term loans—college funds (average)	$1372
	Financial aid recipients	88%	Long-term loans—external funds (average)	$2965

Undergraduate Facts				
	Part-time	5%	*Freshman Data:* 1,105 applied, 81% were accepted, 47% (422) of those entered	
	State residents	62%	From top tenth of high school class	38%
	Transfers	17%	SAT-takers scoring 600 or over on verbal	16%
	African-Americans	1%	SAT-takers scoring 700 or over on verbal	2%
	Native Americans	1%	SAT-takers scoring 600 or over on math	31%
	Hispanics	2%	SAT-takers scoring 700 or over on math	6%
	Asian-Americans	7%	ACT-takers scoring 26 or over	47%
	International students	7%	ACT-takers scoring 30 or over	16%
	Freshmen returning for sophomore year	77%	*Majors with most degrees conferred:* business, nursing, liberal arts/general studies.	
	Students completing degree within 5 years	58%		
	Grads pursuing further study	22%		

Majors Accounting, anthropology, art education, art/fine arts, arts administration, biology/biological sciences, botany/plant sciences, business, chemistry, child psychology/child development, communication, computer science, creative writing, (pre)dentistry sequence, early childhood education, earth science, ecology/environmental studies, economics, education, elementary education, English, equestrian studies, finance/banking, French, German, health education, history, humanities, information science, international business, Japanese, journalism, (pre)law sequence, liberal arts/general studies, mathematics, medical technology, (pre)medicine sequence, modern languages, music, music education, natural sciences, nursing, philosophy, physical education, physics, political science/government, psychology, public relations, radio and television studies, religious studies, science, science education, secondary education, sociology, Spanish, studio art, systems science, theater arts/drama, (pre)veterinary medicine sequence.

Applying *Required:* essay, high school transcript, 2 recommendations, SAT or ACT. *Recommended:* 3 years of high school math and science, some high school foreign language, interview. *Application deadlines:* 8/1, 4/1 priority date for financial aid. *Contact:* Mr. Thomas Meicho, Dean of Admissions, 450 Linfield Avenue, McMinnville, OR 97128, 503-472-4121 Ext. 213.

From the College Distinctive features of Linfield College include the opportunity for student research in the Science Division and Linfield Research Institute, the annual Oregon Nobel Laureate Symposium, award-winning theater and music programs, popular study abroad programs, a new physical education/recreation complex, and nationally competitive athletic programs.

Loyola College

Baltimore, Maryland

Founded 1852
Urban setting
Independent, Roman Catholic (Jesuit)
Coed
Awards B, M, D

Enrollment 6,249 total; 3,330 undergraduates (708 freshmen)

Faculty 448 total; 213 full-time (88% have doctorate/terminal degree); student-faculty ratio is 15:1; grad assistants teach no undergraduate courses.

Libraries 264,145 bound volumes, 360,238 titles on microform, 2,008 periodical subscriptions

Computing *Terminals/PCs available for student use:* 166, located in computer center, library, dormitories; PC not required.

Of Special Interest *Core academic program:* yes. Computer course required for mathematical science, physics, engineering science, all business majors. Academic exchange with Johns Hopkins University, College of Notre Dame of Maryland, Goucher College, Towson State University, Morgan State University, Peabody Conservatory of Music. Sponsors and participates in study-abroad programs. Army ROTC, cooperative Air Force ROTC.

On Campus Drama/theater group; student-run newspaper and radio station. No national or local fraternities or sororities on campus.

Athletics Member NCAA (Division I). *Intercollegiate sports:* basketball (M, W), cross-country running (M), field hockey (W), golf (M), lacrosse (M, W), soccer (M), swimming and diving (M, W), tennis (M, W), volleyball (W). *Scholarships:* M, W.

Costs (1991–92) & Aid				
	Comprehensive fee	$15,890	Need-based scholarships (average)	$3760
	Tuition	$10,320	Non-need scholarships (average)	$4410
	Mandatory fees	$170	Short-term loans	N/Avail
	Room and board	$5400	Long-term loans—college funds	N/Avail
	Financial aid recipients	55%	Long-term loans—external funds (average)	$3035

Undergraduate Facts				
	Part-time	6%	*Freshman Data:* 3,922 applied, 67% were accepted, 27% (708) of those entered	
	State residents	47%		
	Transfers	4%	From top tenth of high school class	31%
	African-Americans	3%	SAT-takers scoring 600 or over on verbal	13%
	Native Americans	0%	SAT-takers scoring 700 or over on verbal	1%
	Hispanics	2%	SAT-takers scoring 600 or over on math	30%
	Asian-Americans	2%	SAT-takers scoring 700 or over on math	5%
	International students	2%	ACT-takers scoring 26 or over	N/App
	Freshmen returning for sophomore year	89%	ACT-takers scoring 30 or over	N/App
	Students completing degree within 5 years	73%	*Majors with most degrees conferred:* business, psychology, communication.	
	Grads pursuing further study	19%		

Majors Accounting, art/fine arts, biology/biological sciences, business, business economics, chemistry, classics, communication, computer engineering, computer science, creative writing, economics, education, electrical engineering, elementary education, engineering (general), engineering sciences, English, finance/banking, French, German, history, interdisciplinary studies, Latin, management information systems, marketing/retailing/merchandising, mathematics, military science, philosophy, photography, physics, political science/government, psychology, sociology, Spanish, speech pathology and audiology, theater arts/drama, theology.

Applying *Required:* essay, high school transcript, 3 years of high school math and science, 2 years of high school foreign language, SAT. *Recommended:* interview. 1 recommendation required for some. *Application deadlines:* 2/1, same for early action, continuous to 3/1 for financial aid. *Contact:* Mr. William Bossemeyer, Director of Admissions, 4501 North Charles Street, Baltimore, MD 21210, 301-323-1010 Ext. 5012.

Luther College

Decorah, Iowa

Founded 1861
Small-town setting
Independent/affiliated with Evangelical Lutheran Church in America
Coed
Awards B

Enrollment 2,350 total—all undergraduates (581 freshmen)

Faculty 185 total; 150 full-time (73% have doctorate/terminal degree); student-faculty ratio is 14:1.

Libraries 282,000 bound volumes, 17,000 titles on microform, 1,500 periodical subscriptions

Computing *Terminals/PCs available for student use:* 210, located in computer center, library, dormitories, all classroom buildings; PC not required.

Of Special Interest *Core academic program:* yes. Computer course required for accounting, management, science majors. Phi Beta Kappa chapter. Academic exchange program: no. Sponsors and participates in study-abroad programs.

On Campus Drama/theater group; student-run newspaper and radio station. *Social organizations:* 1 national fraternity, 9 local fraternities, 6 local sororities; 13% of eligible undergraduate men and 13% of eligible undergraduate women are members.

Athletics Member NCAA (Division III). *Intercollegiate sports:* baseball (M), basketball (M, W), cross-country running (M, W), football (M), golf (M, W), soccer (M, W), softball (W), swimming and diving (M, W), tennis (M, W), track and field (M, W), volleyball (W), wrestling (M).

Costs (1991–92) & Aid				
	Comprehensive fee	$13,900	Need-based scholarships (average)	$1531
	Tuition	$10,600	Non-need scholarships (average)	$1099
	Mandatory fees	N/App	Short-term loans (average)	$100
	Room and board	$3300	Long-term loans—college funds (average)	$1500
	Financial aid recipients	80%	Long-term loans—external funds (average)	$2200

Undergraduate Facts				
	Part-time	3%	*Freshman Data:* 1,301 applied, 89% were accepted, 50% (581) of those entered	
	State residents	37%		
	Transfers	3%	From top tenth of high school class	33%
	African-Americans	1%	SAT-takers scoring 600 or over on verbal	15%
	Native Americans	0%	SAT-takers scoring 700 or over on verbal	2%
	Hispanics	1%	SAT-takers scoring 600 or over on math	40%
	Asian-Americans	2%	SAT-takers scoring 700 or over on math	10%
	International students	6%	ACT-takers scoring 26 or over	37%
	Freshmen returning for sophomore year	88%	ACT-takers scoring 30 or over	9%
	Students completing degree within 5 years	78%	*Majors with most degrees conferred:* biology/ biological sciences, business, English.	
	Grads pursuing further study	20%		

Majors Accounting, African studies, anthropology, art education, art/fine arts, arts administration, biology/biological sciences, black/African-American studies, business, chemistry, classics, communication, computer science, cytotechnology, dance, (pre)dentistry sequence, economics, education, elementary education, engineering sciences, English, environmental biology, forestry, French, German, Greek, health education, Hebrew, history, interdisciplinary studies, international business, international studies, Latin, Latin American studies, (pre)law sequence, management information systems, marine biology, mathematics, medical technology, (pre)medicine sequence, modern languages, museum studies, music, music business, music education, nursing, occupational therapy, optometry, philosophy, physical education, physical therapy, physics, political science/government, psychobiology, psychology, religious studies, Scandinavian languages/studies, secondary education, social work, sociology, Spanish, special education, speech/rhetoric/public address/debate, sports administration, sports medicine, theater arts/drama, (pre)veterinary medicine sequence.

Applying *Required:* essay, high school transcript, 2 years of high school foreign language, 1 recommendation, 3 years of high school social science, SAT or ACT. *Recommended:* 3 years of high school math and science, interview. *Application deadlines:* 6/1, 3/1 priority date for financial aid. *Contact:* Dr. Dennis Johnson, Dean for Enrollment Management, 700 College Drive, Decorah, IA 52101, 319-387-1287 or toll-free 800-458-8437.

Macalester College

St. Paul, Minnesota

Founded 1874
Urban setting
Independent, Presbyterian
Coed
Awards B

Enrollment	1,858 total—all undergraduates (403 freshmen)
Faculty	185 total; 125 full-time (91% have doctorate/terminal degree); student-faculty ratio is 12:1.
Libraries	328,090 bound volumes, 53,388 titles on microform, 1,378 periodical subscriptions
Computing	*Terminals/PCs available for student use:* 400, located in library, dormitories, academic departments; PC not required but available for purchase. Campus network links student PCs. Students may purchase computers from college at an educational cost.
Of Special Interest	*Core academic program:* yes. Phi Beta Kappa chapter. Academic exchange with College of St. Catherine, College of St. Thomas, Augsburg College, Hamline University, Minneapolis College of Art and Design. Sponsors and participates in study-abroad programs. Cooperative Naval ROTC, cooperative Air Force ROTC.
On Campus	Drama/theater group; student-run newspaper and radio station. No national or local fraternities or sororities on campus.
Athletics	Member NCAA (Division III). *Intercollegiate sports:* basketball (M, W), crew (M, W), cross-country running (M, W), fencing (M, W), football (M), golf (M, W), rugby (M, W), skiing (cross-country) (M, W), soccer (M, W), softball (W), swimming and diving (M, W), tennis (M, W), track and field (M, W), volleyball (M, W), water polo (M, W).

Costs (1991–92) & Aid				
	Comprehensive fee	$17,314	Need-based scholarships (average)	$6409
	Tuition	$13,230	Non-need scholarships (average)	$2483
	Mandatory fees	$114	Short-term loans	N/Avail
	Room and board	$3970	Long-term loans—college funds	N/Avail
	Financial aid recipients	70%	Long-term loans—external funds (average)	$2530

Undergraduate Facts				
	Part-time	7%	*Freshman Data:* 2,360 applied, 58% were accepted, 30% (403) of those entered	
	State residents	24%		
	Transfers	2%	From top tenth of high school class	56%
	African-Americans	4%	SAT-takers scoring 600 or over on verbal	57%
	Native Americans	1%	SAT-takers scoring 700 or over on verbal	13%
	Hispanics	3%	SAT-takers scoring 600 or over on math	61%
	Asian-Americans	4%	SAT-takers scoring 700 or over on math	20%
	International students	12%	ACT-takers scoring 26 or over	86%
	Freshmen returning for sophomore year	92%	ACT-takers scoring 30 or over	42%
	Students completing degree within 5 years	N/R	*Majors with most degrees conferred:* political science/government, psychology, economics.	
	Grads pursuing further study	N/R		

Majors Anthropology, art/fine arts, art history, biology/biological sciences, chemistry, classics, computer science, East Asian studies, economics, English, environmental sciences, French, geography, geology, German, Greek, history, humanities, international studies, Latin, (pre)law sequence, linguistics, mathematics, (pre)medicine sequence, music, philosophy, physics, political science/government, psychology, religious studies, Russian, Russian and Slavic studies, science education, social science, sociology, Spanish, speech/rhetoric/public address/debate, studio art, theater arts/drama, urban studies, women's studies.

Applying *Required:* essay, high school transcript, 3 recommendations, SAT or ACT. *Recommended:* 3 years of high school math and science, 3 years of high school foreign language, campus interview, Achievements. *Application deadlines:* 2/1, 12/1 for early decision, 3/1 priority date for financial aid. *Contact:* Mr. William M. Shain, Dean of Admissions, 1600 Grand Avenue, St. Paul, MN 55105, 612-696-6357 or toll-free 800-231-7974.

✱ Marlboro College

Marlboro, Vermont

Founded 1947
Rural setting
Independent
Coed
Awards B, M

Enrollment 268 total—all undergraduates (51 freshmen)

Faculty 42 total; 38 full-time (62% have doctorate/terminal degree); student-faculty ratio is 8:1.

Libraries 57,000 bound volumes, 4,500 titles on microform, 192 periodical subscriptions

Computing *Terminals/PCs available for student use:* 15, located in computer center; PC not required.

Of Special Interest *Core academic program:* no. Academic exchange with School for International Training, Brattleboro School of Music. Participates in study-abroad programs.

On Campus Drama/theater group. No national or local fraternities or sororities on campus.

Athletics *Intercollegiate sports:* skiing (cross-country) (M, W), skiing (downhill) (M, W), soccer (M, W), softball (M, W), volleyball (M, W).

Costs (1991–92) & Aid				
Comprehensive fee	$20,570	Need-based scholarships (average)	$7000
Tuition	$15,000	Non-need scholarships	N/Avail
Mandatory fees	$420	Short-term loans (average)	$50
Room and board	$5150	Long-term loans—college funds (average)	$500
Financial aid recipients	65%	Long-term loans—external funds (average)	$3000

Undergraduate Facts			
Part-time	5%	*Freshman Data:* 189 applied, 74% were accepted, 36% (51) of those entered	
State residents	13%		
Transfers	30%	From top tenth of high school class	N/R
African-Americans	1%	SAT-takers scoring 600 or over on verbal	37%
Native Americans	0%	SAT-takers scoring 700 or over on verbal	3%
Hispanics	1%	SAT-takers scoring 600 or over on math	16%
Asian-Americans	0%	SAT-takers scoring 700 or over on math	2%
International students	6%	ACT-takers scoring 26 or over	N/R
Freshmen returning for sophomore year	80%	ACT-takers scoring 30 or over	N/R
Students completing degree within 5 years	40%		
Grads pursuing further study	N/R		

Majors African studies, American studies, anthropology, applied mathematics, art/fine arts, art history, Asian/Oriental studies, astronomy, astrophysics, behavioral sciences, biblical studies, biochemistry, biology/biological sciences, botany/plant sciences, cell biology, ceramic art and design, chemistry, child psychology/child development, classics, comparative literature, computer science, conservation, creative writing, dance, (pre)dentistry sequence, earth science, East Asian studies, East European and Soviet studies, ecology/environmental studies, economics, energy management technologies, English, environmental biology, environmental design, environmental education, environmental sciences, ethnic studies, European studies, experimental psychology, film studies, folklore, forestry, French, German, Greek, history, history of philosophy, human ecology, humanities, interdisciplinary studies, international economics, international studies, Italian, jazz, Latin, (pre)law sequence, linguistics, literature, marine biology, mathematics, (pre)medicine sequence, medieval studies, microbiology, modern languages, molecular biology, music, music history, natural sciences, painting/drawing, peace studies, philosophy, photography, physical sciences, physics, piano/organ, planetary and space sciences, political science/government, Portuguese, psychology, religious studies, Romance languages, Russian, sacred music, Scandinavian languages/studies, sculpture, social science, social work, sociology, solar technologies, Spanish, stringed instruments, studio art, theater arts/drama, (pre)veterinary medicine sequence, voice, wind and percussion instruments, women's studies, wood sciences.

Applying *Required:* essay, high school transcript, 1 recommendation, campus interview, sample of expository prose, SAT or ACT. *Recommended:* 3 years of high school math and science, some high school foreign language, Achievements, English Composition Test. *Application deadlines:* rolling, 12/1 for early decision, 1/15 for early action, 5/1 priority date for financial aid. *Contact:* Mr. Wayne Wood, Director of Admissions, South Road, Marlboro, VT 05344, 802-257-4333 Ext. 237 or toll-free 800-343-0049 (out-of-state).

Marquette University

Milwaukee, Wisconsin

Founded 1881
Urban setting
Independent, Roman Catholic (Jesuit)
Coed
Awards A, B, M, D

Enrollment 11,345 total; 8,409 undergraduates (1,600 freshmen)

Faculty 990 total; 573 full-time (92% have doctorate/terminal degree); student-faculty ratio is 14:1; grad assistants teach a few undergraduate courses.

Libraries 884,070 bound volumes, 701,103 titles on microform, 8,473 periodical subscriptions

Computing *Terminals/PCs available for student use:* 500, located in computer center, library, dormitories, labs, clusters; PC not required. Campus network links student PCs.

Of Special Interest *Core academic program:* yes. Computer course required for business administration, engineering, journalism, broadcast and electronic communication majors. Phi Beta Kappa, Sigma Xi chapters. Academic exchange with Milwaukee Institute of Art and Design. Sponsors and participates in study-abroad programs. Army ROTC, Naval ROTC, cooperative Air Force ROTC.

On Campus Drama/theater group; student-run newspaper and radio station. *Social organizations:* 9 national fraternities, 6 national sororities; 10% of eligible undergraduate men and 10% of eligible undergraduate women are members.

Athletics Member NCAA (Division I). *Intercollegiate sports:* baseball (M), basketball (M, W), crew (M, W), cross-country running (M, W), football (M), golf (M), ice hockey (M), lacrosse (M), rugby (M), sailing (M, W), skiing (downhill) (M, W), soccer (M, W), softball (W), swimming and diving (M, W), tennis (M, W), track and field (M, W), volleyball (M, W), wrestling (M). *Scholarships:* M, W.

Costs (1992–93) & Aid

Comprehensive fee	$14,284	
Tuition	$9900	
Mandatory fees	$34	
Room and board	$4350	
Financial aid recipients	85%	
Need-based scholarships		Avail
Non-need scholarships (average)		$1800
Short-term loans (average)		$200
Long-term loans—college funds (average)		$1000
Long-term loans—external funds (average)		$3500

Undergraduate Facts

Part-time	11%
State residents	55%
Transfers	N/R
African-Americans	4%
Native Americans	1%
Hispanics	3%
Asian-Americans	5%
International students	2%
Freshmen returning for sophomore year	88%
Students completing degree within 5 years	74%
Grads pursuing further study	22%

Freshman Data: 6,081 applied, 81% were accepted, 33% (1,600) of those entered

From top tenth of high school class	36%
SAT-takers scoring 600 or over on verbal	10%
SAT-takers scoring 700 or over on verbal	1%
SAT-takers scoring 600 or over on math	32%
SAT-takers scoring 700 or over on math	5%
ACT-takers scoring 26 or over	42%
ACT-takers scoring 30 or over	9%

Majors with most degrees conferred: marketing/retailing/merchandising, political science/government, accounting.

Majors Accounting, advertising, anthropology, bilingual/bicultural education, biochemistry, biology/biological sciences, biomedical engineering, broadcasting, business, business economics, chemistry, civil engineering, computer engineering, computer science, criminal justice, dental services, (pre)dentistry sequence, economics, education, electrical engineering, electronics engineering, elementary education, engineering (general), English, finance/banking, French, German, history, human development, humanities, human resources, industrial engineering, interdisciplinary studies, international business, international studies, journalism, Latin, (pre)law sequence, management information systems, marketing/retailing/merchandising, mathematics, mechanical engineering, medical laboratory technology, (pre)medicine sequence, middle school education, molecular biology, natural sciences, nursing, philosophy, physics, political science/government, psychology, public relations, secondary education, social science, social work, sociology, Spanish, speech pathology and audiology, speech/rhetoric/public address/debate, statistics, technical writing, theater arts/drama, theology.

Applying *Required:* high school transcript, SAT or ACT. *Recommended:* 3 years of high school science, 2 years of high school foreign language, interview. 3 years of high school math required for some. *Application deadlines:* rolling, 3/1 priority date for financial aid. *Contact:* Mr. Leo B. Flynn, Director of Admissions, 1217 West Wisconsin Avenue, Milwaukee, WI 53233, 414-288-7302 or toll-free 800-222-6544.

Maryville University of St. Louis

St. Louis, Missouri

Founded 1872
Suburban setting
Independent
Coed
Awards B, M

Enrollment 3,546 total; 2,902 undergraduates (125 freshmen)

Faculty 247 total; 77 full-time (78% have doctorate/terminal degree); student-faculty ratio is 14:1; grad assistants teach no undergraduate courses.

Libraries 90,000 bound volumes, 113,000 titles on microform, 600 periodical subscriptions

Computing *Terminals/PCs available for student use:* 46, located in computer center, library; PC not required.

Of Special Interest *Core academic program:* yes. Computer course required for business, health care management, information systems majors. Academic exchange with Fontbonne College, Lindenwood College, Webster University, Missouri Baptist College. Sponsors and participates in study-abroad programs. Cooperative Army ROTC.

On Campus Student-run newspaper. No national or local fraternities or sororities on campus.

Athletics Member NCAA (Division III). *Intercollegiate sports:* basketball (M, W), cross-country running (M, W), golf (M, W), soccer (M, W), tennis (M, W), track and field (M, W), volleyball (W).

Costs (1991–92) & Aid				
	Comprehensive fee	$11,650	Need-based scholarships (average)	$2306
	Tuition	$7800	Non-need scholarships (average)	$1476
	Mandatory fees	N/App	Short-term loans	N/Avail
	Room and board	$3850	Long-term loans—college funds	N/Avail
	Financial aid recipients	50%	Long-term loans—external funds	Avail

Undergraduate Facts				
	Part-time	64%	*Freshman Data:* 338 applied, 65% were accepted, 57% (125) of those entered	
	State residents	91%		
	Transfers	50%	From top tenth of high school class	33%
	African-Americans	5%	SAT-takers scoring 600 or over on verbal	N/R
	Native Americans	N/R	SAT-takers scoring 700 or over on verbal	N/R
	Hispanics	1%	SAT-takers scoring 600 or over on math	N/R
	Asian-Americans	4%	SAT-takers scoring 700 or over on math	N/R
	International students	5%	ACT-takers scoring 26 or over	39%
	Freshmen returning for sophomore year	70%	ACT-takers scoring 30 or over	11%
	Students completing degree within 5 years	50%	*Majors with most degrees conferred:* business, computer information systems, nursing.	
	Grads pursuing further study	12%		

Majors Accounting, actuarial science, art education, art/fine arts, biology/biological sciences, business, chemistry, communication, computer information systems, early childhood education, education, elementary education, English, health services administration, history, humanities, interior design, international studies, literature, management information systems, marketing/retailing/merchandising, mathematics, medical technology, (pre)medicine sequence, music, music education, music therapy, nursing, philosophy, physical therapy, political science/government, psychology, religious studies, science, science education, secondary education, sociology, studio art, voice.

Applying *Required:* high school transcript. *Recommended:* SAT. Essay, recommendations, campus interview, audition, portfolio, ACT required for some. *Application deadlines:* rolling, 3/1 priority date for financial aid. *Contact:* Mr. Ron Kronacher, Director of Admissions, Gander Hall, St. Louis, MO 63141, 314-576-9350 or toll-free 800-627-9855.

Mary Washington College

Fredericksburg, Virginia

Founded 1908
Small-town setting
State-supported
Coed
Awards B, M

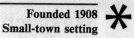

Enrollment 3,489 total; 3,426 undergraduates (715 freshmen)

Faculty 227 total; 170 full-time (85% have doctorate/terminal degree); student-faculty ratio is 17:1; grad assistants teach no undergraduate courses.

Libraries 330,000 bound volumes, 205,623 titles on microform, 1,700 periodical subscriptions

Computing *Terminals/PCs available for student use:* 110, located in computer center, library, computer labs; PC not required.

Of Special Interest *Core academic program:* yes. Computer course required for math majors. Phi Beta Kappa chapter. Academic exchange program: no. Participates in study-abroad programs.

On Campus Drama/theater group; student-run newspaper and radio station. No national or local fraternities or sororities on campus.

Athletics Member NCAA (Division III). *Intercollegiate sports:* baseball (M), basketball (M, W), crew (M, W), cross-country running (M, W), equestrian sports (M, W), field hockey (W), lacrosse (M, W), rugby (M, W), soccer (M, W), softball (W), swimming and diving (M, W), tennis (M, W), track and field (M, W), volleyball (W).

Costs (1991–92) & Aid				
State resident tuition	$1672	650 Need-based scholarships (average)	$1800
Nonresident tuition	$5130	75 Non-need scholarships (average)	$1820
Mandatory fees	$946	Short-term loans (average)	$50
Room and board	$4250	Long-term loans—college funds	N/Avail
Financial aid recipients	50%	Long-term loans—external funds (average)	$2300

Undergraduate Facts			
Part-time	20%	*Freshman Data:* 4,151 applied, 48% were accepted, 36% (715) of those entered	
State residents	69%		
Transfers	6%	From top tenth of high school class	41%
African-Americans	5%	SAT-takers scoring 600 or over on verbal	18%
Native Americans	0%	SAT-takers scoring 700 or over on verbal	2%
Hispanics	1%	SAT-takers scoring 600 or over on math	32%
Asian-Americans	2%	SAT-takers scoring 700 or over on math	3%
International students	1%	ACT-takers scoring 26 or over	N/App
Freshmen returning for sophomore year	92%	ACT-takers scoring 30 or over	N/App
Students completing degree within 5 years	72%	*Majors with most degrees conferred:* business, psychology, English.	
Grads pursuing further study	20%		

Majors American studies, art/fine arts, art history, biology/biological sciences, business, chemistry, classics, computer science, dance, (pre)dentistry sequence, economics, elementary education, English, environmental sciences, French, geography, geology, German, historic preservation, history, interdisciplinary studies, international studies, Latin, (pre)law sequence, liberal arts/general studies, mathematics, (pre)medicine sequence, modern languages, music, music education, philosophy, physics, political science/government, psychology, religious studies, secondary education, sociology, Spanish, studio art, theater arts/drama, (pre)veterinary medicine sequence.

Applying *Required:* essay, high school transcript, 3 years of high school math and science, 3 years of high school foreign language, SAT. *Recommended:* 3 Achievements, English Composition Test. *Application deadlines:* 2/1, 11/1 for early decision, 1/15 for early action, 3/1 for financial aid. *Contact:* Dr. Martin A. Wilder Jr., Vice-President for Admissions and Financial Aid, 1301 College Avenue, Fredericksburg, VA 22401, 703-899-4681 or toll-free 800-468-5614.

Massachusetts Institute of Technology
Cambridge, Massachusetts

Founded 1861
Urban setting
Independent
Coed
Awards B, M, D

Enrollment 9,628 total; 4,389 undergraduates (1,050 freshmen)

Faculty 985 total; 964 full-time (90% have doctorate/terminal degree); student-faculty ratio is 4:1; grad assistants teach a few undergraduate courses.

Libraries 2.1 million bound volumes, 1.6 million titles on microform, 21,402 periodical subscriptions

Computing *Terminals/PCs available for student use:* 1,200, located in computer center, student center, library, dormitories; PC not required. Campus network links student PCs.

Of Special Interest *Core academic program:* yes. Computer course required for electrical engineering, chemical engineering, civil engineering, aeronautics, astronautics majors. Phi Beta Kappa, Sigma Xi chapters. Academic exchange with Wellesley College, Harvard University. Participates in study-abroad programs. Army ROTC, Naval ROTC, Air Force ROTC.

On Campus Drama/theater group; student-run newspaper and radio station. *Social organizations:* 33 national fraternities, 4 national sororities, local fraternities, social clubs; 50% of eligible undergraduate men and 30% of eligible undergraduate women are members.

Athletics Member NCAA (Division III), NAIA. *Intercollegiate sports:* baseball (M), basketball (M, W), crew (M, W), cross-country running (M, W), fencing (M, W), field hockey (W), football (M), golf (M), gymnastics (M, W), ice hockey (M, W), lacrosse (M, W), riflery (M, W), rugby (M, W), sailing (M, W), skiing (cross-country) (M, W), skiing (downhill) (M, W), soccer (M, W), softball (W), squash (M), swimming and diving (M, W), tennis (M, W), track and field (M, W), volleyball (M, W), water polo (M), wrestling (M).

Costs (1991–92) & Aid				
	Comprehensive fee	$22,230	Need-based scholarships (average)	$10,870
	Tuition	$16,900	Non-need scholarships	N/Avail
	Mandatory fees	N/App	Short-term loans (average)	$600
	Room and board	$5330	Long-term loans—college funds (average)	$3850
	Financial aid recipients	60%	Long-term loans—external funds (average)	$3060

Undergraduate Facts				
	Part-time	1%	*Freshman Data:* 6,481 applied, 31% were accepted, 52% (1,050) of those entered	
	State residents	8%		
	Transfers	2%	From top tenth of high school class	94%
	African-Americans	6%	SAT-takers scoring 600 or over on verbal	68%
	Native Americans	1%	SAT-takers scoring 700 or over on verbal	18%
	Hispanics	8%	SAT-takers scoring 600 or over on math	99%
	Asian-Americans	21%	SAT-takers scoring 700 or over on math	81%
	International students	9%	ACT-takers scoring 26 or over	98%
	Freshmen returning for sophomore year	97%	ACT-takers scoring 30 or over	82%
	Students completing degree within 5 years	90%	*Majors with most degrees conferred:* electrical engineering, mechanical engineering, biology/biological sciences.	
	Grads pursuing further study	50%		

Majors Aerospace engineering, aerospace sciences, American studies, anthropology, applied mathematics, archaeology, architectural engineering, architecture, art history, astronomy, astrophysics, atmospheric sciences, bacteriology, biochemistry, bioengineering, biology/biological sciences, biomedical engineering, biophysics, business, business economics, cell biology, ceramic engineering, chemical engineering, chemistry, Chinese, city/community/regional planning, civil engineering, communication, computer engineering, computer information systems, computer programming, computer science, construction engineering, construction management, creative writing, (pre)dentistry sequence, drafting and design, earth science, economics, electrical engineering, electronics engineering, engineering (general), engineering and applied sciences, engineering design, engineering management, engineering physics, environmental design, environmental engineering, environmental sciences, film studies, fluid and thermal sciences, food sciences, French, genetics, geochemistry, geological engineering, geology, geophysical engineering, geophysics, German, health science, history, history of science, humanities, information science, interdisciplinary studies, international studies, Latin American studies, (pre)law sequence, liberal arts/general studies, linguistics, literature, manufacturing engineering, marine biology, marine engineering, materials engineering, materials sciences, mathematics, mechanical engineering, (pre)medicine sequence, medieval studies, metallurgical engineering, metallurgical technology, metallurgy, meteorology, microbiology, mining and mineral engineering, molecular biology, music, naval architecture, naval sciences, nuclear engineering, nuclear physics, nutrition, ocean engineering, pharmacy/pharmaceutical sciences, philosophy, photography, physical sciences, physics, physiology, planetary and space sciences, plastics engineering, political science/government, psychology, radio and television studies, robotics, Russian, Russian and Slavic studies, science, Spanish, statistics, systems science, technology and public affairs, theater arts/drama, transportation engineering, urban studies, (pre)veterinary medicine sequence, women's studies.

Applying *Required:* essay, high school transcript, 3 recommendations, interview, SAT or ACT, 3 Achievements. *Recommended:* 3 years of high school math and science, 1 year of high school foreign language. *Application deadlines:* 1/1, 11/1 for early action, 2/1 priority date for financial aid. *Contact:* Mr. Michael C. Behnke, Director of Admissions, 77 Massachusetts Avenue, Room 3-107, Cambridge, MA 02139, 617-253-4791.

Messiah College

Grantham, Pennsylvania

Founded 1909
Small-town setting
Independent/affiliated with Brethren in Christ Church
Coed
Awards B

Enrollment	2,259 total—all undergraduates (560 freshmen)
Faculty	182 total; 127 full-time (66% have doctorate/terminal degree); student-faculty ratio is 18:1.
Libraries	180,000 bound volumes, 5,000 titles on microform, 1,000 periodical subscriptions
Computing	*Terminals/PCs available for student use:* 250, located in computer center, library; PC not required. Campus network links student PCs.
Of Special Interest	*Core academic program:* yes. Computer course required for business, accounting, math, science, engineering majors. Sigma Xi chapter. Academic exchange with 13 members of the Christian College Consortium. Sponsors and participates in study-abroad programs.
On Campus	Mandatory chapel; drama/theater group; student-run newspaper and radio station. No national or local fraternities or sororities on campus.
Athletics	Member NCAA (Division III). *Intercollegiate sports:* baseball (M), basketball (M, W), cross-country running (M, W), field hockey (W), golf (M), soccer (M, W), softball (W), tennis (M, W), track and field (M, W), volleyball (W), wrestling (M).

Costs (1991–92) & Aid	Comprehensive fee	$13,080	Need-based scholarships (average)	$1500
	Tuition	$8620	Non-need scholarships (average)	$1275
	Mandatory fees	$80	Short-term loans	N/Avail
	Room and board	$4380	Long-term loans—college funds	N/Avail
	Financial aid recipients	86%	Long-term loans—external funds (average)	$2500

Under- graduate Facts	Part-time	3%	*Freshman Data:* 1,456 applied, 81% were accepted, 48% (560) of those entered	
	State residents	49%		
	Transfers	5%	From top tenth of high school class	48%
	African-Americans	3%	SAT-takers scoring 600 or over on verbal	32%
	Native Americans	0%	SAT-takers scoring 700 or over on verbal	9%
	Hispanics	2%	SAT-takers scoring 600 or over on math	50%
	Asian-Americans	3%	SAT-takers scoring 700 or over on math	17%
	International students	1%	ACT-takers scoring 26 or over	98%
	Freshmen returning for sophomore year	86%	ACT-takers scoring 30 or over	2%
	Students completing degree within 5 years	70%	*Majors with most degrees conferred:* business, natural sciences, education.	
	Grads pursuing further study	N/R		

Majors Accounting, art/fine arts, art history, behavioral sciences, biblical studies, business, chemistry, civil engineering technology, clinical psychology, communication, computer information systems, computer science, dietetics, early childhood education, education, elementary education, English, experimental psychology, family services, French, geography, German, history, home economics, humanities, human resources, journalism, (pre)law sequence, liberal arts/general studies, marketing/retailing/merchandising, mathematics, medical technology, (pre)medicine sequence, modern languages, music, music education, natural sciences, nursing, pastoral studies, physical education, physics, psychology, radio and television studies, recreation and leisure services, religious education, religious studies, secondary education, social science, social work, sociology, Spanish, speech/rhetoric/public address/debate, sports medicine, stringed instruments, theology, (pre)veterinary medicine sequence, voice.

Applying *Required:* essay, high school transcript, 2 recommendations, SAT or ACT. *Recommended:* 3 years of high school math and science. Some high school foreign language required for some. *Application deadlines:* rolling, 4/1 priority date for financial aid. *Contact:* Mr. Ron E. Long, Vice President for Communications, Old Main Building, Grantham, PA 17027, 717-766-2511 Ext. 6000 or toll-free 800-382-1349 (in-state), 800-233-4220 (out-of-state).

✻ Miami University

Oxford, Ohio

Founded 1809
Small-town setting
State-supported
Coed
Awards B, M, D

Enrollment	16,331 total; 14,688 undergraduates (3,290 freshmen)
Faculty	873 total; 763 full-time; student-faculty ratio is 21:1; grad assistants teach a few undergraduate courses.
Libraries	1.1 million bound volumes, 1.7 million titles on microform, 6,000 periodical subscriptions
Computing	*Terminals/PCs available for student use:* 500, located in library, academic buildings; PC not required.
Of Special Interest	*Core academic program:* yes. Computer course required for business, applied science majors. Phi Beta Kappa, Sigma Xi chapters. Academic exchange with Greater Cincinnati Consortium of Colleges and Universities. Sponsors and participates in study-abroad programs. Naval ROTC, Air Force ROTC.
On Campus	Drama/theater group; student-run newspaper and radio station. *Social organizations:* 28 national fraternities, 22 national sororities; 33% of eligible undergraduate men and 35% of eligible undergraduate women are members.
Athletics	Member NCAA (Division I). *Intercollegiate sports:* archery (M, W), basketball (M, W), cross-country running (M, W), equestrian sports (M, W), field hockey (W), football (M), golf (M), gymnastics (M, W), ice hockey (M), lacrosse (M), riflery (M, W), rugby (M), sailing (M, W), soccer (M, W), swimming and diving (M, W), tennis (M, W), track and field (M, W), volleyball (W), wrestling (M). *Scholarships:* M, W.

Costs (1991–92) & Aid				
	State resident tuition	$3764	Need-based scholarships	Avail
	Nonresident tuition	$8054	1400 Non-need scholarships (average)	$950
	Mandatory fees	N/App	Short-term loans (average)	$300
	Room and board	$3620	Long-term loans—college funds (average)	$1275
	Financial aid recipients	40%	Long-term loans—external funds (average)	$2100

Undergraduate Facts				
	Part-time	5%	*Freshman Data:* 8,773 applied, 82% were accepted, 46% (3,290) of those entered	
	State residents	73%		
	Transfers	2%	From top tenth of high school class	45%
	African-Americans	3%	SAT-takers scoring 600 or over on verbal	16%
	Native Americans	0%	SAT-takers scoring 700 or over on verbal	1%
	Hispanics	1%	SAT-takers scoring 600 or over on math	47%
	Asian-Americans	1%	SAT-takers scoring 700 or over on math	6%
	International students	1%	ACT-takers scoring 26 or over	52%
	Freshmen returning for sophomore year	92%	ACT-takers scoring 30 or over	10%
	Students completing degree within 5 years	72%	*Majors with most degrees conferred:* marketing/retailing/merchandising, finance/banking, accounting.	
	Grads pursuing further study	N/R		

Majors Accounting, aerospace sciences, American studies, anthropology, art education, art/fine arts, black/African-American studies, botany/plant sciences, broadcasting, business, business economics, business education, chemistry, child care/child and family studies, classics, communication, computer science, consumer services, creative writing, dietetics, early childhood education, earth science, economics, education, elementary education, English, environmental design, family and consumer studies, family services, finance/banking, food services management, French, geography, geology, German, Greek, health education, history, home economics, home economics education, interdisciplinary studies, interior design, international studies, journalism, landscape architecture/design, Latin, linguistics, marketing/retailing/merchandising, mathematics, medical technology, microbiology, music, music education, nursing, paper and pulp sciences, philosophy, physical education, physics, political science/government, psychology, public administration, public relations, Russian, science education, secondary education, secretarial studies/office management, sociology, Spanish, special education, speech pathology and audiology, speech/rhetoric/public address/debate, speech therapy, sports medicine, studio art, systems science, theater arts/drama, urban studies, zoology.

Applying *Required:* high school transcript, 3 years of high school math and science, 2 years of high school foreign language, SAT or ACT. *Recommended:* essay. *Application deadlines:* 1/31, 11/1 for early decision, 3/1 priority date for financial aid. *Contact:* Mr. James S. McCoy, Assistant Vice President for Enrollment Services, Oxford, OH 45056, 513-529-2531.

Michigan State University

East Lansing, Michigan

Founded 1855
Small-town setting
State-supported
Coed
Awards B, M, D

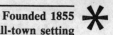

Enrollment	42,088 total; 33,684 undergraduates (6,116 freshmen)
Faculty	4,123 total; 3,550 full-time (94% have doctorate/terminal degree); grad assistants teach a few undergraduate courses.
Libraries	2.8 million bound volumes, 220,005 titles on microform, 28,142 periodical subscriptions
Computing	*Terminals/PCs available for student use:* 2,500, located in computer center, library, dormitories; PC not required. Campus network links student PCs.
Of Special Interest	*Core academic program:* yes. Computer course required for agriculture, business, communication, engineering, natural science majors. Phi Beta Kappa, Sigma Xi chapters. Sponsors and participates in study-abroad programs. Army ROTC, Air Force ROTC.
On Campus	Drama/theater group; student-run newspaper and radio station. *Social organizations:* 31 national fraternities, 22 national sororities; 10% of eligible undergraduate men and 10% of eligible undergraduate women are members.
Athletics	Member NCAA (Division I). *Intercollegiate sports:* baseball (M), basketball (M, W), cross-country running (M, W), equestrian sports (M, W), fencing (M), field hockey (W), football (M), golf (M, W), gymnastics (M, W), ice hockey (M), lacrosse (M), soccer (M), swimming and diving (M, W), tennis (M, W), track and field (M, W), volleyball (W), wrestling (M). *Scholarships:* M, W.

Costs (1991–92) & Aid				
	State resident tuition	$3139	26201 Need-based scholarships (average)	$385
	Nonresident tuition	$8359	1500 Non-need scholarships (average)	$1000
	Mandatory fees	$335	Short-term loans (average)	$785
	Room and board	$3375	Long-term loans—college funds	N/Avail
	Financial aid recipients	60%	Long-term loans—external funds (average)	$2273

Undergraduate Facts				
	Part-time	10%	*Freshman Data:* 18,856 applied, 78% were accepted, 41% (6,116) of those entered	
	State residents	91%		
	Transfers	6%	From top tenth of high school class	25%
	African-Americans	8%	SAT-takers scoring 600 or over on verbal	9%
	Native Americans	1%	SAT-takers scoring 700 or over on verbal	1%
	Hispanics	2%	SAT-takers scoring 600 or over on math	23%
	Asian-Americans	3%	SAT-takers scoring 700 or over on math	5%
	International students	1%	ACT-takers scoring 26 or over	16%
	Freshmen returning for sophomore year	89%	ACT-takers scoring 30 or over	2%
	Students completing degree within 5 years	61%	*Majors with most degrees conferred:* accounting, communication, finance/banking.	
	Grads pursuing further study	N/R		

Majors Accounting, advertising, agricultural business, agricultural economics, agricultural engineering, agricultural sciences, agronomy/soil and crop sciences, American studies, animal sciences, anthropology, art/fine arts, art history, astrophysics, biochemistry, biology/biological sciences, botany/plant sciences, business, chemical engineering, chemistry, child psychology/child development, Chinese, civil engineering, classics, communication, computer engineering, computer science, construction management, criminal justice, dietetics, early childhood education, earth science, economics, education, electrical engineering, elementary education, engineering (general), engineering mechanics, engineering technology, English, entomology, environmental education, environmental sciences, family and consumer studies, family services, fashion merchandising, finance/banking, fish and game management, food sciences, food services management, food services technology, forestry, French, geography, geology, geophysics, German, health education, history, home economics education, horticulture, hotel and restaurant management, human ecology, humanities, human resources, interior design, Italian, Japanese, journalism, laboratory technologies, landscape architecture/design, Latin, (pre)law sequence, linguistics, manufacturing technology, marketing/retailing/merchandising, materials engineering, materials sciences, mathematics, mechanical engineering, medical technology, microbiology, music, music education, music therapy, natural resource management, nursing, nutrition, parks management, philosophy, physical education, physical sciences, physics, physiology, political science/government, psychology, public administration, public affairs and policy studies, purchasing/inventory management, religious studies, Russian, science, social science, social work, sociology, Spanish, special education, speech pathology and audiology, statistics, studio art, telecommunications, textiles and clothing, theater arts/drama, tourism and travel, transportation technologies, urban studies, (pre)veterinary medicine sequence, veterinary sciences, wildlife management, zoology.

Applying *Required:* high school transcript, SAT or ACT. *Application deadlines:* 8/1, continuous processing for financial aid. *Contact:* Dr. William H. Turner, Director of Admissions, 250 Administration Building, East Lansing, MI 48824, 517-355-8332.

From the College Michigan State's distinguishing characteristics include students, programs, and activities rich in diversity; a beautiful park-like campus; the nation's largest, most comprehensive residence hall system; two small residential colleges; a distinctive Honors College; the nation's most competitive scholarship program; and early undergraduate research opportunities.

Michigan Technological University

Houghton, Michigan

Founded 1885
Small-town setting
State-supported
Coed
Awards A, B, M, D

Enrollment 6,921 total; 6,355 undergraduates (1,295 freshmen)

Faculty 369 total; 342 full-time (78% have doctorate/terminal degree); student-faculty ratio is 15:1; grad assistants teach a few undergraduate courses.

Libraries 780,902 bound volumes, 3,842 periodical subscriptions

Computing *Terminals/PCs available for student use:* 410, located in computer center, dormitories, computer labs; PC not required but available for purchase.

Of Special Interest *Core academic program:* yes. Computer course required. Sigma Xi chapter. Academic exchange with Central Michigan University, Northwestern Michigan College, Delta College. Sponsors and participates in study-abroad programs. Army ROTC, Air Force ROTC.

On Campus Drama/theater group; student-run newspaper and radio station. *Social organizations:* 11 national fraternities, 4 national sororities, 4 local fraternities, 4 local sororities, social clubs; 11% of eligible undergraduate men and 15% of eligible undergraduate women are members.

Athletics Member NCAA (Division II). *Intercollegiate sports:* basketball (M, W), cross-country running (M, W), football (M), ice hockey (M), skiing (cross-country) (M, W), swimming and diving (M, W), tennis (M, W), track and field (M, W), volleyball (W). *Scholarships:* M, W.

Costs (1991–92) & Aid				
State resident tuition	$2781	1106 Need-based scholarships (average)	$797
Nonresident tuition	$6420	2668 Non-need scholarships (average)	$988
Mandatory fees	$135	Short-term loans (average)	$234
Room and board	$3390	Long-term loans—college funds (average)	$1098
Financial aid recipients	73%	Long-term loans—external funds (average)	$1857

Undergraduate Facts			
Part-time	7%	*Freshman Data:* 2,746 applied, 96% were accepted, 49% (1,295) of those entered	
State residents	80%		
Transfers	23%	From top tenth of high school class	37%
African-Americans	1%	SAT-takers scoring 600 or over on verbal	11%
Native Americans	1%	SAT-takers scoring 700 or over on verbal	1%
Hispanics	1%	SAT-takers scoring 600 or over on math	51%
Asian-Americans	1%	SAT-takers scoring 700 or over on math	13%
International students	4%	ACT-takers scoring 26 or over	43%
Freshmen returning for sophomore year	84%	ACT-takers scoring 30 or over	10%
Students completing degree within 5 years	52%		
Grads pursuing further study	N/R		

Majors Accounting, applied mathematics, biochemistry, bioengineering, biology/biological sciences, biomedical engineering, biotechnology, business, business economics, chemical engineering, chemistry, civil engineering, computer engineering, computer information systems, computer programming, computer science, construction engineering, (pre)dentistry sequence, earth science, ecology/environmental studies, electrical engineering, electronics engineering, engineering (general), engineering mechanics, engineering physics, English, environmental engineering, forestry, geological engineering, geology, geophysical engineering, history, labor and industrial relations, liberal arts/general studies, management information systems, marketing/retailing/merchandising, materials sciences, mathematics, mechanical engineering, medical technology, (pre)medicine sequence, metallurgical engineering, microbiology, mining and mineral engineering, physical sciences, physics, polymer science, science education, secondary education, social science, statistics, surveying engineering, technical writing, transportation engineering, (pre)veterinary medicine sequence, water resources, wood sciences.

Applying *Required:* high school transcript. *Recommended:* 3 years of high school science, some high school foreign language, interview, SAT or ACT, Achievements, English Composition Test (with essay). 3 years of high school math required for some. *Application deadlines:* rolling, 3/1 for financial aid. *Contact:* Mr. Joseph Galetto, Director of Enrollment Management, 1400 Townsend Drive, Houghton, MI 49931, 906-487-2335.

Middlebury College

Middlebury, Vermont

Founded 1800
Rural setting
Independent
Coed

Awards B, M, D (M, D in summer institutes only)

Enrollment	1,960 total—all undergraduates (555 freshmen)
Faculty	220 total; 180 full-time (90% have doctorate/terminal degree); student-faculty ratio is 11:1.
Libraries	650,044 bound volumes, 70,098 titles on microform, 1,984 periodical subscriptions
Computing	*Terminals/PCs available for student use:* 200, located in computer center, library, dormitories; PC not required.
Of Special Interest	*Core academic program:* yes. Computer course required for math majors. Phi Beta Kappa chapter. Academic exchange with Swarthmore College, Berea College, Bucknell University, Eckerd College, St. Olaf College, American University (Washington Semester), Williams College (Mystic Seaport Program in American Maritime Studies), Institute for Architecture and Urban Studies. Sponsors and participates in study-abroad programs. Cooperative Army ROTC.
On Campus	Drama/theater group; student-run newspaper and radio station. No national or local fraternities or sororities on campus.
Athletics	Member NCAA (Division III). *Intercollegiate sports:* baseball (M), basketball (M, W), cross-country running (M, W), field hockey (W), football (M), golf (M), ice hockey (M, W), lacrosse (M, W), skiing (cross-country) (M, W), skiing (downhill) (M, W), soccer (M, W), squash (W), swimming and diving (M, W), tennis (M, W), track and field (M, W).

Costs (1991–92) & Aid	Comprehensive fee	$21,200	Need-based scholarships (average)	$11,473
	Tuition	N/App	Non-need scholarships	N/Avail
	Mandatory fees	N/App	Short-term loans	N/Avail
	Room and board	N/App	Long-term loans—college funds (average)	$1950
	Financial aid recipients	35%	Long-term loans—external funds	Avail

Undergraduate Facts	Part-time	1%	*Freshman Data:* 3,925 applied, 31% were accepted, 46% (555) of those entered	
	State residents	5%		
	Transfers	1%	From top tenth of high school class	65%
	African-Americans	4%	SAT-takers scoring 600 or over on verbal	N/R
	Native Americans	1%	SAT-takers scoring 700 or over on verbal	N/R
	Hispanics	3%	SAT-takers scoring 600 or over on math	N/R
	Asian-Americans	4%	SAT-takers scoring 700 or over on math	N/R
	International students	3%	ACT-takers scoring 26 or over	N/R
	Freshmen returning for sophomore year	98%	ACT-takers scoring 30 or over	N/R
	Students completing degree within 5 years	90%	*Majors with most degrees conferred:* English, political science/government, history.	
	Grads pursuing further study	N/R		

Majors American studies, anthropology, art/fine arts, biochemistry, biology/biological sciences, chemistry, Chinese, classics, computer science, dance, (pre)dentistry sequence, East Asian studies, East European and Soviet studies, ecology/environmental studies, economics, English, environmental sciences, film studies, French, geography, geology, German, history, international economics, international studies, Italian, Japanese, (pre)law sequence, literature, mathematics, (pre)medicine sequence, molecular biology, music, philosophy, physics, political science/government, psychology, religious studies, Russian, Russian and Slavic studies, sociology, Spanish, theater arts/drama, (pre)veterinary medicine sequence, women's studies.

Applying *Required:* high school transcript, ACT or SAT and 3 College Board Achievement Tests (including English Composition Test) or 5 College Board Achievement Tests (including English Composition Test with or without essay). *Recommended:* 4 years of high school math, 4 years of high school foreign language, interview. *Application deadlines:* 1/15, 11/15 for early decision, 2/1 priority date for financial aid. *Contact:* Mr. Geoff Smith, Director of Admissions, 131 South Main, Middlebury, VT 05753, 802-388-3711 Ext. 5153.

✻ Millikin University

Decatur, Illinois

Founded 1901
Suburban setting
Independent/affiliated with Presbyterian Church (U.S.A.)
Coed
Awards B

Enrollment 1,841 total—all undergraduates (425 freshmen)

Faculty 185 total; 118 full-time (61% have doctorate/terminal degree); student-faculty ratio is 15:1.

Libraries 169,798 bound volumes, 17,800 titles on microform, 963 periodical subscriptions

Computing *Terminals/PCs available for student use:* 110, located in computer center, specialized labs; PC not required. Campus network links student PCs.

Of Special Interest *Core academic program:* yes. Computer course required for business, math education majors. Academic exchange program: no. Participates in study-abroad programs.

On Campus Drama/theater group; student-run newspaper and radio station. *Social organizations:* 5 national fraternities, 4 national sororities; 27% of eligible undergraduate men and 25% of eligible undergraduate women are members.

Athletics Member NCAA (Division III). *Intercollegiate sports:* baseball (M), basketball (M, W), cross-country running (M, W), football (M), golf (M), soccer (M), softball (W), swimming and diving (M, W), tennis (M, W), track and field (M, W), volleyball (W), wrestling (M).

Costs (1992–93) & Aid				
	Comprehensive fee	$14,637	Need-based scholarships (average)	$3565
	Tuition	$10,590	Non-need scholarships (average)	$2525
	Mandatory fees	$91	Short-term loans (average)	$250
	Room and board	$3956	Long-term loans—college funds (average)	$2350
	Financial aid recipients	87%	Long-term loans—external funds (average)	$2332

Undergraduate Facts				
	Part-time	5%	*Freshman Data:* 1,181 applied, 92% were accepted, 39% (425) of those entered	
	State residents	89%		
	Transfers	20%	From top tenth of high school class	26%
	African-Americans	3%	SAT-takers scoring 600 or over on verbal	7%
	Native Americans	1%	SAT-takers scoring 700 or over on verbal	1%
	Hispanics	1%	SAT-takers scoring 600 or over on math	20%
	Asian-Americans	1%	SAT-takers scoring 700 or over on math	4%
	International students	1%	ACT-takers scoring 26 or over	29%
	Freshmen returning for sophomore year	83%	ACT-takers scoring 30 or over	7%
	Students completing degree within 5 years	58%	*Majors with most degrees conferred:* accounting, nursing, elementary education.	
	Grads pursuing further study	14%		

Majors Accounting, American studies, art education, art/fine arts, arts administration, art therapy, behavioral sciences, biology/biological sciences, business, business economics, chemistry, commercial art, communication, computer management, computer science, creative writing, economics, education, elementary education, English, environmental biology, finance/banking, French, German, history, human resources, human services, international business, international studies, jazz, (pre)law sequence, liberal arts/general studies, marketing/retailing/merchandising, mathematics, medical technology, (pre)medicine sequence, modern languages, music, music education, nursing, philosophy, physical education, physical sciences, physics, political science/government, psychology, religious studies, sacred music, science, science education, secondary education, social science, sociology, Spanish, theater arts/drama, (pre)veterinary medicine sequence, voice.

Applying *Required:* high school transcript, 3 recommendations, SAT or ACT. *Recommended:* 3 years of high school math and science, some high school foreign language, interview. *Application deadlines:* rolling, 8/1 priority date for financial aid. *Contact:* Mr. James Kettelkamp, Dean of Admissions, 1184 West Main Street, Decatur, IL 62522, 217-424-6210 or toll-free 800-373-7733.

Millsaps College

Jackson, Mississippi

Founded 1890
Urban setting
Independent, United Methodist
Coed
Awards B, M

Enrollment	1,421 total; 1,280 undergraduates (273 freshmen)
Faculty	105 total; 90 full-time (84% have doctorate/terminal degree); student-faculty ratio is 14:1; grad assistants teach no undergraduate courses.
Libraries	249,875 bound volumes, 16,007 titles on microform, 895 periodical subscriptions
Computing	*Terminals/PCs available for student use:* 125, located in computer center, dormitories, student labs; PC not required. Campus network links student PCs.
Of Special Interest	*Core academic program:* yes. Computer course required for business majors. Phi Beta Kappa chapter. Academic exchange with Georgetown University, American University, Drew University, Institute of European Studies. Participates in study-abroad programs. Cooperative Army ROTC.
On Campus	Drama/theater group; student-run newspaper. *Social organizations:* 6 national fraternities, 5 national sororities; 62% of eligible undergraduate men and 61% of eligible undergraduate women are members.
Athletics	Member NCAA (Division III). *Intercollegiate sports:* baseball (M), basketball (M, W), cross-country running (M, W), football (M), golf (M), soccer (M, W), tennis (M, W), volleyball (W).

Costs (1991–92) & Aid				
	Comprehensive fee	$13,345	Need-based scholarships (average)	$5276
	Tuition	$9510	Non-need scholarships (average)	$4100
	Mandatory fees	$200	Short-term loans (average)	$500
	Room and board	$3635	Long-term loans—college funds (average)	$2500
	Financial aid recipients	64%	Long-term loans—external funds (average)	$3000

Undergraduate Facts				
	Part-time	13%	*Freshman Data:* 772 applied, 88% were accepted, 40% (273) of those entered	
	State residents	65%		
	Transfers	5%	From top tenth of high school class	32%
	African-Americans	5%	SAT-takers scoring 600 or over on verbal	25%
	Native Americans	0%	SAT-takers scoring 700 or over on verbal	2%
	Hispanics	2%	SAT-takers scoring 600 or over on math	19%
	Asian-Americans	1%	SAT-takers scoring 700 or over on math	1%
	International students	1%	ACT-takers scoring 26 or over	43%
	Freshmen returning for sophomore year	83%	ACT-takers scoring 30 or over	8%
	Students completing degree within 5 years	53%	*Majors with most degrees conferred:* English, business, accounting.	
	Grads pursuing further study	42%		

Majors Accounting, art/fine arts, biology/biological sciences, business, chemistry, classics, computer science, economics, education, elementary education, English, French, geology, Greek, history, Latin, mathematics, music, music education, philosophy, physics, piano/organ, political science/government, psychology, religious studies, sacred music, sociology, Spanish, theater arts/drama, voice.

Applying *Required:* essay, high school transcript, SAT or ACT. *Recommended:* 3 years of high school math and science, recommendations, interview, Achievements. *Application deadlines:* 4/1, 3/1 priority date for financial aid. *Contact:* Mr. Gary L. Fretwell, Vice President, Enrollment and Student Services, 1701 North State Street, Jackson, MS 39210, 601-974-1050.

✱ **Mills College**

Oakland, California

Founded 1852
Urban setting
Independent
Women
Awards B, M

Enrollment	1,064 total; 772 undergraduates (152 freshmen)	
Faculty	151 total; 70 full-time (77% have doctorate/terminal degree); student-faculty ratio is 8:1; grad assistants teach a few undergraduate courses.	
Libraries	201,916 bound volumes, 7,657 titles on microform, 650 periodical subscriptions	
Computing	*Terminals/PCs available for student use:* 117, located in computer center, student center, library, dormitories, student lounge, academic buildings; PC not required. Campus network links student PCs.	
Of Special Interest	*Core academic program:* yes. Computer course required for math majors. Phi Beta Kappa chapter. Academic exchange with University of California at Berkeley, California State University at Hayward, Sonoma State University, 9 other California colleges, American University (Washington Semester), Agnes Scott College, Barnard College, Fisk University, Hollins College, Howard University, Manhattanville College, Mount Holyoke College, Simmons College, Spelman College, Swarthmore. Participates in study-abroad programs.	
On Campus	Drama/theater group; student-run newspaper. No national or local sororities on campus.	
Athletics	Member NCAA (Division III). *Intercollegiate sports:* basketball, crew, cross-country running, tennis, volleyball.	

Costs (1991–92) & Aid	Comprehensive fee	$19,210	Need-based scholarships (average)	$6817
	Tuition	$13,400	Non-need scholarships (average)	$6651
	Mandatory fees	$110	Short-term loans	N/Avail
	Room and board	$5700	Long-term loans—college funds	N/Avail
	Financial aid recipients	70%	Long-term loans—external funds (average)	$3767

Undergraduate Facts	Part-time	4%	*Freshman Data:* 484 applied, 78% were accepted, 40% (152) of those entered	
	State residents	69%		
	Transfers	25%	From top tenth of high school class	30%
	African-Americans	8%	SAT-takers scoring 600 or over on verbal	26%
	Native Americans	1%	SAT-takers scoring 700 or over on verbal	3%
	Hispanics	4%	SAT-takers scoring 600 or over on math	24%
	Asian-Americans	9%	SAT-takers scoring 700 or over on math	2%
	International students	6%	ACT-takers scoring 26 or over	30%
	Freshmen returning for sophomore year	77%	ACT-takers scoring 30 or over	10%
	Students completing degree within 5 years	63%	*Majors with most degrees conferred:* political, legal, and economic analysis, English, communication.	
	Grads pursuing further study	20%		

Majors American studies, anthropology, art/fine arts, art history, biochemistry, biology/biological sciences, business economics, chemistry, child psychology/child development, communication, comparative literature, computer science, creative writing, dance, early childhood education, economics, education, elementary education, English, environmental sciences, ethnic studies, French, Germanic languages and literature, Hispanic studies, history, international studies, liberal arts/general studies, mathematics, (pre)medicine sequence, music, philosophy, political, legal, and economic analysis, psychology, social science, sociology, statistics, studio art, theater arts/drama, women's studies.

Applying *Required:* essay, high school transcript, 3 recommendations, submit graded paper in place of essay, SAT. *Recommended:* 3 years of high school math and science, 2 years of high school foreign language, interview, 3 Achievements, English Composition Test (with essay). ACT required for some. *Application deadlines:* rolling, 2/15 priority date for financial aid. *Contact:* Ms. Genevieve Ann Flaherty, Dean, Admission and Financial Aid, 5000 MacArthur Boulevard, Oakland, CA 94613, 510-430-2135 or toll-free 800-87-MILLS.

Milwaukee School of Engineering

Milwaukee, Wisconsin

Founded 1903
Urban setting
Independent
Coed
Awards A, B, M

Enrollment 3,183 total; 2,834 undergraduates (551 freshmen)

Faculty 205 total; 105 full-time (35% have doctorate/terminal degree); student-faculty ratio is 17:1; grad assistants teach no undergraduate courses.

Libraries 60,000 bound volumes, 675 periodical subscriptions

Computing *Terminals/PCs available for student use:* 150, located in computer center, student center, library, classrooms, labs; PC not required. Campus network links student PCs.

Of Special Interest *Core academic program:* yes. Computer course required. Academic exchange program: no. Study-abroad programs: no. Air Force ROTC, cooperative Army ROTC.

On Campus Drama/theater group; student-run newspaper and radio station. *Social organizations:* 2 national fraternities, 4 local fraternities, 2 local sororities; 10% of eligible undergraduate men and 15% of eligible undergraduate women are members.

Athletics Member NAIA. *Intercollegiate sports:* baseball (M), basketball (M, W), cross-country running (M, W), golf (M), ice hockey (M), soccer (M), softball (W), volleyball (W), wrestling (M).

Costs (1992–93) & Aid				
	Comprehensive fee	$12,960	Need-based scholarships	Avail
	Tuition	$9960	Non-need scholarships (average)	$3200
	Mandatory fees	N/App	Short-term loans	Avail
	Room and board	$3000	Long-term loans—college funds (average)	$2500
	Financial aid recipients	84%	Long-term loans—external funds (average)	$2500

Undergraduate Facts				
	Part-time	5%	*Freshman Data:* 1,190 applied, 85% were accepted, 55% (551) of those entered	
	State residents	75%		
	Transfers	25%	From top tenth of high school class	35%
	African-Americans	3%	SAT-takers scoring 600 or over on verbal	N/R
	Native Americans	1%	SAT-takers scoring 700 or over on verbal	N/R
	Hispanics	2%	SAT-takers scoring 600 or over on math	N/R
	Asian-Americans	3%	SAT-takers scoring 700 or over on math	N/R
	International students	3%	ACT-takers scoring 26 or over	42%
	Freshmen returning for sophomore year	73%	ACT-takers scoring 30 or over	10%
	Students completing degree within 5 years	55%	*Majors with most degrees conferred:* electrical engineering, mechanical engineering, architectural engineering.	
	Grads pursuing further study	8%		

Majors Architectural engineering, biomedical engineering, business, computer engineering, electrical engineering, electrical engineering technology, industrial administration, industrial engineering, manufacturing technology, mechanical engineering, mechanical engineering technology, technical writing.

Applying *Required:* essay, high school transcript, SAT or ACT. *Recommended:* 3 years of high school math, 2 years of high school foreign language, 1 recommendation, interview. 3 years of high school science required for some. *Application deadlines:* rolling, 4/1 priority date for financial aid. *Contact:* Mr. T. Owen Smith, Dean of Admissions, Milwaukee, WI 53201, 414-277-7202 or toll-free 800-332-6763.

Monmouth College

Monmouth, Illinois

Founded 1853
Small-town setting
Independent/affiliated with Presbyterian Church
Coed
Awards B

Enrollment 725 total—all undergraduates (282 freshmen)

Faculty 77 total; 55 full-time (93% have doctorate/terminal degree); student-faculty ratio is 10:1.

Libraries 185,000 bound volumes, 67,000 titles on microform, 800 periodical subscriptions

Computing *Terminals/PCs available for student use:* 88, located in computer center, library; PC not required.

Of Special Interest *Core academic program:* yes. Academic exchange with members of the Associated Colleges of the Midwest. Sponsors and participates in study-abroad programs. Army ROTC.

On Campus Drama/theater group; student-run newspaper and radio station. *Social organizations:* 5 national fraternities, 3 national sororities; 50% of eligible undergraduate men and 60% of eligible undergraduate women are members.

Athletics Member NCAA (Division III). *Intercollegiate sports:* baseball (M), basketball (M, W), cross-country running (M, W), football (M), golf (M), soccer (M, W), softball (W), tennis (M, W), track and field (M, W), volleyball (W), wrestling (M).

Costs (1991–92) & Aid				
	Comprehensive fee	$15,800	Need-based scholarships	Avail
	Tuition	$12,450	Non-need scholarships (average)	$4000
	Mandatory fees	N/App	Short-term loans	N/Avail
	Room and board	$3350	Long-term loans—college funds	N/Avail
	Financial aid recipients	88%	Long-term loans—external funds (average)	$2000

Undergraduate Facts				
	Part-time	2%	*Freshman Data:* 706 applied, 88% were accepted, 45% (282) of those entered	
	State residents	75%		
	Transfers	11%	From top tenth of high school class	30%
	African-Americans	10%	SAT-takers scoring 600 or over on verbal	N/R
	Native Americans	0%	SAT-takers scoring 700 or over on verbal	N/R
	Hispanics	2%	SAT-takers scoring 600 or over on math	N/R
	Asian-Americans	3%	SAT-takers scoring 700 or over on math	N/R
	International students	6%	ACT-takers scoring 26 or over	49%
	Freshmen returning for sophomore year	92%	ACT-takers scoring 30 or over	17%
	Students completing degree within 5 years	82%		
	Grads pursuing further study	32%		

Majors Accounting, art/fine arts, biology/biological sciences, business, chemistry, classics, communication, computer science, economics, education, elementary education, English, environmental sciences, French, geology, Greek, history, humanities, Latin, liberal arts/general studies, mathematics, medical technology, modern languages, music, natural sciences, nursing, philosophy, physical education, physics, political science/government, psychology, religious studies, secondary education, sociology, Spanish, special education, speech/rhetoric/public address/debate, theater arts/drama.

Applying *Required:* essay, high school transcript, 3 years of high school math, 2 years of high school foreign language, 2 recommendations, SAT or ACT. *Recommended:* 3 years of high school science, interview. *Application deadlines:* 3/1, 2/1 for early decision, 3/15 priority date for financial aid. *Contact:* Dr. David Long, Dean of Admissions, 700 East Broadway, Monmouth, IL 61462, 309-457-2131 or toll-free 800-747-2687.

Morehouse College

Atlanta, Georgia

Founded 1867
Urban setting
Independent
Men
Awards B

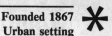

Enrollment	2,992 total—all undergraduates (747 freshmen)	
Faculty	150 total; 115 full-time.	
Libraries	560,000 bound volumes, 110,000 titles on microform, 1,000 periodical subscriptions	
Computing	*Terminals/PCs available for student use:* 118, located in computer center, library, dormitories.	
Of Special Interest	*Core academic program:* yes. Computer course required for math, engineering, accounting, finance, management majors. Phi Beta Kappa chapter. Academic exchange with members of the Atlanta University Center, University Center of Georgia. Sponsors and participates in study-abroad programs. Army ROTC, Naval ROTC, cooperative Air Force ROTC.	
On Campus	Mandatory chapel; drama/theater group; student-run newspaper and radio station. *Social organizations:* 5 national fraternities; 2% of eligible undergraduates are members.	
Athletics	Member NCAA (Division II). *Intercollegiate sports:* basketball, cross-country running, football, swimming and diving, tennis, track and field. *Scholarships.*	

Costs (1991–92) & Aid				
	Comprehensive fee	$11,426	Need-based scholarships (average)	$4500
	Tuition	$5800	Non-need scholarships (average)	$1800
	Mandatory fees	$892	Short-term loans	N/Avail
	Room and board	$4734	Long-term loans—college funds	N/Avail
	Financial aid recipients	68%	Long-term loans—external funds	Avail

Undergraduate Facts				
	Part-time	5%	*Freshman Data:* 3,390 applied, 43% were accepted, 51% (747) of those entered	
	State residents	18%		
	Transfers	5%	From top tenth of high school class	40%
	African-Americans	98%	SAT-takers scoring 600 or over on verbal	N/R
	Native Americans	N/R	SAT-takers scoring 700 or over on verbal	N/R
	Hispanics	N/R	SAT-takers scoring 600 or over on math	N/R
	Asian-Americans	N/R	SAT-takers scoring 700 or over on math	N/R
	International students	2%	ACT-takers scoring 26 or over	N/R
	Freshmen returning for sophomore year	77%	ACT-takers scoring 30 or over	N/R
	Students completing degree within 5 years	N/R		
	Grads pursuing further study	N/R		

Majors Accounting, actuarial science, art/fine arts, biology/biological sciences, business, chemistry, communication, computer science, (pre)dentistry sequence, economics, education, English, finance/banking, French, German, history, insurance, interdisciplinary studies, (pre)law sequence, marketing/retailing/merchandising, mathematics, (pre)medicine sequence, music, philosophy, physical education, physics, political science/government, psychology, real estate, religious studies, sociology, Spanish, urban studies.

Applying *Required:* essay, high school transcript, 3 years of high school math, SAT or ACT. *Recommended:* 3 years of high school science, some high school foreign language. Recommendations, interview required for some. *Application deadlines:* 3/15, 4/1 for financial aid. *Contact:* Mr. Sterling H. Hudson, Director of Admissions, 830 Westview Drive, Atlanta, GA 30314, 404-681-2800 Ext. 2632.

Mount Holyoke College

South Hadley, Massachusetts

Founded 1837
Small-town setting
Independent
Women
Awards B, M

Enrollment	1,910 total; 1,897 undergraduates (465 freshmen)
Faculty	226 total; 194 full-time (83% have doctorate/terminal degree); student-faculty ratio is 10:1; grad assistants teach no undergraduate courses.
Libraries	590,567 bound volumes, 15,120 titles on microform, 1,811 periodical subscriptions
Computing	*Terminals/PCs available for student use:* 245, located in computer center, library, dormitories, classroom buildings; PC not required. Campus network links student PCs.
Of Special Interest	*Core academic program:* yes. Computer course required for math majors. Phi Beta Kappa, Sigma Xi chapters. Academic exchange with members of the Twelve College Exchange Program and Five Colleges, Inc., Spelman College, Mills College. Participates in study-abroad programs. Cooperative Army ROTC, cooperative Air Force ROTC.
On Campus	Drama/theater group; student-run newspaper and radio station. No national or local sororities on campus.
Athletics	Member NCAA (Division III). *Intercollegiate sports:* basketball, crew, cross-country running, equestrian sports, field hockey, golf, lacrosse, soccer, squash, swimming and diving, tennis, track and field, volleyball.

Costs (1991–92) & Aid				
	Comprehensive fee	$20,950	Need-based scholarships (average)	$10,800
	Tuition	$15,950	Non-need scholarships	N/Avail
	Mandatory fees	$100	Short-term loans	N/Avail
	Room and board	$4900	Long-term loans—college funds (average)	$2000
	Financial aid recipients	60%	Long-term loans—external funds (average)	$2500

Undergraduate Facts				
	Part-time	1%	*Freshman Data:* 1,806 applied, 65% were accepted, 40% (465) of those entered	
	State residents	19%		
	Transfers	9%	From top tenth of high school class	47%
	African-Americans	4%	SAT-takers scoring 600 or over on verbal	27%
	Native Americans	0%	SAT-takers scoring 700 or over on verbal	5%
	Hispanics	3%	SAT-takers scoring 600 or over on math	33%
	Asian-Americans	6%	SAT-takers scoring 700 or over on math	6%
	International students	11%	ACT-takers scoring 26 or over	48%
	Freshmen returning for sophomore year	96%	ACT-takers scoring 30 or over	4%
	Students completing degree within 5 years	80%	*Majors with most degrees conferred:* English, political science/government, biology/biological sciences.	
	Grads pursuing further study	25%		

Majors American studies, anthropology, art history, Asian/Oriental studies, astronomy, biochemistry, biology/biological sciences, black/African-American studies, chemistry, classics, computer science, dance, economics, education, English, European studies, French, geography, geology, German, Greek, history, international studies, Italian, Judaic studies, Latin, Latin American studies, mathematics, medieval studies, music, philosophy, physics, political science/government, psychobiology, psychology, religious studies, Romance languages, Russian, Russian and Slavic studies, sociology, Spanish, statistics, studio art, theater arts/drama, women's studies.

Applying *Required:* essay, high school transcript, 3 years of high school math, 2 recommendations, interview, SAT and 3 College Board Achievement Tests (including College Board English Composition Test) or SAT and ACT. *Recommended:* 3 years of high school science, 4 years of high school foreign language. *Application deadlines:* 2/1, 11/15 for early decision, 2/1 for financial aid. *Contact:* Ms. Anita Smith, Director of Admissions, College Street, South Hadley, MA 01075, 413-538-2023.

Mount St. Mary's College

Los Angeles, California

Founded 1925
Urban setting
Independent, Roman Catholic
Primarily women
Awards A, B, M

Enrollment 1,235 total; 949 undergraduates (200 freshmen)

Faculty 146 total; 59 full-time (85% have doctorate/terminal degree); student-faculty ratio is 11:1; grad assistants teach no undergraduate courses.

Libraries 140,000 bound volumes, 4,760 titles on microform, 690 periodical subscriptions

Computing *Terminals/PCs available for student use:* 70, located in computer center, student center, library, resource center; PC not required.

Of Special Interest *Core academic program:* yes. Computer course required for business, math majors. Academic exchange with University of Southern California, University of California, Los Angeles, Sisters of St. Joseph College Consortium. Sponsors and participates in study-abroad programs. Cooperative Army ROTC, cooperative Naval ROTC, cooperative Air Force ROTC.

On Campus Student-run newspaper. *Social organizations:* 1 local sorority.

Athletics Member NAIA. *Intercollegiate sports:* cross-country running (W), tennis (W), volleyball (W).

Costs (1991–92) & Aid	Comprehensive fee	$14,935	Need-based scholarships (average)	$4500
	Tuition	$9950	Non-need scholarships	Avail
	Mandatory fees	$300	Short-term loans (average)	$300
	Room and board	$4685	Long-term loans—college funds (average)	$1500
	Financial aid recipients	77%	Long-term loans—external funds (average)	$2500

Undergraduate Facts				
	Part-time	10%	*Freshman Data:* 574 applied, 79% were accepted, 44% (200) of those entered	
	State residents	87%		
	Transfers	13%	From top tenth of high school class	37%
	African-Americans	9%	SAT-takers scoring 600 or over on verbal	11%
	Native Americans	0%	SAT-takers scoring 700 or over on verbal	2%
	Hispanics	33%	SAT-takers scoring 600 or over on math	13%
	Asian-Americans	19%	SAT-takers scoring 700 or over on math	3%
	International students	2%	ACT-takers scoring 26 or over	6%
	Freshmen returning for sophomore year	86%	ACT-takers scoring 30 or over	0%
	Students completing degree within 5 years	66%	*Majors with most degrees conferred:* business, nursing, physical therapy.	
	Grads pursuing further study	N/R		

Majors Accounting, American studies, art education, art/fine arts, biochemistry, biology/biological sciences, business, business education, chemistry, child psychology/child development, (pre)dentistry sequence, education, elementary education, English, French, gerontology, health services administration, history, international business, (pre)law sequence, marketing/retailing/merchandising, mathematics, (pre)medicine sequence, music, music education, nursing, philosophy, physical therapy, political science/government, psychology, religious studies, secondary education, social science, sociology, Spanish, voice.

Applying *Required:* essay, high school transcript, SAT or ACT. *Recommended:* 3 years of high school math and science, some high school foreign language, recommendations. Campus interview required for some. *Application deadlines:* rolling, 10/31 for early action, 3/1 priority date for financial aid. *Contact:* Mrs. Bernadette Robert, Acting Director of Admissions, 12001 Chalon Road, Los Angeles, CA 90049, 213-476-2237 Ext. 3320 or toll-free 800-222-MSMC (in-state), 800-633-8709 (out-of-state).

✱ Muhlenberg College

Allentown, Pennsylvania

Founded 1848
Suburban setting
Independent/affiliated with Lutheran Church
Coed
Awards B

Enrollment 1,636 total—all undergraduates (464 freshmen)

Faculty 151 total; 108 full-time (86% have doctorate/terminal degree); student-faculty ratio is 13:1.

Libraries 300,000 bound volumes, 20,000 titles on microform, 1,608 periodical subscriptions

Computing *Terminals/PCs available for student use:* 100, located in computer center, library, 5 computer labs; PC not required. Campus network links student PCs.

Of Special Interest *Core academic program:* yes. Computer course required for math majors. Phi Beta Kappa chapter. Academic exchange with 6 members of the Lehigh Valley Association of Independent Colleges. Sponsors and participates in study-abroad programs. Cooperative Army ROTC, cooperative Air Force ROTC.

On Campus Drama/theater group; student-run newspaper and radio station. *Social organizations:* 6 national fraternities, 4 national sororities; 55% of eligible undergraduate men and 45% of eligible undergraduate women are members.

Athletics Member NCAA (Division III). *Intercollegiate sports:* baseball (M), basketball (M, W), cross-country running (M, W), field hockey (W), football (M), golf (M), lacrosse (W), soccer (M, W), softball (W), tennis (M, W), track and field (M, W), volleyball (W), wrestling (M).

Costs (1991–92) & Aid

Comprehensive fee	$19,765	Need-based scholarships (average)		$7854
Tuition	$15,000	Non-need scholarships (average)		$4200
Mandatory fees	$505	Short-term loans		N/Avail
Room and board	$4260	Long-term loans—college funds		N/Avail
Financial aid recipients	63%	Long-term loans—external funds (average)		$3000

Undergraduate Facts

Part-time	4%	*Freshman Data:* 2,360 applied, 80% were accepted, 25% (464) of those entered	
State residents	32%		
Transfers	6%	From top tenth of high school class	25%
African-Americans	2%	SAT-takers scoring 600 or over on verbal	10%
Native Americans	0%	SAT-takers scoring 700 or over on verbal	1%
Hispanics	2%	SAT-takers scoring 600 or over on math	34%
Asian-Americans	3%	SAT-takers scoring 700 or over on math	4%
International students	2%	ACT-takers scoring 26 or over	N/R
Freshmen returning for sophomore year	91%	ACT-takers scoring 30 or over	N/R
Students completing degree within 5 years	80%	*Majors with most degrees conferred:* biology/ biological sciences, psychology, English.	
Grads pursuing further study	28%		

Majors Accounting, African studies, American studies, art/fine arts, Asian/Oriental studies, biology/biological sciences, business, chemistry, classics, communication, computer information systems, computer science, (pre)dentistry sequence, economics, elementary education, English, environmental sciences, French, German, Greek, history, humanities, human resources, information science, international studies, Latin, Latin American studies, (pre)law sequence, mathematics, (pre)medicine sequence, ministries, music, natural sciences, philosophy, physics, political science/government, psychology, religious studies, Russian and Slavic studies, secondary education, social science, social work, sociology, Spanish, theater arts/drama, (pre)veterinary medicine sequence, women's studies.

Applying *Required:* essay, high school transcript, 3 years of high school math, 2 years of high school foreign language, 2 recommendations, SAT, 2 Achievements, English Composition Test. *Recommended:* 3 years of high school science, campus interview. *Application deadlines:* 2/15, 1/15 for early decision, 2/15 priority date for financial aid. *Contact:* Mr. Christopher Hooker-Haring, Director of Admissions, 2400 Chew Street, Allentown, PA 18104, 215-821-3200.

Nebraska Wesleyan University

Lincoln, Nebraska

Founded 1887
Suburban setting
Independent, United Methodist
Coed
Awards A, B

Enrollment 1,655 total—all undergraduates (344 freshmen)

Faculty 143 total; 87 full-time (78% have doctorate/terminal degree); student-faculty ratio is 13:1.

Libraries 159,036 bound volumes, 3,521 titles on microform, 745 periodical subscriptions

Computing *Terminals/PCs available for student use:* 100, located in library, dormitories, computer lab; PC not required.

Of Special Interest *Core academic program:* yes. Computer course required. Academic exchange with American University. Sponsors and participates in study-abroad programs. Cooperative Army ROTC, cooperative Naval ROTC, cooperative Air Force ROTC.

On Campus Drama/theater group; student-run newspaper. *Social organizations:* 4 national fraternities, 2 national sororities, 1 local sorority; 39% of eligible undergraduate men and 41% of eligible undergraduate women are members.

Athletics Member NCAA (Division III), NAIA. *Intercollegiate sports:* basketball (M, W), cross-country running (M, W), football (M), golf (M, W), softball (W), tennis (M, W), track and field (M, W), volleyball (W).

Costs (1991–92) & Aid				
Comprehensive fee	$11,177	Need-based scholarships (average)	$2041
Tuition	$7980	Non-need scholarships (average)	$905
Mandatory fees	$247	Short-term loans	N/Avail
Room and board	$2950	Long-term loans—college funds	N/Avail
Financial aid recipients	90%	Long-term loans—external funds (average)	$3337

Undergraduate Facts			
Part-time	16%	*Freshman Data:* 839 applied, 88% were accepted, 46% (344) of those entered	
State residents	92%		
Transfers	4%	From top tenth of high school class	25%
African-Americans	2%	SAT-takers scoring 600 or over on verbal	N/R
Native Americans	1%	SAT-takers scoring 700 or over on verbal	N/R
Hispanics	1%	SAT-takers scoring 600 or over on math	N/R
Asian-Americans	1%	SAT-takers scoring 700 or over on math	N/R
International students	1%	ACT-takers scoring 26 or over	29%
Freshmen returning for sophomore year	83%	ACT-takers scoring 30 or over	4%
Students completing degree within 5 years	59%	*Majors with most degrees conferred:* business, psychology, biology/biological sciences.	
Grads pursuing further study	N/R		

Majors Art education, art/fine arts, biology/biological sciences, business, business education, chemistry, communication, computer information systems, computer science, economics, education, elementary education, English, French, German, history, interdisciplinary studies, international studies, mathematics, middle school education, music, music education, nursing, philosophy, physical education, physics, political science/government, psychobiology, psychology, religious studies, science education, secondary education, social work, sociology, Spanish, special education, speech/rhetoric/public address/debate, theater arts/drama.

Applying *Required:* high school transcript, SAT or ACT. *Application deadlines:* rolling, 4/15 priority date for financial aid. *Contact:* Mr. Ken Sieg, Director of Admissions, 5000 St. Paul Avenue, Lincoln, NE 68504, 402-465-2218.

From the College Nebraska Wesleyan's faculty members are dedicated to providing every student opportunities for success. Superior research equipment and facilities enable students to gain experience as early as the freshman year. These factors contribute to the acceptance of two thirds of graduates to graduate/professional programs within three years of graduation.

New College of the University of South Florida
Sarasota, Florida

Founded 1960
Suburban setting
State-supported
Coed
Awards B

Enrollment 530 total—all undergraduates (109 freshmen)

Faculty 53 total—all full-time (98% have doctorate/terminal degree); student-faculty ratio is 10:1.

Libraries 210,000 bound volumes, 380,834 titles on microform, 1,598 periodical subscriptions

Computing *Terminals/PCs available for student use:* 40, located in computer center, student center, library, natural sciences building; PC not required.

Of Special Interest *Core academic program:* no. Academic exchange with 82 members of the National Student Exchange. Sponsors and participates in study-abroad programs. Cooperative Army ROTC, cooperative Air Force ROTC.

On Campus Drama/theater group; student-run newspaper. No national or local fraternities or sororities on campus.

Athletics None

Costs (1991–92) & Aid				
	State resident tuition	$1675	28 Need-based scholarships (average)	$575
	Nonresident tuition	$6690	235 Non-need scholarships (average)	$1088
	Mandatory fees	N/App	Short-term loans (average)	$500
	Room and board	$3375	Long-term loans—college funds	N/Avail
	Financial aid recipients	75%	Long-term loans—external funds (average)	$3000

Undergraduate Facts				
	Part-time	0%	*Freshman Data:* 703 applied, 33% were accepted, 47% (109) of those entered	
	State residents	56%		
	Transfers	34%	From top tenth of high school class	49%
	African-Americans	2%	SAT-takers scoring 600 or over on verbal	61%
	Native Americans	0%	SAT-takers scoring 700 or over on verbal	15%
	Hispanics	4%	SAT-takers scoring 600 or over on math	68%
	Asian-Americans	4%	SAT-takers scoring 700 or over on math	22%
	International students	3%	ACT-takers scoring 26 or over	83%
	Freshmen returning for sophomore year	85%	ACT-takers scoring 30 or over	30%
	Students completing degree within 5 years	47%	*Majors with most degrees conferred:* psychology, biology/biological sciences, literature.	
	Grads pursuing further study	30%		

Majors Anatomy, anthropology, applied art, archaeology, art/fine arts, art history, behavioral sciences, biology/biological sciences, cell biology, ceramic art and design, chemistry, child psychology/child development, classics, comparative literature, creative writing, (pre)dentistry sequence, ecology/environmental studies, economics, English, environmental biology, environmental sciences, European studies, evolutionary biology, experimental psychology, French, genetics, German, Germanic languages and literature, gerontology, Greek, history, history of philosophy, interdisciplinary studies, international economics, international studies, Latin, Latin American studies, (pre)law sequence, liberal arts/general studies, literature, marine biology, marine sciences, mathematics, (pre)medicine sequence, medieval studies, modern languages, molecular biology, music, music history, natural sciences, painting/drawing, philosophy, physics, physiology, political science/government, psychobiology, psychology, public affairs and policy studies, religious studies, Russian, Russian and Slavic studies, science, sculpture, social science, sociology, Spanish, studio art, (pre)veterinary medicine sequence, Western civilization and culture.

Applying *Required:* essay, high school transcript, 2 years of high school foreign language, 2 recommendations, original graded paper, SAT or ACT. *Recommended:* 3 years of high school math and science, interview. Campus interview required for some. *Application deadlines:* rolling, 2/1 priority date for financial aid. *Contact:* Mr. David Anderson, Acting Director of Admissions, 5700 North Tamiami Trail, Sarasota, FL 34243, 813-355-2963.

From the College The New College campus consists of historic bay-front mansions and dormitories designed by I. M. Pei. The campus is adjacent to the Asolo State Theatre and the Ringling Museum of Art. Located in Sarasota, New College offers students a variety of cultural and recreational opportunities in addition to an innovative and challenging educational experience.

New Jersey Institute of Technology
Newark, New Jersey

Founded 1881
Urban setting
State-related
Coed
Awards B, M, D

Enrollment 7,417 total; 4,896 undergraduates (559 freshmen)

Faculty 491 total; 322 full-time (94% have doctorate/terminal degree); student-faculty ratio is 15:1; grad assistants teach a few undergraduate courses.

Libraries 147,777 bound volumes, 185 titles on microform, 1,704 periodical subscriptions

Computing *Terminals/PCs available for student use:* 1,000, located in computer center, student center, library, dormitories. Campus network links student PCs. Computers are provided for freshmen. Sophomores, juniors, and seniors may lease computers with an option to buy. All students pay a computer maintenance fee.

Of Special Interest *Core academic program:* yes. Computer course required. Sigma Xi chapter. Academic exchange with Essex County College, Rutgers, The State University of New Jersey, University of Medicine and Dentistry of New Jersey. Study-abroad programs: no. Air Force ROTC.

On Campus Drama/theater group; student-run newspaper and radio station. *Social organizations:* 9 national fraternities, 1 national sorority, 6 local fraternities, 4 local sororities; 19% of eligible undergraduate men and 21% of eligible undergraduate women are members.

Athletics Member NCAA (Division III). *Intercollegiate sports:* baseball (M), basketball (M, W), bowling (M, W), cross-country running (M, W), fencing (M, W), golf (M, W), skiing (downhill) (M, W), soccer (M), softball (W), tennis (M, W), volleyball (M, W).

Costs (1991–92) & Aid				
	State resident tuition	$3628	169 Need-based scholarships (average)	$2000
	Nonresident tuition	$7568	600 Non-need scholarships (average)	$1000
	Mandatory fees	$660	Short-term loans	N/Avail
	Room and board	$4772	Long-term loans—college funds (average)	$1200
	Financial aid recipients	75%	Long-term loans—external funds (average)	$1700

Undergraduate Facts				
	Part-time	34%	*Freshman Data:* 1,541 applied, 67% were accepted, 54% (559) of those entered	
	State residents	90%		
	Transfers	35%	From top tenth of high school class	25%
	African-Americans	11%	SAT-takers scoring 600 or over on verbal	6%
	Native Americans	1%	SAT-takers scoring 700 or over on verbal	1%
	Hispanics	11%	SAT-takers scoring 600 or over on math	46%
	Asian-Americans	16%	SAT-takers scoring 700 or over on math	11%
	International students	5%	ACT-takers scoring 26 or over	N/App
	Freshmen returning for sophomore year	80%	ACT-takers scoring 30 or over	N/App
	Students completing degree within 5 years	70%	*Majors with most degrees conferred:* electrical engineering, engineering technology, mechanical engineering.	
	Grads pursuing further study	5%		

Majors Actuarial science, applied mathematics, architecture, chemical engineering, chemistry, civil engineering, computer engineering, computer science, computer technologies, construction technologies, electrical engineering, electrical engineering technology, engineering sciences, engineering technology, industrial engineering, interdisciplinary studies, manufacturing engineering, manufacturing technology, materials engineering, materials sciences, mechanical engineering, mechanical engineering technology, physics, statistics, technology and public affairs.

Applying *Required:* essay, high school transcript, 4 years of high school math, SAT, 1 Achievement. *Recommended:* some high school foreign language. *Application deadlines:* 4/1, 12/1 for early decision, 3/15 priority date for financial aid. *Contact:* Mr. William Anderson, Assistant Vice President for Academic Affairs, 323 Martin Luther King Boulevard, Newark, NJ 07102, 201-596-3300 or toll-free 800-222-NJIT (in-state).

From the College All full-time freshmen receive their own NJIT/AT-286 personal computer to use during their undergraduate years. Each computer package includes 1 megabyte of memory, two floppy-disk drives, an enhanced keyboard, a graphics card, a power supply, a serial and a parallel port, a monochrome monitor, and ten diskettes. Various software packages are also included. Upon graduation, students may purchase the computer and software packages for a nominal fee.

New Mexico Institute of Mining and Technology
Socorro, New Mexico

Founded 1889
Small-town setting
State-supported
Coed
Awards A, B, M, D

Enrollment	1,434 total; 1,126 undergraduates (239 freshmen)	
Faculty	101 total; 98 full-time (98% have doctorate/terminal degree); student-faculty ratio is 11:1; grad assistants teach a few undergraduate courses.	
Libraries	141,000 bound volumes, 71,000 titles on microform, 1,025 periodical subscriptions	
Computing	*Terminals/PCs available for student use:* 50, located in computer center, technical communications lab, most academic departments; PC not required. Campus network links student PCs.	
Of Special Interest	*Core academic program:* yes. Computer course required. Sigma Xi chapter. Academic exchange with St. John's College (NM), State University of New York College at New Paltz. Study-abroad programs: no.	
On Campus	Drama/theater group; student-run newspaper and radio station. No national or local fraternities or sororities on campus.	
Athletics	None	

Costs (1991–92) & Aid				
	State resident tuition	$1070	191 Need-based scholarships (average)	$840
	Nonresident tuition	$4642	250 Non-need scholarships (average)	$1012
	Mandatory fees	$459	Short-term loans (average)	$275
	Room and board	$2720	Long-term loans—college funds	N/Avail
	Financial aid recipients	72%	Long-term loans—external funds (average)	$2370

Undergraduate Facts				
	Part-time	24%	*Freshman Data:* 662 applied, 78% were accepted, 46% (239) of those entered	
	State residents	61%		
	Transfers	29%	From top tenth of high school class	33%
	African-Americans	1%	SAT-takers scoring 600 or over on verbal	N/R
	Native Americans	2%	SAT-takers scoring 700 or over on verbal	N/R
	Hispanics	15%	SAT-takers scoring 600 or over on math	N/R
	Asian-Americans	2%	SAT-takers scoring 700 or over on math	N/R
	International students	13%	ACT-takers scoring 26 or over	69%
	Freshmen returning for sophomore year	69%	ACT-takers scoring 30 or over	1%
	Students completing degree within 5 years	N/R	*Majors with most degrees conferred:* physics, computer science, petroleum/natural gas engineering.	
	Grads pursuing further study	N/R		

Majors Accounting, applied mathematics, astrophysics, atmospheric sciences, behavioral sciences, biology/biological sciences, business, chemical engineering, chemistry, computer programming, computer science, (pre)dentistry sequence, electrical engineering, electronics engineering, engineering sciences, environmental biology, environmental engineering, environmental sciences, experimental psychology, geochemistry, geological engineering, geology, geophysics, liberal arts/general studies, materials engineering, mathematics, mechanical engineering, medical technology, (pre)medicine sequence, metallurgical engineering, mining and mineral engineering, petroleum/natural gas engineering, physics, psychology, science, science education, secondary education, technical writing, (pre)veterinary medicine sequence.

Applying *Required:* high school transcript, 3 years of high school math and science, SAT or ACT. *Recommended:* some high school foreign language, interview, Achievements. 2 recommendations required for some. *Application deadlines:* 8/15, 3/1 priority date for financial aid. *Contact:* Ms. Louise E. Chamberlin, Director of Admissions, Brown Hall, Socorro, NM 87801, 505-835-5424 or toll-free 800-428-TECH.

New York University

New York, New York

Founded 1831
Urban setting
Independent
Coed
Awards A, B, M, D

Enrollment	33,340 total; 15,092 undergraduates (2,548 freshmen)
Faculty	4,330 total; 1,260 full-time (94% have doctorate/terminal degree); student-faculty ratio is 13:1; grad assistants teach a few undergraduate courses.
Libraries	3.5 million bound volumes, 2.9 million titles on microform, 28,817 periodical subscriptions
Computing	*Terminals/PCs available for student use:* 500, located in computer center, student center, library, dormitories; PC not required but available for purchase. Campus network links student PCs.
Of Special Interest	*Core academic program:* yes. Computer course required for business, math, science majors. Phi Beta Kappa, Sigma Xi chapters. Academic exchange program: no. Sponsors and participates in study-abroad programs. Cooperative Army ROTC, cooperative Air Force ROTC.
On Campus	Drama/theater group; student-run newspaper and radio station. *Social organizations:* 11 national fraternities, 3 national sororities, 7 local sororities; 7% of eligible undergraduate men and 6% of eligible undergraduate women are members.
Athletics	Member NCAA (Division III). *Intercollegiate sports:* basketball (M, W), cross-country running (M, W), fencing (M, W), golf (M), soccer (M), swimming and diving (M, W), tennis (M, W), track and field (M, W), volleyball (M, W), wrestling (M).

Costs (1991–92) & Aid				
	Comprehensive fee	$22,444	Need-based scholarships (average)	$4200
	Tuition	$15,620	Non-need scholarships (average)	$7000
	Mandatory fees	$50	Short-term loans (average)	$300
	Room and board	$6774	Long-term loans—college funds (average)	$2500
	Financial aid recipients	66%	Long-term loans—external funds (average)	$2900

Undergraduate Facts				
	Part-time	20%	*Freshman Data:* 9,957 applied, 64% were accepted, 40% (2,548) of those entered	
	State residents	50%		
	Transfers	11%	From top tenth of high school class	61%
	African-Americans	8%	SAT-takers scoring 600 or over on verbal	34%
	Native Americans	1%	SAT-takers scoring 700 or over on verbal	5%
	Hispanics	8%	SAT-takers scoring 600 or over on math	53%
	Asian-Americans	17%	SAT-takers scoring 700 or over on math	12%
	International students	5%	ACT-takers scoring 26 or over	N/R
	Freshmen returning for sophomore year	82%	ACT-takers scoring 30 or over	N/R
	Students completing degree within 5 years	66%		
	Grads pursuing further study	76%		

Majors Accounting, actuarial science, adult and continuing education, anthropology, applied mathematics, archaeology, art education, art/fine arts, art history, art therapy, Asian/Oriental studies, audio engineering, behavioral sciences, biochemistry, biology/biological sciences, black/African-American studies, broadcasting, business, business economics, chemistry, child psychology/child development, city/community/regional planning, classics, communication, comparative literature, computer information systems, computer science, creative writing, dance, dance therapy, (pre)dentistry sequence, dietetics, early childhood education, East Asian studies, ecology/environmental studies, economics, education, educational media, elementary education, English, European studies, experimental psychology, film and video, film studies, finance/banking, food services management, French, German, Germanic languages and literature, graphic arts, Greek, Hebrew, Hispanic studies, history, hotel and restaurant management, humanities, interdisciplinary studies, international business, Islamic studies, Italian, jazz, journalism, Judaic studies, Latin, Latin American studies, (pre)law sequence, liberal arts/general studies, linguistics, literature, marketing/retailing/merchandising, mathematics, (pre)medicine sequence, medieval studies, middle school education, modern languages, museum studies, music, music business, music education, music history, natural sciences, Near and Middle Eastern studies, nursing, nutrition, occupational safety and health, occupational therapy, operations research, peace studies, philosophy, photography, physical therapy, physics, piano/organ, political science/government, Portuguese, psychobiology, psychology, radio and television studies, recreation and leisure services, recreation therapy, rehabilitation therapy, religious studies, retail management, Romance languages, Russian, Russian and Slavic studies, science education, sculpture, secondary education, Slavic languages, social science, social work, sociology, Spanish, special education, speech pathology and audiology, speech therapy, statistics, studio art, theater arts/drama, urban studies, (pre)veterinary medicine sequence, voice, women's studies.

Applying *Required:* essay, high school transcript, 3 years of high school math and science, 2 years of high school foreign language, 1 recommendation, SAT or ACT. *Recommended:* interview, Achievements, English Composition Test. Campus interview, Achievements required for some. *Application deadlines:* 2/1, 12/15 for early decision, 2/15 priority date for financial aid. *Contact:* Director of Admissions, 22 Washington Square North, New York, NY 10011, 212-998-4500.

North Carolina State University

Raleigh, North Carolina

Founded 1887
Urban setting
State-supported
Coed
Awards A, B, M, D

Enrollment	27,236 total; 18,369 undergraduates (3,243 freshmen)
Faculty	1,448 total; 1,228 full-time (91% have doctorate/terminal degree); student-faculty ratio is 14:1; grad assistants teach a few undergraduate courses.
Libraries	2 million bound volumes, 3 million titles on microform, 19,385 periodical subscriptions
Computing	*Terminals/PCs available for student use:* 3,200, located in computer center, student center, library, dormitories; PC not required. Campus network links student PCs.
Of Special Interest	*Core academic program:* yes. Computer course required for engineering, botany, math education, psychology, geology, meteorology, math, statistics, textiles majors. Sigma Xi chapter. Academic exchange with 5 members of the Cooperating Raleigh Colleges, Duke University, University of North Carolina at Chapel Hill. Sponsors and participates in study-abroad programs. Army ROTC, Naval ROTC, Air Force ROTC.
On Campus	Drama/theater group; student-run newspaper and radio station. *Social organizations:* 25 national fraternities, 9 national sororities; 14% of eligible undergraduate men and 15% of eligible undergraduate women are members.
Athletics	Member NCAA (Division I). *Intercollegiate sports:* baseball (M), basketball (M, W), cross-country running (M, W), fencing (M, W), football (M), golf (M, W), gymnastics (M, W), ice hockey (M), lacrosse (M), racquetball (M, W), riflery (M, W), rugby (M, W), sailing (M, W), skiing (downhill) (M, W), soccer (M, W), swimming and diving (M, W), tennis (M, W), track and field (M, W), volleyball (M, W), weight lifting (M, W), wrestling (M). *Scholarships:* M, W.

Costs (1991-92) & Aid				
	State resident tuition	$1254	Need-based scholarships (average)	$700
	Nonresident tuition	$7122	Non-need scholarships (average)	$1000
	Mandatory fees	N/App	Short-term loans (average)	$100
	Room and board	$3150	Long-term loans—college funds	Avail
	Financial aid recipients	36%	Long-term loans—external funds (average)	$1950

Undergraduate Facts				
	Part-time	11%	*Freshman Data:* 9,318 applied, 66% were accepted, 52% (3,243) of those entered	
	State residents	88%		
	Transfers	6%	From top tenth of high school class	45%
	African-Americans	10%	SAT-takers scoring 600 or over on verbal	12%
	Native Americans	1%	SAT-takers scoring 700 or over on verbal	2%
	Hispanics	1%	SAT-takers scoring 600 or over on math	33%
	Asian-Americans	3%	SAT-takers scoring 700 or over on math	7%
	International students	1%	ACT-takers scoring 26 or over	N/R
	Freshmen returning for sophomore year	91%	ACT-takers scoring 30 or over	N/R
	Students completing degree within 5 years	59%	*Majors with most degrees conferred:* business, electrical engineering, mechanical engineering.	
	Grads pursuing further study	N/R		

Majors Accounting, aerospace engineering, agricultural business, agricultural economics, agricultural education, agricultural engineering, agricultural sciences, agronomy/soil and crop sciences, animal sciences, anthropology, applied mathematics, architecture, biochemistry, biology/biological sciences, botany/plant sciences, business, chemical engineering, chemistry, civil engineering, communication, computer engineering, computer science, conservation, construction engineering, construction management, criminal justice, (pre)dentistry sequence, economics, education, electrical engineering, English, entomology, environmental design, fish and game management, food sciences, forestry, French, geology, geophysics, history, horticulture, humanities, human resources, industrial design, industrial engineering, journalism, landscape architecture/design, liberal arts/general studies, materials engineering, mathematics, mechanical engineering, medical technology, (pre)medicine sequence, meteorology, microbiology, natural resource management, nuclear engineering, nutrition, ornamental horticulture, paper and pulp sciences, parks management, philosophy, physics, political science/government, poultry sciences, psychology, public affairs and policy studies, recreational facilities management, science education, secondary education, social science, social work, sociology, Spanish, speech therapy, statistics, technical writing, textile engineering, textiles and clothing, tourism and travel, (pre)veterinary medicine sequence, vocational education, wildlife biology, wood sciences, zoology.

Applying *Required:* high school transcript, 3 years of high school math and science, 4 years of high school English, 2 years of high school social studies, SAT or ACT. *Recommended:* essay, 2 years of high school foreign language, English Composition Test, College Board Achievement Test in math. Recommendations, interview required for some. *Application deadlines:* 2/1, 11/1 for early action, 3/1 priority date for financial aid. *Contact:* Ms. Kay P. Leager, Associate Director of Admissions, Box 7103, 112 Peele Hall, Raleigh, NC 27695, 919-515-2434.

North Central College

Naperville, Illinois

Founded 1861
Suburban setting
Independent, United Methodist
Coed
Awards B, M

Enrollment 2,551 total; 2,158 undergraduates (344 freshmen)

Faculty 120 total; 98 full-time (71% have doctorate/terminal degree); student-faculty ratio is 14:1; grad assistants teach no undergraduate courses.

Libraries 106,590 bound volumes, 764 periodical subscriptions

Computing *Terminals/PCs available for student use:* 105, located in computer center, library, dormitories, labs; PC not required. Campus network links student PCs.

Of Special Interest *Core academic program:* yes. Academic exchange with Aurora University, Illinois Benedictine College. Sponsors and participates in study-abroad programs. Cooperative Army ROTC, cooperative Air Force ROTC.

On Campus Drama/theater group; student-run newspaper and radio station. No national or local fraternities or sororities on campus.

Athletics Member NCAA (Division III). *Intercollegiate sports:* basketball (M, W), cross-country running (M, W), football (M), golf (M, W), soccer (M), swimming and diving (M, W), tennis (M, W), track and field (M, W), volleyball (W), wrestling (M).

Costs (1991–92) & Aid				
	Comprehensive fee	$13,695	Need-based scholarships (average)	$2890
	Tuition	$9870	Non-need scholarships (average)	$3520
	Mandatory fees	$90	Short-term loans	N/Avail
	Room and board	$3735	Long-term loans—college funds (average)	$1929
	Financial aid recipients	80%	Long-term loans—external funds (average)	$2934

Undergraduate Facts				
	Part-time	38%	*Freshman Data:* 1,032 applied, 79% were accepted, 42% (344) of those entered	
	State residents	75%		
	Transfers	37%	From top tenth of high school class	35%
	African-Americans	6%	SAT-takers scoring 600 or over on verbal	N/R
	Native Americans	1%	SAT-takers scoring 700 or over on verbal	N/R
	Hispanics	2%	SAT-takers scoring 600 or over on math	N/R
	Asian-Americans	2%	SAT-takers scoring 700 or over on math	N/R
	International students	1%	ACT-takers scoring 26 or over	45%
	Freshmen returning for sophomore year	80%	ACT-takers scoring 30 or over	9%
	Students completing degree within 5 years	60%	*Majors with most degrees conferred:* business, broadcasting, computer science.	
	Grads pursuing further study	15%		

Majors Accounting, actuarial science, anthropology, art education, art/fine arts, biology/biological sciences, broadcasting, business, business education, chemistry, classics, communication, computer information systems, computer science, (pre)dentistry sequence, early childhood education, economics, education, elementary education, English, finance/banking, French, German, graphic arts, Greek, health education, history, humanities, international business, Japanese, Latin, (pre)law sequence, liberal arts/general studies, literature, management information systems, marketing/retailing/merchandising, mathematics, (pre)medicine sequence, modern languages, music, natural sciences, philosophy, physical education, physical fitness/human movement, physics, piano/organ, political science/government, psychology, public relations, reading education, religious studies, science education, secondary education, social science, sociology, Spanish, speech/rhetoric/public address/debate, sports medicine, theater arts/drama, (pre)veterinary medicine sequence, voice.

Applying *Required:* high school transcript, SAT or ACT. *Recommended:* essay, 3 years of high school math and science, some high school foreign language, recommendations. Interview required for some. *Application deadlines:* rolling, 7/1 priority date for financial aid. *Contact:* Mr. Rick Spencer, Vice-President for Admissions, Financial Aid, and Enrollment, 30 North Brainard Street, Naperville, IL 60566-7063, 708-420-3477.

Northeast Missouri State University
Kirksville, Missouri

Founded 1867
Small-town setting
State-supported
Coed
Awards B, M

Enrollment 5,939 total; 5,710 undergraduates (1,413 freshmen)

Faculty 464 total; 337 full-time (68% have doctorate/terminal degree); student-faculty ratio is 16:1; grad assistants teach a few undergraduate courses.

Libraries 629,617 bound volumes, 1.1 million titles on microform, 1,912 periodical subscriptions

Computing *Terminals/PCs available for student use:* 734, located in computer center, library, dormitories, academic buildings; PC not required. Campus network links student PCs.

Of Special Interest *Core academic program:* yes. Computer course required. Academic exchange with Gulf Coast Research Laboratory, Reis Biological Station. Sponsors and participates in study-abroad programs. Army ROTC.

On Campus Drama/theater group; student-run newspaper and radio station. *Social organizations:* 16 national fraternities, 9 national sororities, 1 local sorority; 28% of eligible undergraduate men and 15% of eligible undergraduate women are members.

Athletics Member NCAA (Division II). *Intercollegiate sports:* baseball (M), basketball (M, W), cross-country running (M, W), football (M), golf (M, W), rugby (M), soccer (M, W), softball (W), swimming and diving (M, W), tennis (M, W), track and field (M, W), volleyball (W), wrestling (M). *Scholarships:* M, W.

Costs (1991–92) & Aid				
	State resident tuition	$1800	375 Need-based scholarships (average)	$287
	Nonresident tuition	$3504	2003 Non-need scholarships (average)	$1232
	Mandatory fees	N/App	Short-term loans (average)	$347
	Room and board	$2584	Long-term loans—college funds (average)	$1558
	Financial aid recipients	76%	Long-term loans—external funds (average)	$2947

Undergraduate Facts				
	Part-time	5%	*Freshman Data:* 5,418 applied, 71% were accepted, 37% (1,413) of those entered	
	State residents	73%		
	Transfers	4%	From top tenth of high school class	35%
	African-Americans	4%	SAT-takers scoring 600 or over on verbal	N/R
	Native Americans	1%	SAT-takers scoring 700 or over on verbal	N/R
	Hispanics	1%	SAT-takers scoring 600 or over on math	N/R
	Asian-Americans	1%	SAT-takers scoring 700 or over on math	N/R
	International students	3%	ACT-takers scoring 26 or over	47%
	Freshmen returning for sophomore year	81%	ACT-takers scoring 30 or over	17%
	Students completing degree within 5 years	60%	*Majors with most degrees conferred:* business, accounting, English.	
	Grads pursuing further study	31%		

Majors Accounting, agricultural economics, agricultural sciences, agronomy/soil and crop sciences, animal sciences, applied art, art/fine arts, biology/biological sciences, business, chemistry, commercial art, communication, computer science, criminal justice, (pre)dentistry sequence, economics, English, equestrian studies, finance/banking, French, German, health science, history, journalism, law enforcement/police sciences, (pre)law sequence, linguistics, marketing/retailing/merchandising, mathematics, (pre)medicine sequence, music, music business, nursing, philosophy, physics, piano/organ, political science/government, psychology, religious studies, sociology, Spanish, speech pathology and audiology, speech/rhetoric/public address/debate, studio art, theater arts/drama, (pre)veterinary medicine sequence, voice.

Applying *Required:* essay, high school transcript, ACT. *Recommended:* 3 years of high school math and science, 2 years of high school foreign language, SAT, PSAT. Recommendations required for some. *Application deadlines:* 3/1, 11/5 for early action, 4/30 priority date for financial aid. *Contact:* Ms. Kathy Rieck, Dean of Admission and Records, 205 McClain Hall, Kirksville, MO 63501, 816-785-4114 or toll-free 800-892-7792 (in-state).

From the College Northeast Missouri State University holds the educational philosophy that the acquisition of knowledge and skills is best facilitated in an active learning environment. Northeast has implemented this philosophy through pairing a competitive academic climate with small class size. Students engage in active learning outside the classroom through University-sponsored experiences and numerous undergraduate research opportunities.

Northwestern University

Evanston, Illinois

Founded 1851
Suburban setting
Independent
Coed
Awards B, M, D

Enrollment	14,198 total; 7,458 undergraduates (1,946 freshmen)
Faculty	915 total; 773 full-time (100% have doctorate/terminal degree); student-faculty ratio is 8:1; grad assistants teach a few undergraduate courses.
Libraries	3.5 million bound volumes, 2.5 million titles on microform, 38,000 periodical subscriptions
Computing	*Terminals/PCs available for student use:* 210, located in computer center, student center, library, dormitories, academic buildings; PC not required.
Of Special Interest	*Core academic program:* yes. Computer course required for engineering majors. Phi Beta Kappa, Sigma Xi chapters. Academic exchange with 11 members of the Committee on Institutional Cooperation. Sponsors and participates in study-abroad programs. Naval ROTC, cooperative Army ROTC, cooperative Air Force ROTC.
On Campus	Drama/theater group; student-run newspaper and radio station. *Social organizations:* 22 national fraternities, 12 national sororities; 43% of eligible undergraduate men and 44% of eligible undergraduate women are members.
Athletics	Member NCAA (Division I). *Intercollegiate sports:* baseball (M), basketball (M, W), fencing (M, W), field hockey (W), football (M), golf (M), lacrosse (W), soccer (M), softball (W), swimming and diving (M, W), tennis (M, W), volleyball (W), wrestling (M). *Scholarships:* M, W.

Costs (1991–92) & Aid	Comprehensive fee	$19,197	Need-based scholarships (average)	$7500
	Tuition	$14,370	Non-need scholarships	N/Avail
	Mandatory fees	N/App	Short-term loans (average)	$50
	Room and board	$4827	Long-term loans—college funds (average)	$2600
	Financial aid recipients	60%	Long-term loans—external funds (average)	$2745

Undergraduate Facts				
	Part-time	1%	*Freshman Data:* 11,406 applied, 48% were accepted, 36% (1,946) of those entered	
	State residents	27%		
	Transfers	1%	From top tenth of high school class	80%
	African-Americans	8%	SAT-takers scoring 600 or over on verbal	44%
	Native Americans	1%	SAT-takers scoring 700 or over on verbal	5%
	Hispanics	2%	SAT-takers scoring 600 or over on math	77%
	Asian-Americans	12%	SAT-takers scoring 700 or over on math	31%
	International students	2%	ACT-takers scoring 26 or over	90%
	Freshmen returning for sophomore year	96%	ACT-takers scoring 30 or over	49%
	Students completing degree within 5 years	88%	*Majors with most degrees conferred:* economics, political science/government, journalism.	
	Grads pursuing further study	28%		

Majors American studies, anthropology, applied mathematics, art education, art/fine arts, art history, Asian/Oriental studies, astronomy, astrophysics, behavioral sciences, biochemistry, bioengineering, biology/biological sciences, biomedical engineering, black/African-American studies, broadcasting, cell biology, chemical engineering, chemistry, child psychology/child development, city/community/regional planning, civil engineering, classics, cognitive science, communication, comparative literature, computer engineering, computer science, dental services, (pre)dentistry sequence, economics, education, electrical engineering, engineering and applied sciences, engineering sciences, English, environmental engineering, environmental sciences, film studies, French, geography, geology, German, Germanic languages and literature, Greek, Hispanic studies, history, human development, humanities, industrial engineering, interdisciplinary studies, Italian, journalism, Judaic studies, Latin, Latin American studies, linguistics, literature, materials engineering, materials sciences, mathematics, mechanical engineering, (pre)medicine sequence, microbiology, modern languages, molecular biology, music, music education, music history, natural sciences, neurosciences, philosophy, physics, piano/organ, political science/government, Portuguese, psychology, radio and television studies, religious studies, Romance languages, Russian, Russian and Slavic studies, sacred music, science education, secondary education, Slavic languages, social science, sociology, Spanish, speech pathology and audiology, speech/rhetoric/public address/debate, speech therapy, statistics, stringed instruments, studio art, theater arts/drama, urban studies, voice, wind and percussion instruments, women's studies.

Applying *Required:* essay, high school transcript, 1 recommendation, SAT or ACT. *Recommended:* 3 years of high school math and science, some high school foreign language, interview, English Composition Test (with essay). Audition for music majors, Achievements, English Composition Test required for some. *Application deadlines:* 1/1, 11/1 for early decision, 2/15 priority date for financial aid. *Contact:* Ms. Carol Lunkenheimer, Director of Admissions, 1801 Hinman Avenue, Evanston, IL 60208, 708-491-4100.

✶ Oberlin College

Oberlin, Ohio

Founded 1833
Small-town setting
Independent
Coed
Awards B, M

Enrollment	2,912 total; 2,843 undergraduates (638 freshmen)
Faculty	248 total; student-faculty ratio is 12:1; grad assistants teach no undergraduate courses.
Libraries	1 million bound volumes, 292,288 titles on microform, 2,765 periodical subscriptions
Computing	*Terminals/PCs available for student use:* 195, located in computer center, student center, library, dormitories, classroom buildings; PC not required.
Of Special Interest	*Core academic program:* yes. Phi Beta Kappa, Sigma Xi chapters. Academic exchange with 11 members of the Great Lakes Colleges Association, Fisk University, Gallaudet University. Sponsors and participates in study-abroad programs.
On Campus	Drama/theater group; student-run newspaper and radio station. No national or local fraternities or sororities on campus.
Athletics	Member NCAA (Division III). *Intercollegiate sports:* baseball (M), basketball (M, W), cross-country running (M, W), equestrian sports (M, W), fencing (M, W), field hockey (W), football (M), ice hockey (M), lacrosse (M, W), racquetball (M, W), soccer (M, W), squash (M, W), swimming and diving (M, W), tennis (M, W), track and field (M, W), volleyball (M, W).

Costs (1991–92) & Aid				
	Comprehensive fee	$21,972	Need-based scholarships (average)	$9200
	Tuition	$16,375	Non-need scholarships (average)	$2000
	Mandatory fees	$442	Short-term loans (average)	$200
	Room and board	$5155	Long-term loans—college funds (average)	$1550
	Financial aid recipients	50%	Long-term loans—external funds (average)	$3100

Undergraduate Facts				
	Part-time	3%	*Freshman Data:* 3,392 applied, 68% were accepted, 28% (638) of those entered	
	State residents	N/R		
	Transfers	2%	From top tenth of high school class	55%
	African-Americans	8%	SAT-takers scoring 600 or over on verbal	55%
	Native Americans	1%	SAT-takers scoring 700 or over on verbal	11%
	Hispanics	3%	SAT-takers scoring 600 or over on math	69%
	Asian-Americans	9%	SAT-takers scoring 700 or over on math	21%
	International students	6%	ACT-takers scoring 26 or over	N/R
	Freshmen returning for sophomore year	94%	ACT-takers scoring 30 or over	N/R
	Students completing degree within 5 years	84%		
	Grads pursuing further study	N/R		

Majors Anthropology, archaeology, art/fine arts, art history, astronomy, biochemistry, biology/biological sciences, black/African-American studies, chemistry, classics, comparative literature, computer science, creative writing, dance, East Asian studies, ecology/environmental studies, economics, English, environmental sciences, French, geology, German, Greek, history, international studies, jazz, Judaic studies, Latin, Latin American studies, legal studies, mathematics, music, music education, music history, Near and Middle Eastern studies, neurosciences, philosophy, physics, piano/organ, political science/government, psychobiology, psychology, religious studies, Romance languages, Russian, Russian and Slavic studies, sociology, Spanish, stringed instruments, studio art, theater arts/drama, voice, wind and percussion instruments, women's studies.

Applying *Required:* essay, high school transcript, 2 recommendations, SAT or ACT. *Recommended:* 4 years of high school math, 3 years of high school science, 3 years of high school foreign language, interview, 3 Achievements, English Composition Test (with essay). *Application deadlines:* 1/15, 1/2 for early decision, continuous to 2/1 for financial aid. *Contact:* Mr. Thomas C. Hayden, Director of Admissions, 101 N. Professor St., Oberlin, OH 44074, 216-775-8411 or toll-free 800-622-OBIE.

Occidental College

Los Angeles, California

Founded 1887
Urban setting
Independent
Coed
Awards B, M

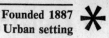

Enrollment	1,601 total; 1,570 undergraduates (395 freshmen)
Faculty	164 total; 134 full-time (94% have doctorate/terminal degree); student-faculty ratio is 11:1; grad assistants teach no undergraduate courses.
Libraries	520,000 bound volumes, 217,944 titles on microform, 2,075 periodical subscriptions
Computing	*Terminals/PCs available for student use:* 200, located in library, dormitories, classrooms; PC not required but available for purchase.
Of Special Interest	*Core academic program:* yes. Computer course required for economics, marine biology, cognitive science majors. Phi Beta Kappa chapter. Academic exchange with California Institute of Technology, Art Center College of Design. Sponsors and participates in study-abroad programs. Cooperative Army ROTC, cooperative Air Force ROTC.
On Campus	Drama/theater group; student-run newspaper. *Social organizations:* 4 national fraternities, 3 local sororities; 15% of eligible undergraduate men and 15% of eligible undergraduate women are members.
Athletics	Member NCAA (Division III), NAIA. *Intercollegiate sports:* badminton (M, W), baseball (M), basketball (M, W), cross-country running (M, W), equestrian sports (M, W), fencing (M, W), field hockey (W), football (M), golf (M, W), lacrosse (M), rugby (M), skiing (downhill) (M, W), soccer (M, W), softball (W), swimming and diving (M, W), tennis (M, W), track and field (M, W), volleyball (W), water polo (M).

Costs (1991–92) & Aid	Comprehensive fee	$19,727	Need-based scholarships (average)	$7825
	Tuition	$14,517	Non-need scholarships (average)	$6146
	Mandatory fees	$267	Short-term loans (average)	$513
	Room and board	$4943	Long-term loans—college funds (average)	$3120
	Financial aid recipients	65%	Long-term loans—external funds (average)	$2553

Undergraduate Facts				
	Part-time	1%	*Freshman Data:* 2,111 applied, 63% were accepted, 30% (395) of those entered	
	State residents	62%		
	Transfers	4%	From top tenth of high school class	57%
	African-Americans	6%	SAT-takers scoring 600 or over on verbal	26%
	Native Americans	1%	SAT-takers scoring 700 or over on verbal	5%
	Hispanics	12%	SAT-takers scoring 600 or over on math	50%
	Asian-Americans	15%	SAT-takers scoring 700 or over on math	11%
	International students	3%	ACT-takers scoring 26 or over	N/R
	Freshmen returning for sophomore year	86%	ACT-takers scoring 30 or over	N/R
	Students completing degree within 5 years	73%	*Majors with most degrees conferred:* English, biology/biological sciences, psychology.	
	Grads pursuing further study	N/R		

Majors American studies, anthropology, applied art, art education, art/fine arts, art history, Asian/Oriental studies, behavioral sciences, biochemistry, biology/biological sciences, chemistry, Chinese, classics, cognitive science, comparative literature, (pre)dentistry sequence, earth science, East Asian studies, East European and Soviet studies, ecology/environmental studies, economics, education, English, environmental sciences, film studies, French, geochemistry, geology, geophysics, German, Germanic languages and literature, Hispanic studies, history, history of science, interdisciplinary studies, international studies, Japanese, Latin American studies, (pre)law sequence, liberal arts/general studies, linguistics, literature, marine biology, mathematics, (pre)medicine sequence, microbiology, modern languages, molecular biology, music, music education, music history, neurosciences, painting/drawing, philosophy, physical fitness/human movement, physical sciences, physics, political science/government, psychobiology, psychology, public affairs and policy studies, religious studies, Romance languages, Russian, Russian and Slavic studies, sculpture, secondary education, sociology, Spanish, sports medicine, studio art, theater arts/drama, urban studies, (pre)veterinary medicine sequence, women's studies.

Applying *Required:* essay, high school transcript, 2 years of high school foreign language, 3 recommendations, SAT or ACT. *Recommended:* 3 years of high school math and science, interview, Achievements, English Composition Test (with essay). *Application deadlines:* 2/1, 11/15 for early decision, 2/1 for financial aid. *Contact:* Mrs. Charlene Liebau, Dean of Admissions, 1600 Campus Road, Los Angeles, CA 90041, 213-259-2700 or toll-free 800-825-5262.

✱ Oglethorpe University

Atlanta, Georgia

Founded 1835
Urban setting
Independent
Coed
Awards B, M

Enrollment 1,147 total; 1,061 undergraduates (200 freshmen)

Faculty 99 total; 41 full-time (95% have doctorate/terminal degree); student-faculty ratio is 11:1; grad assistants teach no undergraduate courses.

Libraries 88,469 bound volumes, 1 title on microform, 809 periodical subscriptions

Computing *Terminals/PCs available for student use:* 24, located in computer center; PC not required.

Of Special Interest *Core academic program:* yes. Computer course required for business administration, economics, accounting majors. Academic exchange with University Center in Georgia. Sponsors and participates in study-abroad programs. Cooperative Army ROTC, cooperative Naval ROTC, cooperative Air Force ROTC.

On Campus Drama/theater group; student-run newspaper. *Social organizations:* 4 national fraternities, 2 national sororities; 33% of eligible undergraduate men and 25% of eligible undergraduate women are members.

Athletics Member NCAA (Division III). *Intercollegiate sports:* baseball (M), basketball (M, W), cross-country running (M, W), soccer (M, W), tennis (M, W), track and field (M, W), volleyball (W).

Costs (1991–92) & Aid				
	Comprehensive fee	$13,950	Need-based scholarships (average)	$2112
	Tuition	$10,250	Non-need scholarships (average)	$3885
	Mandatory fees	N/App	Short-term loans (average)	$248
	Room and board	$3700	Long-term loans—college funds (average)	$1145
	Financial aid recipients	83%	Long-term loans—external funds (average)	$2953

Undergraduate Facts				
	Part-time	30%	*Freshman Data:* 752 applied, 84% were accepted, 32% (200) of those entered	
	State residents	62%		
	Transfers	7%	From top tenth of high school class	47%
	African-Americans	7%	SAT-takers scoring 600 or over on verbal	24%
	Native Americans	1%	SAT-takers scoring 700 or over on verbal	5%
	Hispanics	1%	SAT-takers scoring 600 or over on math	50%
	Asian-Americans	4%	SAT-takers scoring 700 or over on math	9%
	International students	4%	ACT-takers scoring 26 or over	63%
	Freshmen returning for sophomore year	73%	ACT-takers scoring 30 or over	12%
	Students completing degree within 5 years	59%	*Majors with most degrees conferred:* business, accounting, psychology.	
	Grads pursuing further study	32%		

Majors Accounting, American studies, art/fine arts, behavioral sciences, biology/biological sciences, business, business economics, chemistry, commercial art, communication, computer management, computer science, creative writing, (pre)dentistry sequence, early childhood education, economics, education, elementary education, English, French, history, interdisciplinary studies, international studies, (pre)law sequence, liberal arts/general studies, mathematics, medical technology, (pre)medicine sequence, music, philosophy, physics, political science/government, psychology, science, secondary education, social work, sociology, studio art, (pre)veterinary medicine sequence.

Applying *Required:* high school transcript, 3 years of high school math, 1 recommendation, SAT or ACT. *Recommended:* 3 years of high school science, some high school foreign language, interview, minimum 2.5 GPA. Interview required for some. *Application deadlines:* 8/1, 12/1 for early decision, 5/1 priority date for financial aid. *Contact:* Mr. Dennis T. Matthews, Director of Admissions, 4484 Peachtree Road, Atlanta, GA 30319, 404-364-8307.

Ohio Northern University

Ada, Ohio

Founded 1871
Small-town setting
Independent, United Methodist
Coed
Awards B, D

Enrollment	2,791 total; 2,343 undergraduates (601 freshmen)
Faculty	175 total; 155 full-time (77% have doctorate/terminal degree); student-faculty ratio is 13:1; grad assistants teach no undergraduate courses.
Libraries	378,801 bound volumes, 268,907 titles on microform, 4,003 periodical subscriptions
Computing	*Terminals/PCs available for student use:* 100, located in computer center, library, dormitories, academic buildings; PC not required.
Of Special Interest	*Core academic program:* yes. Computer course required. Sigma Xi chapter. Academic exchange program: no. Participates in study-abroad programs. Cooperative Army ROTC, cooperative Air Force ROTC.
On Campus	Drama/theater group; student-run newspaper and radio station. *Social organizations:* 8 national fraternities, 4 national sororities; 35% of eligible undergraduate men and 35% of eligible undergraduate women are members.
Athletics	Member NCAA (Division III). *Intercollegiate sports:* baseball (M), basketball (M, W), cross-country running (M, W), football (M), golf (M), soccer (M, W), softball (W), swimming and diving (M, W), tennis (M, W), track and field (M, W), volleyball (W), wrestling (M).

Costs (1992–93) & Aid				
	Comprehensive fee	$17,070	Need-based scholarships (average)	$3657
	Tuition	$13,455	Non-need scholarships (average)	$3726
	Mandatory fees	N/App	Short-term loans (average)	$1200
	Room and board	$3615	Long-term loans—college funds	N/Avail
	Financial aid recipients	90%	Long-term loans—external funds (average)	$2900

Undergraduate Facts				
	Part-time	4%	*Freshman Data:* 1,993 applied, 78% were accepted, 39% (601) of those entered	
	State residents	76%		
	Transfers	5%	From top tenth of high school class	33%
	African-Americans	3%	SAT-takers scoring 600 or over on verbal	N/R
	Native Americans	0%	SAT-takers scoring 700 or over on verbal	N/R
	Hispanics	0%	SAT-takers scoring 600 or over on math	N/R
	Asian-Americans	1%	SAT-takers scoring 700 or over on math	N/R
	International students	2%	ACT-takers scoring 26 or over	27%
	Freshmen returning for sophomore year	81%	ACT-takers scoring 30 or over	5%
	Students completing degree within 5 years	65%	*Majors with most degrees conferred:* pharmacy/ pharmaceutical sciences, elementary education, biology/biological sciences.	
	Grads pursuing further study	23%		

Majors Accounting, art/fine arts, biochemistry, biology/biological sciences, broadcasting, business, ceramic art and design, chemistry, civil engineering, communication, computer science, criminal justice, (pre)dentistry sequence, economics, electrical engineering, elementary education, English, finance/banking, French, graphic arts, health education, history, industrial arts, international studies, (pre)law sequence, marketing/retailing/merchandising, mathematics, mechanical engineering, medical technology, (pre)medicine sequence, music, music education, painting/drawing, pharmacy/pharmaceutical sciences, philosophy, physical education, physics, political science/government, psychology, public relations, religious studies, sociology, Spanish, speech/rhetoric/public address/debate, sports administration, sports medicine, theater arts/drama, (pre)veterinary medicine sequence.

Applying *Required:* high school transcript, 3 years of high school math, SAT or ACT. *Recommended:* essay, 2 years of high school foreign language, recommendations, campus interview. *Application deadlines:* 8/15, 6/1 priority date for financial aid. *Contact:* Ms. Karen Condeni, Dean of Admissions and Financial Aid, Lehr Memorial Building, Ada, OH 45810, 419-772-2260.

From the College While its facilities are among the best in the Midwest for a school its size, what truly sets Ohio Northern apart from other universities is its concern for each student. Attention to the individual, both in and out of the classroom, is the standard.

✻ Ohio Wesleyan University

Delaware, Ohio

Founded 1842
Small-town setting
Independent, United Methodist
Coed
Awards B

Enrollment 2,057 total—all undergraduates (521 freshmen)

Faculty 162 total; 132 full-time (95% have doctorate/terminal degree); student-faculty ratio is 14:1.

Libraries 456,000 bound volumes, 175 titles on microform, 1,198 periodical subscriptions

Computing *Terminals/PCs available for student use:* 135, located in computer center, library, dormitories, academic departments; PC not required. Campus network links student PCs.

Of Special Interest *Core academic program:* yes. Computer course required for math, science, psychology, economics majors. Phi Beta Kappa, Sigma Xi chapters. Academic exchange with 11 members of the Great Lakes Colleges Association, New York City Arts Program. Sponsors and participates in study-abroad programs. Cooperative Air Force ROTC.

On Campus Drama/theater group; student-run newspaper and radio station. *Social organizations:* 11 national fraternities, 7 national sororities; 55% of eligible undergraduate men and 45% of eligible undergraduate women are members.

Athletics Member NCAA (Division III). *Intercollegiate sports:* basketball (M, W), cross-country running (M, W), equestrian sports (M, W), field hockey (W), football (M), golf (M), lacrosse (M, W), rugby (M), sailing (M, W), soccer (M, W), swimming and diving (M, W), tennis (M, W), track and field (M, W), volleyball (W).

Costs (1992–93) & Aid				
	Comprehensive fee	$19,774	Need-based scholarships (average)	$8776
	Tuition	$14,644	Non-need scholarships (average)	$8312
	Mandatory fees	N/App	Short-term loans (average)	$150
	Room and board	$5130	Long-term loans—college funds (average)	$2000
	Financial aid recipients	54%	Long-term loans—external funds (average)	$2726

Undergraduate Facts				
	Part-time	3%	*Freshman Data:* 2,345 applied, 77% were accepted, 29% (521) of those entered	
	State residents	44%		
	Transfers	9%	From top tenth of high school class	33%
	African-Americans	5%	SAT-takers scoring 600 or over on verbal	23%
	Native Americans	1%	SAT-takers scoring 700 or over on verbal	1%
	Hispanics	1%	SAT-takers scoring 600 or over on math	44%
	Asian-Americans	2%	SAT-takers scoring 700 or over on math	12%
	International students	9%	ACT-takers scoring 26 or over	40%
	Freshmen returning for sophomore year	86%	ACT-takers scoring 30 or over	12%
	Students completing degree within 5 years	75%	*Majors with most degrees conferred:* business, biology/biological sciences, political science/government.	
	Grads pursuing further study	31%		

Majors Accounting, anthropology, art education, art/fine arts, art history, art therapy, astronomy, bacteriology, biology/biological sciences, black/African-American studies, botany/plant sciences, broadcasting, business, chemistry, classics, computer science, creative writing, (pre)dentistry sequence, earth science, economics, education, elementary education, engineering sciences, English, environmental sciences, French, geography, geology, German, health education, history, humanities, international business, international studies, journalism, (pre)law sequence, literature, mathematics, (pre)medicine sequence, music, music education, nursing, philosophy, physical education, physics, political science/government, psychology, public administration, religious studies, sacred music, secondary education, sociology, Spanish, statistics, studio art, theater arts/drama, urban studies, (pre)veterinary medicine sequence, women's studies, zoology.

Applying *Required:* essay, high school transcript, 3 years of high school math, 2 recommendations, SAT or ACT. *Recommended:* 3 years of high school science, 3 years of high school foreign language, interview, English Composition Test. *Application deadlines:* 3/1, 1/4 for early decision, 3/15 priority date for financial aid. *Contact:* Mr. O'Neal Turner, Director of Admission, Slocum Hall, Delaware, OH 43015, 614-368-3024 or toll-free 800-862-0612 (in-state), 800-922-8953 (out-of-state).

Pacific Lutheran University

Tacoma, Washington

Independent/affiliated with Evangelical Lutheran Church in America

Founded 1890
Suburban setting
Coed
Awards B, M

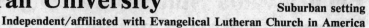

Enrollment 3,571 total; 3,008 undergraduates (505 freshmen)

Faculty 304 total; 233 full-time (90% have doctorate/terminal degree); student-faculty ratio is 14:1; grad assistants teach no undergraduate courses.

Libraries 333,010 bound volumes, 54,151 titles on microform, 2,110 periodical subscriptions

Computing *Terminals/PCs available for student use:* 100, located in computer center, science building; PC not required. Campus network links student PCs.

Of Special Interest *Core academic program:* yes. Computer course required for business, math, engineering majors. Academic exchange program: no. Sponsors and participates in study-abroad programs. Army ROTC.

On Campus Drama/theater group; student-run newspaper and radio station. No national or local fraternities or sororities on campus.

Athletics Member NAIA. *Intercollegiate sports:* baseball (M), basketball (M, W), crew (M, W), cross-country running (M, W), football (M), golf (M), lacrosse (M), skiing (cross-country) (M, W), skiing (downhill) (M, W), soccer (M, W), softball (W), swimming and diving (M, W), tennis (M, W), track and field (M, W), volleyball (M, W), wrestling (M). *Scholarships:* M, W.

Costs (1991–92) & Aid				
	Comprehensive fee	$14,965	Need-based scholarships (average)	$2534
	Tuition	$11,075	Non-need scholarships (average)	$2150
	Mandatory fees	N/App	Short-term loans (average)	$250
	Room and board	$3890	Long-term loans—college funds	N/Avail
	Financial aid recipients	73%	Long-term loans—external funds (average)	$3200

Undergraduate Facts				
	Part-time	16%	*Freshman Data:* 1,647 applied, 80% were accepted, 38% (505) of those entered	
	State residents	68%		
	Transfers	32%	From top tenth of high school class	38%
	African-Americans	2%	SAT-takers scoring 600 or over on verbal	14%
	Native Americans	1%	SAT-takers scoring 700 or over on verbal	2%
	Hispanics	1%	SAT-takers scoring 600 or over on math	27%
	Asian-Americans	4%	SAT-takers scoring 700 or over on math	6%
	International students	4%	ACT-takers scoring 26 or over	N/R
	Freshmen returning for sophomore year	78%	ACT-takers scoring 30 or over	N/R
	Students completing degree within 5 years	66%	*Majors with most degrees conferred:* business, education, biology/biological sciences.	
	Grads pursuing further study	N/R		

Majors Accounting, anthropology, art education, art/fine arts, art history, biochemistry, biology/biological sciences, broadcasting, business, business education, chemistry, classics, communication, computer engineering, computer science, (pre)dentistry sequence, early childhood education, earth science, ecology/environmental studies, economics, education, electrical engineering, elementary education, engineering physics, English, finance/banking, French, geology, German, history, international business, international studies, jazz, journalism, (pre)law sequence, legal studies, literature, management information systems, marketing/retailing/merchandising, mathematics, medical technology, (pre)medicine sequence, modern languages, music, music education, nursing, philosophy, physical education, physics, piano/organ, political science/government, psychology, public relations, publishing, radio and television studies, reading education, recreational facilities management, recreation and leisure services, recreation therapy, religious studies, sacred music, Scandinavian languages/studies, secondary education, social work, sociology, Spanish, special education, speech/rhetoric/ public address/debate, sports administration, sports medicine, stringed instruments, studio art, theater arts/drama, (pre)veterinary medicine sequence, voice.

Applying *Required:* essay, high school transcript, 2 years of high school foreign language, 2 recommendations, SAT or ACT. *Recommended:* 3 years of high school math and science, English Composition Test (with essay). Interview required for some. *Application deadlines:* 5/1, 11/15 for early action, 3/1 priority date for financial aid. *Contact:* Mr. David Gunovich, Interim Director of Admissions, Tacoma, WA 98447, 206-535-7151 or toll-free 800-274-6758.

From the College International study is a Pacific Lutheran University specialty. Study abroad places over 200 students annually in foreign settings; on-campus programs include Scandinavian, Chinese, and Global studies as well as new language offerings in Japanese and Chinese. Another highlight is the completion of a new campus music center.

Pennsylvania State University
University Park Campus
State College, Pennsylvania

Founded 1855
Small-town setting
State-related
Coed
Awards A, B, M, D

Enrollment 38,989 total; 32,475 undergraduates (4,712 freshmen)

Faculty 2,177 total; 1,778 full-time (88% have doctorate/terminal degree); student-faculty ratio is 19:1; grad assistants teach a few undergraduate courses.

Libraries 2.3 million bound volumes, 2.2 million titles on microform, 26,233 periodical subscriptions

Computing *Terminals/PCs available for student use:* 1,737, located in computer center, library, dormitories, classrooms; PC not required. Campus network links student PCs.

Of Special Interest *Core academic program:* yes. Computer course required for some engineering majors. Phi Beta Kappa, Sigma Xi chapters. Sponsors study-abroad programs. Army ROTC, Naval ROTC, Air Force ROTC.

On Campus Drama/theater group; student-run newspaper and radio station. *Social organizations:* 55 national fraternities, 25 national sororities; 15% of eligible undergraduate men and 17% of eligible undergraduate women are members.

Athletics Member NCAA (Division I). *Intercollegiate sports:* baseball (M), basketball (M, W), cross-country running (M, W), equestrian sports (M, W), fencing (M, W), field hockey (W), football (M), golf (M, W), gymnastics (M, W), ice hockey (M), lacrosse (M, W), rugby (M, W), skiing (downhill) (M, W), soccer (M, W), swimming and diving (M, W), tennis (M, W), track and field (M, W), volleyball (M, W), water polo (M), weight lifting (M), wrestling (M). *Scholarships:* M, W.

Costs (1991–92) & Aid
State resident tuition	$4332	Need-based scholarships — Avail
Nonresident tuition	$9118	Non-need scholarships — Avail
Mandatory fees	$70	Short-term loans — Avail
Room and board	$3670	Long-term loans — Avail
Financial aid recipients	73%	

Undergraduate Facts
Part-time	7%
State residents	82%
Transfers	2%
African-Americans	3%
Native Americans	1%
Hispanics	1%
Asian-Americans	4%
International students	1%
Freshmen returning for sophomore year	84%
Students completing degree within 5 years	57%
Grads pursuing further study	N/R

Freshman Data: 22,820 applied, 54% were accepted, 38% (4,712) of those entered
From top tenth of high school class	43%
SAT-takers scoring 600 or over on verbal	15%
SAT-takers scoring 700 or over on verbal	2%
SAT-takers scoring 600 or over on math	45%
SAT-takers scoring 700 or over on math	10%
ACT-takers scoring 26 or over	N/R
ACT-takers scoring 30 or over	N/R

Majors with most degrees conferred: accounting, elementary education, liberal arts/general studies.

Majors Accounting, actuarial science, advertising, aerospace engineering, agricultural business, agricultural economics, agricultural education, agricultural engineering, agricultural sciences, agronomy/soil and crop sciences, American studies, animal sciences, anthropology, architectural engineering, architecture, art education, art/fine arts, art history, astronomy, biochemistry, biology/biological sciences, botany/plant sciences, broadcasting, business, business economics, cell biology, ceramic engineering, ceramic sciences, chemical engineering, chemistry, child care/child and family studies, civil engineering, classics, communication, community services, comparative literature, computer engineering, computer science, criminal justice, dairy sciences, earth science, East Asian studies, ecology/environmental studies, economics, electrical engineering, elementary education, engineering sciences, English, entomology, environmental engineering, family and consumer studies, film and video, film studies, finance/banking, fish and game management, food sciences, forestry, forest technology, French, geography, geological engineering, geology, German, health education, health services administration, history, home economics education, horticulture, hotel and restaurant management, human development, industrial engineering, insurance, interdisciplinary studies, international business, international studies, Italian, journalism, labor and industrial relations, labor studies, landscape architecture/design, landscaping/grounds maintenance, Latin American studies, law enforcement/police sciences, (pre)law sequence, liberal arts/general studies, linguistics, literature, management information systems, marketing/retailing/merchandising, mathematics, mechanical engineering, (pre)medicine sequence, medieval studies, metallurgy, meteorology, microbiology, mining and mineral engineering, molecular biology, music, music education, nuclear engineering, nursing, nutrition, operations research, parks management, petroleum/natural gas engineering, philosophy, physical fitness/human movement, physics, political science/government, pollution control technologies, polymer science, poultry sciences, psychology, public affairs and policy studies, real estate, recreation and leisure services, religious studies, Russian, science, secondary education, social work, sociology, Spanish, special education, speech pathology and audiology, speech/rhetoric/public address/debate, theater arts/drama, (pre)veterinary medicine sequence, vocational education, wildlife management.

Applying *Required:* high school transcript, 3 years of high school math and science, SAT or ACT. Some high school foreign language required for some. *Application deadlines:* rolling, 3/15 priority date for financial aid. *Contact:*, Director of Undergraduate Admissions, 201 Shields Building, University Park, PA 16802, 814-865-5478.

Pepperdine University

Malibu, California

Founded 1937
Small-town setting
Independent/affiliated with Church of Christ
Coed
Awards B, M, D ✱

Enrollment	6,800 total; 2,707 undergraduates (691 freshmen)
Faculty	294 total; 143 full-time (99% have doctorate/terminal degree); student-faculty ratio is 13:1; grad assistants teach no undergraduate courses.
Libraries	465,695 bound volumes, 438,896 titles on microform, 3,248 periodical subscriptions
Computing	*Terminals/PCs available for student use:* 256, located in computer center, library, dormitories, electronic classrooms; PC not required. Campus network links student PCs.
Of Special Interest	*Core academic program:* yes. Computer course required for business, math, social science, communications, biology, chemistry majors. Academic exchange program: no. Sponsors and participates in study-abroad programs. Cooperative Army ROTC, cooperative Naval ROTC, cooperative Air Force ROTC.
On Campus	Mandatory chapel; drama/theater group; student-run newspaper and radio station. *Social organizations:* 6 local fraternities, 7 local sororities; 25% of eligible undergraduate men and 30% of eligible undergraduate women are members.
Athletics	Member NCAA (Division I). *Intercollegiate sports:* baseball (M), basketball (M, W), cross-country running (M, W), golf (M, W), ice hockey (M), lacrosse (M), rugby (M), soccer (W), swimming and diving (W), tennis (M, W), volleyball (M, W), water polo (M). *Scholarships:* M, W.

Costs (1992–93 estimated) & Aid	Comprehensive fee	$22,560	Need-based scholarships (average)	$5687
	Tuition	$16,000	Non-need scholarships (average)	$3900
	Mandatory fees	$60	Short-term loans (average)	$200
	Room and board	$6500	Long-term loans—college funds (average)	$2500
	Financial aid recipients	65%	Long-term loans—external funds (average)	$2625
Undergraduate Facts	Part-time	5%	*Freshman Data:* 3,105 applied, 57% were accepted, 691 entered	
	State residents	53%		
	Transfers	5%	From top tenth of high school class	85%
	African-Americans	4%	SAT-takers scoring 600 or over on verbal	13%
	Native Americans	1%	SAT-takers scoring 700 or over on verbal	2%
	Hispanics	7%	SAT-takers scoring 600 or over on math	21%
	Asian-Americans	6%	SAT-takers scoring 700 or over on math	1%
	International students	10%	ACT-takers scoring 26 or over	53%
	Freshmen returning for sophomore year	84%	ACT-takers scoring 30 or over	8%
	Students completing degree within 5 years	68%	*Majors with most degrees conferred:* business, communication, international studies.	
	Grads pursuing further study	52%		

Majors Accounting, advertising, American studies, art/fine arts, biology/biological sciences, broadcasting, business, chemistry, communication, computer science, economics, education, elementary education, English, French, German, history, humanities, interdisciplinary studies, international studies, journalism, liberal arts/general studies, literature, mathematics, music, music education, natural sciences, nutrition, philosophy, physical education, political science/government, psychology, public relations, recreation and leisure services, religious education, religious studies, secondary education, social science, sociology, Spanish, sports medicine, telecommunications, theater arts/drama.

Applying *Required:* essay, high school transcript, 3 years of high school math, 2 recommendations, SAT. *Recommended:* 3 years of high school science, 2 years of high school foreign language, interview, ACT, Achievements. English Composition Test required for some. *Application deadlines:* 2/1, 11/15 for early action, 3/1 priority date for financial aid. *Contact:* Mr. Paul Long, Dean of Admission, 24255 Pacific Coast Highway, Malibu, CA 90265, 310-456-4392.

Pitzer College

Claremont, California

Founded 1963
Small-town setting
Independent
Coed
Awards B

Enrollment	750 total—all undergraduates (190 freshmen)
Faculty	88 total; 60 full-time (100% have doctorate/terminal degree); student-faculty ratio is 10:1.
Libraries	1.9 million bound volumes, 1 million titles on microform, 10,900 periodical subscriptions
Computing	*Terminals/PCs available for student use:* 45, located in computer center, library.
Of Special Interest	*Core academic program:* yes. Computer course required for economics, organizational studies majors. Sigma Xi chapter. Academic exchange with The Claremont Colleges, Colby College. Sponsors and participates in study-abroad programs.
On Campus	Drama/theater group; student-run newspaper and radio station. No national or local fraternities or sororities on campus.
Athletics	Member NCAA (Division III). *Intercollegiate sports:* badminton (M, W), baseball (M), basketball (M, W), cross-country running (M, W), fencing (M, W), football (M), golf (M), soccer (M, W), softball (W), swimming and diving (M, W), tennis (M, W), track and field (M, W), volleyball (W), water polo (M), wrestling (M).

Costs (1991–92) & Aid				
	Comprehensive fee	$21,284	Need-based scholarships (average)	$9500
	Tuition	$14,992	Non-need scholarships	Avail
	Mandatory fees	$1290	Short-term loans (average)	$100
	Room and board	$5002	Long-term loans—college funds (average)	$4100
	Financial aid recipients	49%	Long-term loans—external funds (average)	$2400

Undergraduate Facts				
	Part-time	5%	*Freshman Data:* 1,090 applied, 54% were accepted, 32% (190) of those entered	
	State residents	44%		
	Transfers	5%	From top tenth of high school class	36%
	African-Americans	6%	SAT-takers scoring 600 or over on verbal	24%
	Native Americans	2%	SAT-takers scoring 700 or over on verbal	5%
	Hispanics	11%	SAT-takers scoring 600 or over on math	29%
	Asian-Americans	8%	SAT-takers scoring 700 or over on math	6%
	International students	6%	ACT-takers scoring 26 or over	64%
	Freshmen returning for sophomore year	92%	ACT-takers scoring 30 or over	3%
	Students completing degree within 5 years	75%	*Majors with most degrees conferred:* psychology, English.	
	Grads pursuing further study	34%		

Majors American studies, anthropology, art/fine arts, Asian/Oriental studies, biology/biological sciences, chemistry, classics, economics, English, environmental sciences, European studies, film studies, folklore, French, German, history, international studies, Latin American studies, linguistics, mathematics, Mexican-American/Chicano studies, music, natural sciences, philosophy, physics, political science/government, psychobiology, psychology, religious studies, social science, sociology, Spanish, theater arts/drama, women's studies.

Applying *Required:* essay, high school transcript, 2 recommendations, SAT or ACT. *Recommended:* 3 years of high school math and science, 2 years of high school foreign language, interview, 3 Achievements, English Composition Test. *Application deadlines:* 2/1, 12/1 for early action, 2/1 for financial aid. *Contact:* Dr. Paul B. Ranslow, Dean of Admission and College Relations, 1050 North Mills Avenue, Claremont, CA 91711-6110, 714-621-8129.

Polytechnic University, Brooklyn Campus
Brooklyn, New York

Founded 1854
Urban setting
Independent
Coed
Awards B, M, D

Enrollment	2,130 total; 1,118 undergraduates (243 freshmen)
Faculty	393 total; 195 full-time (94% have doctorate/terminal degree); student-faculty ratio is 14:1; grad assistants teach a few undergraduate courses.
Libraries	310,000 bound volumes, 1,561 periodical subscriptions
Computing	*Terminals/PCs available for student use:* 160, located in computer center, library, computer labs; PC not required but available for purchase.
Of Special Interest	*Core academic program:* yes. Computer course required. Sigma Xi chapter. Academic exchange program: no. Participates in study-abroad programs. Army ROTC, cooperative Air Force ROTC.
On Campus	Student-run newspaper. *Social organizations:* 2 national fraternities, 3 local fraternities, 1 coed fraternity; 10% of eligible undergraduate men and 1% of eligible undergraduate women are members.
Athletics	Member NCAA (Division III). *Intercollegiate sports:* baseball (M), basketball (M, W), cross-country running (M), lacrosse (M), soccer (M), tennis (M, W), volleyball (W).

Costs (1991–92) & Aid				
	Comprehensive fee	$19,060	Need-based scholarships	Avail
	Tuition	$13,600	Non-need scholarships (average)	$7523
	Mandatory fees	$400	Short-term loans	N/Avail
	Room and board	$5060	Long-term loans—college funds (average)	$1024
	Financial aid recipients	88%	Long-term loans—external funds (average)	$2690

Undergraduate Facts				
	Part-time	16%	*Freshman Data:* 707 applied, 74% were accepted, 46% (243) of those entered	
	State residents	85%		
	Transfers	28%	From top tenth of high school class	42%
	African-Americans	10%	SAT-takers scoring 600 or over on verbal	11%
	Native Americans	N/R	SAT-takers scoring 700 or over on verbal	2%
	Hispanics	10%	SAT-takers scoring 600 or over on math	54%
	Asian-Americans	30%	SAT-takers scoring 700 or over on math	19%
	International students	12%	ACT-takers scoring 26 or over	N/R
	Freshmen returning for sophomore year	87%	ACT-takers scoring 30 or over	N/R
	Students completing degree within 5 years	60%	*Majors with most degrees conferred:* electrical engineering, mechanical engineering, aerospace engineering.	
	Grads pursuing further study	4%		

Majors Actuarial science, aerospace engineering, applied mathematics, chemical engineering, chemistry, civil engineering, computer engineering, computer information systems, computer science, electrical engineering, humanities, industrial engineering, journalism, manufacturing engineering, mathematics, mechanical engineering, metallurgical engineering, physics, social science, technical writing.

Applying *Required:* high school transcript, 3 years of high school math and science, recommendations, SAT or ACT. *Recommended:* essay, interview. *Application deadlines:* rolling, 12/1 for early decision, same for early action, 2/1 priority date for financial aid. *Contact:* Mr. Peter G. Jordan, Director of Undergraduate Admissions, 6 Metrotech Center, Brooklyn, NY 11201, 718-260-3100 or toll-free 800-POLYTECH.

Polytechnic University, Farmingdale Campus
Farmingdale, New York

Founded 1854
Suburban setting
Independent
Coed
Awards B, M, D

Enrollment	822 total; 433 undergraduates (94 freshmen)
Faculty	393 total; 195 full-time (94% have doctorate/terminal degree); student-faculty ratio is 14:1; grad assistants teach a few undergraduate courses.
Libraries	310,000 bound volumes, 1,561 periodical subscriptions
Computing	*Terminals/PCs available for student use:* 86, located in computer center, library, computer labs; PC not required but available for purchase. Campus network links student PCs.
Of Special Interest	*Core academic program:* yes. Computer course required. Academic exchange with 15 members of the Long Island Regional Advisory Council for Higher Education. Participates in study-abroad programs. Army ROTC, cooperative Air Force ROTC.
On Campus	Student-run newspaper. *Social organizations:* 1 national fraternity, 2 coed fraternities; 25% of eligible undergraduate men and 5% of eligible undergraduate women are members.
Athletics	Member NCAA (Division III). *Intercollegiate sports:* baseball (M), basketball (M), cross-country running (M), lacrosse (M), soccer (M), tennis (M), volleyball (W).

Costs (1991–92) & Aid				
	Comprehensive fee	$18,350	Need-based scholarships	Avail
	Tuition	$13,600	Non-need scholarships (average)	$8800
	Mandatory fees	$400	Short-term loans	N/Avail
	Room and board	$4350	Long-term loans—college funds (average)	$1024
	Financial aid recipients	89%	Long-term loans—external funds (average)	$2690

Undergraduate Facts				
	Part-time	19%	*Freshman Data:* 402 applied, 74% were accepted, 32% (94) of those entered	
	State residents	95%		
	Transfers	32%	From top tenth of high school class	69%
	African-Americans	4%	SAT-takers scoring 600 or over on verbal	20%
	Native Americans	0%	SAT-takers scoring 700 or over on verbal	5%
	Hispanics	5%	SAT-takers scoring 600 or over on math	69%
	Asian-Americans	15%	SAT-takers scoring 700 or over on math	23%
	International students	5%	ACT-takers scoring 26 or over	N/R
	Freshmen returning for sophomore year	90%	ACT-takers scoring 30 or over	N/R
	Students completing degree within 5 years	60%	*Majors with most degrees conferred:* electrical engineering, mechanical engineering, aerospace engineering.	
	Grads pursuing further study	4%		

Majors Aerospace engineering, chemical engineering, civil engineering, computer engineering, computer information systems, computer science, electrical engineering, industrial engineering, mathematics, mechanical engineering, metallurgical engineering.

Applying *Required:* high school transcript, 3 years of high school math and science, recommendations, SAT or ACT. *Recommended:* essay, interview. *Application deadlines:* rolling, 11/1 for early decision, same for early action, 2/1 priority date for financial aid. *Contact:* Mr. William N. Blades, Director of Admissions, Long Island Center, Farmingdale, NY 11735, 516-755-4200 or toll-free 800-POLYTECH.

Pomona College

Claremont, California

Founded 1887
Small-town setting
Independent
Coed
Awards B

Enrollment	1,375 total—all undergraduates (360 freshmen)
Faculty	154 total—all full-time (100% have doctorate/terminal degree); student-faculty ratio is 9:1.
Libraries	1.8 million bound volumes, 1 million titles on microform, 6,830 periodical subscriptions
Computing	*Terminals/PCs available for student use:* 160, located in computer center, student center, library, dormitories, classroom buildings; PC not required.
Of Special Interest	*Core academic program:* yes. Computer course required for chemistry, biochemistry, economics, geology, physics, math, sociology majors. Phi Beta Kappa, Sigma Xi chapters. Academic exchange with other members of The Claremont Colleges, Swarthmore College, Colby College, Smith College, Fisk University, Spelman College. Sponsors and participates in study-abroad programs.
On Campus	Drama/theater group; student-run newspaper and radio station. *Social organizations:* 3 local fraternities, 4 local coed fraternities; 8% of eligible undergraduate men and 2% of eligible undergraduate women are members.
Athletics	Member NCAA (Division III). *Intercollegiate sports:* baseball (M), basketball (M, W), cross-country running (M, W), football (M), golf (M), soccer (M, W), softball (W), swimming and diving (M, W), tennis (M, W), track and field (M, W), volleyball (W), water polo (M).

Costs (1991–92) & Aid	Comprehensive fee	$21,080	Need-based scholarships (average)	$10,400
	Tuition	$14,800	Non-need scholarships	N/Avail
	Mandatory fees	$130	Short-term loans (average)	$100
	Room and board	$6150	Long-term loans—college funds (average)	$2500
	Financial aid recipients	55%	Long-term loans—external funds (average)	$2600

Undergraduate Facts	Part-time	0%	*Freshman Data:* 2,854 applied, 37% were accepted, 34% (360) of those entered	
	State residents	42%		
	Transfers	2%	From top tenth of high school class	79%
	African-Americans	5%	SAT-takers scoring 600 or over on verbal	71%
	Native Americans	1%	SAT-takers scoring 700 or over on verbal	16%
	Hispanics	11%	SAT-takers scoring 600 or over on math	86%
	Asian-Americans	15%	SAT-takers scoring 700 or over on math	47%
	International students	2%	ACT-takers scoring 26 or over	N/R
	Freshmen returning for sophomore year	99%	ACT-takers scoring 30 or over	N/R
	Students completing degree within 5 years	92%	*Majors with most degrees conferred:* English, political science/government, psychology.	
	Grads pursuing further study	24%		

Majors American studies, anthropology, art/fine arts, art history, Asian/Oriental studies, astronomy, biochemistry, biology/biological sciences, black/African-American studies, cell biology, chemistry, Chinese, classics, computer science, East Asian studies, ecology/environmental studies, economics, English, film studies, French, geology, German, Germanic languages and literature, Hispanic studies, history, humanities, interdisciplinary studies, international studies, Japanese, liberal arts/general studies, linguistics, literature, mathematics, (pre)medicine sequence, Mexican-American/Chicano studies, microbiology, modern languages, molecular biology, music, philosophy, physics, political science/government, psychology, public affairs and policy studies, religious studies, Romance languages, Russian, sociology, Spanish, studio art, theater arts/drama, women's studies.

Applying *Required:* essay, high school transcript, 3 years of high school math, 3 years of high school foreign language, 3 recommendations, SAT or ACT. *Recommended:* 3 years of high school science, interview, portfolio or tapes for art and performing arts, 3 Achievements, English Composition Test (with essay). *Application deadlines:* 1/15, 11/15 for early decision, 2/1 for financial aid. *Contact:* Mr. Bruce Poch, Dean of Admissions, 333 North College Way, Claremont, CA 91711, 714-621-8134.

✷ Presbyterian College

Clinton, South Carolina

Founded 1880
Small-town setting
Independent, Presbyterian
Coed
Awards B

Enrollment 1,148 total—all undergraduates (291 freshmen)

Faculty 98 total; 73 full-time (81% have doctorate/terminal degree); student-faculty ratio is 14:1.

Libraries 140,000 bound volumes, 4,500 titles on microform, 750 periodical subscriptions

Computing *Terminals/PCs available for student use:* 100, located in computer center, library, academic buildings; PC not required.

Of Special Interest *Core academic program:* yes. Computer course required for math, physics majors. Academic exchange with Gulf Coast Marine Laboratory, American University. Sponsors and participates in study-abroad programs. Army ROTC.

On Campus Drama/theater group; student-run newspaper and radio station. *Social organizations:* 6 national fraternities, 3 national sororities, Women's Social Hall; 46% of eligible undergraduate men and 42% of eligible undergraduate women are members.

Athletics Member NCAA (Division II), NAIA. *Intercollegiate sports:* baseball (M), basketball (M, W), cross-country running (M), football (M), golf (M), riflery (M, W), soccer (M, W), tennis (M, W), track and field (M), volleyball (W). *Scholarships:* M, W.

Costs (1991–92) & Aid				
	Comprehensive fee	$13,510	Need-based scholarships (average)	$3191
	Tuition	$9512	Non-need scholarships (average)	$2186
	Mandatory fees	$814	Short-term loans	N/Avail
	Room and board	$3184	Long-term loans—college funds (average)	$2352
	Financial aid recipients	75%	Long-term loans—external funds (average)	$3290

Undergraduate Facts				
	Part-time	5%	*Freshman Data:* 1,105 applied, 74% were accepted, 35% (291) of those entered	
	State residents	47%		
	Transfers	5%	From top tenth of high school class	40%
	African-Americans	5%	SAT-takers scoring 600 or over on verbal	17%
	Native Americans	N/R	SAT-takers scoring 700 or over on verbal	2%
	Hispanics	1%	SAT-takers scoring 600 or over on math	28%
	Asian-Americans	1%	SAT-takers scoring 700 or over on math	4%
	International students	1%	ACT-takers scoring 26 or over	47%
	Freshmen returning for sophomore year	88%	ACT-takers scoring 30 or over	7%
	Students completing degree within 5 years	77%	*Majors with most degrees conferred:* business, psychology, biology/biological sciences.	
	Grads pursuing further study	30%		

Majors Accounting, art/fine arts, biology/biological sciences, business, chemistry, (pre)dentistry sequence, economics, education, elementary education, English, French, German, history, (pre)law sequence, mathematics, (pre)medicine sequence, modern languages, music, music education, philosophy, physics, political science/government, psychology, religious studies, social science, sociology, Spanish, special education, theater arts/drama, (pre)veterinary medicine sequence.

Applying *Required:* essay, high school transcript, 3 years of high school math, some high school foreign language, 1 recommendation, SAT or ACT. *Recommended:* 3 years of high school science, interview. *Application deadlines:* 4/1, 3/1 priority date for financial aid. *Contact:* Ms. Margaret Williamson, Dean of Admissions and Financial Aid, South Broad Street, Clinton, SC 29325, 803-833-2820 Ext. 8229 or toll-free 800-476-7272.

From the College Presbyterian College—with 16 national and international scholarship recipients in recent years, including a Rhodes Scholar—emphasizes a high-quality, values-centered education. One example is a new program in applied ethics. Students respect the strong honor code and participate in an active, community-based volunteer service program.

Princeton University

Princeton, New Jersey

Founded 1746
Suburban setting
Independent
Coed
Awards B, M, D

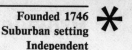

Enrollment	6,412 total; 4,538 undergraduates (1,132 freshmen)
Faculty	890 total; 795 full-time; student-faculty ratio is 5:1; grad assistants teach a few undergraduate courses.
Libraries	4.3 million bound volumes, 2.7 million titles on microform, 36,850 periodical subscriptions
Computing	*Terminals/PCs available for student use:* 438, located in computer center, library, dormitories, academic departments.
Of Special Interest	*Core academic program:* yes. Computer course required for engineering majors. Phi Beta Kappa, Sigma Xi chapters. Academic exchange with Rutgers, The State University of New Jersey, Westminster Choir College, Princeton Theological Seminary. Participates in study-abroad programs. Army ROTC, cooperative Air Force ROTC.
On Campus	Drama/theater group; student-run newspaper and radio station. *Social organizations:* 11 eating clubs; 70% of eligible undergraduate men and 70% of eligible undergraduate women are members.
Athletics	Member NCAA (Division I), NAIA. *Intercollegiate sports:* baseball (M), basketball (M, W), crew (M, W), cross-country running (M, W), fencing (M, W), field hockey (W), football (M), golf (M, W), ice hockey (M, W), lacrosse (M, W), soccer (M, W), softball (W), squash (M, W), swimming and diving (M, W), table tennis (M, W), tennis (M, W), track and field (M, W), volleyball (M, W), wrestling (M).

Costs (1992–93) & Aid				
	Comprehensive fee	$23,267	Need-based scholarships (average)	$10,600
	Tuition	$17,750	Non-need scholarships	N/Avail
	Mandatory fees	N/App	Short-term loans	N/Avail
	Room and board	$5517	Long-term loans—college funds (average)	$3000
	Financial aid recipients	41%	Long-term loans—external funds (average)	$3000
Undergraduate Facts	Part-time	0%	*Freshman Data:* 12,717 applied, 16% were accepted, 56% (1,132) of those entered	
	State residents	13%		
	Transfers	1%	From top tenth of high school class	90%
	African-Americans	7%	SAT-takers scoring 600 or over on verbal	75%
	Native Americans	1%	SAT-takers scoring 700 or over on verbal	27%
	Hispanics	5%	SAT-takers scoring 600 or over on math	94%
	Asian-Americans	10%	SAT-takers scoring 700 or over on math	60%
	International students	6%	ACT-takers scoring 26 or over	N/App
	Freshmen returning for sophomore year	98%	ACT-takers scoring 30 or over	N/App
	Students completing degree within 5 years	94%	*Majors with most degrees conferred:* history, English, political science/government.	
	Grads pursuing further study	N/R		

Majors Aerospace engineering, African studies, American studies, anthropology, applied mathematics, archaeology, architectural engineering, architecture, art/fine arts, art history, astrophysics, bioengineering, biology/biological sciences, black/African-American studies, chemical engineering, chemistry, civil engineering, classics, cognitive science, comparative literature, computer science, creative writing, East Asian studies, ecology/environmental studies, economics, electrical engineering, energy management technologies, engineering and applied sciences, engineering management, engineering physics, English, environmental engineering, environmental sciences, European studies, evolutionary biology, geological engineering, geology, geophysics, Germanic languages and literature, history, humanities, international studies, Latin American studies, linguistics, management engineering, mathematics, mechanical engineering, molecular biology, music, Near and Middle Eastern studies, philosophy, physics, political science/government, psychology, public affairs and policy studies, religious studies, robotics, Romance languages, Russian and Slavic studies, Slavic languages, sociology, statistics, theater arts/drama, transportation engineering, women's studies.

Applying *Required:* essay, high school transcript, recommendations, SAT. *Recommended:* 4 years of high school math, 3 years of high school science, 4 years of high school foreign language, interview, 3 Achievements. Achievements required for some. *Application deadlines:* 1/2, 11/1 for early action, 2/1 for financial aid. *Contact:* Mr. Fred A. Hargadon, Dean of Admission, West College, Princeton, NJ 08544, 609-258-6150.

✳ Providence College

Providence, Rhode Island

Founded 1917
Urban setting
Independent, Roman Catholic
Coed
Awards A, B, M, D

Enrollment 6,204 total; 3,814 undergraduates (967 freshmen)

Faculty 296 total; 250 full-time (79% have doctorate/terminal degree); student-faculty ratio is 15:1; grad assistants teach no undergraduate courses.

Libraries 301,067 bound volumes, 25,709 titles on microform, 1,877 periodical subscriptions

Computing *Terminals/PCs available for student use:* 144, located in computer center, classrooms; PC not required.

Of Special Interest *Core academic program:* yes. Computer course required for engineering, health services, math, business-related majors. Academic exchange program: no. Sponsors and participates in study-abroad programs. Army ROTC.

On Campus Drama/theater group; student-run newspaper and radio station. No national or local fraternities or sororities on campus.

Athletics Member NCAA (Division I). *Intercollegiate sports:* baseball (M), basketball (M, W), cross-country running (M, W), field hockey (W), golf (M), ice hockey (M, W), lacrosse (M), racquetball (M, W), rugby (M, W), soccer (M, W), softball (W), swimming and diving (M, W), tennis (M, W), track and field (M, W), volleyball (W). *Scholarships:* M, W.

Costs (1991–92) & Aid				
	Comprehensive fee	$17,140	Need-based scholarships (average)	$5150
	Tuition	$11,740	Non-need scholarships (average)	$10,000
	Mandatory fees	$100	Short-term loans	N/Avail
	Room and board	$5300	Long-term loans—college funds	N/Avail
	Financial aid recipients	51%	Long-term loans—external funds (average)	$3000

Undergraduate Facts				
	Part-time	41%	*Freshman Data:* 5,414 applied, 60% were accepted, 30% (967) of those entered	
	State residents	15%		
	Transfers	2%	From top tenth of high school class	22%
	African-Americans	2%	SAT-takers scoring 600 or over on verbal	9%
	Native Americans	0%	SAT-takers scoring 700 or over on verbal	1%
	Hispanics	2%	SAT-takers scoring 600 or over on math	27%
	Asian-Americans	1%	SAT-takers scoring 700 or over on math	3%
	International students	1%	ACT-takers scoring 26 or over	62%
	Freshmen returning for sophomore year	95%	ACT-takers scoring 30 or over	6%
	Students completing degree within 5 years	87%		
	Grads pursuing further study	N/R		

Majors Accounting, American studies, art/fine arts, art history, biology/biological sciences, business, business economics, chemistry, computer science, economics, education, elementary education, English, finance/banking, French, health services administration, history, humanities, instrumentation technology, Italian, Latin American studies, liberal arts/general studies, marketing/retailing/merchandising, mathematics, modern languages, music, painting/drawing, philosophy, photography, political science/government, psychology, religious studies, secondary education, social science, social work, sociology, Spanish, special education, studio art, systems science, theater arts/drama.

Applying *Required:* essay, high school transcript, SAT or ACT. *Recommended:* 3 years of high school math, 3 years of high school foreign language, recommendations, campus interview, 3 Achievements, English Composition Test. 3 years of high school science required for some. *Application deadlines:* 2/1, 12/15 for early action, 2/15 priority date for financial aid. *Contact:* Mr. Michael G. Backes, Dean of Admissions, Eaton Street and River Avenue, Providence, RI 02918, 401-865-2535.

Purdue University

West Lafayette, Indiana

Founded 1869
Suburban setting
State-supported
Coed
Awards A, B, M, D

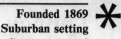

Enrollment	36,163 total; 29,663 undergraduates (5,954 freshmen)
Faculty	2,208 total; 2,110 full-time (99% have doctorate/terminal degree); student-faculty ratio is 18:1; grad assistants teach about a quarter of the undergraduate courses.
Libraries	1.9 million bound volumes, 1.8 million titles on microform, 16,400 periodical subscriptions
Computing	*Terminals/PCs available for student use:* 500, located in computer center, student center, dormitories; PC not required. Campus network links student PCs.
Of Special Interest	*Core academic program:* no. Computer course required for engineering, management, agriculture, consumer and family sciences majors. Phi Beta Kappa, Sigma Xi chapters. Academic exchange program: no. Sponsors and participates in study-abroad programs. Army ROTC, Naval ROTC, Air Force ROTC.
On Campus	Drama/theater group; student-run newspaper and radio station. *Social organizations:* 45 national fraternities, 24 national sororities, 1 local sorority; 24% of eligible undergraduate men and 24% of eligible undergraduate women are members.
Athletics	Member NCAA (Division I). *Intercollegiate sports:* archery (M, W), baseball (M), basketball (M, W), crew (M, W), cross-country running (M, W), equestrian sports (M, W), fencing (M, W), football (M), golf (M, W), gymnastics (M, W), ice hockey (M), lacrosse (M, W), racquetball (M, W), riflery (M, W), rugby (M, W), sailing (M, W), soccer (M, W), squash (M, W), swimming and diving (M, W), tennis (M, W), track and field (M, W), volleyball (W), water polo (M, W), wrestling (M). *Scholarships:* M, W.

Costs (1991–92) & Aid				
	State resident tuition	$2324	Need-based scholarships	Avail
	Nonresident tuition	$7440	Non-need scholarships (average)	$1000
	Mandatory fees	N/App	Short-term loans	N/Avail
	Room and board	$3010	Long-term loans—college funds	Avail
	Financial aid recipients	40%	Long-term loans—external funds	Avail

Undergraduate Facts				
	Part-time	9%	*Freshman Data:* 21,909 applied, 83% were accepted, 33% (5,954) of those entered	
	State residents	72%		
	Transfers	N/R	From top tenth of high school class	35%
	African-Americans	3%	SAT-takers scoring 600 or over on verbal	15%
	Native Americans	1%	SAT-takers scoring 700 or over on verbal	2%
	Hispanics	2%	SAT-takers scoring 600 or over on math	32%
	Asian-Americans	3%	SAT-takers scoring 700 or over on math	7%
	International students	2%	ACT-takers scoring 26 or over	82%
	Freshmen returning for sophomore year	88%	ACT-takers scoring 30 or over	40%
	Students completing degree within 5 years	68%	*Majors with most degrees conferred:* engineering (general), communication, pharmacy/pharmaceutical sciences.	
	Grads pursuing further study	20%		

Majors Accounting, actuarial science, advertising, agricultural business/economics/sciences/technologies, agronomy, aircraft/missile maintenance, American studies, animal sciences, anthropology, applied mathematics, art/fine arts, art history, athletic training, atmospheric sciences, aviation administration/technology, biochemistry, biological sciences, biomedical sciences, black/African-American studies, botany, business, business economics, cell biology, ceramic art/design, chemistry, child care/child and family, child psychology/development, clinical psychology, commercial art, communication, community services, comparative literature, computer programming/science/technologies, conservation, construction management/technologies, consumer services, creative writing, criminal justice, (pre)dentistry sequence, dietetics, drafting/design, earth science, ecology/environmental studies, economics, education (agricultural, art, early childhood, elementary, health, home economics, physical, reading, science, secondary, special, vocational), educational media, electrical/electronics technologies, electrical engineering technology, engineering (aerospace, agricultural, biomedical, chemical, civil, computer, construction, electrical, forest, general, geological, industrial, management, manufacturing, materials, mechanical, metallurgical, nuclear, surveying, systems), engineering management/sciences/technology, English, entomology, environmental health sciences, environmental sciences, evolutionary biology, family/consumer studies, farm/ranch management, fashion design and technology/merchandising, film studies, finance/banking, fish/game management, flight training, food marketing/sciences, food services management, forestry, forest technology, French, genetics, geochemistry, geology, geophysics, German, Germanic languages/literature, graphic arts, health science, history, home economics, horticulture, hospitality services, hotel/restaurant management, human resources, illustration, industrial administration/arts/design, industrial engineering technology, interdisciplinary studies, interior design, journalism, landscape architecture/design, landscaping/grounds maintenance, (pre)law sequence, linguistics, management information systems, manufacturing technology, marketing/retailing/merchandising, materials sciences, mathematics, mechanical engineering technology, medical technology, (pre)medicine sequence, medieval studies, metallurgy, meteorology, microbiology, molecular biology, natural resource management, neurosciences, nuclear physics, nursing, nutrition, occupational safety/health, painting/drawing, paleontology, parks management, pharmacology, pharmacy/pharmaceutical sciences, philosophy, photography, physical fitness/human movement, physical sciences, physics, physiology, political science/government, poultry sciences, psychology, public relations, radio/television, radiological sciences, range management, recreational facilities management, recreation/leisure services, religious studies, retail management, robotics, Russian, science, social work, sociology, soil conservation, Spanish, speech pathology and audiology/therapy, statistics, technology and public affairs, telecommunications, textile arts, textiles/clothing, theater arts/drama, tourism/travel, (pre)veterinary medicine sequence, veterinary sciences, wildlife biology/management, wood sciences.

Applying *Required:* high school transcript, SAT or ACT. *Recommended:* 3 years of high school math and science, some high school foreign language, recommendations, campus interview. 3 years of high school math and science required for some. *Application deadlines:* rolling, 3/1 priority date for financial aid. *Contact:* Mr. William J. Murray, Director of Admissions, Schleman Hall, West Lafayette, IN 47907, 317-494-1776.

✱ Quincy College

Quincy, Illinois

Founded 1860
Small-town setting
Independent, Roman Catholic
Coed
Awards A, B, M

Enrollment	1,374 total; 1,313 undergraduates (362 freshmen)
Faculty	99 total; 68 full-time (63% have doctorate/terminal degree); student-faculty ratio is 13:1; grad assistants teach no undergraduate courses.
Libraries	220,847 bound volumes, 154,101 titles on microform, 715 periodical subscriptions
Computing	*Terminals/PCs available for student use:* 129, located in computer center, library, dormitories; PC not required.
Of Special Interest	*Core academic program:* yes. Computer course required for political science, sociology, accounting, management, marketing majors. Academic exchange program: no. Participates in study-abroad programs.
On Campus	Drama/theater group; student-run newspaper and radio station. No national or local fraternities or sororities on campus.
Athletics	Member NCAA (Division II). *Intercollegiate sports:* baseball (M), basketball (M, W), football (M), soccer (M, W), softball (W), tennis (M, W), volleyball (M, W). *Scholarships:* M, W.

Costs (1991–92) & Aid				
	Comprehensive fee	$12,044	Need-based scholarships (average)	$2284
	Tuition	$8404	Non-need scholarships (average)	$4064
	Mandatory fees	$200	Short-term loans (average)	$150
	Room and board	$3440	Long-term loans—college funds (average)	$2258
	Financial aid recipients	95%	Long-term loans—external funds (average)	$2788

Undergraduate Facts				
	Part-time	15%	*Freshman Data:* 1,249 applied, 69% were accepted, 42% (362) of those entered	
	State residents	71%		
	Transfers	7%	From top tenth of high school class	23%
	African-Americans	3%	SAT-takers scoring 600 or over on verbal	N/R
	Native Americans	1%	SAT-takers scoring 700 or over on verbal	N/R
	Hispanics	1%	SAT-takers scoring 600 or over on math	N/R
	Asian-Americans	1%	SAT-takers scoring 700 or over on math	N/R
	International students	1%	ACT-takers scoring 26 or over	36%
	Freshmen returning for sophomore year	88%	ACT-takers scoring 30 or over	8%
	Students completing degree within 5 years	64%	*Majors with most degrees conferred:* political science/government, business, elementary education.	
	Grads pursuing further study	22%		

Majors Accounting, art education, art/fine arts, art history, biology/biological sciences, business, chemistry, communication, computer science, (pre)dentistry sequence, elementary education, English, finance/banking, history, humanities, human resources, interdisciplinary studies, international studies, (pre)law sequence, liberal arts/general studies, management information systems, marketing/retailing/merchandising, mathematics, medical technology, (pre)medicine sequence, music, music business, music education, philosophy, physical education, political science/government, psychology, radio and television studies, religious education, secondary education, social work, sociology, special education, sports administration, studio art, theology, (pre)veterinary medicine sequence.

Applying *Required:* high school transcript, 1 recommendation, SAT or ACT. *Recommended:* 3 years of high school math and science, some high school foreign language, interview. *Application deadlines:* rolling, continuous processing for financial aid. *Contact:* Mr. Patrick Olwig, Director of Admissions, 1800 College Avenue, Quincy, IL 62301, 217-222-8020 Ext. 5215 or toll-free 800-688-4295.

Randolph-Macon Woman's College

Lynchburg, Virginia

Founded 1891
Suburban setting
Independent, Methodist
Women
Awards B

Enrollment	769 total—all undergraduates (215 freshmen)
Faculty	91 total; 67 full-time (94% have doctorate/terminal degree); student-faculty ratio is 10:1.
Libraries	159,500 bound volumes, 350 titles on microform, 840 periodical subscriptions
Computing	*Terminals/PCs available for student use:* 70, located in computer center, library, dormitories; PC not required.
Of Special Interest	*Core academic program:* yes. Phi Beta Kappa chapter. Academic exchange with members of the Tri-College Consortium, Seven-College Exchange Program, American University (Washington Semester). Sponsors and participates in study-abroad programs. Cooperative Army ROTC.
On Campus	Drama/theater group; student-run newspaper and radio station. No national or local sororities on campus.
Athletics	Member NCAA (Division III). *Intercollegiate sports:* basketball, equestrian sports, fencing, field hockey, lacrosse, soccer, softball, swimming and diving, tennis, volleyball.

Costs (1992–93) & Aid				
	Comprehensive fee	$18,070	Need-based scholarships (average)	$5682
	Tuition	$12,450	Non-need scholarships (average)	$2253
	Mandatory fees	$120	Short-term loans	N/Avail
	Room and board	$5500	Long-term loans—college funds	N/Avail
	Financial aid recipients	70%	Long-term loans—external funds (average)	$2924

Undergraduate Facts				
	Part-time	7%	*Freshman Data:* 700 applied, 85% were accepted, 36% (215) of those entered	
	State residents	41%		
	Transfers	8%	From top tenth of high school class	31%
	African-Americans	4%	SAT-takers scoring 600 or over on verbal	15%
	Native Americans	0%	SAT-takers scoring 700 or over on verbal	1%
	Hispanics	2%	SAT-takers scoring 600 or over on math	18%
	Asian-Americans	2%	SAT-takers scoring 700 or over on math	2%
	International students	6%	ACT-takers scoring 26 or over	N/R
	Freshmen returning for sophomore year	75%	ACT-takers scoring 30 or over	N/R
	Students completing degree within 5 years	70%	*Majors with most degrees conferred:* English, art/fine arts, political science/government.	
	Grads pursuing further study	33%		

Majors Anthropology, art/fine arts, art history, biology/biological sciences, chemistry, classics, communication, creative writing, dance, economics, English, French, German, Germanic languages and literature, Greek, history, international studies, Latin, literature, mathematics, music, music history, philosophy, physics, political science/government, psychology, religious studies, Russian and Slavic studies, sociology, Spanish, studio art, theater arts/drama, voice.

Applying *Required:* essay, high school transcript, 3 years of high school math, 3 years of high school foreign language, 3 recommendations, SAT or ACT, 3 Achievements, English Composition Test. *Recommended:* 3 years of high school science, interview. *Application deadlines:* 3/1, 11/15 for early decision, 3/1 priority date for financial aid. *Contact:* Ms. Jean H. Stewart, Senior Associate Director of Admissions, 2500 Rivermont Avenue, Lynchburg, VA 24503, 804-846-9680.

✷ Reed College

Portland, Oregon

Founded 1909
Suburban setting
Independent
Coed
Awards B, M

Enrollment	1,299 total; 1,274 undergraduates (296 freshmen)
Faculty	132 total; 101 full-time (79% have doctorate/terminal degree); student-faculty ratio is 11:1; grad assistants teach no undergraduate courses.
Libraries	345,491 bound volumes, 32,250 titles on microform, 1,510 periodical subscriptions
Computing	*Terminals/PCs available for student use:* 135, located in computer center, library, some academic departments; PC not required. Campus network links student PCs. Student PCs can link with departmental networks.
Of Special Interest	*Core academic program:* yes. Computer course required for physics, math, biology, psychology majors. Phi Beta Kappa chapter. Academic exchange with Oregon Independent Colleges Association. Sponsors and participates in study-abroad programs. Cooperative Army ROTC.
On Campus	Drama/theater group; student-run newspaper and radio station. No national or local fraternities or sororities on campus.
Athletics	*Intercollegiate sports:* basketball (M), crew (M, W), fencing (M, W), rugby (M, W), sailing (M, W), skiing (cross-country) (M, W), skiing (downhill) (M, W), soccer (M, W).

Costs (1992–93 estimated) & Aid	Comprehensive fee	$22,830	Need-based scholarships (average)	$10,200
	Tuition	$18,060	Non-need scholarships	N/Avail
	Mandatory fees	$130	Short-term loans (average)	$100
	Room and board	$4640	Long-term loans—college funds (average)	$2300
	Financial aid recipients	50%	Long-term loans—external funds (average)	$2300

Undergraduate Facts	Part-time	5%	*Freshman Data:* 1,744 applied, 65% were accepted, 26% (296) of those entered	
	State residents	19%		
	Transfers	5%	From top tenth of high school class	56%
	African-Americans	2%	SAT-takers scoring 600 or over on verbal	68%
	Native Americans	0%	SAT-takers scoring 700 or over on verbal	22%
	Hispanics	2%	SAT-takers scoring 600 or over on math	73%
	Asian-Americans	6%	SAT-takers scoring 700 or over on math	29%
	International students	3%	ACT-takers scoring 26 or over	N/R
	Freshmen returning for sophomore year	90%	ACT-takers scoring 30 or over	N/R
	Students completing degree within 5 years	58%	*Majors with most degrees conferred:* biology/ biological sciences, English, history.	
	Grads pursuing further study	57%		

Majors American studies, anthropology, art/fine arts, art history, biochemistry, biology/biological sciences, biophysics, chemistry, Chinese, classics, dance, economics, English, French, German, Germanic languages and literature, history, international studies, linguistics, literature, mathematics, medieval studies, music, philosophy, physics, political science/government, psychology, religious studies, Russian, sociology, Spanish, studio art, theater arts/drama.

Applying *Required:* essay, high school transcript, 2 recommendations, SAT or ACT. *Recommended:* 3 years of high school math and science, some high school foreign language, interview, 3 Achievements, English Composition Test (with essay). 3 Achievements required for some. *Application deadlines:* 2/15, 12/1 for early decision, 3/1 for financial aid. *Contact:* Mr. Robert Mansueto, Director of Admission, 3203 Southeast Woodstock Boulevard, Portland, OR 97202-8199, 503-777-7511 or toll-free 800-547-4750 (out-of-state).

From the College Foremost an intellectual community, Reed offers an integrated curriculum. From freshman humanities to the senior thesis, there is a balance of breadth and depth through structure and flexibility. Reed ranks first among the nation's undergraduate institutions in percentage of graduates earning Ph.D.'s. Reed also ranks first in faculty commitment to teaching in a national survey of professors.

Rensselaer Polytechnic Institute

Troy, New York

Founded 1824
Suburban setting
Independent
Coed
Awards B, M, D

Enrollment	6,842 total; 4,450 undergraduates (972 freshmen)
Faculty	465 total; 395 full-time (98% have doctorate/terminal degree); student-faculty ratio is 11:1; grad assistants teach a few undergraduate courses.
Libraries	565,752 bound volumes, 541,219 titles on microform, 4,835 periodical subscriptions
Computing	*Terminals/PCs available for student use:* 457, located in computer center, library, dormitories, academic buildings; PC not required. Campus network links student PCs.
Of Special Interest	*Core academic program:* yes. Computer course required for engineering, math, physics, science and technology, management, economics majors. Sigma Xi chapter. Academic exchange with 14 members of the Hudson-Mohawk Association of Colleges and Universities, Williams College, Harvey Mudd College. Sponsors and participates in study-abroad programs. Army ROTC, Naval ROTC, Air Force ROTC.
On Campus	Drama/theater group; student-run newspaper and radio station. *Social organizations:* 28 national fraternities, 4 national sororities, 1 local fraternity, 1 local sorority, 1 coed fraternity; 35% of eligible undergraduate men and 25% of eligible undergraduate women are members.
Athletics	Member NCAA (Division III). *Intercollegiate sports:* baseball (M), basketball (M, W), crew (M, W), cross-country running (M, W), equestrian sports (M, W), field hockey (W), football (M), golf (M), ice hockey (M, W), lacrosse (M, W), rugby (M), skiing (cross-country) (M, W), skiing (downhill) (M, W), soccer (M, W), softball (W), swimming and diving (M, W), tennis (M, W), track and field (M, W), wrestling (M). *Scholarships:* M.

Costs (1991–92) & Aid				
	Comprehensive fee	$20,775	Need-based scholarships (average)	$6511
	Tuition	$15,150	Non-need scholarships (average)	$2635
	Mandatory fees	$475	Short-term loans	N/Avail
	Room and board	$5150	Long-term loans—college funds (average)	$2750
	Financial aid recipients	75%	Long-term loans—external funds (average)	$4750

Undergraduate Facts				
	Part-time	0%	*Freshman Data:* 4,746 applied, 78% were accepted, 26% (972) of those entered	
	State residents	37%		
	Transfers	4%	From top tenth of high school class	59%
	African-Americans	4%	SAT-takers scoring 600 or over on verbal	25%
	Native Americans	1%	SAT-takers scoring 700 or over on verbal	3%
	Hispanics	4%	SAT-takers scoring 600 or over on math	83%
	Asian-Americans	13%	SAT-takers scoring 700 or over on math	32%
	International students	5%	ACT-takers scoring 26 or over	N/R
	Freshmen returning for sophomore year	85%	ACT-takers scoring 30 or over	N/R
	Students completing degree within 5 years	N/R	*Majors with most degrees conferred:* mechanical engineering, electrical engineering, computer science.	
	Grads pursuing further study	N/R		

Majors Aerospace engineering, architecture, biochemistry, biology/biological sciences, biomedical engineering, biophysics, business, chemical engineering, chemistry, civil engineering, communication, computer engineering, computer science, (pre)dentistry sequence, economics, electrical engineering, engineering physics, engineering sciences, environmental engineering, geology, industrial engineering, interdisciplinary studies, (pre)law sequence, management engineering, materials engineering, mathematics, mechanical engineering, (pre)medicine sequence, nuclear engineering, philosophy, physics, psychology, science, science education, technical writing, technology and public affairs.

Applying *Required:* high school transcript, 3 years of high school math and science, 1 recommendation, SAT or ACT. *Recommended:* some high school foreign language, campus interview, 3 Achievements, English Composition Test. Essay, 3 Achievements required for some. *Application deadlines:* 1/15, 1/1 for early decision, 2/15 priority date for financial aid. *Contact:* Mr. Conrad J. Sharrow, Dean of Undergraduate Admissions, Sage and Eaton Streets, Troy, NY 12180, 518-276-6216 or toll-free 800-448-6562.

From the College One of America's leading technological universities, Rensselaer is committed to teaching, education, and research. Undergraduates have numerous opportunities to conduct research through the University-funded Undergraduate Research Program. Washington Roebling, chief engineer of the Brooklyn Bridge, and Nancy Fitzroy, the first woman to be named president of the American Society of Mechanical Engineers, are among successful Rensselaer graduates.

Rhodes College

Memphis, Tennessee

Founded 1848
Suburban setting
Independent, Presbyterian
Coed
Awards B

Enrollment 1,429 total—all undergraduates (381 freshmen)

Faculty 147 total; 113 full-time (95% have doctorate/terminal degree); student-faculty ratio is 12:1.

Libraries 220,000 bound volumes, 6,200 titles on microform, 1,170 periodical subscriptions

Computing *Terminals/PCs available for student use:* 110, located in computer center, library, classroom buildings; PC not required but available for purchase. Campus network links student PCs.

Of Special Interest *Core academic program:* yes. Computer course required for math, economics, business, political science majors. Phi Beta Kappa chapter. Academic exchange with Memphis College of Art, Gulf Coast Research Laboratory, Oak Ridge National Laboratory. Sponsors and participates in study-abroad programs. Cooperative Army ROTC, cooperative Air Force ROTC.

On Campus Drama/theater group; student-run newspaper. *Social organizations:* 6 national fraternities, 7 national sororities; 55% of eligible undergraduate men and 63% of eligible undergraduate women are members.

Athletics Member NCAA (Division III). *Intercollegiate sports:* baseball (M), basketball (M, W), cross-country running (M, W), equestrian sports (M, W), football (M), golf (M), lacrosse (M), soccer (M, W), swimming and diving (M, W), tennis (M, W), track and field (M, W), volleyball (W).

Costs (1992–93) & Aid				
	Comprehensive fee	$18,659	Need-based scholarships (average)	$7073
	Tuition	$13,792	Non-need scholarships (average)	$7092
	Mandatory fees	$158	Short-term loans	N/Avail
	Room and board	$4709	Long-term loans—college funds (average)	$1102
	Financial aid recipients	67%	Long-term loans—external funds (average)	$2956

Undergraduate Facts				
	Part-time	5%	*Freshman Data:* 2,003 applied, 68% were accepted, 28% (381) of those entered	
	State residents	38%		
	Transfers	5%	From top tenth of high school class	57%
	African-Americans	5%	SAT-takers scoring 600 or over on verbal	49%
	Native Americans	0%	SAT-takers scoring 700 or over on verbal	7%
	Hispanics	1%	SAT-takers scoring 600 or over on math	65%
	Asian-Americans	3%	SAT-takers scoring 700 or over on math	18%
	International students	3%	ACT-takers scoring 26 or over	72%
	Freshmen returning for sophomore year	87%	ACT-takers scoring 30 or over	26%
	Students completing degree within 5 years	75%	*Majors with most degrees conferred:* business, biology/biological sciences, English.	
	Grads pursuing further study	32%		

Majors Anthropology, art/fine arts, biochemistry, biology/biological sciences, business, chemistry, classics, computer science, economics, English, French, German, history, interdisciplinary studies, international business, international economics, international studies, Latin American studies, mathematics, music, philosophy, physics, political science/government, psychology, religious studies, Russian and Slavic studies, sociology, Spanish, studio art, theater arts/drama, urban studies.

Applying *Required:* essay, high school transcript, 3 years of high school math, 2 years of high school foreign language, 2 recommendations, SAT or ACT. *Recommended:* 3 years of high school science, interview. *Application deadlines:* 2/1, 11/15 for early decision, 3/1 priority date for financial aid. *Contact:* Mr. David Wottle, Dean of Admissions and Financial Aid, 2000 North Parkway, Memphis, TN 38112, 901-726-3700 or toll-free 800-844-5969 (out-of-state).

Rice University

Houston, Texas

Founded 1912
Urban setting
Independent
Coed
Awards B, M, D

Enrollment 4,079 total; 2,697 undergraduates (624 freshmen)

Faculty 542 total; 424 full-time (98% have doctorate/terminal degree); student-faculty ratio is 9:1; grad assistants teach a few undergraduate courses.

Libraries 1.5 million bound volumes, 1.8 million titles on microform, 13,100 periodical subscriptions

Computing *Terminals/PCs available for student use:* 200, located in computer center, dormitories, academic department buildings; PC not required.

Of Special Interest *Core academic program:* yes. Computer course required for business, electrical engineering, mechanical engineering, chemical engineering, space physics majors. Phi Beta Kappa, Sigma Xi chapters. Academic exchange with 5 members of the Swarthmore College Exchange. Sponsors and participates in study-abroad programs. Naval ROTC, cooperative Army ROTC.

On Campus Drama/theater group; student-run newspaper and radio station. No national or local fraternities or sororities on campus.

Athletics Member NCAA (Division I). *Intercollegiate sports:* baseball (M), basketball (M, W), crew (M, W), cross-country running (M, W), football (M), golf (M), lacrosse (M), riflery (M, W), rugby (M), sailing (M, W), soccer (M, W), swimming and diving (M, W), tennis (M, W), track and field (M, W), volleyball (W). *Scholarships:* M, W.

Costs (1991–92) & Aid

Comprehensive fee	$12,900	
Tuition	$7700	
Mandatory fees	$300	
Room and board	$4900	
Financial aid recipients	80%	
Need-based scholarships (average)		$4191
Non-need scholarships (average)		$4016
Short-term loans (average)		$300
Long-term loans—college funds		N/Avail
Long-term loans—external funds (average)		$3910

Undergraduate Facts

Part-time	0%
State residents	47%
Transfers	1%
African-Americans	6%
Native Americans	1%
Hispanics	6%
Asian-Americans	8%
International students	2%
Freshmen returning for sophomore year	95%
Students completing degree within 5 years	88%
Grads pursuing further study	60%

Freshman Data: 6,028 applied, 21% were accepted, 50% (624) of those entered

From top tenth of high school class	86%
SAT-takers scoring 600 or over on verbal	76%
SAT-takers scoring 700 or over on verbal	25%
SAT-takers scoring 600 or over on math	88%
SAT-takers scoring 700 or over on math	60%
ACT-takers scoring 26 or over	N/App
ACT-takers scoring 30 or over	N/App

Majors Anthropology, architecture, art/fine arts, art history, Asian/Oriental studies, behavioral sciences, biochemistry, biology/biological sciences, business, chemical engineering, chemistry, civil engineering, classics, computer engineering, computer science, ecology/environmental studies, economics, electrical engineering, English, environmental engineering, evolutionary biology, French, geology, geophysics, German, history, linguistics, materials sciences, mathematics, mechanical engineering, music, neurosciences, philosophy, physical education, physics, political science/government, psychology, public affairs and policy studies, religious studies, Russian and Slavic studies, sociology, Spanish, statistics.

Applying *Required:* essay, high school transcript, 3 years of high school math, 2 years of high school foreign language, 2 recommendations, SAT, 3 Achievements, English Composition Test. *Recommended:* interview. 3 years of high school science required for some. *Application deadlines:* 1/2, 11/1 for early decision, 12/1 for early action, 6/1 priority date for financial aid. *Contact:* Mr. Ron W. Moss, Director of Admissions, 6100 South Main Street, Houston, TX 77251, 713-527-4036 or toll-free 800-527-OWLS (out-of-state).

Ripon College

Ripon, Wisconsin

Founded 1851
Small-town setting
Independent
Coed
Awards B

Enrollment	838 total—all undergraduates (165 freshmen)
Faculty	97 total; 75 full-time (88% have doctorate/terminal degree); student-faculty ratio is 11:1.
Libraries	150,312 bound volumes, 17,526 titles on microform, 700 periodical subscriptions
Computing	*Terminals/PCs available for student use:* 82, located in computer center, library, dormitories, classroom buildings; PC not required.
Of Special Interest	*Core academic program:* yes. Computer course required for math, science, business majors. Phi Beta Kappa chapter. Academic exchange with American University, Newberry Library, Oak Ridge National Laboratory, University of Chicago, Associated Colleges of the Midwest Wilderness Field Station. Sponsors and participates in study-abroad programs. Army ROTC.
On Campus	Drama/theater group; student-run newspaper and radio station. *Social organizations:* 3 national fraternities, 2 national sororities, 3 local fraternities, 1 local sorority; 65% of eligible undergraduate men and 30% of eligible undergraduate women are members.
Athletics	Member NCAA (Division III). *Intercollegiate sports:* baseball (M), basketball (M, W), cross-country running (M, W), fencing (M, W), football (M), golf (M), ice hockey (M), lacrosse (M, W), riflery (M, W), rugby (M), soccer (M, W), softball (W), swimming and diving (M, W), tennis (M, W), track and field (M, W), volleyball (W), wrestling (M).

Costs (1991–92) & Aid	Comprehensive fee	$16,050	Need-based scholarships (average)	$3667
	Tuition	$12,740	Non-need scholarships (average)	$2156
	Mandatory fees	$160	Short-term loans (average)	$50
	Room and board	$3150	Long-term loans—college funds	N/Avail
	Financial aid recipients	86%	Long-term loans—external funds (average)	$1783

Undergraduate Facts	Part-time	3%	*Freshman Data:* 530 applied, 86% were accepted, 36% (165) of those entered	
	State residents	55%		
	Transfers	13%	From top tenth of high school class	34%
	African-Americans	1%	SAT-takers scoring 600 or over on verbal	22%
	Native Americans	1%	SAT-takers scoring 700 or over on verbal	3%
	Hispanics	2%	SAT-takers scoring 600 or over on math	33%
	Asian-Americans	2%	SAT-takers scoring 700 or over on math	8%
	International students	4%	ACT-takers scoring 26 or over	36%
	Freshmen returning for sophomore year	91%	ACT-takers scoring 30 or over	11%
	Students completing degree within 5 years	64%	*Majors with most degrees conferred:* history, economics, biology/biological sciences.	
	Grads pursuing further study	20%		

Majors Anthropology, art/fine arts, behavioral sciences, biochemistry, biology/biological sciences, business, chemistry, computer science, (pre)dentistry sequence, economics, education, elementary education, English, French, German, history, interdisciplinary studies, (pre)law sequence, literature, mathematics, (pre)medicine sequence, modern languages, music, music education, natural sciences, philosophy, physical education, physical sciences, physics, political science/government, psychobiology, psychology, Romance languages, science, secondary education, sociology, Spanish, speech/rhetoric/public address/debate, theater arts/drama, (pre)veterinary medicine sequence.

Applying *Required:* essay, high school transcript, 1 recommendation, SAT or ACT. *Recommended:* 3 years of high school math and science, some high school foreign language, interview. *Application deadlines:* 3/15, 12/1 for early decision, 3/1 priority date for financial aid. *Contact:* Mr. Paul J. Weeks, Dean of Admissions, 300 Seward Street, Ripon, WI 54971, 414-748-8102 or toll-free 800-242-0324 (in-state), 800-558-0248 (out-of-state).

From the College Ripon College has an unrivaled commitment to the liberal arts and a dedicated teaching faculty to ensure its fulfillment. The traditional, residential nature of Ripon creates a distinctive academic and social community. This atmosphere offers the best educational value and scholarship and financial aid programs represent the commitment to making Ripon affordable.

Rochester Institute of Technology

Rochester, New York

Founded 1829
Suburban setting
Independent
Coed
Awards A, B, M, D

Enrollment	13,018 total; 11,150 undergraduates (1,400 freshmen)
Faculty	1,076 total; 636 full-time (70% have doctorate/terminal degree); student-faculty ratio is 13:1; grad assistants teach no undergraduate courses.
Libraries	324,000 bound volumes, 4,803 titles on microform, 6,394 periodical subscriptions
Computing	*Terminals/PCs available for student use:* 800, located in computer center, library, dormitories, College of Fine Arts; PC not required. Campus network links student PCs.
Of Special Interest	*Core academic program:* yes. Computer course required for most majors. Academic exchange with members of the Rochester Area Colleges. Sponsors and participates in study-abroad programs. Army ROTC, Air Force ROTC, cooperative Naval ROTC.
On Campus	Drama/theater group; student-run newspaper and radio station. *Social organizations:* 10 national fraternities, 3 national sororities, local fraternities, local sororities; 6% of eligible undergraduate men and 6% of eligible undergraduate women are members.
Athletics	Member NCAA (Division III). *Intercollegiate sports:* baseball (M), basketball (M, W), cross-country running (M, W), ice hockey (M, W), lacrosse (M, W), soccer (M, W), softball (W), swimming and diving (M, W), tennis (M, W), track and field (M, W), volleyball (W), wrestling (M).

Costs (1991–92) & Aid				
	Comprehensive fee	$17,118	Need-based scholarships (average)	$3900
	Tuition	$11,823	Non-need scholarships (average)	$2065
	Mandatory fees	$195	Short-term loans (average)	$100
	Room and board	$5100	Long-term loans—college funds (average)	$2000
	Financial aid recipients	69%	Long-term loans—external funds (average)	$2500

Undergraduate Facts				
	Part-time	19%	*Freshman Data:* 4,558 applied, 81% were accepted, 38% (1,400) of those entered	
	State residents	68%		
	Transfers	33%	From top tenth of high school class	22%
	African-Americans	5%	SAT-takers scoring 600 or over on verbal	9%
	Native Americans	1%	SAT-takers scoring 700 or over on verbal	1%
	Hispanics	2%	SAT-takers scoring 600 or over on math	37%
	Asian-Americans	5%	SAT-takers scoring 700 or over on math	7%
	International students	4%	ACT-takers scoring 26 or over	42%
	Freshmen returning for sophomore year	84%	ACT-takers scoring 30 or over	12%
	Students completing degree within 5 years	55%	*Majors with most degrees conferred:* photography, computer graphics, computer science.	
	Grads pursuing further study	15%		

Majors Accounting, advertising, aerospace engineering, applied art, applied mathematics, art/fine arts, biochemistry, biology/biological sciences, biomedical sciences, biomedical technologies, biotechnology, business, ceramic art and design, chemistry, civil engineering technology, commercial art, communication, communication equipment technology, computer engineering, computer graphics, computer information systems, computer programming, computer science, computer technologies, criminal justice, data processing, (pre)dentistry sequence, dietetics, ecology/environmental studies, economics, electrical and electronics technologies, electrical engineering, electrical engineering technology, electronics engineering, engineering (general), engineering technology, environmental design, environmental sciences, film and video, finance/banking, food marketing, food services management, graphic arts, hotel and restaurant management, human services, illustration, industrial design, industrial engineering, interior design, international business, jewelry and metalsmithing, law enforcement/police sciences, (pre)law sequence, management information systems, manufacturing technology, marketing/retailing/merchandising, mathematics, mechanical engineering, mechanical engineering technology, medical illustration, medical technology, (pre)medicine sequence, nuclear medical technology, nutrition, painting/drawing, photography, physics, polymer science, printing technologies, printmaking, publishing, radio and television studies, science, social work, statistics, studio art, telecommunications, textile arts, tourism and travel, (pre)veterinary medicine sequence.

Applying *Required:* essay, high school transcript, SAT or ACT. *Recommended:* recommendations, interview. 3 years of high school math and science, portfolio for art majors required for some. *Application deadlines:* 7/1, 12/1 for early decision, 3/15 priority date for financial aid. *Contact:* Mr. Daniel Shelley, Director of Admissions, 1 Lomb Memorial Drive, Rochester, NY 14623, 716-475-6631.

Rockhurst College

Kansas City, Missouri

Founded 1910
Urban setting
Independent, Roman Catholic (Jesuit)
Coed
Awards A, B, M

Enrollment 2,740 total; 2,081 undergraduates (251 freshmen)

Faculty 142 total; 87 full-time (72% have doctorate/terminal degree); student-faculty ratio is 20:1; grad assistants teach no undergraduate courses.

Libraries 96,830 bound volumes, 15,212 titles on microform, 675 periodical subscriptions

Computing *Terminals/PCs available for student use:* 55, located in computer center, library, dormitories, computer science labs; PC not required. Campus network links student PCs.

Of Special Interest *Core academic program:* yes. Computer course required for accounting majors. Academic exchange with members of the Kansas City Regional Council for Higher Education. Sponsors and participates in study-abroad programs. Cooperative Army ROTC.

On Campus Drama/theater group; student-run newspaper and radio station. *Social organizations:* 3 national fraternities; 30% of eligible undergraduate men are members.

Athletics Member NAIA. *Intercollegiate sports:* basketball (M, W), cross-country running (M, W), golf (M, W), soccer (M, W), tennis (M, W), volleyball (W). *Scholarships:* M, W.

Costs (1991–92) & Aid				
Comprehensive fee	$11,990	Need-based scholarships (average)	$3286
Tuition	$8200	Non-need scholarships (average)	$1615
Mandatory fees	$180	Short-term loans (average)	$500
Room and board	$3610	Long-term loans—college funds (average)	$2128
Financial aid recipients	53%	Long-term loans—external funds (average)	$3241

Undergraduate Facts			
Part-time	47%	*Freshman Data:* 790 applied, 91% were accepted, 35% (251) of those entered	
State residents	63%		
Transfers	27%	From top tenth of high school class	20%
African-Americans	8%	SAT-takers scoring 600 or over on verbal	12%
Native Americans	1%	SAT-takers scoring 700 or over on verbal	3%
Hispanics	4%	SAT-takers scoring 600 or over on math	28%
Asian-Americans	2%	SAT-takers scoring 700 or over on math	2%
International students	1%	ACT-takers scoring 26 or over	25%
Freshmen returning for sophomore year	78%	ACT-takers scoring 30 or over	3%
Students completing degree within 5 years	N/R	*Majors with most degrees conferred:* accounting, marketing/retailing/merchandising, business.	
Grads pursuing further study	N/R		

Majors Accounting, biology/biological sciences, business, business economics, chemistry, communication, computer information systems, computer management, computer programming, computer science, (pre)dentistry sequence, economics, education, elementary education, English, finance/banking, French, health science, history, humanities, human resources, human services, international business, international studies, labor and industrial relations, (pre)law sequence, liberal arts/general studies, marketing/retailing/merchandising, mathematics, medical technology, (pre)medicine sequence, nursing, occupational therapy, philosophy, physical therapy, physics, political science/government, psychology, public relations, religious studies, science education, secondary education, social science, social work, sociology, Spanish, theology, (pre)veterinary medicine sequence.

Applying *Required:* high school transcript, 1 recommendation, SAT or ACT. *Recommended:* 3 years of high school math and science, some high school foreign language, interview. *Application deadlines:* 6/30, 11/1 for early decision, 4/1 priority date for financial aid. *Contact:* Ms. Barbara O'Connell, Director of Admissions, 1100 Rockhurst Road, Kansas City, MO 64110, 816-926-4100 or toll-free 800-842-6776.

Rollins College

Winter Park, Florida

Founded 1885
Suburban setting
Independent
Coed
Awards B, M

Enrollment 2,119 total; 1,466 undergraduates (402 freshmen)

Faculty 135 total—all full-time (92% have doctorate/terminal degree); student-faculty ratio is 12:1; grad assistants teach no undergraduate courses.

Libraries 248,673 bound volumes, 22,459 titles on microform, 1,661 periodical subscriptions

Computing *Terminals/PCs available for student use:* 100, located in computer center, library, dormitories, writing center; PC not required but available for purchase.

Of Special Interest *Core academic program:* yes. Computer course required for math majors. Sigma Xi chapter. Academic exchange with American University (Washington Semester). Sponsors and participates in study-abroad programs.

On Campus Drama/theater group; student-run newspaper and radio station. *Social organizations:* 5 national fraternities, 4 national sororities, 1 local fraternity, 1 local sorority; 35% of eligible undergraduate men and 35% of eligible undergraduate women are members.

Athletics Member NCAA (Division II). *Intercollegiate sports:* baseball (M), basketball (M, W), crew (M, W), cross-country running (M, W), golf (M, W), sailing (M, W), soccer (M, W), softball (W), tennis (M, W), volleyball (W). *Scholarships:* M, W.

Costs (1991–92) & Aid				
Comprehensive fee	$18,195	Need-based scholarships (average)	$7100
Tuition	$13,500	Non-need scholarships (average)	$6800
Mandatory fees	$400	Short-term loans (average)	$200
Room and board	$4295	Long-term loans—college funds (average)	$1000
Financial aid recipients	57%	Long-term loans—external funds (average)	$3700

Undergraduate Facts

Part-time	1%	*Freshman Data:* 2,050 applied, 65% were accepted, 30% (402) of those entered	
State residents	35%		
Transfers	15%	From top tenth of high school class	35%
African-Americans	4%	SAT-takers scoring 600 or over on verbal	12%
Native Americans	0%	SAT-takers scoring 700 or over on verbal	1%
Hispanics	8%	SAT-takers scoring 600 or over on math	26%
Asian-Americans	4%	SAT-takers scoring 700 or over on math	4%
International students	5%	ACT-takers scoring 26 or over	32%
Freshmen returning for sophomore year	88%	ACT-takers scoring 30 or over	6%
Students completing degree within 5 years	80%	*Majors with most degrees conferred:* economics, psychology, English.	
Grads pursuing further study	25%		

Majors Anthropology, art/fine arts, art history, biology/biological sciences, chemistry, classics, clinical psychology, computer science, (pre)dentistry sequence, economics, education, elementary education, English, environmental sciences, French, German, history, interdisciplinary studies, international studies, Latin American studies, (pre)law sequence, mathematics, (pre)medicine sequence, music, music history, philosophy, physics, political science/government, psychology, religious studies, sociology, Spanish, studio art, theater arts/drama, (pre)veterinary medicine sequence.

Applying *Required:* essay, high school transcript, 3 years of high school math, 1 recommendation, SAT or ACT. *Recommended:* 3 years of high school science, 2 years of high school foreign language, interview, 3 Achievements, English Composition Test (with essay). Interview required for some. *Application deadlines:* 2/15, 11/15 for early decision, 2/1 priority date for financial aid. *Contact:* Mr. David Erdmann, Dean, Admissions and Student Financial Planning, 1000 Holt Avenue, Winter Park, FL 32789-4499, 407-646-2161.

Rose-Hulman Institute of Technology
Terre Haute, Indiana

Founded 1874
Rural setting
Independent
Men
Awards B, M

Enrollment 1,420 total; 1,350 undergraduates (369 freshmen)

Faculty 97 total; 92 full-time (93% have doctorate/terminal degree); student-faculty ratio is 15:1; grad assistants teach no undergraduate courses.

Libraries 52,000 bound volumes, 392 periodical subscriptions

Computing *Terminals/PCs available for student use:* 300, located in computer center, student center, academic buildings.

Of Special Interest *Core academic program:* yes. Computer course required. Academic exchange with Indiana State University. Sponsors study-abroad programs. Army ROTC, Air Force ROTC.

On Campus Drama/theater group; student-run newspaper and radio station. *Social organizations:* 8 national fraternities; 40% of eligible undergraduates are members.

Athletics Member NCAA (Division III). *Intercollegiate sports:* baseball, basketball, cross-country running, football, golf, riflery, soccer, tennis, track and field, wrestling.

Costs (1992–93) & Aid				
	Comprehensive fee	$15,700	Need-based scholarships (average)	$2000
	Tuition	$11,840	Non-need scholarships (average)	$2000
	Mandatory fees	$60	Short-term loans (average)	$200
	Room and board	$3800	Long-term loans—college funds	N/Avail
	Financial aid recipients	89%	Long-term loans—external funds (average)	$1500

Undergraduate Facts				
	Part-time	0%	*Freshman Data:* 3,153 applied, 63% were accepted, 19% (369) of those entered	
	State residents	59%		
	Transfers	1%	From top tenth of high school class	62%
	African-Americans	1%	SAT-takers scoring 600 or over on verbal	22%
	Native Americans	1%	SAT-takers scoring 700 or over on verbal	2%
	Hispanics	1%	SAT-takers scoring 600 or over on math	77%
	Asian-Americans	2%	SAT-takers scoring 700 or over on math	27%
	International students	4%	ACT-takers scoring 26 or over	100%
	Freshmen returning for sophomore year	72%	ACT-takers scoring 30 or over	60%
	Students completing degree within 5 years	72%		
	Grads pursuing further study	20%		

Majors Chemical engineering, chemistry, civil engineering, computer engineering, computer science, economics, electrical engineering, mathematics, mechanical engineering, optics, physics.

Applying *Required:* high school transcript, 4 years of high school math, 1 recommendation, SAT. *Recommended:* 3 years of high school science, ACT. *Application deadlines:* rolling, 3/1 priority date for financial aid. *Contact:* Mr. Charles G. Howard, Dean of Admissions, 5500 Wabash Avenue, Terre Haute, IN 47803, 812-877-8213 or toll-free 800-552-0725 (in-state), 800-248-7448 (out-of-state).

Rutgers, The State University of New Jersey, College of Engineering
Piscataway, New Jersey

Founded 1864
Small-town setting
State-supported
Coed
Awards B

Enrollment 48,693 university total; 2,460 undergraduates (599 freshmen)

Faculty 122 full-time (90% have doctorate/terminal degree); student-faculty ratio is 12:1; grad assistants teach a few undergraduate courses.

Libraries 4.3 million bound volumes, 2.3 million titles on microform, 15,934 periodical subscriptions

Computing *Terminals/PCs available for student use:* 600, located in computer center, library, dormitories, various locations on campus; PC not required but available for purchase. Campus network links student PCs.

Of Special Interest *Core academic program:* yes. Computer course required. Sigma Xi chapter. Academic exchange with members of the National Student Exchange. Sponsors and participates in study-abroad programs. Army ROTC, Air Force ROTC.

On Campus Drama/theater group; student-run newspaper and radio station. *Social organizations:* 31 national fraternities, 10 national sororities, 3 local fraternities, 5 local sororities; 10% of eligible undergraduate men and 10% of eligible undergraduate women are members.

Athletics Member NCAA (Division I). *Intercollegiate sports:* baseball (M), basketball (M, W), crew (M, W), cross-country running (M, W), fencing (M, W), field hockey (W), football (M), golf (M, W), gymnastics (W), lacrosse (M, W), soccer (M, W), softball (W), swimming and diving (M, W), tennis (M, W), track and field (M, W), volleyball (W), wrestling (M). *Scholarships:* M, W.

Costs (1991–92) & Aid				
State resident tuition	$3456	186 Need-based scholarships (average)	$1274
Nonresident tuition	$7032	412 Non-need scholarships (average)	$1641
Mandatory fees	$668	Short-term loans (average)	$200
Room and board	$4018	Long-term loans—college funds (average)	$699
Financial aid recipients	59%	Long-term loans—external funds (average)	$2190

Undergraduate Facts			
Part-time	2%	*Freshman Data:* 2,737 applied, 74% were accepted, 30% (599) of those entered	
State residents	86%		
Transfers	5%	From top tenth of high school class	38%
African-Americans	6%	SAT-takers scoring 600 or over on verbal	12%
Native Americans	0%	SAT-takers scoring 700 or over on verbal	2%
Hispanics	6%	SAT-takers scoring 600 or over on math	68%
Asian-Americans	20%	SAT-takers scoring 700 or over on math	22%
International students	6%	ACT-takers scoring 26 or over	N/R
Freshmen returning for sophomore year	91%	ACT-takers scoring 30 or over	N/R
Students completing degree within 5 years	68%	*Majors with most degrees conferred:* electrical engineering, mechanical engineering, civil engineering.	
Grads pursuing further study	N/R		

Majors Aerospace engineering, agricultural engineering, biomedical engineering, ceramic engineering, chemical engineering, civil engineering, computer engineering, electrical engineering, engineering and applied sciences, industrial engineering, mechanical engineering.

Applying *Required:* high school transcript, 4 years of high school math, 1 course each in chemistry and physics, SAT or ACT. 3 Achievements required for some. *Application deadlines:* 1/15, 3/1 priority date for financial aid. *Contact:* Dr. Elizabeth Mitchell, Assistant V.P. for University Undergraduate Admissions, PO Box 2101, New Brunswick, NJ 08903-2101, 908-932-3770; *Office location:* Davidson Road.

Rutgers, The State University of New Jersey, College of Pharmacy
New Brunswick, New Jersey

Founded 1927
Small-town setting
State-supported
Coed
Awards B, D

Enrollment	48,693 university total; 847 school total; 820 undergraduates (171 freshmen)
Faculty	47 full-time (90% have doctorate/terminal degree); student-faculty ratio is 12:1; grad assistants teach no undergraduate courses.
Libraries	4.3 million bound volumes, 2.3 million titles on microform, 15,934 periodical subscriptions
Computing	*Terminals/PCs available for student use:* 600, located in computer center, library, dormitories, various locations on campus; PC not required but available for purchase. Campus network links student PCs.
Of Special Interest	*Core academic program:* yes. Sigma Xi chapter. Academic exchange with members of the National Student Exchange. Sponsors and participates in study-abroad programs. Army ROTC, Air Force ROTC.
On Campus	Drama/theater group; student-run newspaper and radio station. *Social organizations:* 31 national fraternities, 10 national sororities, 3 local fraternities, 5 local sororities; 10% of eligible undergraduate men and 10% of eligible undergraduate women are members.
Athletics	Member NCAA (Division I). *Intercollegiate sports:* baseball (M), basketball (M, W), crew (M, W), cross-country running (M, W), fencing (M, W), field hockey (W), football (M), golf (M, W), gymnastics (W), lacrosse (M, W), soccer (M, W), softball (W), swimming and diving (M, W), tennis (M, W), track and field (M, W), volleyball (W), wrestling (M). *Scholarships:* M, W.

Costs (1991–92) & Aid				
	State resident tuition	$3456	98 Need-based scholarships (average)	$794
	Nonresident tuition	$7032	148 Non-need scholarships (average)	$1585
	Mandatory fees	$668	Short-term loans (average)	$200
	Room and board	$4018	Long-term loans—college funds (average)	$850
	Financial aid recipients	65%	Long-term loans—external funds (average)	$2334

Undergraduate Facts				
	Part-time	1%	*Freshman Data:* 794 applied, 46% were accepted, 47% (171) of those entered	
	State residents	85%		
	Transfers	2%	From top tenth of high school class	56%
	African-Americans	6%	SAT-takers scoring 600 or over on verbal	8%
	Native Americans	0%	SAT-takers scoring 700 or over on verbal	0%
	Hispanics	7%	SAT-takers scoring 600 or over on math	54%
	Asian-Americans	27%	SAT-takers scoring 700 or over on math	9%
	International students	2%	ACT-takers scoring 26 or over	N/R
	Freshmen returning for sophomore year	87%	ACT-takers scoring 30 or over	N/R
	Students completing degree within 5 years	59%		
	Grads pursuing further study	N/R		

Major Pharmacy/pharmaceutical sciences.

Applying *Required:* high school transcript, 3 years of high school math, 2 years of high school foreign language, 1 course each in biology and chemistry, SAT or ACT. 3 Achievements required for some. *Application deadlines:* 1/15, 3/1 priority date for financial aid. *Contact:* Dr. Elizabeth Mitchell, Assistant V.P. for University Undergraduate Admissions, Davidson Road, New Brunswick, NJ 08903, 908-932-3770.

Rutgers, The State University of New Jersey, Cook College
New Brunswick, New Jersey

Founded 1921
Small-town setting
State-supported
Coed
Awards B

Enrollment	48,693 university total; 2,874 undergraduates (485 freshmen)
Faculty	90 full-time (90% have doctorate/terminal degree); student-faculty ratio is 16:1; grad assistants teach a few undergraduate courses.
Libraries	4.3 million bound volumes, 2.3 million titles on microform, 15,934 periodical subscriptions
Computing	*Terminals/PCs available for student use:* 600, located in computer center, student center, library, various locations on campus; PC not required but available for purchase. Campus network links student PCs.
Of Special Interest	*Core academic program:* yes. Computer course required for agricultural science, animal science, biochemistry, bioresource engineering, earth and atmospheric science, environmental and business economics, environmental planning and design, food science, natural resource management and applied ecology, plant science, public health, and teacher educati. Sigma Xi chapter. Academic exchange program: no. Sponsors and participates in study-abroad programs. Army ROTC, Air Force ROTC.
On Campus	Drama/theater group; student-run newspaper and radio station. *Social organizations:* 31 national fraternities, 10 national sororities, 3 local fraternities, 5 local sororities; 10% of eligible undergraduate men and 10% of eligible undergraduate women are members.
Athletics	Member NCAA (Division I). *Intercollegiate sports:* baseball (M), basketball (M, W), crew (M, W), cross-country running (M, W), fencing (M, W), field hockey (W), football (M), golf (M, W), gymnastics (W), lacrosse (M, W), soccer (M, W), softball (W), swimming and diving (M, W), tennis (M, W), track and field (M, W), volleyball (W), wrestling (M). *Scholarships:* M, W.

Costs (1991–92) & Aid				
	State resident tuition	$3456	243 Need-based scholarships (average)	$1222
	Nonresident tuition	$7032	240 Non-need scholarships (average)	$2141
	Mandatory fees	$710	Short-term loans (average)	$200
	Room and board	$4018	Long-term loans—college funds (average)	$745
	Financial aid recipients	48%	Long-term loans—external funds (average)	$2262

Undergraduate Facts				
	Part-time	11%	*Freshman Data:* 3,394 applied, 63% were accepted, 23% (485) of those entered	
	State residents	90%		
	Transfers	8%	From top tenth of high school class	31%
	African-Americans	5%	SAT-takers scoring 600 or over on verbal	11%
	Native Americans	0%	SAT-takers scoring 700 or over on verbal	1%
	Hispanics	5%	SAT-takers scoring 600 or over on math	37%
	Asian-Americans	8%	SAT-takers scoring 700 or over on math	4%
	International students	1%	ACT-takers scoring 26 or over	N/R
	Freshmen returning for sophomore year	92%	ACT-takers scoring 30 or over	N/R
	Students completing degree within 5 years	70%	*Majors with most degrees conferred:* environmental sciences, business economics, biology/biological sciences.	
	Grads pursuing further study	N/R		

Majors Agricultural economics, agricultural education, agricultural engineering, agricultural sciences, agronomy/soil and crop sciences, animal sciences, atmospheric sciences, biochemistry, biology/biological sciences, biomedical sciences, biotechnology, botany/plant sciences, business economics, cell biology, chemistry, chemistry, foods, and nutrition, communication, computer science, conservation, (pre)dentistry sequence, earth science, ecology/environmental studies, entomology, environmental and business economics, environmental design, environmental education, environmental health sciences, environmental sciences, fish and game management, food sciences, forestry, genetics, geography, geology, health, physical education, and sports studies, horticulture, human ecology, interdisciplinary studies, international studies, journalism, landscape architecture/design, (pre)law sequence, (pre)medicine sequence, meteorology, microbiology, natural resource management, nutrition, oceanography, physical education, physical fitness/human movement, physiology, public health, radiological sciences, recreation and leisure services, sports administration, (pre)veterinary medicine sequence, vocational education, water resources, wildlife management.

Applying *Required:* high school transcript, 3 years of high school math, SAT or ACT. 3 Achievements required for some. *Application deadlines:* 1/15, 3/1 priority date for financial aid. *Contact:* Dr. Elizabeth Mitchell, Assistant V.P. for University Undergraduate Admissions, Davidson Road, New Brunswick, NJ 08903, 908-932-3770.

Rutgers, The State University of New Jersey, Douglass College
New Brunswick, New Jersey

Founded 1918
Small-town setting
State-supported
Women
Awards B

Enrollment	48,693 university total; 3,268 undergraduates (694 freshmen)
Faculty	765 full-time (90% have doctorate/terminal degree); student-faculty ratio is 17:1; grad assistants teach a few undergraduate courses.
Libraries	4.3 million bound volumes, 2.3 million titles on microform, 15,934 periodical subscriptions
Computing	*Terminals/PCs available for student use:* 600, located in computer center, library, dormitories, computer stations; PC not required but available for purchase. Campus network links student PCs.
Of Special Interest	*Core academic program:* yes. Computer course required for math, psychology, statistics, business majors. Phi Beta Kappa, Sigma Xi chapters. Academic exchange with members of the National Student Exchange. Sponsors and participates in study-abroad programs. Army ROTC, Air Force ROTC.
On Campus	Drama/theater group; student-run newspaper and radio station. *Social organizations:* 10 national sororities, 5 local sororities; 10% of eligible undergraduates are members.
Athletics	Member NCAA (Division I). *Intercollegiate sports:* basketball, crew, cross-country running, fencing, field hockey, golf, gymnastics, lacrosse, soccer, softball, swimming and diving, tennis, track and field, volleyball. *Scholarships.*

Costs (1991–92) & Aid				
	State resident tuition	$3114	469 Need-based scholarships (average)	$865
	Nonresident tuition	$6338	367 Non-need scholarships (average)	$2280
	Mandatory fees	$668	Short-term loans (average)	$200
	Room and board	$4018	Long-term loans—college funds (average)	$661
	Financial aid recipients	51%	Long-term loans—external funds (average)	$2239

Undergraduate Facts				
	Part-time	5%	*Freshman Data:* 4,427 applied, 66% were accepted, 24% (694) of those entered	
	State residents	92%		
	Transfers	5%	From top tenth of high school class	28%
	African-Americans	11%	SAT-takers scoring 600 or over on verbal	11%
	Native Americans	0%	SAT-takers scoring 700 or over on verbal	2%
	Hispanics	5%	SAT-takers scoring 600 or over on math	27%
	Asian-Americans	11%	SAT-takers scoring 700 or over on math	3%
	International students	1%	ACT-takers scoring 26 or over	N/R
	Freshmen returning for sophomore year	92%	ACT-takers scoring 30 or over	N/R
	Students completing degree within 5 years	76%	*Majors with most degrees conferred:* psychology, English, political science/government.	
	Grads pursuing further study	N/R		

Majors Accounting, African studies, American studies, anthropology, art/fine arts, art history, Asian/Oriental studies, atmospheric sciences, biochemistry, biology/biological sciences, biomedical sciences, biometrics, biotechnology, botany/plant sciences, business, cell biology, chemistry, chemistry, foods, and nutrition, Chinese, classics, communication, comparative literature, computer science, dance, East European and Soviet studies, ecology/environmental studies, economics, English, entomology, finance/banking, food sciences, French, genetics, geography, geology, German, Greek, health, physical education, and sports studies, Hispanic studies, history, interdisciplinary studies, Italian, journalism, Judaic studies, labor studies, Latin, Latin American studies, (pre)law sequence, linguistics, marketing/retailing/merchandising, mathematics, medical technology, (pre)medicine sequence, microbiology, music, Near and Middle Eastern studies, nutrition, philosophy, physical education, physical fitness/human movement, physics, physiology, political science/government, Portuguese, psychology, public health, recreation and leisure services, religious studies, Russian, Russian and Slavic studies, sociology, Spanish, sports administration, statistics, theater arts/drama, urban studies, women's studies.

Applying *Required:* high school transcript, 3 years of high school math, 2 years of high school foreign language, 2 years of high school science, SAT or ACT. 3 Achievements required for some. *Application deadlines:* 1/15, 3/1 priority date for financial aid. *Contact:* Dr. Elizabeth Mitchell, Assistant V.P. for University Undergraduate Admissions, PO Box 2101, New Brunswick, NJ 08903-2101, 908-932-3770; *Office location:* Davidson Road.

From the College The Douglass Project for Rutgers Women in Math, Science, and Engineering, offering cocurricular support for women in these nontraditional majors, received the AAUW Equity in Education Award for 1990. Douglass will also offer a Certificate Program in International Studies in fall 1992, which will benefit students contemplating careers in education, government, international business, journalism, and law.

Rutgers, The State University of New Jersey, Rutgers College
New Brunswick, New Jersey

Founded 1766
Small-town setting
State-supported
Coed
Awards B

Enrollment	48,693 university total; 8,554 undergraduates (1,599 freshmen)
Faculty	765 full-time (90% have doctorate/terminal degree); student-faculty ratio is 17:1; grad assistants teach a few undergraduate courses.
Libraries	4.3 million bound volumes, 2.3 million titles on microform, 15,934 periodical subscriptions
Computing	*Terminals/PCs available for student use:* 600, located in computer center, library, various locations on campus; PC not required but available for purchase. Campus network links student PCs.
Of Special Interest	*Core academic program:* yes. Computer course required for math, business majors. Phi Beta Kappa, Sigma Xi chapters. Academic exchange with members of the National Student Exchange. Sponsors and participates in study-abroad programs. Army ROTC, Air Force ROTC.
On Campus	Drama/theater group; student-run newspaper and radio station. *Social organizations:* 31 national fraternities, 10 national sororities, 3 local fraternities, 5 local sororities; 10% of eligible undergraduate men and 10% of eligible undergraduate women are members.
Athletics	Member NCAA (Division I). *Intercollegiate sports:* baseball (M), basketball (M, W), crew (M, W), cross-country running (M, W), fencing (M, W), field hockey (W), football (M), golf (M, W), gymnastics (W), lacrosse (M, W), soccer (M, W), softball (W), swimming and diving (M, W), tennis (M, W), track and field (M, W), volleyball (W), wrestling (M). *Scholarships:* M, W.

Costs (1991–92) & Aid				
	State resident tuition	$3114	637 Need-based scholarships (average)	$1123
	Nonresident tuition	$6338	1700 Non-need scholarships (average)	$1745
	Mandatory fees	$732	Short-term loans (average)	$200
	Room and board	$4018	Long-term loans—college funds (average)	$718
	Financial aid recipients	62%	Long-term loans—external funds (average)	$2311

Undergraduate Facts				
	Part-time	4%	*Freshman Data:* 13,673 applied, 46% were accepted, 26% (1,599) of those entered	
	State residents	88%		
	Transfers	6%	From top tenth of high school class	44%
	African-Americans	8%	SAT-takers scoring 600 or over on verbal	23%
	Native Americans	0%	SAT-takers scoring 700 or over on verbal	2%
	Hispanics	10%	SAT-takers scoring 600 or over on math	52%
	Asian-Americans	11%	SAT-takers scoring 700 or over on math	13%
	International students	2%	ACT-takers scoring 26 or over	N/R
	Freshmen returning for sophomore year	91%	ACT-takers scoring 30 or over	N/R
	Students completing degree within 5 years	77%	*Majors with most degrees conferred:* economics, psychology, English.	
	Grads pursuing further study	N/R		

Majors Accounting, African studies, American studies, anthropology, art/fine arts, art history, Asian/Oriental studies, biochemistry, biology/biological sciences, biomedical sciences, biometrics, black/African-American studies, botany/plant sciences, business, cell biology, chemistry, chemistry, foods, and nutrition, Chinese, classics, communication, comparative literature, computer science, criminal justice, dance, (pre)dentistry sequence, East European and Soviet studies, ecology/environmental studies, economics, English, entomology, finance/banking, French, genetics, geography, geology, German, Greek, health, physical education, and sports studies, Hispanic studies, history, interdisciplinary studies, Italian, journalism, Judaic studies, labor studies, Latin, Latin American studies, (pre)law sequence, linguistics, marketing/retailing/merchandising, mathematics, (pre)medicine sequence, microbiology, music, Near and Middle Eastern studies, nutrition, philosophy, physical education, physical fitness/human movement, physics, physiology, political science/government, Portuguese, psychology, public health, recreation and leisure services, religious studies, Russian, Russian and Slavic studies, sociology, Spanish, sports administration, statistics, theater arts/drama, urban studies, women's studies.

Applying *Required:* high school transcript, 3 years of high school math, 2 years of high school foreign language, SAT or ACT. 3 Achievements required for some. *Application deadlines:* 1/15, 3/1 priority date for financial aid. *Contact:* Dr. Elizabeth Mitchell, Assistant V.P. for University Undergraduate Admissions, Davidson Road, New Brunswick, NJ 08903, 908-932-3770.

✳ **St. John's College**

Annapolis, Maryland

Founded 1696
Small-town setting
Independent
Coed
Awards B, M

Enrollment 481 total; 417 undergraduates (112 freshmen)

Faculty 69 total; 61 full-time (56% have doctorate/terminal degree); student-faculty ratio is 8:1; grad assistants teach no undergraduate courses.

Libraries 92,036 bound volumes, 75 titles on microform, 131 periodical subscriptions

Computing *Terminals/PCs available for student use:* 10, located in computer center, library; PC not required.

Of Special Interest *Core academic program:* yes. Academic exchange program: no. Study-abroad programs: no.

On Campus Drama/theater group; student-run newspaper. No national or local fraternities or sororities on campus.

Athletics None

Costs (1992–93) & Aid				
	Comprehensive fee	$20,600	Need-based scholarships (average)	$7970
	Tuition	$15,400	Non-need scholarships	N/Avail
	Mandatory fees	N/App	Short-term loans	N/Avail
	Room and board	$5200	Long-term loans—college funds (average)	$2500
	Financial aid recipients	50%	Long-term loans—external funds (average)	$2625

Undergraduate Facts				
	Part-time	2%	*Freshman Data:* 277 applied, 84% were accepted, 48% (112) of those entered	
	State residents	15%		
	Transfers	9%	From top tenth of high school class	23%
	African-Americans	3%	SAT-takers scoring 600 or over on verbal	N/R
	Native Americans	0%	SAT-takers scoring 700 or over on verbal	N/R
	Hispanics	2%	SAT-takers scoring 600 or over on math	N/R
	Asian-Americans	5%	SAT-takers scoring 700 or over on math	N/R
	International students	3%	ACT-takers scoring 26 or over	N/R
	Freshmen returning for sophomore year	84%	ACT-takers scoring 30 or over	N/R
	Students completing degree within 5 years	65%		
	Grads pursuing further study	25%		

Majors Interdisciplinary studies, liberal arts/general studies, Western civilization and culture.

Applying *Required:* essay, high school transcript, 3 years of high school math, 2 years of high school foreign language, 2 recommendations. *Recommended:* 3 years of high school science, interview, SAT or ACT. *Application deadlines:* rolling, 2/25 priority date for financial aid. *Contact:* Mr. John Christensen, Director of Admissions, Charles Carroll Barrister House, Annapolis, MD 21404, 301-263-2371 Ext. 222 or toll-free 800-727-9238.

From the College Great Books Program: St. John's offers an integrated liberal arts and sciences curriculum structured around seminar discussions of major works of Western civilization. These discussions are supported by tutorials in mathematics, music, language, and the physical sciences. Only original sources are read, and all classes are small discussion groups.

St. John's College

Santa Fe, New Mexico

Founded 1964
Small-town setting
Independent
Coed
Awards B, M

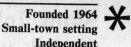

Enrollment	450 total; 400 undergraduates (112 freshmen)
Faculty	55 total; 50 full-time (71% have doctorate/terminal degree); grad assistants teach no undergraduate courses.
Libraries	52,615 bound volumes, 178 periodical subscriptions
Computing	*Terminals/PCs available for student use:* 2, located in science and lab building; PC not required.
Of Special Interest	*Core academic program:* yes. Academic exchange with St. John's College (MD). Study-abroad programs: no.
On Campus	Drama/theater group; student-run newspaper. No national or local fraternities or sororities on campus.
Athletics	*Intercollegiate sports:* fencing (M, W), soccer (M, W).

Costs (1991–92) & Aid				
	Comprehensive fee	$19,008	Need-based scholarships	Avail
	Tuition	$14,262	Non-need scholarships	Avail
	Mandatory fees	$50	Short-term loans	N/Avail
	Room and board	$4696	Long-term loans—college funds (average)	$5100
	Financial aid recipients	54%	Long-term loans—external funds (average)	$2650

Undergraduate Facts				
	Part-time	2%	*Freshman Data:* 270 applied, 74% were accepted, 56% (112) of those entered	
	State residents	15%		
	Transfers	25%	From top tenth of high school class	30%
	African-Americans	1%	SAT-takers scoring 600 or over on verbal	54%
	Native Americans	1%	SAT-takers scoring 700 or over on verbal	11%
	Hispanics	5%	SAT-takers scoring 600 or over on math	43%
	Asian-Americans	3%	SAT-takers scoring 700 or over on math	11%
	International students	2%	ACT-takers scoring 26 or over	57%
	Freshmen returning for sophomore year	85%	ACT-takers scoring 30 or over	15%
	Students completing degree within 5 years	60%		
	Grads pursuing further study	26%		

Major Liberal arts/general studies.

Applying *Required:* essay, high school transcript, 3 years of high school math and science, 2 years of high school foreign language, 2 recommendations. *Recommended:* interview, SAT or ACT. *Application deadlines:* rolling, 3/1 priority date for financial aid. *Contact:* Mr. Larry Clendenin, Director of Admissions, 1160 Camino Cruz Blanca, Santa Fe, NM 87501-4599, 505-982-3691 Ext. 231 or toll-free 800-331-5232 (out-of-state).

From the College St. John's is known for its Great Books Program, a classic arts and science curriculum based on the reading of original works. All classes are small and discussion-based; performance is evaluated on the basis of written papers and classroom participation. Students are evaluated orally once each semester, and grades are de-emphasized.

Saint John's University
Coordinate with College of Saint Benedict
Collegeville, Minnesota

Founded 1857
Rural setting
Independent, Roman Catholic
Men
Awards B, M

Enrollment 1,956 total; 1,873 undergraduates (415 freshmen)

Faculty 145 total; 110 full-time (90% have doctorate/terminal degree); student-faculty ratio is 14:1; grad assistants teach no undergraduate courses.

Libraries 475,000 bound volumes, 78,000 titles on microform, 2,100 periodical subscriptions

Computing *Terminals/PCs available for student use:* 185, located in computer center, library, academic buildings; PC not required.

Of Special Interest *Core academic program:* yes. Computer course required for math, accounting, business administration majors. Academic exchange with College of Saint Benedict. Sponsors and participates in study-abroad programs. Army ROTC.

On Campus Drama/theater group; student-run newspaper and radio station. No national or local fraternities on campus.

Athletics Member NCAA (Division III), NAIA. *Intercollegiate sports:* baseball, basketball, crew, cross-country running, football, golf, ice hockey, lacrosse, riflery, rugby, skiing (cross-country), skiing (downhill), soccer, swimming and diving, tennis, track and field, wrestling.

Costs (1991–92) & Aid

Comprehensive fee	$13,250	
Tuition	$9485	
Mandatory fees	$80	
Room and board	$3685	
Financial aid recipients	75%	
Need-based scholarships (average)		$2522
Non-need scholarships (average)		$1200
Short-term loans		N/Avail
Long-term loans—college funds		N/Avail
Long-term loans—external funds (average)		$2253

Undergraduate Facts

Part-time	3%
State residents	75%
Transfers	3%
African-Americans	2%
Native Americans	N/R
Hispanics	1%
Asian-Americans	1%
International students	2%
Freshmen returning for sophomore year	86%
Students completing degree within 5 years	70%
Grads pursuing further study	20%

Freshman Data: 824 applied, 93% were accepted, 54% (415) of those entered

From top tenth of high school class	20%
SAT-takers scoring 600 or over on verbal	10%
SAT-takers scoring 700 or over on verbal	2%
SAT-takers scoring 600 or over on math	28%
SAT-takers scoring 700 or over on math	2%
ACT-takers scoring 26 or over	28%
ACT-takers scoring 30 or over	4%

Majors Accounting, art education, art/fine arts, art history, biology/biological sciences, business, chemistry, classics, communication, computer science, (pre)dentistry sequence, dietetics, economics, education, elementary education, English, forestry, French, German, Greek, history, humanities, Latin, (pre)law sequence, liberal arts/general studies, mathematics, medical technology, (pre)medicine sequence, medieval studies, music, music education, natural sciences, nursing, nutrition, occupational therapy, peace studies, philosophy, physical therapy, physics, political science/government, psychology, religious education, religious studies, sacred music, social science, social work, sociology, Spanish, theater arts/drama, theology, (pre)veterinary medicine sequence.

Applying *Required:* essay, high school transcript, SAT or ACT. *Recommended:* 3 years of high school math and science, some high school foreign language, PSAT. Recommendations, interview required for some. *Application deadlines:* rolling, 12/1 for early decision, 4/1 priority date for financial aid. *Contact:* Mr. Roger C. Young, Director of Admissions, Collegeville, MN 56321, 612-363-2196 or toll-free 800-24 JOHNS.

Saint Joseph's University

Philadelphia, Pennsylvania

Founded 1851
Suburban setting
Independent, Roman Catholic (Jesuit)
Coed
Awards A, B, M

Enrollment 6,643 total; 3,815 undergraduates (620 freshmen)

Faculty 364 total; 157 full-time (89% have doctorate/terminal degree); student-faculty ratio is 18:1; grad assistants teach no undergraduate courses.

Libraries 299,000 bound volumes, 660,000 titles on microform, 1,750 periodical subscriptions

Computing *Terminals/PCs available for student use:* 200, located in computer center, library, dormitories, academic buildings, classrooms; PC not required. Campus network links student PCs.

Of Special Interest *Core academic program:* yes. Computer course required for math, business majors. Sigma Xi chapter. Academic exchange with members of the Jesuit Student Exchange. Sponsors and participates in study-abroad programs. Air Force ROTC, cooperative Army ROTC, cooperative Naval ROTC.

On Campus Drama/theater group; student-run newspaper and radio station. *Social organizations:* 4 national fraternities, 3 national sororities; 10% of eligible undergraduate men and 20% of eligible undergraduate women are members.

Athletics Member NCAA (Division I). *Intercollegiate sports:* baseball (M), basketball (M, W), crew (M, W), cross-country running (M, W), golf (M), soccer (M), tennis (M, W), track and field (M, W). *Scholarships:* M, W.

Costs (1991–92) & Aid				
Comprehensive fee	$14,750	Need-based scholarships	Avail
Tuition	$10,000	Non-need scholarships	Avail
Mandatory fees	N/App	Short-term loans	N/Avail
Room and board	$4750	Long-term loans—college funds	N/Avail
Financial aid recipients	80%	Long-term loans—external funds	Avail

Undergraduate Facts			
Part-time	33%	*Freshman Data:* 2,307 applied, 79% were accepted, 34% (620) of those entered	
State residents	58%		
Transfers	5%	From top tenth of high school class	38%
African-Americans	8%	SAT-takers scoring 600 or over on verbal	N/R
Native Americans	0%	SAT-takers scoring 700 or over on verbal	N/R
Hispanics	3%	SAT-takers scoring 600 or over on math	N/R
Asian-Americans	2%	SAT-takers scoring 700 or over on math	N/R
International students	3%	ACT-takers scoring 26 or over	N/R
Freshmen returning for sophomore year	90%	ACT-takers scoring 30 or over	N/R
Students completing degree within 5 years	72%	*Majors with most degrees conferred:* marketing/retailing/merchandising, food marketing, finance/banking.	
Grads pursuing further study	36%		

Majors Accounting, art/fine arts, biology/biological sciences, business, chemistry, computer science, criminal justice, (pre)dentistry sequence, economics, education, elementary education, English, finance/banking, food marketing, French, German, health services administration, history, humanities, human services, international business, international studies, labor studies, (pre)law sequence, management information systems, marketing/retailing/merchandising, mathematics, (pre)medicine sequence, philosophy, physics, political science/government, psychology, public administration, purchasing/inventory management, secondary education, sociology, Spanish, theology.

Applying *Required:* essay, high school transcript, 3 years of high school math, 2 years of high school foreign language, 1 recommendation, SAT or ACT. *Recommended:* 3 years of high school science, campus interview, English Composition Test (with essay). *Application deadlines:* 3/1, 12/1 for early decision, 2/15 priority date for financial aid. *Contact:* Mr. Randy H. Miller, Director of Admissions, 5600 City Avenue, Philadelphia, PA 19131, 215-660-1300.

St. Lawrence University

Canton, New York

Founded 1856
Rural setting
Independent
Coed
Awards B, M

Enrollment	2,119 total; 1,997 undergraduates (422 freshmen)
Faculty	177 total; 160 full-time (95% have doctorate/terminal degree); student-faculty ratio is 12:1; grad assistants teach no undergraduate courses.
Libraries	404,000 bound volumes, 274,083 titles on microform, 2,487 periodical subscriptions
Computing	*Terminals/PCs available for student use:* 600, located in computer center, library, dormitories, computer labs; PC not required. Campus network links student PCs.
Of Special Interest	*Core academic program:* yes. Computer course required for some majors. Phi Beta Kappa chapter. Academic exchange with Clarkson University, State University of New York College of Technology at Canton, State University of New York College at Potsdam. Sponsors and participates in study-abroad programs. Cooperative Air Force ROTC.
On Campus	Drama/theater group; student-run newspaper and radio station. *Social organizations:* 7 national fraternities, 4 national sororities, 1 local sorority; 40% of eligible undergraduate men and 50% of eligible undergraduate women are members.
Athletics	Member NCAA (Division III). *Intercollegiate sports:* baseball (M), basketball (M, W), crew (M), cross-country running (M, W), equestrian sports (M, W), field hockey (W), football (M), ice hockey (M, W), lacrosse (M, W), rugby (M), skiing (cross-country) (M, W), skiing (downhill) (M, W), soccer (M, W), swimming and diving (M, W), tennis (M, W), track and field (M, W), volleyball (W), wrestling (M).

Costs (1991–92) & Aid	Comprehensive fee	$20,801	Need-based scholarships (average)	$11,244
	Tuition	$15,620	Non-need scholarships (average)	$5000
	Mandatory fees	$131	Short-term loans (average)	$100
	Room and board	$5050	Long-term loans—college funds (average)	$2500
	Financial aid recipients	55%	Long-term loans—external funds (average)	$3000

Undergraduate Facts	Part-time	7%	*Freshman Data:* 2,192 applied, 72% were accepted, 27% (422) of those entered	
	State residents	50%		
	Transfers	2%	From top tenth of high school class	N/R
	African-Americans	3%	SAT-takers scoring 600 or over on verbal	10%
	Native Americans	1%	SAT-takers scoring 700 or over on verbal	1%
	Hispanics	1%	SAT-takers scoring 600 or over on math	38%
	Asian-Americans	1%	SAT-takers scoring 700 or over on math	5%
	International students	3%	ACT-takers scoring 26 or over	N/R
	Freshmen returning for sophomore year	91%	ACT-takers scoring 30 or over	N/R
	Students completing degree within 5 years	80%	*Majors with most degrees conferred:* political science/government, economics, English.	
	Grads pursuing further study	22%		

Majors Anthropology, art/fine arts, Asian/Oriental studies, biology/biological sciences, biophysics, Canadian studies, chemistry, computer science, creative writing, ecology/environmental studies, economics, English, environmental sciences, French, geology, geophysics, German, history, literature, mathematics, modern languages, music, philosophy, physical education, physics, political science/government, psychology, recreation and leisure services, religious studies, Romance languages, sociology, Spanish, theater arts/drama.

Applying *Required:* essay, high school transcript, 3 years of high school math and science, 3 years of high school foreign language, 2 recommendations, SAT or ACT, 1 Achievement, English Composition Test. *Recommended:* interview, 2 Achievements, English Composition Test (with essay). *Application deadlines:* 2/1, 12/15 for early decision, 2/15 for financial aid. *Contact:* Mr. Joel Wincowski, Dean of Admissions and Financial Aid, Vilas Hall, Admissions, Canton, NY 13617, 315-379-5261.

St. Louis College of Pharmacy

St. Louis, Missouri

Founded 1864
Urban setting
Independent
Coed
Awards B, M, D

Enrollment	771 total; 755 undergraduates (133 freshmen)
Faculty	82 total; 52 full-time (83% have doctorate/terminal degree); student-faculty ratio is 12:1; grad assistants teach no undergraduate courses.
Libraries	38,900 bound volumes, 2 titles on microform, 456 periodical subscriptions
Computing	*Terminals/PCs available for student use:* 41, located in library, computer lab; PC not required.
Of Special Interest	*Core academic program:* yes. Academic exchange program: no. Study-abroad programs: no. Cooperative Army ROTC, cooperative Air Force ROTC.
On Campus	Drama/theater group; student-run newspaper. *Social organizations:* 4 national fraternities, 2 national sororities; 70% of eligible undergraduate men and 65% of eligible undergraduate women are members.
Athletics	None

Costs (1991–92) & Aid				
	Comprehensive fee	$11,160	Need-based scholarships (average)	$1200
	Tuition	$7400	Non-need scholarships (average)	$1150
	Mandatory fees	$60	Short-term loans	N/Avail
	Room and board	$3700	Long-term loans—college funds (average)	$750
	Financial aid recipients	84%	Long-term loans—external funds (average)	$2750

Undergraduate Facts				
	Part-time	3%	*Freshman Data:* 219 applied, 83% were accepted, 73% (133) of those entered	
	State residents	43%		
	Transfers	6%	From top tenth of high school class	32%
	African-Americans	6%	SAT-takers scoring 600 or over on verbal	N/R
	Native Americans	0%	SAT-takers scoring 700 or over on verbal	N/R
	Hispanics	1%	SAT-takers scoring 600 or over on math	N/R
	Asian-Americans	5%	SAT-takers scoring 700 or over on math	N/R
	International students	2%	ACT-takers scoring 26 or over	36%
	Freshmen returning for sophomore year	88%	ACT-takers scoring 30 or over	8%
	Students completing degree within 5 years	87%		
	Grads pursuing further study	6%		

Major Pharmacy/pharmaceutical sciences.

Applying *Required:* high school transcript, SAT or ACT. *Recommended:* 3 years of high school math and science, some high school foreign language, interview. *Application deadlines:* rolling, 6/30 priority date for financial aid. *Contact:* Ms. Diane Drilling, Director of Admissions, 4588 Parkview Place, St. Louis, MO 63110, 314-367-8700 Ext. 227.

✱ Saint Louis University

St. Louis, Missouri

Founded 1818
Urban setting
Independent, Roman Catholic (Jesuit)
Coed
Awards A, B, M, D

Enrollment 11,814 total; 7,508 undergraduates (914 freshmen)

Faculty 1,469 total; 1,068 full-time (79% have doctorate/terminal degree); student-faculty ratio is 15:1; grad assistants teach a few undergraduate courses.

Libraries 2.1 million bound volumes, 35,000 titles on microform, 11,412 periodical subscriptions

Computing *Terminals/PCs available for student use:* 200, located in computer center, dormitories, academic buildings; PC not required. Campus network links student PCs.

Of Special Interest *Core academic program:* yes. Computer course required for business, science, math majors. Phi Beta Kappa, Sigma Xi chapters. Academic exchange with Washington University. Sponsors and participates in study-abroad programs. Air Force ROTC, cooperative Army ROTC.

On Campus Drama/theater group; student-run newspaper and radio station. *Social organizations:* 3 national fraternities, 1 national sorority, 3 local fraternities, 2 local sororities; 16% of eligible undergraduate men and 12% of eligible undergraduate women are members.

Athletics Member NCAA (Division I). *Intercollegiate sports:* baseball (M), basketball (M, W), field hockey (W), golf (M), ice hockey (M), rugby (M), soccer (M), softball (W), swimming and diving (M, W), tennis (M, W), volleyball (W). *Scholarships:* M, W.

Costs (1992–93) & Aid				
	Comprehensive fee	$14,300	Need-based scholarships (average)	$3000
	Tuition	$9880	Non-need scholarships (average)	$6500
	Mandatory fees	N/App	Short-term loans	N/Avail
	Room and board	$4420	Long-term loans—college funds	N/Avail
	Financial aid recipients	80%	Long-term loans—external funds (average)	$2625

Undergraduate Facts				
	Part-time	16%	*Freshman Data:* 2,814 applied, 85% were accepted, 38% (914) of those entered	
	State residents	65%		
	Transfers	16%	From top tenth of high school class	27%
	African-Americans	8%	SAT-takers scoring 600 or over on verbal	11%
	Native Americans	1%	SAT-takers scoring 700 or over on verbal	1%
	Hispanics	3%	SAT-takers scoring 600 or over on math	29%
	Asian-Americans	6%	SAT-takers scoring 700 or over on math	6%
	International students	3%	ACT-takers scoring 26 or over	55%
	Freshmen returning for sophomore year	78%	ACT-takers scoring 30 or over	15%
	Students completing degree within 5 years	72%	*Majors with most degrees conferred:* business, psychology, biology/biological sciences.	
	Grads pursuing further study	62%		

Majors Accounting, aerospace engineering, aircraft and missile maintenance, American studies, art/fine arts, atmospheric sciences, aviation administration, aviation technology, biology/biological sciences, business, business economics, chemistry, classics, communication, community services, computer science, criminal justice, (pre)dentistry sequence, early childhood education, earth science, economics, electrical engineering, elementary education, English, finance/banking, flight training, French, geology, geophysics, German, Greek, history, humanities, international business, labor and industrial relations, Latin, Latin American studies, (pre)law sequence, management information systems, marketing/retailing/merchandising, mathematics, medical records services, medical technology, (pre)medicine sequence, meteorology, middle school education, modern languages, nuclear medical technology, nursing, occupational therapy, philosophy, physical therapy, physician's assistant studies, physics, political science/government, psychology, religious studies, Russian, secondary education, social work, sociology, Spanish, special education, speech pathology and audiology, speech/rhetoric/public address/debate, speech therapy, theology, tourism and travel, urban studies, (pre)veterinary medicine sequence.

Applying *Required:* high school transcript, SAT or ACT. *Recommended:* 3 years of high school math, some high school foreign language. *Application deadlines:* rolling, 4/1 priority date for financial aid. *Contact:* Mr. Kent R. Hopkins, Director of Admissions, 221 North Grand Boulevard, St. Louis, MO 63103, 314-658-2500 or toll-free 800-325-6666 (out-of-state).

St. Mary's College of Maryland

St. Mary's City, Maryland

Founded 1840
Rural setting
State-supported
Coed
Awards B

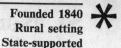

Enrollment 1,339 total—all undergraduates (227 freshmen)

Faculty 142 total; 96 full-time (95% have doctorate/terminal degree); student-faculty ratio is 13:1.

Libraries 129,818 bound volumes, 31,057 titles on microform, 1,579 periodical subscriptions

Computing *Terminals/PCs available for student use:* 67, located in computer center, library, computer labs; PC not required. Campus network links student PCs.

Of Special Interest *Core academic program:* yes. Computer course required for math majors. Academic exchange program: no. Sponsors and participates in study-abroad programs.

On Campus Drama/theater group; student-run newspaper and radio station. No national or local fraternities or sororities on campus.

Athletics Member NCAA (Division III). *Intercollegiate sports:* baseball (M), basketball (M, W), crew (M, W), fencing (M, W), field hockey (W), lacrosse (M, W), rugby (M), sailing (M, W), soccer (M, W), swimming and diving (M, W), tennis (M, W), volleyball (W), wrestling (M).

Costs (1991–92) & Aid				
State resident tuition	$2500	142 Need-based scholarships (average)	$1800
Nonresident tuition	$4400	166 Non-need scholarships (average)	$2680
Mandatory fees	$710	Short-term loans (average)	$129
Room and board	$4100	Long-term loans—college funds (average)	$870
Financial aid recipients	53%	Long-term loans—external funds (average)	$2476

Undergraduate Facts			
Part-time	5%	*Freshman Data:* 1,549 applied, 39% were accepted, 37% (227) of those entered	
State residents	88%		
Transfers	N/R	From top tenth of high school class	37%
African-Americans	9%	SAT-takers scoring 600 or over on verbal	41%
Native Americans	0%	SAT-takers scoring 700 or over on verbal	7%
Hispanics	1%	SAT-takers scoring 600 or over on math	55%
Asian-Americans	4%	SAT-takers scoring 700 or over on math	10%
International students	2%	ACT-takers scoring 26 or over	N/R
Freshmen returning for sophomore year	91%	ACT-takers scoring 30 or over	N/R
Students completing degree within 5 years	60%	*Majors with most degrees conferred:* economics, psychology, political science/government.	
Grads pursuing further study	23%		

Majors Anthropology, art/fine arts, biology/biological sciences, chemistry, economics, English, history, human development, literature, mathematics, modern languages, music, natural sciences, philosophy, physics, political science/government, psychology, public affairs and policy studies, sociology, theater arts/drama.

Applying *Required:* essay, high school transcript, 3 years of high school math, 2 years of high school foreign language, SAT. *Recommended:* 3 years of high school science, 4 years of high school foreign language, 3 recommendations, campus interview. ACT required for some. *Application deadlines:* 1/15, 12/15 for early decision, 3/15 priority date for financial aid. *Contact:* Mr. Richard Edgar, Director of Admissions, St. Mary's City, MD 20686, 301-862-0292 or toll-free 800-492-7181.

* St. Norbert College

De Pere, Wisconsin

Founded 1898
Suburban setting
Independent, Roman Catholic
Coed
Awards B, M

Enrollment 1,877 total; 1,866 undergraduates (457 freshmen)

Faculty 149 total; 118 full-time (78% have doctorate/terminal degree); student-faculty ratio is 15:1; grad assistants teach no undergraduate courses.

Libraries 160,845 bound volumes, 23,583 titles on microform, 736 periodical subscriptions

Computing *Terminals/PCs available for student use:* 55, located in computer center, academic buildings; PC not required. Campus network links student PCs.

Of Special Interest *Core academic program:* yes. Computer course required for business, accounting, math, social science, natural sciences majors. Academic exchange with St. Edwards University, Higher Education Consortium for Urban Affairs. Sponsors and participates in study-abroad programs. Army ROTC.

On Campus Drama/theater group; student-run newspaper and radio station. *Social organizations:* 3 national fraternities, 2 local fraternities, 3 local sororities, 13 social clubs; 49% of eligible undergraduate men and 54% of eligible undergraduate women are members.

Athletics Member NCAA (Division III). *Intercollegiate sports:* baseball (M), basketball (M, W), cross-country running (M, W), football (M), golf (M, W), ice hockey (M), soccer (M, W), softball (W), tennis (M, W), track and field (M, W), volleyball (W).

Costs (1992–93) & Aid				
	Comprehensive fee	$14,815	Need-based scholarships (average)	$3704
	Tuition	$10,730	Non-need scholarships (average)	$2892
	Mandatory fees	$75	Short-term loans	N/Avail
	Room and board	$4010	Long-term loans—college funds	N/Avail
	Financial aid recipients	88%	Long-term loans—external funds (average)	$2872

Undergraduate Facts				
	Part-time	3%	*Freshman Data:* 1,183 applied, 90% were accepted, 43% (457) of those entered	
	State residents	72%		
	Transfers	10%	From top tenth of high school class	26%
	African-Americans	1%	SAT-takers scoring 600 or over on verbal	15%
	Native Americans	1%	SAT-takers scoring 700 or over on verbal	0%
	Hispanics	1%	SAT-takers scoring 600 or over on math	25%
	Asian-Americans	1%	SAT-takers scoring 700 or over on math	5%
	International students	1%	ACT-takers scoring 26 or over	32%
	Freshmen returning for sophomore year	83%	ACT-takers scoring 30 or over	5%
	Students completing degree within 5 years	72%	*Majors with most degrees conferred:* business, communication, elementary education.	
	Grads pursuing further study	N/R		

Majors Accounting, anthropology, applied art, art education, art/fine arts, biology/biological sciences, business, chemistry, communication, computer information systems, computer science, (pre)dentistry sequence, early childhood education, economics, education, elementary education, English, environmental sciences, French, German, graphic arts, history, humanities, international business, international economics, international studies, (pre)law sequence, mathematics, medical technology, (pre)medicine sequence, middle school education, music, music education, natural sciences, philosophy, physics, political science/government, psychology, religious education, religious studies, secondary education, social science, sociology, Spanish, theater arts/drama, (pre)veterinary medicine sequence, voice.

Applying *Required:* essay, high school transcript, 3 years of high school math, recommendations, SAT or ACT. *Recommended:* 3 years of high school science, 2 years of high school foreign language, interview. *Application deadlines:* rolling, 3/1 priority date for financial aid. *Contact:* Mr. Scott J. Goplin, Dean of Admission, 100 Grant Street, De Pere, WI 54115, 414-337-3005 or toll-free 800-236-4878.

St. Olaf College

Northfield, Minnesota

Founded 1874
Small-town setting
Independent, Lutheran
Coed
Awards B

Enrollment	3,057 total—all undergraduates (743 freshmen)
Faculty	359 total; 230 full-time (79% have doctorate/terminal degree); student-faculty ratio is 12:1.
Libraries	393,397 bound volumes, 180,000 titles on microform, 1,700 periodical subscriptions
Computing	*Terminals/PCs available for student use:* 321, located in computer center, library, dormitories, all academic buildings; PC not required. Campus network links student PCs.
Of Special Interest	*Core academic program:* yes. Computer course required for some majors. Phi Beta Kappa chapter. Academic exchange with Carleton College, Augsburg College, various art institutions. Sponsors and participates in study-abroad programs.
On Campus	Drama/theater group; student-run newspaper and radio station. No national or local fraternities or sororities on campus.
Athletics	Member NCAA (Division III). *Intercollegiate sports:* baseball (M), basketball (M, W), cross-country running (M, W), football (M), golf (M, W), ice hockey (M), skiing (cross-country) (M, W), skiing (downhill) (M, W), soccer (M, W), softball (W), swimming and diving (M, W), tennis (M, W), track and field (M, W), volleyball (W), wrestling (M).

Costs (1992–93) & Aid				
	Comprehensive fee	$16,250	Need-based scholarships (average)	$4218
	Tuition	$12,750	Non-need scholarships	Avail
	Mandatory fees	N/App	Short-term loans (average)	$1550
	Room and board	$3500	Long-term loans—college funds (average)	$2000
	Financial aid recipients	57%	Long-term loans—external funds (average)	$2463

Undergraduate Facts				
	Part-time	3%	*Freshman Data:* 2,041 applied, 74% were accepted, 49% (743) of those entered	
	State residents	55%		
	Transfers	4%	From top tenth of high school class	40%
	African-Americans	1%	SAT-takers scoring 600 or over on verbal	22%
	Native Americans	1%	SAT-takers scoring 700 or over on verbal	4%
	Hispanics	1%	SAT-takers scoring 600 or over on math	43%
	Asian-Americans	3%	SAT-takers scoring 700 or over on math	13%
	International students	2%	ACT-takers scoring 26 or over	51%
	Freshmen returning for sophomore year	89%	ACT-takers scoring 30 or over	12%
	Students completing degree within 5 years	82%	*Majors with most degrees conferred:* psychology, economics, biology/biological sciences.	
	Grads pursuing further study	20%		

Majors American studies, art education, art/fine arts, art history, Asian/Oriental studies, biology/biological sciences, black/African-American studies, chemistry, classics, computer science, dance, (pre)dentistry sequence, East Asian studies, East European and Soviet studies, economics, education, elementary education, English, French, German, Greek, health science, Hispanic studies, history, home economics education, Latin, (pre)law sequence, literature, mathematics, (pre)medicine sequence, medieval studies, music, music education, nursing, philosophy, physical education, physics, piano/organ, political science/government, psychology, religious studies, Russian, Russian and Slavic studies, sacred music, Scandinavian languages/studies, secondary education, social work, sociology, Spanish, speech/rhetoric/public address/debate, stringed instruments, theater arts/drama, urban studies, (pre)veterinary medicine sequence, voice, Western civilization and culture, wind and percussion instruments, women's studies.

Applying *Required:* essay, high school transcript, 2 recommendations, SAT or ACT, PSAT. *Recommended:* 3 years of high school math and science, 2 years of high school foreign language, interview. *Application deadlines:* 2/15, 11/15 for early decision, 3/1 priority date for financial aid. *Contact:* Mr. John Ruohoniemi, Director of Admissions, 1520 St. Olaf Avenue, Northfield, MN 55057, 507-646-3025.

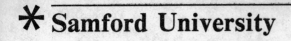

Samford University

Birmingham, Alabama

Founded 1841
Suburban setting
Independent, Baptist
Coed
Awards A, B, M, D

Enrollment 4,248 total; 3,194 undergraduates (591 freshmen)

Faculty 323 total; 160 full-time (83% have doctorate/terminal degree); student-faculty ratio is 15:1; grad assistants teach no undergraduate courses.

Libraries 515,913 bound volumes, 236,588 titles on microform, 3,896 periodical subscriptions

Computing *Terminals/PCs available for student use:* 250, located in computer center, library, schools of business, nursing, education, science, pharmacy and music; PC not required.

Of Special Interest *Core academic program:* yes. Computer course required for business, math majors. Academic exchange with University of Alabama at Birmingham, Birmingham-Southern College. Sponsors and participates in study-abroad programs. Air Force ROTC, cooperative Army ROTC.

On Campus Mandatory chapel; drama/theater group; student-run newspaper and radio station. *Social organizations:* 5 national fraternities, 6 national sororities; 30% of eligible undergraduate men and 30% of eligible undergraduate women are members.

Athletics Member NCAA (Division I). *Intercollegiate sports:* basketball (M), cross-country running (M, W), football (M), golf (M, W), softball (W), tennis (M, W), track and field (M, W), volleyball (W). *Scholarships:* M, W.

Costs (1991–92) & Aid				
	Comprehensive fee	$9894	Need-based scholarships (average)	$1500
	Tuition	$6540	Non-need scholarships (average)	$1500
	Mandatory fees	N/App	Short-term loans	N/Avail
	Room and board	$3354	Long-term loans—college funds	N/Avail
	Financial aid recipients	83%	Long-term loans—external funds (average)	$2700

Undergraduate Facts				
	Part-time	14%	*Freshman Data:* 1,320 applied, 73% were accepted, 61% (591) of those entered	
	State residents	50%		
	Transfers	30%	From top tenth of high school class	38%
	African-Americans	7%	SAT-takers scoring 600 or over on verbal	13%
	Native Americans	1%	SAT-takers scoring 700 or over on verbal	1%
	Hispanics	1%	SAT-takers scoring 600 or over on math	19%
	Asian-Americans	1%	SAT-takers scoring 700 or over on math	2%
	International students	1%	ACT-takers scoring 26 or over	30%
	Freshmen returning for sophomore year	93%	ACT-takers scoring 30 or over	8%
	Students completing degree within 5 years	74%	*Majors with most degrees conferred:* pharmacy/ pharmaceutical sciences, business, education.	
	Grads pursuing further study	68%		

Majors Accounting, adult and continuing education, art education, art/fine arts, biology/biological sciences, business, business economics, chemistry, commercial art, communication, computer science, cytotechnology, (pre)dentistry sequence, early childhood education, economics, education, educational administration, elementary education, engineering physics, English, environmental sciences, family and consumer studies, fashion merchandising, finance/banking, food services management, French, geography, German, graphic arts, health education, history, home economics, home economics education, human resources, insurance, interior design, international business, international studies, journalism, law enforcement/police sciences, (pre)law sequence, liberal arts/general studies, literature, marine biology, marketing/retailing/merchandising, mathematics, medical records services, medical technology, (pre)medicine sequence, ministries, music, music education, nuclear medical technology, nursing, nutrition, occupational therapy, painting/drawing, paralegal studies, pastoral studies, pharmacy/pharmaceutical sciences, physical education, physics, piano/organ, political science/government, psychology, public administration, public affairs and policy studies, radiological technology, real estate, recreation and leisure services, religious education, religious studies, sacred music, science education, secondary education, sociology, Spanish, speech/rhetoric/public address/debate, sports medicine, stringed instruments, theater arts/drama, theology, (pre)veterinary medicine sequence, voice.

Applying *Required:* essay, high school transcript, 2 recommendations, SAT or ACT. *Recommended:* 3 years of high school math and science, some high school foreign language, campus interview. *Application deadlines:* rolling, 12/1 for early decision, 3/1 priority date for financial aid. *Contact:* Dr. Don Belcher, Dean of Admissions and Financial Aid, Samford Hall, Birmingham, AL 35229, 205-870-2901 or toll-free 800-888-7218.

Santa Clara University

Santa Clara, California

Founded 1851
Suburban setting
Independent, Roman Catholic (Jesuit)
Coed
Awards B, M, D

Enrollment 7,761 total; 3,998 undergraduates (927 freshmen)

Faculty 551 total; 333 full-time (90% have doctorate/terminal degree); student-faculty ratio is 13:1; grad assistants teach no undergraduate courses.

Libraries 544,778 bound volumes, 36,735 titles on microform, 5,478 periodical subscriptions

Computing *Terminals/PCs available for student use:* 332, located in computer center, student center, library; PC not required.

Of Special Interest *Core academic program:* yes. Computer course required for business, engineering majors. Phi Beta Kappa, Sigma Xi chapters. Academic exchange program: no. Participates in study-abroad programs. Army ROTC, cooperative Naval ROTC, cooperative Air Force ROTC.

On Campus Drama/theater group; student-run newspaper and radio station. *Social organizations:* 4 national fraternities, 3 national sororities; 16% of eligible undergraduate men and 17% of eligible undergraduate women are members.

Athletics Member NCAA (Division I). *Intercollegiate sports:* baseball (M), basketball (M, W), crew (M, W), cross-country running (M, W), football (M), golf (M), lacrosse (M), rugby (M), soccer (M, W), tennis (M, W), volleyball (M, W), water polo (M). *Scholarships:* M, W.

Costs (1992–93) & Aid
Comprehensive fee	$17,706	
Tuition	$12,150	
Mandatory fees	N/App	
Room and board	$5556	
Financial aid recipients	56%	
Need-based scholarships (average)		$4874
Non-need scholarships (average)		$7011
Short-term loans (average)		$500
Long-term loans—college funds (average)		$2500
Long-term loans—external funds (average)		$2748

Undergraduate Facts
Part-time	3%
State residents	62%
Transfers	19%
African-Americans	2%
Native Americans	1%
Hispanics	10%
Asian-Americans	17%
International students	7%
Freshmen returning for sophomore year	92%
Students completing degree within 5 years	75%
Grads pursuing further study	23%

Freshman Data: 3,430 applied, 71% were accepted, 38% (927) of those entered

From top tenth of high school class	40%
SAT-takers scoring 600 or over on verbal	12%
SAT-takers scoring 700 or over on verbal	1%
SAT-takers scoring 600 or over on math	42%
SAT-takers scoring 700 or over on math	8%
ACT-takers scoring 26 or over	N/R
ACT-takers scoring 30 or over	N/R

Majors with most degrees conferred: finance/banking, marketing/retailing/merchandising, English.

Majors Accounting, anthropology, art/fine arts, biology/biological sciences, business, business economics, chemistry, civil engineering, classics, communication, computer engineering, computer information systems, computer science, dance, (pre)dentistry sequence, economics, education, electrical engineering, engineering (general), engineering physics, English, finance/banking, French, German, history, humanities, information science, interdisciplinary studies, international business, Italian, (pre)law sequence, liberal arts/general studies, marketing/retailing/merchandising, mathematics, mechanical engineering, (pre)medicine sequence, modern languages, music, philosophy, physics, political science/government, psychology, religious studies, retail management, science, sociology, Spanish, theater arts/drama, (pre)veterinary medicine sequence.

Applying *Required:* essay, high school transcript, 3 years of high school math, 3 years of high school foreign language, 1 recommendation, SAT or ACT. *Recommended:* interview. 3 years of high school science required for some. *Application deadlines:* 2/1, 2/1 priority date for financial aid. *Contact:* Mr. Daniel J. Saracino, Dean of Admissions, 500 El Camino Real, Santa Clara, CA 95053, 408-554-4700.

Sarah Lawrence College

Bronxville, New York

Founded 1926
Small-town setting
Independent
Coed
Awards B, M

Enrollment 1,150 total; 1,000 undergraduates (230 freshmen)

Faculty 225 total; 161 full-time (95% have doctorate/terminal degree); student-faculty ratio is 6:1; grad assistants teach no undergraduate courses.

Libraries 200,000 bound volumes, 3,000 titles on microform, 1,000 periodical subscriptions

Computing *Terminals/PCs available for student use:* 20, located in computer center; PC not required.

Of Special Interest *Core academic program:* yes. Academic exchange program: no. Sponsors and participates in study-abroad programs.

On Campus Drama/theater group; student-run newspaper. No national or local fraternities or sororities on campus.

Athletics *Intercollegiate sports:* basketball (M), crew (M, W), equestrian sports (M, W), soccer (M), tennis (M, W), volleyball (W).

Costs (1991-92) & Aid				
	Comprehensive fee	$23,150	Need-based scholarships (average)	$9273
	Tuition	$16,400	Non-need scholarships	N/Avail
	Mandatory fees	$350	Short-term loans	N/Avail
	Room and board	$6400	Long-term loans—college funds (average)	$1605
	Financial aid recipients	46%	Long-term loans—external funds (average)	$3117

Undergraduate Facts				
	Part-time	10%	*Freshman Data:* 1,296 applied, 49% were accepted, 36% (230) of those entered	
	State residents	17%		
	Transfers	10%	From top tenth of high school class	32%
	African-Americans	9%	SAT-takers scoring 600 or over on verbal	43%
	Native Americans	1%	SAT-takers scoring 700 or over on verbal	8%
	Hispanics	8%	SAT-takers scoring 600 or over on math	33%
	Asian-Americans	6%	SAT-takers scoring 700 or over on math	5%
	International students	8%	ACT-takers scoring 26 or over	N/R
	Freshmen returning for sophomore year	96%	ACT-takers scoring 30 or over	N/R
	Students completing degree within 5 years	80%	*Majors with most degrees conferred:* literature, history, psychology.	
	Grads pursuing further study	40%		

Majors American studies, anthropology, art/fine arts, art history, Asian/Oriental studies, biology/biological sciences, black/African-American studies, ceramic art and design, chemistry, child psychology/child development, classics, comparative literature, computer science, creative writing, dance, (pre)dentistry sequence, early childhood education, East European and Soviet studies, ecology/environmental studies, economics, English, European studies, film studies, French, geology, German, Greek, history, human development, humanities, interdisciplinary studies, international studies, Italian, Latin, liberal arts/general studies, literature, marine biology, mathematics, (pre)medicine sequence, modern languages, music, music history, natural sciences, painting/drawing, philosophy, photography, physics, piano/organ, political science/government, psychology, public affairs and policy studies, religious studies, Romance languages, Russian, science, sculpture, social science, sociology, Spanish, studio art, theater arts/drama, voice, women's studies.

Applying *Required:* essay, high school transcript, 3 recommendations, SAT, ACT or any 3 College Board Achievement Tests. *Recommended:* 3 years of high school math and science, some high school foreign language, interview, English Composition Test (with essay). *Application deadlines:* 2/1, 1/1 for early decision, 2/1 for financial aid. *Contact:* Ms. Robin G. Mamlet, Director of Admissions, 1 Meadway, Bronxville, NY 10708, 914-395-2510 or toll-free 800-888-2858.

Scripps College

Claremont, California

Founded 1926
Small-town setting
Independent
Women
Awards B

Enrollment	632 total—all undergraduates (146 freshmen)
Faculty	95 total; 60 full-time (97% have doctorate/terminal degree); student-faculty ratio is 9:1.
Libraries	1.9 million bound volumes, 1.1 million titles on microform, 6,800 periodical subscriptions
Computing	*Terminals/PCs available for student use:* 30, located in computer center, classrooms; PC not required.
Of Special Interest	*Core academic program:* yes. Computer course required. Phi Beta Kappa, Sigma Xi chapters. Academic exchange with 5 members of The Claremont Colleges, Colby College, Spelman College, California Institute of Technology. Sponsors and participates in study-abroad programs. Cooperative Army ROTC, cooperative Air Force ROTC.
On Campus	Drama/theater group; student-run newspaper and radio station. No national or local sororities on campus.
Athletics	Member NCAA (Division III). *Intercollegiate sports:* basketball, cross-country running, golf, soccer, softball, swimming and diving, tennis, track and field, volleyball.

Costs (1991–92) & Aid				
	Comprehensive fee	$21,450	Need-based scholarships	Avail
	Tuition	$14,700	Non-need scholarships	Avail
	Mandatory fees	$100	Short-term loans (average)	$500
	Room and board	$6650	Long-term loans—college funds (average)	$1737
	Financial aid recipients	50%	Long-term loans—external funds (average)	$2800

Undergraduate Facts				
	Part-time	2%	*Freshman Data:* 750 applied, 67% were accepted, 29% (146) of those entered	
	State residents	51%		
	Transfers	4%	From top tenth of high school class	50%
	African-Americans	3%	SAT-takers scoring 600 or over on verbal	32%
	Native Americans	1%	SAT-takers scoring 700 or over on verbal	5%
	Hispanics	10%	SAT-takers scoring 600 or over on math	42%
	Asian-Americans	11%	SAT-takers scoring 700 or over on math	3%
	International students	2%	ACT-takers scoring 26 or over	N/R
	Freshmen returning for sophomore year	84%	ACT-takers scoring 30 or over	N/R
	Students completing degree within 5 years	65%	*Majors with most degrees conferred:* psychology, English, biology/biological sciences.	
	Grads pursuing further study	33%		

Majors Accounting, American studies, anthropology, art/fine arts, art history, Asian/Oriental studies, astronomy, biochemistry, biology/biological sciences, black/African-American studies, chemistry, Chinese, classics, comparative literature, dance, economics, English, European studies, film studies, folklore, French, geology, German, Germanic languages and literature, Hispanic studies, history, international studies, Italian, Japanese, Latin, Latin American studies, legal studies, linguistics, literature, mathematics, Mexican-American/Chicano studies, modern languages, music, philosophy, physics, political science/government, psychobiology, psychology, religious studies, Russian, sociology, Spanish, studio art, theater arts/drama, women's studies.

Applying *Required:* essay, high school transcript, 3 recommendations, graded writing sample, SAT or ACT. *Recommended:* 3 years of high school math and science, 3 years of high school foreign language, interview, 3 Achievements, English Composition Test. *Application deadlines:* 2/1, 11/15 for early decision, 2/1 priority date for financial aid. *Contact:* Ms. Leslie Miles, Dean of Admissions and Financial Aid, 1030 Columbia Avenue, Claremont, CA 91711, 714-621-8149.

Shepherd College

Shepherdstown, West Virginia

Founded 1871
Small-town setting
State-supported
Coed
Awards A, B

Enrollment	3,501 total—all undergraduates (844 freshmen)
Faculty	184 total; 124 full-time (68% have doctorate/terminal degree); student-faculty ratio is 18:1.
Libraries	154,746 bound volumes, 133,783 titles on microform, 930 periodical subscriptions
Computing	*Terminals/PCs available for student use:* 202, located in computer center, 3 microcomputer labs; PC not required.
Of Special Interest	*Core academic program:* yes. Computer course required. Academic exchange program: no. Participates in study-abroad programs. Cooperative Air Force ROTC.
On Campus	Drama/theater group; student-run newspaper and radio station. *Social organizations:* 5 national fraternities, 5 national sororities, 1 local fraternity; 25% of eligible undergraduate men and 25% of eligible undergraduate women are members.
Athletics	Member NCAA (Division II), NAIA. *Intercollegiate sports:* baseball (M), basketball (M, W), cross-country running (M, W), football (M), golf (M, W), soccer (M), softball (W), tennis (M, W), volleyball (M, W). *Scholarships:* M, W.

Costs (1991–92) & Aid				
	State resident tuition	$1894	Need-based scholarships	Avail
	Nonresident tuition	$4314	435 Non-need scholarships (average)	$535
	Mandatory fees	N/App	Short-term loans (average)	$250
	Room and board	$3500	Long-term loans—college funds	N/Avail
	Financial aid recipients	39%	Long-term loans—external funds (average)	$1588

Undergraduate Facts				
	Part-time	35%	*Freshman Data:* 2,140 applied, 48% were accepted, 82% (844) of those entered	
	State residents	68%		
	Transfers	30%	From top tenth of high school class	N/R
	African-Americans	5%	SAT-takers scoring 600 or over on verbal	21%
	Native Americans	1%	SAT-takers scoring 700 or over on verbal	1%
	Hispanics	3%	SAT-takers scoring 600 or over on math	21%
	Asian-Americans	2%	SAT-takers scoring 700 or over on math	1%
	International students	1%	ACT-takers scoring 26 or over	67%
	Freshmen returning for sophomore year	76%	ACT-takers scoring 30 or over	20%
	Students completing degree within 5 years	68%	*Majors with most degrees conferred:* business, education, nursing.	
	Grads pursuing further study	50%		

Majors Accounting, applied art, applied mathematics, art education, art/fine arts, art therapy, biology/biological sciences, botany/plant sciences, broadcasting, business, business economics, business education, chemistry, child care/child and family studies, commercial art, communication, computer information systems, computer management, computer programming, computer science, data processing, (pre)dentistry sequence, early childhood education, earth science, economics, education, elementary education, English, European studies, fashion merchandising, finance/banking, food services management, graphic arts, health education, history, home economics, home economics education, hotel and restaurant management, international studies, (pre)law sequence, library science, literature, management information systems, marketing/retailing/merchandising, mathematics, (pre)medicine sequence, music, music education, music history, natural resource management, nursing, painting/drawing, photography, physical education, physical fitness/human movement, physical sciences, piano/organ, political science/government, psychology, public administration, recreational facilities management, recreation and leisure services, recreation therapy, science, science education, secondary education, secretarial studies/office management, social work, sociology, speech/rhetoric/public address/debate, sports medicine, studio art, textiles and clothing, theater arts/drama, tourism and travel, (pre)veterinary medicine sequence, voice, Western civilization and culture, wildlife management, wind and percussion instruments, zoology.

Applying *Required:* essay, high school transcript, 3 years of high school math and science, 3 recommendations, SAT or ACT, English Composition Test. *Recommended:* 2 years of high school foreign language, campus interview. *Application deadlines:* 2/1, 11/15 for early action, continuous to 3/1 for financial aid. *Contact:* Mr. Karl L. Wolf, Director of Admissions, King Street, McMunan Hall, Shepherdstown, WV 25443, 304-876-2511 Ext. 212 or toll-free 800-344-5231.

From the College Since Shepherd College is located only an hour's drive from the Baltimore and Washington beltways, it offers numerous internships and co-op programs with government agencies, scientific research centers, and corporations in the area. It is also the home of the Contemporary American Theater Festival and has outstanding programs in art and music.

Siena College

Loudonville, New York

Founded 1937
Suburban setting
Independent, Roman Catholic
Coed
Awards B

Enrollment 3,570 total—all undergraduates (613 freshmen)

Faculty 261 total; 173 full-time (84% have doctorate/terminal degree); student-faculty ratio is 16:1.

Libraries 233,277 bound volumes, 28,484 titles on microform, 1,457 periodical subscriptions

Computing *Terminals/PCs available for student use:* 350, located in computer center, academic buildings; PC not required.

Of Special Interest *Core academic program:* yes. Computer course required for accounting, physics, math, business-related majors. Academic exchange with members of the Hudson-Mohawk Association of Colleges and Universities. Participates in study-abroad programs. Army ROTC, cooperative Air Force ROTC.

On Campus Drama/theater group; student-run newspaper and radio station. No national or local fraternities or sororities on campus.

Athletics Member NCAA (Division I). *Intercollegiate sports:* baseball (M), basketball (M, W), crew (M, W), cross-country running (M, W), equestrian sports (M, W), fencing (M, W), field hockey (W), football (M), golf (M), ice hockey (M), lacrosse (M, W), rugby (M), skiing (downhill) (M, W), soccer (M, W), tennis (M, W), track and field (M, W), volleyball (W). *Scholarships:* M, W.

Costs (1991–92) & Aid				
	Comprehensive fee	$13,525	Need-based scholarships (average)	$1773
	Tuition	$8850	Non-need scholarships (average)	$3305
	Mandatory fees	$210	Short-term loans	N/Avail
	Room and board	$4465	Long-term loans—college funds	N/Avail
	Financial aid recipients	75%	Long-term loans—external funds (average)	$2952

Undergraduate Facts

Part-time	24%	*Freshman Data:* 2,635 applied, 72% were accepted, 32% (613) of those entered
State residents	86%	
Transfers	6%	From top tenth of high school class — 25%
African-Americans	2%	SAT-takers scoring 600 or over on verbal — 7%
Native Americans	0%	SAT-takers scoring 700 or over on verbal — 1%
Hispanics	2%	SAT-takers scoring 600 or over on math — 32%
Asian-Americans	1%	SAT-takers scoring 700 or over on math — 4%
International students	1%	ACT-takers scoring 26 or over — 32%
Freshmen returning for sophomore year	96%	ACT-takers scoring 30 or over — 3%
Students completing degree within 5 years	80%	*Majors with most degrees conferred:* accounting, marketing/retailing/merchandising, biology/biological sciences.
Grads pursuing further study	24%	

Majors Accounting, American studies, biology/biological sciences, business economics, chemistry, computer science, (pre)dentistry sequence, economics, English, finance/banking, French, history, marketing/retailing/merchandising, mathematics, philosophy, physics, political science/government, psychology, religious studies, secondary education, social work, sociology, Spanish.

Applying *Required:* essay, high school transcript, 3 years of high school math, 1 recommendation, SAT or ACT. *Recommended:* 2 years of high school foreign language, Achievements. 3 years of high school science, campus interview required for some. *Application deadlines:* 3/1, 12/1 for early action, 2/1 priority date for financial aid. *Contact:* Ms. Joann McKenna, Director of Admissions, 515 Loudon Road, Loudonville, NY 12211-1462, 518-783-2423.

Simon's Rock College of Bard

Great Barrington, Massachusetts

Founded 1964
Small-town setting
Independent
Coed
Awards A, B

Enrollment	286 total—all undergraduates (127 freshmen)
Faculty	46 total; 34 full-time (75% have doctorate/terminal degree); student-faculty ratio is 9:1.
Libraries	55,000 bound volumes, 330 periodical subscriptions
Computing	*Terminals/PCs available for student use:* 20, located in computer center, dormitories; PC not required.
Of Special Interest	*Core academic program:* yes. Computer course required. Academic exchange with Bard College. Participates in study-abroad programs.
On Campus	Drama/theater group; student-run newspaper. No national or local fraternities or sororities on campus.
Athletics	*Intercollegiate sports:* basketball (M, W), soccer (M, W), tennis (M, W).

Costs (1991–92) & Aid				
	Comprehensive fee	$21,150	Need-based scholarships (average)	$7100
	Tuition	$14,160	Non-need scholarships (average)	$1000
	Mandatory fees	$1640	Short-term loans	N/Avail
	Room and board	$5350	Long-term loans—college funds	Avail
	Financial aid recipients	70%	Long-term loans—external funds	Avail

Undergraduate Facts				
	Part-time	N/R	*Freshman Data:* 311 applied, 58% were accepted, 70% (127) of those entered	
	State residents	N/R		
	Transfers	N/R	From top tenth of high school class	N/R
	African-Americans	5%	SAT-takers scoring 600 or over on verbal	47%
	Native Americans	N/R	SAT-takers scoring 700 or over on verbal	11%
	Hispanics	2%	SAT-takers scoring 600 or over on math	48%
	Asian-Americans	5%	SAT-takers scoring 700 or over on math	13%
	International students	4%	ACT-takers scoring 26 or over	N/R
	Freshmen returning for sophomore year	85%	ACT-takers scoring 30 or over	N/R
	Students completing degree within 5 years	N/R		
	Grads pursuing further study	N/R		

Majors American studies, art/fine arts, ecology/environmental studies, English, environmental sciences, French, literature, (pre)medicine sequence, natural sciences, social science, Spanish, statistics.

Applying *Required:* essay, high school transcript, 3 recommendations, campus interview, parent application, SAT or ACT, PSAT. *Application deadlines:* 6/15, 6/15 priority date for financial aid. *Contact:* Mr. Brian R. Hopewell, Director of Admissions and Alumni Affairs, 84 Alford Road, Great Barrington, MA 01230-9702, 413-528-0771 Ext. 313.

From the College Tenth and eleventh graders who can't wait to get to college don't have to wait any longer. Simon's Rock offers bright, motivated, young students the opportunity to begin their college studies at age 16. Special scholarships are available for high-achieving sophomores. Simon's Rock is rated #1 among Northeast regional liberal arts colleges by *U.S. News & World Report.*

Simpson College

Indianola, Iowa

Founded 1860
Small-town setting
Independent, Methodist
Coed
Awards B

Enrollment 1,752 total—all undergraduates (289 freshmen)

Faculty 137 total; 69 full-time (74% have doctorate/terminal degree); student-faculty ratio is 15:1.

Libraries 138,309 bound volumes, 9,869 titles on microform, 573 periodical subscriptions

Computing *Terminals/PCs available for student use:* 180, located in computer center, student center, library; PC not required.

Of Special Interest *Core academic program:* yes. Computer course required for sociology, business, pre-engineering, math, psychology majors. Academic exchange with Drew University, American University. Sponsors and participates in study-abroad programs.

On Campus Drama/theater group; student-run newspaper. *Social organizations:* 3 national fraternities, 4 national sororities, 1 local fraternity; 40% of eligible undergraduate men and 41% of eligible undergraduate women are members.

Athletics Member NCAA (Division III). *Intercollegiate sports:* baseball (M), basketball (M, W), cross-country running (M, W), football (M), golf (M, W), softball (W), tennis (M, W), track and field (M, W), volleyball (W), wrestling (M).

Costs (1991–92) & Aid	Comprehensive fee	$12,960	Need-based scholarships (average)	$3857
	Tuition	$9500	Non-need scholarships (average)	$4559
	Mandatory fees	$85	Short-term loans (average)	$200
	Room and board	$3375	Long-term loans—college funds (average)	$2054
	Financial aid recipients	90%	Long-term loans—external funds (average)	$3069

Undergraduate Facts				
	Part-time	37%	*Freshman Data:* 899 applied, 81% were accepted, 40% (289) of those entered	
	State residents	95%		
	Transfers	6%	From top tenth of high school class	32%
	African-Americans	1%	SAT-takers scoring 600 or over on verbal	N/R
	Native Americans	0%	SAT-takers scoring 700 or over on verbal	N/R
	Hispanics	1%	SAT-takers scoring 600 or over on math	N/R
	Asian-Americans	1%	SAT-takers scoring 700 or over on math	N/R
	International students	1%	ACT-takers scoring 26 or over	38%
	Freshmen returning for sophomore year	80%	ACT-takers scoring 30 or over	9%
	Students completing degree within 5 years	61%		
	Grads pursuing further study	N/R		

Majors Accounting, advertising, art education, art/fine arts, arts administration, athletic training, biology/biological sciences, business, chemistry, commercial art, communication, computer management, computer science, corrections, criminal justice, (pre)dentistry sequence, early childhood education, ecology/environmental studies, economics, education, elementary education, engineering (general), English, environmental biology, French, German, health services administration, history, international business, international studies, (pre)law sequence, mathematics, medical laboratory technology, medical technology, (pre)medicine sequence, music, music education, philosophy, physical education, physical therapy, political science/government, psychology, religious studies, science, secondary education, social science, sociology, Spanish, sports administration, theater arts/drama, (pre)veterinary medicine sequence.

Applying *Required:* high school transcript, 1 recommendation, SAT or ACT. *Recommended:* 3 years of high school math and science, 3 years of high school foreign language, interview, top half of graduating class. *Application deadlines:* rolling, 4/20 priority date for financial aid. *Contact:* Mr. John Kellogg, Vice President, Admissions and College Marketing, 701 North C Street, Indianola, IA 50125, 515-961-1624 or toll-free 800-362-2454 (in-state), 800-247-2121 (out-of-state).

From the College Simpson combines the best of a liberal arts education with outstanding career preparation and extracurricular programs. Located 12 miles from Des Moines, Simpson offers the friendliness of a small town and the advantages of a metropolitan area. Activities range from an award-winning vocal music program to nationally recognized NCAA Division III teams.

✱ Skidmore College

Saratoga Springs, New York

Founded 1903
Small-town setting
Independent
Coed
Awards B

Enrollment	2,156 total—all undergraduates (626 freshmen)
Faculty	208 total; 193 full-time (92% have doctorate/terminal degree); student-faculty ratio is 11:1.
Libraries	377,180 bound volumes, 160,000 titles on microform, 1,600 periodical subscriptions
Computing	*Terminals/PCs available for student use:* 200, located in computer center, library, dormitories, classroom buildings; PC not required. Campus network links student PCs.
Of Special Interest	*Core academic program:* yes. Phi Beta Kappa chapter. Academic exchange with members of the Hudson-Mohawk Association of Colleges and Universities, American University (Washington Semester). Sponsors and participates in study-abroad programs. Cooperative Army ROTC, cooperative Naval ROTC, cooperative Air Force ROTC.
On Campus	Drama/theater group; student-run newspaper and radio station. No national or local fraternities or sororities on campus.
Athletics	Member NCAA (Division III). *Intercollegiate sports:* baseball (M), basketball (M, W), crew (M, W), equestrian sports (M, W), field hockey (W), golf (M), ice hockey (M, W), lacrosse (M, W), soccer (M, W), swimming and diving (W), tennis (M, W), volleyball (W).

Costs (1992-93 estimated) & Aid				
	Comprehensive fee	$22,135	Need-based scholarships (average)	$9260
	Tuition	$16,650	Non-need scholarships	N/Avail
	Mandatory fees	$215	Short-term loans	Avail
	Room and board	$5270	Long-term loans—college funds	N/Avail
	Financial aid recipients	47%	Long-term loans—external funds (average)	$2600

Undergraduate Facts				
	Part-time	N/R	*Freshman Data:* 4,252 applied, 61% were accepted, 24% (626) of those entered	
	State residents	31%		
	Transfers	4%	From top tenth of high school class	32%
	African-Americans	3%	SAT-takers scoring 600 or over on verbal	23%
	Native Americans	1%	SAT-takers scoring 700 or over on verbal	1%
	Hispanics	4%	SAT-takers scoring 600 or over on math	48%
	Asian-Americans	3%	SAT-takers scoring 700 or over on math	8%
	International students	2%	ACT-takers scoring 26 or over	N/R
	Freshmen returning for sophomore year	91%	ACT-takers scoring 30 or over	N/R
	Students completing degree within 5 years	80%	*Majors with most degrees conferred:* sociology, English, business.	
	Grads pursuing further study	31%		

Majors American studies, anthropology, art education, art/fine arts, art history, biochemistry, biology/biological sciences, business, business economics, chemistry, classics, computer science, creative writing, dance, (pre)dentistry sequence, economics, elementary education, English, French, geology, German, history, literature, mathematics, (pre)medicine sequence, music, philosophy, physical education, physics, political science/government, psychology, social work, sociology, Spanish, studio art, theater arts/drama, (pre)veterinary medicine sequence.

Applying *Required:* essay, high school transcript, 3 years of high school math and science, 3 years of high school foreign language, 2 recommendations, SAT or ACT. *Recommended:* interview, 3 Achievements, English Composition Test (with essay). *Application deadlines:* 2/1, 12/15 for early decision, 2/1 for financial aid. *Contact:* Ms. Mary Lou Bates, Director of Admissions, North Broadway, Saratoga Springs, NY 12866, 518-584-5000 Ext. 2213.

Smith College

Northampton, Massachusetts

Founded 1871
Small-town setting
Independent
Women
Awards B, M, D

Enrollment	2,974 total; 2,607 undergraduates (604 freshmen)
Faculty	283 total; 249 full-time (96% have doctorate/terminal degree); student-faculty ratio is 10:1; grad assistants teach no undergraduate courses.
Libraries	1 million bound volumes, 59,632 titles on microform, 3,158 periodical subscriptions
Computing	*Terminals/PCs available for student use:* 230, located in computer center, resource centers; PC not required but available for purchase. Campus network links student PCs.
Of Special Interest	*Core academic program:* no. Computer course required for some majors. Phi Beta Kappa, Sigma Xi chapters. Academic exchange with Pomona College, Howard University, North Carolina Central University, Spelman College, Tougaloo College, members of Five Colleges Inc., Twelve College Exchange Program. Sponsors and participates in study-abroad programs. Cooperative Army ROTC, cooperative Air Force ROTC.
On Campus	Drama/theater group; student-run newspaper and radio station. No national or local sororities on campus.
Athletics	Member NCAA (Division III). *Intercollegiate sports:* basketball, crew, cross-country running, equestrian sports, field hockey, lacrosse, skiing (downhill), soccer, softball, squash, swimming and diving, tennis, track and field, volleyball.

Costs (1991–92) & Aid				
	Comprehensive fee	$21,870	Need-based scholarships (average)	$9805
	Tuition	$15,650	Non-need scholarships	N/Avail
	Mandatory fees	$120	Short-term loans (average)	$30
	Room and board	$6100	Long-term loans—college funds (average)	$2962
	Financial aid recipients	52%	Long-term loans—external funds (average)	$2900

Undergraduate Facts				
	Part-time	4%	*Freshman Data:* 2,178 applied, 69% were accepted, 40% (604) of those entered	
	State residents	21%		
	Transfers	9%	From top tenth of high school class	55%
	African-Americans	4%	SAT-takers scoring 600 or over on verbal	41%
	Native Americans	0%	SAT-takers scoring 700 or over on verbal	5%
	Hispanics	3%	SAT-takers scoring 600 or over on math	50%
	Asian-Americans	11%	SAT-takers scoring 700 or over on math	7%
	International students	5%	ACT-takers scoring 26 or over	N/R
	Freshmen returning for sophomore year	91%	ACT-takers scoring 30 or over	N/R
	Students completing degree within 5 years	87%	*Majors with most degrees conferred:* political science/government, English.	
	Grads pursuing further study	20%		

Majors American studies, anthropology, architecture, art/fine arts, art history, astronomy, biochemistry, biology/biological sciences, black/African-American studies, chemistry, child psychology/child development, classics, clinical psychology, comparative literature, computer science, dance, early childhood education, economics, education, English, film studies, French, geology, Germanic languages and literature, Greek, history, interdisciplinary studies, international studies, Italian, Latin, Latin American studies, mathematics, medieval studies, music, Near and Middle Eastern studies, philosophy, physics, political science/government, Portuguese, psychology, religious studies, Russian, Russian and Slavic studies, sociology, Spanish, studio art, theater arts/drama, women's studies.

Applying *Required:* essay, high school transcript, 2 recommendations, SAT or ACT, 3 Achievements, English Composition Test. *Recommended:* 3 years of high school math and science, 3 years of high school foreign language, interview, English Composition Test (with essay). *Application deadlines:* 1/15, 11/15 for early decision, 1/15 for financial aid. *Contact:* Ms. Juliet Brigham, Director of Admissions, College Hall 30, Northampton, MA 01063, 413-585-2500; *Office location:* Garrison Hall, West Street.

South Dakota School of Mines and Technology
Rapid City, South Dakota

Founded 1885
Suburban setting
State-supported
Coed
Awards B, M, D

Enrollment 2,450 total; 2,132 undergraduates (834 freshmen)

Faculty 139 total; 88 full-time (80% have doctorate/terminal degree); student-faculty ratio is 16:1; grad assistants teach a few undergraduate courses.

Libraries 106,000 bound volumes, 194,414 titles on microform, 961 periodical subscriptions

Computing *Terminals/PCs available for student use:* 290, located in computer center, student center, library, classroom buildings; PC not required. Campus network links student PCs.

Of Special Interest *Core academic program:* yes. Computer course required. Sigma Xi chapter. Academic exchange program: no. Study-abroad programs: no. Army ROTC.

On Campus Drama/theater group; student-run newspaper and radio station. *Social organizations:* 4 national fraternities, 2 national sororities; 20% of eligible undergraduate men and 19% of eligible undergraduate women are members.

Athletics Member NAIA. *Intercollegiate sports:* basketball (M, W), cross-country running (M, W), football (M), tennis (M), track and field (M, W), volleyball (W). *Scholarships:* M, W.

Costs (1991–92) & Aid				
	State resident tuition	$1399	883 Need-based scholarships (average)	$1103
	Nonresident tuition	$3220	382 Non-need scholarships (average)	$631
	Mandatory fees	$760	Short-term loans (average)	$451
	Room and board	$2300	Long-term loans—college funds (average)	$1402
	Financial aid recipients	52%	Long-term loans—external funds (average)	$1560

Undergraduate Facts				
	Part-time	25%	*Freshman Data:* 1,081 applied, 95% were accepted, 81% (834) of those entered	
	State residents	81%		
	Transfers	10%	From top tenth of high school class	29%
	African-Americans	2%	SAT-takers scoring 600 or over on verbal	N/R
	Native Americans	1%	SAT-takers scoring 700 or over on verbal	N/R
	Hispanics	1%	SAT-takers scoring 600 or over on math	N/R
	Asian-Americans	1%	SAT-takers scoring 700 or over on math	N/R
	International students	3%	ACT-takers scoring 26 or over	43%
	Freshmen returning for sophomore year	71%	ACT-takers scoring 30 or over	7%
	Students completing degree within 5 years	36%		
	Grads pursuing further study	9%		

Majors Chemical engineering, chemistry, civil engineering, computer science, electrical engineering, geological engineering, geology, industrial engineering, interdisciplinary studies, mathematics, mechanical engineering, metallurgical engineering, mining and mineral engineering, physics.

Applying *Required:* high school transcript, SAT or ACT. *Recommended:* 3 years of high school math and science, some high school foreign language. *Application deadlines:* rolling, 3/15 priority date for financial aid. *Contact:* Mr. Gary Bjordal, Director of Admissions, 501 East Saint Joseph Street, Rapid City, SD 57701, 605-394-2400 or toll-free 800-742-8606 (in-state).

Southern Methodist University

Dallas, Texas

Founded 1911
Suburban setting
Independent/affiliated with United Methodist Church
Coed
Awards B, M, D

Enrollment	8,547 total; 5,309 undergraduates (1,229 freshmen)
Faculty	584 total; 477 full-time (85% have doctorate/terminal degree); student-faculty ratio is 14:1; grad assistants teach a few undergraduate courses.
Libraries	2.5 million bound volumes, 6,356 periodical subscriptions
Computing	*Terminals/PCs available for student use:* 250, located in computer center, various locations on campus.
Of Special Interest	*Core academic program:* yes. Computer course required for engineering, business majors. Phi Beta Kappa, Sigma Xi chapters. Academic exchange program: no. Sponsors and participates in study-abroad programs. Cooperative Army ROTC, cooperative Air Force ROTC.
On Campus	Student-run newspaper and radio station. *Social organizations:* 15 national fraternities, 12 national sororities; 38% of eligible undergraduate men and 45% of eligible undergraduate women are members.
Athletics	Member NCAA (Division I). *Intercollegiate sports:* basketball (M, W), cross-country running (M, W), football (M), golf (M, W), soccer (M, W), swimming and diving (M, W), tennis (M, W), track and field (M, W). *Scholarships:* M, W.

Costs (1991–92) & Aid				
	Comprehensive fee	$16,600	Need-based scholarships (average)	$2900
	Tuition	$10,440	Non-need scholarships (average)	$4100
	Mandatory fees	$1328	Short-term loans	Avail
	Room and board	$4832	Long-term loans—college funds (average)	$8000
	Financial aid recipients	60%	Long-term loans—external funds (average)	$2942

Undergraduate Facts				
	Part-time	5%	*Freshman Data:* 4,971 applied, 68% were accepted, 37% (1,229) of those entered	
	State residents	55%		
	Transfers	17%	From top tenth of high school class	40%
	African-Americans	4%	SAT-takers scoring 600 or over on verbal	N/R
	Native Americans	1%	SAT-takers scoring 700 or over on verbal	N/R
	Hispanics	6%	SAT-takers scoring 600 or over on math	N/R
	Asian-Americans	4%	SAT-takers scoring 700 or over on math	N/R
	International students	1%	ACT-takers scoring 26 or over	N/R
	Freshmen returning for sophomore year	87%	ACT-takers scoring 30 or over	N/R
	Students completing degree within 5 years	67%		
	Grads pursuing further study	N/R		

Majors Accounting, advertising, anthropology, archaeology, art/fine arts, art history, behavioral sciences, biology/biological sciences, biomedical engineering, black/African-American studies, broadcasting, business, chemistry, communication, computer engineering, computer science, creative writing, dance, economics, electrical engineering, English, European studies, film studies, finance/banking, French, geology, geophysics, German, history, humanities, Italian, journalism, Latin American studies, (pre)law sequence, management information systems, mathematics, mechanical engineering, (pre)medicine sequence, Mexican-American/Chicano studies, modern languages, music, music education, music history, music therapy, operations research, philosophy, physics, piano/organ, political science/government, psychology, radio and television studies, real estate, religious studies, Russian, Russian and Slavic studies, social science, sociology, Spanish, statistics, studio art, theater arts/drama, voice, wind and percussion instruments.

Applying *Required:* essay, high school transcript, 3 years of high school math and science, 1 recommendation, SAT or ACT. *Recommended:* 2 years of high school foreign language, interview. Achievements required for some. *Application deadlines:* 1/15, 11/1 for early action, 3/1 priority date for financial aid. *Contact:* Mr. Andrew L. Bryant, Director of Admissions, 6425 Boaz Street, Dallas, TX 75275, 214-692-2065 or toll-free 800-323-0672.

Southwestern University

Georgetown, Texas

Founded 1840
Suburban setting
Independent, Methodist
Coed
Awards B

Enrollment 1,231 total—all undergraduates (324 freshmen)

Faculty 127 total; 83 full-time (90% have doctorate/terminal degree); student-faculty ratio is 13:1.

Libraries 211,000 bound volumes, 20,369 titles on microform, 1,054 periodical subscriptions

Computing *Terminals/PCs available for student use:* 170, located in computer center, library, dormitories, academic departments; PC not required.

Of Special Interest *Core academic program:* yes. Computer course required. Academic exchange program: no. Sponsors and participates in study-abroad programs.

On Campus Drama/theater group; student-run newspaper. *Social organizations:* 4 national fraternities, 3 national sororities; 48% of eligible undergraduate men and 41% of eligible undergraduate women are members.

Athletics Member NAIA. *Intercollegiate sports:* baseball (M), basketball (M, W), cross-country running (M, W), fencing (M), golf (M, W), lacrosse (M, W), soccer (M, W), softball (W), tennis (M, W), volleyball (M, W).

Costs (1991–92) & Aid				
	Comprehensive fee	$13,581	Need-based scholarships (average)	$4730
	Tuition	$9400	Non-need scholarships (average)	$3870
	Mandatory fees	N/App	Short-term loans	N/Avail
	Room and board	$4181	Long-term loans—college funds (average)	$1925
	Financial aid recipients	67%	Long-term loans—external funds (average)	$2589

Undergraduate Facts				
	Part-time	4%	*Freshman Data:* 1,209 applied, 65% were accepted, 41% (324) of those entered	
	State residents	89%		
	Transfers	7%	From top tenth of high school class	47%
	African-Americans	3%	SAT-takers scoring 600 or over on verbal	24%
	Native Americans	0%	SAT-takers scoring 700 or over on verbal	3%
	Hispanics	9%	SAT-takers scoring 600 or over on math	41%
	Asian-Americans	4%	SAT-takers scoring 700 or over on math	9%
	International students	2%	ACT-takers scoring 26 or over	50%
	Freshmen returning for sophomore year	84%	ACT-takers scoring 30 or over	9%
	Students completing degree within 5 years	62%	*Majors with most degrees conferred:* business, psychology, biology/biological sciences.	
	Grads pursuing further study	27%		

Majors Accounting, American studies, animal sciences, art education, art/fine arts, art history, biology/biological sciences, business, chemistry, communication, computer science, (pre)dentistry sequence, economics, English, experimental psychology, French, German, history, international studies, (pre)law sequence, literature, mathematics, (pre)medicine sequence, modern languages, music, music education, music history, philosophy, physical education, physics, piano/organ, political science/government, psychology, religious studies, sacred music, social science, sociology, Spanish, studio art, theater arts/drama, (pre)veterinary medicine sequence, women's studies.

Applying *Required:* essay, high school transcript, 1 recommendation, SAT or ACT. *Recommended:* 4 years of high school math, 3 years of high school science, 2 years of high school foreign language, interview. Interview required for some. *Application deadlines:* 2/15, 1/1 for early decision, 3/1 priority date for financial aid. *Contact:* Mr. John W. Lind, Vice-President for Admission, University at Maple, Georgetown, TX 78626, 512-863-1202 or toll-free 800-252-3166.

Spelman College

Atlanta, Georgia

Founded 1881
Urban setting
Independent
Women
Awards B

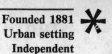

Enrollment	1,850 total—all undergraduates (544 freshmen)
Faculty	162 total; 116 full-time (87% have doctorate/terminal degree); student-faculty ratio is 16:1.
Libraries	379,912 bound volumes, 385,538 titles on microform, 1,439 periodical subscriptions
Computing	*Terminals/PCs available for student use:* 102, located in computer center, library, academic buildings; PC not required.
Of Special Interest	*Core academic program:* yes. Computer course required. Academic exchange with members of the Atlanta University Center, Bryn Mawr College, Grinnel College, Haverford College, Mount Holyoke College. Sponsors and participates in study-abroad programs. Cooperative Army ROTC, cooperative Naval ROTC, cooperative Air Force ROTC.
On Campus	Drama/theater group; student-run newspaper. *Social organizations:* 2 national sororities; 15% of eligible undergraduates are members.
Athletics	*Intercollegiate sports:* basketball, tennis, track and field, volleyball.

Costs (1991–92) & Aid				
	Comprehensive fee	$11,727	Need-based scholarships (average)	$992
	Tuition	$5800	Non-need scholarships (average)	$2211
	Mandatory fees	$1157	Short-term loans	N/Avail
	Room and board	$4770	Long-term loans—college funds (average)	$1521
	Financial aid recipients	84%	Long-term loans—external funds (average)	$3007

Undergraduate Facts				
	Part-time	4%	*Freshman Data:* 3,236 applied, 42% were accepted, 40% (544) of those entered	
	State residents	21%		
	Transfers	7%	From top tenth of high school class	49%
	African-Americans	98%	SAT-takers scoring 600 or over on verbal	3%
	Native Americans	0%	SAT-takers scoring 700 or over on verbal	1%
	Hispanics	0%	SAT-takers scoring 600 or over on math	10%
	Asian-Americans	0%	SAT-takers scoring 700 or over on math	1%
	International students	2%	ACT-takers scoring 26 or over	23%
	Freshmen returning for sophomore year	90%	ACT-takers scoring 30 or over	2%
	Students completing degree within 5 years	54%	*Majors with most degrees conferred:* psychology, economics, English.	
	Grads pursuing further study	39%		

Majors Art/fine arts, biochemistry, biology/biological sciences, chemistry, child psychology/child development, computer science, economics, engineering (general), English, French, history, mathematics, music, natural sciences, philosophy, physics, political science/government, psychology, religious studies, sociology, Spanish, theater arts/drama.

Applying *Required:* essay, high school transcript, 2 recommendations, SAT or ACT. *Recommended:* 3 years of high school math and science, 2 years of high school foreign language. Interview required for some. *Application deadlines:* 2/1, 11/1 for early decision, continuous to 4/1 for financial aid. *Contact:* Ms. Aline Rivers, Executive Director of Enrollment Management, 350 Spelman Lane, SW, Atlanta, GA 30314, 404-681-3643 Ext. 1480 or toll-free 800-241-3421 (out-of-state).

Stanford University

Stanford, California

Founded 1891
Suburban setting
Independent
Coed
Awards B, M, D

Enrollment 13,549 total; 6,527 undergraduates (1,526 freshmen)

Faculty 1,406 total—all full-time (98% have doctorate/terminal degree); student-faculty ratio is 10:1; grad assistants teach a few undergraduate courses.

Libraries 5.7 million bound volumes, 3.3 million titles on microform, 56,800 periodical subscriptions

Computing *Terminals/PCs available for student use:* N/R.

Of Special Interest *Core academic program:* yes. Computer course required for electrical engineering, math majors. Phi Beta Kappa, Sigma Xi chapters. Academic exchange with Howard University. Sponsors and participates in study-abroad programs. Cooperative Army ROTC, cooperative Naval ROTC, cooperative Air Force ROTC.

On Campus Drama/theater group; student-run newspaper and radio station. *Social organizations:* 18 national fraternities, 8 national sororities, 6 eating clubs; 10% of eligible undergraduate men and 10% of eligible undergraduate women are members.

Athletics Member NCAA (Division I), NAIA. *Intercollegiate sports:* baseball (M), basketball (M, W), crew (M, W), cross-country running (M, W), equestrian sports (M, W), fencing (M, W), field hockey (M, W), football (M), golf (M, W), gymnastics (M, W), ice hockey (M, W), lacrosse (M, W), racquetball (M, W), rugby (M, W), sailing (M, W), skiing (cross-country) (M, W), skiing (downhill) (M, W), soccer (M, W), squash (M, W), swimming and diving (M, W), tennis (M, W), track and field (M, W), volleyball (M, W), water polo (M, W), wrestling (M). *Scholarships:* M, W.

Costs (1991–92) & Aid				
	Comprehensive fee	$21,360	Need-based scholarships (average)	$7644
	Tuition	$15,102	Non-need scholarships	N/Avail
	Mandatory fees	$99	Short-term loans	Avail
	Room and board	$6159	Long-term loans—college funds (average)	$2298
	Financial aid recipients	62%	Long-term loans—external funds (average)	$2781

Undergraduate Facts				
	Part-time	0%	*Freshman Data:* 13,530 applied, 20% were accepted, 56% (1,526) of those entered	
	State residents	39%		
	Transfers	8%	From top tenth of high school class	92%
	African-Americans	8%	SAT-takers scoring 600 or over on verbal	73%
	Native Americans	1%	SAT-takers scoring 700 or over on verbal	23%
	Hispanics	10%	SAT-takers scoring 600 or over on math	91%
	Asian-Americans	20%	SAT-takers scoring 700 or over on math	59%
	International students	4%	ACT-takers scoring 26 or over	N/R
	Freshmen returning for sophomore year	98%	ACT-takers scoring 30 or over	N/R
	Students completing degree within 5 years	N/R	*Majors with most degrees conferred:* economics, history, political science/government.	
	Grads pursuing further study	N/R		

Majors American studies, anthropology, art/fine arts, art history, Asian/Oriental studies, biology/biological sciences, black/African-American studies, chemical engineering, chemistry, Chinese, civil engineering, classics, communication, computer science, earth science, East Asian studies, economics, electrical engineering, engineering (general), English, European studies, French, geology, geophysics, German, history, humanities, industrial engineering, interdisciplinary studies, international studies, Italian, Japanese, journalism, Latin American studies, linguistics, materials engineering, materials sciences, mathematics, mechanical engineering, medieval studies, microbiology, music, music history, petroleum/natural gas engineering, philosophy, physics, political science/government, Portuguese, psychology, public affairs and policy studies, religious studies, Russian, Slavic languages, sociology, Spanish, studio art, theater arts/drama, urban studies, women's studies.

Applying *Required:* essay, high school transcript, 3 recommendations, SAT or ACT. *Recommended:* Achievements, English Composition Test. *Application deadlines:* 12/15, 2/1 priority date for financial aid. *Contact:* Mr. John Bunnell, Associate Dean of Admissions, Old Union Building, Room 232, Stanford, CA 94305, 415-723-2091.

State University of New York at Binghamton
Binghamton, New York

Founded 1946
Suburban setting
State-supported
Coed
Awards B, M, D

Enrollment 11,883 total; 8,928 undergraduates (1,699 freshmen)

Faculty 687 total; 508 full-time (95% have doctorate/terminal degree); student-faculty ratio is 17:1; grad assistants teach a few undergraduate courses.

Libraries 1.4 million bound volumes, 1.1 million titles on microform, 10,879 periodical subscriptions

Computing *Terminals/PCs available for student use:* 700, located in library, dormitories, computer labs.

Of Special Interest *Core academic program:* yes. Computer course required for management, math, accounting, industrial technology majors. Phi Beta Kappa, Sigma Xi chapters. Academic exchange with Broome Community College, New York State Visiting Student Program. Sponsors and participates in study-abroad programs. Cooperative Army ROTC, cooperative Naval ROTC, cooperative Air Force ROTC.

On Campus Drama/theater group; student-run newspaper and radio station. *Social organizations:* 13 national fraternities, 9 national sororities, 3 local fraternities, 2 local sororities; 13% of eligible undergraduate men and 12% of eligible undergraduate women are members.

Athletics Member NCAA (Division III). *Intercollegiate sports:* badminton (M, W), basketball (M, W), bowling (M), crew (M, W), cross-country running (M, W), equestrian sports (M, W), fencing (M, W), golf (M, W), ice hockey (M), lacrosse (M, W), racquetball (M, W), rugby (M), skiing (downhill) (M, W), soccer (M, W), swimming and diving (M, W), tennis (M, W), track and field (M, W), volleyball (M, W), wrestling (M).

Costs (1991–92) & Aid				
	State resident tuition	$2150	1200 Need-based scholarships (average)	$700
	Nonresident tuition	$5750	30 Non-need scholarships (average)	$2380
	Mandatory fees	$293	Short-term loans (average)	$200
	Room and board	$4388	Long-term loans—college funds	N/Avail
	Financial aid recipients	50%	Long-term loans—external funds (average)	$1880

Undergraduate Facts				
	Part-time	9%	*Freshman Data:* 15,084 applied, 40% were accepted, 28% (1,699) of those entered	
	State residents	92%		
	Transfers	7%	From top tenth of high school class	71%
	African-Americans	6%	SAT-takers scoring 600 or over on verbal	26%
	Native Americans	1%	SAT-takers scoring 700 or over on verbal	2%
	Hispanics	5%	SAT-takers scoring 600 or over on math	62%
	Asian-Americans	9%	SAT-takers scoring 700 or over on math	16%
	International students	1%	ACT-takers scoring 26 or over	N/R
	Freshmen returning for sophomore year	92%	ACT-takers scoring 30 or over	N/R
	Students completing degree within 5 years	84%	*Majors with most degrees conferred:* English, psychology, biology/biological sciences.	
	Grads pursuing further study	40%		

Majors Accounting, African studies, American studies, anthropology, Arabic, art/fine arts, art history, biochemistry, biology/biological sciences, black/African-American studies, business, chemistry, classics, comparative literature, computer information systems, computer science, creative writing, (pre)dentistry sequence, ecology/environmental studies, economics, electrical engineering, English, environmental sciences, film studies, French, geography, geology, geophysics, German, Germanic languages and literature, Greek, Hebrew, history, human resources, industrial engineering technology, interdisciplinary studies, Italian, Judaic studies, Latin, Latin American studies, (pre)law sequence, legal studies, liberal arts/general studies, linguistics, literature, marketing/retailing/merchandising, mathematics, mechanical engineering, (pre)medicine sequence, medieval studies, music, Near and Middle Eastern studies, nursing, painting/drawing, philosophy, physics, piano/organ, political science/government, psychobiology, psychology, religious studies, Romance languages, Russian and Slavic studies, social science, sociology, Spanish, stringed instruments, studio art, theater arts/drama, (pre)veterinary medicine sequence, voice, wind and percussion instruments.

Applying *Required:* high school transcript, SAT or ACT. *Recommended:* essay, 3 years of high school math and science, some high school foreign language, portfolio, audition. 3 years of high school math and science, some high school foreign language, 1 recommendation required for some. *Application deadlines:* 2/1, 11/1 for early decision, 2/15 priority date for financial aid. *Contact:* Mr. Geoffrey D. Gould, Director of Admissions, Student Services Lecture Building, Binghamton, NY 13902-6000, 607-777-2171.

State University of New York at Buffalo
Buffalo, New York

Founded 1846
Suburban setting
State-supported
Coed
Awards B, M, D

Enrollment	23,573 total; 15,439 undergraduates (2,015 freshmen)
Faculty	1,091 total; 870 full-time (95% have doctorate/terminal degree); student-faculty ratio is 14:1; grad assistants teach a few undergraduate courses.
Libraries	2.7 million bound volumes, 4.0 million titles on microform, 23,292 periodical subscriptions
Computing	*Terminals/PCs available for student use:* 750, located in computer center, library, dormitories, academic buildings; PC not required.
Of Special Interest	*Core academic program:* yes. Computer course required for management, engineering majors. Phi Beta Kappa, Sigma Xi chapters. Academic exchange with all institutions in the western New York area, Association of Colleges and Universities of the State of New York. Sponsors and participates in study-abroad programs. Cooperative Army ROTC.
On Campus	Drama/theater group; student-run newspaper and radio station. *Social organizations:* 18 national fraternities, 6 national sororities, 4 local fraternities, 3 local sororities; 8% of eligible undergraduate men and 4% of eligible undergraduate women are members.
Athletics	Member NCAA (Division II). *Intercollegiate sports:* basketball (M, W), crew (M, W), cross-country running (M, W), field hockey (W), football (M), ice hockey (M), lacrosse (M), rugby (M, W), soccer (M, W), swimming and diving (M, W), tennis (M, W), track and field (M, W), volleyball (W), wrestling (M). *Scholarships:* M, W.

Costs (1991–92) & Aid				
	State resident tuition	$2150	1070 Need-based scholarships (average)	$600
	Nonresident tuition	$5750	770 Non-need scholarships (average)	$930
	Mandatory fees	$370	Short-term loans (average)	$300
	Room and board	$4376	Long-term loans—college funds (average)	$668
	Financial aid recipients	75%	Long-term loans—external funds (average)	$3086

Undergraduate Facts				
	Part-time	15%	*Freshman Data:* 14,906 applied, 45% were accepted, 30% (2,015) of those entered	
	State residents	97%		
	Transfers	9%	From top tenth of high school class	39%
	African-Americans	6%	SAT-takers scoring 600 or over on verbal	13%
	Native Americans	1%	SAT-takers scoring 700 or over on verbal	2%
	Hispanics	3%	SAT-takers scoring 600 or over on math	52%
	Asian-Americans	7%	SAT-takers scoring 700 or over on math	12%
	International students	2%	ACT-takers scoring 26 or over	N/R
	Freshmen returning for sophomore year	87%	ACT-takers scoring 30 or over	N/R
	Students completing degree within 5 years	55%	*Majors with most degrees conferred:* business, social science, psychology.	
	Grads pursuing further study	N/R		

Majors Accounting, aerospace engineering, American studies, anthropology, architecture, art education, art/fine arts, art history, biochemistry, biology/biological sciences, biophysics, black/African-American studies, business, cell biology, chemical engineering, chemistry, civil engineering, classics, communication, computer science, dance, (pre)dentistry sequence, early childhood education, ecology/environmental studies, economics, electrical engineering, engineering (general), engineering physics, engineering sciences, English, environmental biology, environmental design, film studies, French, geography, geology, German, gerontology, health science, history, human services, industrial engineering, interdisciplinary studies, international studies, Italian, Judaic studies, (pre)law sequence, legal studies, linguistics, mathematics, mechanical engineering, medical technology, (pre)medicine sequence, modern languages, molecular biology, music, music education, Native American studies, nuclear medical technology, nursing, occupational therapy, painting/drawing, pharmacology, pharmacy/pharmaceutical sciences, philosophy, photography, physical fitness/human movement, physical therapy, physics, political science/government, psychology, public affairs and policy studies, radio and television studies, religious studies, Russian, science education, secondary education, social science, sociology, Spanish, speech pathology and audiology, statistics, studio art, theater arts/drama, urban studies, (pre)veterinary medicine sequence, women's studies.

Applying *Required:* high school transcript, SAT or ACT. *Recommended:* 3 years of high school math and science, 3 years of high school foreign language. Recommendations, portfolio, audition required for some. *Application deadlines:* 1/5, 3/16 priority date for financial aid. *Contact:* Mr. Kevin M. Durkin, Director of Admissions, Hayes Annex A, Main Street Campus, Buffalo, NY 14214, 716-831-2111.

State University of New York College at Geneseo
Geneseo, New York

Founded 1867
Rural setting
State-supported
Coed
Awards B, M

Enrollment 5,630 total; 5,140 undergraduates (1,202 freshmen)

Faculty 327 total; 238 full-time (84% have doctorate/terminal degree); student-faculty ratio is 19:1; grad assistants teach no undergraduate courses.

Libraries 419,225 bound volumes, 964,672 titles on microform, 3,014 periodical subscriptions

Computing *Terminals/PCs available for student use:* 300, located in computer center, student center, library, dormitories, academic departments; PC not required but available for purchase.

Of Special Interest *Core academic program:* yes. Computer course required for business, chemistry, math, accounting, economics, political science, physics majors. Academic exchange with Rochester Area Colleges. Sponsors and participates in study-abroad programs. Cooperative Army ROTC, cooperative Naval ROTC, cooperative Air Force ROTC.

On Campus Drama/theater group; student-run newspaper and radio station. *Social organizations:* 6 national fraternities, 4 national sororities, 4 local fraternities, 6 local sororities; 19% of eligible undergraduate men and 15% of eligible undergraduate women are members.

Athletics Member NCAA (Division III). *Intercollegiate sports:* basketball (M, W), crew (M, W), cross-country running (M, W), ice hockey (M), lacrosse (M, W), racquetball (M, W), rugby (M, W), soccer (M, W), softball (W), squash (M, W), swimming and diving (M, W), track and field (M, W), volleyball (M, W).

Costs (1991–92) & Aid				
State resident tuition	$2150	Need-based scholarships		Avail
Nonresident tuition	$5750	191 Non-need scholarships (average)		$658
Mandatory fees	$295	Short-term loans (average)		$300
Room and board	$3442	Long-term loans—college funds		N/Avail
Financial aid recipients	85%	Long-term loans—external funds (average)		$1400

Undergraduate Facts			
Part-time	3%	*Freshman Data:* 8,930 applied, 39% were accepted, 34% (1,202) of those entered	
State residents	98%		
Transfers	10%	From top tenth of high school class	79%
African-Americans	2%	SAT-takers scoring 600 or over on verbal	27%
Native Americans	1%	SAT-takers scoring 700 or over on verbal	2%
Hispanics	3%	SAT-takers scoring 600 or over on math	65%
Asian-Americans	4%	SAT-takers scoring 700 or over on math	11%
International students	1%	ACT-takers scoring 26 or over	63%
Freshmen returning for sophomore year	92%	ACT-takers scoring 30 or over	8%
Students completing degree within 5 years	68%		
Grads pursuing further study	27%		

Majors Accounting, American studies, anthropology, applied art, art/fine arts, art history, biochemistry, biology/biological sciences, black/African-American studies, broadcasting, business, chemistry, communication, comparative literature, computer science, (pre)dentistry sequence, early childhood education, economics, education, elementary education, English, French, geochemistry, geography, geology, geophysics, history, (pre)law sequence, management information systems, mathematics, medical technology, (pre)medicine sequence, music, music history, natural sciences, philosophy, physics, political science/government, psychology, radio and television studies, sociology, Spanish, special education, speech pathology and audiology, speech/rhetoric/public address/debate, speech therapy, studio art, theater arts/drama, (pre)veterinary medicine sequence.

Applying *Required:* essay, high school transcript, SAT or ACT. *Recommended:* 4 years of high school math and science, 3 years of high school foreign language, recommendations, campus interview. *Application deadlines:* 2/15, 11/15 for early decision, 2/15 priority date for financial aid. *Contact:* Ms. Janet Graeter, Dean of Admissions, Erwin Building, Geneseo, NY 14454, 716-245-5571.

State University of New York College of Environmental Science and Forestry
Syracuse, New York

Founded 1911
Urban setting
State-supported
Coed
Awards B, M, D

Enrollment 1,551 total; 1,279 undergraduates (79 freshmen)

Faculty 122 total; 110 full-time (98% have doctorate/terminal degree); student-faculty ratio is 20:1; grad assistants teach a few undergraduate courses.

Libraries 106,192 bound volumes, 91,000 titles on microform, 1,109 periodical subscriptions

Computing *Terminals/PCs available for student use:* 100, located in computer center, library, academic buildings; PC not required.

Of Special Interest *Core academic program:* yes. Computer course required for forest engineering, paper science and engineering, forestry, landscape architecture, environmental studies, natural resource management majors. Academic exchange with Syracuse University. Participates in study-abroad programs. Cooperative Army ROTC, cooperative Air Force ROTC.

On Campus Drama/theater group; student-run newspaper and radio station. *Social organizations:* 25 national fraternities, 13 national sororities, 1 local fraternity; 25% of eligible undergraduate men and 25% of eligible undergraduate women are members.

Athletics None

Costs (1992–93 estimated) & Aid				
	State resident tuition	$2650	100 Need-based scholarships (average)	$500
	Nonresident tuition	$6250	100 Non-need scholarships (average)	$1350
	Mandatory fees	$287	Short-term loans (average)	$200
	Room and board	$5845	Long-term loans—college funds	N/Avail
	Financial aid recipients	85%	Long-term loans—external funds (average)	$2200

Undergraduate Facts				
	Part-time	16%	*Freshman Data:* 630 applied, 20% were accepted, 61% (79) of those entered	
	State residents	80%		
	Transfers	95%	From top tenth of high school class	60%
	African-Americans	3%	SAT-takers scoring 600 or over on verbal	25%
	Native Americans	1%	SAT-takers scoring 700 or over on verbal	0%
	Hispanics	1%	SAT-takers scoring 600 or over on math	50%
	Asian-Americans	1%	SAT-takers scoring 700 or over on math	10%
	International students	1%	ACT-takers scoring 26 or over	N/R
	Freshmen returning for sophomore year	N/R	ACT-takers scoring 30 or over	N/R
	Students completing degree within 5 years	N/R	*Majors with most degrees conferred:* environmental biology, landscape architecture/design, environmental sciences.	
	Grads pursuing further study	10%		

Majors Biochemistry, biology/biological sciences, botany/plant sciences, chemistry, (pre)dentistry sequence, ecology/environmental studies, entomology, environmental biology, environmental design, environmental education, environmental engineering, environmental sciences, fish and game management, forest engineering, forestry, landscape architecture/design, land use management and reclamation, (pre)law sequence, (pre)medicine sequence, molecular biology, natural resource management, paper and pulp sciences, polymer science, science education, (pre)veterinary medicine sequence, wildlife biology, wildlife management, wood sciences, zoology.

Applying *Required:* essay, high school transcript, 4 years of high school math and science, SAT or ACT. *Recommended:* recommendations, interview. *Application deadlines:* rolling, 11/15 for early decision, 3/15 priority date for financial aid. *Contact:* Ms. Susan Sanford, Associate Director of Admissions, 1 Forestry Drive, Syracuse, NY 13210, 315-470-6600 or toll-free 800-777-7373.

State University of New York Maritime College
Throgs Neck, New York

Founded 1874
Suburban setting
State-supported
Coed
Awards B, M

Enrollment 784 total; 679 undergraduates (256 freshmen)

Faculty 109 total; 67 full-time (49% have doctorate/terminal degree); student-faculty ratio is 14:1; grad assistants teach a few undergraduate courses.

Libraries 77,000 bound volumes, 7,287 titles on microform, 450 periodical subscriptions

Computing *Terminals/PCs available for student use:* 65, located in computer center, library, student lounge; PC not required. Campus network links student PCs.

Of Special Interest *Core academic program:* yes. Computer course required. Academic exchange program: no. Study-abroad programs: no. Naval ROTC, cooperative Air Force ROTC.

On Campus Dress code; student-run newspaper. *Social organizations:* 1 local fraternity; 4% of eligible undergraduate men are members.

Athletics Member NCAA (Division III). *Intercollegiate sports:* basketball (M, W), crew (M, W), cross-country running (M, W), ice hockey (M), lacrosse (M), riflery (M, W), rugby (M), sailing (M, W), soccer (M), swimming and diving (M, W), tennis (M, W), volleyball (M, W), wrestling (M).

Costs (1991–92) & Aid				
State resident tuition	$2150	Need-based scholarships		Avail
Nonresident tuition	$5750	Non-need scholarships		Avail
Mandatory fees	$330	Short-term loans (average)		$200
Room and board	$4080	Long-term loans—college funds		N/Avail
Financial aid recipients	58%	Long-term loans—external funds (average)		$2300

Undergraduate Facts			
Part-time	7%	*Freshman Data:* 874 applied, 57% were accepted, 51% (256) of those entered	
State residents	72%		
Transfers	17%	From top tenth of high school class	19%
African-Americans	4%	SAT-takers scoring 600 or over on verbal	7%
Native Americans	0%	SAT-takers scoring 700 or over on verbal	3%
Hispanics	7%	SAT-takers scoring 600 or over on math	18%
Asian-Americans	5%	SAT-takers scoring 700 or over on math	1%
International students	3%	ACT-takers scoring 26 or over	N/R
Freshmen returning for sophomore year	79%	ACT-takers scoring 30 or over	N/R
Students completing degree within 5 years	N/R	*Majors with most degrees conferred:* business, marine engineering, electrical engineering.	
Grads pursuing further study	N/R		

Majors Business, electrical engineering, humanities, marine engineering, maritime sciences, mechanical engineering, meteorology, naval architecture, naval sciences, oceanography.

Applying *Required:* high school transcript, 3 years of high school math and science, 1 recommendation, medical history, SAT or ACT. *Recommended:* essay, some high school foreign language, interview, Achievements, English Composition Test (with essay). *Application deadlines:* rolling, 12/1 for early decision, 5/1 priority date for financial aid. *Contact:* Mr. Peter Cooney, Director of Admissions, Fort Schuyler, Throgs Neck, NY 10465, 212-409-7200 Ext. 220 or toll-free 800-654-1874 (in-state), 800-642-1874 (out-of-state).

✻ Stetson University

DeLand, Florida

Founded 1883
Small-town setting
Independent, Baptist
Coed
Awards B, M, D

Enrollment 2,351 total; 2,055 undergraduates (472 freshmen)

Faculty 188 total; 152 full-time (88% have doctorate/terminal degree); student-faculty ratio is 12:1; grad assistants teach no undergraduate courses.

Libraries 300,000 bound volumes, 4,000 titles on microform, 1,300 periodical subscriptions

Computing *Terminals/PCs available for student use:* 120, located in computer center, library, science hall; PC not required but available for purchase.

Of Special Interest *Core academic program:* yes. Computer course required for business administration, math, physics, chemistry, biology, psychology, sociology, political science, economics, physical education, education majors. Phi Beta Kappa chapter. Academic exchange with Eckerd College, Rollins College, Austin College, Berea College, Hamline University, Gustavus Adolphus College, Macalester College, University of Redlands, St. Olaf College. Sponsors and participates in study-abroad programs. Cooperative Army ROTC.

On Campus Drama/theater group; student-run newspaper and radio station. *Social organizations:* 7 national fraternities, 7 national sororities; 44% of eligible undergraduate men and 42% of eligible undergraduate women are members.

Athletics Member NCAA (Division I). *Intercollegiate sports:* basketball (M, W), cross-country running (M, W), golf (M, W), soccer (M), tennis (M, W), volleyball (M, W). *Scholarships:* M, W.

Costs (1992–93) & Aid

Comprehensive fee	$15,145	
Tuition	$10,660	
Mandatory fees	$450	
Room and board	$4035	
Financial aid recipients	80%	
Need-based scholarships (average)		$6815
Non-need scholarships (average)		$1550
Short-term loans (average)		$100
Long-term loans—college funds (average)		$2100
Long-term loans—external funds (average)		$2750

Undergraduate Facts

Part-time	3%		
State residents	77%		
Transfers	23%		
African-Americans	2%		
Native Americans	1%		
Hispanics	3%		
Asian-Americans	2%		
International students	3%		
Freshmen returning for sophomore year	80%		
Students completing degree within 5 years	60%		
Grads pursuing further study	40%		

Freshman Data: 1,572 applied, 84% were accepted, 36% (472) of those entered

From top tenth of high school class	44%
SAT-takers scoring 600 or over on verbal	9%
SAT-takers scoring 700 or over on verbal	1%
SAT-takers scoring 600 or over on math	24%
SAT-takers scoring 700 or over on math	3%
ACT-takers scoring 26 or over	33%
ACT-takers scoring 30 or over	7%

Majors with most degrees conferred: business, education, psychology.

Majors Accounting, American studies, art/fine arts, biology/biological sciences, business, business economics, chemistry, computer science, (pre)dentistry sequence, economics, education, elementary education, English, finance/banking, French, geography, German, history, humanities, (pre)law sequence, marketing/retailing/merchandising, mathematics, medical technology, (pre)medicine sequence, music, music education, philosophy, physical education, physics, piano/organ, political science/government, psychology, religious studies, Russian and Slavic studies, sacred music, social science, sociology, Spanish, speech/rhetoric/public address/debate, theater arts/drama, (pre)veterinary medicine sequence, voice.

Applying *Required:* essay, high school transcript, 3 years of high school math and science, some high school foreign language, recommendations, SAT or ACT. *Recommended:* interview, Achievements, English Composition Test (with essay). *Application deadlines:* 3/1, 11/15 for early decision, 3/15 priority date for financial aid. *Contact:* Ms. Linda Glover, Dean of Admissions, Griffith Hall, DeLand, FL 32720, 904-822-7100 or toll-free 800-688-0101.

Stevens Institute of Technology

Hoboken, New Jersey

Founded 1870
Urban setting
Independent
Coed
Awards B, M, D

Enrollment 3,240 total; 1,293 undergraduates (356 freshmen)

Faculty 250 total; 140 full-time (93% have doctorate/terminal degree); student-faculty ratio is 9:1; grad assistants teach no undergraduate courses.

Libraries 150,000 bound volumes, 20 titles on microform, 1,000 periodical subscriptions

Computing *Terminals/PCs available for student use:* 1,400, located in computer center, student center, library, dormitories; AT&T 6386 or any other IBM-compatible PC required for freshmen and available for purchase or lease. Campus network links student PCs.

Of Special Interest *Core academic program:* yes. Computer course required. Sigma Xi chapter. Academic exchange with New York University. Sponsors study-abroad programs. Cooperative Army ROTC, cooperative Air Force ROTC.

On Campus Drama/theater group; student-run newspaper and radio station. *Social organizations:* 10 national fraternities, 3 national sororities; 35% of eligible undergraduate men and 30% of eligible undergraduate women are members.

Athletics Member NCAA (Division III). *Intercollegiate sports:* archery (M, W), baseball (M, W), basketball (M), bowling (M), cross-country running (M), fencing (M, W), golf (M), lacrosse (M), rugby (M), sailing (M, W), skiing (cross-country) (M, W), skiing (downhill) (M, W), soccer (M, W), squash (M), tennis (M, W), volleyball (M, W), wrestling (M).

Costs (1992–93) & Aid				
	Comprehensive fee	$20,600	Need-based scholarships	Avail
	Tuition	$15,400	Non-need scholarships (average)	$3500
	Mandatory fees	$150	Short-term loans	N/Avail
	Room and board	$5050	Long-term loans—college funds	Avail
	Financial aid recipients	80%	Long-term loans—external funds	N/Avail

Undergraduate Facts				
	Part-time	0%	*Freshman Data:* 1,574 applied, 81% were accepted, 28% (356) of those entered	
	State residents	55%		
	Transfers	10%	From top tenth of high school class	51%
	African-Americans	5%	SAT-takers scoring 600 or over on verbal	20%
	Native Americans	1%	SAT-takers scoring 700 or over on verbal	4%
	Hispanics	15%	SAT-takers scoring 600 or over on math	70%
	Asian-Americans	20%	SAT-takers scoring 700 or over on math	24%
	International students	9%	ACT-takers scoring 26 or over	N/App
	Freshmen returning for sophomore year	81%	ACT-takers scoring 30 or over	N/App
	Students completing degree within 5 years	73%	*Majors with most degrees conferred:* electrical engineering, mechanical engineering, civil engineering.	
	Grads pursuing further study	15%		

Majors Applied mathematics, biochemistry, biology/biological sciences, chemical engineering, chemistry, civil engineering, computer engineering, computer information systems, computer science, construction engineering, construction management, (pre)dentistry sequence, electrical engineering, engineering (general), engineering and applied sciences, engineering management, engineering physics, engineering sciences, English, environmental engineering, geological engineering, history, history of science, humanities, (pre)law sequence, liberal arts/general studies, management engineering, management information systems, manufacturing engineering, marine engineering, materials engineering, materials sciences, mathematics, mechanical engineering, (pre)medicine sequence, metallurgical engineering, metallurgy, nuclear engineering, ocean engineering, optics, philosophy, physics, plastics engineering, polymer science, robotics, science, statistics, systems science, technology and public affairs, transportation engineering, water resources.

Applying *Required:* high school transcript, 4 years of high school math, 3 years of high school science, interview, SAT. *Recommended:* essay, some high school foreign language, recommendations, Achievements, English Composition Test. *Application deadlines:* 3/1, 11/1 for early decision, 3/1 priority date for financial aid. *Contact:* Mr. Peter Persuitti, Dean, Admissions and Financial Aid, Castle Point Station, Hoboken, NJ 07030, 201-420-5194.

From the College Stevens is experiencing an unprecedented revitalization period encompassing all aspects of campus life—laboratories, classrooms, athletic facilities, and residence halls. An $18.8-million laboratory modernization will include the James C. Nicoll, Jr. Environmental Process Laboratory, a significant addition to the Center for Environmental Engineering, the Analytical Characterization Facility for advanced materials research, and the new Electrical Engineering Senior Design Laboratory. A new $12.5-million recreation and athletic complex is also being planned.

* Swarthmore College

Swarthmore, Pennsylvania

Founded 1864
Small-town setting
Independent
Coed
Awards B

Enrollment	1,320 total—all undergraduates (319 freshmen)
Faculty	157 total; 142 full-time (93% have doctorate/terminal degree); student-faculty ratio is 9:1.
Libraries	776,000 bound volumes, 230,000 titles on microform, 2,700 periodical subscriptions
Computing	*Terminals/PCs available for student use:* 135, located in computer center, library, labs; PC not required.
Of Special Interest	*Core academic program:* yes. Phi Beta Kappa, Sigma Xi chapters. Academic exchange with University of Pennsylvania, Haverford College, Bryn Mawr College, Tufts University, Pomona College, Rice University, Middlebury College, Howard University. Sponsors and participates in study-abroad programs. Cooperative Army ROTC, cooperative Naval ROTC, cooperative Air Force ROTC.
On Campus	Drama/theater group; student-run newspaper and radio station. *Social organizations:* 2 national fraternities; 5% of eligible undergraduate men are members.
Athletics	Member NCAA (Division III). *Intercollegiate sports:* badminton (W), baseball (M), basketball (M, W), cross-country running (M, W), field hockey (W), football (M), golf (M), lacrosse (M, W), rugby (M, W), soccer (M, W), softball (W), swimming and diving (M, W), tennis (M, W), track and field (M, W), volleyball (W), wrestling (M).

Costs (1991–92) & Aid				
	Comprehensive fee	$22,160	Need-based scholarships (average)	$10,700
	Tuition	$16,465	Non-need scholarships (average)	$11,750
	Mandatory fees	$175	Short-term loans (average)	$100
	Room and board	$5520	Long-term loans—college funds (average)	$1980
	Financial aid recipients	55%	Long-term loans—external funds (average)	$1930

Undergraduate Facts				
	Part-time	0%	*Freshman Data:* 3,582 applied, 26% were accepted, 34% (319) of those entered	
	State residents	15%		
	Transfers	10%	From top tenth of high school class	80%
	African-Americans	7%	SAT-takers scoring 600 or over on verbal	78%
	Native Americans	0%	SAT-takers scoring 700 or over on verbal	29%
	Hispanics	4%	SAT-takers scoring 600 or over on math	90%
	Asian-Americans	9%	SAT-takers scoring 700 or over on math	49%
	International students	6%	ACT-takers scoring 26 or over	N/App
	Freshmen returning for sophomore year	98%	ACT-takers scoring 30 or over	N/App
	Students completing degree within 5 years	88%	*Majors with most degrees conferred:* economics, literature, history.	
	Grads pursuing further study	30%		

Majors Anthropology, art/fine arts, art history, Asian/Oriental studies, astronomy, astrophysics, biochemistry, biology/biological sciences, chemistry, civil engineering, classics, computer engineering, economics, electrical engineering, engineering (general), English, environmental sciences, French, German, Greek, history, international studies, Latin, linguistics, literature, mathematics, mechanical engineering, medieval studies, music, philosophy, physics, political science/government, psychobiology, psychology, religious studies, Russian, sociology, Spanish, theater arts/drama.

Applying *Required:* essay, high school transcript, 2 recommendations, SAT, 3 Achievements, English Composition Test. *Recommended:* 3 years of high school math and science, some high school foreign language, interview. *Application deadlines:* 2/1, 11/15 for early decision, 2/15 priority date for financial aid. *Contact:* Mr. Robert A. Barr Jr., Dean of Admissions, 500 College Avenue, Swarthmore, PA 19081, 215-328-8308.

Syracuse University

Syracuse, New York

Founded 1870
Urban setting
Independent
Coed
Awards B, M, D

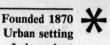

Enrollment 15,960 total; 11,495 undergraduates (2,525 freshmen)

Faculty 1,489 total; 955 full-time (83% have doctorate/terminal degree); student-faculty ratio is 9:1; grad assistants teach a few undergraduate courses.

Libraries 2.3 million bound volumes, 3.6 million titles on microform, 18,044 periodical subscriptions

Computing *Terminals/PCs available for student use:* 330, located in computer center, student center, dormitories, academic buildings; PC not required. Campus network links student PCs.

Of Special Interest *Core academic program:* yes. Computer course required for engineering, management majors. Phi Beta Kappa, Sigma Xi chapters. Academic exchange with State University of New York College of Environmental Science and Forestry. Sponsors and participates in study-abroad programs. Army ROTC, Air Force ROTC.

On Campus Drama/theater group; student-run newspaper and radio station. *Social organizations:* 29 national fraternities, 20 national sororities, 1 local fraternity, 2 local sororities, minority organizations; 24% of eligible undergraduate men and 33% of eligible undergraduate women are members.

Athletics Member NCAA (Division I). *Intercollegiate sports:* basketball (M, W), crew (M, W), cross-country running (M, W), field hockey (W), football (M), gymnastics (M), lacrosse (M), soccer (M), swimming and diving (M, W), tennis (W), track and field (M, W), volleyball (W), wrestling (M). *Scholarships:* M, W.

Costs (1991–92) & Aid				
	Comprehensive fee	$18,817	Need-based scholarships (average)	$4600
	Tuition	$12,640	Non-need scholarships	Avail
	Mandatory fees	$317	Short-term loans	Avail
	Room and board	$5860	Long-term loans—college funds	N/Avail
	Financial aid recipients	60%	Long-term loans—external funds (average)	$3000

Undergraduate Facts				
	Part-time	8%	*Freshman Data:* 11,510 applied, 72% were accepted, 31% (2,525) of those entered	
	State residents	36%		
	Transfers	16%	From top tenth of high school class	28%
	African-Americans	9%	SAT-takers scoring 600 or over on verbal	14%
	Native Americans	1%	SAT-takers scoring 700 or over on verbal	2%
	Hispanics	4%	SAT-takers scoring 600 or over on math	36%
	Asian-Americans	5%	SAT-takers scoring 700 or over on math	7%
	International students	2%	ACT-takers scoring 26 or over	N/R
	Freshmen returning for sophomore year	91%	ACT-takers scoring 30 or over	N/R
	Students completing degree within 5 years	70%	*Majors with most degrees conferred:* business, social science, communication.	
	Grads pursuing further study	30%		

Majors Accounting, adult and continuing education, advertising, aerospace engineering, American studies, anthropology, applied art, architecture, art education, art/fine arts, art history, arts administration, Asian/Oriental studies, behavioral sciences, biblical languages, bilingual/bicultural education, biochemistry, bioengineering, biology/biological sciences, biomedical engineering, black/African-American studies, broadcasting, business, ceramic art and design, chemical engineering, chemistry, child care/child and family studies, civil engineering, classics, communication, community services, comparative literature, computer engineering, computer information systems, computer science, consumer services, (pre)dentistry sequence, dietetics, early childhood education, East European and Soviet studies, ecology/environmental studies, economics, education, electrical engineering, elementary education, engineering (general), engineering management, engineering physics, English, environmental design, environmental engineering, environmental sciences, family and consumer studies, family services, fashion design and technology, film studies, finance/banking, food sciences, food services management, French, geography, geology, German, gerontology, graphic arts, health education, history, human development, humanities, illustration, industrial design, information science, interdisciplinary studies, interior design, international studies, Italian, jewelry and metalsmithing, journalism, labor and industrial relations, Latin, Latin American studies, (pre)law sequence, linguistics, management information systems, marketing/retailing/merchandising, mathematics, mechanical engineering, (pre)medicine sequence, medieval studies, modern languages, music, music business, music education, music history, natural sciences, nursing, nutrition, painting/drawing, philosophy, photography, physical education, physics, piano/organ, political science/government, psychology, public affairs and policy studies, public relations, radio and television studies, rehabilitation therapy, religious studies, retail management, Romance languages, Russian, Russian and Slavic studies, science education, sculpture, secondary education, Slavic languages, social science, social work, sociology, South Asian studies, Spanish, special education, speech pathology and audiology, speech/rhetoric/public address/debate, speech therapy, statistics, stringed instruments, studio art, telecommunications, textile arts, textiles and clothing, theater arts/drama, (pre)veterinary medicine sequence, voice, wind and percussion instruments.

Applying *Required:* essay, high school transcript, 3 years of high school math and science, 2 years of high school foreign language, 1 recommendation, SAT or ACT. *Recommended:* campus interview. Audition for drama and music majors, portfolio for art and architecture majors required for some. *Application deadlines:* 2/1, 11/15 for early decision, 1/31 for financial aid. *Contact:* Office of Admissions, 210 Tolley Administration Building, Syracuse, NY 13244, 315-443-3611.

Taylor University

Upland, Indiana

Founded 1846
Rural setting
Independent
Coed
Awards A, B

Enrollment	1,790 total—all undergraduates (468 freshmen)
Faculty	128 total; 96 full-time (66% have doctorate/terminal degree); student-faculty ratio is 18:1.
Libraries	155,000 bound volumes, 18,062 titles on microform, 750 periodical subscriptions
Computing	*Terminals/PCs available for student use:* 182, located in computer center, library, dormitories, computer lab; PC not required.
Of Special Interest	*Core academic program:* yes. Computer course required. Academic exchange with members of the Christian College Coalition and the Christian College Consortium. Sponsors and participates in study-abroad programs. Cooperative Army ROTC, cooperative Naval ROTC, cooperative Air Force ROTC.
On Campus	Dress code; mandatory chapel; drama/theater group; student-run newspaper and radio station. No national or local fraternities or sororities on campus.
Athletics	Member NAIA. *Intercollegiate sports:* baseball (M), basketball (M, W), cross-country running (M, W), football (M), golf (M), soccer (M), softball (W), tennis (M, W), track and field (M, W), volleyball (W).

Costs (1991–92) & Aid				
	Comprehensive fee	$12,895	Need-based scholarships (average)	$1731
	Tuition	$9158	Non-need scholarships (average)	$985
	Mandatory fees	$195	Short-term loans	Avail
	Room and board	$3542	Long-term loans—college funds (average)	$1350
	Financial aid recipients	74%	Long-term loans—external funds	Avail

Undergraduate Facts				
	Part-time	3%	*Freshman Data:* 1,396 applied, 76% were accepted, 44% (468) of those entered	
	State residents	35%		
	Transfers	6%	From top tenth of high school class	42%
	African-Americans	2%	SAT-takers scoring 600 or over on verbal	13%
	Native Americans	N/R	SAT-takers scoring 700 or over on verbal	1%
	Hispanics	1%	SAT-takers scoring 600 or over on math	26%
	Asian-Americans	1%	SAT-takers scoring 700 or over on math	4%
	International students	2%	ACT-takers scoring 26 or over	39%
	Freshmen returning for sophomore year	97%	ACT-takers scoring 30 or over	6%
	Students completing degree within 5 years	85%	*Majors with most degrees conferred:* business, elementary education, psychology.	
	Grads pursuing further study	12%		

Majors Accounting, art education, art/fine arts, athletic training, biblical languages, biblical studies, biology/biological sciences, broadcasting, business, chemistry, communication, computer information systems, computer programming, computer science, creative writing, (pre)dentistry sequence, economics, education, elementary education, English, environmental sciences, French, history, international studies, journalism, (pre)law sequence, liberal arts/general studies, literature, mathematics, medical technology, (pre)medicine sequence, middle school education, ministries, modern languages, music, music education, natural sciences, philosophy, physical education, physics, political science/government, psychology, public relations, recreation and leisure services, religious education, religious studies, robotics, sacred music, science education, secondary education, social science, social work, sociology, Spanish, speech/rhetoric/public address/debate, theater arts/drama, theology, (pre)veterinary medicine sequence, voice.

Applying *Required:* essay, high school transcript, 3 years of high school math and science, recommendations, SAT or ACT. *Recommended:* some high school foreign language, interview. *Application deadlines:* rolling, 3/1 for financial aid. *Contact:* Mr. Herbert Frye, Dean of Admissions, 500 West Leade Avenue, Upland, IN 46989, 317-998-5206 or toll-free 800-882-3456.

Texas A&M University

College Station, Texas

Founded 1876
Small-town setting
State-supported
Coed
Awards B, M, D

Enrollment	40,997 total; 33,024 undergraduates (6,087 freshmen)
Faculty	2,350 total; 1,973 full-time (90% have doctorate/terminal degree); student-faculty ratio is 20:1; grad assistants teach a few undergraduate courses.
Libraries	1.8 million bound volumes, 3.9 million titles on microform, 23,200 periodical subscriptions
Computing	*Terminals/PCs available for student use:* 1,000, located in computer center, library, dormitories, various locations on campus; PC not required. Campus network links student PCs.
Of Special Interest	*Core academic program:* yes. Computer course required. Sigma Xi chapter. Academic exchange with Texas A&M University at Galveston. Sponsors and participates in study-abroad programs. Army ROTC, Naval ROTC, Air Force ROTC.
On Campus	Drama/theater group; student-run newspaper and radio station. *Social organizations:* 26 national fraternities, 11 national sororities; 8% of eligible undergraduate men and 9% of eligible undergraduate women are members.
Athletics	Member NCAA (Division I). *Intercollegiate sports:* baseball (M), basketball (M, W), cross-country running (M, W), equestrian sports (M, W), football (M), golf (M, W), riflery (M, W), soccer (W), swimming and diving (M, W), tennis (M, W), track and field (M, W), volleyball (W). *Scholarships:* M, W.

Costs (1991–92) & Aid				
	State resident tuition	$720	3500 Need-based scholarships (average)	$1100
	Nonresident tuition	$3840	3000 Non-need scholarships (average)	$1500
	Mandatory fees	$690	Short-term loans (average)	$500
	Room and board	$3560	Long-term loans—college funds	N/Avail
	Financial aid recipients	40%	Long-term loans—external funds (average)	$2300

Undergraduate Facts				
	Part-time	7%	*Freshman Data:* 12,069 applied, 85% were accepted, 59% (6,087) of those entered	
	State residents	94%		
	Transfers	15%	From top tenth of high school class	44%
	African-Americans	3%	SAT-takers scoring 600 or over on verbal	10%
	Native Americans	0%	SAT-takers scoring 700 or over on verbal	1%
	Hispanics	8%	SAT-takers scoring 600 or over on math	35%
	Asian-Americans	3%	SAT-takers scoring 700 or over on math	8%
	International students	1%	ACT-takers scoring 26 or over	35%
	Freshmen returning for sophomore year	85%	ACT-takers scoring 30 or over	10%
	Students completing degree within 5 years	60%		
	Grads pursuing further study	N/R		

Majors Accounting, aerospace engineering, agricultural business, agricultural economics, agricultural education, agricultural engineering, agronomy/soil and crop sciences, animal sciences, anthropology, applied mathematics, biochemistry, bioengineering, biology/biological sciences, biomedical sciences, biophysics, botany/plant sciences, business, chemical engineering, chemistry, civil engineering, communication, computer science, construction management, dairy sciences, economics, electrical engineering, elementary education, engineering technology, English, entomology, environmental biology, environmental design, finance/banking, food sciences, forestry, geography, geology, geophysics, health education, history, horticulture, industrial administration, industrial engineering, journalism, landscape architecture/design, management information systems, marketing/retailing/merchandising, mathematics, mechanical engineering, meteorology, microbiology, mining and mineral engineering, modern languages, nuclear engineering, nutrition, ocean engineering, ornamental horticulture, parks management, petroleum/natural gas engineering, philosophy, physical education, physics, political science/government, poultry sciences, psychology, range management, recreation and leisure services, safety and security technologies, secondary education, sociology, speech/rhetoric/public address/debate, theater arts/drama, wildlife management, zoology.

Applying *Required:* high school transcript, 3 years of high school math, SAT or ACT. *Recommended:* 2 years of high school foreign language, 2 Achievements. Recommendations required for some. *Application deadlines:* 3/1, 4/15 priority date for financial aid. *Contact:* Mr. Gary R. Engelgau, Executive Director, Admissions and Records, Room 100, Heaton Hall, College Station, TX 77843, 409-845-1040.

From the College The *Chronicle of Higher Education Almanac* lists Texas A&M University as seventh in the enrollment of National Merit Scholars, seventh in the size of endowments, and eighth in total research and development spending among U.S. colleges and universities. Requests for additional information are welcome.

Texas Christian University

Fort Worth, Texas

Founded 1873
Suburban setting
Independent/affiliated with Christian Church (Disciples of Christ)
Coed
Awards B, M, D

Enrollment 6,538 total; 5,501 undergraduates (1,217 freshmen)

Faculty 468 total; 308 full-time (87% have doctorate/terminal degree); student-faculty ratio is 18:1; grad assistants teach a few undergraduate courses.

Libraries 1.4 million bound volumes, 382,041 titles on microform, 3,723 periodical subscriptions

Computing *Terminals/PCs available for student use:* 1,269, located in computer center, library, writing center; PC not required.

Of Special Interest *Core academic program:* yes. Computer course required for business, nursing, education, communication, arts and science, some fine arts majors. Phi Beta Kappa, Sigma Xi chapters. Academic exchange program: no. Sponsors and participates in study-abroad programs. Army ROTC, Air Force ROTC.

On Campus Drama/theater group; student-run newspaper and radio station. *Social organizations:* 10 national fraternities, 12 national sororities, 2 local fraternities; 29% of eligible undergraduate men and 38% of eligible undergraduate women are members.

Athletics Member NCAA (Division I). *Intercollegiate sports:* baseball (M), basketball (M, W), cross-country running (M, W), football (M), golf (M, W), riflery (W), soccer (M, W), swimming and diving (M, W), tennis (M, W), track and field (M, W). *Scholarships:* M, W.

Costs (1991–92) & Aid

Comprehensive fee	$10,890	
Tuition	$7320	
Mandatory fees	$846	
Room and board	$2724	
Financial aid recipients	52%	
Need-based scholarships (average)		$3771
Non-need scholarships (average)		$2855
Short-term loans (average)		$200
Long-term loans—college funds (average)		$1000
Long-term loans—external funds (average)		$2200

Undergraduate Facts

Part-time	12%
State residents	71%
Transfers	22%
African-Americans	4%
Native Americans	1%
Hispanics	4%
Asian-Americans	2%
International students	3%
Freshmen returning for sophomore year	75%
Students completing degree within 5 years	62%
Grads pursuing further study	31%

Freshman Data: 3,712 applied, 78% were accepted, 42% (1,217) of those entered

From top tenth of high school class	29%
SAT-takers scoring 600 or over on verbal	N/R
SAT-takers scoring 700 or over on verbal	N/R
SAT-takers scoring 600 or over on math	N/R
SAT-takers scoring 700 or over on math	N/R
ACT-takers scoring 26 or over	N/R
ACT-takers scoring 30 or over	N/R

Majors with most degrees conferred: business, communication, education.

Majors Accounting, advertising, applied art, art education, art/fine arts, art history, astrophysics, biochemistry, biology/biological sciences, broadcasting, business, chemistry, commercial art, communication, computer science, criminal justice, dance, (pre)dentistry sequence, dietetics, economics, education, elementary education, engineering (general), English, environmental sciences, fashion merchandising, film studies, finance/banking, French, geology, history, interior design, journalism, Latin American studies, (pre)law sequence, liberal arts/general studies, marketing/retailing/merchandising, mathematics, medical technology, (pre)medicine sequence, modern languages, music, music education, music history, neurosciences, nursing, nutrition, painting/drawing, philosophy, physical education, physical fitness/human movement, physics, piano/organ, political science/government, psychology, public relations, radio and television studies, reading education, real estate, religious studies, sacred music, secondary education, social work, sociology, Spanish, special education, speech pathology and audiology, speech/rhetoric/public address/debate, stringed instruments, studio art, theater arts/drama, urban studies, (pre)veterinary medicine sequence, voice, wind and percussion instruments.

Applying *Required:* essay, high school transcript, 3 years of high school math and science, 2 years of high school foreign language, 2 recommendations, SAT or ACT. *Recommended:* interview. *Application deadlines:* 2/15, 11/15 for early action, 5/1 priority date for financial aid. *Contact:* Ms. Sandra Ware, Associate Dean of Admissions, Sadler Hall, Fort Worth, TX 76129, 817-921-7490 or toll-free 800-828-3764.

Thomas Aquinas College

Santa Paula, California

Founded 1971
Rural setting
Independent, Roman Catholic
Coed
Awards B

Enrollment	201 total—all undergraduates (66 freshmen)
Faculty	20 total; 19 full-time (75% have doctorate/terminal degree); student-faculty ratio is 10:1.
Libraries	31,000 bound volumes, 42 periodical subscriptions
Computing	*Terminals/PCs available for student use:* 6, located in student center, dormitories; PC not required.
Of Special Interest	*Core academic program:* yes. Academic exchange program: no. Study-abroad programs: no.
On Campus	Dress code. No national or local fraternities or sororities on campus.
Athletics	None

Costs (1991–92) & Aid				
	Comprehensive fee	$16,300	Need-based scholarships (average)	$5000
	Tuition	$11,700	Non-need scholarships	N/Avail
	Mandatory fees	N/App	Short-term loans	N/Avail
	Room and board	$4600	Long-term loans—college funds (average)	$2700
	Financial aid recipients	78%	Long-term loans—external funds (average)	$2970

Undergraduate Facts				
	Part-time	0%	*Freshman Data:* 129 applied, 61% were accepted, 84% (66) of those entered	
	State residents	34%		
	Transfers	0%	From top tenth of high school class	34%
	African-Americans	0%	SAT-takers scoring 600 or over on verbal	36%
	Native Americans	0%	SAT-takers scoring 700 or over on verbal	5%
	Hispanics	3%	SAT-takers scoring 600 or over on math	34%
	Asian-Americans	4%	SAT-takers scoring 700 or over on math	7%
	International students	10%	ACT-takers scoring 26 or over	47%
	Freshmen returning for sophomore year	73%	ACT-takers scoring 30 or over	5%
	Students completing degree within 5 years	67%		
	Grads pursuing further study	N/R		

Majors Interdisciplinary studies, liberal arts/general studies, Western civilization and culture.

Applying *Required:* essay, high school transcript, 2 years of high school foreign language, 3 recommendations, SAT or ACT. *Recommended:* 3 years of high school math and science. Interview required for some. *Application deadlines:* rolling, 9/1 priority date for financial aid. *Contact:* Mr. Thomas J. Susanka Jr., Director of Admissions, 10000 North Ojai Road, Santa Paula, CA 93060, 805-525-4417 Ext. 359 or toll-free 800-634-9797.

From the College The College's integrated curriculum is based on the Great Books, the original works of the principal philosophers, theologians, scientists, mathematicians, poets, and writers of Western civilization. There are no lectures. Small groups of students meeting in tutorials, seminars, and laboratories are guided by faculty in analyzing and discussing these original texts. The academic program is guided by the philosophic and religious traditions of the Catholic Church.

✷ Transylvania University

Lexington, Kentucky

Founded 1780
Urban setting
Independent/affiliated with Christian Church (Disciples of Christ)
Coed
Awards B

Enrollment 1,038 total—all undergraduates (236 freshmen)

Faculty 102 total; 65 full-time (79% have doctorate/terminal degree); student-faculty ratio is 10:1.

Libraries 127,000 bound volumes, 64 titles on microform, 580 periodical subscriptions

Computing *Terminals/PCs available for student use:* 160, located in computer center, library, dormitories; PC not required.

Of Special Interest *Core academic program:* yes. Academic exchange with University of Kentucky, May Term Consortium, Washington Center for Internships and Academic Seminars. Sponsors and participates in study-abroad programs. Cooperative Army ROTC, cooperative Air Force ROTC.

On Campus Drama/theater group; student-run newspaper and radio station. *Social organizations:* 4 national fraternities, 4 national sororities; 56% of eligible undergraduate men and 63% of eligible undergraduate women are members.

Athletics Member NAIA. *Intercollegiate sports:* basketball (M, W), field hockey (W), golf (M), soccer (M), softball (W), swimming and diving (M, W), tennis (M, W). *Scholarships:* M, W.

Costs (1991–92) & Aid				
	Comprehensive fee	$13,667	Need-based scholarships	Avail
	Tuition	$9221	Non-need scholarships (average)	$4311
	Mandatory fees	$398	Short-term loans	N/Avail
	Room and board	$4048	Long-term loans—college funds (average)	$1615
	Financial aid recipients	74%	Long-term loans—external funds (average)	$2775

Undergraduate Facts				
	Part-time	9%	*Freshman Data:* 763 applied, 95% were accepted, 32% (236) of those entered	
	State residents	81%		
	Transfers	10%	From top tenth of high school class	57%
	African-Americans	2%	SAT-takers scoring 600 or over on verbal	25%
	Native Americans	0%	SAT-takers scoring 700 or over on verbal	4%
	Hispanics	1%	SAT-takers scoring 600 or over on math	45%
	Asian-Americans	2%	SAT-takers scoring 700 or over on math	8%
	International students	1%	ACT-takers scoring 26 or over	58%
	Freshmen returning for sophomore year	84%	ACT-takers scoring 30 or over	21%
	Students completing degree within 5 years	65%	*Majors with most degrees conferred:* business, biology/biological sciences, psychology.	
	Grads pursuing further study	40%		

Majors Anthropology, art education, biology/biological sciences, business, chemistry, computer science, economics, education, elementary education, English, French, history, mathematics, music, music education, philosophy, physical education, physics, political science/government, psychology, religious studies, secondary education, sociology, Spanish, studio art, theater arts/drama.

Applying *Required:* essay, high school transcript, 3 years of high school math, 2 recommendations, minimum 2.25 GPA, SAT or ACT. *Recommended:* 3 years of high school science, some high school foreign language, interview. Interview required for some. *Application deadlines:* 3/15, 11/1 for early decision, 4/1 priority date for financial aid. *Contact:* Ms. Patricia L. Bain, Director of Admissions, 300 North Broadway, Lexington, KY 40508-1797, 606-233-8242 or toll-free 800-872-6798.

From the College Transylvania, founded in 1780, is the nation's sixteenth-oldest college. Alumni include 2 U.S. vice presidents, 50 U.S. senators, and 36 governors. Transylvania has been ranked in the top five among southern regional liberal arts colleges in each of the last four annual surveys conducted by *U.S. News & World Report.*

Trenton State College

Trenton, New Jersey

Founded 1855
Suburban setting
State-supported
Coed
Awards B, M

Enrollment	6,971 total; 6,018 undergraduates (862 freshmen)
Faculty	523 total; 322 full-time (82% have doctorate/terminal degree); student-faculty ratio is 15:1; grad assistants teach no undergraduate courses.
Libraries	505,000 bound volumes, 555,000 titles on microform, 1,480 periodical subscriptions
Computing	*Terminals/PCs available for student use:* 550, located in computer center, student center, library, academic buildings; PC not required.
Of Special Interest	*Core academic program:* yes. Computer course required for business, engineering technology, education, chemistry, criminal justice, math, physics majors. Academic exchange with members of the National Student Exchange. Sponsors and participates in study-abroad programs. Cooperative Army ROTC, cooperative Air Force ROTC.
On Campus	Drama/theater group; student-run newspaper and radio station. *Social organizations:* 12 national fraternities, 12 national sororities, 5 local fraternities, 3 local sororities; 10% of eligible undergraduate men and 7% of eligible undergraduate women are members.
Athletics	Member NCAA (Division III). *Intercollegiate sports:* baseball (M), basketball (M, W), cross-country running (M, W), field hockey (W), football (M), golf (M), lacrosse (W), soccer (M, W), softball (W), swimming and diving (M, W), tennis (M, W), track and field (M, W), wrestling (M).

Costs (1991–92) & Aid				
	State resident tuition	$3079	100 Need-based scholarships (average)	$600
	Nonresident tuition	$4400	676 Non-need scholarships (average)	$1500
	Mandatory fees	$320	Short-term loans (average)	$100
	Room and board	$4750	Long-term loans—college funds	N/Avail
	Financial aid recipients	48%	Long-term loans—external funds (average)	$1750

Undergraduate Facts				
	Part-time	18%	*Freshman Data:* 4,842 applied, 45% were accepted, 40% (862) of those entered	
	State residents	91%		
	Transfers	24%	From top tenth of high school class	52%
	African-Americans	9%	SAT-takers scoring 600 or over on verbal	18%
	Native Americans	1%	SAT-takers scoring 700 or over on verbal	2%
	Hispanics	4%	SAT-takers scoring 600 or over on math	39%
	Asian-Americans	2%	SAT-takers scoring 700 or over on math	8%
	International students	1%	ACT-takers scoring 26 or over	N/App
	Freshmen returning for sophomore year	92%	ACT-takers scoring 30 or over	N/App
	Students completing degree within 5 years	67%	*Majors with most degrees conferred:* psychology, English, art/fine arts.	
	Grads pursuing further study	7%		

Majors Accounting, applied art, applied mathematics, art education, art/fine arts, art therapy, biology/biological sciences, broadcasting, business, business economics, chemistry, commercial art, communication, computer information systems, computer science, criminal justice, (pre)dentistry sequence, early childhood education, economics, education, electrical and electronics technologies, electrical engineering technology, electronics engineering technology, elementary education, engineering technology, English, finance/banking, graphic arts, health education, history, industrial engineering technology, interior design, journalism, (pre)law sequence, marketing/retailing/merchandising, mathematics, mechanical engineering technology, (pre)medicine sequence, music, music education, nursing, philosophy, physical education, physics, political science/government, psychology, public administration, reading education, secondary education, secretarial studies/office management, sociology, special education, speech pathology and audiology, statistics, (pre)veterinary medicine sequence.

Applying *Required:* essay, high school transcript, 3 years of high school math and science, SAT. *Recommended:* 2 years of high school foreign language, recommendations. Interview required for some. *Application deadlines:* 2/15, 11/1 for early decision, 4/15 priority date for financial aid. *Contact:* Mr. John Iacovelli, Director of Admissions and Financial Aid, Green Hall, Trenton, NJ 08650-4700, 609-771-2131 or toll-free 800-624-0967 (in-state).

✱ **Trinity College**

Hartford, Connecticut

Founded 1823
Urban setting
Independent
Coed
Awards B, M

Enrollment	2,212 total; 2,013 undergraduates (483 freshmen)	
Faculty	219 total; 153 full-time (98% have doctorate/terminal degree); student-faculty ratio is 10:1; grad assistants teach no undergraduate courses.	
Libraries	811,000 bound volumes, 203,000 titles on microform, 2,162 periodical subscriptions	
Computing	*Terminals/PCs available for student use:* 150, located in computer center, academic departments; PC not required. Campus network links student PCs.	
Of Special Interest	*Core academic program:* yes. Computer course required for engineering majors. Phi Beta Kappa, Sigma Xi chapters. Academic exchange with members of the Twelve College Exchange Program, Hartford Consortium for Higher Education. Sponsors and participates in study-abroad programs. Cooperative Army ROTC.	
On Campus	Drama/theater group; student-run newspaper and radio station. *Social organizations:* 7 national fraternities, 2 national sororities; 33% of eligible undergraduate men and 11% of eligible undergraduate women are members.	
Athletics	Member NCAA (Division III). *Intercollegiate sports:* baseball (M), basketball (M, W), crew (M, W), cross-country running (M, W), equestrian sports (M, W), fencing (M, W), field hockey (W), football (M), golf (M), ice hockey (M), lacrosse (M, W), rugby (M, W), skiing (downhill) (M, W), soccer (M, W), squash (M, W), swimming and diving (M, W), tennis (M, W), track and field (M, W), volleyball (M, W), water polo (M, W), wrestling (M).	

Costs (1991–92) & Aid				
	Comprehensive fee	$21,770	Need-based scholarships (average)	$11,150
	Tuition	$16,220	Non-need scholarships	Avail
	Mandatory fees	$730	Short-term loans (average)	$100
	Room and board	$4820	Long-term loans—college funds (average)	$2500
	Financial aid recipients	40%	Long-term loans—external funds (average)	$2625

Undergraduate Facts				
	Part-time	11%	*Freshman Data:* 2,791 applied, 62% were accepted, 28% (483) of those entered	
	State residents	34%		
	Transfers	3%	From top tenth of high school class	40%
	African-Americans	7%	SAT-takers scoring 600 or over on verbal	29%
	Native Americans	0%	SAT-takers scoring 700 or over on verbal	3%
	Hispanics	4%	SAT-takers scoring 600 or over on math	55%
	Asian-Americans	6%	SAT-takers scoring 700 or over on math	10%
	International students	3%	ACT-takers scoring 26 or over	49%
	Freshmen returning for sophomore year	95%	ACT-takers scoring 30 or over	10%
	Students completing degree within 5 years	N/R	*Majors with most degrees conferred:* English, history, economics.	
	Grads pursuing further study	N/R		

Majors American studies, art/fine arts, art history, Asian/Oriental studies, biochemistry, biology/biological sciences, biomedical engineering, black/African-American studies, chemistry, classics, comparative literature, computer science, dance, East European and Soviet studies, ecology/environmental studies, economics, education, electrical engineering, engineering (general), English, French, German, Greek, history, Italian, Judaic studies, Latin, Latin American studies, mathematics, mechanical engineering, modern languages, music, neurosciences, philosophy, physical sciences, physics, political science/government, psychology, public affairs and policy studies, religious studies, Romance languages, Russian, Russian and Slavic studies, sociology, Spanish, studio art, theater arts/drama, women's studies.

Applying *Required:* essay, high school transcript, 3 years of high school math, 2 years of high school foreign language, 3 recommendations, SAT or ACT, 1 Achievement, English Composition Test. *Recommended:* 3 years of high school science, interview, English Composition Test (with essay). *Application deadlines:* 1/15, 12/1 for early decision, 2/1 for financial aid. *Contact:* Dr. David M. Borus, Dean of Admissions and Financial Aid, 300 Summit Street, Hartford, CT 06106, 203-297-2180.

From the College Trinity offers its students the distinctive combination of a beautiful hilltop campus in a thriving capital city. Students find hundreds of internship possibilities, volunteer opportunities, and cultural or entertainment activities in Hartford. More than 50 percent of the students pursue internships in business, politics, law, medicine, education, and the arts.

Trinity University

San Antonio, Texas

Founded 1869
Urban setting
Independent/affiliated with Presbyterian Church
Coed
Awards B, M

Enrollment	2,518 total; 2,291 undergraduates (576 freshmen)
Faculty	261 total; 231 full-time (94% have doctorate/terminal degree); grad assistants teach no undergraduate courses.
Libraries	695,327 bound volumes, 236,165 titles on microform, 2,424 periodical subscriptions
Computing	*Terminals/PCs available for student use:* 200, located in computer center, student center; PC not required.
Of Special Interest	*Core academic program:* yes. Computer course required. Phi Beta Kappa, Sigma Xi chapters. Academic exchange program: no. Sponsors and participates in study-abroad programs. Cooperative Army ROTC, cooperative Air Force ROTC.
On Campus	Drama/theater group; student-run newspaper and radio station. *Social organizations:* 5 local fraternities, 6 local sororities; 29% of eligible undergraduate men and 29% of eligible undergraduate women are members.
Athletics	Member NCAA (Division III). *Intercollegiate sports:* basketball (M, W), football (M), golf (M), soccer (M, W), tennis (M, W), track and field (M, W), volleyball (M, W).

Costs (1992–93 estimated) & Aid				
	Comprehensive fee	$14,710	Need-based scholarships (average)	$9888
	Tuition	$10,200	Non-need scholarships (average)	$3134
	Mandatory fees	$140	Short-term loans	Avail
	Room and board	$4370	Long-term loans—college funds	Avail
	Financial aid recipients	71%	Long-term loans—external funds (average)	$2500

Undergraduate Facts				
	Part-time	4%	*Freshman Data:* 2,300 applied, 72% were accepted, 35% (576) of those entered	
	State residents	61%		
	Transfers	5%	From top tenth of high school class	67%
	African-Americans	2%	SAT-takers scoring 600 or over on verbal	34%
	Native Americans	1%	SAT-takers scoring 700 or over on verbal	5%
	Hispanics	9%	SAT-takers scoring 600 or over on math	63%
	Asian-Americans	7%	SAT-takers scoring 700 or over on math	14%
	International students	1%	ACT-takers scoring 26 or over	73%
	Freshmen returning for sophomore year	90%	ACT-takers scoring 30 or over	22%
	Students completing degree within 5 years	72%	*Majors with most degrees conferred:* business, English, economics.	
	Grads pursuing further study	50%		

Majors American studies, anthropology, art/fine arts, art history, Asian/Oriental studies, biochemistry, biology/biological sciences, business, chemistry, classics, communication, computer science, (pre)dentistry sequence, earth science, economics, engineering (general), engineering sciences, English, European studies, French, geology, German, Greek, history, information science, interdisciplinary studies, international studies, journalism, Latin, (pre)law sequence, mathematics, (pre)medicine sequence, music, philosophy, physics, political science/government, psychology, religious studies, Russian, secondary education, sociology, Spanish, speech/rhetoric/public address/debate, studio art, theater arts/drama, urban studies, (pre)veterinary medicine sequence.

Applying *Required:* essay, high school transcript, 3 years of high school math and science, some high school foreign language, recommendations, SAT or ACT. *Recommended:* interview. *Application deadlines:* 2/1, 11/15 for early decision, 2/1 priority date for financial aid. *Contact:* Ms. Sara Krause, Director of Admissions, 715 Stadium Drive, San Antonio, TX 78212, 512-736-7207 or toll-free 800-TRINITY.

Tufts University

Medford, Massachusetts

Founded 1852
Suburban setting
Independent
Coed
Awards B, M, D

Enrollment 7,645 total; 4,393 undergraduates (1,176 freshmen)

Faculty 619 total; 346 full-time (96% have doctorate/terminal degree); student-faculty ratio is 13:1; grad assistants teach a few undergraduate courses.

Libraries 743,000 bound volumes, 845,000 titles on microform, 5,600 periodical subscriptions

Computing *Terminals/PCs available for student use:* 140, located in computer center, student center, library, personal computer labs, CAD lab; PC not required.

Of Special Interest *Core academic program:* yes. Computer course required for engineering majors. Phi Beta Kappa, Sigma Xi chapters. Academic exchange with Boston College, Boston University, Brandeis University, Swarthmore College, American University (Washington Semester). Sponsors and participates in study-abroad programs. Cooperative Army ROTC, cooperative Naval ROTC, cooperative Air Force ROTC.

On Campus Drama/theater group; student-run newspaper and radio station. *Social organizations:* 11 national fraternities, 4 national sororities; 16% of eligible undergraduate men and 4% of eligible undergraduate women are members.

Athletics Member NCAA (Division III). *Intercollegiate sports:* baseball (M), basketball (M, W), crew (M, W), cross-country running (M, W), field hockey (W), football (M), golf (M), ice hockey (M), lacrosse (M, W), sailing (M, W), soccer (M, W), softball (W), squash (M, W), swimming and diving (M, W), tennis (M, W), track and field (M, W), volleyball (W).

Costs (1991–92) & Aid				
	Comprehensive fee	$22,479	Need-based scholarships (average)	$9914
	Tuition	$16,755	Non-need scholarships (average)	$750
	Mandatory fees	$424	Short-term loans (average)	$3300
	Room and board	$5300	Long-term loans—college funds (average)	$1948
	Financial aid recipients	41%	Long-term loans—external funds (average)	$3039

Undergraduate Facts				
	Part-time	0%	*Freshman Data:* 7,308 applied, 47% were accepted, 34% (1,176) of those entered	
	State residents	27%		
	Transfers	5%	From top tenth of high school class	65%
	African-Americans	4%	SAT-takers scoring 600 or over on verbal	46%
	Native Americans	N/R	SAT-takers scoring 700 or over on verbal	5%
	Hispanics	4%	SAT-takers scoring 600 or over on math	83%
	Asian-Americans	9%	SAT-takers scoring 700 or over on math	25%
	International students	7%	ACT-takers scoring 26 or over	N/R
	Freshmen returning for sophomore year	99%	ACT-takers scoring 30 or over	N/R
	Students completing degree within 5 years	90%	*Majors with most degrees conferred:* English, political science/government, international studies.	
	Grads pursuing further study	35%		

Majors American studies, anthropology, archaeology, architectural engineering, art/fine arts, art history, Asian/Oriental studies, astronomy, behavioral sciences, biology/biological sciences, black/African-American studies, chemical engineering, chemistry, child care/child and family studies, child psychology/child development, Chinese, civil engineering, classics, computer engineering, computer science, early childhood education, ecology/environmental studies, economics, electrical engineering, elementary education, engineering and applied sciences, engineering design, engineering physics, engineering sciences, English, environmental engineering, environmental sciences, experimental psychology, French, geology, geophysical engineering, German, Greek, history, international studies, Latin, mathematics, mechanical engineering, mental health/rehabilitation counseling, music, philosophy, physics, political science/government, psychology, public health, Romance languages, Russian, Russian and Slavic studies, secondary education, sociobiology, sociology, Southeast Asian studies, Spanish, special education, theater arts/drama, urban studies, women's studies.

Applying *Required:* essay, high school transcript, 1 recommendation, SAT or ACT, 3 Achievements, English Composition Test. *Recommended:* 3 years of high school math and science, 3 years of high school foreign language. *Application deadlines:* 1/10, 1/1 for early decision, 2/1 for financial aid. *Contact:* Mr. David D. Cuttino, Dean of Undergraduate Admissions, Bendetson Hall, Medford, MA 02155, 617-627-3170.

Tulane University

New Orleans, Louisiana

Founded 1834
Urban setting
Independent
Coed
Awards B, M, D

Enrollment 11,487 total; 7,084 undergraduates (1,367 freshmen)

Faculty 684 total; 492 full-time (98% have doctorate/terminal degree); student-faculty ratio is 13:1; grad assistants teach a few undergraduate courses.

Libraries 1.8 million bound volumes, 2.0 million titles on microform, 17,236 periodical subscriptions

Computing *Terminals/PCs available for student use:* 385, located in computer center, library, dormitories, classrooms, academic buildings; PC not required.

Of Special Interest *Core academic program:* yes. Computer course required for business management, engineering, math majors. Phi Beta Kappa, Sigma Xi chapters. Academic exchange with Xavier University of Louisiana, Loyola University, New Orleans. Sponsors and participates in study-abroad programs. Army ROTC, Naval ROTC, Air Force ROTC.

On Campus Drama/theater group; student-run newspaper and radio station. *Social organizations:* 19 national fraternities, 10 national sororities; 32% of eligible undergraduate men and 38% of eligible undergraduate women are members.

Athletics Member NCAA (Division I). *Intercollegiate sports:* basketball (M, W), cross-country running (M, W), football (M), golf (M, W), tennis (M, W), track and field (M, W), volleyball (W). *Scholarships:* M, W.

Costs (1992–93 estimated) & Aid

Comprehensive fee	$23,785	
Tuition	$17,925	
Mandatory fees	$260	
Room and board	$5600	
Financial aid recipients	50%	
Need-based scholarships (average)	$11,000	
Non-need scholarships (average)	$13,150	
Short-term loans (average)	$200	
Long-term loans—college funds (average)	$1500	
Long-term loans—external funds (average)	$2000	

Undergraduate Facts

Part-time	24%
State residents	17%
Transfers	7%
African-Americans	9%
Native Americans	1%
Hispanics	4%
Asian-Americans	4%
International students	3%
Freshmen returning for sophomore year	90%
Students completing degree within 5 years	75%
Grads pursuing further study	N/R

Freshman Data: 7,491 applied, 73% were accepted, 25% (1,367) of those entered

From top tenth of high school class	44%
SAT-takers scoring 600 or over on verbal	28%
SAT-takers scoring 700 or over on verbal	4%
SAT-takers scoring 600 or over on math	52%
SAT-takers scoring 700 or over on math	13%
ACT-takers scoring 26 or over	N/R
ACT-takers scoring 30 or over	N/R

Majors with most degrees conferred: English, history, psychology.

Majors American studies, anthropology, architecture, art/fine arts, art history, Asian/Oriental studies, biochemistry, biology/biological sciences, biomedical engineering, business, chemical engineering, chemistry, civil engineering, classics, communication, computer engineering, computer information systems, computer science, earth science, ecology/environmental studies, economics, electrical engineering, engineering (general), engineering management, English, French, geology, German, Germanic languages and literature, Greek, history, international studies, Italian, Judaic studies, Latin, Latin American studies, liberal arts/general studies, linguistics, mathematics, mechanical engineering, medieval studies, music, paralegal studies, philosophy, physical education, physics, political science/government, Portuguese, psychology, public affairs and policy studies, religious studies, Russian, Russian and Slavic studies, sociology, Spanish, studio art, theater arts/drama, women's studies.

Applying *Required:* essay, high school transcript, 1 recommendation, SAT or ACT. *Recommended:* 3 years of high school science, some high school foreign language, interview, Achievements, English Composition Test. 3 years of high school math required for some. *Application deadlines:* 1/15, 11/1 for early action, 2/1 priority date for financial aid. *Contact:* Ms. Lois V. Conrad, Dean of Admissions, 6823 Saint Charles Avenue, New Orleans, LA 70118, 504-865-5731.

✴ **Union College**

Schenectady, New York

Founded 1795
Suburban setting
Independent
Coed
Awards B, M, D

Enrollment	2,307 total; 1,940 undergraduates (507 freshmen)
Faculty	199 total; 174 full-time (96% have doctorate/terminal degree); student-faculty ratio is 11:1; grad assistants teach no undergraduate courses.
Libraries	473,321 bound volumes, 16,952 titles on microform, 2,226 periodical subscriptions
Computing	*Terminals/PCs available for student use:* 160, located in computer center, library, labs, academic buildings; PC not required. Campus network links student PCs.
Of Special Interest	*Core academic program:* yes. Computer course required for engineering majors. Phi Beta Kappa, Sigma Xi chapters. Academic exchange with Hudson-Mohawk Association of Colleges and Universities. Sponsors and participates in study-abroad programs. Cooperative Army ROTC, cooperative Naval ROTC, cooperative Air Force ROTC.
On Campus	Drama/theater group; student-run newspaper and radio station. *Social organizations:* 17 national fraternities, 4 national sororities, 2 coed fraternity; 46% of eligible undergraduate men and 25% of eligible undergraduate women are members.
Athletics	Member NCAA (Division III). *Intercollegiate sports:* baseball (M), basketball (M, W), crew (M, W), cross-country running (M, W), fencing (M, W), field hockey (W), football (M), golf (M), ice hockey (M), lacrosse (M, W), rugby (M, W), sailing (M, W), skiing (cross-country) (M, W), skiing (downhill) (M, W), soccer (M, W), softball (W), swimming and diving (M, W), tennis (M, W), track and field (M, W), volleyball (W).

Costs (1991–92) & Aid				
	Comprehensive fee	$20,974	Need-based scholarships (average)	$9466
	Tuition	$15,420	Non-need scholarships	Avail
	Mandatory fees	$159	Short-term loans (average)	$100
	Room and board	$5395	Long-term loans—college funds (average)	$2463
	Financial aid recipients	45%	Long-term loans—external funds (average)	$2626

Undergraduate Facts				
	Part-time	0%	*Freshman Data:* 3,050 applied, 60% were accepted, 28% (507) of those entered	
	State residents	55%		
	Transfers	2%	From top tenth of high school class	40%
	African-Americans	3%	SAT-takers scoring 600 or over on verbal	N/App
	Native Americans	0%	SAT-takers scoring 700 or over on verbal	N/App
	Hispanics	3%	SAT-takers scoring 600 or over on math	N/App
	Asian-Americans	6%	SAT-takers scoring 700 or over on math	N/App
	International students	2%	ACT-takers scoring 26 or over	N/R
	Freshmen returning for sophomore year	95%	ACT-takers scoring 30 or over	N/R
	Students completing degree within 5 years	84%	*Majors with most degrees conferred:* economics, psychology, political science/government.	
	Grads pursuing further study	33%		

Majors American studies, art/fine arts, biology/biological sciences, business economics, chemistry, civil engineering, classics, computer science, East Asian studies, economics, electrical engineering, English, geology, history, humanities, interdisciplinary studies, Latin American studies, mathematics, mechanical engineering, (pre)medicine sequence, modern languages, philosophy, physics, political science/government, psychology, science, social science, sociology, women's studies.

Applying *Required:* essay, high school transcript, 2 recommendations, 3 College Board Achievement Tests (including College Board English Composition Test) or ACT. *Recommended:* 2 years of high school foreign language, interview. 3 years of high school math and science required for some. *Application deadlines:* 2/1, same for early decision, 2/1 priority date for financial aid. *Contact:* Mr. Daniel Lundquist, Dean of Admissions and Financial Aid, Becker Hall, Schenectady, NY 12308, 518-370-6112.

United States Air Force Academy

Colorado Springs, Colorado

Founded 1954
Suburban setting
Federally supported
Coed
Awards B

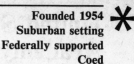

Enrollment 4,440 total—all undergraduates (1,388 freshmen)

Faculty 517 total—all full-time (40% have doctorate/terminal degree); student-faculty ratio is 8:1.

Libraries 601,000 bound volumes, 495,000 titles on microform, 3,800 periodical subscriptions

Computing *Terminals/PCs available for student use:* 2,500, located in students' rooms; UNISYS 386 required for freshmen and available for purchase. Campus network links student PCs.

Of Special Interest *Core academic program:* yes. Computer course required. Sigma Xi chapter. Academic exchange with other United States service academies. Sponsors study-abroad programs.

On Campus Dress code; drama/theater group; student-run radio station. No national or local fraternities or sororities on campus.

Athletics Member NCAA (Division I–men; Division II–women). *Intercollegiate sports:* baseball (M), basketball (M, W), bowling (M, W), cross-country running (M, W), equestrian sports (M, W), fencing (M, W), football (M), golf (M), gymnastics (M, W), ice hockey (M), lacrosse (M), racquetball (M, W), riflery (M, W), rugby (M, W), skiing (cross-country) (M, W), skiing (downhill) (M, W), soccer (M, W), softball (W), squash (M), swimming and diving (M, W), tennis (M, W), track and field (M, W), volleyball (M, W), water polo (M), weight lifting (M), wrestling (M).

Costs	Comprehensive fee		$0	Financial aid	N/App
Under-graduate Facts	Part-time		0%	*Freshman Data:* 11,000 applied, 16% were accepted, 77% (1,388) of those entered	
	State residents		5%		
	Transfers		11%	From top tenth of high school class	76%
	African-Americans		7%	SAT-takers scoring 600 or over on verbal	28%
	Native Americans		1%	SAT-takers scoring 700 or over on verbal	2%
	Hispanics		6%	SAT-takers scoring 600 or over on math	83%
	Asian-Americans		3%	SAT-takers scoring 700 or over on math	26%
	International students		1%	ACT-takers scoring 26 or over	N/R
	Freshmen returning for sophomore year		82%	ACT-takers scoring 30 or over	N/R
	Students completing degree within 5 years		74%		
	Grads pursuing further study		4%		

Majors Aerospace engineering, aerospace sciences, behavioral sciences, biology/biological sciences, business, chemistry, civil engineering, computer science, economics, electrical engineering, engineering (general), engineering mechanics, engineering sciences, English, geography, history, humanities, international studies, legal studies, mathematics, operations research, physics, science, social science.

Applying *Required:* essay, high school transcript, interview, authorized nomination, SAT or ACT. *Recommended:* 4 years of high school math and science, 2 years of high school foreign language, Achievements, English Composition Test. *Application deadline:* 1/31. *Contact:* Lt. Col. Rolland Stoneman, Director of Selection, Headquarters USAFA/RRS, Colorado Springs, CO 80840, 303-472-2520.

From the College The Air Force Academy challenge requires a well-rounded academic, physical, and leadership background. Cadets must accept discipline, be competitive, and have a desire to serve others with a sense of duty and morality. Applicants should prepare early to meet the admissions requirements, competition, and demands they'll face at the Academy.

United States Coast Guard Academy
New London, Connecticut

Founded 1876
Small-town setting
Federally supported
Coed
Awards B

Enrollment 951 total—all undergraduates (276 freshmen)

Faculty 105 total—all full-time (30% have doctorate/terminal degree).

Libraries 151,694 bound volumes, 51,378 titles on microform, 1,023 periodical subscriptions

Computing *Terminals/PCs available for student use:* 130, located in computer center, library, dormitories engineering, science, math, computer science departments; Macintosh SE required for freshmen and available for purchase. Campus network links student PCs.

Of Special Interest *Core academic program:* yes. Computer course required. Academic exchange with Connecticut College. Study-abroad programs: no.

On Campus Dress code; drama/theater group; student-run newspaper. No national or local fraternities or sororities on campus.

Athletics Member NCAA (Division III). *Intercollegiate sports:* baseball (M), basketball (M, W), bowling (M, W), crew (M, W), cross-country running (M, W), football (M), lacrosse (M), riflery (M, W), rugby (M), sailing (M, W), soccer (M, W), softball (W), swimming and diving (M), tennis (M), track and field (M, W), volleyball (W), wrestling (M).

Costs	Comprehensive fee	$0	Financial aid	N/App
Under-graduate Facts	Part-time	0%	*Freshman Data:* 2,314 applied, 21% were accepted, 56% (276) of those entered	
	State residents	5%		
	Transfers	0%	From top tenth of high school class	67%
	African-Americans	2%	SAT-takers scoring 600 or over on verbal	32%
	Native Americans	1%	SAT-takers scoring 700 or over on verbal	0%
	Hispanics	3%	SAT-takers scoring 600 or over on math	79%
	Asian-Americans	5%	SAT-takers scoring 700 or over on math	20%
	International students	2%	ACT-takers scoring 26 or over	N/R
	Freshmen returning for sophomore year	91%	ACT-takers scoring 30 or over	N/R
	Students completing degree within 5 years	N/R	*Majors with most degrees conferred:* political science/government, business.	
	Grads pursuing further study	N/R		

Majors Business, civil engineering, computer science, electrical engineering, marine engineering, marine sciences, mathematics, political science/government.

Applying *Required:* essay, high school transcript, 3 years of high school math, 3 recommendations, SAT or ACT. *Recommended:* 3 years of high school science. *Application deadline:* 12/15. *Contact:* Capt. Thomas D. Combs Jr., Director of Admissions, 15 Mohegan Avenue, New London, CT 06320-4195, 203-444-8500.

United States Merchant Marine Academy
Kings Point, New York

Founded 1943
Rural setting
Federally supported
Coed
Awards B

✱

Enrollment	949 total—all undergraduates (298 freshmen)
Faculty	80 total; 76 full-time (85% have doctorate/terminal degree); student-faculty ratio is 10:1.
Libraries	220,273 bound volumes, 113,531 titles on microform, 1,200 periodical subscriptions
Computing	*Terminals/PCs available for student use:* 1,200, located in computer center, library, dormitories, classrooms, independent study labs; Zenith 386SX required for freshmen and available for purchase. Campus network links student PCs.
Of Special Interest	*Core academic program:* yes. Computer course required. Academic exchange program: no. Study-abroad programs: no.
On Campus	Dress code; drama/theater group; student-run newspaper. No national or local fraternities or sororities on campus.
Athletics	Member NCAA (Division III). *Intercollegiate sports:* baseball (M), basketball (M), crew (M, W), cross-country running (M, W), football (M), golf (M, W), ice hockey (M), lacrosse (M), riflery (M, W), rugby (M), sailing (M, W), soccer (M), swimming and diving (M, W), tennis (M, W), track and field (M, W), volleyball (M, W), wrestling (M).

Costs	Comprehensive fee		$0	Financial aid	N/App
Undergraduate Facts	Part-time		0%	*Freshman Data:* 1,594 applied, 27% were accepted, 69% (298) of those entered	
	State residents		12%		
	Transfers		0%	From top tenth of high school class	40%
	African-Americans		1%	SAT-takers scoring 600 or over on verbal	22%
	Native Americans		1%	SAT-takers scoring 700 or over on verbal	6%
	Hispanics		2%	SAT-takers scoring 600 or over on math	43%
	Asian-Americans		4%	SAT-takers scoring 700 or over on math	2%
	International students		2%	ACT-takers scoring 26 or over	N/R
	Freshmen returning for sophomore year		80%	ACT-takers scoring 30 or over	N/R
	Students completing degree within 5 years		66%		
	Grads pursuing further study		2%		

Majors Marine engineering, marine sciences, maritime sciences.

Applying *Required:* essay, high school transcript, 3 years of high school math, 1 recommendation, SAT or ACT. *Recommended:* 3 years of high school science, some high school foreign language, campus interview. Achievements required for some. *Application deadline:* 3/1. *Contact:* Capt. Emmanuel L. Jenkins, USMS, Director of Admissions, Wiley Hall, Kings Point, NY 11024, 516-773-5391 or toll-free 800-732-6267 (out-of-state).

United States Military Academy

West Point, New York

Founded 1802
Rural setting
Federally supported
Coed
Awards B

Enrollment 4,392 total—all undergraduates (1,248 freshmen)

Faculty 535 total—all full-time (33% have doctorate/terminal degree); student-faculty ratio is 8:1.

Libraries 412,638 bound volumes, 120,954 titles on microform, 2,400 periodical subscriptions

Computing *Terminals/PCs available for student use:* 6,600, located in computer center, library, dormitories; UNISYS 386 required for freshmen and available for purchase. Campus network links student PCs.

Of Special Interest *Core academic program:* yes. Computer course required. Academic exchange with other United States service academies. Study-abroad programs: no.

On Campus Dress code; drama/theater group; student-run radio station. No national or local fraternities or sororities on campus.

Athletics Member NCAA (Division I). *Intercollegiate sports:* baseball (M), basketball (M, W), cross-country running (M, W), football (M), golf (M), gymnastics (M), ice hockey (M), lacrosse (M), riflery (M, W), soccer (M, W), softball (W), swimming and diving (M, W), tennis (M, W), track and field (M, W), volleyball (W), water polo (M), wrestling (M).

Costs	Comprehensive fee		Financial aid	
Under-graduate Facts	Part-time	0%	*Freshman Data:* 12,247 applied, 13% were accepted, 76% (1,248) of those entered	N/App
	State residents	N/R		
	Transfers	0%	From top tenth of high school class	65%
	African-Americans	7%	SAT-takers scoring 600 or over on verbal	33%
	Native Americans	1%	SAT-takers scoring 700 or over on verbal	4%
	Hispanics	4%	SAT-takers scoring 600 or over on math	79%
	Asian-Americans	5%	SAT-takers scoring 700 or over on math	24%
	International students	1%	ACT-takers scoring 26 or over	64%
	Freshmen returning for sophomore year	87%	ACT-takers scoring 30 or over	25%
	Students completing degree within 5 years	71%		
	Grads pursuing further study	N/R		

Majors Aerospace engineering, American studies, applied mathematics, Arabic, automotive engineering, behavioral sciences, biology/biological sciences, business, chemical engineering, chemistry, Chinese, civil engineering, computer science, East Asian studies, East European and Soviet studies, economics, electrical engineering, engineering and applied sciences, engineering management, engineering physics, environmental engineering, European studies, French, geography, German, history, humanities, interdisciplinary studies, international studies, Latin American studies, literature, mathematics, mechanical engineering, (pre)medicine sequence, military science, modern languages, Near and Middle Eastern studies, nuclear engineering, operations research, philosophy, physical sciences, physics, political science/government, Portuguese, psychology, public affairs and policy studies, Russian, science, social science, sociology, Spanish, systems engineering.

Applying *Required:* essay, high school transcript, 4 recommendations, authorized nomination, medical and physical aptitude exams, proof of age (between 17 and 21 at matriculation), proof of U.S. citizenship (except students nominated by agreement between U.S. and another country), unmarried, not pregnant, no legal obligation to support a child, SAT or ACT. *Recommended:* 3 years of high school math and science, 2 years of high school foreign language, interview. *Application deadlines:* rolling, 10/25 for early action. *Contact:* Col. Pierce A. Rushton, Director of Admissions, 606 Thayer Road, West Point, NY 10996, 914-938-3526.

United States Naval Academy

Annapolis, Maryland

Founded 1845
Small-town setting
Federally supported
Primarily men
Awards B

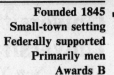

Enrollment	4,265 total—all undergraduates (1,133 freshmen)
Faculty	600 total—all full-time.
Libraries	750,000 bound volumes, 2,100 periodical subscriptions
Computing	*Terminals/PCs available for student use:* 6,100, located in computer center, library, dormitories; IBM-compatible required for freshmen and available for purchase. Campus network links student PCs.
Of Special Interest	*Core academic program:* yes. Computer course required. Sigma Xi chapter. Academic exchange program: no. Study-abroad programs: no.
On Campus	Dress code; drama/theater group; student-run radio station. No national or local fraternities or sororities on campus.
Athletics	Member NCAA (Division I–men; Division II–women). *Intercollegiate sports:* basketball (M, W), crew (M, W), cross-country running (M, W), fencing (M, W), football (M), golf (M), gymnastics (M, W), lacrosse (M), riflery (M), sailing (M, W), soccer (M), squash (M), swimming and diving (M, W), tennis (M), track and field (M, W), volleyball (M, W), water polo (M), wrestling (M).

Costs	Comprehensive fee	$0	Financial aid	N/App
Under-graduate Facts	Part-time	0%	*Freshman Data:* 11,588 applied, 12% were accepted, 82% (1,133) of those entered	
	State residents	2%		
	Transfers	0%	From top tenth of high school class	59%
	African-Americans	6%	SAT-takers scoring 600 or over on verbal	35%
	Native Americans	1%	SAT-takers scoring 700 or over on verbal	5%
	Hispanics	6%	SAT-takers scoring 600 or over on math	86%
	Asian-Americans	5%	SAT-takers scoring 700 or over on math	31%
	International students	1%	ACT-takers scoring 26 or over	N/R
	Freshmen returning for sophomore year	86%	ACT-takers scoring 30 or over	N/R
	Students completing degree within 5 years	N/R		
	Grads pursuing further study	N/R		

Majors Aerospace engineering, chemistry, computer science, economics, electrical engineering, engineering (general), engineering and applied sciences, English, history, marine engineering, mathematics, mechanical engineering, naval architecture, ocean engineering, oceanography, physics, political science/government, systems engineering.

Applying *Required:* essay, high school transcript, 2 recommendations, authorized nomination, SAT or ACT. *Recommended:* 4 years of high school math and science, some high school foreign language, interview. *Application deadline:* 3/1. *Contact:* Capt. D. W. Davis, USNA Candidate Guidance Office, 117 Decatur Road, Annapolis, MD 21402, 410-267-4361 or toll-free 800-638-9156.

University at Albany, State University of New York
Albany, New York

Founded 1844
Suburban setting
State-supported
Coed
Awards B, M, D

Enrollment 15,333 total; 11,072 undergraduates (2,029 freshmen)

Faculty 904 total; 671 full-time (95% have doctorate/terminal degree); student-faculty ratio is 17:1; grad assistants teach a few undergraduate courses.

Libraries 1.6 million bound volumes, 2.4 million titles on microform, 7,000 periodical subscriptions

Computing *Terminals/PCs available for student use:* 500, located in computer center, library, dormitories, special user rooms; PC not required. Campus network links student PCs.

Of Special Interest *Core academic program:* yes. Computer course required for business administration, accounting, applied math majors. Phi Beta Kappa, Sigma Xi chapters. Academic exchange with New York State Visiting Student Program, Hudson-Mohawk Association of Colleges and Universities. Sponsors and participates in study-abroad programs. Army ROTC, cooperative Naval ROTC, cooperative Air Force ROTC.

On Campus Drama/theater group; student-run newspaper and radio station. *Social organizations:* 15 national fraternities, 5 national sororities, 5 local fraternities, 6 local sororities; 20% of eligible undergraduate men and 15% of eligible undergraduate women are members.

Athletics Member NCAA (Division III). *Intercollegiate sports:* baseball (M), basketball (M, W), crew (M, W), cross-country running (M, W), football (M), gymnastics (M, W), lacrosse (M), rugby (M), soccer (M, W), swimming and diving (M, W), tennis (M, W), track and field (M, W), volleyball (W), wrestling (M).

Costs (1991–92) & Aid				
	State resident tuition	$2150	1206 Need-based scholarships (average)	$654
	Nonresident tuition	$5750	Non-need scholarships	Avail
	Mandatory fees	$227	Short-term loans	Avail
	Room and board	$3666	Long-term loans—college funds	N/Avail
	Financial aid recipients	70%	Long-term loans—external funds	Avail

Undergraduate Facts				
	Part-time	5%	*Freshman Data:* 14,834 applied, 57% were accepted, 24% (2,029) of those entered	
	State residents	97%		
	Transfers	33%	From top tenth of high school class	23%
	African-Americans	9%	SAT-takers scoring 600 or over on verbal	13%
	Native Americans	1%	SAT-takers scoring 700 or over on verbal	1%
	Hispanics	6%	SAT-takers scoring 600 or over on math	53%
	Asian-Americans	6%	SAT-takers scoring 700 or over on math	8%
	International students	1%	ACT-takers scoring 26 or over	N/R
	Freshmen returning for sophomore year	90%	ACT-takers scoring 30 or over	N/R
	Students completing degree within 5 years	66%		
	Grads pursuing further study	45%		

Majors Accounting, African studies, anthropology, art/fine arts, Asian/Oriental studies, atmospheric sciences, biochemistry, biology/biological sciences, black/African-American studies, business, chemistry, Chinese, classics, communication, computer science, criminal justice, earth science, East European and Soviet studies, economics, English, French, geography, geology, German, Greek, Hispanic studies, history, interdisciplinary studies, Italian, Japanese, Judaic studies, Latin, Latin American studies, linguistics, mathematics, medical technology, medieval studies, meteorology, molecular biology, music, philosophy, physics, political science/government, psychology, public affairs and policy studies, Romance languages, Russian, secondary education, social work, sociology, Spanish, speech/rhetoric/public address/debate, studio art, theater arts/drama, women's studies.

Applying *Required:* high school transcript, SAT or ACT. *Recommended:* essay, 3 years of high school math and science, some high school foreign language. 3 years of high school math and science, portfolio, audition required for some. *Application deadlines:* 3/1, 3/15 priority date for financial aid. *Contact:* Dr. Micheileen Treadwell, Director of Admissions, 1400 Washington Avenue, Albany, NY 12222, 518-442-5435.

From the College The University is currently ranked eleventh in *Money* magazine's best buys among American colleges and universities. Albany is also the home of the New York State Writers Institute. Administered by William Kennedy, the Pulitzer Prize–winning author of *Ironweed*, the institute supports the literary arts through lectures, readings, and seminars conducted by prominent writers.

University of Alabama in Huntsville
Huntsville, Alabama

Founded 1950
Urban setting
State-supported
Coed
Awards B, M, D

Enrollment	8,624 total; 6,376 undergraduates (777 freshmen)
Faculty	439 total; 276 full-time (87% have doctorate/terminal degree); student-faculty ratio is 20:1; grad assistants teach a few undergraduate courses.
Libraries	300,000 bound volumes, 300,000 titles on microform, 3,000 periodical subscriptions
Computing	*Terminals/PCs available for student use:* 113, located in computer center, student center, library, labs; PC not required.
Of Special Interest	*Core academic program:* yes. Computer course required for engineering, business, math majors. Sigma Xi chapter. Academic exchange with Alabama Agricultural and Mechanical University, Oakwood College, Athens State College, John C. Calhoun State Community College. Participates in study-abroad programs. Cooperative Army ROTC, cooperative Air Force ROTC.
On Campus	Drama/theater group; student-run newspaper. *Social organizations:* 5 national fraternities, 5 national sororities, social clubs; 5% of eligible undergraduate men and 6% of eligible undergraduate women are members.
Athletics	Member NCAA (Division II). *Intercollegiate sports:* basketball (M, W), crew (M, W), ice hockey (M), soccer (M), tennis (M, W), volleyball (W). *Scholarships:* M, W.

Costs (1991–92) & Aid	State resident tuition	$2235	80 Need-based scholarships (average)	$1000
	Nonresident tuition	$4470	450 Non-need scholarships (average)	$1800
	Mandatory fees	N/App	Short-term loans (average)	$200
	Room and board	$4260	Long-term loans—college funds	N/Avail
	Financial aid recipients	28%	Long-term loans—external funds (average)	$1650

Undergraduate Facts	Part-time	59%	*Freshman Data:* 1,094 applied, 82% were accepted, 87% (777) of those entered	
	State residents	97%		
	Transfers	10%	From top tenth of high school class	N/R
	African-Americans	6%	SAT-takers scoring 600 or over on verbal	12%
	Native Americans	1%	SAT-takers scoring 700 or over on verbal	2%
	Hispanics	1%	SAT-takers scoring 600 or over on math	28%
	Asian-Americans	3%	SAT-takers scoring 700 or over on math	7%
	International students	2%	ACT-takers scoring 26 or over	32%
	Freshmen returning for sophomore year	80%	ACT-takers scoring 30 or over	10%
	Students completing degree within 5 years	N/R	*Majors with most degrees conferred:* electrical engineering, nursing, accounting.	
	Grads pursuing further study	N/R		

Majors Accounting, art/fine arts, art history, biology/biological sciences, business, business economics, chemical engineering, chemistry, civil engineering, communication, computer engineering, computer science, economics, education, electrical engineering, elementary education, English, finance/banking, French, German, history, human development, industrial engineering, international business, management information systems, marketing/retailing/merchandising, mathematics, mechanical engineering, music, music education, nursing, optics, physics, political science/government, psychology, purchasing/inventory management, Russian and Slavic studies, secondary education, sociology, systems engineering.

Applying *Required:* high school transcript, SAT or ACT. *Recommended:* 3 years of high school math and science, some high school foreign language. Campus interview required for some. *Application deadlines:* 8/13, 4/1 priority date for financial aid. *Contact:* Ms. Sabrina Williams, Admissions Processing Supervisor, University Center 124, Huntsville, AL 35899, 205-895-6070 or toll-free 800-UAH-CALL (in-state).

From the College The University of Alabama in Huntsville, a space-grant university, is a comprehensive research institution located in one of the nation's leading research parks. UAH offers over fifty majors or programs of study from art and accounting to computer science and optical engineering. The more than 8,500 students enjoy both employment opportunities and campus activities.

University of Arizona

Tucson, Arizona

Founded 1885
Urban setting
State-supported
Coed
Awards B, M, D

Enrollment	35,220 total; 26,826 undergraduates (4,217 freshmen)
Faculty	1,652 total; 1,576 full-time (86% have doctorate/terminal degree); student-faculty ratio is 16:1; grad assistants teach about a quarter of the undergraduate courses.
Libraries	3.8 million bound volumes, 31,919 periodical subscriptions
Computing	*Terminals/PCs available for student use:* N/R; PC not required. Campus network links student PCs.
Of Special Interest	*Core academic program:* yes. Computer course required for business administration, public administration, engineering, mining, science majors. Phi Beta Kappa, Sigma Xi chapters. Academic exchange program: no. Sponsors and participates in study-abroad programs. Army ROTC, Naval ROTC, Air Force ROTC.
On Campus	Drama/theater group; student-run newspaper and radio station. *Social organizations:* 22 national fraternities, 13 national sororities; 12% of eligible undergraduate men and 12% of eligible undergraduate women are members.
Athletics	Member NCAA (Division I). *Intercollegiate sports:* baseball (M), basketball (M, W), cross-country running (M, W), football (M), golf (M, W), gymnastics (W), ice hockey (M), lacrosse (M), rugby (M), soccer (M), softball (W), swimming and diving (M, W), tennis (M, W), track and field (M, W), volleyball (M, W). *Scholarships:* M, W.

Costs (1991–92) & Aid				
	State resident tuition	$1580	8500 Need-based scholarships (average)	$1624
	Nonresident tuition	$6996	5293 Non-need scholarships (average)	$1705
	Mandatory fees	N/App	Short-term loans (average)	$1203
	Room and board	$3701	Long-term loans—college funds (average)	$2330
	Financial aid recipients	60%	Long-term loans—external funds (average)	$2500

Undergraduate Facts				
	Part-time	19%	*Freshman Data:* 13,003 applied, 85% were accepted, 38% (4,217) of those entered	
	State residents	71%		
	Transfers	29%	From top tenth of high school class	29%
	African-Americans	2%	SAT-takers scoring 600 or over on verbal	9%
	Native Americans	1%	SAT-takers scoring 700 or over on verbal	1%
	Hispanics	11%	SAT-takers scoring 600 or over on math	26%
	Asian-Americans	4%	SAT-takers scoring 700 or over on math	5%
	International students	7%	ACT-takers scoring 26 or over	27%
	Freshmen returning for sophomore year	76%	ACT-takers scoring 30 or over	6%
	Students completing degree within 5 years	44%		
	Grads pursuing further study	N/R		

Majors Accounting, aerospace engineering, agricultural economics, agricultural education, agricultural engineering, agricultural technologies, agronomy/soil and crop sciences, animal sciences, anthropology, architecture, art education, art/fine arts, art history, Asian/Oriental studies, astronomy, atmospheric sciences, biochemistry, biology/biological sciences, botany/plant sciences, business, business economics, cell biology, chemical engineering, chemistry, child care/child and family studies, child psychology/child development, city/community/regional planning, civil engineering, classics, communication, computer engineering, computer information systems, computer science, consumer services, creative writing, criminal justice, dance, early childhood education, earth science, East Asian studies, ecology/environmental studies, economics, education, electrical engineering, elementary education, energy management technologies, engineering physics, English, entomology, evolutionary biology, family and consumer studies, farm and ranch management, fashion merchandising, finance/banking, fish and game management, food sciences, food services management, French, geography, geological engineering, geology, German, Greek, health education, health services administration, history, home economics, home economics education, horticulture, humanities, human resources, human services, industrial engineering, information science, interdisciplinary studies, interior design, Italian, jazz, journalism, Judaic studies, Latin, Latin American studies, liberal arts/general studies, linguistics, management information systems, marine biology, marketing/retailing/merchandising, materials engineering, materials sciences, mathematics, mechanical engineering, medical technology, metallurgical engineering, Mexican-American/Chicano studies, microbiology, mining and mineral engineering, molecular biology, music, music education, music history, natural resource management, Near and Middle Eastern studies, nuclear engineering, nursing, nutrition, occupational safety and health, optics, parks management, pharmacy/pharmaceutical sciences, philosophy, photography, physical education, physics, piano/organ, planetary and space sciences, political science/government, Portuguese, psychology, public administration, radio and television studies, range management, real estate, recreation and leisure services, rehabilitation therapy, religious studies, Romance languages, Russian, Russian and Slavic studies, secondary education, social science, sociology, Spanish, speech pathology and audiology, speech/rhetoric/public address/debate, stringed instruments, studio art, systems engineering, textiles and clothing, theater arts/drama, urban studies, (pre)veterinary medicine sequence, veterinary sciences, voice, water resources, wildlife management, wind and percussion instruments, women's studies.

Applying *Required:* high school transcript, 3 years of high school math, SAT or ACT. *Recommended:* 3 years of high school science, some high school foreign language. 3 years of high school science required for some. *Application deadlines:* 4/1, 11/1 for early action, 3/1 priority date for financial aid. *Contact:* Mr. Jerome A. Lucido, Director of Admissions, Nugent Building, Tucson, AZ 85721, 602-621-3939.

University of California at Berkeley
Berkeley, California

Founded 1868
Urban setting
State-supported
Coed
Awards B, M, D

Enrollment	30,372 total; 21,660 undergraduates (3,226 freshmen)
Faculty	1,466 full-time (99% have doctorate/terminal degree); grad assistants teach a few undergraduate courses.
Libraries	7.6 million bound volumes, 4.3 million titles on microform, 104,000 periodical subscriptions
Computing	*Terminals/PCs available for student use:* N/R; PC not required but available for purchase.
Of Special Interest	*Core academic program:* yes. Computer course required for engineering, business majors. Phi Beta Kappa, Sigma Xi chapters. Academic exchange with Holy Name College, Mills College, Howard University, local state and community colleges. Sponsors and participates in study-abroad programs. Army ROTC, Naval ROTC, Air Force ROTC.
On Campus	Drama/theater group; student-run newspaper and radio station. *Social organizations:* national fraternities, national sororities; 14% of eligible undergraduate men and 13% of eligible undergraduate women are members.
Athletics	Member NCAA (Division I). *Intercollegiate sports:* baseball (M), basketball (M, W), crew (M, W), cross-country running (M, W), field hockey (W), football (M), golf (M, W), gymnastics (M, W), rugby (M), skiing (downhill) (M, W), soccer (M, W), softball (W), squash (M, W), swimming and diving (M, W), tennis (M, W), track and field (M, W), volleyball (M, W), water polo (M, W). *Scholarships:* M, W.

Costs (1991–92) & Aid				
	State resident tuition	$0	9889 Need-based scholarships (average)	$1263
	Nonresident tuition	$7699	2065 Non-need scholarships (average)	$653
	Mandatory fees	$2678	Short-term loans (average)	$250
	Room and board	$6050	Long-term loans—college funds (average)	$2309
	Financial aid recipients	48%	Long-term loans—external funds (average)	$2460

Undergraduate Facts				
	Part-time	0%	*Freshman Data:* 20,365 applied, 40% were accepted, 39% (3,226) of those entered	
	State residents	87%		
	Transfers	30%	From top tenth of high school class	95%
	African-Americans	7%	SAT-takers scoring 600 or over on verbal	40%
	Native Americans	1%	SAT-takers scoring 700 or over on verbal	7%
	Hispanics	15%	SAT-takers scoring 600 or over on math	72%
	Asian-Americans	30%	SAT-takers scoring 700 or over on math	39%
	International students	3%	ACT-takers scoring 26 or over	N/R
	Freshmen returning for sophomore year	90%	ACT-takers scoring 30 or over	N/R
	Students completing degree within 5 years	68%	*Majors with most degrees conferred:* biology/biological sciences, English, social science.	
	Grads pursuing further study	N/R		

Majors Anatomy, anthropology, applied mathematics, Arabic, architecture, art/fine arts, art history, Asian/Oriental studies, astrophysics, biochemistry, bioengineering, biology/biological sciences, biophysics, black/African-American studies, botany/plant sciences, business, cell biology, chemical engineering, chemistry, Chinese, civil engineering, classics, communication, comparative literature, computer engineering, computer science, conservation, dance, dietetics, earth science, East Asian studies, ecology/environmental studies, economics, electrical engineering, engineering physics, engineering sciences, English, entomology, environmental design, environmental sciences, ethnic studies, film studies, food sciences, forestry, forest technology, French, genetics, geography, geology, geophysical engineering, geophysics, German, Greek, Hebrew, history, industrial engineering, Italian, Japanese, landscape architecture/design, Latin, Latin American studies, legal studies, linguistics, literature, manufacturing engineering, materials sciences, mathematics, mechanical engineering, Mexican-American/Chicano studies, microbiology, mining and mineral engineering, molecular biology, music, Native American studies, natural resource management, naval architecture, Near and Middle Eastern studies, nuclear engineering, nutrition, operations research, optometry, paleontology, peace studies, petroleum/natural gas engineering, philosophy, physical education, physics, physiology, political science/government, Portuguese, psychology, religious studies, Russian and Slavic studies, Scandinavian languages/studies, Slavic languages, social science, sociology, Southeast Asian studies, Spanish, speech/rhetoric/public address/debate, statistics, theater arts/drama, women's studies, zoology.

Applying *Required:* essay, high school transcript, 3 years of high school math, 2 years of high school foreign language, SAT or ACT, 3 Achievements, English Composition Test. *Recommended:* 3 years of high school science. *Application deadlines:* 11/30, 3/2 priority date for financial aid. *Contact:* Office of Undergraduate Admission, 110 Sproul Hall, Berkeley, CA 94720, 510-642-0569.

University of California, Davis

Davis, California

Founded 1906
Suburban setting
State-supported
Coed
Awards B, M, D

Enrollment	23,302 total; 17,877 undergraduates (2,368 freshmen)
Faculty	1,626 total; 1,398 full-time (98% have doctorate/terminal degree); student-faculty ratio is 19:1; grad assistants teach a few undergraduate courses.
Libraries	2.4 million bound volumes, 3 million titles on microform, 52,000 periodical subscriptions
Computing	*Terminals/PCs available for student use:* 350, located in computer center, dormitories, many areas throughout campus; PC not required.
Of Special Interest	*Core academic program:* yes. Computer course required for engineering, math, statistics, some science majors. Phi Beta Kappa, Sigma Xi chapters. Academic exchange program: no. Sponsors study-abroad programs. Army ROTC.
On Campus	Drama/theater group; student-run newspaper and radio station. *Social organizations:* 29 national fraternities, 15 national sororities, 2 local fraternities, 3 local sororities; 15% of eligible undergraduate men and 13% of eligible undergraduate women are members.
Athletics	Member NCAA (Division II). *Intercollegiate sports:* baseball (M), basketball (M, W), cross-country running (M, W), football (M), golf (M), gymnastics (M, W), soccer (M, W), softball (W), swimming and diving (M, W), tennis (M, W), track and field (M, W), volleyball (M, W), water polo (M), wrestling (M).

Costs (1991–92) & Aid				
	State resident tuition	$0	3254 Need-based scholarships (average)	$1285
	Nonresident tuition	$7699	2509 Non-need scholarships (average)	$886
	Mandatory fees	$2430	Short-term loans (average)	$526
	Room and board	$5015	Long-term loans—college funds (average)	$1821
	Financial aid recipients	34%	Long-term loans—external funds (average)	$2600

Undergraduate Facts				
	Part-time	3%	*Freshman Data:* 16,509 applied, 49% were accepted, 29% (2,368) of those entered	
	State residents	92%		
	Transfers	15%	From top tenth of high school class	90%
	African-Americans	4%	SAT-takers scoring 600 or over on verbal	15%
	Native Americans	1%	SAT-takers scoring 700 or over on verbal	2%
	Hispanics	9%	SAT-takers scoring 600 or over on math	43%
	Asian-Americans	23%	SAT-takers scoring 700 or over on math	11%
	International students	1%	ACT-takers scoring 26 or over	N/R
	Freshmen returning for sophomore year	91%	ACT-takers scoring 30 or over	N/R
	Students completing degree within 5 years	61%	*Major with most degrees conferred:* psychology.	
	Grads pursuing further study	36%		

Majors Aerospace engineering, agricultural business, agricultural economics, agricultural education, agricultural engineering, agricultural sciences, agronomy/soil and crop sciences, American studies, animal sciences, anthropology, applied art, art/fine arts, art history, Asian/Oriental studies, atmospheric sciences, bacteriology, behavioral sciences, biochemistry, biology/biological sciences, biophysics, black/African-American studies, botany/plant sciences, chemical engineering, chemistry, child psychology/child development, Chinese, civil engineering, classics, comparative literature, computer engineering, computer science, dietetics, early childhood education, East Asian studies, ecology/environmental studies, economics, electrical engineering, engineering and applied sciences, English, entomology, environmental design, environmental sciences, ethnic studies, family and consumer studies, farm and ranch management, fish and game management, food sciences, food services management, French, genetics, geography, geology, German, Greek, history, human development, interdisciplinary studies, interior design, international studies, Italian, Japanese, landscape architecture/design, Latin, linguistics, materials engineering, materials sciences, mathematics, mechanical engineering, medieval studies, Mexican-American/Chicano studies, music, music education, music history, Native American studies, natural resource management, nutrition, philosophy, physical education, physical fitness/human movement, physics, physiology, political science/government, polymer science, poultry sciences, psychology, public affairs and policy studies, range management, religious studies, Russian, sociology, Spanish, speech/rhetoric/public address/debate, statistics, studio art, textile arts, textiles and clothing, theater arts/drama, water resources, wildlife biology, women's studies, zoology.

Applying *Required:* essay, high school transcript, 2 years of high school foreign language, SAT, 3 Achievements, English Composition Test (with essay). *Recommended:* 3 years of high school math and science. *Application deadlines:* 11/30, 3/2 priority date for financial aid. *Contact:* Dr. Gary Tudor, Director of Admissions, Mrak Hall, Davis, CA 95616, 916-752-2971.

University of California, Irvine

Irvine, California

Founded 1965
Suburban setting
State-supported
Coed
Awards B, M, D

Enrollment   16,949 total; 13,811 undergraduates (2,550 freshmen)

Faculty   743 total; grad assistants teach about a quarter of the undergraduate courses.

Libraries   1.5 million bound volumes, 1.8 million titles on microform, 19,500 periodical subscriptions

Computing   *Terminals/PCs available for student use:* 500, located in computer center, student center, library, departmental and computer labs; PC not required.

Of Special Interest   *Core academic program:* yes. Computer course required for social science, engineering, math majors. Phi Beta Kappa, Sigma Xi chapters. Academic exchange with other campuses of the University of California System. Sponsors study-abroad programs. Cooperative Army ROTC, cooperative Naval ROTC, cooperative Air Force ROTC.

On Campus   Drama/theater group; student-run newspaper and radio station. *Social organizations:* 16 national fraternities, 12 national sororities, 1 local fraternity, 1 local sorority; 13% of eligible undergraduate men and 13% of eligible undergraduate women are members.

Athletics   Member NCAA (Division I). *Intercollegiate sports:* baseball (M), basketball (M, W), crew (M), cross-country running (M, W), golf (M), sailing (M, W), soccer (M, W), swimming and diving (M, W), tennis (M, W), track and field (M, W), volleyball (M, W), water polo (M). *Scholarships:* M, W.

Costs (1991–92) & Aid			
State resident tuition	$0	2678 Need-based scholarships (average)	$1824
Nonresident tuition	$7699	367 Non-need scholarships (average)	$1325
Mandatory fees	$2524	Short-term loans (average)	$100
Room and board	$4993	Long-term loans—college funds (average)	$1449
Financial aid recipients	40%	Long-term loans—external funds (average)	$2361

Undergraduate Facts			
Part-time	N/R	*Freshman Data:* 14,563 applied, 19% were accepted, 94% (2,550) of those entered	
State residents	96%		
Transfers	29%	From top tenth of high school class	N/R
African-Americans	3%	SAT-takers scoring 600 or over on verbal	N/R
Native Americans	1%	SAT-takers scoring 700 or over on verbal	N/R
Hispanics	10%	SAT-takers scoring 600 or over on math	N/R
Asian-Americans	40%	SAT-takers scoring 700 or over on math	N/R
International students	3%	ACT-takers scoring 26 or over	N/R
Freshmen returning for sophomore year	N/R	ACT-takers scoring 30 or over	N/R
Students completing degree within 5 years	N/R	*Majors with most degrees conferred:* sociology, psychology, economics.	
Grads pursuing further study	N/R		

Majors   Anthropology, art/fine arts, art history, biology/biological sciences, business, chemistry, civil engineering, classics, comparative literature, computer science, dance, ecology/environmental studies, economics, electrical engineering, engineering (general), English, ethnic studies, film studies, French, geography, German, history, human ecology, humanities, information science, linguistics, literature, mathematics, mechanical engineering, music, philosophy, physics, political science/government, psychology, Russian, social science, sociology, Spanish, studio art, theater arts/drama.

Applying   *Required:* essay, high school transcript, 3 years of high school math, 2 years of high school foreign language, SAT or ACT, 3 Achievements, English Composition Test. *Recommended:* 3 years of high school science. *Application deadlines:* rolling, 3/2 priority date for financial aid. *Contact:* Dr. James Dunning, Director of Admissions, 260 Administration Building, Irvine, CA 92717, 714-856-6701.

University of California, Los Angeles
Los Angeles, California

Founded 1919
Urban setting
State-supported
Coed
Awards B, M, D

Enrollment	36,366 total; 24,368 undergraduates (3,984 freshmen)
Faculty	3,250 total; grad assistants teach no undergraduate courses.
Libraries	6.2 million bound volumes, 5.4 million titles on microform, 96,676 periodical subscriptions
Computing	*Terminals/PCs available for student use:* 475, located in computer center, library; PC not required.
Of Special Interest	*Core academic program:* yes. Computer course required for some majors. Phi Beta Kappa, Sigma Xi chapters. Academic exchange with University of Southern California. Sponsors study-abroad programs. Army ROTC, Naval ROTC, Air Force ROTC.
On Campus	Drama/theater group; student-run newspaper and radio station. *Social organizations:* 32 national fraternities, 18 national sororities, 2 local fraternities, 3 local sororities; 16% of eligible undergraduate men and 16% of eligible undergraduate women are members.
Athletics	Member NCAA (Division I). *Intercollegiate sports:* baseball (M), basketball (M, W), cross-country running (M, W), football (M), golf (M, W), gymnastics (M, W), soccer (M), softball (W), swimming and diving (M, W), tennis (M, W), track and field (M, W), volleyball (M, W), water polo (M). *Scholarships:* M, W.

Costs (1991–92) & Aid				
	State resident tuition	$0	8282 Need-based scholarships (average)	$5339
	Nonresident tuition	$7699	1115 Non-need scholarships (average)	$1500
	Mandatory fees	$2336	Short-term loans (average)	$100
	Room and board	$5230	Long-term loans—college funds (average)	$2000
	Financial aid recipients	39%	Long-term loans—external funds (average)	$4000

Undergraduate Facts				
	Part-time	0%	*Freshman Data:* 22,650 applied, 46% were accepted, 38% (3,984) of those entered	
	State residents	94%		
	Transfers	1%	From top tenth of high school class	N/R
	African-Americans	6%	SAT-takers scoring 600 or over on verbal	24%
	Native Americans	1%	SAT-takers scoring 700 or over on verbal	2%
	Hispanics	17%	SAT-takers scoring 600 or over on math	67%
	Asian-Americans	32%	SAT-takers scoring 700 or over on math	26%
	International students	2%	ACT-takers scoring 26 or over	N/R
	Freshmen returning for sophomore year	94%	ACT-takers scoring 30 or over	N/R
	Students completing degree within 5 years	66%	*Majors with most degrees conferred:* economics, psychology, political science/government.	
	Grads pursuing further study	N/R		

Majors Aerospace engineering, African languages, anthropology, applied art, applied mathematics, Arabic, art/fine arts, art history, astronomy, astrophysics, atmospheric sciences, biochemistry, biology/biological sciences, black/African-American studies, business economics, chemical engineering, chemistry, Chinese, civil engineering, classics, communication, computer engineering, computer science, dance, East Asian studies, economics, electrical engineering, engineering (general), engineering and applied sciences, English, film studies, French, geochemistry, geography, geological engineering, geology, geophysical engineering, geophysics, German, Greek, Hebrew, history, international economics, international studies, Italian, Japanese, Judaic studies, Latin, Latin American studies, linguistics, materials engineering, materials sciences, mathematics, mechanical engineering, Mexican-American/Chicano studies, microbiology, music, music education, music history, natural resource management, Near and Middle Eastern studies, nursing, philosophy, physical fitness/human movement, physics, planetary and space sciences, political science/government, Portuguese, psychobiology, psychology, radio and television studies, religious studies, Russian, Russian and Slavic studies, Scandinavian languages/studies, Slavic languages, sociology, Spanish, systems science, theater arts/drama, Western civilization and culture, women's studies.

Applying *Required:* essay, high school transcript, 3 years of high school math, 2 years of high school foreign language, SAT or ACT, 3 Achievements. *Recommended:* 3 years of high school science. *Application deadlines:* 11/30, 3/2 for financial aid. *Contact:* Dr. Rae Lee Siporin, Director of Undergraduate Admissions, 405 Hilgard Avenue, Los Angeles, CA 90024, 213-206-8331.

University of California, Riverside

Riverside, California

Founded 1954
Suburban setting
State-supported
Coed
Awards B, M, D

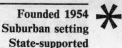

Enrollment	8,890 total; 7,310 undergraduates (1,434 freshmen)
Faculty	718 total; 571 full-time (98% have doctorate/terminal degree); student-faculty ratio is 14:1; grad assistants teach a few undergraduate courses.
Libraries	1.5 million bound volumes, 1.2 million titles on microform, 14,000 periodical subscriptions
Computing	*Terminals/PCs available for student use:* 170, located in computer center, student center, library, dormitories, other campus locations; PC not required. Campus network links student PCs.
Of Special Interest	*Core academic program:* yes. Computer course required for statistics, math, business administration, political science, environmental science, engineering majors. Phi Beta Kappa, Sigma Xi chapters. Academic exchange program: no. Sponsors and participates in study-abroad programs. Cooperative Army ROTC, cooperative Air Force ROTC.
On Campus	Drama/theater group; student-run newspaper and radio station. *Social organizations:* 10 national fraternities, 9 national sororities; 14% of eligible undergraduate men and 17% of eligible undergraduate women are members.
Athletics	Member NCAA (Division II). *Intercollegiate sports:* baseball (M), basketball (M, W), cross-country running (M, W), softball (W), swimming and diving (M, W), tennis (M, W), track and field (M, W), volleyball (W), water polo (M). *Scholarships:* M, W.

Costs (1991–92) & Aid	State resident tuition	$0	Need-based scholarships	Avail
	Nonresident tuition	$7701	Non-need scholarships	Avail
	Mandatory fees	$2373	Short-term loans	Avail
	Room and board	$5360	Long-term loans—college funds	Avail
	Financial aid recipients	45%	Long-term loans—external funds	Avail
Undergraduate Facts	Part-time	4%	*Freshman Data:* 9,675 applied, 73% were accepted, 20% (1,434) of those entered	
	State residents	98%		
	Transfers	20%	From top tenth of high school class	N/R
	African-Americans	3%	SAT-takers scoring 600 or over on verbal	9%
	Native Americans	1%	SAT-takers scoring 700 or over on verbal	1%
	Hispanics	11%	SAT-takers scoring 600 or over on math	30%
	Asian-Americans	28%	SAT-takers scoring 700 or over on math	5%
	International students	1%	ACT-takers scoring 26 or over	N/R
	Freshmen returning for sophomore year	89%	ACT-takers scoring 30 or over	N/R
	Students completing degree within 5 years	58%	*Majors with most degrees conferred:* business, biology/biological sciences, psychology.	
	Grads pursuing further study	45%		

Majors Agronomy/soil and crop sciences, anthropology, art/fine arts, art history, biochemistry, biology/biological sciences, biomedical sciences, botany/plant sciences, business, business economics, chemical engineering, chemistry, classics, comparative literature, computer science, creative writing, dance, economics, electrical engineering, engineering and applied sciences, English, entomology, environmental engineering, environmental sciences, ethnic studies, French, geography, geology, geophysics, German, history, human development, humanities, Latin American studies, (pre)law sequence, liberal arts/general studies, linguistics, mathematics, modern languages, music, philosophy, physical sciences, physics, political science/government, psychobiology, psychology, religious studies, Russian and Slavic studies, sociology, Spanish, statistics, studio art, theater arts/drama, women's studies.

Applying *Required:* essay, high school transcript, 3 years of high school math, 2 years of high school foreign language, SAT or ACT, 3 Achievements, English Composition Test. *Recommended:* 3 years of high school science. *Application deadlines:* 11/30, 3/2 priority date for financial aid. *Contact:* Ms. Marion McCarthy, Associate Admissions Officer, 900 University Avenue, Riverside, CA 92521, 714-787-3411.

University of California, San Diego
La Jolla, California

Founded 1959
Suburban setting
State-supported
Coed
Awards B, M, D

Enrollment 17,966 total; 14,529 undergraduates (2,521 freshmen)

Faculty 1,161 total; 926 full-time (97% have doctorate/terminal degree); student-faculty ratio is 18:1; grad assistants teach a few undergraduate courses.

Libraries 2.1 million bound volumes, 2 million titles on microform, 23,784 periodical subscriptions

Computing *Terminals/PCs available for student use:* 500, located in computer center, student center, library, each academic college; PC not required.

Of Special Interest *Core academic program:* yes. Computer course required for applied mechanics, engineering sciences, quantitative sciences, electrical engineering, psychology, economics majors. Phi Beta Kappa, Sigma Xi chapters. Academic exchange with Dartmouth College, San Diego State University, Spelman College, Morehouse College. Sponsors and participates in study-abroad programs. Cooperative Army ROTC, cooperative Naval ROTC, cooperative Air Force ROTC.

On Campus Drama/theater group; student-run newspaper and radio station. *Social organizations:* 14 national fraternities, 8 national sororities; 12% of eligible undergraduate men and 8% of eligible undergraduate women are members.

Athletics Member NCAA (Division III). *Intercollegiate sports:* baseball (M), basketball (M, W), crew (M, W), cross-country running (M, W), fencing (M, W), golf (M, W), soccer (M, W), softball (W), swimming and diving (M, W), tennis (M, W), track and field (M, W), volleyball (M, W), water polo (M, W).

Costs (1991–92) & Aid				
State resident tuition	$0	2971 Need-based scholarships (average)	$1520
Nonresident tuition	$7699	Non-need scholarships (average)	$1120
Mandatory fees	$2463	Short-term loans (average)	$150
Room and board	$6152	Long-term loans—college funds (average)	$1563
Financial aid recipients	36%	Long-term loans—external funds (average)	$3300

Undergraduate Facts			
Part-time	1%	*Freshman Data:* 19,109 applied, 56% were accepted, 24% (2,521) of those entered	
State residents	92%		
Transfers	25%	From top tenth of high school class	95%
African-Americans	3%	SAT-takers scoring 600 or over on verbal	18%
Native Americans	1%	SAT-takers scoring 700 or over on verbal	2%
Hispanics	10%	SAT-takers scoring 600 or over on math	59%
Asian-Americans	21%	SAT-takers scoring 700 or over on math	15%
International students	2%	ACT-takers scoring 26 or over	N/R
Freshmen returning for sophomore year	91%	ACT-takers scoring 30 or over	N/R
Students completing degree within 5 years	56%	*Majors with most degrees conferred:* biology/biological sciences, economics, political science/government.	
Grads pursuing further study	31%		

Majors Anthropology, applied mathematics, architecture, art/fine arts, art history, Asian/Oriental studies, biochemistry, bioengineering, biology/biological sciences, biophysics, cell biology, chemical engineering, chemistry, Chinese, classics, cognitive science, communication, computer engineering, computer science, creative writing, earth science, ecology/environmental studies, economics, electrical engineering, engineering (general), engineering and applied sciences, engineering physics, engineering sciences, English, ethnic studies, evolutionary biology, experimental psychology, film studies, French, German, Germanic languages and literature, history, information science, interdisciplinary studies, international studies, Italian, Judaic studies, linguistics, literature, mathematics, mechanical engineering, microbiology, molecular biology, music, music history, philosophy, photography, physics, physiology, political science/government, psychology, religious studies, Russian, sociology, Spanish, studio art, systems engineering, systems science, theater arts/drama, urban studies.

Applying *Required:* essay, high school transcript, 3 years of high school math, 2 years of high school foreign language, SAT or ACT, 3 Achievements, English Composition Test. *Recommended:* 3 years of high school science. *Application deadlines:* 11/30, continuous to 5/1 for financial aid. *Contact:* Ms. Victoria Valle Staples, Director, Student Outreach and Recruitment, La Jolla, CA 92093, 619-534-4831; *Office location:* 9500 Gilman Drive.

University of California, Santa Barbara
Santa Barbara, California

Founded 1891
Suburban setting
State-supported
Coed
Awards B, M, D

Enrollment 18,519 total; 16,176 undergraduates (2,977 freshmen)

Faculty 985 total; 705 full-time (95% have doctorate/terminal degree); student-faculty ratio is 19:1; grad assistants teach a few undergraduate courses.

Libraries 2 million bound volumes, 21,400 periodical subscriptions

Computing *Terminals/PCs available for student use:* 2,000, located in computer center, library, departmental labs; PC not required.

Of Special Interest *Core academic program:* yes. Computer course required for engineering, economics/math majors. Phi Beta Kappa, Sigma Xi chapters. Academic exchange program: no. Sponsors and participates in study-abroad programs. Army ROTC.

On Campus Drama/theater group; student-run newspaper and radio station. *Social organizations:* 12 national fraternities, 12 national sororities; 12% of eligible undergraduate men and 18% of eligible undergraduate women are members.

Athletics Member NCAA (Division I). *Intercollegiate sports:* baseball (M), basketball (M, W), crew (M, W), cross-country running (M, W), football (M), golf (M, W), gymnastics (M, W), lacrosse (M), rugby (M, W), soccer (M, W), softball (W), swimming and diving (M, W), tennis (M, W), track and field (M, W), volleyball (M, W), water polo (M). *Scholarships:* M, W.

Costs (1991–92) & Aid
State resident tuition	$0	
Nonresident tuition	$7699	
Mandatory fees	$2403	
Room and board	$5548	
Financial aid recipients	33%	
3803 Need-based scholarships (average)		$1746
68 Non-need scholarships (average)		$1632
Short-term loans (average)		$548
Long-term loans—college funds (average)		$775
Long-term loans—external funds (average)		$2790

Undergraduate Facts
Part-time	2%
State residents	94%
Transfers	28%
African-Americans	3%
Native Americans	1%
Hispanics	11%
Asian-Americans	12%
International students	1%
Freshmen returning for sophomore year	87%
Students completing degree within 5 years	57%
Grads pursuing further study	26%

Freshman Data: 18,078 applied, 68% were accepted, 24% (2,977) of those entered

From top tenth of high school class	N/R
SAT-takers scoring 600 or over on verbal	9%
SAT-takers scoring 700 or over on verbal	1%
SAT-takers scoring 600 or over on math	38%
SAT-takers scoring 700 or over on math	5%
ACT-takers scoring 26 or over	N/R
ACT-takers scoring 30 or over	N/R

Majors Anthropology, archaeology, art/fine arts, art history, Asian/Oriental studies, biochemistry, biology/biological sciences, black/African-American studies, botany/plant sciences, business economics, cell biology, chemical engineering, chemistry, Chinese, classics, communication, comparative literature, computer engineering, computer science, creative writing, criminal justice, dance, East Asian studies, East European and Soviet studies, ecology/environmental studies, economics, electrical engineering, English, environmental biology, environmental engineering, evolutionary biology, film studies, French, geography, geology, geophysics, Germanic languages and literature, Greek, Hispanic studies, history, interdisciplinary studies, Italian, Japanese, Latin, Latin American studies, legal studies, liberal arts/general studies, linguistics, literature, marine biology, mathematics, mechanical engineering, medieval studies, Mexican-American/Chicano studies, microbiology, molecular biology, music, nuclear engineering, pharmacology, philosophy, physics, physiology, political science/government, Portuguese, psychology, religious studies, Russian and Slavic studies, Slavic languages, sociology, Spanish, speech pathology and audiology, statistics, studio art, theater arts/drama, women's studies, zoology.

Applying *Required:* essay, high school transcript, 2 years of high school foreign language, 4 years of high school English, 1 year of high school U.S. History, SAT or ACT, 3 Achievements, English Composition Test. *Recommended:* 3 years of high school math and science, 3 years of high school foreign language. Interview required for some. *Application deadlines:* 11/30, 3/2 priority date for financial aid. *Contact:* Mr. William Villa, Director of Admissions/Relations with Schools, 1234 Cheadle Hall, Santa Barbara, CA 93106, 805-893-2485.

University of California, Santa Cruz
Santa Cruz, California

Founded 1965
Small-town setting
State-supported
Coed
Awards B, M, D

Enrollment	10,136 total; 9,161 undergraduates (1,791 freshmen)
Faculty	559 total; 405 full-time (98% have doctorate/terminal degree); student-faculty ratio is 19:1; grad assistants teach a few undergraduate courses.
Libraries	1 million bound volumes, 531,416 titles on microform, 13,190 periodical subscriptions
Computing	*Terminals/PCs available for student use:* 200, located in computer center, student center, each academic college; PC not required.
Of Special Interest	*Core academic program:* yes. Computer course required for economics majors. Phi Beta Kappa chapter. Academic exchange with other campuses of the University of California System, University of New Hampshire. Sponsors and participates in study-abroad programs.
On Campus	Drama/theater group; student-run newspaper and radio station. No national or local fraternities or sororities on campus.
Athletics	Member NCAA (Division III). *Intercollegiate sports:* basketball (M, W), cross-country running (M, W), fencing (M, W), sailing (M, W), soccer (M), swimming and diving (M, W), tennis (M, W), volleyball (M, W), water polo (M, W).

Costs (1992–93) & Aid				
State resident tuition	$0	2956 Need-based scholarships (average)	$4410
Nonresident tuition	$7699	197 Non-need scholarships (average)	$2817
Mandatory fees	$2573	Short-term loans (average)	$500
Room and board	$5805	Long-term loans—college funds (average)	$1740
Financial aid recipients	54%	Long-term loans—external funds (average)	$3300

Undergraduate Facts			
Part-time	4%	*Freshman Data:* 11,377 applied, 67% were accepted, 23% (1,791) of those entered	
State residents	97%		
Transfers	30%	From top tenth of high school class	98%
African-Americans	3%	SAT-takers scoring 600 or over on verbal	24%
Native Americans	1%	SAT-takers scoring 700 or over on verbal	3%
Hispanics	8%	SAT-takers scoring 600 or over on math	35%
Asian-Americans	8%	SAT-takers scoring 700 or over on math	5%
International students	2%	ACT-takers scoring 26 or over	N/R
Freshmen returning for sophomore year	88%	ACT-takers scoring 30 or over	N/R
Students completing degree within 5 years	44%	*Majors with most degrees conferred:* biology/ biological sciences, psychology, literature.	
Grads pursuing further study	50%		

Majors American studies, anthropology, applied mathematics, art/fine arts, art history, biochemistry, biology/biological sciences, botany/plant sciences, business economics, cell biology, chemistry, classics, clinical psychology, comparative literature, computer engineering, computer science, creative writing, dance, earth science, East Asian studies, ecology/environmental studies, economics, English, environmental sciences, ethnic studies, evolutionary biology, experimental psychology, film studies, French, geology, geophysics, German, Greek, history, information science, Italian, Japanese, Latin American studies, legal studies, linguistics, literature, marine biology, mathematics, medieval studies, molecular biology, music, painting/drawing, peace studies, philosophy, photography, physics, political science/government, psychobiology, psychology, religious studies, Russian, Russian and Slavic studies, sociology, South Asian studies, Southeast Asian studies, Spanish, studio art, theater arts/drama, Western civilization and culture, women's studies.

Applying *Required:* essay, high school transcript, 3 years of high school math, 2 years of high school foreign language, SAT or ACT, 3 Achievements, English Composition Test. *Recommended:* 3 years of high school science. 3 recommendations, interview required for some. *Application deadlines:* 11/30, 3/2 priority date for financial aid. *Contact:* Mr. Joseph P. Allen, Dean of Admissions, Admissions Office, Cook House, Santa Cruz, CA 95064, 408-459-2705.

University of Chicago

Chicago, Illinois

Founded 1891
Urban setting
Independent
Coed
Awards B, M, D

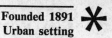

Enrollment	9,432 total; 3,440 undergraduates (850 freshmen)
Faculty	1,490 total—all full-time (100% have doctorate/terminal degree); student-faculty ratio is 3:1; grad assistants teach a few undergraduate courses.
Libraries	5.2 million bound volumes, 1.5 million titles on microform, 48,000 periodical subscriptions
Computing	*Terminals/PCs available for student use:* 600, located in computer center, library, dormitories, classroom buildings; PC not required but available for purchase. Campus network links student PCs.
Of Special Interest	*Core academic program:* yes. Computer course required for applied math, statistics majors. Phi Beta Kappa, Sigma Xi chapters. Academic exchange with Committee on Institutional Cooperation, Associated Colleges of the Midwest. Sponsors and participates in study-abroad programs. Cooperative Army ROTC, cooperative Air Force ROTC.
On Campus	Drama/theater group; student-run newspaper and radio station. *Social organizations:* 9 national fraternities, 2 national sororities; 10% of eligible undergraduate men and 3% of eligible undergraduate women are members.
Athletics	Member NCAA (Division III). *Intercollegiate sports:* baseball (M), basketball (M, W), cross-country running (M, W), fencing (M), football (M), soccer (M, W), softball (W), swimming and diving (M, W), tennis (M, W), track and field (M, W), volleyball (W), wrestling (M).

Costs (1991–92) & Aid	Comprehensive fee	$21,897	Need-based scholarships (average)	$9228
	Tuition	$15,945	Non-need scholarships (average)	$8278
	Mandatory fees	$267	Short-term loans	N/Avail
	Room and board	$5685	Long-term loans—college funds (average)	$1958
	Financial aid recipients	80%	Long-term loans—external funds (average)	$2218

Undergraduate Facts	Part-time	1%	*Freshman Data:* 6,042 applied, 45% were accepted, 31% (850) of those entered	
	State residents	25%		
	Transfers	8%	From top tenth of high school class	69%
	African-Americans	4%	SAT-takers scoring 600 or over on verbal	65%
	Native Americans	1%	SAT-takers scoring 700 or over on verbal	20%
	Hispanics	3%	SAT-takers scoring 600 or over on math	83%
	Asian-Americans	19%	SAT-takers scoring 700 or over on math	39%
	International students	3%	ACT-takers scoring 26 or over	83%
	Freshmen returning for sophomore year	93%	ACT-takers scoring 30 or over	42%
	Students completing degree within 5 years	82%	*Majors with most degrees conferred:* economics, biology/biological sciences, political science/government.	
	Grads pursuing further study	41%		

Majors African studies, anthropology, applied mathematics, Arabic, art/fine arts, art history, Asian/Oriental studies, behavioral sciences, biochemistry, biology/biological sciences, black/African-American studies, chemistry, Chinese, classics, creative writing, East Asian studies, East European and Soviet studies, economics, English, French, geography, geophysics, German, Germanic languages and literature, Greek, history, history of science, humanities, interdisciplinary studies, Italian, Japanese, Latin, Latin American studies, linguistics, mathematics, medieval studies, modern languages, music, music history, Near and Middle Eastern studies, philosophy, physics, political science/government, psychology, public affairs and policy studies, religious studies, Romance languages, Russian, Russian and Slavic studies, Slavic languages, social science, sociology, Southeast Asian studies, Spanish, statistics, studio art.

Applying *Required:* essay, high school transcript, 2 recommendations, SAT or ACT. *Recommended:* 3 years of high school math and science, some high school foreign language, interview. *Application deadlines:* 1/15, 11/15 for early decision, 2/1 priority date for financial aid. *Contact:* Mr. Theodore O'Neill, Dean of Admissions, 1116 East 59th Street, Chicago, IL 60637, 312-702-8650.

From the College The University has just celebrated the centennial of its founding. The renowned Common Core Curriculum remains at the heart of the institution. In addition to attending small discussion classes, students have many opportunities to work on faculty research projects. A film studies center has just opened, and construction is under way for a new college and medical school biology learning center.

University of Colorado at Boulder

Boulder, Colorado

Founded 1876
Suburban setting
State-supported
Coed
Awards B, M, D

Enrollment	25,571 total; 20,495 undergraduates (3,444 freshmen)
Faculty	1,093 total; 1,006 full-time (91% have doctorate/terminal degree); student-faculty ratio is 19:1; grad assistants teach a few undergraduate courses.
Libraries	2.3 million bound volumes, 4 million titles on microform, 25,788 periodical subscriptions
Computing	*Terminals/PCs available for student use:* 820, located in computer center, library, dormitories, classroom buildings; PC not required.
Of Special Interest	*Core academic program:* no. Computer course required for business, engineering majors. Phi Beta Kappa, Sigma Xi chapters. Academic exchange with other units in the University of Colorado System. Sponsors and participates in study-abroad programs. Army ROTC, Naval ROTC, Air Force ROTC.
On Campus	Drama/theater group; student-run newspaper and radio station. *Social organizations:* 27 national fraternities, 15 national sororities; 14% of eligible undergraduate men and 18% of eligible undergraduate women are members.
Athletics	Member NCAA (Division I). *Intercollegiate sports:* baseball (M), basketball (M, W), bowling (M, W), cross-country running (M, W), fencing (M, W), field hockey (W), football (M), golf (M), ice hockey (M), lacrosse (M, W), rugby (M, W), skiing (cross-country) (M, W), skiing (downhill) (M, W), soccer (M, W), swimming and diving (M, W), tennis (M, W), track and field (M, W), volleyball (W), wrestling (M). *Scholarships:* M, W.

Costs (1991–92) & Aid				
	State resident tuition	$1972	4799 Need-based scholarships (average)	$2950
	Nonresident tuition	$9900	1387 Non-need scholarships (average)	$2568
	Mandatory fees	$451	Short-term loans	Avail
	Room and board	$3540	Long-term loans—college funds	Avail
	Financial aid recipients	40%	Long-term loans—external funds	Avail

Undergraduate Facts				
	Part-time	8%	*Freshman Data:* 14,344 applied, 69% were accepted, 35% (3,444) of those entered	
	State residents	67%		
	Transfers	9%	From top tenth of high school class	30%
	African-Americans	2%	SAT-takers scoring 600 or over on verbal	N/R
	Native Americans	1%	SAT-takers scoring 700 or over on verbal	N/R
	Hispanics	5%	SAT-takers scoring 600 or over on math	N/R
	Asian-Americans	5%	SAT-takers scoring 700 or over on math	N/R
	International students	1%	ACT-takers scoring 26 or over	N/R
	Freshmen returning for sophomore year	82%	ACT-takers scoring 30 or over	N/R
	Students completing degree within 5 years	58%		
	Grads pursuing further study	N/R		

Majors Accounting, advertising, aerospace engineering, American studies, anthropology, applied mathematics, architectural engineering, art education, art/fine arts, art history, Asian/Oriental studies, biology/biological sciences, black/African-American studies, broadcasting, business, cell biology, chemical engineering, chemistry, Chinese, civil engineering, classics, communication, computer engineering, computer information systems, computer science, conservation, dance, (pre)dentistry sequence, East European and Soviet studies, ecology/environmental studies, economics, electrical engineering, engineering physics, English, environmental biology, environmental design, film studies, finance/banking, French, geography, geology, German, Greek, history, humanities, human resources, interdisciplinary studies, international business, international studies, Italian, Japanese, journalism, labor and industrial relations, Latin, Latin American studies, linguistics, management information systems, marketing/retailing/merchandising, mathematics, mechanical engineering, (pre)medicine sequence, microbiology, molecular biology, music, music business, music education, music history, operations research, pharmacy/pharmaceutical sciences, philosophy, physical education, physical fitness/human movement, physics, political science/government, psychology, public administration, public relations, radio and television studies, real estate, recreational facilities management, religious studies, Russian, Russian and Slavic studies, sociology, Spanish, speech pathology and audiology, studio art, theater arts/drama, tourism and travel, transportation engineering, (pre)veterinary medicine sequence, women's studies.

Applying *Required:* high school transcript, 3 years of high school math and science, 2 years of high school foreign language, SAT or ACT. *Recommended:* essay, 3 recommendations. 4 years of high school math, 3 years of high school foreign language required for some. *Application deadlines:* 2/15, 4/1 priority date for financial aid. *Contact:* Admissions Counselor, Campus Box 30, Boulder, CO 80309, 303-492-6301; *Office location:* Regent Administrative Center 125.

University of Connecticut

Storrs, Connecticut

Founded 1881
Rural setting
State-supported
Coed
Awards B, M, D

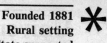

Enrollment 17,127 total; 12,621 undergraduates (2,174 freshmen)

Faculty 1,250 total; 1,211 full-time (90% have doctorate/terminal degree); student-faculty ratio is 14:1; grad assistants teach a few undergraduate courses.

Libraries 1.7 million bound volumes, 2.3 million titles on microform, 9,000 periodical subscriptions

Computing *Terminals/PCs available for student use:* 1,800, located in computer center, student center, library, dormitories, departmental labs; PC not required. Campus network links student PCs.

Of Special Interest *Core academic program:* yes. Computer course required. Phi Beta Kappa, Sigma Xi chapters. Academic exchange with other public institutions in Connecticut. Sponsors and participates in study-abroad programs. Army ROTC, Air Force ROTC.

On Campus Drama/theater group; student-run newspaper and radio station. *Social organizations:* 16 national fraternities, 9 national sororities, local fraternities, local sororities; 10% of eligible undergraduate men and 10% of eligible undergraduate women are members.

Athletics Member NCAA (Division I). *Intercollegiate sports:* baseball (M), basketball (M, W), cross-country running (M, W), field hockey (W), football (M), golf (M), ice hockey (M), soccer (M, W), softball (W), swimming and diving (M, W), tennis (M, W), track and field (M, W), volleyball (W). *Scholarships:* M, W.

Costs (1991–92) & Aid				
State resident tuition	$2786	3586 Need-based scholarships (average)	$1714
Nonresident tuition	$8496	400 Non-need scholarships (average)	$5959
Mandatory fees	$677	Short-term loans	N/Avail
Room and board	$4522	Long-term loans—college funds	N/Avail
Financial aid recipients	48%	Long-term loans—external funds (average)	$3481

Undergraduate Facts

Part-time	6%	*Freshman Data:* 11,609 applied, 62% were accepted, 30% (2,174) of those entered	
State residents	88%		
Transfers	12%	From top tenth of high school class	25%
African-Americans	4%	SAT-takers scoring 600 or over on verbal	9%
Native Americans	1%	SAT-takers scoring 700 or over on verbal	1%
Hispanics	3%	SAT-takers scoring 600 or over on math	29%
Asian-Americans	4%	SAT-takers scoring 700 or over on math	4%
International students	1%	ACT-takers scoring 26 or over	N/App
Freshmen returning for sophomore year	87%	ACT-takers scoring 30 or over	N/App
Students completing degree within 5 years	62%	*Majors with most degrees conferred:* English, economics, psychology.	
Grads pursuing further study	15%		

Majors Accounting, actuarial science, agricultural economics, agricultural education, agricultural sciences, agronomy/soil and crop sciences, animal sciences, anthropology, applied mathematics, art/fine arts, art history, biology/biological sciences, biophysics, ceramic art and design, chemical engineering, chemistry, civil engineering, classics, communication, computer engineering, cytotechnology, (pre)dentistry sequence, dietetics, East European and Soviet studies, economics, education, electrical engineering, elementary education, English, family and consumer studies, finance/banking, French, geography, geology, geophysics, German, graphic arts, health services administration, history, horticulture, human development, insurance, Italian, journalism, landscape architecture/design, Latin American studies, (pre)law sequence, linguistics, management information systems, marketing/retailing/merchandising, mathematics, mechanical engineering, medical laboratory technology, medical technology, (pre)medicine sequence, modern languages, molecular biology, music, music education, music history, natural resource management, nursing, nutrition, painting/drawing, pharmacy/pharmaceutical sciences, philosophy, photography, physical education, physical therapy, physics, physiology, piano/organ, political science/government, Portuguese, psychology, real estate, recreation and leisure services, rehabilitation therapy, Russian, Russian and Slavic studies, sculpture, secondary education, sociology, Spanish, special education, statistics, studio art, theater arts/drama, urban studies, (pre)veterinary medicine sequence, voice, wind and percussion instruments, women's studies.

Applying *Required:* high school transcript, 3 years of high school math, 2 years of high school foreign language, SAT. *Recommended:* essay, recommendations. 3 years of high school science required for some. *Application deadlines:* 4/1, 2/15 priority date for financial aid. *Contact:* Dr. Ann L. Huckenbeck, Director of Admissions, 28 North Eagleville Road, Storrs, CT 06269-3088, 203-486-3137.

From the College The University of Connecticut is a study in contrasts. Students will find small-school opportunities at a major university. They can also find a tremendous liberal arts college amid impressive professional programs. The variety of majors, clubs, and people ensures that everyone is able to find a niche.

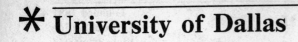

University of Dallas

Irving, Texas

Founded 1956
Suburban setting
Independent, Roman Catholic
Coed
Awards B, M, D

Enrollment 2,995 total; 1,162 undergraduates (284 freshmen)

Faculty 116 total; 77 full-time; student-faculty ratio is 12:1; grad assistants teach no undergraduate courses.

Libraries 278,699 bound volumes, 16,728 titles on microform, 738 periodical subscriptions

Computing *Terminals/PCs available for student use:* 50, located in science buildings; PC not required.

Of Special Interest *Core academic program:* yes. Phi Beta Kappa chapter. Academic exchange program. Sponsors study-abroad programs. Cooperative Army ROTC, cooperative Air Force ROTC.

On Campus Drama/theater group; student-run newspaper. No national or local fraternities or sororities on campus.

Athletics Member NAIA. *Intercollegiate sports:* basketball (M, W), rugby (M), tennis (M, W).

Costs (1991–92) & Aid				
	Comprehensive fee	$13,388	Need-based scholarships (average)	$1506
	Tuition	$8150	Non-need scholarships (average)	$2796
	Mandatory fees	$450	Short-term loans	N/Avail
	Room and board	$4788	Long-term loans—college funds	N/Avail
	Financial aid recipients	81%	Long-term loans—external funds (average)	$2817

Undergraduate Facts				
	Part-time	7%	*Freshman Data:* 612 applied, 89% were accepted, 52% (284) of those entered	
	State residents	64%		
	Transfers	7%	From top tenth of high school class	50%
	African-Americans	2%	SAT-takers scoring 600 or over on verbal	23%
	Native Americans	1%	SAT-takers scoring 700 or over on verbal	3%
	Hispanics	11%	SAT-takers scoring 600 or over on math	33%
	Asian-Americans	7%	SAT-takers scoring 700 or over on math	7%
	International students	4%	ACT-takers scoring 26 or over	50%
	Freshmen returning for sophomore year	81%	ACT-takers scoring 30 or over	13%
	Students completing degree within 5 years	54%	*Majors with most degrees conferred:* English, history, biology/biological sciences.	
	Grads pursuing further study	50%		

Majors Art education, art/fine arts, art history, biochemistry, biology/biological sciences, business, chemistry, classics, economics, education, elementary education, English, French, German, history, (pre)law sequence, mathematics, (pre)medicine sequence, philosophy, physics, political science/government, psychology, secondary education, Spanish, theater arts/drama, theology, (pre)veterinary medicine sequence.

Applying *Required:* essay, high school transcript, 1 recommendation, SAT or ACT. *Recommended:* 3 years of high school math and science, 2 years of high school foreign language, interview. *Application deadlines:* 8/1, 12/1 for early action, 3/1 priority date for financial aid. *Contact:* Ms. Jennifer Hantho, Dean of Admissions and Financial Aid, 1845 East Northgate Drive, Irving, TX 75062, 214-721-5266.

University of Delaware

Newark, Delaware

Founded 1743
Small-town setting
State-related
Coed
Awards A, B, M, D

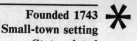

Enrollment 17,323 total; 14,655 undergraduates (3,225 freshmen)

Faculty 963 total; 922 full-time (80% have doctorate/terminal degree); student-faculty ratio is 17:1; grad assistants teach a few undergraduate courses.

Libraries 2 million bound volumes, 2.1 million titles on microform, 23,000 periodical subscriptions

Computing *Terminals/PCs available for student use:* 605, located in computer center, library, dormitories, 32 sites throughout campus; PC not required but available for purchase. Campus network links student PCs.

Of Special Interest *Core academic program:* yes. Computer course required for engineering, business, economics, math, agriculture majors. Phi Beta Kappa, Sigma Xi chapters. Academic exchange with over 100 members of the National Student Exchange. Sponsors and participates in study-abroad programs. Army ROTC, Air Force ROTC.

On Campus Drama/theater group; student-run newspaper and radio station. *Social organizations:* 17 national fraternities, 13 national sororities; 17% of eligible undergraduate men and 12% of eligible undergraduate women are members.

Athletics Member NCAA (Division I). *Intercollegiate sports:* baseball (M), basketball (M, W), cross-country running (M, W), field hockey (W), football (M), golf (M), lacrosse (M, W), soccer (M, W), softball (W), swimming and diving (M, W), tennis (M, W), track and field (M, W), volleyball (W). *Scholarships:* M, W.

Costs (1991–92) & Aid				
State resident tuition	$3220	2080 Need-based scholarships (average)	$2150
Nonresident tuition	$8390	2110 Non-need scholarships (average)	$3000
Mandatory fees	$331	Short-term loans (average)	$100
Room and board	$3540	Long-term loans—college funds	N/Avail
Financial aid recipients	47%	Long-term loans—external funds (average)	$2800

Undergraduate Facts			
Part-time	9%	*Freshman Data:* 13,051 applied, 69% were accepted, 36% (3,225) of those entered	
State residents	39%		
Transfers	3%	From top tenth of high school class	22%
African-Americans	4%	SAT-takers scoring 600 or over on verbal	9%
Native Americans	0%	SAT-takers scoring 700 or over on verbal	1%
Hispanics	1%	SAT-takers scoring 600 or over on math	30%
Asian-Americans	2%	SAT-takers scoring 700 or over on math	4%
International students	1%	ACT-takers scoring 26 or over	N/App
Freshmen returning for sophomore year	84%	ACT-takers scoring 30 or over	N/App
Students completing degree within 5 years	67%	*Majors with most degrees conferred:* business, psychology, English.	
Grads pursuing further study	17%		

Majors Accounting, agricultural business, agricultural economics, agricultural education, agricultural engineering, agricultural sciences, agronomy/soil and crop sciences, American studies, animal sciences, anthropology, applied art, art education, art/fine arts, art history, astronomy, biochemistry, biology/biological sciences, biotechnology, black/African-American studies, botany/plant sciences, business, business economics, chemical engineering, chemistry, child care/child and family studies, child psychology/child development, civil engineering, classics, cognitive science, communication, community services, comparative literature, computer science, criminal justice, (pre)dentistry sequence, dietetics, early childhood education, East Asian studies, ecology/environmental studies, economics, education, electrical engineering, elementary education, English, entomology, environmental engineering, environmental engineering technology, environmental sciences, family and consumer studies, family services, fashion design and technology, fashion merchandising, film studies, finance/banking, food sciences, French, geography, geology, geophysical engineering, geophysics, German, Germanic languages and literature, graphic arts, health education, historic preservation, history, home economics, horticulture, hotel and restaurant management, information science, interior design, international business, international studies, Italian, jazz, journalism, Latin, Latin American studies, (pre)law sequence, legal studies, liberal arts/general studies, linguistics, management information systems, marketing/retailing/merchandising, mathematics, mechanical engineering, medical technology, (pre)medicine sequence, medieval studies, music, music education, nursing, nutrition, ocean engineering, ornamental horticulture, paleontology, parks management, philosophy, physical education, physical fitness/human movement, physics, piano/organ, political science/government, psychology, public administration, recreational facilities management, religious studies, Russian, science education, secondary education, sociology, Spanish, special education, statistics, technical writing, textiles and clothing, theater arts/drama, transportation engineering, (pre)veterinary medicine sequence, voice, wildlife management, women's studies.

Applying *Required:* high school transcript, 2 years of high school foreign language, SAT. *Recommended:* Achievements, English Composition Test (with essay). Essay, 2 recommendations, campus interview required for some. *Application deadlines:* 3/1, 3/15 priority date for financial aid. *Contact:* Dr. Bruce Walker, Dean of Admissions, 116 Hullihen Hall, South College Avenue, Newark, DE 19716, 302-831-8123.

From the College The University of Delaware is centrally located between New York City and Washington, D.C. The wide selection of majors, a nationally recognized Honors Program, and the opportunity to conduct research with faculty are a few of the unique features that make Delaware the institution of choice for 14,500 undergraduates. Sixty percent of students are from outside of Delaware.

University of Denver

Denver, Colorado

Founded 1864
Urban setting
Independent
Coed
Awards B, M, D

Enrollment 8,019 total; 2,778 undergraduates (506 freshmen)

Faculty 395 total; 375 full-time (75% have doctorate/terminal degree); student-faculty ratio is 13:1; grad assistants teach a few undergraduate courses.

Libraries 2.9 million bound volumes, 1.1 million titles on microform, 5,316 periodical subscriptions

Computing *Terminals/PCs available for student use:* 250, located in computer center, library, dormitories, computer labs; PC not required.

Of Special Interest *Core academic program:* yes. Computer course required. Phi Beta Kappa, Sigma Xi chapters. Academic exchange program: no. Sponsors and participates in study-abroad programs. Cooperative Army ROTC, cooperative Air Force ROTC.

On Campus Drama/theater group; student-run newspaper and radio station. *Social organizations:* 10 national fraternities, 6 national sororities; 46% of eligible undergraduate men and 35% of eligible undergraduate women are members.

Athletics Member NCAA (Division II). *Intercollegiate sports:* baseball (M), basketball (M, W), golf (M), gymnastics (W), ice hockey (M), lacrosse (M), soccer (M, W), swimming and diving (M, W), tennis (M, W), volleyball (W). *Scholarships:* M, W.

Costs (1991–92) & Aid				
	Comprehensive fee	$17,196	Need-based scholarships (average)	$7931
	Tuition	$12,852	Non-need scholarships (average)	$8030
	Mandatory fees	$138	Short-term loans (average)	$100
	Room and board	$4206	Long-term loans—college funds (average)	$900
	Financial aid recipients	47%	Long-term loans—external funds (average)	$2250

Undergraduate Facts				
	Part-time	18%	*Freshman Data:* 2,839 applied, 58% were accepted, 31% (506) of those entered	
	State residents	32%		
	Transfers	26%	From top tenth of high school class	30%
	African-Americans	4%	SAT-takers scoring 600 or over on verbal	6%
	Native Americans	1%	SAT-takers scoring 700 or over on verbal	0%
	Hispanics	5%	SAT-takers scoring 600 or over on math	21%
	Asian-Americans	3%	SAT-takers scoring 700 or over on math	4%
	International students	6%	ACT-takers scoring 26 or over	39%
	Freshmen returning for sophomore year	81%	ACT-takers scoring 30 or over	11%
	Students completing degree within 5 years	N/R	*Majors with most degrees conferred:* business, hotel and restaurant management, communication.	
	Grads pursuing further study	N/R		

Majors Accounting, advertising, American studies, animal sciences, anthropology, art/fine arts, art history, biochemistry, biology/biological sciences, business, chemistry, classics, communication, comparative literature, computer science, construction management, creative writing, (pre)dentistry sequence, economics, electrical engineering, engineering (general), English, environmental sciences, finance/banking, French, geography, German, history, hotel and restaurant management, international business, international studies, journalism, Judaic studies, Latin American studies, (pre)law sequence, marketing/retailing/merchandising, mathematics, mechanical engineering, (pre)medicine sequence, music, music education, natural sciences, philosophy, physics, political science/government, psychology, public affairs and policy studies, real estate, religious studies, Russian, science, social science, sociology, Spanish, speech/rhetoric/public address/debate, statistics, theater arts/drama, urban studies, (pre)veterinary medicine sequence, veterinary technology, women's studies.

Applying *Required:* essay, high school transcript, 2 recommendations, activity sheet, SAT or ACT. *Recommended:* 3 years of high school math and science, some high school foreign language, interview. 3 years of high school math and science required for some. *Application deadlines:* rolling, 12/20 for early action, 3/1 priority date for financial aid. *Contact:* Ms. Susan Hunt, Director of Admission Counseling, 2199 South University Boulevard, Denver, CO 80208, 303-871-2036 or toll-free 800-525-9495 (out-of-state).

University of Detroit Mercy

Detroit, Michigan

Founded 1877
Urban setting
Independent, Roman Catholic (Jesuit)
Coed
Awards A, B, M, D

Enrollment 7,888 total; 4,788 undergraduates (431 freshmen)

Faculty 528 total; 308 full-time; student-faculty ratio is 14:1; grad assistants teach a few undergraduate courses.

Libraries 732,677 bound volumes, 128,503 titles on microform, 2,402 periodical subscriptions

Computing *Terminals/PCs available for student use:* 75, located in computer center, student center, library, classroom buildings; PC not required.

Of Special Interest *Core academic program:* yes. Computer course required. Academic exchange with 5 members of the Detroit Area Consortium of Catholic Colleges. Sponsors and participates in study-abroad programs. Cooperative Army ROTC.

On Campus Drama/theater group; student-run newspaper and radio station. *Social organizations:* 7 national fraternities, 7 local fraternities, 3 local sororities; 22% of eligible undergraduate men and 13% of eligible undergraduate women are members.

Athletics Member NCAA (Division I). *Intercollegiate sports:* baseball (M), basketball (M, W), cross-country running (M, W), fencing (M, W), golf (M, W), riflery (M, W), soccer (M), softball (W), tennis (M), track and field (M, W). *Scholarships:* M, W.

Costs (1991–92) & Aid				
Comprehensive fee	$13,369	Need-based scholarships		Avail
Tuition	$10,080	Non-need scholarships		Avail
Mandatory fees	$50	Short-term loans		N/Avail
Room and board	$3239	Long-term loans—college funds		Avail
Financial aid recipients	72%	Long-term loans—external funds		N/Avail

Undergraduate Facts		
Part-time	50%	*Freshman Data:*
State residents	93%	From top tenth of high school class — 26%
Transfers	33%	SAT-takers scoring 600 or over on verbal — 10%
African-Americans	39%	SAT-takers scoring 700 or over on verbal — 1%
Native Americans	1%	SAT-takers scoring 600 or over on math — 32%
Hispanics	1%	SAT-takers scoring 700 or over on math — 5%
Asian-Americans	2%	ACT-takers scoring 26 or over — 32%
International students	4%	ACT-takers scoring 30 or over — 5%
Freshmen returning for sophomore year	81%	*Majors with most degrees conferred:* nursing, engineering (general), architecture.
Students completing degree within 5 years	42%	
Grads pursuing further study	N/R	

Majors Accounting, architecture, Asian/Oriental studies, behavioral sciences, biochemistry, biology/biological sciences, broadcasting, business, chemical engineering, chemistry, child psychology/child development, civil engineering, classics, communication, computer engineering, computer information systems, computer programming, computer science, computer technologies, construction engineering, criminal justice, cytotechnology, dental services, (pre)dentistry sequence, early childhood education, economics, education, electrical engineering, elementary education, engineering (general), English, finance/banking, French, gerontology, health education, health services administration, history, hotel and restaurant management, humanities, human resources, human services, industrial administration, information science, international business, journalism, labor and industrial relations, Latin, (pre)law sequence, legal studies, management information systems, marketing/retailing/merchandising, mathematics, mechanical engineering, medical records services, medical technology, (pre)medicine sequence, military science, nuclear medical technology, nursing, philosophy, physical education, physician's assistant studies, plastics engineering, plastics technology, political science/government, polymer science, psychology, public administration, public relations, radio and television studies, religious studies, science education, secondary education, social science, social work, sociology, Spanish, special education, sports medicine, systems engineering, theater arts/drama.

Applying *Required:* high school transcript, SAT or ACT. *Recommended:* recommendations. 3 years of high school math and science, some high school foreign language, 1 recommendation, interview required for some. *Application deadlines:* 8/15, 4/1 priority date for financial aid. *Contact:* Mr. Randall J. Berd, Director of Admissions, 4001 West McNichols Road, Detroit, MI 48221, 313-993-1245.

University of Florida

Gainesville, Florida

Founded 1853
Small-town setting
State-supported
Coed
Awards B, M, D

Enrollment 34,814 total; 26,860 undergraduates (2,942 freshmen)

Faculty 3,834 total; 3,606 full-time (86% have doctorate/terminal degree); student-faculty ratio is 28:1; grad assistants teach a few undergraduate courses.

Libraries 2.8 million bound volumes, 2.7 million titles on microform, 29,000 periodical subscriptions

Computing *Terminals/PCs available for student use:* 325, located in computer center, dormitories, labs; PC not required.

Of Special Interest *Core academic program:* yes. Computer course required for business-related, insurance, nutrition, building construction, poultry science, physical education, engineering majors. Phi Beta Kappa, Sigma Xi chapters. Academic exchange program: no. Sponsors and participates in study-abroad programs. Army ROTC, Naval ROTC, Air Force ROTC.

On Campus Drama/theater group; student-run newspaper and radio station. *Social organizations:* 30 national fraternities, 20 national sororities; 30% of eligible undergraduate men and 25% of eligible undergraduate women are members.

Athletics Member NCAA (Division I). *Intercollegiate sports:* baseball (M), basketball (M, W), cross-country running (M, W), football (M), golf (M, W), gymnastics (W), swimming and diving (M, W), tennis (M, W), track and field (M, W), volleyball (W). *Scholarships:* M, W.

Costs (1992–93 estimated) & Aid				
	State resident tuition	$1475	Need-based scholarships	Avail
	Nonresident tuition	$5610	7500 Non-need scholarships (average)	$980
	Mandatory fees	N/App	Short-term loans (average)	$500
	Room and board	$3790	Long-term loans—college funds	N/Avail
	Financial aid recipients	58%	Long-term loans—external funds (average)	$2900

Undergraduate Facts				
	Part-time	13%	*Freshman Data:* 10,785 applied, 71% were accepted, 38% (2,942) of those entered	
	State residents	90%		
	Transfers	30%	From top tenth of high school class	N/R
	African-Americans	5%	SAT-takers scoring 600 or over on verbal	19%
	Native Americans	1%	SAT-takers scoring 700 or over on verbal	3%
	Hispanics	6%	SAT-takers scoring 600 or over on math	55%
	Asian-Americans	4%	SAT-takers scoring 700 or over on math	13%
	International students	5%	ACT-takers scoring 26 or over	67%
	Freshmen returning for sophomore year	88%	ACT-takers scoring 30 or over	22%
	Students completing degree within 5 years	55%		
	Grads pursuing further study	N/R		

Majors Accounting, advertising, aerospace engineering, agricultural education, agricultural engineering, agronomy/soil and crop sciences, American studies, animal sciences, anthropology, architecture, art education, art/fine arts, art history, Asian/Oriental studies, astronomy, botany/plant sciences, business, ceramic art and design, ceramic engineering, chemical engineering, chemistry, civil engineering, classics, communication, computer science, conservation, construction technologies, criminal justice, dairy sciences, dance, dietetics, early childhood education, ecology/environmental studies, economics, education, educational administration, electrical engineering, elementary education, engineering (general), engineering and applied sciences, engineering sciences, English, entomology, environmental engineering, finance/banking, food sciences, forestry, French, geography, geology, German, graphic arts, health education, health science, history, horticulture, industrial engineering, insurance, interior design, journalism, Judaic studies, landscape architecture/design, linguistics, marketing/retailing/merchandising, materials engineering, mathematics, mechanical engineering, medical technology, metallurgical engineering, microbiology, music, music education, nuclear engineering, nursing, nutrition, occupational therapy, ornamental horticulture, painting/drawing, pharmacy/pharmaceutical sciences, philosophy, photography, physical education, physical therapy, physician's assistant studies, physics, political science/government, poultry sciences, psychology, public relations, radio and television studies, real estate, recreation and leisure services, religious studies, Romance languages, Russian, sacred music, science education, sculpture, secondary education, sociology, Spanish, special education, speech/rhetoric/public address/debate, sports medicine, statistics, studio art, systems engineering, technical writing, telecommunications, theater arts/drama, wildlife management, zoology.

Applying *Required:* high school transcript, 3 years of high school math and science, 2 years of high school foreign language, SAT or ACT. *Application deadlines:* 2/1, 3/1 priority date for financial aid. *Contact:* Admissions Office, 201 Creser Hall, Gainesville, FL 32611, 904-392-1365.

University of Georgia

Athens, Georgia

Founded 1785
Suburban setting
State-supported
Coed
Awards A, B, M, D

Enrollment 28,691 total; 22,385 undergraduates (2,859 freshmen)

Faculty 1,982 total; 1,825 full-time (94% have doctorate/terminal degree); grad assistants teach about a quarter of the undergraduate courses.

Libraries 3 million bound volumes, 4.7 million titles on microform, 54,851 periodical subscriptions

Computing *Terminals/PCs available for student use:* 800, located in computer center, student center, library, dormitories, various campus facilities; PC not required.

Of Special Interest *Core academic program:* yes. Computer course required for business majors. Phi Beta Kappa, Sigma Xi chapters. Academic exchange with National Student Exchange. Sponsors and participates in study-abroad programs. Army ROTC, Air Force ROTC.

On Campus Drama/theater group; student-run newspaper and radio station. *Social organizations:* 25 national fraternities, 22 national sororities, local fraternities, local sororities; 20% of eligible undergraduate men and 24% of eligible undergraduate women are members.

Athletics Member NCAA (Division I). *Intercollegiate sports:* baseball (M), basketball (M, W), cross-country running (M, W), equestrian sports (M, W), football (M), golf (M, W), gymnastics (W), ice hockey (M), lacrosse (M), rugby (M), soccer (M, W), swimming and diving (M, W), tennis (M, W), track and field (M, W), volleyball (M, W). *Scholarships:* M, W.

Costs (1991–92) & Aid
State resident tuition	$1722	100 Need-based scholarships (average)	$900
Nonresident tuition	$5166	1200 Non-need scholarships (average)	$750
Mandatory fees	$354	Short-term loans (average)	$150
Room and board	$2988	Long-term loans—college funds (average)	$1445
Financial aid recipients	50%	Long-term loans—external funds (average)	$2600

Undergraduate Facts
Part-time	14%	*Freshman Data:* 10,125 applied, 70% were accepted, 40% (2,859) of those entered	
State residents	80%		
Transfers	9%	From top tenth of high school class	N/R
African-Americans	6%	SAT-takers scoring 600 or over on verbal	11%
Native Americans	1%	SAT-takers scoring 700 or over on verbal	1%
Hispanics	1%	SAT-takers scoring 600 or over on math	27%
Asian-Americans	2%	SAT-takers scoring 700 or over on math	4%
International students	1%	ACT-takers scoring 26 or over	N/R
Freshmen returning for sophomore year	86%	ACT-takers scoring 30 or over	N/R
Students completing degree within 5 years	55%	*Majors with most degrees conferred:* political science/government, marketing/retailing/merchandising, finance/banking.	
Grads pursuing further study	N/R		

Majors Accounting, advertising, agricultural business, agricultural economics, agricultural education, agricultural engineering, agricultural sciences, agricultural technologies, agronomy/soil and crop sciences, animal sciences, anthropology, applied art, art education, art/fine arts, art history, astronomy, biochemistry, biology/biological sciences, black/African-American studies, botany/plant sciences, broadcasting, business, business education, chemistry, child care/child and family studies, child psychology/child development, Chinese, classics, communication, comparative literature, computer science, criminal justice, dairy sciences, dance, (pre)dentistry sequence, dietetics, early childhood education, economics, education, elementary education, English, entomology, environmental health sciences, family and consumer studies, fashion merchandising, film studies, finance/banking, fish and game management, food sciences, food services management, forestry, forest technology, French, genetics, geography, geology, German, Germanic languages and literature, graphic arts, Greek, health education, history, home economics, home economics education, horticulture, hotel and restaurant management, human resources, industrial arts, insurance, interdisciplinary studies, interior design, international business, international studies, Italian, Japanese, journalism, labor and industrial relations, landscape architecture/design, landscaping/grounds maintenance, Latin, Latin American studies, (pre)law sequence, linguistics, literature, management information systems, marketing/retailing/merchandising, mathematics, medical technology, (pre)medicine sequence, medieval studies, microbiology, middle school education, music, music education, music history, music therapy, nursing, nutrition, operations research, optometry, painting/drawing, pest control technology, pharmacy/pharmaceutical sciences, philosophy, photography, physical education, physical fitness/human movement, physics, piano/organ, political science/government, poultry sciences, psychology, public relations, publishing, radio and television studies, reading education, real estate, recreation and leisure services, religious studies, Romance languages, Russian, sacred music, science education, sculpture, secondary education, Slavic languages, social science, social work, sociology, Spanish, special education, speech pathology and audiology, speech/rhetoric/public address/debate, statistics, stringed instruments, studio art, systems science, telecommunications, textiles and clothing, theater arts/drama, theology, (pre)veterinary medicine sequence, vocational education, voice, water resources, wildlife biology, wind and percussion instruments, women's studies, zoology.

Applying *Required:* high school transcript, 3 years of high school math and science, 2 years of high school foreign language, SAT or ACT. *Application deadlines:* 2/1, 3/1 priority date for financial aid. *Contact:* Dr. Claire Swann, Director of Admissions, Academic Building, Athens, GA 30602, 404-542-8776.

From the College Students graduating from the University of Georgia, the country's first state-chartered public university, receive a common sense of educational heritage and a nationally competitive preparation that reflects the University's vital role in the past, present, and future of Georgia, the South, America, and, more than ever, the entire globe.

University of Illinois at Urbana-Champaign
Champaign, Illinois

Founded 1867
Suburban setting
State-supported
Coed
Awards B, M, D

Enrollment 36,139 total; 26,366 undergraduates (5,651 freshmen)

Faculty 2,232 total; 2,166 full-time (82% have doctorate/terminal degree); student-faculty ratio is 12:1; grad assistants teach about a quarter of the undergraduate courses.

Libraries 7.5 million bound volumes, 3.3 million titles on microform, 92,550 periodical subscriptions

Computing *Terminals/PCs available for student use:* 8,000, located in computer center, student center, library, dormitories, labs; PC not required. Campus network links student PCs.

Of Special Interest *Core academic program:* yes. Computer course required for all science, engineering, commerce majors. Phi Beta Kappa, Sigma Xi chapters. Academic exchange with members of the Committee on Institutional Cooperation. Sponsors and participates in study-abroad programs. Army ROTC, Naval ROTC, Air Force ROTC.

On Campus Drama/theater group; student-run newspaper and radio station. *Social organizations:* 57 national fraternities, 29 national sororities; 26% of eligible undergraduate men and 28% of eligible undergraduate women are members.

Athletics Member NCAA (Division I). *Intercollegiate sports:* baseball (M), basketball (M, W), cross-country running (M, W), fencing (M), football (M), golf (M, W), gymnastics (M, W), softball (W), swimming and diving (M, W), tennis (M, W), track and field (M, W), volleyball (W), wrestling (M). *Scholarships:* M, W.

Costs (1991–92) & Aid		
State resident tuition	$2236	
Nonresident tuition	$5988	
Mandatory fees	$819	
Room and board	$3902	
Financial aid recipients	83%	
4890 Need-based scholarships (average)		$1520
1238 Non-need scholarships (average)		$1082
Short-term loans (average)		$200
Long-term loans—college funds (average)		$1420
Long-term loans—external funds (average)		$2259

Undergraduate Facts		
Part-time	6%	
State residents	98%	
Transfers	5%	
African-Americans	7%	
Native Americans	1%	
Hispanics	5%	
Asian-Americans	11%	
International students	1%	
Freshmen returning for sophomore year	95%	
Students completing degree within 5 years	74%	
Grads pursuing further study	27%	

Freshman Data: 15,024 applied, 72% were accepted, 52% (5,651) of those entered
From top tenth of high school class — 56%
SAT-takers scoring 600 or over on verbal — 20%
SAT-takers scoring 700 or over on verbal — 2%
SAT-takers scoring 600 or over on math — 59%
SAT-takers scoring 700 or over on math — 17%
ACT-takers scoring 26 or over — 68%
ACT-takers scoring 30 or over — 23%
Majors with most degrees conferred: economics, psychology, finance/banking.

Majors Accounting, actuarial science, advertising, aerospace engineering, agricultural business, agricultural economics, agricultural education, agricultural engineering, agricultural sciences, agronomy/soil and crop sciences, anatomy, animal sciences, anthropology, architecture, art education, art/fine arts, art history, Asian/Oriental studies, astronomy, biochemistry, bioengineering, biology/biological sciences, biophysics, botany/plant sciences, broadcasting, business, business education, ceramic engineering, chemical engineering, chemistry, city/community/regional planning, civil engineering, classics, communication, comparative literature, computer engineering, computer science, dairy sciences, dance, dietetics, early childhood education, East European and Soviet studies, ecology/environmental studies, economics, education, electrical engineering, elementary education, engineering (general), engineering management, engineering mechanics, engineering physics, English, entomology, family and consumer studies, fashion design and technology, finance/banking, food sciences, food services management, forestry, French, genetics, geography, geology, German, Germanic languages and literature, graphic arts, Greek, health education, history, home economics, home economics education, horticulture, hotel and restaurant management, human development, humanities, human resources, industrial design, industrial engineering, interdisciplinary studies, interior design, Italian, journalism, landscape architecture/design, Latin, Latin American studies, (pre)law sequence, liberal arts/general studies, linguistics, literature, marketing/retailing/merchandising, mathematics, mechanical engineering, medieval studies, metallurgical engineering, microbiology, music, music education, music history, nuclear engineering, nutrition, ornamental horticulture, painting/drawing, parks management, philosophy, photography, physical education, physics, physiology, piano/organ, political science/government, Portuguese, psychology, radio and television studies, recreation and leisure services, religious studies, Russian, Russian and Slavic studies, science education, sculpture, secondary education, social science, social work, sociology, Spanish, special education, speech pathology and audiology, speech/rhetoric/public address/debate, statistics, stringed instruments, textiles and clothing, theater arts/drama, (pre)veterinary medicine sequence, vocational education, voice, wind and percussion instruments.

Applying *Required:* high school transcript, SAT or ACT. Essay, 3 years of high school math, 2 years of high school foreign language, interview, audition, statement of professional interest required for some. *Application deadlines:* 1/1, 3/15 priority date for financial aid. *Contact:* Ms. Martha H. Moore, Associate Director of Admissions, 177 Henry Admin. Building, 506 S. Wright, Champaign, IL 61820, 217-333-0306.

University of Iowa

Iowa City, Iowa

Founded 1847
Small-town setting
State-supported
Coed
Awards B, M, D

Enrollment 27,881 total; 18,917 undergraduates (2,907 freshmen)

Faculty 1,705 total; student-faculty ratio is 16:1; grad assistants teach a few undergraduate courses.

Libraries 3 million bound volumes, 3.4 million titles on microform, 18,514 periodical subscriptions

Computing *Terminals/PCs available for student use:* 900, located in computer center, student center, library, dormitories, classroom buildings; PC not required. Campus network links student PCs.

Of Special Interest *Core academic program:* yes. Computer course required for business administration, geography, engineering, education, nursing, exercise science majors. Phi Beta Kappa, Sigma Xi chapters. Academic exchange with Iowa State University of Science and Technology, University of Northern Iowa, the Committee on Institutional Cooperation. Sponsors and participates in study-abroad programs. Army ROTC, Air Force ROTC.

On Campus Drama/theater group; student-run newspaper and radio station. *Social organizations:* 30 national fraternities, 20 national sororities; 17% of eligible undergraduate men and 18% of eligible undergraduate women are members.

Athletics Member NCAA (Division I). *Intercollegiate sports:* badminton (M, W), basketball (M, W), bowling (M, W), crew (M, W), cross-country running (M, W), field hockey (W), football (M), golf (M, W), gymnastics (M, W), ice hockey (M, W), lacrosse (M, W), rugby (M, W), sailing (M, W), soccer (M), softball (W), swimming and diving (M, W), table tennis (M, W), tennis (M, W), track and field (M, W), volleyball (M, W), wrestling (M). *Scholarships:* M, W.

Costs (1991–92) & Aid				
State resident tuition	$1952	3261 Need-based scholarships (average)	$1446
Nonresident tuition	$6470	1278 Non-need scholarships (average)	$1115
Mandatory fees	$140	Short-term loans (average)	$300
Room and board	$2982	Long-term loans—college funds (average)	$1083
Financial aid recipients	70%	Long-term loans—external funds (average)	$1980

Undergraduate Facts			
Part-time	16%	*Freshman Data:* 7,796 applied, 87% were accepted, 43% (2,907) of those entered	
State residents	72%		
Transfers	N/R	From top tenth of high school class	21%
African-Americans	2%	SAT-takers scoring 600 or over on verbal	N/R
Native Americans	1%	SAT-takers scoring 700 or over on verbal	N/R
Hispanics	1%	SAT-takers scoring 600 or over on math	N/R
Asian-Americans	3%	SAT-takers scoring 700 or over on math	N/R
International students	3%	ACT-takers scoring 26 or over	36%
Freshmen returning for sophomore year	83%	ACT-takers scoring 30 or over	9%
Students completing degree within 5 years	51%	*Majors with most degrees conferred:* business, communication, engineering (general).	
Grads pursuing further study	N/R		

Majors Accounting, actuarial science, advertising, African studies, American studies, anatomy, anthropology, applied mathematics, art education, art/fine arts, art history, Asian/Oriental studies, astronomy, biochemistry, biology/biological sciences, biomedical engineering, black/African-American studies, botany/plant sciences, broadcasting, business, business economics, ceramic art and design, chemical engineering, chemistry, child psychology/child development, Chinese, civil engineering, classics, clinical psychology, communication, comparative literature, computer engineering, computer science, creative writing, dance, dental services, (pre)dentistry sequence, earth science, East European and Soviet studies, ecology/environmental studies, economics, education, electrical engineering, elementary education, engineering (general), English, environmental engineering, experimental psychology, film studies, finance/banking, French, geography, geology, German, Greek, health education, history, humanities, human resources, industrial engineering, interdisciplinary studies, international business, international studies, Italian, Japanese, jazz, jewelry and metalsmithing, journalism, labor and industrial relations, Latin, Latin American studies, (pre)law sequence, liberal arts/general studies, linguistics, literature, management engineering, marketing/retailing/merchandising, materials engineering, mathematics, mechanical engineering, medical technology, (pre)medicine sequence, microbiology, museum studies, music, music education, music history, music therapy, nuclear medical technology, nursing, opera, painting/drawing, pharmacy/pharmaceutical sciences, philosophy, photography, physical education, physical fitness/human movement, physical therapy, physician's assistant studies, physics, piano/organ, political science/government, Portuguese, psychology, public relations, radio and television studies, recreational facilities management, recreation and leisure services, recreation therapy, religious studies, Romance languages, Russian, science education, sculpture, secondary education, social science, social work, sociology, Spanish, speech pathology and audiology, speech/rhetoric/public address/debate, speech therapy, sports administration, sports medicine, statistics, stringed instruments, studio art, telecommunications, theater arts/drama, urban studies, (pre)veterinary medicine sequence, voice, wind and percussion instruments, women's studies, zoology.

Applying *Required:* high school transcript, 3 years of high school math and science, 2 years of high school foreign language, SAT or ACT. *Recommended:* campus interview. *Application deadlines:* 5/15, 1/1 priority date for financial aid. *Contact:* Mr. Michael Barron, Director, Admissions, Calvin Hall, Iowa City, IA 52242, 319-335-1548 or toll-free 800-553-4692.

From the College Iowa offers strong undergraduate programs in diverse areas, such as the health sciences, traditional liberal arts, and preprofessional programs. Undergraduates are exposed to outstanding opportunities and facilities, from the world-renowned Writer's Workshop to the top-ranked College of Medicine and University Hospitals and Clinics, the largest university-owned teaching hospital in the United States.

University of Kansas

Lawrence, Kansas

Founded 1866
Suburban setting
State-supported
Coed
Awards B, M, D

Enrollment	29,150 total; 20,007 undergraduates (3,352 freshmen)
Faculty	1,265 total; 1,046 full-time (95% have doctorate/terminal degree); student-faculty ratio is 16:1; grad assistants teach about a quarter of the undergraduate courses.
Libraries	3.0 million bound volumes, 2.3 million titles on microform, 29,000 periodical subscriptions
Computing	*Terminals/PCs available for student use:* 500, located in computer center, library, classrooms, labs; PC not required but available for purchase. Campus network links student PCs.
Of Special Interest	*Core academic program:* yes. Computer course required for business, math, physics, geology, most engineering majors. Phi Beta Kappa, Sigma Xi chapters. Academic exchange program: no. Sponsors and participates in study-abroad programs. Army ROTC, Naval ROTC, Air Force ROTC.
On Campus	Drama/theater group; student-run newspaper and radio station. *Social organizations:* 28 national fraternities, 18 national sororities; 20% of eligible undergraduate men and 22% of eligible undergraduate women are members.
Athletics	Member NCAA (Division I). *Intercollegiate sports:* baseball (M), basketball (M, W), crew (M, W), cross-country running (M, W), fencing (M, W), football (M), golf (M, W), ice hockey (M), lacrosse (M, W), racquetball (M, W), rugby (M, W), soccer (M, W), softball (W), swimming and diving (M, W), tennis (M, W), track and field (M, W), volleyball (M, W), wrestling (M). *Scholarships:* M, W.

Costs (1991–92) & Aid				
	State resident tuition	$1324	3650 Need-based scholarships (average)	$1071
	Nonresident tuition	$5002	2260 Non-need scholarships (average)	$829
	Mandatory fees	$338	Short-term loans (average)	$720
	Room and board	$2684	Long-term loans—college funds	N/Avail
	Financial aid recipients	33%	Long-term loans—external funds (average)	$3026

Undergraduate Facts				
	Part-time	9%	*Freshman Data:* 7,739 applied, 66% were accepted, 66% (3,352) of those entered	
	State residents	68%		
	Transfers	7%	From top tenth of high school class	20%
	African-Americans	3%	SAT-takers scoring 600 or over on verbal	N/App
	Native Americans	1%	SAT-takers scoring 700 or over on verbal	N/App
	Hispanics	2%	SAT-takers scoring 600 or over on math	N/App
	Asian-Americans	3%	SAT-takers scoring 700 or over on math	N/App
	International students	5%	ACT-takers scoring 26 or over	30%
	Freshmen returning for sophomore year	80%	ACT-takers scoring 30 or over	8%
	Students completing degree within 5 years	47%	*Majors with most degrees conferred:* journalism, business, psychology.	
	Grads pursuing further study	N/R		

Majors Accounting, advertising, aerospace engineering, African studies, American studies, anthropology, applied art, archaeology, architectural engineering, architecture, art education, art/fine arts, art history, Asian/Oriental studies, astronomy, atmospheric sciences, biochemistry, biology/biological sciences, black/African-American studies, botany/plant sciences, broadcasting, business, cell biology, ceramic art and design, chemical engineering, chemistry, child care/child and family studies, child psychology/child development, Chinese, civil engineering, classics, commercial art, communication, comparative literature, computer engineering, computer science, creative writing, cytotechnology, dance, (pre)dentistry sequence, early childhood education, East Asian studies, East European and Soviet studies, ecology/environmental studies, economics, education, electrical engineering, elementary education, engineering physics, English, entomology, environmental biology, environmental sciences, film studies, French, genetics, geography, geology, geophysics, German, Germanic languages and literature, graphic arts, health education, history, history of science, human development, humanities, industrial design, interior design, Italian, Japanese, jewelry and metalsmithing, journalism, Latin American studies, (pre)law sequence, liberal arts/general studies, linguistics, mathematics, mechanical engineering, medical records services, medical technology, (pre)medicine sequence, meteorology, microbiology, music, music education, music history, music therapy, nursing, occupational therapy, painting/drawing, paleontology, petroleum/natural gas engineering, pharmacy/pharmaceutical sciences, philosophy, photography, physical education, physics, physiology, piano/organ, political science/government, psychology, radio and television studies, radiological technology, recreation and leisure services, religious studies, respiratory therapy, Russian, Russian and Slavic studies, science education, sculpture, secondary education, Slavic languages, social work, sociology, Spanish, speech pathology and audiology, sports medicine, stringed instruments, studio art, textile arts, theater arts/drama, toxicology, voice, wind and percussion instruments, women's studies, zoology.

Applying *Required:* high school transcript, ACT. *Recommended:* 3 years of high school math and science, some high school foreign language. *Application deadlines:* 4/1, 2/1 for nonresidents, 3/1 priority date for financial aid. *Contact:* Ms. Deborah Castrop, Director of Admissions, 126 Strong Hall, Lawrence, KS 66045, 913-864-3911.

University of Maryland College Park

College Park, Maryland

Founded 1856
Suburban setting
State-supported
Coed
Awards B, M, D

Enrollment	34,623 total; 25,361 undergraduates (3,287 freshmen)
Faculty	2,631 total; 2,086 full-time (79% have doctorate/terminal degree); student-faculty ratio is 15:1; grad assistants teach a few undergraduate courses.
Libraries	2 million bound volumes, 2 million titles on microform, 22,000 periodical subscriptions
Computing	*Terminals/PCs available for student use:* 500, located in computer center, library, dormitories, academic buildings; PC not required but available for purchase.
Of Special Interest	*Core academic program:* yes. Computer course required for accounting, finance, education majors. Phi Beta Kappa, Sigma Xi chapters. Academic exchange with 62 members of the National Student Exchange. Sponsors and participates in study-abroad programs. Air Force ROTC, cooperative Naval ROTC.
On Campus	Drama/theater group; student-run newspaper and radio station. *Social organizations:* 28 national fraternities, 20 national sororities; 9% of eligible undergraduate men and 10% of eligible undergraduate women are members.
Athletics	Member NCAA (Division I). *Intercollegiate sports:* baseball (M), basketball (M, W), cross-country running (M, W), field hockey (W), football (M), golf (M), gymnastics (W), lacrosse (M, W), soccer (M, W), softball (W), swimming and diving (M, W), tennis (M, W), track and field (M, W), volleyball (W), wrestling (M). *Scholarships:* M, W.

Costs (1991–92) & Aid				
	State resident tuition	$1926	3500 Need-based scholarships (average)	$1075
	Nonresident tuition	$6794	400 Non-need scholarships (average)	$2500
	Mandatory fees	$509	Short-term loans (average)	$803
	Room and board	$4990	Long-term loans—college funds (average)	$500
	Financial aid recipients	50%	Long-term loans—external funds (average)	$1900

Undergraduate Facts				
	Part-time	17%	*Freshman Data:* 13,910 applied, 68% were accepted, 35% (3,287) of those entered	
	State residents	75%		
	Transfers	11%	From top tenth of high school class	N/R
	African-Americans	11%	SAT-takers scoring 600 or over on verbal	N/R
	Native Americans	1%	SAT-takers scoring 700 or over on verbal	N/R
	Hispanics	3%	SAT-takers scoring 600 or over on math	N/R
	Asian-Americans	10%	SAT-takers scoring 700 or over on math	N/R
	International students	3%	ACT-takers scoring 26 or over	N/R
	Freshmen returning for sophomore year	88%	ACT-takers scoring 30 or over	N/R
	Students completing degree within 5 years	51%	*Majors with most degrees conferred:* political science/government, psychology, engineering (general).	
	Grads pursuing further study	N/R		

Majors Accounting, advertising, aerospace engineering, agricultural business, agricultural economics, agricultural education, agricultural engineering, agricultural sciences, agronomy/soil and crop sciences, American studies, animal sciences, anthropology, architecture, art education, art/fine arts, art history, astronomy, biochemistry, biology/biological sciences, black/African-American studies, botany/plant sciences, broadcasting, business, business education, chemical engineering, chemistry, child care/child and family studies, civil engineering, classics, community services, computer science, conservation, consumer services, criminal justice, dairy sciences, dance, (pre)dentistry sequence, dietetics, early childhood education, East Asian studies, economics, education, educational administration, electrical engineering, elementary education, engineering (general), English, entomology, family and consumer studies, fashion design and technology, fashion merchandising, finance/banking, fire protection engineering, fire science, food sciences, French, geography, geology, German, Germanic languages and literature, health education, history, home economics, home economics education, horticulture, human ecology, industrial arts, interior design, Italian, journalism, Judaic studies, labor and industrial relations, Latin, law enforcement/police sciences, (pre)law sequence, liberal arts/general studies, linguistics, marketing/retailing/merchandising, mathematics, mechanical engineering, (pre)medicine sequence, microbiology, music, music education, music history, natural resource management, nuclear engineering, nutrition, philosophy, physical education, physical fitness/human movement, physical sciences, physics, political science/government, poultry sciences, psychology, public relations, radio and television studies, recreation and leisure services, Romance languages, Russian, Russian and Slavic studies, science education, secondary education, secretarial studies/office management, Slavic languages, sociology, Spanish, special education, speech pathology and audiology, speech/rhetoric/public address/debate, speech therapy, statistics, studio art, textiles and clothing, theater arts/drama, transportation technologies, urban studies, (pre)veterinary medicine sequence, vocational education, wildlife management, zoology.

Applying *Required:* high school transcript, 3 years of high school math, 2 years of high school foreign language, SAT or ACT. *Recommended:* 3 years of high school science. Essay, recommendations, campus interview required for some. *Application deadlines:* 4/30, 12/1 for early action, 2/15 priority date for financial aid. *Contact:* Dr. Linda Clement, Director of Admissions, 0130 Mitchell Building, College Park, MD 20742, 301-314-8388.

University of Massachusetts at Amherst
Amherst, Massachusetts

Founded 1863
Small-town setting
State-supported
Coed
Awards A, B, M, D

Enrollment 22,070 total; 17,170 undergraduates (3,309 freshmen)

Faculty 1,223 total; 1,138 full-time (93% have doctorate/terminal degree); student-faculty ratio is 18:1; grad assistants teach a few undergraduate courses.

Libraries 2.4 million bound volumes, 1.8 million titles on microform, 13,807 periodical subscriptions

Computing Terminals/PCs available for student use: 200, located in computer center, library, dormitories, academic buildings; PC not required. Campus network links student PCs.

Of Special Interest *Core academic program:* yes. Computer course required for business, engineering, math, science majors. Phi Beta Kappa, Sigma Xi chapters. Academic exchange with members of the National Student Exchange and Five Colleges, Inc. Sponsors and participates in study-abroad programs. Army ROTC, Air Force ROTC.

On Campus Drama/theater group; student-run newspaper and radio station. *Social organizations:* 15 national fraternities, 8 national sororities, 1 local sorority; 5% of eligible undergraduate men and 4% of eligible undergraduate women are members.

Athletics Member NCAA (Division I). *Intercollegiate sports:* baseball (M), basketball (M, W), cross-country running (M, W), field hockey (W), football (M), gymnastics (M, W), lacrosse (M), skiing (downhill) (M, W), soccer (W), softball (W), swimming and diving (M, W), track and field (M, W), volleyball (W), water polo (M). *Scholarships:* M, W.

Costs (1991–92) & Aid
State resident tuition	$2052	9800 Need-based scholarships (average)	$1500
Nonresident tuition	$7920	550 Non-need scholarships (average)	$550
Mandatory fees	$2811	Short-term loans (average)	$150
Room and board	$3587	Long-term loans—college funds (average)	$750
Financial aid recipients	47%	Long-term loans—external funds (average)	$1840

Undergraduate Facts
Part-time	4%	*Freshman Data:* 14,590 applied, 83% were accepted, 27% (3,309) of those entered	
State residents	81%		
Transfers	22%	From top tenth of high school class	14%
African-Americans	2%	SAT-takers scoring 600 or over on verbal	9%
Native Americans	1%	SAT-takers scoring 700 or over on verbal	1%
Hispanics	3%	SAT-takers scoring 600 or over on math	25%
Asian-Americans	3%	SAT-takers scoring 700 or over on math	5%
International students	2%	ACT-takers scoring 26 or over	N/R
Freshmen returning for sophomore year	77%	ACT-takers scoring 30 or over	N/R
Students completing degree within 5 years	60%	*Majors with most degrees conferred:* economics, psychology, communication.	
Grads pursuing further study	N/R		

Majors Accounting, agricultural economics, agronomy/soil and crop sciences, animal sciences, anthropology, art education, art/fine arts, art history, astronomy, biochemistry, black/African-American studies, botany/plant sciences, business, chemical engineering, chemistry, Chinese, civil engineering, classics, communication, comparative literature, computer engineering, computer information systems, computer science, dance, (pre)dentistry sequence, drafting and design, early childhood education, East European and Soviet studies, economics, education, electrical engineering, elementary education, English, entomology, environmental design, environmental sciences, fashion merchandising, finance/banking, fish and game management, food sciences, food services technology, forestry, French, geography, geology, German, history, home economics, hotel and restaurant management, human development, industrial engineering, information science, interdisciplinary studies, Italian, Japanese, journalism, Judaic studies, landscape architecture/design, (pre)law sequence, legal studies, liberal arts/general studies, linguistics, marketing/retailing/merchandising, mathematics, mechanical engineering, medical technology, (pre)medicine sequence, microbiology, music, natural resource management, Near and Middle Eastern studies, nursing, nutrition, pest control technology, philosophy, physical education, physical fitness/human movement, physics, political science/government, Portuguese, psychology, public health, recreation and leisure services, Russian, science, sociology, Spanish, speech pathology and audiology, sports administration, studio art, theater arts/drama, tourism and travel, (pre)veterinary medicine sequence, wildlife biology, women's studies, wood sciences, zoology.

Applying *Required:* essay, high school transcript, 3 years of high school math, 2 years of high school foreign language, SAT or ACT. *Recommended:* recommendations, Achievements, English Composition Test (with essay). *Application deadlines:* 2/15, 3/1 priority date for financial aid. *Contact:* Mr. Timm R. Rinehart, Director, Undergraduate Admissions, University Admissions Center, Amherst, MA 01003, 413-545-0222.

From the College What makes Massachusetts at Amherst special? Great neighbors, for one thing. As part of the Five College Consortium with Amherst, Smith, Mount Holyoke, and Hampshire colleges, students take courses, use the libraries, attend cultural events, and share faculty among the five colleges—all at no extra charge. A free bus system and no red tape make it all work.

University of Miami

Coral Gables, Florida

Founded 1925
Suburban setting
Independent
Coed
Awards B, M, D

Enrollment 13,969 total; 8,638 undergraduates (1,851 freshmen)

Faculty 1,087 total; 672 full-time (96% have doctorate/terminal degree); student-faculty ratio is 8:1; grad assistants teach a few undergraduate courses.

Libraries 1.7 million bound volumes, 2.8 million titles on microform, 15,900 periodical subscriptions

Computing *Terminals/PCs available for student use:* 200, located in computer center, student center, library, dormitories; PC not required.

Of Special Interest *Core academic program:* yes. Computer course required for business, engineering majors. Phi Beta Kappa, Sigma Xi chapters. Academic exchange program: no. Sponsors and participates in study-abroad programs. Army ROTC, Air Force ROTC.

On Campus Drama/theater group; student-run newspaper and radio station. *Social organizations:* 16 national fraternities, 8 national sororities; 18% of eligible undergraduate men and 15% of eligible undergraduate women are members.

Athletics Member NCAA (Division I). *Intercollegiate sports:* baseball (M), basketball (M, W), crew (M, W), cross-country running (M, W), football (M), golf (M, W), swimming and diving (M, W), tennis (M, W), track and field (M, W). *Scholarships:* M, W.

Costs (1992–93) & Aid		
Comprehensive fee	$20,960	
Tuition	$14,870	
Mandatory fees	$180	
Room and board	$5910	
Financial aid recipients	78%	
Need-based scholarships		Avail
Non-need scholarships (average)		$6600
Short-term loans		Avail
Long-term loans—college funds		N/Avail
Long-term loans—external funds (average)		$2827

Undergraduate Facts		
Part-time	8%	
State residents	52%	
Transfers	7%	
African-Americans	7%	
Native Americans	1%	
Hispanics	20%	
Asian-Americans	4%	
International students	10%	
Freshmen returning for sophomore year	N/R	
Students completing degree within 5 years	N/R	
Grads pursuing further study	N/R	
Freshman Data: 7,566 applied, 79% were accepted, 31% (1,851) of those entered		
From top tenth of high school class		37%
SAT-takers scoring 600 or over on verbal		16%
SAT-takers scoring 700 or over on verbal		2%
SAT-takers scoring 600 or over on math		38%
SAT-takers scoring 700 or over on math		9%
ACT-takers scoring 26 or over		28%
ACT-takers scoring 30 or over		9%
Majors with most degrees conferred: psychology, finance/banking, biology/biological sciences.		

Majors Accounting, actuarial science, advertising, aerospace engineering, anthropology, applied mathematics, architectural engineering, architecture, art education, art/fine arts, art history, astronomy, audio engineering, biochemistry, biology/biological sciences, biomedical engineering, broadcasting, business, ceramic art and design, chemistry, civil engineering, communication, computer engineering, computer information systems, computer science, construction management, creative writing, criminal justice, cytotechnology, (pre)dentistry sequence, economics, electrical engineering, electronics engineering, elementary education, engineering sciences, English, environmental engineering, environmental sciences, film and video, film studies, finance/banking, French, geography, geology, graphic arts, health science, health services administration, history, human services, illustration, industrial administration, industrial engineering, insurance, international business, international studies, jazz, journalism, Judaic studies, landscape architecture/design, Latin American studies, (pre)law sequence, legal studies, liberal arts/general studies, manufacturing engineering, marine biology, marine sciences, marketing/retailing/merchandising, materials sciences, mathematics, mechanical engineering, medical technology, (pre)medicine sequence, meteorology, microbiology, music, music business, music education, music therapy, nuclear engineering, nuclear medical technology, nursing, occupational safety and health, ocean engineering, oceanography, painting/drawing, philosophy, photography, physical therapy, physics, piano/organ, political science/government, psychobiology, psychology, public affairs and policy studies, public relations, radio and television studies, real estate, religious studies, science education, secondary education, sociology, Spanish, special education, speech/rhetoric/public address/debate, statistics, stringed instruments, studio art, systems science, telecommunications, theater arts/drama, transportation engineering, voice, wind and percussion instruments.

Applying *Required:* essay, high school transcript, 1 recommendation, SAT or ACT. *Recommended:* 3 years of high school math and science, some high school foreign language, interview. Achievements required for some. *Application deadlines:* 3/1, 11/1 for early decision, 3/1 priority date for financial aid. *Contact:* Ms. Mary K. Conway, Director of Admissions, PO Box 248025, Coral Gables, FL 33124, 305-284-4323; *Office location:* Ashe Building Rm. 132, 1252 Memorial Dr.

✱ University of Michigan

Ann Arbor, Michigan

Founded 1817
Suburban setting
State-supported
Coed
Awards B, M, D

Enrollment	36,228 total; 23,126 undergraduates (4,770 freshmen)
Faculty	3,310 total; 2,691 full-time (95% have doctorate/terminal degree); student-faculty ratio is 7:1; grad assistants teach a few undergraduate courses.
Libraries	6.4 million bound volumes, 4.3 million titles on microform, 70,157 periodical subscriptions
Computing	*Terminals/PCs available for student use:* 4,200, located in computer center, student center, library, dormitories, academic buildings; PC not required. Campus network links student PCs.
Of Special Interest	*Core academic program:* no. Computer course required for engineering, math, business administration majors. Phi Beta Kappa, Sigma Xi chapters. Academic exchange with Michigan State University, University of Wisconsin, Indiana University, Purdue University, Northwestern University, University of Minnesota, Ohio State University, University of Iowa, University of Chicago. Sponsors and participates in study-abroad programs. Army ROTC, Naval ROTC, Air Force ROTC.
On Campus	Drama/theater group; student-run newspaper and radio station. *Social organizations:* 41 national fraternities, 23 national sororities, 1 local fraternity, 1 local sorority; 25% of eligible undergraduate men and 25% of eligible undergraduate women are members.
Athletics	Member NCAA (Division I). *Intercollegiate sports:* baseball (M), basketball (M, W), cross-country running (M, W), field hockey (W), football (M), golf (M, W), gymnastics (M, W), ice hockey (M), softball (W), swimming and diving (M, W), tennis (M, W), track and field (M, W), volleyball (W), wrestling (M). *Scholarships:* M, W.

Costs (1991–92) & Aid				
	State resident tuition	$3710	9200 Need-based scholarships (average)	$2000
	Nonresident tuition	$12,818	1500 Non-need scholarships (average)	$2000
	Mandatory fees	$135	Short-term loans (average)	$575
	Room and board	$4084	Long-term loans—college funds	N/Avail
	Financial aid recipients	35%	Long-term loans—external funds (average)	$3000

Undergraduate Facts				
	Part-time	6%	*Freshman Data:* 17,719 applied, 64% were accepted, 42% (4,770) of those entered	
	State residents	70%		
	Transfers	4%	From top tenth of high school class	65%
	African-Americans	7%	SAT-takers scoring 600 or over on verbal	28%
	Native Americans	1%	SAT-takers scoring 700 or over on verbal	4%
	Hispanics	4%	SAT-takers scoring 600 or over on math	69%
	Asian-Americans	9%	SAT-takers scoring 700 or over on math	27%
	International students	2%	ACT-takers scoring 26 or over	68%
	Freshmen returning for sophomore year	94%	ACT-takers scoring 30 or over	23%
	Students completing degree within 5 years	83%	*Majors with most degrees conferred:* psychology, English, political science/government.	
	Grads pursuing further study	N/R		

Majors Accounting, actuarial science, aerospace engineering, African studies, American studies, anthropology, applied art, applied mathematics, Arabic, architecture, art history, Asian/Oriental studies, astronomy, atmospheric sciences, biblical studies, biology/biological sciences, biomedical sciences, biophysics, black/African-American studies, botany/plant sciences, business, ceramic art and design, chemical engineering, chemistry, Chinese, civil engineering, classics, communication, comparative literature, computer engineering, computer science, creative writing, dance, dental services, (pre)dentistry sequence, East Asian studies, East European and Soviet studies, ecology/environmental studies, economics, education, electrical engineering, elementary education, engineering (general), engineering physics, engineering sciences, English, environmental biology, environmental design, environmental sciences, film and video, fish and game management, forestry, French, geography, geology, German, graphic arts, Greek, Hebrew, history, humanities, industrial design, industrial engineering, information science, interior design, international studies, Islamic studies, Italian, Japanese, jazz, jewelry and metalsmithing, journalism, Judaic studies, landscape architecture/design, Latin, Latin American studies, (pre)law sequence, liberal arts/general studies, linguistics, literature, marine engineering, materials engineering, materials sciences, mathematics, mechanical engineering, medical technology, (pre)medicine sequence, medieval studies, meteorology, Mexican-American/Chicano studies, microbiology, molecular biology, music, music education, music history, natural resource management, naval architecture, Near and Middle Eastern studies, nuclear engineering, nursing, nutrition, oceanography, painting/drawing, pharmacy/pharmaceutical sciences, philosophy, photography, physical education, physical fitness/human movement, physics, piano/organ, political science/government, printmaking, psychology, recreation and leisure services, religious studies, Romance languages, Russian, Russian and Slavic studies, Scandinavian languages/studies, sculpture, secondary education, social science, sociology, South Asian studies, Southeast Asian studies, Spanish, special education, sports administration, statistics, stringed instruments, textile arts, theater arts/drama, voice, wildlife biology, wildlife management, wind and percussion instruments, women's studies, zoology.

Applying *Required:* essay, high school transcript, SAT or ACT. *Recommended:* 3 years of high school science, some high school foreign language. 3 years of high school math, recommendations, interview required for some. *Application deadlines:* 2/1, 2/15 priority date for financial aid. *Contact:* Mr. Richard H. Shaw Jr., Director, Undergraduate Admissions, 5115 East Jefferson, Ann Arbor, MI 48109-1316, 313-764-7433.

University of Michigan–Dearborn

Dearborn, Michigan

Founded 1959
Suburban setting
State-supported
Coed
Awards B, M

Enrollment	7,044 total; 5,977 undergraduates (697 freshmen)
Faculty	384 total; 197 full-time (84% have doctorate/terminal degree); grad assistants teach no undergraduate courses.
Libraries	292,380 bound volumes, 387,834 titles on microform, 1,614 periodical subscriptions
Computing	*Terminals/PCs available for student use:* 350, located in computer center, engineering, computer and writing labs; PC not required.
Of Special Interest	*Core academic program:* yes. Computer course required for business administration, engineering majors. Academic exchange with University of Michigan (Ann Arbor). Sponsors and participates in study-abroad programs. Army ROTC, cooperative Naval ROTC, cooperative Air Force ROTC.
On Campus	Drama/theater group; student-run newspaper and radio station. *Social organizations:* 7 national fraternities, 4 national sororities, 1 local fraternity, 1 local sorority; 6% of eligible undergraduate men and 5% of eligible undergraduate women are members.
Athletics	Member NAIA. *Intercollegiate sport:* basketball (W). *Scholarships:* W.

Costs (1991–92) & Aid	State resident tuition	$2765	Need-based scholarships	Avail
	Nonresident tuition	$8958	Non-need scholarships	Avail
	Mandatory fees	$100	Short-term loans	Avail
	Room and board	N/App	Long-term loans—college funds	N/Avail
	Financial aid recipients	N/R	Long-term loans—external funds	Avail

Undergraduate Facts	Part-time	42%	*Freshman Data:* 1,753 applied, 71% were accepted, 56% (697) of those entered	
	State residents	99%		
	Transfers	50%	From top tenth of high school class	35%
	African-Americans	6%	SAT-takers scoring 600 or over on verbal	10%
	Native Americans	1%	SAT-takers scoring 700 or over on verbal	0%
	Hispanics	2%	SAT-takers scoring 600 or over on math	28%
	Asian-Americans	4%	SAT-takers scoring 700 or over on math	7%
	International students	1%	ACT-takers scoring 26 or over	N/R
	Freshmen returning for sophomore year	N/R	ACT-takers scoring 30 or over	N/R
	Students completing degree within 5 years	N/R		
	Grads pursuing further study	N/R		

Majors American studies, anthropology, art education, art history, behavioral sciences, bilingual/bicultural education, biochemistry, biology/biological sciences, business, business education, chemistry, child care/child and family studies, child psychology/child development, comparative literature, computer information systems, computer programming, computer science, early childhood education, ecology/environmental studies, economics, education, electrical engineering, elementary education, engineering (general), English, environmental sciences, finance/banking, health services administration, history, humanities, industrial engineering, information science, interdisciplinary studies, international studies, liberal arts/general studies, literature, manufacturing engineering, marketing/retailing/merchandising, mathematics, mechanical engineering, microbiology, music, music history, natural sciences, philosophy, physical sciences, physics, political science/government, psychology, public administration, science education, secondary education, social science, sociology.

Applying *Required:* high school transcript, SAT or ACT. *Recommended:* 3 years of high school math and science, some high school foreign language. Recommendations, interview required for some. *Application deadlines:* rolling, 5/1 priority date for financial aid. *Contact:* Ms. Carol S. Mack, Director of Admissions, 4901 Evergreen Road, Dearborn, MI 48128, 313-593-5100.

University of Minnesota, Morris

Morris, Minnesota

Founded 1959
Small-town setting
State-supported
Coed
Awards B

Enrollment	1,915 total—all undergraduates (510 freshmen)
Faculty	145 total; 131 full-time (83% have doctorate/terminal degree); student-faculty ratio is 15:1.
Libraries	152,000 bound volumes, 880 periodical subscriptions
Computing	*Terminals/PCs available for student use:* 120, located in computer center, library, dormitories; PC not required.
Of Special Interest	*Core academic program:* yes. Computer course required. Academic exchange with other units of the University of Minnesota system. Sponsors and participates in study-abroad programs.
On Campus	Drama/theater group; student-run newspaper and radio station. *Social organizations:* 2 national fraternities, 2 local sororities; 87% of eligible undergraduate men and 90% of eligible undergraduate women are members.
Athletics	Member NAIA. *Intercollegiate sports:* basketball (M, W), football (M), golf (M, W), tennis (M, W), track and field (M, W), volleyball (W), wrestling (M).

Costs (1991–92) & Aid				
	State resident tuition	$2475	1739 Need-based scholarships (average)	$1021
	Nonresident tuition	$7301	670 Non-need scholarships (average)	$1066
	Mandatory fees	$249	Short-term loans	Avail
	Room and board	$2949	Long-term loans—college funds (average)	$1684
	Financial aid recipients	87%	Long-term loans—external funds (average)	$2634

Undergraduate Facts				
	Part-time	3%	*Freshman Data:* 1,605 applied, 50% were accepted, 64% (510) of those entered	
	State residents	87%		
	Transfers	4%	From top tenth of high school class	62%
	African-Americans	4%	SAT-takers scoring 600 or over on verbal	42%
	Native Americans	3%	SAT-takers scoring 700 or over on verbal	8%
	Hispanics	1%	SAT-takers scoring 600 or over on math	56%
	Asian-Americans	3%	SAT-takers scoring 700 or over on math	16%
	International students	1%	ACT-takers scoring 26 or over	52%
	Freshmen returning for sophomore year	90%	ACT-takers scoring 30 or over	12%
	Students completing degree within 5 years	N/R	*Majors with most degrees conferred:* business economics, education, chemistry.	
	Grads pursuing further study	N/R		

Majors Art history, biology/biological sciences, business economics, chemistry, communication, computer science, (pre)dentistry sequence, economics, education, elementary education, English, European studies, French, geology, German, health education, history, human services, Latin American studies, (pre)law sequence, mathematics, (pre)medicine sequence, music, philosophy, physics, political science/government, psychology, secondary education, social science, sociology, Spanish, speech/rhetoric/public address/debate, studio art, theater arts/drama, (pre)veterinary medicine sequence.

Applying *Required:* high school transcript, 3 years of high school math and science, 2 years of high school foreign language, ACT. *Recommended:* recommendations, interview. Essay required for some. *Application deadlines:* 3/15, 12/1 for early decision, 4/1 priority date for financial aid. *Contact:* Mr. Robert J. Vikander, Director, Admissions and Financial Aid, Behmler Hall, Morris, MN 56267, 612-589-2211 Ext. 6035 or toll-free 800-992-8863.

University of Minnesota, Twin Cities Campus
Minneapolis, Minnesota

Founded 1851
Urban setting
State-supported
Coed
Awards B, M, D

Enrollment	39,315 total; 25,515 undergraduates (3,264 freshmen)
Faculty	2,839 total; 2,568 full-time (89% have doctorate/terminal degree); grad assistants teach about a quarter of the undergraduate courses.
Libraries	4.8 million bound volumes, 3.3 million titles on microform, 33,659 periodical subscriptions
Computing	*Terminals/PCs available for student use:* 700, located in computer center, student center, library, dormitories; PC not required. Campus network links student PCs.
Of Special Interest	*Core academic program:* yes. Computer course required for business, statistics, social work, sociology, engineering, architecture majors. Phi Beta Kappa, Sigma Xi chapters. Academic exchange with National Student Exchange. Sponsors and participates in study-abroad programs. Army ROTC, Naval ROTC, Air Force ROTC.
On Campus	Drama/theater group; student-run newspaper and radio station. *Social organizations:* 33 national fraternities, 18 national sororities, 2 local sororities; 3% of eligible undergraduate men and 3% of eligible undergraduate women are members.
Athletics	Member NCAA (Division I). *Intercollegiate sports:* basketball (M, W), cross-country running (M, W), football (M), golf (M, W), gymnastics (M, W), ice hockey (M), skiing (downhill) (M, W), swimming and diving (M, W), tennis (M, W), track and field (M, W), volleyball (W), wrestling (M). *Scholarships:* M, W.

Costs (1991–92) & Aid				
	State resident tuition	$2829	5018 Need-based scholarships (average)	$1636
	Nonresident tuition	$8344	1104 Non-need scholarships (average)	$3304
	Mandatory fees	$354	Short-term loans	Avail
	Room and board	$3288	Long-term loans—college funds (average)	$1084
	Financial aid recipients	57%	Long-term loans—external funds (average)	$3250

Undergraduate Facts				
	Part-time	33%	*Freshman Data:* 10,306 applied, 61% were accepted, 52% (3,264) of those entered	
	State residents	73%	From top tenth of high school class	N/R
	Transfers	21%	SAT-takers scoring 600 or over on verbal	N/R
	African-Americans	8%	SAT-takers scoring 700 or over on verbal	N/R
	Native Americans	2%	SAT-takers scoring 600 or over on math	N/R
	Hispanics	N/R	SAT-takers scoring 700 or over on math	N/R
	Asian-Americans	16%	ACT-takers scoring 26 or over	N/R
	International students	7%	ACT-takers scoring 30 or over	N/R
	Freshmen returning for sophomore year	80%	*Majors with most degrees conferred:* social science, engineering (general), business.	
	Students completing degree within 5 years	27%		
	Grads pursuing further study	15%		

Majors Accounting, aerospace engineering, African studies, agricultural business, agricultural education, agricultural engineering, agricultural sciences, American studies, animal sciences, anthropology, applied art, architecture, art education, art history, astronomy, astrophysics, bilingual/bicultural education, biochemistry, biology/biological sciences, biometrics, black/African-American studies, botany/plant sciences, business, business education, cell biology, chemical engineering, chemistry, child psychology/child development, Chinese, civil engineering, classics, communication, computer science, dance, dental services, (pre)dentistry sequence, early childhood education, earth science, East Asian studies, ecology/environmental studies, economics, education, electrical engineering, elementary education, engineering (general), English, environmental design, environmental sciences, film studies, fish and game management, food sciences, forestry, forest technology, French, funeral service, genetics, geography, geological engineering, geology, geophysics, German, Greek, Hebrew, Hispanic studies, history, home economics, home economics education, human development, humanities, industrial engineering, interdisciplinary studies, interior design, international studies, Italian, Japanese, journalism, Judaic studies, landscape architecture/design, Latin, Latin American studies, (pre)law sequence, linguistics, marketing/retailing/merchandising, materials engineering, materials sciences, mathematics, mechanical engineering, medical technology, (pre)medicine sequence, metallurgical engineering, microbiology, modern languages, music, music education, music therapy, Native American studies, natural resource management, Near and Middle Eastern studies, nursing, nutrition, occupational therapy, parks management, pharmacy/pharmaceutical sciences, philosophy, physical education, physical fitness/human movement, physical sciences, physical therapy, physics, physiology, political science/government, Portuguese, psychology, public relations, recreational facilities management, recreation and leisure services, religious studies, retail management, Russian, Russian and Slavic studies, Scandinavian languages/studies, science, science education, secondary education, social science, sociology, South Asian studies, Spanish, speech pathology and audiology, speech therapy, statistics, studio art, technical writing, textiles and clothing, theater arts/drama, urban studies, (pre)veterinary medicine sequence, vocational education, women's studies.

Applying *Required:* high school transcript, 3 years of high school math and science, ACT, PSAT. Some high school foreign language, SAT required for some. *Application deadlines:* rolling, continuous processing for financial aid. *Contact:* Mr. John R. Printz, Acting Director of Admissions, 240 Williamson, Minneapolis, MN 55455, 612-625-2006 or toll-free 800-752-1000; *Office location:* 231 Pillsbury Drive.

University of Missouri–Columbia

Columbia, Missouri

Founded 1839
Small-town setting
State-supported
Coed
Awards B, M, D

Enrollment 24,660 total; 18,446 undergraduates (3,413 freshmen)

Faculty 1,804 total; 1,552 full-time (78% have doctorate/terminal degree); grad assistants teach a few undergraduate courses.

Libraries 2.6 million bound volumes, 4.9 million titles on microform, 17,395 periodical subscriptions

Computing *Terminals/PCs available for student use:* 588, located in computer center, student center, library, dormitories; PC not required. Campus network links student PCs.

Of Special Interest *Core academic program:* yes. Computer course required for some majors. Phi Beta Kappa, Sigma Xi chapters. Academic exchange with Mid-Missouri Associated Colleges and Universities, National Student Exchange. Sponsors and participates in study-abroad programs. Army ROTC, Air Force ROTC.

On Campus Drama/theater group; student-run newspaper and radio station. *Social organizations:* 35 national fraternities, 23 national sororities; 25% of eligible undergraduate men and 25% of eligible undergraduate women are members.

Athletics Member NCAA (Division I). *Intercollegiate sports:* baseball (M), basketball (M, W), cross-country running (M, W), football (M), golf (M, W), gymnastics (W), softball (W), swimming and diving (M, W), tennis (M, W), track and field (M, W), volleyball (W), wrestling (M). *Scholarships:* M, W.

Costs (1991–92) & Aid			
State resident tuition	$2016	624 Need-based scholarships (average)	$2140
Nonresident tuition	$6290	5383 Non-need scholarships (average)	$1379
Mandatory fees	$296	Short-term loans (average)	$550
Room and board	$3004	Long-term loans—college funds (average)	$1699
Financial aid recipients	67%	Long-term loans—external funds (average)	$2386

Undergraduate Facts			
Part-time	9%	*Freshman Data:* 7,614 applied, 73% were accepted, 61% (3,413) of those entered	
State residents	87%		
Transfers	8%	From top tenth of high school class	31%
African-Americans	4%	SAT-takers scoring 600 or over on verbal	N/R
Native Americans	1%	SAT-takers scoring 700 or over on verbal	N/R
Hispanics	1%	SAT-takers scoring 600 or over on math	N/R
Asian-Americans	2%	SAT-takers scoring 700 or over on math	N/R
International students	2%	ACT-takers scoring 26 or over	39%
Freshmen returning for sophomore year	81%	ACT-takers scoring 30 or over	13%
Students completing degree within 5 years	N/R	*Majors with most degrees conferred:* business, journalism, psychology.	
Grads pursuing further study	N/R		

Majors Accounting, advertising, aerospace engineering, agricultural economics, agricultural education, agricultural engineering, agricultural sciences, agricultural technologies, agronomy/soil and crop sciences, animal sciences, anthropology, archaeology, art education, art/fine arts, art history, Asian/Oriental studies, atmospheric sciences, behavioral sciences, biochemistry, biology/biological sciences, broadcasting, business, business economics, business education, chemical engineering, chemistry, child care/child and family studies, child psychology/child development, civil engineering, classics, communication, computer engineering, computer science, cytotechnology, (pre)dentistry sequence, dietetics, early childhood education, East Asian studies, economics, education, electrical engineering, elementary education, English, environmental design, family and consumer studies, finance/banking, fish and game management, food sciences, forestry, French, geography, geology, German, guidance and counseling, health education, history, home economics education, horticulture, hotel and restaurant management, human development, human resources, industrial arts, industrial engineering, insurance, interdisciplinary studies, international studies, journalism, Latin American studies, liberal arts/general studies, linguistics, marketing/retailing/merchandising, mathematics, mechanical engineering, medical laboratory technology, (pre)medicine sequence, microbiology, music, music education, nuclear medical technology, nursing, nutrition, occupational therapy, parks management, philosophy, photography, physical education, physical therapy, physics, political science/government, psychology, publishing, radio and television studies, radiological sciences, reading education, real estate, recreation and leisure services, religious studies, respiratory therapy, Romance languages, Russian, Russian and Slavic studies, science education, secondary education, social work, sociology, South Asian studies, Spanish, special education, speech pathology and audiology, speech/rhetoric/public address/debate, speech therapy, statistics, textiles and clothing, theater arts/drama, tourism and travel, (pre)veterinary medicine sequence, vocational education.

Applying *Required:* high school transcript, 3 years of high school math, ACT. *Recommended:* 3 years of high school science, some high school foreign language. *Application deadlines:* 5/15, 3/1 for financial aid. *Contact:* Ms. Georgeanne Porter, Director, Undergraduate Admissions, 130 Jesse Hall, Columbia, MO 65211, 314-882-7786 or toll-free 800-225-6075 (in-state).

University of Missouri–Kansas City

Kansas City, Missouri

Founded 1929
Urban setting
State-supported
Coed
Awards B, M, D

Enrollment 11,159 total; 6,253 undergraduates (521 freshmen)

Faculty 540 total; 400 full-time (78% have doctorate/terminal degree); student-faculty ratio is 12:1; grad assistants teach a few undergraduate courses.

Libraries 869,099 bound volumes, 469,831 titles on microform, 8,717 periodical subscriptions

Computing *Terminals/PCs available for student use:* 180, located in computer center, library, dormitories; PC not required.

Of Special Interest *Core academic program:* yes. Computer course required for business administration, accounting, education, engineering majors. Sigma Xi chapter. Academic exchange with other campuses of the University of Missouri System, members of the Kansas City Regional Council for Higher Education. Sponsors and participates in study-abroad programs. Army ROTC.

On Campus Drama/theater group; student-run newspaper. *Social organizations:* 4 national fraternities, 3 national sororities, 1 local sorority; 5% of eligible undergraduate men and 4% of eligible undergraduate women are members.

Athletics Member NCAA (Division I). *Intercollegiate sports:* basketball (M, W), cross-country running (M, W), golf (M, W), riflery (M, W), soccer (M), softball (W), tennis (M, W), volleyball (W). *Scholarships:* M, W.

Costs (1992–93) & Aid

State resident tuition	$2769	833 Need-based scholarships (average)	$1330
Nonresident tuition	$7629	5850 Non-need scholarships (average)	$881
Mandatory fees	$60	Short-term loans (average)	$525
Room and board	$4325	Long-term loans—college funds (average)	$1327
Financial aid recipients	40%	Long-term loans—external funds (average)	$2860

Undergraduate Facts

Part-time	38%	*Freshman Data:* 1,695 applied, 50% were accepted, 62% (521) of those entered	
State residents	80%		
Transfers	N/R	From top tenth of high school class	40%
African-Americans	7%	SAT-takers scoring 600 or over on verbal	N/App
Native Americans	1%	SAT-takers scoring 700 or over on verbal	N/App
Hispanics	2%	SAT-takers scoring 600 or over on math	N/App
Asian-Americans	4%	SAT-takers scoring 700 or over on math	N/App
International students	7%	ACT-takers scoring 26 or over	57%
Freshmen returning for sophomore year	66%	ACT-takers scoring 30 or over	23%
Students completing degree within 5 years	31%	*Majors with most degrees conferred:* business, biology/biological sciences, elementary education.	
Grads pursuing further study	N/R		

Majors Accounting, American studies, anthropology, applied art, art/fine arts, art history, biology/biological sciences, business, business education, chemistry, civil engineering, communication, computer science, creative writing, criminal justice, dance, dental services, earth science, economics, education, electrical engineering, elementary education, English, French, geography, geology, German, health education, history, interdisciplinary studies, Judaic studies, liberal arts/general studies, mathematics, mechanical engineering, medical technology, music, music education, music therapy, nursing, painting/drawing, pharmacy/pharmaceutical sciences, philosophy, physical education, physics, piano/organ, political science/government, psychology, radio and television studies, science education, sculpture, secondary education, sociology, Spanish, speech pathology and audiology, speech/rhetoric/public address/debate, stringed instruments, studio art, theater arts/drama, urban studies, voice, wind and percussion instruments.

Applying *Required:* high school transcript, 3 years of high school math, 4 years of high school English, 2 years each of science and social science, 1 year of fine arts, ACT. *Application deadlines:* rolling, 3/15 priority date for financial aid. *Contact:* Ms. Sally C. Bryant, Director of Admissions, 4747 Troost Avenue, Kansas City, MO 64110, 816-235-1111.

University of Missouri–Rolla

Rolla, Missouri

Founded 1870
Small-town setting
State-supported
Coed
Awards B, M, D

Enrollment	5,582 total; 4,349 undergraduates (748 freshmen)
Faculty	358 total; 333 full-time (91% have doctorate/terminal degree); student-faculty ratio is 12:1; grad assistants teach a few undergraduate courses.
Libraries	432,152 bound volumes, 23,500 titles on microform, 1,537 periodical subscriptions
Computing	*Terminals/PCs available for student use:* 400, located in computer center, library, dormitories, classroom buildings; PC not required.
Of Special Interest	*Core academic program:* yes. Computer course required. Sigma Xi chapter. Academic exchange with University of Missouri–Columbia. Participates in study-abroad programs. Army ROTC, Air Force ROTC.
On Campus	Drama/theater group; student-run newspaper and radio station. *Social organizations:* 21 national fraternities, 4 national sororities, 2 eating clubs; 29% of eligible undergraduate men and 19% of eligible undergraduate women are members.
Athletics	Member NCAA (Division II). *Intercollegiate sports:* baseball (M), basketball (M, W), cross-country running (M, W), football (M), golf (M), riflery (M), soccer (M, W), softball (W), swimming and diving (M), tennis (M), track and field (M, W). *Scholarships:* M, W.

Costs (1991–92) & Aid				
	State resident tuition	$2016	1091 Need-based scholarships (average)	$1743
	Nonresident tuition	$6039	1271 Non-need scholarships (average)	$1326
	Mandatory fees	$420	Short-term loans (average)	$350
	Room and board	$3374	Long-term loans—college funds (average)	$850
	Financial aid recipients	73%	Long-term loans—external funds (average)	$2096

Undergraduate Facts				
	Part-time	12%	*Freshman Data:* 1,618 applied, 98% were accepted, 47% (748) of those entered	
	State residents	82%	From top tenth of high school class	43%
	Transfers	11%	SAT-takers scoring 600 or over on verbal	22%
	African-Americans	4%	SAT-takers scoring 700 or over on verbal	1%
	Native Americans	1%	SAT-takers scoring 600 or over on math	63%
	Hispanics	1%	SAT-takers scoring 700 or over on math	24%
	Asian-Americans	4%	ACT-takers scoring 26 or over	61%
	International students	5%	ACT-takers scoring 30 or over	30%
	Freshmen returning for sophomore year	65%	*Majors with most degrees conferred:* electrical engineering, mechanical engineering, engineering management.	
	Students completing degree within 5 years	36%		
	Grads pursuing further study	N/R		

Majors Aerospace engineering, applied mathematics, biology/biological sciences, business, ceramic engineering, chemical engineering, chemistry, civil engineering, computer science, (pre)dentistry sequence, economics, electrical engineering, engineering management, engineering mechanics, English, geological engineering, geology, geophysics, history, mathematics, mechanical engineering, (pre)medicine sequence, metallurgical engineering, mining and mineral engineering, nuclear engineering, nursing, petroleum/natural gas engineering, philosophy, physics, psychology.

Applying *Required:* high school transcript. *Recommended:* 3 years of high school math and science, some high school foreign language, ACT. SAT or ACT required for some. *Application deadlines:* 7/1, 3/31 priority date for financial aid. *Contact:* Mr. Robert B. Lewis, Director of Admissions, 102 Parker Hall, Rolla, MO 65401, 314-341-4164.

University of New Hampshire

Durham, New Hampshire

Founded 1866
Small-town setting
State-supported
Coed
Awards A, B, M, D

Enrollment	11,219 total; 10,398 undergraduates (2,489 freshmen)
Faculty	825 total; 613 full-time (85% have doctorate/terminal degree); student-faculty ratio is 17:1; grad assistants teach a few undergraduate courses.
Libraries	940,000 bound volumes, 176,710 titles on microform, 6,000 periodical subscriptions
Computing	*Terminals/PCs available for student use:* 300, located in computer center, student center, library, dormitories; PC not required but available for purchase.
Of Special Interest	*Core academic program:* yes. Computer course required for math, physics, engineering, business administration, economics majors. Phi Beta Kappa, Sigma Xi chapters. Academic exchange with San Diego State University, National Student Exchange, New Hampshire College and University Council, New England Land-Grant University Exchange, University of California, Santa Cruz. Sponsors and participates in study-abroad programs. Army ROTC, Air Force ROTC.
On Campus	Drama/theater group; student-run newspaper and radio station. *Social organizations:* 13 national fraternities, 7 national sororities, 2 local fraternities; 18% of eligible undergraduate men and 15% of eligible undergraduate women are members.
Athletics	Member NCAA (Division I). *Intercollegiate sports:* badminton (M, W), baseball (M), basketball (M, W), crew (M, W), cross-country running (M, W), equestrian sports (M, W), fencing (M, W), field hockey (W), football (M), golf (M), gymnastics (W), ice hockey (M, W), lacrosse (M, W), rugby (M, W), skiing (cross-country) (M, W), skiing (downhill) (M, W), soccer (M, W), squash (M, W), swimming and diving (M, W), tennis (M), track and field (M, W), volleyball (M, W). *Scholarships:* M, W.

Costs (1991–92) & Aid				
	State resident tuition	$3290	Need-based scholarships	Avail
	Nonresident tuition	$9840	Non-need scholarships	Avail
	Mandatory fees	$397	Short-term loans	N/Avail
	Room and board	$3600	Long-term loans—college funds (average)	$942
	Financial aid recipients	55%	Long-term loans—external funds (average)	$2831

Undergraduate Facts				
	Part-time	6%	*Freshman Data:* 9,627 applied, 75% were accepted, 35% (2,489) of those entered	
	State residents	55%		
	Transfers	5%	From top tenth of high school class	31%
	African-Americans	1%	SAT-takers scoring 600 or over on verbal	8%
	Native Americans	N/R	SAT-takers scoring 700 or over on verbal	1%
	Hispanics	N/R	SAT-takers scoring 600 or over on math	28%
	Asian-Americans	1%	SAT-takers scoring 700 or over on math	4%
	International students	1%	ACT-takers scoring 26 or over	N/App
	Freshmen returning for sophomore year	84%	ACT-takers scoring 30 or over	N/App
	Students completing degree within 5 years	65%	*Majors with most degrees conferred:* business, English, communication.	
	Grads pursuing further study	N/R		

Majors Agricultural business, agronomy/soil and crop sciences, animal sciences, anthropology, art education, art/fine arts, art history, biochemistry, biology/biological sciences, botany/plant sciences, business, cell biology, chemical engineering, chemistry, child care/child and family studies, city/community/regional planning, civil engineering, classics, communication, computer engineering, computer science, conservation, dance, dietetics, earth science, ecology/environmental studies, economics, electrical engineering, electrical engineering technology, engineering technology, English, entomology, environmental sciences, equestrian studies, evolutionary biology, family and consumer studies, forestry, French, geography, geology, German, Greek, health services administration, history, home economics education, horticulture, hotel and restaurant management, humanities, interdisciplinary studies, international studies, journalism, Latin, linguistics, marine biology, mathematics, mechanical engineering, medical technology, microbiology, molecular biology, music, music education, music history, natural resource management, nursing, nutrition, occupational therapy, parks management, philosophy, physical education, physics, piano/organ, political science/government, psychology, recreation and leisure services, recreation therapy, Russian, science, social work, sociology, Spanish, special education, speech pathology and audiology, speech therapy, sports administration, statistics, stringed instruments, studio art, theater arts/drama, (pre)veterinary medicine sequence, vocational education, voice, water resources, wildlife management, wind and percussion instruments, zoology.

Applying *Required:* essay, high school transcript, 1 recommendation, SAT. *Recommended:* 4 years of high school math and science, 3 years of high school foreign language, campus interview, Achievements, English Composition Test. *Application deadlines:* 2/1, 12/1 for early action, 2/15 priority date for financial aid. *Contact:* Mr. Stanwood C. Fish, Dean of Admissions, Grant House, Durham, NH 03824, 603-862-1360; *Office location:* 4 Garrison Avenue.

University of North Carolina at Chapel Hill
Chapel Hill, North Carolina

Founded 1795
Small-town setting
State-supported
Coed
Awards B, M, D

Enrollment 23,794 total; 15,439 undergraduates (3,142 freshmen)

Faculty 2,430 total; student-faculty ratio is 15:1; grad assistants teach a few undergraduate courses.

Libraries 3.5 million bound volumes, 2.3 million titles on microform, 34,662 periodical subscriptions

Computing *Terminals/PCs available for student use:* 460, located in computer center, student center, dormitories; PC not required but available for purchase.

Of Special Interest *Core academic program:* yes. Computer course required for some majors. Phi Beta Kappa, Sigma Xi chapters. Academic exchange with North Carolina Central University, Duke University, North Carolina State University, University of North Carolina at Greensboro, University of North Carolina at Charlotte. Sponsors and participates in study-abroad programs. Naval ROTC, Air Force ROTC, cooperative Army ROTC.

On Campus Drama/theater group; student-run newspaper and radio station. *Social organizations:* 23 national fraternities, 13 national sororities; 20% of eligible undergraduate men and 20% of eligible undergraduate women are members.

Athletics Member NCAA (Division I). *Intercollegiate sports:* basketball (M, W), cross-country running (M, W), fencing (M, W), field hockey (W), football (M), golf (M, W), gymnastics (W), lacrosse (M), soccer (M, W), swimming and diving (M, W), tennis (M, W), track and field (M, W), volleyball (M, W), wrestling (M). *Scholarships:* M, W.

Costs (1991–92) & Aid				
	State resident tuition	$1248	2700 Need-based scholarships (average)	$1224
	Nonresident tuition	$7116	82 Non-need scholarships (average)	$2100
	Mandatory fees	N/App	Short-term loans (average)	$150
	Room and board	$3700	Long-term loans—college funds (average)	$900
	Financial aid recipients	32%	Long-term loans—external funds (average)	$2200

Undergraduate Facts				
	Part-time	7%	*Freshman Data:* 15,337 applied, 36% were accepted, 58% (3,142) of those entered	
	State residents	82%		
	Transfers	8%	From top tenth of high school class	76%
	African-Americans	10%	SAT-takers scoring 600 or over on verbal	23%
	Native Americans	1%	SAT-takers scoring 700 or over on verbal	4%
	Hispanics	1%	SAT-takers scoring 600 or over on math	47%
	Asian-Americans	3%	SAT-takers scoring 700 or over on math	12%
	International students	1%	ACT-takers scoring 26 or over	N/R
	Freshmen returning for sophomore year	92%	ACT-takers scoring 30 or over	N/R
	Students completing degree within 5 years	N/R	*Majors with most degrees conferred:* biology/biological sciences, business, political science/government.	
	Grads pursuing further study	N/R		

Majors Accounting, actuarial science, advertising, African studies, American studies, anthropology, applied mathematics, archaeology, art education, art/fine arts, art history, astronomy, biology/biological sciences, black/African-American studies, broadcasting, business, chemistry, classics, comparative literature, computer science, criminal justice, dental services, early childhood education, East Asian studies, economics, education, elementary education, engineering and applied sciences, English, environmental engineering, film studies, folklore, French, geography, geology, Germanic languages and literature, Greek, health services administration, history, industrial administration, interdisciplinary studies, international studies, Italian, journalism, Latin, Latin American studies, linguistics, literature, materials sciences, mathematics, medical technology, music, music education, naval sciences, nursing, nutrition, operations research, peace studies, pharmacy/pharmaceutical sciences, philosophy, physical education, physical therapy, physics, political science/government, polymer science, Portuguese, psychology, public affairs and policy studies, public health, public relations, radio and television studies, radiological technology, recreation and leisure services, religious studies, Russian, Russian and Slavic studies, secondary education, sociology, Spanish, speech/rhetoric/public address/debate, statistics, studio art, theater arts/drama, urban studies, women's studies.

Applying *Required:* high school transcript, 3 years of high school math and science, 2 years of high school foreign language, 4 years of high school English, 2 years of high school social studies, SAT or ACT. *Recommended:* essay, recommendations. *Application deadlines:* 1/15, 10/15 for early action, 3/1 priority date for financial aid. *Contact:* James Walters, Director of Undergraduate Admissions, Monogram Building, Chapel Hill, NC 27599, 919-966-3621.

University of Notre Dame

Notre Dame, Indiana

Founded 1842
Suburban setting
Independent, Roman Catholic
Coed
Awards B, M, D

Enrollment	9,900 total; 7,500 undergraduates (1,880 freshmen)
Faculty	840 total; 620 full-time (98% have doctorate/terminal degree); student-faculty ratio is 12:1; grad assistants teach a few undergraduate courses.
Libraries	1.9 million bound volumes, 1.2 million titles on microform, 16,300 periodical subscriptions
Computing	*Terminals/PCs available for student use:* 444, located in computer center, student center, library, various academic departments; PC not required.
Of Special Interest	*Core academic program:* yes. Computer course required for engineering, business majors. Phi Beta Kappa, Sigma Xi chapters. Academic exchange with Saint Mary's College (IN). Sponsors and participates in study-abroad programs. Army ROTC, Naval ROTC, Air Force ROTC.
On Campus	Drama/theater group; student-run newspaper and radio station. No national or local fraternities or sororities on campus.
Athletics	Member NCAA (Division I). *Intercollegiate sports:* baseball (M), basketball (M, W), crew (M, W), cross-country running (M, W), fencing (M, W), football (M), golf (M, W), gymnastics (M, W), ice hockey (M), lacrosse (M), rugby (M), sailing (M, W), skiing (downhill) (M, W), soccer (M, W), softball (W), swimming and diving (M, W), tennis (M, W), track and field (M, W), volleyball (M, W), water polo (M), wrestling (M). *Scholarships:* M, W.

Costs (1991–92) & Aid				
	Comprehensive fee	$17,207	Need-based scholarships (average)	$4000
	Tuition	$13,505	Non-need scholarships	N/Avail
	Mandatory fees	$137	Short-term loans	N/Avail
	Room and board	$3565	Long-term loans—college funds	N/Avail
	Financial aid recipients	65%	Long-term loans—external funds (average)	$3100

Undergraduate Facts				
	Part-time	0%	*Freshman Data:* 8,300 applied, 42% were accepted, 54% (1,880) of those entered	
	State residents	9%		
	Transfers	5%	From top tenth of high school class	76%
	African-Americans	4%	SAT-takers scoring 600 or over on verbal	40%
	Native Americans	1%	SAT-takers scoring 700 or over on verbal	5%
	Hispanics	5%	SAT-takers scoring 600 or over on math	79%
	Asian-Americans	4%	SAT-takers scoring 700 or over on math	30%
	International students	2%	ACT-takers scoring 26 or over	N/R
	Freshmen returning for sophomore year	98%	ACT-takers scoring 30 or over	N/R
	Students completing degree within 5 years	94%		
	Grads pursuing further study	39%		

Majors Accounting, aerospace engineering, American studies, anthropology, architecture, art/fine arts, art history, biochemistry, biology/biological sciences, black/African-American studies, business, chemical engineering, chemistry, civil engineering, classics, communication, computer engineering, computer science, (pre)dentistry sequence, earth science, economics, electrical engineering, engineering (general), engineering sciences, English, film and video, finance/banking, French, geology, German, Germanic languages and literature, Greek, history, interdisciplinary studies, international studies, Italian, Japanese, Latin, Latin American studies, literature, marketing/retailing/merchandising, mathematics, mechanical engineering, (pre)medicine sequence, medieval studies, modern languages, music, painting/drawing, peace studies, philosophy, photography, physics, political science/government, psychology, Romance languages, Russian, sculpture, secondary education, sociology, Spanish, studio art, theater arts/drama, theology, Western civilization and culture.

Applying *Required:* essay, high school transcript, 3 years of high school math, 2 years of high school foreign language, 1 recommendation, SAT. *Recommended:* 3 years of high school science. ACT required for some. *Application deadlines:* 1/10, 11/1 for early action, continuous to 2/28 for financial aid. *Contact:* Mr. Kevin M. Rooney, Director of Admissions, 113 Main Building, Notre Dame, IN 46556, 219-239-7505.

University of Pennsylvania

Philadelphia, Pennsylvania

Founded 1740
Urban setting
Independent
Coed
Awards A, B, M, D

Enrollment	22,220 total; 9,541 undergraduates (2,315 freshmen)
Faculty	4,152 total; 1,892 full-time (99% have doctorate/terminal degree); student-faculty ratio is 7:1; grad assistants teach a few undergraduate courses.
Libraries	3.8 million bound volumes, 32,118 periodical subscriptions
Computing	*Terminals/PCs available for student use:* 750, located in computer center, library, dormitories; PC not required. Campus network links student PCs.
Of Special Interest	*Core academic program:* no. Computer course required for some math, business, engineering majors. Phi Beta Kappa, Sigma Xi chapters. Academic exchange with Bryn Mawr College, Haverford College, Swarthmore College. Sponsors and participates in study-abroad programs. Army ROTC, Naval ROTC, cooperative Air Force ROTC.
On Campus	Drama/theater group; student-run newspaper and radio station. *Social organizations:* 31 national fraternities, 11 national sororities; 31% of eligible undergraduate men and 28% of eligible undergraduate women are members.
Athletics	Member NCAA (Division I). *Intercollegiate sports:* badminton (M, W), basketball (M, W), crew (M, W), cross-country running (M, W), equestrian sports (M, W), fencing (M, W), field hockey (W), football (M), golf (M, W), gymnastics (M, W), ice hockey (M, W), lacrosse (M, W), riflery (M, W), sailing (M, W), skiing (cross-country) (M, W), skiing (downhill) (M, W), soccer (M, W), softball (W), squash (M, W), swimming and diving (M, W), tennis (M, W), track and field (M, W), volleyball (M, W), wrestling (M).

Costs (1991–92) & Aid				
	Comprehensive fee	$21,924	Need-based scholarships	Avail
	Tuition	$14,347	Non-need scholarships	N/Avail
	Mandatory fees	$1547	Short-term loans (average)	$250
	Room and board	$6030	Long-term loans—college funds (average)	$900
	Financial aid recipients	45%	Long-term loans—external funds (average)	$3150

Undergraduate Facts				
	Part-time	6%	*Freshman Data:* 9,789 applied, 47% were accepted, 50% (2,315) of those entered	
	State residents	21%		
	Transfers	3%	From top tenth of high school class	82%
	African-Americans	6%	SAT-takers scoring 600 or over on verbal	53%
	Native Americans	1%	SAT-takers scoring 700 or over on verbal	9%
	Hispanics	4%	SAT-takers scoring 600 or over on math	88%
	Asian-Americans	14%	SAT-takers scoring 700 or over on math	45%
	International students	8%	ACT-takers scoring 26 or over	N/R
	Freshmen returning for sophomore year	97%	ACT-takers scoring 30 or over	N/R
	Students completing degree within 5 years	88%	*Majors with most degrees conferred:* finance/banking, history, English.	
	Grads pursuing further study	28%		

Majors Accounting, actuarial science, adult and continuing education, African languages, African studies, American studies, anthropology, applied art, Arabic, archaeology, art/fine arts, art history, Asian/Oriental studies, astronomy, astrophysics, behavioral sciences, biochemistry, bioengineering, biology/biological sciences, biomedical engineering, biophysics, black/African-American studies, botany/plant sciences, business, chemical engineering, chemistry, child psychology/child development, Chinese, city/community/regional planning, civil engineering, classics, clinical psychology, communication, comparative literature, computer engineering, computer programming, computer science, creative writing, (pre)dentistry sequence, early childhood education, East Asian studies, East European and Soviet studies, ecology/environmental studies, economics, education, electrical engineering, electrical engineering technology, elementary education, engineering (general), engineering and applied sciences, English, environmental design, environmental sciences, ethnic studies, European studies, experimental psychology, finance/banking, folklore, French, geology, German, Germanic languages and literature, Greek, Hebrew, Hispanic studies, history, history of science, insurance, interdisciplinary studies, international business, international economics, international studies, Italian, Japanese, Judaic studies, labor and industrial relations, Latin, Latin American studies, (pre)law sequence, legal studies, liberal arts/general studies, linguistics, literature, marine technology, marketing/retailing/merchandising, materials engineering, materials sciences, mathematics, mechanical engineering, mechanical engineering technology, (pre)medicine sequence, metallurgical engineering, metallurgy, microbiology, military science, modern languages, molecular biology, music, music history, natural sciences, naval sciences, Near and Middle Eastern studies, nursing, painting/drawing, peace studies, philosophy, physics, political science/government, Portuguese, psychobiology, psychology, real estate, religious studies, robotics, Romance languages, Russian, Russian and Slavic studies, Scandinavian languages/studies, secondary education, Slavic languages, social work, sociology, South Asian studies, Southeast Asian studies, Spanish, statistics, systems engineering, systems science, theater arts/drama, transportation engineering, urban studies, (pre)veterinary medicine sequence, women's studies.

Applying *Required:* essay, high school transcript, 2 recommendations, SAT or ACT, 3 Achievements, English Composition Test. *Recommended:* 3 years of high school math and science, 3 years of high school foreign language, interview. *Application deadlines:* 1/1, 11/1 for early decision, 2/15 priority date for financial aid. *Contact:* Mr. Willis J. Stetson Jr., Dean of Admissions, 116 College Hall, Philadelphia, PA 19104, 215-898-7502.

University of Pittsburgh

Pittsburgh, Pennsylvania

Founded 1787
Urban setting
State-related
Coed
Awards B, M, D

Enrollment	27,973 total; 18,250 undergraduates (2,937 freshmen)
Faculty	3,173 total; 2,674 full-time (89% have doctorate/terminal degree); student-faculty ratio is 16:1; grad assistants teach a few undergraduate courses.
Libraries	2.9 million bound volumes, 2.6 million titles on microform, 23,045 periodical subscriptions
Computing	*Terminals/PCs available for student use:* 553, located in computer center various computing labs, and workstations throughout campus; PC not required.
Of Special Interest	*Core academic program:* yes. Computer course required for math, business, engineering, information science, health records administration majors. Phi Beta Kappa, Sigma Xi chapters. Academic exchange with 10 members of the Pittsburgh Council on Higher Education. Participates in study-abroad programs. Army ROTC, Air Force ROTC, cooperative Naval ROTC.
On Campus	Drama/theater group; student-run newspaper and radio station. *Social organizations:* 22 national fraternities, 14 national sororities; 12% of eligible undergraduate men and 9% of eligible undergraduate women are members.
Athletics	Member NCAA (Division I). *Intercollegiate sports:* baseball (M), basketball (M, W), cross-country running (M, W), football (M), gymnastics (M, W), soccer (M), swimming and diving (M, W), tennis (M, W), track and field (M, W), volleyball (W), wrestling (M). *Scholarships:* M, W.

Costs (1991–92) & Aid				
	State resident tuition	$4290	3483 Need-based scholarships (average)	$1350
	Nonresident tuition	$9140	1663 Non-need scholarships (average)	$2230
	Mandatory fees	$376	Short-term loans (average)	$100
	Room and board	$3790	Long-term loans—college funds	N/Avail
	Financial aid recipients	73%	Long-term loans—external funds (average)	$3100

Undergraduate Facts				
	Part-time	26%	*Freshman Data:* 7,773 applied, 81% were accepted, 46% (2,937) of those entered	
	State residents	93%		
	Transfers	N/R	From top tenth of high school class	N/R
	African-Americans	8%	SAT-takers scoring 600 or over on verbal	N/R
	Native Americans	0%	SAT-takers scoring 700 or over on verbal	N/R
	Hispanics	1%	SAT-takers scoring 600 or over on math	N/R
	Asian-Americans	2%	SAT-takers scoring 700 or over on math	N/R
	International students	1%	ACT-takers scoring 26 or over	N/R
	Freshmen returning for sophomore year	84%	ACT-takers scoring 30 or over	N/R
	Students completing degree within 5 years	53%	*Majors with most degrees conferred:* psychology, communication, political science/government.	
	Grads pursuing further study	39%		

Majors Accounting, anthropology, applied mathematics, architectural technologies, art/fine arts, astronomy, biochemistry, biology/biological sciences, biophysics, black/African-American studies, business, business education, chemical engineering, chemistry, child care/child and family studies, child psychology/child development, Chinese, civil engineering, classics, communication, computer science, creative writing, criminal justice, dietetics, economics, electrical engineering, engineering physics, English, film studies, French, geology, German, history, history of philosophy, humanities, industrial engineering, information science, Italian, Japanese, legal studies, liberal arts/general studies, linguistics, literature, materials engineering, materials sciences, mathematics, mechanical engineering, medical records services, medical technology, metallurgical engineering, microbiology, music, natural sciences, neurosciences, nursing, nutrition, occupational therapy, pharmacy/pharmaceutical sciences, philosophy, physical education, physics, political science/government, psychology, public administration, religious studies, Russian, Slavic languages, social science, social work, sociology, Spanish, speech/rhetoric/public address/debate, statistics, studio art, theater arts/drama, urban studies, vocational education.

Applying *Required:* essay, high school transcript, SAT or ACT. *Recommended:* 3 years of high school math and science, 3 years of high school foreign language, recommendations, interview. *Application deadlines:* rolling, 3/1 priority date for financial aid. *Contact:* Dr. Betsy A. Porter, Director, Admissions and Financial Aid, Bruce Hall, Pittsburgh, PA 15260, 412-624-7164.

University of Pittsburgh at Johnstown
Johnstown, Pennsylvania

Founded 1927
Suburban setting
State-related
Coed
Awards A, B

Enrollment 3,243 total—all undergraduates (658 freshmen)

Faculty 201 total; 143 full-time (68% have doctorate/terminal degree); student-faculty ratio is 20:1.

Libraries 125,603 bound volumes, 12,948 titles on microform, 665 periodical subscriptions

Computing *Terminals/PCs available for student use:* 130, located in computer center, library, labs; PC not required.

Of Special Interest *Core academic program:* yes. Computer course required for business, engineering, math majors. Academic exchange with members of the Pittsburgh Council on Higher Education. Sponsors and participates in study-abroad programs.

On Campus Drama/theater group; student-run newspaper and radio station. *Social organizations:* 4 national fraternities, 4 national sororities, 1 local fraternity, 1 local sorority; 15% of eligible undergraduate men and 16% of eligible undergraduate women are members.

Athletics Member NCAA (Division II). *Intercollegiate sports:* baseball (M), basketball (M, W), cross-country running (W), ice hockey (M), rugby (M), skiing (downhill) (M, W), soccer (M), tennis (M, W), track and field (W), volleyball (W), wrestling (M). *Scholarships:* M, W.

Costs (1991–92) & Aid				
State resident tuition	$4290	673 Need-based scholarships (average)	$584
Nonresident tuition	$9140	164 Non-need scholarships (average)	$2848
Mandatory fees	$376	Short-term loans (average)	$50
Room and board	$3394	Long-term loans—college funds (average)	$591
Financial aid recipients	87%	Long-term loans—external funds (average)	$2271

Undergraduate Facts			
Part-time	17%	*Freshman Data:* 1,516 applied, 82% were accepted, 53% (658) of those entered	
State residents	99%		
Transfers	15%	From top tenth of high school class	19%
African-Americans	2%	SAT-takers scoring 600 or over on verbal	N/R
Native Americans	1%	SAT-takers scoring 700 or over on verbal	N/R
Hispanics	1%	SAT-takers scoring 600 or over on math	N/R
Asian-Americans	1%	SAT-takers scoring 700 or over on math	N/R
International students	1%	ACT-takers scoring 26 or over	N/R
Freshmen returning for sophomore year	89%	ACT-takers scoring 30 or over	N/R
Students completing degree within 5 years	N/R	*Majors with most degrees conferred:* business economics, education, engineering technology.	
Grads pursuing further study	N/R		

Majors Accounting, American studies, biology/biological sciences, business, business economics, chemistry, civil engineering technology, communication, computer science, creative writing, (pre)dentistry sequence, ecology/environmental studies, economics, education, electrical engineering technology, elementary education, engineering technology, English, finance/banking, geography, geology, history, humanities, journalism, (pre)law sequence, literature, mathematics, mechanical engineering technology, medical technology, (pre)medicine sequence, natural sciences, political science/government, psychology, science education, secondary education, social science, sociology, theater arts/drama, (pre)veterinary medicine sequence.

Applying *Required:* essay, high school transcript, 2 years of high school foreign language, SAT or ACT. *Recommended:* 3 years of high school math. Campus interview required for some. *Application deadlines:* rolling, 4/1 priority date for financial aid. *Contact:* Mr. Thomas J. Wonders, Director, Admissions and Student Aid, 133 Biddle Hall, Johnstown, PA 15904, 814-269-7076.

University of Puget Sound

Tacoma, Washington

Founded 1888
Suburban setting
Independent, Methodist
Coed
Awards B, M

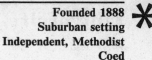

Enrollment 3,210 total; 2,881 undergraduates (697 freshmen)

Faculty 225 total; 195 full-time (87% have doctorate/terminal degree); student-faculty ratio is 13:1; grad assistants teach no undergraduate courses.

Libraries 317,653 bound volumes, 97,151 titles on microform, 1,709 periodical subscriptions

Computing *Terminals/PCs available for student use:* 150, located in computer center, computer labs; PC not required.

Of Special Interest *Core academic program:* yes. Computer course required for accounting, business, public administration, pre-engineering, math majors. Phi Beta Kappa, Sigma Xi chapters. Academic exchange program: no. Sponsors and participates in study-abroad programs. Cooperative Army ROTC.

On Campus Drama/theater group; student-run newspaper and radio station. *Social organizations:* 6 national fraternities, 6 national sororities; 33% of eligible undergraduate men and 33% of eligible undergraduate women are members.

Athletics Member NAIA. *Intercollegiate sports:* baseball (M), basketball (M, W), crew (M, W), cross-country running (M, W), football (M), golf (M), lacrosse (M, W), sailing (M, W), skiing (downhill) (M, W), soccer (M, W), softball (W), swimming and diving (M, W), tennis (M, W), track and field (M, W), volleyball (W). *Scholarships:* M, W.

Costs (1991–92) & Aid				
	Comprehensive fee	$16,670	Need-based scholarships (average)	$2500
	Tuition	$12,570	Non-need scholarships (average)	$3900
	Mandatory fees	$120	Short-term loans (average)	$100
	Room and board	$3980	Long-term loans—college funds (average)	$2000
	Financial aid recipients	70%	Long-term loans—external funds (average)	$3265

Undergraduate Facts				
	Part-time	10%	*Freshman Data:* 3,212 applied, 78% were accepted, 28% (697) of those entered	
	State residents	60%		
	Transfers	16%	From top tenth of high school class	40%
	African-Americans	2%	SAT-takers scoring 600 or over on verbal	15%
	Native Americans	1%	SAT-takers scoring 700 or over on verbal	2%
	Hispanics	1%	SAT-takers scoring 600 or over on math	33%
	Asian-Americans	6%	SAT-takers scoring 700 or over on math	6%
	International students	1%	ACT-takers scoring 26 or over	45%
	Freshmen returning for sophomore year	82%	ACT-takers scoring 30 or over	12%
	Students completing degree within 5 years	56%		
	Grads pursuing further study	N/R		

Majors Accounting, art/fine arts, art history, Asian/Oriental studies, biology/biological sciences, business, chemistry, communication, computer science, (pre)dentistry sequence, economics, English, finance/banking, French, geology, German, history, international business, (pre)law sequence, mathematics, (pre)medicine sequence, modern languages, music, music business, music education, natural sciences, occupational therapy, philosophy, physical education, physics, political science/government, psychology, public administration, religious studies, sociology, Spanish, sports medicine, theater arts/drama, (pre)veterinary medicine sequence.

Applying *Required:* essay, high school transcript, 2 recommendations, SAT or ACT. *Recommended:* 4 years of high school math, 3 years of high school science, 2 years of high school foreign language, interview. *Application deadlines:* 3/1, 11/15 for early decision, 2/15 priority date for financial aid. *Contact:* Dr. George H. Mills, Dean of Admission, 1500 North Warner Street, Tacoma, WA 98416, 206-756-3211.

From the College According to Fiske's *The Best Buys in College Education* (1991), "When it comes to good liberal arts education and personalized attention, few colleges in the Pacific Northwest have a better reputation for delivering the goods than the University of Puget Sound."

University of Redlands

Redlands, California

Founded 1907
Small-town setting
Independent
Coed
Awards B, M

Enrollment	2,300 total; 1,450 undergraduates (485 freshmen)
Faculty	134 total; 114 full-time (80% have doctorate/terminal degree); student-faculty ratio is 13:1; grad assistants teach no undergraduate courses.
Libraries	277,000 bound volumes, 45,000 titles on microform, 1,024 periodical subscriptions
Computing	*Terminals/PCs available for student use:* 84, located in computer center, some individual departments; PC not required.
Of Special Interest	*Core academic program:* yes. Computer course required for business, education, engineering, math majors. Phi Beta Kappa chapter. Academic exchange with members of the Association for Innovation in Higher Education. Sponsors and participates in study-abroad programs. Cooperative Army ROTC, cooperative Air Force ROTC.
On Campus	Drama/theater group; student-run newspaper and radio station. *Social organizations:* 6 local fraternities, 4 local sororities; 14% of eligible undergraduate men and 16% of eligible undergraduate women are members.
Athletics	Member NCAA (Division III), NAIA. *Intercollegiate sports:* baseball (M), basketball (M, W), cross-country running (M, W), football (M), golf (M, W), soccer (M, W), softball (W), swimming and diving (M, W), tennis (M, W), track and field (M, W), volleyball (W), water polo (M, W).

Costs (1991–92) & Aid				
	Comprehensive fee	$18,672	Need-based scholarships	Avail
	Tuition	$13,390	Non-need scholarships	Avail
	Mandatory fees	$212	Short-term loans (average)	$50
	Room and board	$5070	Long-term loans—college funds (average)	$5000
	Financial aid recipients	80%	Long-term loans—external funds (average)	$2339

Undergraduate Facts				
	Part-time	3%	*Freshman Data:* 1,490 applied, 90% were accepted, 36% (485) of those entered	
	State residents	60%		
	Transfers	18%	From top tenth of high school class	34%
	African-Americans	4%	SAT-takers scoring 600 or over on verbal	14%
	Native Americans	1%	SAT-takers scoring 700 or over on verbal	3%
	Hispanics	6%	SAT-takers scoring 600 or over on math	23%
	Asian-Americans	8%	SAT-takers scoring 700 or over on math	3%
	International students	3%	ACT-takers scoring 26 or over	N/R
	Freshmen returning for sophomore year	80%	ACT-takers scoring 30 or over	N/R
	Students completing degree within 5 years	N/R	*Majors with most degrees conferred:* liberal arts/general studies, social science, business.	
	Grads pursuing further study	N/R		

Majors Accounting, anthropology, applied mathematics, art education, art/fine arts, art history, Asian/Oriental studies, behavioral sciences, biology/biological sciences, business, ceramic art and design, chemistry, computer science, creative writing, economics, education, electrical engineering, elementary education, engineering (general), English, environmental sciences, ethnic studies, French, German, history, humanities, international studies, (pre)law sequence, liberal arts/general studies, literature, mathematics, mechanical engineering, (pre)medicine sequence, music, music education, philosophy, physical education, physics, piano/organ, political science/government, psychology, religious studies, secondary education, social science, sociology, Spanish, speech pathology and audiology, speech therapy, stringed instruments, studio art, voice, wind and percussion instruments, women's studies.

Applying *Required:* essay, high school transcript, 2 recommendations, SAT or ACT. *Recommended:* some high school foreign language, interview. 3 years of high school math and science required for some. *Application deadlines:* 4/1, 3/1 priority date for financial aid. *Contact:* Mr. Paul Driscoll, Dean of Admissions, PO Box 3080, Redlands, CA 92373, 714-335-4074; *Office location:* 1200 East Colton Avenue.

University of Richmond

Richmond, Virginia

Founded 1830
Suburban setting
Independent/affiliated with Baptist Church
Coed
Awards B, M

Enrollment	4,688 total; 2,883 undergraduates (804 freshmen)
Faculty	380 total; 252 full-time (91% have doctorate/terminal degree); student-faculty ratio is 12:1; grad assistants teach no undergraduate courses.
Libraries	515,984 bound volumes, 125,374 titles on microform, 6,259 periodical subscriptions
Computing	*Terminals/PCs available for student use:* 200, located in computer center, library, dormitories; PC not required but available for purchase. Campus network links student PCs.
Of Special Interest	*Core academic program:* yes. Computer course required for business majors. Phi Beta Kappa, Sigma Xi chapters. Academic exchange with American University. Sponsors and participates in study-abroad programs. Army ROTC.
On Campus	Drama/theater group; student-run newspaper and radio station. *Social organizations:* 10 national fraternities, 7 national sororities; 55% of eligible undergraduate men and 60% of eligible undergraduate women are members.
Athletics	Member NCAA (Division I). *Intercollegiate sports:* baseball (M), basketball (M, W), cross-country running (M, W), field hockey (W), football (M), golf (M), lacrosse (M, W), rugby (M), soccer (M, W), swimming and diving (M, W), tennis (M, W), track and field (M, W), water polo (M). *Scholarships:* M, W.

Costs (1992–93) & Aid				
	Comprehensive fee	$15,460	Need-based scholarships (average)	$3763
	Tuition	$12,620	Non-need scholarships (average)	$6412
	Mandatory fees	N/App	Short-term loans (average)	$100
	Room and board	$2840	Long-term loans—college funds (average)	$1021
	Financial aid recipients	53%	Long-term loans—external funds (average)	$3650

Undergraduate Facts				
	Part-time	2%	*Freshman Data:* 4,423 applied, 56% were accepted, 33% (804) of those entered	
	State residents	23%		
	Transfers	3%	From top tenth of high school class	35%
	African-Americans	4%	SAT-takers scoring 600 or over on verbal	29%
	Native Americans	1%	SAT-takers scoring 700 or over on verbal	2%
	Hispanics	1%	SAT-takers scoring 600 or over on math	70%
	Asian-Americans	2%	SAT-takers scoring 700 or over on math	14%
	International students	1%	ACT-takers scoring 26 or over	N/R
	Freshmen returning for sophomore year	92%	ACT-takers scoring 30 or over	N/R
	Students completing degree within 5 years	83%	*Majors with most degrees conferred:* business, English, political science/government.	
	Grads pursuing further study	25%		

Majors Accounting, American studies, art/fine arts, art history, arts administration, biology/biological sciences, business, chemistry, classics, computer science, criminal justice, early childhood education, economics, education, elementary education, English, European studies, finance/banking, French, German, Greek, health education, health science, history, interdisciplinary studies, international business, international studies, journalism, Latin, Latin American studies, marketing/retailing/merchandising, mathematics, military science, music, music education, music history, philosophy, physical education, physical fitness/human movement, physics, piano/organ, political science/government, psychology, religious studies, Russian and Slavic studies, secondary education, sociology, Spanish, speech/rhetoric/public address/debate, stringed instruments, studio art, theater arts/drama, urban studies, voice, wind and percussion instruments, women's studies.

Applying *Required:* essay, high school transcript, 3 years of high school math, 1 recommendation, SAT or ACT, 3 Achievements, English Composition Test. *Recommended:* 3 years of high school science, 2 years of high school foreign language, English Composition Test (with essay). *Application deadlines:* 2/1, 11/1 for early decision, 2/1 for financial aid. *Contact:* Mr. Thomas N. Pollard Jr., Dean of Admissions, Sarah Brunet Hall, Richmond Way, Richmond, VA 23173, 804-289-8640.

University of Rochester

Rochester, New York

Founded 1850
Suburban setting
Independent
Coed
Awards B, M, D

Enrollment 8,753 total; 5,149 undergraduates (1,226 freshmen)

Faculty 577 total; 505 full-time (99% have doctorate/terminal degree); student-faculty ratio is 11:1; grad assistants teach a few undergraduate courses.

Libraries 2.7 million bound volumes, 3.6 million titles on microform, 14,000 periodical subscriptions

Computing *Terminals/PCs available for student use:* 700, located in computer center, library, dormitories, academic buildings, many other locations throughout campus; PC not required. Campus network links student PCs.

Of Special Interest *Core academic program:* yes. Computer course required for engineering majors. Phi Beta Kappa, Sigma Xi chapters. Academic exchange with Rochester Area Colleges. Sponsors and participates in study-abroad programs. Naval ROTC, cooperative Army ROTC, cooperative Air Force ROTC.

On Campus Drama/theater group; student-run newspaper and radio station. *Social organizations:* 17 national fraternities, 10 national sororities; 30% of eligible undergraduate men and 21% of eligible undergraduate women are members.

Athletics Member NCAA (Division III). *Intercollegiate sports:* baseball (M), basketball (M, W), crew (M, W), cross-country running (M, W), equestrian sports (M, W), field hockey (W), football (M), golf (M, W), ice hockey (M), lacrosse (M, W), rugby (M), skiing (cross-country) (M, W), skiing (downhill) (M, W), soccer (M, W), softball (W), squash (M, W), swimming and diving (M, W), tennis (M, W), track and field (M, W), volleyball (M, W).

Costs (1991–92) & Aid				
	Comprehensive fee	$21,271	Need-based scholarships (average)	$7987
	Tuition	$15,150	Non-need scholarships (average)	$2732
	Mandatory fees	$371	Short-term loans (average)	$500
	Room and board	$5750	Long-term loans—college funds (average)	$2175
	Financial aid recipients	76%	Long-term loans—external funds (average)	$3075

Undergraduate Facts				
	Part-time	3%	*Freshman Data:* 7,280 applied, 70% were accepted, 24% (1,226) of those entered	
	State residents	47%		
	Transfers	12%	From top tenth of high school class	53%
	African-Americans	6%	SAT-takers scoring 600 or over on verbal	23%
	Native Americans	N/R	SAT-takers scoring 700 or over on verbal	3%
	Hispanics	4%	SAT-takers scoring 600 or over on math	63%
	Asian-Americans	9%	SAT-takers scoring 700 or over on math	19%
	International students	6%	ACT-takers scoring 26 or over	68%
	Freshmen returning for sophomore year	94%	ACT-takers scoring 30 or over	23%
	Students completing degree within 5 years	74%	*Majors with most degrees conferred:* psychology, political science/government, biology/biological sciences.	
	Grads pursuing further study	34%		

Majors Anthropology, applied mathematics, art history, astronomy, biochemistry, biology/biological sciences, cell biology, chemical engineering, chemistry, classics, cognitive science, computer science, economics, electrical engineering, engineering and applied sciences, engineering sciences, English, evolutionary biology, film studies, French, genetics, geology, German, health science, history, interdisciplinary studies, Japanese, linguistics, mathematics, mechanical engineering, microbiology, music, music education, music history, neurosciences, nursing, optics, philosophy, physics, political science/government, psychology, religious studies, Russian, science, Spanish, statistics, studio art, women's studies.

Applying *Required:* essay, high school transcript, 1 recommendation, SAT or ACT. *Recommended:* 3 years of high school math and science, 2 years of high school foreign language, interview, Achievements, English Composition Test (with essay). Audition, portfolio required for some. *Application deadlines:* 1/15, 2/1 for early decision, 2/1 priority date for financial aid. *Contact:* Mr. Wayne A. Locust, Director of Admissions, Meliora Hall, Intercampus Drive, Rochester, NY 14627-0001, 716-275-3221.

University of Scranton

Scranton, Pennsylvania

Founded 1888
Urban setting
Independent, Roman Catholic (Jesuit)
Coed
Awards A, B, M

Enrollment 5,113 total; 4,410 undergraduates (911 freshmen)

Faculty 387 total; 255 full-time (73% have doctorate/terminal degree); student-faculty ratio is 17:1; grad assistants teach no undergraduate courses.

Libraries 245,000 bound volumes, 52,000 titles on microform, 1,800 periodical subscriptions

Computing *Terminals/PCs available for student use:* 308, located in computer center, library, dormitories, various academic departments; PC not required. Campus network links student PCs.

Of Special Interest *Core academic program:* yes. Computer course required for business, math, electronics engineering majors. Sigma Xi chapter. Academic exchange with 27 members of the Jesuit Educational System. Participates in study-abroad programs. Army ROTC, cooperative Air Force ROTC.

On Campus Drama/theater group; student-run newspaper and radio station. No national or local fraternities or sororities on campus.

Athletics Member NCAA (Division III). *Intercollegiate sports:* baseball (M), basketball (M, W), bowling (M, W), crew (M, W), cross-country running (M, W), equestrian sports (M, W), field hockey (W), golf (M), ice hockey (M), lacrosse (M, W), rugby (M), skiing (downhill) (M, W), soccer (M, W), softball (W), swimming and diving (M, W), tennis (M, W), track and field (M, W), volleyball (M, W), wrestling (M).

Costs (1991–92) & Aid				
	Comprehensive fee	$14,128	Need-based scholarships (average)	$2600
	Tuition	$9056	Non-need scholarships (average)	$3050
	Mandatory fees	$570	Short-term loans	N/Avail
	Room and board	$4502	Long-term loans—college funds	N/Avail
	Financial aid recipients	80%	Long-term loans—external funds (average)	$3000

Undergraduate Facts				
	Part-time	12%	*Freshman Data:* 4,441 applied, 59% were accepted, 34% (911) of those entered	
	State residents	53%		
	Transfers	7%	From top tenth of high school class	33%
	African-Americans	1%	SAT-takers scoring 600 or over on verbal	11%
	Native Americans	0%	SAT-takers scoring 700 or over on verbal	1%
	Hispanics	1%	SAT-takers scoring 600 or over on math	30%
	Asian-Americans	1%	SAT-takers scoring 700 or over on math	3%
	International students	1%	ACT-takers scoring 26 or over	N/R
	Freshmen returning for sophomore year	94%	ACT-takers scoring 30 or over	N/R
	Students completing degree within 5 years	85%		
	Grads pursuing further study	26%		

Majors Accounting, advertising, biochemistry, biology/biological sciences, biophysics, broadcasting, business, business economics, chemistry, classics, communication, computer engineering, computer information systems, computer science, criminal justice, (pre)dentistry sequence, economics, education, electronics engineering, elementary education, English, film and video, finance/banking, French, German, gerontology, Greek, health services administration, history, human services, international business, international studies, journalism, Latin, law enforcement/police sciences, (pre)law sequence, marketing/retailing/merchandising, mathematics, medical technology, (pre)medicine sequence, modern languages, neurosciences, nursing, philosophy, physical therapy, physics, political science/government, psychology, public administration, public relations, radio and television studies, religious studies, Romance languages, secondary education, sociology, Spanish, theology, (pre)veterinary medicine sequence.

Applying *Required:* high school transcript, 3 years of high school math, 2 years of high school foreign language, SAT or ACT. *Recommended:* 2 recommendations, campus interview. 3 years of high school science required for some. *Application deadlines:* 3/1, 11/1 for early action, 2/15 priority date for financial aid. *Contact:* Rev. Bernard R. McIlhenny, SJ, Dean of Admissions, Room 406, Saint Thomas Hall, Scranton, PA 18510-4501, 717-941-7540.

University of Southern California

Los Angeles, California

Founded 1880
Urban setting
Independent
Coed
Awards B, M, D

Enrollment	27,624 total; 14,668 undergraduates (2,388 freshmen)
Faculty	3,402 total; 2,168 full-time (88% have doctorate/terminal degree); student-faculty ratio is 17:1; grad assistants teach about a quarter of the undergraduate courses.
Libraries	2.7 million bound volumes, 2.9 million titles on microform, 16,000 periodical subscriptions
Computing	*Terminals/PCs available for student use:* 4,500, located in computer center, student center, library, dormitories; PC not required. Campus network links student PCs.
Of Special Interest	*Core academic program:* yes. Computer course required for business administration, some engineering majors. Phi Beta Kappa, Sigma Xi chapters. Academic exchange with Hebrew Union College–Jewish Institute of Religion, California Institute of Technology, University of California, Los Angeles. Sponsors and participates in study-abroad programs. Army ROTC, Naval ROTC, Air Force ROTC.
On Campus	Drama/theater group; student-run newspaper and radio station. *Social organizations:* 26 national fraternities, 12 national sororities; 22% of eligible undergraduate men and 22% of eligible undergraduate women are members.
Athletics	Member NCAA (Division I). *Intercollegiate sports:* baseball (M), basketball (M, W), crew (M, W), cross-country running (M, W), football (M), golf (M, W), lacrosse (M), rugby (M), sailing (M, W), soccer (M), swimming and diving (M, W), tennis (M, W), track and field (M, W), volleyball (M, W), water polo (M). *Scholarships:* M, W.

Costs (1991–92) & Aid				
	Comprehensive fee	$21,560	Need-based scholarships (average)	$7006
	Tuition	$15,020	Non-need scholarships (average)	$5500
	Mandatory fees	$280	Short-term loans (average)	$250
	Room and board	$6260	Long-term loans—college funds (average)	$2351
	Financial aid recipients	62%	Long-term loans—external funds (average)	$2983

Undergraduate Facts				
	Part-time	10%	*Freshman Data:* 10,409 applied, 73% were accepted, 32% (2,388) of those entered	
	State residents	65%		
	Transfers	6%	From top tenth of high school class	42%
	African-Americans	6%	SAT-takers scoring 600 or over on verbal	N/R
	Native Americans	1%	SAT-takers scoring 700 or over on verbal	N/R
	Hispanics	10%	SAT-takers scoring 600 or over on math	N/R
	Asian-Americans	20%	SAT-takers scoring 700 or over on math	N/R
	International students	7%	ACT-takers scoring 26 or over	N/R
	Freshmen returning for sophomore year	84%	ACT-takers scoring 30 or over	N/R
	Students completing degree within 5 years	56%		
	Grads pursuing further study	20%		

Majors Accounting, aerospace engineering, American studies, anthropology, architecture, art education, art/fine arts, art history, astronomy, biology/biological sciences, biomedical engineering, broadcasting, business, chemical engineering, chemistry, civil engineering, classics, communication, comparative literature, computer science, dance, dental services, East Asian studies, economics, education, electrical engineering, engineering (general), English, ethnic studies, film studies, food marketing, French, geography, geology, German, gerontology, Greek, history, humanities, industrial engineering, interdisciplinary studies, international studies, Italian, jazz, journalism, Latin, linguistics, mathematics, mechanical engineering, metallurgical engineering, music, music education, natural sciences, nursing, occupational therapy, petroleum/natural gas engineering, philosophy, physical education, physical sciences, physical therapy, physics, piano/organ, political science/government, psychobiology, psychology, public administration, public affairs and policy studies, public relations, radio and television studies, religious studies, Russian, safety and security technologies, social science, sociology, Spanish, stringed instruments, studio art, systems engineering, theater arts/drama, voice, wind and percussion instruments, women's studies.

Applying *Required:* essay, high school transcript, SAT or ACT. *Recommended:* 3 years of high school math and science, 2 years of high school foreign language, recommendations, interview, Achievements. Recommendations required for some. *Application deadlines:* 2/1, continuous to 2/15 for financial aid. *Contact:* Mr. Duncan Murdoch, Director of Admissions, 700 Childs Way, Los Angeles, CA 90089-0911, 213-740-8775.

University of Tennessee, Knoxville

Knoxville, Tennessee

Founded 1794
Urban setting
State-supported
Coed
Awards B, M, D

Enrollment	25,598 total; 19,385 undergraduates (3,061 freshmen)
Faculty	1,157 total; 1,113 full-time (80% have doctorate/terminal degree); student-faculty ratio is 17:1; grad assistants teach a few undergraduate courses.
Libraries	1.7 million bound volumes, 1.8 million titles on microform, 19,061 periodical subscriptions
Computing	*Terminals/PCs available for student use:* 2,500, located in computer center, student center, library, dormitories, classrooms; PC not required.
Of Special Interest	*Core academic program:* no. Computer course required for agricultural economics, agricultural education, animal sciences, food sciences, forestry, ornamental horticulture, business, advertising, child and family studies, adult and continuing education majors. Phi Beta Kappa, Sigma Xi chapters. Academic exchange with Knoxville College, Academic Common Market. Sponsors and participates in study-abroad programs. Army ROTC, Air Force ROTC.
On Campus	Drama/theater group; student-run newspaper and radio station. *Social organizations:* 26 national fraternities, 18 national sororities; 9% of eligible undergraduate men and 10% of eligible undergraduate women are members.
Athletics	Member NCAA (Division I). *Intercollegiate sports:* baseball (M), basketball (M, W), cross-country running (M, W), football (M), golf (M, W), swimming and diving (M, W), tennis (M, W), track and field (M, W), volleyball (W). *Scholarships:* M, W.

Costs (1992–93 estimated) & Aid				
	State resident tuition	$1878	2480 Need-based scholarships (average)	$1000
	Nonresident tuition	$5410	2000 Non-need scholarships (average)	$1000
	Mandatory fees	$233	Short-term loans (average)	$50
	Room and board	$3361	Long-term loans—college funds (average)	$750
	Financial aid recipients	35%	Long-term loans—external funds (average)	$3000

Undergraduate Facts				
	Part-time	15%	*Freshman Data:* 6,994 applied, 73% were accepted, 60% (3,061) of those entered	
	State residents	85%		
	Transfers	5%	From top tenth of high school class	26%
	African-Americans	5%	SAT-takers scoring 600 or over on verbal	10%
	Native Americans	1%	SAT-takers scoring 700 or over on verbal	1%
	Hispanics	1%	SAT-takers scoring 600 or over on math	24%
	Asian-Americans	1%	SAT-takers scoring 700 or over on math	5%
	International students	4%	ACT-takers scoring 26 or over	27%
	Freshmen returning for sophomore year	79%	ACT-takers scoring 30 or over	6%
	Students completing degree within 5 years	41%	*Majors with most degrees conferred:* finance/banking, psychology, accounting.	
	Grads pursuing further study	N/R		

Majors Accounting, adult and continuing education, advertising, aerospace engineering, agricultural business, agricultural economics, agricultural education, agricultural engineering, agronomy/soil and crop sciences, American studies, animal sciences, anthropology, applied art, architecture, art education, art/fine arts, art history, Asian/Oriental studies, astronomy, biochemistry, biology/biological sciences, biomedical engineering, black/African-American studies, botany/plant sciences, broadcasting, business, business economics, business education, cell biology, ceramic art and design, chemical engineering, chemistry, child care/child and family studies, child psychology/child development, civil engineering, classics, communication, comparative literature, computer engineering, computer science, construction engineering, creative writing, cytotechnology, dance, (pre)dentistry sequence, dietetics, early childhood education, East Asian studies, East European and Soviet studies, ecology/environmental studies, economics, education, electrical engineering, elementary education, energy management technologies, engineering and applied sciences, engineering mechanics, engineering physics, engineering sciences, English, environmental sciences, family and consumer studies, fashion merchandising, finance/banking, fish and game management, food sciences, forestry, French, geography, geology, German, graphic arts, Greek, health education, history, home economics education, horticulture, hotel and restaurant management, human ecology, human services, illustration, industrial engineering, interior design, international business, Italian, jazz, journalism, landscape architecture/design, Latin, Latin American studies, liberal arts/general studies, linguistics, literature, management information systems, marketing/retailing/merchandising, mathematics, mechanical engineering, medical laboratory technology, medical records services, medical technology, (pre)medicine sequence, medieval studies, metallurgical engineering, metallurgy, microbiology, music, music education, music history, nuclear engineering, nursing, nutrition, ornamental horticulture, painting/drawing, philosophy, physical education, physical fitness/human movement, physics, piano/organ, political science/government, psychology, public administration, public health, public relations, recreation and leisure services, religious studies, retail management, Romance languages, Russian, Russian and Slavic studies, sacred music, science education, sculpture, secondary education, social work, sociology, Spanish, special education, speech pathology and audiology, speech/rhetoric/public address/debate, sports administration, statistics, stringed instruments, studio art, systems engineering, textiles and clothing, theater arts/drama, transportation engineering, urban studies, (pre)veterinary medicine sequence, vocational education, voice, wildlife management, wind and percussion instruments, women's studies, zoology.

Applying *Required:* high school transcript, 3 years of high school math, 2 years of high school foreign language, SAT or ACT. Recommendations, interview required for some. *Application deadlines:* 7/1, 2/15 priority date for financial aid. *Contact:* Mr. Gerald Bowker, Dean of Admissions and Records, 320 Student Services Building, Knoxville, TN 37996, 615-974-2105 or toll-free 800-221-8657 (in-state).

University of Texas at Austin

Austin, Texas

Founded 1883
Urban setting
State-supported
Coed
Awards B, M, D

Enrollment 49,961 total; 37,025 undergraduates (7,551 freshmen)

Faculty 2,341 total; 2,196 full-time (84% have doctorate/terminal degree); student-faculty ratio is 20:1; grad assistants teach about a quarter of the undergraduate courses.

Libraries 5.8 million bound volumes, 4 million titles on microform, 79,400 periodical subscriptions

Computing *Terminals/PCs available for student use:* 12,000, located in computer center, student center, library, dormitories; PC not required.

Of Special Interest *Core academic program:* yes. Computer course required for engineering, business, education majors. Phi Beta Kappa, Sigma Xi chapters. Academic exchange program: no. Sponsors and participates in study-abroad programs. Army ROTC, Naval ROTC, Air Force ROTC.

On Campus Drama/theater group; student-run newspaper and radio station. *Social organizations:* 28 national fraternities, 15 national sororities; 14% of eligible undergraduate men and 14% of eligible undergraduate women are members.

Athletics Member NCAA (Division I). *Intercollegiate sports:* baseball (M), basketball (M, W), cross-country running (M, W), football (M), golf (M, W), swimming and diving (M, W), tennis (M, W), track and field (M, W), volleyball (W). *Scholarships:* M, W.

Costs (1991–92) & Aid				
	State resident tuition	$650	8270 Need-based scholarships (average)	$1835
	Nonresident tuition	$3890	9603 Non-need scholarships (average)	$1633
	Mandatory fees	$525	Short-term loans (average)	$250
	Room and board	$3800	Long-term loans—college funds (average)	$3400
	Financial aid recipients	47%	Long-term loans—external funds (average)	$2990

Undergraduate Facts				
	Part-time	13%	*Freshman Data:* 14,342 applied, 69% were accepted, 76% (7,551) of those entered	
	State residents	91%		
	Transfers	5%	From top tenth of high school class	60%
	African-Americans	4%	SAT-takers scoring 600 or over on verbal	N/R
	Native Americans	1%	SAT-takers scoring 700 or over on verbal	N/R
	Hispanics	13%	SAT-takers scoring 600 or over on math	N/R
	Asian-Americans	8%	SAT-takers scoring 700 or over on math	N/R
	International students	4%	ACT-takers scoring 26 or over	N/R
	Freshmen returning for sophomore year	85%	ACT-takers scoring 30 or over	N/R
	Students completing degree within 5 years	91%	*Majors with most degrees conferred:* psychology, electrical engineering, biology/biological sciences.	
	Grads pursuing further study	N/R		

Majors Accounting, advertising, aerospace engineering, African languages, African studies, American studies, anthropology, archaeology, architectural engineering, architecture, art education, art/fine arts, art history, Asian/Oriental studies, astronomy, biochemistry, biology/biological sciences, black/African-American studies, botany/plant sciences, broadcasting, business, chemical engineering, chemistry, child psychology/child development, civil engineering, classics, communication, computer science, dance, data processing, (pre)dentistry sequence, dietetics, early childhood education, East European and Soviet studies, economics, education, electrical engineering, elementary education, engineering sciences, English, ethnic studies, European studies, film studies, finance/banking, French, geography, geology, geophysics, German, Greek, Hebrew, history, home economics, home economics education, humanities, insurance, interdisciplinary studies, interior design, international business, international studies, Italian, Japanese, journalism, Latin, Latin American studies, (pre)law sequence, liberal arts/general studies, linguistics, management information systems, marketing/retailing/merchandising, mathematics, mechanical engineering, (pre)medicine sequence, Mexican-American/Chicano studies, microbiology, molecular biology, music, music education, Near and Middle Eastern studies, nursing, nutrition, painting/drawing, pharmacy/pharmaceutical sciences, philosophy, photography, physical education, physics, political science/government, Portuguese, psychology, radio and television studies, real estate, Russian, Russian and Slavic studies, Scandinavian languages/studies, Slavic languages, social work, sociology, Spanish, special education, statistics, studio art, textiles and clothing, theater arts/drama, (pre)veterinary medicine sequence, zoology.

Applying *Required:* high school transcript, 3 years of high school math, 2 years of high school foreign language, SAT or ACT. 1 Achievement, English Composition Test required for some. *Application deadlines:* 3/1, 3/15 priority date for financial aid. *Contact:* Ms. Shirley F. Binder, Director of Admissions, Red River and Martin Luther King Blvd., Austin, TX 78712, 512-471-1711.

University of the South

Sewanee, Tennessee

Founded 1857
Small-town setting
Independent, Episcopal
Coed
Awards B, M, D

Enrollment 1,181 total; 1,109 undergraduates (329 freshmen)

Faculty 121 total; 103 full-time (94% have doctorate/terminal degree); student-faculty ratio is 11:1; grad assistants teach no undergraduate courses.

Libraries 411,988 bound volumes, 197,048 titles on microform, 2,611 periodical subscriptions

Computing *Terminals/PCs available for student use:* 35, located in computer center, library; PC not required. Campus network links student PCs.

Of Special Interest *Core academic program:* yes. Computer course required for math, science, psychology majors. Phi Beta Kappa, Sigma Xi chapters. Academic exchange program: no. Sponsors and participates in study-abroad programs.

On Campus Dress code; drama/theater group; student-run newspaper and radio station. *Social organizations:* 11 national fraternities, 6 local sororities; 69% of eligible undergraduate men and 72% of eligible undergraduate women are members.

Athletics Member NCAA (Division III). *Intercollegiate sports:* baseball (M), basketball (M, W), crew (M, W), cross-country running (M, W), equestrian sports (M, W), fencing (M, W), field hockey (W), football (M), golf (M), lacrosse (M, W), rugby (M, W), skiing (cross-country) (M, W), skiing (downhill) (M, W), soccer (M, W), softball (W), swimming and diving (M, W), tennis (M, W), track and field (M, W), volleyball (W).

Costs (1991–92) & Aid				
	Comprehensive fee	$17,015	Need-based scholarships (average)	$8497
	Tuition	$13,350	Non-need scholarships (average)	$4438
	Mandatory fees	$155	Short-term loans	N/Avail
	Room and board	$3510	Long-term loans—college funds (average)	$2700
	Financial aid recipients	48%	Long-term loans—external funds (average)	$2700

Undergraduate Facts				
	Part-time	3%	*Freshman Data:* 1,178 applied, 75% were accepted, 37% (329) of those entered	
	State residents	19%		
	Transfers	4%	From top tenth of high school class	40%
	African-Americans	2%	SAT-takers scoring 600 or over on verbal	29%
	Native Americans	0%	SAT-takers scoring 700 or over on verbal	4%
	Hispanics	1%	SAT-takers scoring 600 or over on math	48%
	Asian-Americans	1%	SAT-takers scoring 700 or over on math	7%
	International students	3%	ACT-takers scoring 26 or over	67%
	Freshmen returning for sophomore year	98%	ACT-takers scoring 30 or over	12%
	Students completing degree within 5 years	78%	*Majors with most degrees conferred:* English, political science/government, art/fine arts.	
	Grads pursuing further study	35%		

Majors American studies, anthropology, applied art, art/fine arts, art history, Asian/Oriental studies, biology/biological sciences, chemistry, classics, comparative literature, computer science, (pre)dentistry sequence, economics, English, environmental sciences, European studies, forestry, French, geology, German, Greek, history, international studies, Latin, (pre)law sequence, literature, mathematics, (pre)medicine sequence, medieval studies, music, music history, natural resource management, painting/drawing, philosophy, physics, political science/government, psychology, religious studies, Russian, Russian and Slavic studies, social science, Spanish, studio art, theater arts/drama.

Applying *Required:* essay, high school transcript, 3 years of high school math, 2 years of high school foreign language, 2 recommendations, SAT or ACT. *Recommended:* 3 years of high school science, campus interview, Achievements, English Composition Test. *Application deadlines:* 2/1, 11/15 for early decision, 3/1 priority date for financial aid. *Contact:* Mr. Robert M. Hedrick, Director of Admission, 735 University Avenue, Sewanee, TN 37375, 615-598-1238.

University of Tulsa

Tulsa, Oklahoma

Founded 1894
Urban setting
Independent/affiliated with Presbyterian Church
Coed
Awards B, M, D

Enrollment 4,785 total; 3,315 undergraduates (706 freshmen)

Faculty 414 total; 332 full-time (93% have doctorate/terminal degree); student-faculty ratio is 12:1; grad assistants teach a few undergraduate courses.

Libraries 725,336 bound volumes, 2.1 million titles on microform, 4,300 periodical subscriptions

Computing *Terminals/PCs available for student use:* 225, located in computer center, library, dormitories, academic buildings; PC not required.

Of Special Interest *Core academic program:* yes. Computer course required. Phi Beta Kappa, Sigma Xi chapters. Academic exchange program: no. Sponsors and participates in study-abroad programs. Army ROTC.

On Campus Drama/theater group; student-run newspaper and radio station. *Social organizations:* 7 national fraternities, 7 national sororities; 23% of eligible undergraduate men and 24% of eligible undergraduate women are members.

Athletics Member NCAA (Division I). *Intercollegiate sports:* basketball (M), cross-country running (M, W), football (M), golf (M, W), soccer (M, W), tennis (M, W), track and field (M, W), volleyball (W). *Scholarships:* M, W.

Costs (1991–92) & Aid				
Comprehensive fee	$12,250	Need-based scholarships (average)	$2000
Tuition	$8650	Non-need scholarships (average)	$2000
Mandatory fees	N/App	Short-term loans (average)	$200
Room and board	$3600	Long-term loans—college funds (average)	$1000
Financial aid recipients	77%	Long-term loans—external funds (average)	$1500

Undergraduate Facts

Part-time	13%	*Freshman Data:* 1,678 applied, 95% were accepted, 44% (706) of those entered	
State residents	51%		
Transfers	9%	From top tenth of high school class	31%
African-Americans	4%	SAT-takers scoring 600 or over on verbal	19%
Native Americans	3%	SAT-takers scoring 700 or over on verbal	1%
Hispanics	2%	SAT-takers scoring 600 or over on math	46%
Asian-Americans	2%	SAT-takers scoring 700 or over on math	9%
International students	9%	ACT-takers scoring 26 or over	43%
Freshmen returning for sophomore year	80%	ACT-takers scoring 30 or over	12%
Students completing degree within 5 years	50%	*Majors with most degrees conferred:* accounting, finance/banking, marketing/retailing/merchandising.	
Grads pursuing further study	N/R		

Majors Accounting, advertising, anthropology, applied mathematics, art education, art/fine arts, art history, athletic training, biology/biological sciences, broadcasting, business, cell biology, ceramic art and design, chemical engineering, chemistry, commercial art, communication, comparative literature, computer information systems, computer science, (pre)dentistry sequence, earth science, ecology/environmental studies, economics, education, electrical engineering, elementary education, engineering physics, English, environmental biology, finance/banking, French, geological engineering, geology, geophysics, health education, health science, history, international studies, journalism, (pre)law sequence, legal studies, literature, management information systems, marketing/retailing/merchandising, mathematics, mechanical engineering, (pre)medicine sequence, music, music education, nursing, painting/drawing, petroleum/natural gas engineering, philosophy, physical sciences, physics, piano/organ, political science/government, printmaking, psychology, public relations, radio and television studies, religious studies, science, science education, sculpture, secondary education, sociology, Spanish, special education, speech pathology and audiology, stringed instruments, studio art, systems engineering, theater arts/drama, (pre)veterinary medicine sequence, voice, wind and percussion instruments.

Applying *Required:* high school transcript, 1 recommendation, SAT or ACT. *Recommended:* essay, 3 years of high school math and science, 2 years of high school foreign language, interview. *Application deadlines:* rolling, 3/1 priority date for financial aid. *Contact:* Mr. John C. Corso, Associate Vice President for Student Services, 600 South College, Tulsa, OK 74104, 918-631-2307 or toll-free 800-331-3050 (out-of-state); *Office location:* McClure Hall, 6th and Evanston.

University of Vermont

Burlington, Vermont

Founded 1791
Small-town setting
State-supported
Coed
Awards A, B, M, D

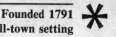

Enrollment 9,492 total; 8,029 undergraduates (1,845 freshmen)

Faculty 1,017 total; 873 full-time (87% have doctorate/terminal degree); student-faculty ratio is 15:1; grad assistants teach a few undergraduate courses.

Libraries 1.4 million bound volumes, 10,318 periodical subscriptions

Computing *Terminals/PCs available for student use:* 396, located in computer center, library, dormitories; PC required for all first year and transfer students entering either the College of Engineering and Mathematics or the School of Business Administration.

Of Special Interest *Core academic program:* no. Computer course required for mathematical science, business administration, engineering, wildlife biology majors. Phi Beta Kappa, Sigma Xi chapters. Academic exchange program: no. Sponsors and participates in study-abroad programs. Army ROTC, cooperative Air Force ROTC.

On Campus Drama/theater group; student-run newspaper and radio station. *Social organizations:* 14 national fraternities, 6 national sororities, 2 local fraternities; 6% of eligible undergraduate men and 10% of eligible undergraduate women are members.

Athletics Member NCAA (Division I), NAIA. *Intercollegiate sports:* basketball (M, W), crew (M, W), cross-country running (M, W), fencing (M, W), field hockey (W), golf (M), gymnastics (M, W), ice hockey (M, W), lacrosse (M, W), rugby (M), skiing (cross-country) (M, W), skiing (downhill) (M, W), soccer (M, W), swimming and diving (M, W), tennis (M, W), track and field (M, W), volleyball (M, W), wrestling (M). *Scholarships:* M, W.

Costs (1991–92) & Aid				
State resident tuition	$5314	Need-based scholarships	Avail
Nonresident tuition	$13,914	58 Non-need scholarships (average)	$7900
Mandatory fees	$414	Short-term loans	N/Avail
Room and board	$4142	Long-term loans—college funds (average)	$1080
Financial aid recipients	37%	Long-term loans—external funds (average)	$3300

Undergraduate Facts			
Part-time	6%	*Freshman Data:* 8,154 applied, 72% were accepted, 31% (1,845) of those entered	
State residents	50%		
Transfers	4%	From top tenth of high school class	32%
African-Americans	1%	SAT-takers scoring 600 or over on verbal	10%
Native Americans	1%	SAT-takers scoring 700 or over on verbal	1%
Hispanics	1%	SAT-takers scoring 600 or over on math	36%
Asian-Americans	3%	SAT-takers scoring 700 or over on math	5%
International students	1%	ACT-takers scoring 26 or over	N/R
Freshmen returning for sophomore year	87%	ACT-takers scoring 30 or over	N/R
Students completing degree within 5 years	N/R	*Majors with most degrees conferred:* business, political science/government, English.	
Grads pursuing further study	N/R		

Majors Accounting, agricultural economics, agricultural sciences, agricultural technologies, agronomy/soil and crop sciences, animal sciences, anthropology, applied mathematics, art education, art/fine arts, art history, Asian/Oriental studies, biochemistry, bioengineering, biology/biological sciences, biomedical engineering, botany/plant sciences, business, Canadian studies, chemistry, child care/child and family studies, civil engineering, classics, computer science, consumer services, dairy sciences, (pre)dentistry sequence, dietetics, early childhood education, East European and Soviet studies, ecology/environmental studies, economics, education, electrical engineering, elementary education, engineering (general), engineering management, English, environmental biology, environmental education, environmental sciences, European studies, family and consumer studies, fashion merchandising, finance/banking, fish and game management, food sciences, forestry, French, geography, geology, German, Greek, health education, history, home economics, home economics education, horticulture, human development, industrial arts, Latin, Latin American studies, (pre)law sequence, marketing/retailing/merchandising, mathematics, mechanical engineering, medical technology, (pre)medicine sequence, microbiology, modern languages, music, music education, music history, natural resource management, nursing, nutrition, parks management, philosophy, physical education, physical therapy, physics, political science/government, psychology, reading education, recreational facilities management, recreation and leisure services, religious studies, Romance languages, Russian, Russian and Slavic studies, science education, secondary education, social work, sociology, soil conservation, Spanish, special education, speech pathology and audiology, statistics, studio art, textiles and clothing, theater arts/drama, (pre)veterinary medicine sequence, vocational education, wildlife biology, wildlife management, zoology.

Applying *Required:* essay, high school transcript, 3 years of high school math, 2 years of high school foreign language, SAT or ACT. *Recommended:* 2 recommendations, interview. *Application deadlines:* 2/1, 11/1 for early decision, 3/1 for financial aid. *Contact:* Ms. Carol Hogan, Director of Admissions, Clement House, Burlington, VT 05405, 802-656-3370.

University of Virginia

Charlottesville, Virginia

Founded 1819
Suburban setting
State-supported
Coed
Awards B, M, D

Enrollment	17,606 total; 11,306 undergraduates (2,539 freshmen)
Faculty	1,000 total; 871 full-time (90% have doctorate/terminal degree); student-faculty ratio is 11:1; grad assistants teach about a quarter of the undergraduate courses.
Libraries	3.3 million bound volumes, 4.6 million titles on microform, 21,173 periodical subscriptions
Computing	*Terminals/PCs available for student use:* 1,503, located in computer center, library, microcomputer labs; PC not required. Campus network links student PCs.
Of Special Interest	*Core academic program:* yes. Computer course required for engineering, commerce majors. Phi Beta Kappa, Sigma Xi chapters. Academic exchange program: no. Sponsors and participates in study-abroad programs. Army ROTC, Naval ROTC, Air Force ROTC.
On Campus	Drama/theater group; student-run newspaper and radio station. *Social organizations:* 39 national fraternities, 22 national sororities; 28% of eligible undergraduate men and 30% of eligible undergraduate women are members.
Athletics	Member NCAA (Division I). *Intercollegiate sports:* baseball (M), basketball (M, W), cross-country running (M, W), field hockey (W), football (M), golf (M), lacrosse (M, W), soccer (M, W), softball (W), swimming and diving (M, W), tennis (M, W), track and field (M, W), volleyball (W), wrestling (M). *Scholarships:* M, W.

Costs (1991–92) & Aid				
	State resident tuition	$2740	2119 Need-based scholarships (average)	$3914
	Nonresident tuition	$8950	250 Non-need scholarships (average)	$3500
	Mandatory fees	$614	Short-term loans (average)	$200
	Room and board	$3309	Long-term loans—college funds (average)	$1650
	Financial aid recipients	33%	Long-term loans—external funds (average)	$2306

Undergraduate Facts				
	Part-time	1%	*Freshman Data:* 14,334 applied, 34% were accepted, 52% (2,539) of those entered	
	State residents	65%		
	Transfers	4%	From top tenth of high school class	74%
	African-Americans	12%	SAT-takers scoring 600 or over on verbal	41%
	Native Americans	0%	SAT-takers scoring 700 or over on verbal	6%
	Hispanics	1%	SAT-takers scoring 600 or over on math	73%
	Asian-Americans	8%	SAT-takers scoring 700 or over on math	28%
	International students	2%	ACT-takers scoring 26 or over	N/App
	Freshmen returning for sophomore year	96%	ACT-takers scoring 30 or over	N/App
	Students completing degree within 5 years	90%	*Majors with most degrees conferred:* business, English, history.	
	Grads pursuing further study	N/R		

Majors Aerospace engineering, anthropology, applied mathematics, architecture, astronomy, biology/biological sciences, black/African-American studies, business, chemical engineering, chemistry, city/community/regional planning, civil engineering, classics, comparative literature, computer science, economics, electrical engineering, engineering sciences, English, environmental sciences, French, German, history, interdisciplinary studies, international studies, Italian, mathematics, mechanical engineering, music, nuclear engineering, nursing, philosophy, physical education, physics, political science/government, psychology, religious studies, Slavic languages, sociology, Spanish, speech pathology and audiology, speech/rhetoric/public address/debate, studio art, systems engineering, theater arts/drama.

Applying *Required:* essay, high school transcript, 4 years of high school math, 2 years of high school foreign language, 1 recommendation, SAT, 3 Achievements, English Composition Test. *Recommended:* 3 years of high school science. *Application deadlines:* 1/2, 11/1 for early decision, 3/1 priority date for financial aid. *Contact:* Mr. John A. Blackburn, Dean of Admissions, Miller Hall, McCormick Road, Charlottesville, VA 22906, 804-924-7751.

University of Washington

Seattle, Washington

Founded 1861
Urban setting
State-supported
Coed
Awards B, M, D

Enrollment	34,269 total; 25,092 undergraduates (3,641 freshmen)
Faculty	2,834 total; 1,850 full-time (87% have doctorate/terminal degree); student-faculty ratio is 9:1; grad assistants teach about a quarter of the undergraduate courses.
Libraries	5 million bound volumes, 5 million titles on microform, 50,000 periodical subscriptions
Computing	*Terminals/PCs available for student use:* 1,312, located in computer center, student center, academic departments; PC not required.
Of Special Interest	*Core academic program:* yes. Computer course required for engineering, math, statistics majors. Phi Beta Kappa, Sigma Xi chapters. Academic exchange program: no. Sponsors and participates in study-abroad programs. Army ROTC, Naval ROTC, Air Force ROTC.
On Campus	Drama/theater group; student-run newspaper and radio station. *Social organizations:* 32 national fraternities, 18 national sororities; 18% of eligible undergraduate men and 14% of eligible undergraduate women are members.
Athletics	Member NCAA (Division I). *Intercollegiate sports:* baseball (M), basketball (M, W), crew (M, W), cross-country running (M, W), football (M), golf (M, W), gymnastics (W), soccer (M, W), softball (W), swimming and diving (M, W), tennis (M, W), track and field (M, W), volleyball (W), wrestling (M). *Scholarships:* M, W.

Costs (1991–92) & Aid				
	State resident tuition	$2178	5910 Need-based scholarships (average)	$1150
	Nonresident tuition	$6075	250 Non-need scholarships (average)	$1200
	Mandatory fees	N/App	Short-term loans (average)	$600
	Room and board	$3306	Long-term loans—college funds	N/Avail
	Financial aid recipients	30%	Long-term loans—external funds (average)	$2669

Undergraduate Facts				
	Part-time	19%	*Freshman Data:* 11,068 applied, 67% were accepted, 49% (3,641) of those entered	
	State residents	90%		
	Transfers	33%	From top tenth of high school class	54%
	African-Americans	4%	SAT-takers scoring 600 or over on verbal	13%
	Native Americans	1%	SAT-takers scoring 700 or over on verbal	2%
	Hispanics	3%	SAT-takers scoring 600 or over on math	36%
	Asian-Americans	18%	SAT-takers scoring 700 or over on math	8%
	International students	2%	ACT-takers scoring 26 or over	36%
	Freshmen returning for sophomore year	90%	ACT-takers scoring 30 or over	11%
	Students completing degree within 5 years	N/R		
	Grads pursuing further study	N/R		

Majors Accounting, advertising, aerospace engineering, anthropology, Arabic, architecture, art/fine arts, art history, Asian/Oriental studies, astronomy, atmospheric sciences, audio engineering, biochemistry, biology/biological sciences, black/African-American studies, botany/plant sciences, broadcasting, business, business economics, Canadian studies, cell biology, ceramic art and design, ceramic engineering, chemical engineering, chemistry, Chinese, city/community/regional planning, civil engineering, classics, communication, comparative literature, computer engineering, computer information systems, computer science, construction management, creative writing, criminal justice, dance, dental services, (pre)dentistry sequence, East Asian studies, East European and Soviet studies, ecology/environmental studies, economics, education, electrical engineering, elementary education, engineering (general), English, environmental engineering, environmental health sciences, ethnic studies, finance/banking, food sciences, forest engineering, forestry, French, geography, geology, German, Germanic languages and literature, graphic arts, Greek, health services administration, Hebrew, history, history of science, human resources, industrial design, industrial engineering, interdisciplinary studies, international business, international studies, Italian, Japanese, journalism, Judaic studies, landscape architecture/design, Latin, Latin American studies, liberal arts/general studies, linguistics, management information systems, marketing/retailing/merchandising, materials engineering, mathematics, mechanical engineering, medical technology, (pre)medicine sequence, metallurgical engineering, Mexican-American/Chicano studies, microbiology, molecular biology, music, music education, music history, Native American studies, Near and Middle Eastern studies, nursing, occupational therapy, ocean engineering, oceanography, painting/drawing, paper and pulp sciences, peace studies, pharmacy/pharmaceutical sciences, philosophy, photography, physical therapy, physics, piano/organ, political science/government, Portuguese, psychology, religious studies, Romance languages, Russian, Russian and Slavic studies, Scandinavian languages/studies, sculpture, secondary education, Slavic languages, social work, sociology, South Asian studies, Spanish, speech pathology and audiology, statistics, stringed instruments, studio art, technical writing, theater arts/drama, (pre)veterinary medicine sequence, voice, wildlife management, women's studies, wood sciences, zoology.

Applying *Required:* high school transcript, 3 years of high school math, 2 years of high school foreign language, SAT or ACT. *Application deadlines:* 2/1, 2/28 priority date for financial aid. *Contact:* Ms. Stephanie Preston, Assistant Director of Admissions, 1410 Northeast Campus Parkway, Seattle, WA 98195, 206-543-9686.

University of Wisconsin–Madison

Madison, Wisconsin

Founded 1848
Urban setting
State-supported
Coed
Awards B, M, D

Enrollment 43,196 total; 28,900 undergraduates (4,642 freshmen)

Faculty 2,325 total; 2,245 full-time (95% have doctorate/terminal degree); student-faculty ratio is 12:1; grad assistants teach about a quarter of the undergraduate courses.

Libraries 4.8 million bound volumes, 2 million titles on microform, 51,000 periodical subscriptions

Computing *Terminals/PCs available for student use:* 1,800, located in computer center, student center, library, dormitories; PC not required. Campus network links student PCs.

Of Special Interest *Core academic program:* no. Computer course required for business, engineering, education majors. Phi Beta Kappa, Sigma Xi chapters. Academic exchange program: no. Sponsors and participates in study-abroad programs. Army ROTC, Naval ROTC, Air Force ROTC.

On Campus Drama/theater group; student-run newspaper and radio station. *Social organizations:* 27 national fraternities, 10 national sororities; 8% of eligible undergraduate men and 8% of eligible undergraduate women are members.

Athletics Member NCAA (Division I). *Intercollegiate sports:* badminton (W), basketball (M, W), crew (M, W), cross-country running (M, W), football (M), golf (M, W), ice hockey (M, W), rugby (M), sailing (M), soccer (M, W), swimming and diving (M, W), tennis (M, W), track and field (M, W), volleyball (M, W), wrestling (M). *Scholarships:* M, W.

Costs (1991–92) & Aid

State resident tuition	$2188	
Nonresident tuition	$7169	
Mandatory fees	N/App	
Room and board	$3247	
Financial aid recipients	37%	
8529 Need-based scholarships (average)		$830
3825 Non-need scholarships (average)		$1614
Short-term loans (average)		$300
Long-term loans—college funds (average)		$1243
Long-term loans—external funds (average)		$2406

Undergraduate Facts

Part-time	9%
State residents	70%
Transfers	5%
African-Americans	2%
Native Americans	N/R
Hispanics	2%
Asian-Americans	4%
International students	4%
Freshmen returning for sophomore year	89%
Students completing degree within 5 years	62%
Grads pursuing further study	N/R

Freshman Data: 13,895 applied, 75% were accepted, 45% (4,642) of those entered

From top tenth of high school class	33%
SAT-takers scoring 600 or over on verbal	17%
SAT-takers scoring 700 or over on verbal	2%
SAT-takers scoring 600 or over on math	51%
SAT-takers scoring 700 or over on math	15%
ACT-takers scoring 26 or over	48%
ACT-takers scoring 30 or over	13%

Majors with most degrees conferred: political science/government, psychology, English.

Majors Accounting, actuarial science, advertising, African languages, agricultural business, agricultural economics, agricultural education, agricultural engineering, agronomy/soil and crop sciences, American studies, animal sciences, anthropology, applied art, applied mathematics, art education, art/fine arts, art history, Asian/Oriental studies, astronomy, bacteriology, biochemistry, black/African-American studies, botany/plant sciences, broadcasting, business, cartography, cell biology, chemical engineering, chemistry, child care/child and family studies, child psychology/child development, Chinese, civil engineering, classics, communication, comparative literature, computer engineering, computer science, construction management, consumer services, dairy sciences, dietetics, early childhood education, earth science, economics, electrical engineering, elementary education, engineering and applied sciences, engineering mechanics, engineering physics, English, entomology, environmental engineering, experimental psychology, family and consumer studies, farm and ranch management, fashion merchandising, finance/banking, food sciences, forestry, French, genetics, geography, geology, geophysics, German, Greek, Hebrew, Hispanic studies, history, history of science, home economics, home economics education, horticulture, industrial engineering, insurance, interior design, international studies, Italian, Japanese, journalism, labor and industrial relations, landscape architecture/design, Latin, Latin American studies, linguistics, mathematics, mechanical engineering, medical technology, metallurgical engineering, mining and mineral engineering, molecular biology, music, music education, natural resource management, nuclear engineering, nursing, nutrition, occupational therapy, pharmacology, pharmacy/pharmaceutical sciences, philosophy, physical education, physical therapy, physician's assistant studies, physics, political science/government, Portuguese, poultry sciences, psychology, public relations, radio and television studies, real estate, recreation and leisure services, Russian, Scandinavian languages/studies, science education, secondary education, Slavic languages, social science, social work, sociology, Southeast Asian studies, Spanish, special education, speech therapy, statistics, surveying engineering, textiles and clothing, theater arts/drama, toxicology, urban studies, water resources, wildlife management, women's studies, zoology.

Applying *Required:* high school transcript, 3 years of high school math, 2 years of high school foreign language, SAT or ACT. *Recommended:* 3 years of high school science. *Application deadlines:* 2/1, 3/1 priority date for financial aid. *Contact:* Mr. Millard Storey, Director of Admissions, 750 University Avenue, Madison, WI 53706, 608-262-3961.

Ursinus College

Collegeville, Pennsylvania

Founded 1869
Suburban setting
Independent/affiliated with United Church of Christ
Coed
Awards B

Enrollment 1,017 total—all undergraduates (239 freshmen)

Faculty 110 total; 83 full-time (92% have doctorate/terminal degree); student-faculty ratio is 12:1.

Libraries 175,000 bound volumes, 155,000 titles on microform, 900 periodical subscriptions

Computing *Terminals/PCs available for student use:* 100, located in computer center, library, dormitories, academic building; PC not required.

Of Special Interest *Core academic program:* yes. Computer course required for economics/business administration, psychology, math, chemistry, physics majors. Phi Beta Kappa, Sigma Xi chapters. Academic exchange with Howard University. Sponsors and participates in study-abroad programs.

On Campus Drama/theater group; student-run newspaper and radio station. *Social organizations:* 1 national fraternity, 7 local fraternities, 5 local sororities; 38% of eligible undergraduate men and 39% of eligible undergraduate women are members.

Athletics Member NCAA (Division III). *Intercollegiate sports:* basketball (M, W), cross-country running (M, W), field hockey (W), football (M), golf (M, W), gymnastics (W), lacrosse (M, W), soccer (M), swimming and diving (M, W), tennis (M, W), track and field (M, W), volleyball (W), wrestling (M).

Costs (1991–92) & Aid				
	Comprehensive fee	$17,030	Need-based scholarships (average)	$4100
	Tuition	$12,400	Non-need scholarships (average)	$4100
	Mandatory fees	$130	Short-term loans	N/Avail
	Room and board	$4500	Long-term loans—college funds	N/Avail
	Financial aid recipients	74%	Long-term loans—external funds (average)	$2500

Undergraduate Facts				
	Part-time	2%	*Freshman Data:* 1,105 applied, 78% were accepted, 28% (239) of those entered	
	State residents	61%		
	Transfers	3%	From top tenth of high school class	37%
	African-Americans	3%	SAT-takers scoring 600 or over on verbal	9%
	Native Americans	0%	SAT-takers scoring 700 or over on verbal	1%
	Hispanics	2%	SAT-takers scoring 600 or over on math	29%
	Asian-Americans	3%	SAT-takers scoring 700 or over on math	5%
	International students	2%	ACT-takers scoring 26 or over	N/R
	Freshmen returning for sophomore year	88%	ACT-takers scoring 30 or over	N/R
	Students completing degree within 5 years	75%		
	Grads pursuing further study	25%		

Majors Accounting, anthropology, applied mathematics, art/fine arts, biology/biological sciences, business, chemistry, classics, communication, computer science, creative writing, (pre)dentistry sequence, East Asian studies, ecology/environmental studies, economics, education, English, French, German, health education, health science, history, international studies, Japanese, (pre)law sequence, liberal arts/general studies, mathematics, (pre)medicine sequence, modern languages, music, philosophy, physical education, physics, political science/government, psychology, religious studies, Romance languages, secondary education, sociology, Spanish, sports medicine, (pre)veterinary medicine sequence.

Applying *Required:* essay, high school transcript, 3 years of high school math, 2 years of high school foreign language, 3 recommendations, SAT or ACT. *Recommended:* campus interview, 3 Achievements, English Composition Test (with essay). 3 years of high school science required for some. *Application deadlines:* 2/15, 12/15 for early decision, 2/15 priority date for financial aid. *Contact:* Mr. Richard Di Feliciantonio, Director of Admissions, Main Street, Collegeville, PA 19426, 215-489-4111 Ext. 2224.

Utica College of Syracuse University
Utica, New York

Founded 1946
Suburban setting
Independent
Coed
Awards B

Enrollment 1,707 total—all undergraduates (377 freshmen)

Faculty 140 total; 110 full-time (88% have doctorate/terminal degree); student-faculty ratio is 13:1.

Libraries 133,016 bound volumes, 26,001 titles on microform, 1,314 periodical subscriptions

Computing *Terminals/PCs available for student use:* 111, located in computer center, library, dormitories, classroom building; PC not required.

Of Special Interest *Core academic program:* yes. Computer course required for accounting, business administration, actuarial science, math, psychology, chemistry, criminal justice, electrical engineering majors. Academic exchange with members of the New York State Visiting Student Program. Sponsors and participates in study-abroad programs. Army ROTC, cooperative Air Force ROTC.

On Campus Drama/theater group; student-run newspaper and radio station. *Social organizations:* 7 national fraternities, 4 national sororities, 2 local fraternities, 3 local sororities; 18% of eligible undergraduate men and 4% of eligible undergraduate women are members.

Athletics Member NCAA (Division III). *Intercollegiate sports:* baseball (M), basketball (M, W), cross-country running (M, W), golf (M), lacrosse (M), soccer (M, W), softball (W), swimming and diving (M, W), tennis (M, W), volleyball (M).

Costs (1992–93 estimated) & Aid	Comprehensive fee	$15,741	Need-based scholarships	Avail
	Tuition	$10,968	Non-need scholarships	Avail
	Mandatory fees	$90	Short-term loans	N/Avail
	Room and board	$4683	Long-term loans—college funds	N/Avail
	Financial aid recipients	92%	Long-term loans—external funds	Avail

Undergraduate Facts				
Part-time	36%	*Freshman Data:* 1,604 applied, 70% were accepted, 34% (377) of those entered	
State residents	91%		
Transfers	29%	From top tenth of high school class	36%
African-Americans	17%	SAT-takers scoring 600 or over on verbal	15%
Native Americans	1%	SAT-takers scoring 700 or over on verbal	2%
Hispanics	2%	SAT-takers scoring 600 or over on math	27%
Asian-Americans	1%	SAT-takers scoring 700 or over on math	3%
International students	1%	ACT-takers scoring 26 or over	34%
Freshmen returning for sophomore year	76%	ACT-takers scoring 30 or over	10%
Students completing degree within 5 years	71%	*Majors with most degrees conferred:* business, criminal justice, occupational therapy.	
Grads pursuing further study	11%		

Majors Accounting, actuarial science, anthropology, art/fine arts, biology/biological sciences, business, business economics, chemistry, child psychology/child development, communication, computer science, construction management, corrections, criminal justice, (pre)dentistry sequence, economics, English, gerontology, history, human development, international business, international studies, journalism, law enforcement/police sciences, (pre)law sequence, liberal arts/general studies, mathematics, (pre)medicine sequence, nursing, occupational therapy, philosophy, physics, political science/government, psychology, public relations, recreation therapy, secondary education, social science, sociology, speech/rhetoric/public address/debate, theater arts/drama, (pre)veterinary medicine sequence.

Applying *Required:* high school transcript. *Recommended:* essay, 3 years of high school math and science, some high school foreign language, recommendations, interview, SAT or ACT. *Application deadlines:* rolling, 12/1 for early decision, 4/15 priority date for financial aid. *Contact:* Mr. Philip J. Alletto, Director of Admissions,1600 Burrstone Road, Hubbard Hall, Utica, NY 13502, 315-792-3006 or toll-free 800-782-8884.

From the College Syracuse University founded Utica College in 1946. Today Utica remains one of thirteen undergraduate colleges of SU and the only one not located on the main campus. Utica College students are Syracuse University students and receive that prestigious degree upon graduation. Utica's small, private campus is 1 hour from the University.

Valparaiso University

Valparaiso, Indiana

Founded 1859
Small-town setting
Independent/affiliated with Lutheran Church–Missouri Synod
Coed
Awards B, M, D

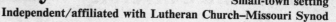

Enrollment	3,872 total; 3,170 undergraduates (641 freshmen)
Faculty	310 total; 230 full-time (70% have doctorate/terminal degree); student-faculty ratio is 14:1; grad assistants teach no undergraduate courses.
Libraries	257,000 bound volumes, 102,000 titles on microform, 1,440 periodical subscriptions
Computing	*Terminals/PCs available for student use:* 215, located in computer center, library, computer labs; PC not required. Campus network links student PCs.
Of Special Interest	*Core academic program:* yes. Computer course required for engineering, business majors. Academic exchange with Associated Colleges of the Midwest. Sponsors and participates in study-abroad programs. Cooperative Army ROTC.
On Campus	Drama/theater group; student-run newspaper and radio station. *Social organizations:* 12 national fraternities, 8 local sororities; 42% of eligible undergraduate men and 39% of eligible undergraduate women are members.
Athletics	Member NCAA (Division I). *Intercollegiate sports:* baseball (M), basketball (M, W), cross-country running (M, W), football (M), golf (M), gymnastics (W), soccer (M, W), softball (W), swimming and diving (M, W), tennis (M, W), volleyball (W), wrestling (M). *Scholarships:* M, W.

Costs (1991–92) & Aid				
	Comprehensive fee	$12,730	Need-based scholarships (average)	$2370
	Tuition	$9670	Non-need scholarships (average)	$2650
	Mandatory fees	$320	Short-term loans	N/Avail
	Room and board	$2740	Long-term loans—college funds (average)	$300
	Financial aid recipients	75%	Long-term loans—external funds (average)	$3750

Undergraduate Facts				
	Part-time	8%	*Freshman Data:* 2,144 applied, 86% were accepted, 35% (641) of those entered	
	State residents	35%		
	Transfers	3%	From top tenth of high school class	41%
	African-Americans	2%	SAT-takers scoring 600 or over on verbal	N/R
	Native Americans	1%	SAT-takers scoring 700 or over on verbal	N/R
	Hispanics	1%	SAT-takers scoring 600 or over on math	N/R
	Asian-Americans	1%	SAT-takers scoring 700 or over on math	N/R
	International students	3%	ACT-takers scoring 26 or over	34%
	Freshmen returning for sophomore year	93%	ACT-takers scoring 30 or over	19%
	Students completing degree within 5 years	N/R	*Majors with most degrees conferred:* business, communication, nursing.	
	Grads pursuing further study	19%		

Majors Accounting, advertising, American studies, art education, art/fine arts, art history, Asian/Oriental studies, astronomy, athletic training, behavioral sciences, biblical languages, biblical studies, biochemistry, biology/biological sciences, biomedical sciences, broadcasting, business, business economics, cartography, chemistry, child psychology/child development, city/community/regional planning, civil engineering, classics, communication, computer engineering, computer information systems, computer science, criminal justice, (pre)dentistry sequence, dietetics, East Asian studies, economics, education, electrical engineering, elementary education, engineering (general), engineering sciences, English, film studies, finance/banking, food marketing, French, geography, geology, German, Greek, health science, Hebrew, history, home economics, home economics education, humanities, human resources, interdisciplinary studies, interior design, international economics, journalism, labor and industrial relations, land use management and reclamation, Latin, Latin American studies, (pre)law sequence, liberal arts/general studies, literature, marketing/retailing/merchandising, mathematics, mechanical engineering, medical technology, (pre)medicine sequence, meteorology, modern languages, music, music business, music education, music history, natural sciences, nursing, philosophy, physical education, physics, piano/organ, political science/government, psychology, public relations, radio and television studies, reading education, religious studies, retail management, Romance languages, sacred music, science, science education, secondary education, social science, social work, sociology, Spanish, special education, speech pathology and audiology, speech therapy, stringed instruments, studio art, theater arts/drama, theology, tourism and travel, urban studies, (pre)veterinary medicine sequence, voice, wind and percussion instruments.

Applying *Required:* high school transcript, SAT or ACT. *Recommended:* essay, some high school foreign language, 2 recommendations. 3 years of high school math and science, interview required for some. *Application deadlines:* rolling, 3/1 priority date for financial aid. *Contact:* Mr. Douglas B. Watkins, Director of Admissions, Kretzman Hall, Valparaiso, IN 46383, 219-464-5011 or toll-free 800-348-2611 (out-of-state).

//** Vanderbilt University**

Nashville, Tennessee

Founded 1873
Urban setting
Independent
Coed
Awards B, M, D

Enrollment 9,581 total; 5,547 undergraduates (1,597 freshmen)

Faculty 822 total; 633 full-time (95% have doctorate/terminal degree); student-faculty ratio is 8:1; grad assistants teach a few undergraduate courses.

Libraries 1.9 million bound volumes, 1.8 million titles on microform, 16,448 periodical subscriptions

Computing *Terminals/PCs available for student use:* 400, located in computer center, student center, library, dormitories, labs; PC not required. Campus network links student PCs.

Of Special Interest *Core academic program:* yes. Computer course required for engineering majors. Phi Beta Kappa, Sigma Xi chapters. Academic exchange with Fisk University, Howard University. Sponsors and participates in study-abroad programs. Army ROTC, Naval ROTC, cooperative Air Force ROTC.

On Campus Drama/theater group; student-run newspaper and radio station. *Social organizations:* 17 national fraternities, 12 national sororities; 47% of eligible undergraduate men and 50% of eligible undergraduate women are members.

Athletics Member NCAA (Division I). *Intercollegiate sports:* basketball (M, W), crew (M, W), cross-country running (M, W), equestrian sports (M, W), fencing (M, W), football (M), golf (M, W), ice hockey (M), lacrosse (M, W), riflery (M, W), rugby (M, W), sailing (M, W), skiing (downhill) (M, W), soccer (M, W), squash (M, W), swimming and diving (W), table tennis (M), tennis (M, W), volleyball (M), water polo (M), weight lifting (M). *Scholarships:* M, W.

Costs (1991–92) & Aid				
	Comprehensive fee	$20,655	Need-based scholarships (average)	$7176
	Tuition	$14,975	Non-need scholarships (average)	$10,223
	Mandatory fees	$260	Short-term loans (average)	$500
	Room and board	$5420	Long-term loans—college funds (average)	$1235
	Financial aid recipients	33%	Long-term loans—external funds (average)	$2416

Undergraduate Facts				
	Part-time	1%	*Freshman Data:* 6,627 applied, 65% were accepted, 37% (1,597) of those entered	
	State residents	16%		
	Transfers	1%	From top tenth of high school class	62%
	African-Americans	4%	SAT-takers scoring 600 or over on verbal	36%
	Native Americans	1%	SAT-takers scoring 700 or over on verbal	5%
	Hispanics	2%	SAT-takers scoring 600 or over on math	72%
	Asian-Americans	4%	SAT-takers scoring 700 or over on math	23%
	International students	2%	ACT-takers scoring 26 or over	86%
	Freshmen returning for sophomore year	90%	ACT-takers scoring 30 or over	21%
	Students completing degree within 5 years	77%	*Majors with most degrees conferred:* economics, English, human development.	
	Grads pursuing further study	52%		

Majors American studies, anthropology, art/fine arts, astronomy, biology/biological sciences, biomedical engineering, black/African-American studies, chemical engineering, chemistry, civil engineering, classics, cognitive science, communication, computer science, early childhood education, East Asian studies, East European and Soviet studies, ecology/environmental studies, economics, electrical engineering, elementary education, engineering sciences, English, European studies, French, geology, German, history, human development, interdisciplinary studies, Latin American studies, mathematics, mechanical engineering, molecular biology, music, philosophy, physics, piano/organ, political science/government, Portuguese, psychology, public affairs and policy studies, religious studies, Russian, secondary education, sociology, Spanish, special education, stringed instruments, theater arts/drama, urban studies, voice, wind and percussion instruments.

Applying *Required:* essay, high school transcript, 3 years of high school math, 2 recommendations, SAT or ACT, 3 Achievements, English Composition Test. *Recommended:* interview. 3 years of high school science, some high school foreign language required for some. *Application deadlines:* 1/15, 11/1 for early decision, 4/15 priority date for financial aid. *Contact:* Dr. Neill Sanders, Dean, Undergraduate Admissions, 401 24th Avenue, South, Nashville, TN 37240, 615-322-2561.

From the College Vanderbilt University, a national research university of distinction, has been honored repeatedly for its exceptional undergraduate advising system. Generous financial aid programs support the University's commitment to making a Vanderbilt education affordable for all qualified students. Other distinctions include the Summer Undergraduate Research Program, in which students collaborate with faculty on original research.

Vassar College

Poughkeepsie, New York

Founded 1861
Suburban setting
Independent
Coed
Awards B, M

Enrollment	2,345 total; 2,218 undergraduates (594 freshmen)
Faculty	234 total; 213 full-time (95% have doctorate/terminal degree); student-faculty ratio is 11:1; grad assistants teach no undergraduate courses.
Libraries	700,000 bound volumes, 350,000 titles on microform, 3,900 periodical subscriptions
Computing	*Terminals/PCs available for student use:* 295, located in academic buildings; PC required for freshmen. Campus network links student PCs.
Of Special Interest	*Core academic program:* no. Computer course required for math majors. Phi Beta Kappa, Sigma Xi chapters. Academic exchange with Howard University, Fisk University, Hampton University, Spelman College, Morehouse College, members of the Twelve College Exchange Program, Marist College. Sponsors and participates in study-abroad programs.
On Campus	Drama/theater group; student-run newspaper and radio station. No national or local fraternities or sororities on campus.
Athletics	Member NCAA (Division III). *Intercollegiate sports:* baseball (M), basketball (M, W), crew (M, W), cross-country running (M, W), fencing (M, W), field hockey (W), golf (M, W), lacrosse (M, W), rugby (M, W), sailing (M, W), soccer (M, W), squash (M, W), swimming and diving (M, W), tennis (M, W), volleyball (M, W).

Costs (1991–92) & Aid				
	Comprehensive fee	$21,770	Need-based scholarships (average)	$11,000
	Tuition	$16,250	Non-need scholarships	N/Avail
	Mandatory fees	$260	Short-term loans (average)	$100
	Room and board	$5260	Long-term loans—college funds (average)	$2650
	Financial aid recipients	60%	Long-term loans—external funds (average)	$2870

Undergraduate Facts				
	Part-time	5%	*Freshman Data:* 3,856 applied, 48% were accepted, 32% (594) of those entered	
	State residents	32%		
	Transfers	1%	From top tenth of high school class	51%
	African-Americans	7%	SAT-takers scoring 600 or over on verbal	54%
	Native Americans	1%	SAT-takers scoring 700 or over on verbal	8%
	Hispanics	5%	SAT-takers scoring 600 or over on math	66%
	Asian-Americans	8%	SAT-takers scoring 700 or over on math	18%
	International students	13%	ACT-takers scoring 26 or over	N/R
	Freshmen returning for sophomore year	99%	ACT-takers scoring 30 or over	N/R
	Students completing degree within 5 years	N/R	*Majors with most degrees conferred:* English, psychology, political science/government.	
	Grads pursuing further study	21%		

Majors African studies, American studies, anthropology, art/fine arts, art history, Asian/Oriental studies, astronomy, biochemistry, biology/biological sciences, chemistry, classics, computer science, East Asian studies, economics, elementary education, English, film studies, French, geography, geology, German, Greek, Hispanic studies, history, interdisciplinary studies, international studies, Italian, Latin, Latin American studies, linguistics, mathematics, medieval studies, music, neurosciences, philosophy, physics, political science/government, psychobiology, psychology, religious studies, Russian, sociology, studio art, technology and public affairs, theater arts/drama, urban studies, women's studies.

Applying *Required:* essay, high school transcript, 2 recommendations, SAT or ACT, 3 Achievements. *Recommended:* 3 years of high school math and science, 3 years of high school foreign language, interview. *Application deadlines:* 1/15, 12/1 for early decision, 1/15 for financial aid. *Contact:* Mr. Thomas Matos, Director of Admissions, Raymond Avenue, Poughkeepsie, NY 12601, 914-437-5364.

✴ Villanova University

Villanova, Pennsylvania

Founded 1842
Suburban setting
Independent, Roman Catholic
Coed
Awards A, B, M, D

Enrollment 11,858 total; 6,858 undergraduates (1,640 freshmen)

Faculty 917 total; 572 full-time (88% have doctorate/terminal degree); student-faculty ratio is 14:1; grad assistants teach no undergraduate courses.

Libraries 583,000 bound volumes, 1,419 titles on microform, 2,855 periodical subscriptions

Computing *Terminals/PCs available for student use:* 200, located in computer center, departmental labs, classrooms; PC not required.

Of Special Interest *Core academic program:* yes. Computer course required for engineering, business, science majors. Phi Beta Kappa, Sigma Xi chapters. Academic exchange with Rosemont College, Cabrini College, Bryn Mawr College. Sponsors and participates in study-abroad programs. Army ROTC, Naval ROTC, cooperative Air Force ROTC.

On Campus Drama/theater group; student-run newspaper and radio station. *Social organizations:* 13 national fraternities, 9 national sororities, 1 local fraternity; 35% of eligible undergraduate men and 45% of eligible undergraduate women are members.

Athletics Member NCAA (Division I). *Intercollegiate sports:* baseball (M), basketball (M, W), crew (M, W), cross-country running (M, W), field hockey (W), football (M), golf (M), ice hockey (M), lacrosse (M, W), rugby (M), sailing (M, W), soccer (M, W), softball (W), swimming and diving (M, W), tennis (M, W), track and field (M, W), volleyball (M, W), water polo (M), weight lifting (M, W). *Scholarships:* M, W.

Costs (1991–92) & Aid				
	Comprehensive fee	$17,390	Need-based scholarships (average)	$3100
	Tuition	$11,790	Non-need scholarships (average)	$9560
	Mandatory fees	$180	Short-term loans	N/Avail
	Room and board	$5420	Long-term loans—college funds	N/Avail
	Financial aid recipients	53%	Long-term loans—external funds (average)	$2914

Undergraduate Facts				
	Part-time	18%	*Freshman Data:* 7,042 applied, 75% were accepted, 31% (1,640) of those entered	
	State residents	30%		
	Transfers	6%	From top tenth of high school class	34%
	African-Americans	2%	SAT-takers scoring 600 or over on verbal	14%
	Native Americans	0%	SAT-takers scoring 700 or over on verbal	1%
	Hispanics	2%	SAT-takers scoring 600 or over on math	48%
	Asian-Americans	3%	SAT-takers scoring 700 or over on math	8%
	International students	2%	ACT-takers scoring 26 or over	N/R
	Freshmen returning for sophomore year	93%	ACT-takers scoring 30 or over	N/R
	Students completing degree within 5 years	84%	*Majors with most degrees conferred:* political science/government, communication, business.	
	Grads pursuing further study	19%		

Majors Accounting, Arabic, art history, astronomy, astrophysics, biochemistry, biology/biological sciences, business, business economics, chemical engineering, chemistry, civil engineering, classics, communication, computer science, criminal justice, (pre)dentistry sequence, economics, education, electrical engineering, elementary education, English, ethnic studies, European studies, finance/banking, French, geography, German, history, humanities, human services, interdisciplinary studies, international business, Islamic studies, (pre)law sequence, liberal arts/general studies, marketing/retailing/merchandising, mathematics, mechanical engineering, (pre)medicine sequence, meteorology, military science, natural sciences, naval sciences, Near and Middle Eastern studies, nursing, peace studies, philosophy, physics, political science/government, psychology, religious studies, secondary education, sociology, Spanish, special education, (pre)veterinary medicine sequence, women's studies.

Applying *Required:* essay, high school transcript, 3 years of high school math and science, SAT or ACT. *Recommended:* recommendations. 4 years of high school math and science, 2 years of high school foreign language, 2 Achievements required for some. *Application deadlines:* 1/15, 12/15 for early action, 2/15 priority date for financial aid. *Contact:* Mr. Stephen Merritt, Director of Admissions, Austin Hall, Villanova, PA 19085, 215-645-4000.

Virginia Polytechnic Institute and State University
Blacksburg, Virginia

Founded 1872
Small-town setting
State-supported
Coed
Awards A, B, M, D

Enrollment 23,912 total; 19,308 undergraduates (4,416 freshmen)

Faculty 1,909 total; 1,444 full-time (87% have doctorate/terminal degree); student-faculty ratio is 17:1; grad assistants teach a few undergraduate courses.

Libraries 1.7 million bound volumes, 5.2 million titles on microform, 16,265 periodical subscriptions

Computing *Terminals/PCs available for student use:* 2,000, located in computer center, library, dormitories, academic buildings; PC required for engineering, computer science and statistics students and available for purchase. Campus network links student PCs.

Of Special Interest *Core academic program:* yes. Computer course required for engineering, business, chemistry, physics, economics, geophysics, forestry, wildlife, crop soil and environmental sciences, poultry sciences, math and business education, nuclear science, statistics, clothing and textiles majors. Phi Beta Kappa, Sigma Xi chapters. Academic exchange program: no. Sponsors and participates in study-abroad programs. Army ROTC, Naval ROTC, Air Force ROTC.

On Campus Drama/theater group; student-run newspaper and radio station. *Social organizations:* 32 national fraternities, 16 national sororities, 1 local fraternity; 15% of eligible undergraduate men and 20% of eligible undergraduate women are members.

Athletics Member NCAA (Division I). *Intercollegiate sports:* archery (M, W), baseball (M), basketball (M, W), bowling (M, W), cross-country running (M, W), equestrian sports (M, W), fencing (M, W), field hockey (W), football (M), golf (M), gymnastics (M, W), lacrosse (M, W), rugby (M), skiing (cross-country) (M, W), skiing (downhill) (M, W), soccer (M, W), swimming and diving (M, W), tennis (M, W), track and field (M, W), volleyball (M, W), weight lifting (M, W), wrestling (M). *Scholarships:* M, W.

Costs (1991–92) & Aid
State resident tuition	$2856	Need-based scholarships	Avail
Nonresident tuition	$7704	1590 Non-need scholarships (average)	$1082
Mandatory fees	$448	Short-term loans (average)	$300
Room and board	$3010	Long-term loans—college funds (average)	$126
Financial aid recipients	50%	Long-term loans—external funds (average)	$2200

Undergraduate Facts
Part-time	3%	*Freshman Data:* 15,985 applied, 70% were accepted, 39% (4,416) of those entered	
State residents	77%		
Transfers	15%	From top tenth of high school class	34%
African-Americans	5%	SAT-takers scoring 600 or over on verbal	13%
Native Americans	1%	SAT-takers scoring 700 or over on verbal	1%
Hispanics	1%	SAT-takers scoring 600 or over on math	43%
Asian-Americans	6%	SAT-takers scoring 700 or over on math	10%
International students	1%	ACT-takers scoring 26 or over	N/R
Freshmen returning for sophomore year	88%	ACT-takers scoring 30 or over	N/R
Students completing degree within 5 years	67%	*Majors with most degrees conferred:* electrical engineering, mechanical engineering, marketing/retailing/merchandising.	
Grads pursuing further study	N/R		

Majors Accounting, aerospace engineering, agricultural business, agricultural economics, agricultural education, agricultural engineering, agricultural sciences, agronomy/soil and crop sciences, animal sciences, architecture, art/fine arts, art history, biochemistry, biology/biological sciences, biomedical engineering, biotechnology, black/African-American studies, broadcasting, business, business economics, business education, chemical engineering, chemistry, child care/child and family studies, civil engineering, classics, communication, computer engineering, computer science, construction management, dairy sciences, (pre)dentistry sequence, dietetics, early childhood education, economics, education, electrical engineering, elementary education, engineering sciences, English, environmental sciences, family and consumer studies, farm and ranch management, fashion design and technology, fashion merchandising, finance/banking, fish and game management, food sciences, forestry, French, geography, geology, geophysics, German, health education, history, home economics, home economics education, horticulture, hotel and restaurant management, human development, human resources, human services, industrial arts, industrial engineering, interior design, international business, international studies, journalism, landscape architecture/design, (pre)law sequence, liberal arts/general studies, management information systems, marketing/retailing/merchandising, materials engineering, mathematics, mechanical engineering, medical technology, (pre)medicine sequence, medieval studies, mining and mineral engineering, music, music education, music history, nutrition, ocean engineering, operations research, parks management, philosophy, physical education, physical fitness/human movement, physics, political science/government, poultry sciences, psychology, public administration, public relations, religious studies, Russian and Slavic studies, science education, secondary education, sociology, Spanish, speech/rhetoric/public address/debate, sports administration, statistics, studio art, textiles and clothing, theater arts/drama, urban studies, (pre)veterinary medicine sequence, vocational education, wildlife management, women's studies, wood sciences.

Applying *Required:* high school transcript, 3 years of high school math, SAT, 2 Achievements, English Composition Test. *Recommended:* 3 years of high school science, 2 years of high school foreign language. 4 years of high school math, 3 years of high school science required for some. *Application deadlines:* 2/1, 11/1 for early decision, 2/15 for financial aid. *Contact:* Office of Undergraduate Admissions, 104 Burruss Hall, Blacksburg, VA 24061-0202, 703-231-6267.

Wabash College

Crawfordsville, Indiana

Founded 1832
Small-town setting
Independent
Men
Awards B

Enrollment 817 total—all undergraduates (224 freshmen)

Faculty 76 total; 69 full-time (97% have doctorate/terminal degree); student-faculty ratio is 11:1.

Libraries 236,007 bound volumes, 7,740 titles on microform, 1,010 periodical subscriptions

Computing *Terminals/PCs available for student use:* 74, located in computer center, library, 3 classrooms; PC not required.

Of Special Interest *Core academic program:* yes. Computer course required for physics majors. Phi Beta Kappa, Sigma Xi chapters. Academic exchange with members of the Great Lakes Colleges Association. Participates in study-abroad programs.

On Campus Drama/theater group; student-run newspaper and radio station. *Social organizations:* 10 national fraternities; 75% of eligible undergraduates are members.

Athletics Member NCAA (Division III). *Intercollegiate sports:* baseball, basketball, cross-country running, football, golf, ice hockey, rugby, sailing, soccer, swimming and diving, tennis, track and field, water polo, wrestling.

Costs (1991–92) & Aid				
	Comprehensive fee	$14,365	Need-based scholarships (average)	$9435
	Tuition	$10,500	Non-need scholarships (average)	$6150
	Mandatory fees	$200	Short-term loans (average)	$1000
	Room and board	$3665	Long-term loans—college funds (average)	$2500
	Financial aid recipients	85%	Long-term loans—external funds (average)	$2245

Undergraduate Facts				
	Part-time	1%	*Freshman Data:* 634 applied, 79% were accepted, 45% (224) of those entered	
	State residents	75%		
	Transfers	2%	From top tenth of high school class	40%
	African-Americans	6%	SAT-takers scoring 600 or over on verbal	17%
	Native Americans	1%	SAT-takers scoring 700 or over on verbal	2%
	Hispanics	2%	SAT-takers scoring 600 or over on math	48%
	Asian-Americans	2%	SAT-takers scoring 700 or over on math	13%
	International students	5%	ACT-takers scoring 26 or over	N/R
	Freshmen returning for sophomore year	89%	ACT-takers scoring 30 or over	N/R
	Students completing degree within 5 years	75%		
	Grads pursuing further study	N/R		

Majors Art/fine arts, biology/biological sciences, chemistry, classics, (pre)dentistry sequence, economics, English, French, German, Greek, history, Latin, (pre)law sequence, mathematics, (pre)medicine sequence, music, philosophy, physics, political science/government, psychology, religious studies, secondary education, Spanish, speech/rhetoric/public address/debate, theater arts/drama, (pre)veterinary medicine sequence.

Applying *Required:* essay, high school transcript, 3 years of high school math, 1 recommendation, SAT or ACT. *Recommended:* 3 years of high school science, 2 years of high school foreign language, interview. *Application deadlines:* rolling, 3/1 priority date for financial aid. *Contact:* Mr. Gregory Birk, Director of Admissions, 502 West Wabash Avenue, Crawfordsville, IN 47933-0352, 317-364-4253 or toll-free 800-345-5385 (in-state).

Wake Forest University

Winston-Salem, North Carolina

Founded 1834
Suburban setting
Independent
Coed
Awards B, M, D

Enrollment	5,679 total; 3,650 undergraduates (856 freshmen)
Faculty	324 total; 268 full-time (81% have doctorate/terminal degree); student-faculty ratio is 12:1; grad assistants teach no undergraduate courses.
Libraries	1.1 million bound volumes, 993,382 titles on microform, 18,678 periodical subscriptions
Computing	*Terminals/PCs available for student use:* 161, located in computer center, student center, library, dormitories, classrooms; PC not required. Campus network links student PCs.
Of Special Interest	*Core academic program:* yes. Computer course required for math, business, economics, accounting, education majors. Phi Beta Kappa, Sigma Xi chapters. Academic exchange with Salem College (NC). Sponsors and participates in study-abroad programs. Army ROTC.
On Campus	Drama/theater group; student-run newspaper and radio station. *Social organizations:* 14 national fraternities, 4 national sororities, 6 local sororities; 42% of eligible undergraduate men and 51% of eligible undergraduate women are members.
Athletics	Member NCAA (Division I). *Intercollegiate sports:* baseball (M), basketball (M, W), cross-country running (M, W), field hockey (W), football (M), golf (M, W), soccer (M), tennis (M, W), track and field (M, W). *Scholarships:* M, W.

Costs (1991–92) & Aid				
	Comprehensive fee	$14,140	Need-based scholarships (average)	$4400
	Tuition	$10,800	Non-need scholarships (average)	$7100
	Mandatory fees	N/App	Short-term loans	N/Avail
	Room and board	$3340	Long-term loans—college funds (average)	$2000
	Financial aid recipients	62%	Long-term loans—external funds (average)	$3300

Undergraduate Facts				
	Part-time	4%	*Freshman Data:* 5,348 applied, 39% were accepted, 41% (856) of those entered	
	State residents	38%		
	Transfers	3%	From top tenth of high school class	73%
	African-Americans	7%	SAT-takers scoring 600 or over on verbal	33%
	Native Americans	1%	SAT-takers scoring 700 or over on verbal	5%
	Hispanics	1%	SAT-takers scoring 600 or over on math	70%
	Asian-Americans	1%	SAT-takers scoring 700 or over on math	17%
	International students	1%	ACT-takers scoring 26 or over	N/App
	Freshmen returning for sophomore year	93%	ACT-takers scoring 30 or over	N/App
	Students completing degree within 5 years	84%	*Majors with most degrees conferred:* business, psychology, English.	
	Grads pursuing further study	N/R		

Majors Accounting, anthropology, art/fine arts, biology/biological sciences, business, chemistry, classics, communication, computer science, economics, education, English, French, German, Greek, health science, history, Latin, (pre)law sequence, mathematics, (pre)medicine sequence, music, philosophy, physical education, physician's assistant studies, physics, political science/government, psychology, religious studies, Russian, sociology, Spanish, speech/rhetoric/public address/debate, theater arts/drama.

Applying *Required:* essay, high school transcript, 3 years of high school math, 2 years of high school foreign language, 1 recommendation, SAT. *Recommended:* 3 years of high school science, 3 Achievements, English Composition Test. *Application deadlines:* 1/15, 11/15 for early decision, 3/1 priority date for financial aid. *Contact:* Mr. William G. Starling, Director of Admissions, 2601 Wake Forest Road, Winston-Salem, NC 27109, 919-759-5201.

✴ Wartburg College

Waverly, Iowa

Founded 1852
Small-town setting
Independent, Lutheran
Coed
Awards B

Enrollment 1,453 total—all undergraduates (381 freshmen)

Faculty 122 total; 81 full-time; student-faculty ratio is 16:1.

Libraries 135,000 bound volumes, 5,042 titles on microform, 660 periodical subscriptions

Computing *Terminals/PCs available for student use:* 70, located in computer center, science building; PC not required.

Of Special Interest *Core academic program:* yes. Computer course required for math, science, business, accounting majors. Academic exchange with members of the May Term Consortium. Sponsors and participates in study-abroad programs.

On Campus Drama/theater group; student-run newspaper and radio station. No national or local fraternities or sororities on campus.

Athletics Member NCAA (Division III). *Intercollegiate sports:* basketball (M, W), cross-country running (M, W), football (M), golf (M, W), soccer (M, W), tennis (M, W), track and field (M, W), volleyball (W), wrestling (M).

Costs (1991–92) & Aid				
	Comprehensive fee	$12,720	Need-based scholarships (average)	$4000
	Tuition	$9400	Non-need scholarships (average)	$1300
	Mandatory fees	$240	Short-term loans	N/Avail
	Room and board	$3080	Long-term loans—college funds (average)	$2000
	Financial aid recipients	89%	Long-term loans—external funds (average)	$2590

Undergraduate Facts				
	Part-time	7%	*Freshman Data:* 1,178 applied, 88% were accepted, 37% (381) of those entered	
	State residents	73%		
	Transfers	5%	From top tenth of high school class	32%
	African-Americans	2%	SAT-takers scoring 600 or over on verbal	N/R
	Native Americans	0%	SAT-takers scoring 700 or over on verbal	N/R
	Hispanics	0%	SAT-takers scoring 600 or over on math	N/R
	Asian-Americans	0%	SAT-takers scoring 700 or over on math	N/R
	International students	7%	ACT-takers scoring 26 or over	30%
	Freshmen returning for sophomore year	74%	ACT-takers scoring 30 or over	6%
	Students completing degree within 5 years	N/R		
	Grads pursuing further study	20%		

Majors Accounting, art education, art/fine arts, biology/biological sciences, broadcasting, business, business economics, chemistry, communication, computer information systems, computer science, (pre)dentistry sequence, economics, education, elementary education, English, finance/banking, French, German, health education, history, international business, journalism, law enforcement/police sciences, (pre)law sequence, liberal arts/general studies, marine biology, marketing/retailing/merchandising, mathematics, medical technology, (pre)medicine sequence, music, music education, music therapy, occupational therapy, painting/drawing, pastoral studies, philosophy, physical education, physical therapy, physics, piano/organ, political science/government, psychology, public relations, recreation and leisure services, religious education, religious studies, science, science education, secondary education, social work, sociology, Spanish, special education, studio art, theology, (pre)veterinary medicine sequence.

Applying *Required:* high school transcript, recommendations, SAT or ACT. *Recommended:* 3 years of high school math and science, 2 years of high school foreign language, interview. Interview required for some. *Application deadlines:* rolling, 3/1 priority date for financial aid. *Contact:* Ms. Deanndrea Katko-Roquet, Director of Admissions, 222 Ninth Street, NW, Waverly, IA 50677, 319-352-8264 or toll-free 800-772-2085.

Washington and Jefferson College

Washington, Pennsylvania

Founded 1781
Small-town setting
Independent
Coed
Awards B

Enrollment	1,126 total—all undergraduates (257 freshmen)
Faculty	100 total; 85 full-time (75% have doctorate/terminal degree); student-faculty ratio is 12:1.
Libraries	195,000 bound volumes, 5,400 titles on microform, 739 periodical subscriptions
Computing	*Terminals/PCs available for student use:* 200, located in computer center, classrooms.
Of Special Interest	*Core academic program:* yes. Computer course required for science majors. Phi Beta Kappa chapter. Academic exchange with American University. Sponsors and participates in study-abroad programs.
On Campus	Drama/theater group; student-run newspaper and radio station. *Social organizations:* 10 national fraternities, 4 national sororities; 53% of eligible undergraduate men and 67% of eligible undergraduate women are members.
Athletics	Member NCAA (Division III). *Intercollegiate sports:* baseball (M), basketball (M, W), cross-country running (M, W), football (M), golf (M), lacrosse (M), soccer (M, W), softball (W), swimming and diving (M, W), tennis (M, W), track and field (M, W), volleyball (W), wrestling (M).

Costs (1991–92) & Aid				
	Comprehensive fee	$16,140	Need-based scholarships	Avail
	Tuition	$12,600	Non-need scholarships (average)	$5000
	Mandatory fees	$250	Short-term loans	N/Avail
	Room and board	$3290	Long-term loans	Avail
	Financial aid recipients	53%		

Undergraduate Facts				
	Part-time	3%	*Freshman Data:* 1,120 applied, 88% were accepted, 26% (257) of those entered	
	State residents	70%		
	Transfers	5%	From top tenth of high school class	43%
	African-Americans	5%	SAT-takers scoring 600 or over on verbal	9%
	Native Americans	1%	SAT-takers scoring 700 or over on verbal	1%
	Hispanics	1%	SAT-takers scoring 600 or over on math	20%
	Asian-Americans	1%	SAT-takers scoring 700 or over on math	2%
	International students	1%	ACT-takers scoring 26 or over	35%
	Freshmen returning for sophomore year	96%	ACT-takers scoring 30 or over	2%
	Students completing degree within 5 years	84%		
	Grads pursuing further study	45%		

Majors Accounting, art education, biology/biological sciences, business, chemistry, computer science, (pre)dentistry sequence, economics, education, English, French, German, history, (pre)law sequence, mathematics, medical technology, (pre)medicine sequence, philosophy, physics, political science/government, psychology, secondary education, sociology, Spanish, (pre)veterinary medicine sequence.

Applying *Required:* high school transcript, 3 years of high school math and science, 2 years of high school foreign language, SAT or ACT, 3 Achievements, English Composition Test. *Recommended:* essay, recommendations, interview, English Composition Test (with essay). *Application deadlines:* 3/1, 11/1 for early decision, 3/15 priority date for financial aid. *Contact:* Mr. Thomas P. O'Connor, Director of Admissions, 27 South Lincoln Street, Washington, PA 15301, 412-223-6025.

Washington and Lee University

Lexington, Virginia

Founded 1749
Small-town setting
Independent
Coed
Awards B, D

Enrollment	1,988 total; 1,602 undergraduates (421 freshmen)
Faculty	138 total; student-faculty ratio is 11:1; grad assistants teach no undergraduate courses.
Libraries	402,742 bound volumes, 116,388 titles on microform, 1,492 periodical subscriptions
Computing	*Terminals/PCs available for student use:* 140, located in computer center, library academic buildings, upperclass residence hall; PC not required.
Of Special Interest	*Core academic program:* yes. Computer course required for some majors. Phi Beta Kappa chapter. Academic exchange with 6 members of the Seven-College Exchange Program, Bates College. Sponsors and participates in study-abroad programs.
On Campus	Drama/theater group; student-run newspaper and radio station. *Social organizations:* 16 national fraternities, 4 national sororities; 82% of eligible undergraduate men and 62% of eligible undergraduate women are members.
Athletics	Member NCAA (Division III). *Intercollegiate sports:* baseball (M), basketball (M, W), cross-country running (M, W), fencing (M, W), field hockey (W), football (M), golf (M), ice hockey (M, W), lacrosse (M, W), rugby (M), soccer (M, W), softball (W), swimming and diving (M, W), tennis (M, W), track and field (M), volleyball (M, W), water polo (M), wrestling (M).

Costs (1991–92) & Aid				
	Comprehensive fee	$15,763	Need-based scholarships (average)	$6870
	Tuition	$11,575	Non-need scholarships (average)	$5140
	Mandatory fees	$120	Short-term loans (average)	$100
	Room and board	$4068	Long-term loans—college funds (average)	$2140
	Financial aid recipients	21%	Long-term loans—external funds (average)	$2750

Undergraduate Facts				
	Part-time	1%	*Freshman Data:* 3,300 applied, 30% were accepted, 43% (421) of those entered	
	State residents	14%		
	Transfers	3%	From top tenth of high school class	60%
	African-Americans	3%	SAT-takers scoring 600 or over on verbal	57%
	Native Americans	0%	SAT-takers scoring 700 or over on verbal	7%
	Hispanics	1%	SAT-takers scoring 600 or over on math	79%
	Asian-Americans	1%	SAT-takers scoring 700 or over on math	25%
	International students	1%	ACT-takers scoring 26 or over	N/R
	Freshmen returning for sophomore year	92%	ACT-takers scoring 30 or over	N/R
	Students completing degree within 5 years	N/R	*Majors with most degrees conferred:* history, economics, English.	
	Grads pursuing further study	N/R		

Majors Accounting, anthropology, art/fine arts, biology/biological sciences, business, chemical engineering, chemistry, classics, computer science, (pre)dentistry sequence, East Asian studies, economics, engineering physics, English, environmental sciences, French, geology, geophysics, German, history, interdisciplinary studies, journalism, (pre)law sequence, mathematics, (pre)medicine sequence, music, philosophy, physics, political science/government, psychology, public affairs and policy studies, religious studies, Romance languages, Russian and Slavic studies, sociology, Spanish, theater arts/drama, (pre)veterinary medicine sequence.

Applying *Required:* essay, high school transcript, 3 years of high school math, 2 years of high school foreign language, 3 recommendations, ACT or SAT and 3 College Board Achievement Tests (including College Board English Composition Test). *Recommended:* 3 years of high school science, interview. *Application deadlines:* 1/15, 12/1 for early decision, 2/1 priority date for financial aid. *Contact:* Mr. William M. Hartog, Dean of Admissions, Gilliam Admissions House, Lexington, VA 24450, 703-463-8710.

Washington College

Chestertown, Maryland

Founded 1782
Small-town setting
Independent
Coed
Awards B, M

Enrollment 981 total; 880 undergraduates (182 freshmen)

Faculty 77 total; 58 full-time (98% have doctorate/terminal degree); student-faculty ratio is 13:1; grad assistants teach no undergraduate courses.

Libraries 194,476 bound volumes, 130,197 titles on microform, 799 periodical subscriptions

Computing *Terminals/PCs available for student use:* 75, located in computer center, library, dormitories, labs, study center; PC not required but available for purchase. Campus network links student PCs.

Of Special Interest *Core academic program:* yes. Computer course required for math, economics, business management majors. Academic exchange with American University. Sponsors and participates in study-abroad programs. Cooperative Army ROTC, cooperative Naval ROTC, cooperative Air Force ROTC.

On Campus Drama/theater group; student-run newspaper. *Social organizations:* 3 national fraternities, 3 national sororities; 25% of eligible undergraduate men and 25% of eligible undergraduate women are members.

Athletics Member NCAA (Division III). *Intercollegiate sports:* baseball (M), basketball (M, W), crew (M, W), field hockey (W), lacrosse (M, W), rugby (M), sailing (M, W), soccer (M), softball (W), swimming and diving (M, W), tennis (M, W), volleyball (W).

Costs (1991–92) & Aid				
	Comprehensive fee	$17,242	Need-based scholarships (average)	$5500
	Tuition	$12,312	Non-need scholarships (average)	$4000
	Mandatory fees	N/App	Short-term loans	N/Avail
	Room and board	$4930	Long-term loans—college funds (average)	$3300
	Financial aid recipients	55%	Long-term loans—external funds (average)	$2900

Undergraduate Facts				
	Part-time	7%	*Freshman Data:* 1,021 applied, 73% were accepted, 24% (182) of those entered	
	State residents	54%		
	Transfers	20%	From top tenth of high school class	27%
	African-Americans	3%	SAT-takers scoring 600 or over on verbal	12%
	Native Americans	N/R	SAT-takers scoring 700 or over on verbal	2%
	Hispanics	2%	SAT-takers scoring 600 or over on math	11%
	Asian-Americans	1%	SAT-takers scoring 700 or over on math	1%
	International students	2%	ACT-takers scoring 26 or over	N/R
	Freshmen returning for sophomore year	85%	ACT-takers scoring 30 or over	N/R
	Students completing degree within 5 years	65%		
	Grads pursuing further study	30%		

Majors American studies, anthropology, art/fine arts, biology/biological sciences, business, chemistry, (pre)dentistry sequence, economics, English, French, German, history, humanities, international studies, Latin American studies, (pre)law sequence, mathematics, (pre)medicine sequence, music, philosophy, physics, political science/government, psychology, sociology, Spanish, theater arts/drama, (pre)veterinary medicine sequence.

Applying *Required:* essay, high school transcript, 3 years of high school math, 2 years of high school foreign language, 2 recommendations, SAT or ACT. *Recommended:* 3 years of high school science, interview, Achievements, English Composition Test. *Application deadlines:* 3/1, 12/1 for early decision, 2/15 priority date for financial aid. *Contact:* Mr. Kevin Coveney, Vice President of Admissions and Enrollment Management, Washington Avenue, Chestertown, MD 21620, 301-778-7700 or toll-free 800-422-1782.

Washington University

St. Louis, Missouri

Founded 1853
Suburban setting
Independent
Coed
Awards B, M, D

Enrollment 9,599 total; 5,040 undergraduates (1,182 freshmen)

Faculty 929 total; 640 full-time (96% have doctorate/terminal degree); student-faculty ratio is 7:1; grad assistants teach a few undergraduate courses.

Libraries 2.3 million bound volumes, 2.4 million titles on microform, 19,000 periodical subscriptions

Computing *Terminals/PCs available for student use:* 2,000, located in computer center, student center, library, dormitories, every school; PC not required. Campus network links student PCs.

Of Special Interest *Core academic program:* yes. Computer course required for some majors. Phi Beta Kappa, Sigma Xi chapters. Academic exchange program. Sponsors and participates in study-abroad programs. Army ROTC, cooperative Air Force ROTC.

On Campus Drama/theater group; student-run newspaper and radio station. *Social organizations:* 12 national fraternities, 7 national sororities; 31% of eligible undergraduate men and 30% of eligible undergraduate women are members.

Athletics Member NCAA (Division III). *Intercollegiate sports:* basketball (M, W), crew (M, W), cross-country running (M, W), fencing (M, W), football (M), golf (M), ice hockey (M), lacrosse (M), rugby (M), soccer (M, W), swimming and diving (M, W), tennis (M, W), track and field (M, W), volleyball (W).

Costs (1992–93) & Aid				
	Comprehensive fee	$22,312	Need-based scholarships (average)	$7800
	Tuition	$16,750	Non-need scholarships (average)	$7400
	Mandatory fees	$168	Short-term loans (average)	$200
	Room and board	$5394	Long-term loans—college funds (average)	$1800
	Financial aid recipients	55%	Long-term loans—external funds (average)	$2800

Undergraduate Facts				
	Part-time	3%	*Freshman Data:* 7,493 applied, 66% were accepted, 24% (1,182) of those entered	
	State residents	19%		
	Transfers	3%	From top tenth of high school class	63%
	African-Americans	7%	SAT-takers scoring 600 or over on verbal	34%
	Native Americans	1%	SAT-takers scoring 700 or over on verbal	5%
	Hispanics	2%	SAT-takers scoring 600 or over on math	75%
	Asian-Americans	10%	SAT-takers scoring 700 or over on math	28%
	International students	4%	ACT-takers scoring 26 or over	79%
	Freshmen returning for sophomore year	94%	ACT-takers scoring 30 or over	34%
	Students completing degree within 5 years	82%		
	Grads pursuing further study	N/R		

Majors Accounting, advertising, anthropology, applied art, applied mathematics, Arabic, archaeology, architecture, art/fine arts, art history, Asian/Oriental studies, biochemistry, biology/biological sciences, black/African-American studies, business, ceramic art and design, chemical engineering, chemistry, Chinese, civil engineering, classics, commercial art, comparative literature, computer engineering, computer science, dance, data processing, earth science, economics, education, electrical engineering, elementary education, engineering (general), engineering and applied sciences, engineering physics, engineering sciences, English, fashion design and technology, finance/banking, French, German, Germanic languages and literature, graphic arts, Greek, Hebrew, history, illustration, interdisciplinary studies, international studies, Italian, Japanese, jewelry and metalsmithing, Judaic studies, Latin, Latin American studies, (pre)law sequence, liberal arts/general studies, linguistics, literature, marketing/retailing/merchandising, mathematics, mechanical engineering, (pre)medicine sequence, medieval studies, modern languages, music, painting/drawing, philosophy, photography, physical sciences, physics, planetary and space sciences, political science/government, psychology, religious studies, Romance languages, Russian, Scandinavian languages/studies, sculpture, secondary education, social work, Spanish, studio art, systems engineering, systems science, technology and public affairs, theater arts/drama, (pre)veterinary medicine sequence, women's studies.

Applying *Required:* essay, high school transcript, 1 recommendation, SAT or ACT. *Recommended:* 4 years of high school math and science, 2 years of high school foreign language, 3 Achievements, English Composition Test (with essay). *Application deadlines:* 2/1, 12/1 for early decision, 12/15 for early action, 2/15 for financial aid. *Contact:* Mr. Harold Wingood, Assistant Provost/Dean of Admissions, Campus Box 1089, 1 Brookings Drive, St. Louis, MO 63130, 314-935-6000 or toll-free 800-582-0700 (in-state), 800-638-0700 (out-of-state).

Webb Institute of Naval Architecture
Glen Cove, New York

Founded 1889
Suburban setting
Independent
Primarily men
Awards B

Enrollment 80 total—all undergraduates (25 freshmen)

Faculty 14 total; 9 full-time (50% have doctorate/terminal degree); student-faculty ratio is 7:1.

Libraries 46,737 bound volumes, 1,516 titles on microform, 197 periodical subscriptions

Computing *Terminals/PCs available for student use:* 46, located in computer center, dormitories, classrooms; PC not required.

Of Special Interest *Core academic program:* yes. Computer course required. Academic exchange program: no. Study-abroad programs: no.

On Campus No national or local fraternities or sororities on campus.

Athletics *Intercollegiate sports:* basketball (M, W), sailing (M, W), soccer (M, W), tennis (M, W).

Costs (1991–92) & Aid				
	Comprehensive fee	$4500	Need-based scholarships (average)	$400
	Tuition	$0	Non-need scholarships	N/Avail
	Mandatory fees	N/App	Short-term loans	N/Avail
	Room and board	$4500	Long-term loans—college funds	N/Avail
	Financial aid recipients	19%	Long-term loans—external funds (average)	$2450

Undergraduate Facts				
	Part-time	0%	*Freshman Data:* 77 applied, 36% were accepted, 89% (25) of those entered	
	State residents	29%		
	Transfers	8%	From top tenth of high school class	76%
	African-Americans	1%	SAT-takers scoring 600 or over on verbal	72%
	Native Americans	0%	SAT-takers scoring 700 or over on verbal	12%
	Hispanics	1%	SAT-takers scoring 600 or over on math	100%
	Asian-Americans	5%	SAT-takers scoring 700 or over on math	60%
	International students	1%	ACT-takers scoring 26 or over	N/App
	Freshmen returning for sophomore year	92%	ACT-takers scoring 30 or over	N/App
	Students completing degree within 5 years	63%		
	Grads pursuing further study	22%		

Majors Marine engineering, naval architecture.

Applying *Required:* high school transcript, 2 recommendations, interview, SAT, 3 Achievements, English Composition Test. *Application deadlines:* 2/15, 10/15 for early decision, 7/1 priority date for financial aid. *Contact:* Mr. William G. Murray, Director of Admissions, Crescent Beach Road, Glen Cove, NY 11542, 516-671-2213.

✻ Wellesley College

Wellesley, Massachusetts

Founded 1870
Suburban setting
Independent
Women
Awards B (double B with MIT)

Enrollment	2,319 total—all undergraduates (580 freshmen)
Faculty	325 total; 239 full-time (93% have doctorate/terminal degree); student-faculty ratio is 10:1.
Libraries	669,915 bound volumes, 60,898 titles on microform, 2,575 periodical subscriptions
Computing	*Terminals/PCs available for student use:* 150, located in computer center, library, dormitories, science center, economics library; PC not required but available for purchase. Campus network links student PCs.
Of Special Interest	*Core academic program:* yes. Phi Beta Kappa, Sigma Xi chapters. Academic exchange with Brandeis University, Babson College, Massachusetts Institute of Technology, members of the Twelve College Exchange Program, Spelman College, Mills College. Sponsors and participates in study-abroad programs. Cooperative Army ROTC, cooperative Air Force ROTC.
On Campus	Drama/theater group; student-run newspaper and radio station. No national or local sororities on campus.
Athletics	Member NCAA (Division III). *Intercollegiate sports:* basketball, crew, cross-country running, fencing, field hockey, lacrosse, rugby, sailing, skiing (downhill), soccer, softball, squash, swimming and diving, tennis, track and field, volleyball.

Costs (1991–92) & Aid				
	Comprehensive fee	$21,848	Need-based scholarships (average)	$9375
	Tuition	$15,966	Non-need scholarships	N/Avail
	Mandatory fees	$375	Short-term loans (average)	$200
	Room and board	$5507	Long-term loans—college funds (average)	$2120
	Financial aid recipients	70%	Long-term loans—external funds (average)	$3037

Undergraduate Facts				
	Part-time	8%	*Freshman Data:* 2,611 applied, 48% were accepted, 46% (580) of those entered	
	State residents	21%		
	Transfers	10%	From top tenth of high school class	79%
	African-Americans	7%	SAT-takers scoring 600 or over on verbal	50%
	Native Americans	1%	SAT-takers scoring 700 or over on verbal	7%
	Hispanics	5%	SAT-takers scoring 600 or over on math	67%
	Asian-Americans	22%	SAT-takers scoring 700 or over on math	16%
	International students	6%	ACT-takers scoring 26 or over	N/App
	Freshmen returning for sophomore year	95%	ACT-takers scoring 30 or over	N/App
	Students completing degree within 5 years	86%	*Majors with most degrees conferred:* political science/government, economics, English.	
	Grads pursuing further study	34%		

Majors American studies, anthropology, archaeology, architecture, art/fine arts, art history, astronomy, biochemistry, biology/biological sciences, black/African-American studies, chemistry, Chinese, classics, computer science, East Asian studies, economics, English, European studies, French, geology, German, Greek, history, Italian, Japanese, Judaic studies, Latin, Latin American studies, linguistics, mathematics, (pre)medicine sequence, medieval studies, music, philosophy, physics, political science/government, psychobiology, psychology, religious studies, Russian, sociology, Spanish, studio art, theater arts/drama, women's studies.

Applying *Required:* essay, high school transcript, 3 recommendations, SAT, 3 Achievements, English Composition Test. *Recommended:* 3 years of high school math and science, some high school foreign language, interview. *Application deadlines:* 2/1, 11/1 for early decision, 2/1 for financial aid. *Contact:* Ms. Janet Lavin, Director of Admission, 240 Green Hall, Wellesley, MA 02181, 617-235-0320 Ext. 2267; *Office location:* 106 Central Street.

Wells College

Aurora, New York

Founded 1868
Rural setting
Independent
Women
Awards B

Enrollment	400 total—all undergraduates (94 freshmen)	
Faculty	58 total; 49 full-time (96% have doctorate/terminal degree); student-faculty ratio is 7:1.	
Libraries	229,000 bound volumes, 6,412 titles on microform, 644 periodical subscriptions	
Computing	*Terminals/PCs available for student use:* 50, located in computer center, Zabriskie Hall of Science, Morgan Hall, Macmillan Hall; PC not required.	
Of Special Interest	*Core academic program:* yes. Computer course required for economics, math majors. Phi Beta Kappa chapter. Academic exchange with members of the Association of Colleges and Universities of the State of New York, Cornell University, American University (Washington Semester), Elmira College in elementary education. Sponsors and participates in study-abroad programs. Cooperative Army ROTC, cooperative Air Force ROTC.	
On Campus	Drama/theater group; student-run newspaper. No national or local sororities on campus.	
Athletics	Member NCAA (Division III). *Intercollegiate sports:* field hockey, lacrosse, soccer, swimming and diving, tennis.	

Costs (1991–92) & Aid				
	Comprehensive fee	$17,400	Need-based scholarships (average)	$6980
	Tuition	$12,500	Non-need scholarships	Avail
	Mandatory fees	$300	Short-term loans	Avail
	Room and board	$4600	Long-term loans—college funds (average)	$3000
	Financial aid recipients	79%	Long-term loans—external funds (average)	$2500

Undergraduate Facts				
	Part-time	4%	*Freshman Data:* 307 applied, 85% were accepted, 36% (94) of those entered	
	State residents	58%		
	Transfers	6%	From top tenth of high school class	30%
	African-Americans	5%	SAT-takers scoring 600 or over on verbal	20%
	Native Americans	1%	SAT-takers scoring 700 or over on verbal	3%
	Hispanics	2%	SAT-takers scoring 600 or over on math	23%
	Asian-Americans	2%	SAT-takers scoring 700 or over on math	3%
	International students	0%	ACT-takers scoring 26 or over	54%
	Freshmen returning for sophomore year	85%	ACT-takers scoring 30 or over	13%
	Students completing degree within 5 years	58%	*Majors with most degrees conferred:* psychology, English, biology/biological sciences.	
	Grads pursuing further study	30%		

Majors American studies, art/fine arts, art history, biology/biological sciences, chemistry, computer science, dance, economics, engineering sciences, English, European studies, French, German, history, Italian, mathematics, music, philosophy, political science/government, psychobiology, psychology, religious studies, Romance languages, Russian, secondary education, sociology, Spanish, studio art, theater arts/drama, (pre)veterinary medicine sequence, Western civilization and culture.

Applying *Required:* essay, high school transcript, 2 recommendations, SAT or ACT, Achievements. *Recommended:* 3 years of high school math and science, 3 years of high school foreign language, interview. *Application deadlines:* 3/1, 12/15 for early decision, 2/15 priority date for financial aid. *Contact:* Ms. Mary Ann Kalbaugh, Dean of Admissions, MacMillan Hall, Aurora, NY 13026, 315-364-3264.

✽ Wesleyan University

Middletown, Connecticut

Founded 1831
Small-town setting
Independent
Coed
Awards B, M, D

Enrollment	3,297 total; 2,664 undergraduates (698 freshmen)
Faculty	341 total; 286 full-time (90% have doctorate/terminal degree); student-faculty ratio is 11:1; grad assistants teach no undergraduate courses.
Libraries	1.1 million bound volumes, 198,000 titles on microform, 3,363 periodical subscriptions
Computing	*Terminals/PCs available for student use:* 300, located in computer center, library; PC not required. Campus network links student PCs.
Of Special Interest	*Core academic program:* no. Computer course required for science, math, economics majors. Phi Beta Kappa, Sigma Xi chapters. Academic exchange with members of the Twelve College Exchange Program. Sponsors and participates in study-abroad programs. Cooperative Army ROTC, cooperative Naval ROTC, cooperative Air Force ROTC.
On Campus	Drama/theater group; student-run newspaper and radio station. *Social organizations:* 6 national fraternities, 3 national sororities, 2 local fraternities, 6 eating clubs; 8% of eligible undergraduate men and 2% of eligible undergraduate women are members.
Athletics	Member NCAA (Division III). *Intercollegiate sports:* basketball (M, W), crew (M, W), cross-country running (M, W), equestrian sports (M, W), field hockey (W), football (M), golf (M), ice hockey (M, W), lacrosse (M, W), rugby (M, W), sailing (M, W), skiing (cross-country) (M, W), soccer (M, W), squash (M, W), swimming and diving (M, W), tennis (M, W), track and field (M, W), volleyball (M, W), water polo (M, W), wrestling (M).

Costs (1991–92) & Aid				
	Comprehensive fee	$21,820	Need-based scholarships (average)	$10,173
	Tuition	$16,250	Non-need scholarships	N/Avail
	Mandatory fees	$580	Short-term loans (average)	$250
	Room and board	$4990	Long-term loans—college funds (average)	$2500
	Financial aid recipients	45%	Long-term loans—external funds (average)	$2500

Undergraduate Facts				
	Part-time	0%	*Freshman Data:* 4,477 applied, 44% were accepted, 36% (698) of those entered	
	State residents	6%		
	Transfers	8%	From top tenth of high school class	65%
	African-Americans	10%	SAT-takers scoring 600 or over on verbal	66%
	Native Americans	1%	SAT-takers scoring 700 or over on verbal	14%
	Hispanics	5%	SAT-takers scoring 600 or over on math	80%
	Asian-Americans	11%	SAT-takers scoring 700 or over on math	34%
	International students	2%	ACT-takers scoring 26 or over	N/R
	Freshmen returning for sophomore year	91%	ACT-takers scoring 30 or over	N/R
	Students completing degree within 5 years	89%	*Majors with most degrees conferred:* English, political science/government, history.	
	Grads pursuing further study	22%		

Majors African studies, American studies, anthropology, art/fine arts, art history, Asian/Oriental studies, astronomy, behavioral sciences, biochemistry, biology/biological sciences, black/African-American studies, chemistry, Chinese, classics, computer science, dance, earth science, East Asian studies, East European and Soviet studies, ecology/environmental studies, economics, English, environmental sciences, film studies, French, German, Germanic languages and literature, Greek, history, humanities, interdisciplinary studies, Italian, Japanese, Latin American studies, liberal arts/general studies, mathematics, medieval studies, molecular biology, music, neurosciences, philosophy, physics, political science/government, psychobiology, psychology, religious studies, Romance languages, Russian, Russian and Slavic studies, social science, sociology, Spanish, studio art, technology and public affairs, theater arts/drama, women's studies.

Applying *Required:* essay, high school transcript, 3 recommendations, SAT or ACT, 3 Achievements, English Composition Test. *Recommended:* 4 years of high school math and science, 4 years of high school foreign language, interview. *Application deadlines:* 1/15, 11/15 for early decision, 2/1 for financial aid. *Contact:* Ms. Barbara-Jan Wilson, Dean of Admissions and Financial Aid, High Street, Middletown, CT 06459, 203-347-9411 Ext. 2427.

Wheaton College

Wheaton, Illinois

Founded 1860
Suburban setting
Independent, nondenominational
Coed
Awards B, M

Enrollment	2,520 total; 2,214 undergraduates (545 freshmen)
Faculty	254 total; 146 full-time (83% have doctorate/terminal degree); student-faculty ratio is 15:1; grad assistants teach no undergraduate courses.
Libraries	356,289 bound volumes, 127,119 titles on microform, 2,164 periodical subscriptions
Computing	*Terminals/PCs available for student use:* 40, located in computer center, computer labs; PC not required.
Of Special Interest	*Core academic program:* yes. Computer course required for business, economics, math majors. Academic exchange with members of the Christian College Consortium. Sponsors and participates in study-abroad programs. Army ROTC.
On Campus	Dress code; mandatory chapel; drama/theater group; student-run newspaper and radio station. No national or local fraternities or sororities on campus.
Athletics	Member NCAA (Division III). *Intercollegiate sports:* basketball (M, W), cross-country running (M, W), football (M), golf (M), soccer (M, W), softball (W), swimming and diving (M, W), tennis (M, W), track and field (M, W), volleyball (W), wrestling (M).

Costs (1991–92) & Aid				
	Comprehensive fee	$13,348	Need-based scholarships (average)	$3364
	Tuition	$9548	Non-need scholarships (average)	$747
	Mandatory fees	N/App	Short-term loans	N/Avail
	Room and board	$3800	Long-term loans—college funds (average)	$1001
	Financial aid recipients	55%	Long-term loans—external funds (average)	$2347

Undergraduate Facts				
	Part-time	2%	*Freshman Data:* 1,311 applied, 71% were accepted, 59% (545) of those entered	
	State residents	22%		
	Transfers	3%	From top tenth of high school class	50%
	African-Americans	1%	SAT-takers scoring 600 or over on verbal	32%
	Native Americans	N/R	SAT-takers scoring 700 or over on verbal	3%
	Hispanics	1%	SAT-takers scoring 600 or over on math	56%
	Asian-Americans	5%	SAT-takers scoring 700 or over on math	17%
	International students	1%	ACT-takers scoring 26 or over	65%
	Freshmen returning for sophomore year	92%	ACT-takers scoring 30 or over	25%
	Students completing degree within 5 years	78%	*Majors with most degrees conferred:* business, economics, literature, psychology.	
	Grads pursuing further study	N/R		

Majors Archaeology, art education, art/fine arts, art history, biblical languages, biblical studies, biology/biological sciences, broadcasting, business economics, chemistry, classics, communication, computer science, (pre)dentistry sequence, economics, elementary education, environmental sciences, French, geology, German, history, interdisciplinary studies, journalism, (pre)law sequence, literature, mathematics, (pre)medicine sequence, modern languages, music, music business, music education, music history, philosophy, physical education, physics, piano/organ, political science/government, psychology, religious education, religious studies, science education, secondary education, sociology, Spanish, speech/rhetoric/public address/debate, stringed instruments, studio art, theater arts/drama, voice, wind and percussion instruments.

Applying *Required:* essay, high school transcript, 2 recommendations, interview, SAT or ACT. *Recommended:* 3 years of high school math and science, 2 years of high school foreign language, Achievements, English Composition Test. *Application deadlines:* 2/15, 12/1 for early action, 3/15 priority date for financial aid. *Contact:* Mr. Dan Crabtree, Director of Admissions, 501 East College Avenue, Wheaton, IL 60187, 708-752-5011 or toll-free 800-222-2419 (out-of-state).

✳ Whitman College

Walla Walla, Washington

Founded 1859
Small-town setting
Independent
Coed
Awards B

Enrollment	1,189 total—all undergraduates (324 freshmen)
Faculty	150 total; 94 full-time (86% have doctorate/terminal degree); student-faculty ratio is 11:1.
Libraries	254,903 bound volumes, 11,000 titles on microform, 1,850 periodical subscriptions
Computing	*Terminals/PCs available for student use:* 105, located in computer center, student center, library, academic buildings; PC not required.
Of Special Interest	*Core academic program:* yes. Phi Beta Kappa, Sigma Xi chapters. Academic exchange with American University, Associated Colleges of the Midwest, Great Lakes Colleges Association. Sponsors and participates in study-abroad programs.
On Campus	Drama/theater group; student-run newspaper and radio station. *Social organizations:* 5 national fraternities, 4 national sororities, 1 local sorority; 50% of eligible undergraduate men and 50% of eligible undergraduate women are members.
Athletics	Member NAIA. *Intercollegiate sports:* baseball (M), basketball (M, W), cross-country running (M, W), golf (M), skiing (cross-country) (M, W), skiing (downhill) (M, W), soccer (M, W), swimming and diving (M, W), tennis (M, W), track and field (M, W), volleyball (W).

Costs (1991–92) & Aid	Comprehensive fee	$17,550	Need-based scholarships (average)	$6575
	Tuition	$13,110	Non-need scholarships	Avail
	Mandatory fees	$100	Short-term loans (average)	$123
	Room and board	$4340	Long-term loans—college funds (average)	$2780
	Financial aid recipients	77%	Long-term loans—external funds (average)	$3621

Undergraduate Facts				
	Part-time	1%	*Freshman Data:* 1,111 applied, 85% were accepted, 34% (324) of those entered	
	State residents	47%		
	Transfers	10%	From top tenth of high school class	39%
	African-Americans	1%	SAT-takers scoring 600 or over on verbal	28%
	Native Americans	1%	SAT-takers scoring 700 or over on verbal	4%
	Hispanics	1%	SAT-takers scoring 600 or over on math	36%
	Asian-Americans	6%	SAT-takers scoring 700 or over on math	8%
	International students	3%	ACT-takers scoring 26 or over	N/R
	Freshmen returning for sophomore year	92%	ACT-takers scoring 30 or over	N/R
	Students completing degree within 5 years	77%	*Majors with most degrees conferred:* English, political science/government, economics.	
	Grads pursuing further study	54%		

Majors Anthropology, art/fine arts, art history, biology/biological sciences, chemistry, computer science, economics, English, French, geology, German, history, mathematics, music, philosophy, physics, political science/government, psychology, sociology, Spanish, theater arts/drama.

Applying *Required:* essay, high school transcript, 1 recommendation, SAT or ACT. *Recommended:* 3 years of high school math and science, 2 years of high school foreign language, interview. *Application deadlines:* 2/15, 12/1 for early decision, 2/15 for financial aid. *Contact:* Ms. Madeleine Eagon, Director of Admissions, Memorial Building, Walla Walla, WA 99362, 509-527-5882.

Whittier College

Whittier, California

Founded 1887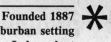
Suburban setting
Independent
Coed
Awards B, M, D

Enrollment	1,838 total; 1,020 undergraduates (270 freshmen)
Faculty	103 total; 79 full-time (92% have doctorate/terminal degree); student-faculty ratio is 13:1; grad assistants teach no undergraduate courses.
Libraries	325,000 bound volumes, 250 titles on microform, 1,270 periodical subscriptions
Computing	*Terminals/PCs available for student use:* 75, located in computer center, library, dormitories, writing lab, academic departments; PC not required.
Of Special Interest	*Core academic program:* yes. Computer course required for business, math, physics majors. Academic exchange program: no. Sponsors and participates in study-abroad programs. Cooperative Army ROTC, cooperative Naval ROTC, cooperative Air Force ROTC.
On Campus	Drama/theater group; student-run newspaper and radio station. *Social organizations:* 4 local fraternities, 5 local sororities; 12% of eligible undergraduate men and 10% of eligible undergraduate women are members.
Athletics	Member NCAA (Division III). *Intercollegiate sports:* baseball (M), basketball (M, W), cross-country running (M, W), football (M), golf (M, W), lacrosse (M, W), soccer (M, W), softball (W), swimming and diving (M, W), tennis (M, W), track and field (M, W), volleyball (W), water polo (M, W).

Costs (1991–92) & Aid				
	Comprehensive fee	$19,588	Need-based scholarships (average)	$8115
	Tuition	$14,170	Non-need scholarships (average)	$5728
	Mandatory fees	$452	Short-term loans (average)	$1000
	Room and board	$4966	Long-term loans—college funds (average)	$1620
	Financial aid recipients	72%	Long-term loans—external funds (average)	$2559

Undergraduate Facts				
	Part-time	2%	*Freshman Data:* 1,349 applied, 61% were accepted, 33% (270) of those entered	
	State residents	59%		
	Transfers	6%	From top tenth of high school class	40%
	African-Americans	5%	SAT-takers scoring 600 or over on verbal	11%
	Native Americans	1%	SAT-takers scoring 700 or over on verbal	1%
	Hispanics	15%	SAT-takers scoring 600 or over on math	23%
	Asian-Americans	6%	SAT-takers scoring 700 or over on math	3%
	International students	5%	ACT-takers scoring 26 or over	N/R
	Freshmen returning for sophomore year	80%	ACT-takers scoring 30 or over	N/R
	Students completing degree within 5 years	46%		
	Grads pursuing further study	36%		

Majors Anthropology, applied art, art/fine arts, athletic training, biochemistry, biology/biological sciences, business, chemistry, child psychology/child development, Chinese, computer science, (pre)dentistry sequence, early childhood education, ecology/environmental studies, economics, education, elementary education, English, environmental sciences, French, geology, history, humanities, international studies, Latin American studies, (pre)law sequence, liberal arts/general studies, mathematics, (pre)medicine sequence, modern languages, music, philosophy, physical education, physical sciences, physical therapy, physics, political science/government, psychology, religious studies, Romance languages, science, secondary education, social science, social work, sociology, Spanish, speech pathology and audiology, sports medicine, theater arts/drama, urban studies, (pre)veterinary medicine sequence.

Applying *Required:* essay, high school transcript, 2 years of high school foreign language, 2 recommendations, SAT or ACT. *Recommended:* 3 years of high school math and science, interview, Achievements. *Application deadlines:* 5/1, 12/10 for early decision, 2/14 priority date for financial aid. *Contact:* Mr. Doug Locker, Director of School Relations, 13406 East Philadelphia Street, Whittier, CA 90608, 310-907-4238 Ext. 238.

Willamette University

Salem, Oregon

Founded 1842
Urban setting
Independent, United Methodist
Coed
Awards B, M, D

Enrollment 2,360 total; 1,622 undergraduates (395 freshmen)

Faculty 179 total; 119 full-time (85% have doctorate/terminal degree); student-faculty ratio is 13:1; grad assistants teach no undergraduate courses.

Libraries 336,394 bound volumes, 71,066 titles on microform, 2,884 periodical subscriptions

Computing *Terminals/PCs available for student use:* 110, located in computer center, library, science center; PC not required. Campus network links student PCs.

Of Special Interest *Core academic program:* yes. Computer course required for business economics, math, chemistry majors. Academic exchange with American University, Drew University. Sponsors and participates in study-abroad programs.

On Campus Drama/theater group; student-run newspaper. *Social organizations:* 6 national fraternities, 3 national sororities; 33% of eligible undergraduate men and 34% of eligible undergraduate women are members.

Athletics Member NCAA (Division III), NAIA. *Intercollegiate sports:* baseball (M), basketball (M, W), cross-country running (M, W), football (M), golf (M), lacrosse (M), rugby (M), soccer (M, W), swimming and diving (M, W), tennis (M, W), track and field (M, W), volleyball (W).

Costs (1991–92) & Aid
Comprehensive fee	$16,430	
Tuition	$12,400	
Mandatory fees	$80	
Room and board	$3950	
Financial aid recipients	75%	
Need-based scholarships (average)		$4500
Non-need scholarships (average)		$2500
Short-term loans (average)		$400
Long-term loans—college funds (average)		$2000
Long-term loans—external funds (average)		$3400

Undergraduate Facts
Part-time	2%
State residents	50%
Transfers	10%
African-Americans	1%
Native Americans	1%
Hispanics	2%
Asian-Americans	5%
International students	6%
Freshmen returning for sophomore year	87%
Students completing degree within 5 years	65%
Grads pursuing further study	30%

Freshman Data: 1,370 applied, 84% were accepted, 34% (395) of those entered

From top tenth of high school class	47%
SAT-takers scoring 600 or over on verbal	23%
SAT-takers scoring 700 or over on verbal	4%
SAT-takers scoring 600 or over on math	46%
SAT-takers scoring 700 or over on math	10%
ACT-takers scoring 26 or over	71%
ACT-takers scoring 30 or over	16%

Majors American studies, art/fine arts, art history, Asian/Oriental studies, biology/biological sciences, business economics, chemistry, computer science, (pre)dentistry sequence, East European and Soviet studies, economics, education, elementary education, English, environmental sciences, European studies, French, German, Hispanic studies, history, humanities, international studies, (pre)law sequence, mathematics, (pre)medicine sequence, music, music education, music therapy, philosophy, physical education, physics, piano/organ, political science/government, psychology, religious studies, Russian and Slavic studies, secondary education, social science, sociology, Spanish, speech/rhetoric/public address/debate, stringed instruments, studio art, theater arts/drama, (pre)veterinary medicine sequence, voice, wind and percussion instruments.

Applying *Required:* essay, high school transcript, 3 years of high school math, 2 years of high school foreign language, 1 recommendation, SAT or ACT. *Recommended:* interview. 3 years of high school science, interview required for some. *Application deadlines:* 2/15, 12/15 for early decision, 2/15 priority date for financial aid. *Contact:* Mr. James M. Sumner, Dean of Admissions, 900 State Street, Salem, OR 97301, 503-370-6303.

William Jewell College

Liberty, Missouri

Founded 1849
Small-town setting
Independent, Baptist
Coed
Awards B

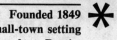

Enrollment	1,366 total—all undergraduates (303 freshmen)
Faculty	143 total; 98 full-time; student-faculty ratio is 14:1.
Libraries	198,630 bound volumes, 789 periodical subscriptions
Computing	*Terminals/PCs available for student use:* 53, located in computer center, library, academic departments; PC not required.
Of Special Interest	*Core academic program:* yes. Computer course required for accounting, business administration majors. Academic exchange with Drew University, American University, 10 members of the American Baptist Association of Colleges and Universities. Sponsors and participates in study-abroad programs.
On Campus	Drama/theater group; student-run newspaper and radio station. *Social organizations:* 4 national fraternities, 4 national sororities; 45% of eligible undergraduate men and 55% of eligible undergraduate women are members.
Athletics	Member NAIA. *Intercollegiate sports:* baseball (M), basketball (M, W), cross-country running (M, W), football (M), golf (M), soccer (M, W), softball (W), swimming and diving (W), tennis (M, W), track and field (M, W), volleyball (W), wrestling (M). *Scholarships:* M, W.

Costs (1991–92) & Aid				
	Comprehensive fee	$10,980	Need-based scholarships (average)	$800
	Tuition	$8300	Non-need scholarships (average)	$2900
	Mandatory fees	N/App	Short-term loans	N/Avail
	Room and board	$2680	Long-term loans—college funds	N/Avail
	Financial aid recipients	87%	Long-term loans—external funds (average)	$2500

Undergraduate Facts				
	Part-time	4%	*Freshman Data:* 622 applied, 81% were accepted, 60% (303) of those entered	
	State residents	79%		
	Transfers	20%	From top tenth of high school class	33%
	African-Americans	2%	SAT-takers scoring 600 or over on verbal	18%
	Native Americans	1%	SAT-takers scoring 700 or over on verbal	5%
	Hispanics	1%	SAT-takers scoring 600 or over on math	32%
	Asian-Americans	1%	SAT-takers scoring 700 or over on math	5%
	International students	1%	ACT-takers scoring 26 or over	31%
	Freshmen returning for sophomore year	87%	ACT-takers scoring 30 or over	8%
	Students completing degree within 5 years	60%	*Majors with most degrees conferred:* business, psychology, education.	
	Grads pursuing further study	27%		

Majors Accounting, art/fine arts, biology/biological sciences, business, chemistry, communication, computer science, data processing, (pre)dentistry sequence, economics, education, elementary education, English, French, history, international business, (pre)law sequence, mathematics, medical laboratory technology, (pre)medicine sequence, music, music education, nursing, philosophy, physical education, physics, political science/government, psychology, religious studies, secondary education, sociology, Spanish, (pre)veterinary medicine sequence, voice.

Applying *Required:* essay, high school transcript, 2 recommendations, SAT or ACT. *Recommended:* 3 years of high school math and science, 2 years of high school foreign language, interview. *Application deadlines:* rolling, 3/15 priority date for financial aid. *Contact:* Mr. T. Edwin Norris, Director of Admission, 500 College Hill, Liberty, MO 64068, 816-781-7700 Ext. 5137 or toll-free 800-753-7009.

*Williams College

Williamstown, Massachusetts

Founded 1793
Small-town setting
Independent
Coed
Awards B, M

Enrollment	2,125 total; 2,083 undergraduates (520 freshmen)
Faculty	271 total; 247 full-time (90% have doctorate/terminal degree); student-faculty ratio is 9:1; grad assistants teach no undergraduate courses.
Libraries	684,588 bound volumes, 311,630 titles on microform, 2,979 periodical subscriptions
Computing	*Terminals/PCs available for student use:* 185, located in computer center, student center, library, academic building; PC not required.
Of Special Interest	*Core academic program:* yes. Phi Beta Kappa, Sigma Xi chapters. Academic exchange with members of the Twelve College Exchange Program, North Adams State College, Bennington College, Rensselaer Polytechnic Institute. Sponsors and participates in study-abroad programs.
On Campus	Drama/theater group; student-run newspaper and radio station. No national or local fraternities or sororities on campus.
Athletics	Member NCAA (Division III). *Intercollegiate sports:* baseball (M), basketball (M, W), crew (M, W), cross-country running (M, W), equestrian sports (M, W), field hockey (W), football (M), golf (M), ice hockey (M, W), lacrosse (M, W), rugby (M, W), sailing (M, W), skiing (cross-country) (M, W), skiing (downhill) (M, W), soccer (M, W), softball (W), squash (M, W), swimming and diving (M, W), tennis (M, W), track and field (M, W), volleyball (M, W), water polo (M, W), wrestling (M).

Costs (1991–92) & Aid				
	Comprehensive fee	$21,940	Need-based scholarships (average)	$10,000
	Tuition	$16,635	Non-need scholarships	N/Avail
	Mandatory fees	$95	Short-term loans (average)	$100
	Room and board	$5210	Long-term loans—college funds (average)	$2500
	Financial aid recipients	38%	Long-term loans—external funds (average)	$2625

Undergraduate Facts				
	Part-time	0%	*Freshman Data:* 4,190 applied, 29% were accepted, 42% (520) of those entered	
	State residents	12%		
	Transfers	2%	From top tenth of high school class	84%
	African-Americans	8%	SAT-takers scoring 600 or over on verbal	73%
	Native Americans	1%	SAT-takers scoring 700 or over on verbal	32%
	Hispanics	5%	SAT-takers scoring 600 or over on math	83%
	Asian-Americans	10%	SAT-takers scoring 700 or over on math	47%
	International students	3%	ACT-takers scoring 26 or over	91%
	Freshmen returning for sophomore year	96%	ACT-takers scoring 30 or over	59%
	Students completing degree within 5 years	94%	*Majors with most degrees conferred:* English, history, political science/government.	
	Grads pursuing further study	20%		

Majors American studies, anthropology, art history, Asian/Oriental studies, astronomy, astrophysics, biochemistry, biology/biological sciences, chemistry, classics, computer science, economics, English, French, geology, German, Greek, history, mathematics, molecular biology, music, philosophy, physics, political science/government, psychology, religious studies, Romance languages, Russian, sociology, Spanish, studio art, theater arts/drama.

Applying *Required:* essay, high school transcript, 4 years of high school math, 4 years of high school foreign language, 2 recommendations, SAT or ACT, 3 Achievements. *Recommended:* 3 years of high school science, interview, English Composition Test (with essay). *Application deadlines:* 1/1, 11/15 for early decision, 2/1 for financial aid. *Contact:* Mr. Philip F. Smith, Dean of Admission, 988 Main Street, Williamstown, MA 01267, 413-597-2211.

From the College A four-week Winter Study program is available for individualized projects, research, and novel fields of interest. In addition, study-abroad programs are offered in many areas of the world. Oxford-style tutorials encourage student research and scholarly debate; over $1-million in national grants is received annually for scientific research. Williams also offers over twenty Division III sports for men and women.

William Smith College
Coordinate with Hobart College
Geneva, New York

Founded 1908
Small-town setting
Independent
Women
Awards B

Enrollment 1,845 total—all undergraduates; 830 at William Smith College (214 freshmen), 1,015 at Hobart College (296 freshmen)

Faculty 180 total; 146 full-time (97% have doctorate/terminal degree); student-faculty ratio is 13:1.

Libraries 300,000 bound volumes, 42,000 titles on microform, 1,809 periodical subscriptions

Computing *Terminals/PCs available for student use:* 372, located in computer center, library, writing annex; PC not required.

Of Special Interest *Core academic program:* yes. Computer course required for math majors. Phi Beta Kappa chapter. Academic exchange with Rochester Area Colleges. Sponsors and participates in study-abroad programs.

On Campus Drama/theater group; student-run newspaper and radio station.

Athletics Member NCAA (Division III). *Intercollegiate sports:* basketball, crew, cross-country running, field hockey, ice hockey, lacrosse, sailing, skiing (downhill), soccer, swimming and diving, tennis.

Costs (1991–92) & Aid				
	Comprehensive fee	$21,542	Need-based scholarships (average)	$8866
	Tuition	$16,077	Non-need scholarships	N/Avail
	Mandatory fees	$299	Short-term loans	N/Avail
	Room and board	$5166	Long-term loans—college funds	N/Avail
	Financial aid recipients	42%	Long-term loans—external funds (average)	$2825

Undergraduate Facts				
	Part-time	1%	*Freshman Data:* 1,350 applied, 70% were accepted, 23% (214) of those entered	
	State residents	41%		
	Transfers	5%	From top tenth of high school class	40%
	African-Americans	6%	SAT-takers scoring 600 or over on verbal	17%
	Native Americans	0%	SAT-takers scoring 700 or over on verbal	1%
	Hispanics	3%	SAT-takers scoring 600 or over on math	31%
	Asian-Americans	2%	SAT-takers scoring 700 or over on math	3%
	International students	4%	ACT-takers scoring 26 or over	N/R
	Freshmen returning for sophomore year	95%	ACT-takers scoring 30 or over	N/R
	Students completing degree within 5 years	82%	*Majors with most degrees conferred:* English, economics, psychology.	
	Grads pursuing further study	35%		

Majors American studies, anthropology, architecture, art/fine arts, art history, Asian/Oriental studies, biology/biological sciences, black/African-American studies, chemistry, classics, comparative literature, computer science, dance, (pre)dentistry sequence, economics, English, environmental sciences, French, geology, German, Greek, history, Latin, (pre)law sequence, mathematics, (pre)medicine sequence, modern languages, music, philosophy, physics, political science/government, psychology, religious studies, Russian, Russian and Slavic studies, sociology, Spanish, studio art, theater arts/drama, urban studies, women's studies.

Applying *Required:* essay, high school transcript, 3 years of high school math, 2 years of high school foreign language, 2 recommendations, SAT or ACT, 3 Achievements, English Composition Test. *Recommended:* 3 years of high school science, interview. *Application deadlines:* 2/15, 1/1 for early decision, 2/15 priority date for financial aid. *Contact:* Ms. Mara O'Laughlin, Director of Admissions, 629 South Main Street, Geneva, NY 14456, 315-781-3472 or toll-free 800-245-0100.

Note: Hobart and William Smith students share a central administration, faculty, and campus and attend all classes together. At the same time, they have separate deans, admission offices, physical education programs, student governments, and alumni and alumnae associations.

✱ Wittenberg University

Springfield, Ohio

Founded 1845
Suburban setting
Independent/affiliated with Evangelical Lutheran Church
Coed
Awards B

Enrollment 2,280 total—all undergraduates (590 freshmen)

Faculty 182 total; 155 full-time (97% have doctorate/terminal degree); student-faculty ratio is 14:1.

Libraries 350,000 bound volumes, 58,248 titles on microform, 1,400 periodical subscriptions

Computing *Terminals/PCs available for student use:* 216, located in computer center, library, dormitories, classrooms; PC not required.

Of Special Interest *Core academic program:* yes. Computer course required for math, business, psychology, science majors. Phi Beta Kappa, Sigma Xi chapters. Academic exchange with 21 members of the Southwestern Ohio Council for Higher Education. Sponsors and participates in study-abroad programs. Cooperative Army ROTC, cooperative Air Force ROTC.

On Campus Drama/theater group; student-run newspaper and radio station. *Social organizations:* 7 national fraternities, 8 national sororities; 35% of eligible undergraduate men and 49% of eligible undergraduate women are members.

Athletics Member NCAA (Division III). *Intercollegiate sports:* baseball (M), basketball (M, W), cross-country running (M, W), field hockey (W), football (M), golf (M, W), ice hockey (M), lacrosse (M, W), rugby (M, W), soccer (M, W), softball (W), swimming and diving (M, W), tennis (M, W), track and field (M, W), volleyball (W).

Costs (1991–92) & Aid

Comprehensive fee	$17,535	
Tuition	$12,792	
Mandatory fees	$699	
Room and board	$4044	
Financial aid recipients	60%	
Need-based scholarships (average)		$7600
Non-need scholarships (average)		$4000
Short-term loans (average)		$50
Long-term loans—college funds (average)		$1000
Long-term loans—external funds (average)		$2200

Undergraduate Facts

Part-time	2%
State residents	47%
Transfers	5%
African-Americans	8%
Native Americans	N/R
Hispanics	2%
Asian-Americans	4%
International students	8%
Freshmen returning for sophomore year	87%
Students completing degree within 5 years	70%
Grads pursuing further study	21%

Freshman Data: 2,440 applied, 78% were accepted, 31% (590) of those entered

From top tenth of high school class	40%
SAT-takers scoring 600 or over on verbal	19%
SAT-takers scoring 700 or over on verbal	3%
SAT-takers scoring 600 or over on math	39%
SAT-takers scoring 700 or over on math	6%
ACT-takers scoring 26 or over	38%
ACT-takers scoring 30 or over	9%

Majors with most degrees conferred: business, biology/biological sciences, education.

Majors Accounting, adult and continuing education, American studies, art education, art/fine arts, art history, Asian/Oriental studies, behavioral sciences, biblical studies, biochemistry, biology/biological sciences, business, business economics, cartography, ceramic art and design, chemistry, child psychology/child development, Chinese, communication, comparative literature, computer science, creative writing, dance, (pre)dentistry sequence, earth science, East Asian studies, East European and Soviet studies, ecology/environmental studies, economics, education, elementary education, English, finance/banking, French, geography, geology, German, Germanic languages and literature, graphic arts, health education, history, humanities, interdisciplinary studies, international business, international studies, Japanese, journalism, (pre)law sequence, liberal arts/general studies, literature, marine biology, marketing/retailing/merchandising, mathematics, (pre)medicine sequence, microbiology, modern languages, music, music education, music history, natural sciences, occupational therapy, painting/drawing, philosophy, physical education, physical sciences, physics, piano/organ, political science/government, psychology, religious studies, Russian, Russian and Slavic studies, sacred music, science, science education, sculpture, secondary education, social science, sociology, Spanish, special education, stringed instruments, studio art, theater arts/drama, theology, urban studies, (pre)veterinary medicine sequence, voice.

Applying *Required:* essay, high school transcript, 3 years of high school math and science, 3 years of high school foreign language, 1 recommendation, SAT or ACT. *Recommended:* interview, Achievements, English Composition Test (with essay). Interview required for some. *Application deadlines:* 3/15, 12/15 for early decision, 1/15 for early action, 3/15 priority date for financial aid. *Contact:* Mr. Kenneth G. Benne, Dean of Admissions, Ward Street at North Wittenberg Avenue, Springfield, OH 45501, 513-327-6314 or toll-free 800-762-5911 (in-state), 800-543-5977 (out-of-state).

From the College East Asian studies, Russian studies, and international marketing are examples of contemporary academic programs that reflect Wittenberg's future-oriented curriculum. In addition to a greater global understanding, students explore solutions to societal issues through a freshman course called Common Learning. Faculty advisers interact closely with students throughout this process. Unique community service programs add balance to the opportunities available to a responsible student body.

Wofford College

Spartanburg, South Carolina

Founded 1854
Urban setting
Independent/affiliated with United Methodist Church
Coed
Awards B

Enrollment 1,117 total—all undergraduates (295 freshmen)

Faculty 88 total; 69 full-time (94% have doctorate/terminal degree); student-faculty ratio is 15:1.

Libraries 183,000 bound volumes, 34,245 titles on microform, 614 periodical subscriptions

Computing *Terminals/PCs available for student use:* 110, located in computer center, library, all academic buildings; PC not required.

Of Special Interest *Core academic program:* yes. Computer course required for economics, business economics, finance, accounting, math, physics majors. Phi Beta Kappa chapter. Academic exchange with Converse College. Sponsors and participates in study-abroad programs. Army ROTC.

On Campus Drama/theater group; student-run newspaper. *Social organizations:* 8 national fraternities, 3 national sororities; 48% of eligible undergraduate men and 44% of eligible undergraduate women are members.

Athletics Member NCAA (Division II). *Intercollegiate sports:* baseball (M), basketball (M, W), cross-country running (M, W), fencing (M, W), football (M), golf (M), riflery (M, W), soccer (M), tennis (M, W), volleyball (W). *Scholarships:* M, W.

Costs (1991–92) & Aid				
	Comprehensive fee	$13,940	Need-based scholarships (average)	$2313
	Tuition	$9790	Non-need scholarships (average)	$4349
	Mandatory fees	N/App	Short-term loans	N/Avail
	Room and board	$4150	Long-term loans—college funds (average)	$2183
	Financial aid recipients	74%	Long-term loans—external funds (average)	$2947

Undergraduate Facts				
	Part-time	4%	*Freshman Data:* 1,052 applied, 88% were accepted, 32% (295) of those entered	
	State residents	71%		
	Transfers	4%	From top tenth of high school class	41%
	African-Americans	8%	SAT-takers scoring 600 or over on verbal	14%
	Native Americans	N/R	SAT-takers scoring 700 or over on verbal	2%
	Hispanics	1%	SAT-takers scoring 600 or over on math	32%
	Asian-Americans	2%	SAT-takers scoring 700 or over on math	4%
	International students	1%	ACT-takers scoring 26 or over	N/R
	Freshmen returning for sophomore year	91%	ACT-takers scoring 30 or over	N/R
	Students completing degree within 5 years	70%	*Majors with most degrees conferred:* English, biology/biological sciences, business economics	
	Grads pursuing further study	32%		

Majors Accounting, art history, biology/biological sciences, business economics, chemistry, computer science, (pre)dentistry sequence, economics, English, finance/banking, French, German, history, humanities, international studies, (pre)law sequence, mathematics, (pre)medicine sequence, philosophy, physics, political science/government, psychology, religious studies, sociology, Spanish, (pre)veterinary medicine sequence.

Applying *Required:* essay, high school transcript, SAT or ACT. *Recommended:* 3 years of high school math and science, some high school foreign language, recommendations, interview, Achievements, English Composition Test. *Application deadlines:* 2/1, 12/1 for early action, continuous to 3/15 for financial aid. *Contact:* Mr. Charles H. Gray Jr., Director of Admissions, 429 North Church Street, Spartanburg, SC 29303-3663, 803-597-4130 Ext. 275.

From the College Upon moving into the Franklin W. Olin Building in 1992, Wofford will have expanded opportunities to use technology in computer science, mathematics, foreign language, and teacher education instruction. Other new facilities are a tennis complex and residence hall. The College recently celebrated the fiftieth anniversary of its Phi Beta Kappa chapter and will host the 1992 NCAA Division II golf championship.

Worcester Polytechnic Institute

Worcester, Massachusetts

Founded 1865
Urban setting
Independent
Coed
Awards B, M, D

Enrollment	3,902 total; 2,656 undergraduates (685 freshmen)
Faculty	342 total; 226 full-time (96% have doctorate/terminal degree); student-faculty ratio is 11:1; grad assistants teach no undergraduate courses.
Libraries	300,000 bound volumes, 785,000 titles on microform, 1,400 periodical subscriptions
Computing	*Terminals/PCs available for student use:* 770, located in computer center, library, computer labs; PC not required. Campus network links student PCs.
Of Special Interest	*Core academic program:* no. Computer course required for some majors. Sigma Xi chapter. Academic exchange with 10 members of the Worcester Consortium for Higher Education. Sponsors and participates in study-abroad programs. Army ROTC, Air Force ROTC, cooperative Naval ROTC.
On Campus	Drama/theater group; student-run newspaper. *Social organizations:* 10 national fraternities, 3 national sororities; 40% of eligible undergraduate men and 40% of eligible undergraduate women are members.
Athletics	Member NCAA (Division III). *Intercollegiate sports:* baseball (M), basketball (M, W), bowling (M, W), crew (M, W), cross-country running (M, W), fencing (M, W), field hockey (W), football (M), golf (M), ice hockey (M), lacrosse (M, W), riflery (M, W), rugby (M, W), sailing (M, W), skiing (downhill) (M, W), soccer (M, W), softball (W), swimming and diving (M, W), tennis (M, W), track and field (M, W), volleyball (M, W), water polo (M, W), wrestling (M).

Costs (1991–92) & Aid				
	Comprehensive fee	$18,715	Need-based scholarships (average)	$4600
	Tuition	$13,985	Non-need scholarships	Avail
	Mandatory fees	$140	Short-term loans (average)	$50
	Room and board	$4590	Long-term loans—college funds (average)	$2000
	Financial aid recipients	70%	Long-term loans—external funds (average)	$4000

Undergraduate Facts				
	Part-time	2%	*Freshman Data:* 2,694 applied, 81% were accepted, 32% (685) of those entered	
	State residents	53%		
	Transfers	3%	From top tenth of high school class	52%
	African-Americans	1%	SAT-takers scoring 600 or over on verbal	23%
	Native Americans	1%	SAT-takers scoring 700 or over on verbal	3%
	Hispanics	1%	SAT-takers scoring 600 or over on math	83%
	Asian-Americans	5%	SAT-takers scoring 700 or over on math	27%
	International students	7%	ACT-takers scoring 26 or over	95%
	Freshmen returning for sophomore year	98%	ACT-takers scoring 30 or over	50%
	Students completing degree within 5 years	75%	*Majors with most degrees conferred:* mechanical engineering, electrical engineering, civil engineering.	
	Grads pursuing further study	17%		

Majors Actuarial science, aerospace engineering, applied mathematics, biochemistry, bioengineering, biology/biological sciences, biomedical engineering, biomedical sciences, biotechnology, business, cell biology, chemical engineering, chemistry, city/community/regional planning, civil engineering, computer engineering, computer information systems, computer management, construction engineering, construction management, (pre)dentistry sequence, ecology/environmental studies, economics, electrical engineering, electronics engineering, embryology, engineering (general), engineering and applied sciences, engineering design, engineering management, engineering mechanics, engineering physics, engineering sciences, environmental engineering, environmental sciences, fire protection engineering, fluid and thermal sciences, genetics, geophysical engineering, history of science, humanities, industrial engineering, information science, interdisciplinary studies, (pre)law sequence, management engineering, manufacturing engineering, materials engineering, materials sciences, mathematics, mechanical engineering, (pre)medicine sequence, metallurgical engineering, metallurgy, microbiology, molecular biology, natural sciences, nuclear engineering, nuclear physics, operations research, optics, physics, science, statistics, systems engineering, technology and public affairs, transportation engineering, (pre)veterinary medicine sequence.

Applying *Required:* high school transcript, 4 years of high school math, 2 recommendations, SAT or ACT, 3 Achievements, English Composition Test. *Recommended:* essay, 3 years of high school science, interview. *Application deadlines:* 2/15, 12/1 for early decision, 3/1 for financial aid. *Contact:* Mr. Robert G. Voss, Executive Director of Admissions and Financial Aid, 100 Institute Road, Worcester, MA 01609, 508-831-5286.

Yale University

New Haven, Connecticut

Founded 1701
Urban setting
Independent
Coed
Awards B, M, D

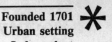

Enrollment	10,778 total; 5,180 undergraduates (1,290 freshmen)
Faculty	715 total; grad assistants teach a few undergraduate courses.
Libraries	9.8 million bound volumes, 3.4 million titles on microform, 51,985 periodical subscriptions
Computing	*Terminals/PCs available for student use:* N/R; PC not required. Campus network links student PCs.
Of Special Interest	*Core academic program:* yes. Computer course required for engineering, math, applied physics majors. Phi Beta Kappa, Sigma Xi chapters. Academic exchange program: no. Sponsors and participates in study-abroad programs. Cooperative Army ROTC, cooperative Air Force ROTC.
On Campus	Drama/theater group; student-run newspaper and radio station. *Social organizations:* student clubs.
Athletics	Member NCAA (Division I). *Intercollegiate sports:* baseball (M), basketball (M, W), crew (M, W), cross-country running (M, W), fencing (M, W), field hockey (W), football (M), golf (M, W), gymnastics (W), ice hockey (M, W), lacrosse (M, W), soccer (M, W), softball (W), squash (M, W), swimming and diving (M, W), tennis (M, W), track and field (M, W), volleyball (W).

Costs (1991–92) & Aid				
	Comprehensive fee	$22,200	Need-based scholarships (average)	$10,882
	Tuition	$16,300	Non-need scholarships	N/Avail
	Mandatory fees	N/App	Short-term loans (average)	$200
	Room and board	$5900	Long-term loans—college funds (average)	$2692
	Financial aid recipients	38%	Long-term loans—external funds (average)	$3090

Undergraduate Facts				
	Part-time	0%	*Freshman Data:* 10,974 applied, 22% were accepted, 54% (1,290) of those entered	
	State residents	10%		
	Transfers	1%	From top tenth of high school class	95%
	African-Americans	7%	SAT-takers scoring 600 or over on verbal	80%
	Native Americans	1%	SAT-takers scoring 700 or over on verbal	36%
	Hispanics	5%	SAT-takers scoring 600 or over on math	92%
	Asian-Americans	14%	SAT-takers scoring 700 or over on math	57%
	International students	4%	ACT-takers scoring 26 or over	N/R
	Freshmen returning for sophomore year	99%	ACT-takers scoring 30 or over	N/R
	Students completing degree within 5 years	93%	*Majors with most degrees conferred:* history, English, economics.	
	Grads pursuing further study	27%		

Majors African studies, American studies, anthropology, applied mathematics, archaeology, architecture, art/fine arts, art history, Asian/Oriental studies, astronomy, biochemistry, biology/biological sciences, biophysics, black/African-American studies, chemical engineering, chemistry, Chinese, classics, comparative literature, computer science, East Asian studies, East European and Soviet studies, ecology/environmental studies, economics, electrical engineering, engineering mechanics, engineering sciences, English, European studies, film studies, French, geology, geophysics, German, Greek, history, history of science, humanities, interdisciplinary studies, Italian, Japanese, Judaic studies, Latin, Latin American studies, linguistics, literature, mathematics, mechanical engineering, music, Near and Middle Eastern studies, philosophy, physics, political science/government, psychology, religious studies, Russian, Russian and Slavic studies, sociology, Spanish, theater arts/drama, women's studies.

Applying *Required:* essay, high school transcript, 3 recommendations, SAT or ACT, 3 Achievements. *Recommended:* 3 years of high school math and science, some high school foreign language, interview. *Application deadlines:* 12/31, 11/1 for early action, 1/15 for financial aid. *Contact:* Ms. Margit A. Dahl, Dean of Undergraduate Admissions, 149 Elm, New Haven, CT 06520, 203-432-1921.

Yeshiva University

New York, New York

Founded 1886
Urban setting
Independent
Coed
Awards B, M, D

Enrollment 4,804 total; 1,852 undergraduates (603 freshmen)

Faculty 164 total; 117 full-time (63% have doctorate/terminal degree); student-faculty ratio is 8:1; grad assistants teach a few undergraduate courses.

Libraries 900,000 bound volumes, 16,570 titles on microform, 7,790 periodical subscriptions

Computing *Terminals/PCs available for student use:* 142, located in computer center, library, classrooms; PC not required.

Of Special Interest *Core academic program:* yes. Computer course required for accounting, finance, marketing, management information systems majors. Academic exchange with Fashion Institute of Technology (Stern College students only). Sponsors and participates in study-abroad programs.

On Campus Drama/theater group; student-run newspaper and radio station. No national or local fraternities or sororities on campus.

Athletics Member NCAA (Division III). *Intercollegiate sports:* basketball (M, W), cross-country running (M), fencing (M), golf (M), tennis (M, W), track and field (M), volleyball (M), wrestling (M).

Costs (1991–92) & Aid				
	Comprehensive fee	$16,595	Need-based scholarships (average)	$3730
	Tuition	$10,875	Non-need scholarships (average)	$3500
	Mandatory fees	$300	Short-term loans	N/Avail
	Room and board	$5420	Long-term loans—college funds (average)	$1500
	Financial aid recipients	75%	Long-term loans—external funds (average)	$2831

Undergraduate Facts				
	Part-time	5%	*Freshman Data:* 1,252 applied, 81% were accepted, 60% (603) of those entered	
	State residents	57%		
	Transfers	28%	From top tenth of high school class	N/R
	African-Americans	N/R	SAT-takers scoring 600 or over on verbal	42%
	Native Americans	N/R	SAT-takers scoring 700 or over on verbal	6%
	Hispanics	N/R	SAT-takers scoring 600 or over on math	62%
	Asian-Americans	N/R	SAT-takers scoring 700 or over on math	24%
	International students	5%	ACT-takers scoring 26 or over	N/App
	Freshmen returning for sophomore year	80%	ACT-takers scoring 30 or over	N/App
	Students completing degree within 5 years	45%	*Majors with most degrees conferred:* psychology, accounting, biology/biological sciences.	
	Grads pursuing further study	80%		

Majors Accounting, biology/biological sciences, chemistry, classics, communication, computer science, (pre)dentistry sequence, early childhood education, economics, education, elementary education, English, finance/banking, French, Hebrew, history, interdisciplinary studies, Judaic studies, (pre)law sequence, management information systems, marketing/retailing/merchandising, mathematics, (pre)medicine sequence, music, philosophy, physics, political science/government, psychology, sociology, special education, speech pathology and audiology, speech/rhetoric/public address/debate, theater arts/drama.

Applying *Required:* high school transcript, 2 years of high school foreign language, 2 recommendations, interview, SAT. *Recommended:* essay. 1 Achievement required for some. *Application deadlines:* 4/15, continuous to 4/15 for financial aid. *Contact:* Mr. Michael Kranzler, Associate Director of Admissions, 500 West 185th Street, New York, NY 10033-3299, 212-960-5400 Ext. 277.

Competitive Colleges Directories

The directories that follow show which of the competitive colleges share certain characteristics in which students are very often interested. To get in-depth information on any of the colleges in these directories, turn back to the individual college listings in the Comparative Profiles section.

Colleges Costing $7000 or Less   346

Colleges with the Most Financial Aid Recipients   346

Ten Largest Colleges   347

Ten Smallest Colleges   347

Colleges Accepting Fewer than Half of Their Applicants   347

Colleges Requiring All Students to Take a Computer Course   348

Single-Sex Colleges   348

Predominantly African-American Colleges   349

Colleges with Religious Affiliation   349

Public Colleges   350

Colleges with the Most Students Completing a Degree   351

Colleges Costing $7000 or Less

Deep Springs College	$0‡
United States Air Force Academy	$0‡
United States Coast Guard Academy	$0‡
United States Merchant Marine Academy	$0
United States Military Academy	$0‡
United States Naval Academy	$0‡
New Mexico Institute of Mining and Technology	$4249†
Cooper Union for the Advancement of Science and Art	$4339*‡
University of Kansas	$4346†
Northeast Missouri State University	$4384†
North Carolina State University	$4404†
South Dakota School of Mines and Technology	$4459†
Webb Institute of Naval Architecture	$4500
Iowa State University of Science and Technology	$4938†‡
University of North Carolina at Chapel Hill	$4948†
Texas A&M University (College Station)	$4970†
University of Texas at Austin	$4975†
New College of the University of South Florida	$5050†
University of Georgia	$5064†
University of Iowa	$5074†
Florida State University	$5171†
University of Florida	$5265†‡
Brigham Young University	$5280‡
University of Arizona	$5281†
University of Missouri–Columbia	$5316†
Purdue University (West Lafayette)	$5334†
Shepherd College	$5394†
University of Wisconsin–Madison	$5435†
University of Tennessee, Knoxville	$5472†‡
University of Washington	$5484†
University of Minnesota, Morris	$5673†
University of Missouri–Rolla	$5810†
State University of New York College at Geneseo	$5887†
University of Colorado at Boulder	$5963†
Colorado State University	$5986†
Auburn University	$6008*†
University at Albany, State University of New York	$6043†
Georgia Institute of Technology	$6083†
Michigan Technological University	$6306†
Virginia Polytechnic Institute and State University	$6314†
University of Minnesota, Twin Cities Campus	$6471†
University of Alabama in Huntsville	$6495†
State University of New York Maritime College	$6560†
University of Virginia	$6663†
State University of New York at Binghamton	$6831†
Michigan State University	$6849†
Mary Washington College	$6868†
State University of New York at Buffalo	$6896†
University of Illinois at Urbana–Champaign	$6957†

* Full room and board not available; estimated cost figured in.
† Cost for in-state students.
‡ Figures are for 1992–93.

Colleges with the Most Financial Aid Recipients

Central University of Iowa	98%
Buena Vista College	96%
College of Insurance	95%
Quincy College	95%
Utica College of Syracuse University	92%
Bethel College (MN)	91%
Houghton College	91%
Alma College	90%
Bellarmine College	90%
Berry College	90%
Bradley University	90%
Carroll College (WI)	90%
Nebraska Wesleyan University	90%
Ohio Northern University	90%
Simpson College (IA)	90%
Polytechnic University, Farmingdale Campus	89%
Rose-Hulman Institute of Technology	89%
Wartburg College	89%
Calvin College	88%
Linfield College	88%
Monmouth College (IL)	88%
Polytechnic University, Brooklyn Campus	88%
St. Norbert College	88%
Clarkson University	87%
Millikin University	87%
University of Minnesota, Morris	87%
University of Pittsburgh at Johnstown	87%
William Jewell College	87%
Goshen College	86%
Messiah College	86%
Ripon College	86%
Augustana College (SD)	85%
Coe College	85%
Fordham University	85%
John Carroll University	85%
Kentucky Wesleyan College	85%
La Salle University	85%
Marquette University	85%
State University of New York College at Geneseo	85%
State University of New York College of Environmental Science and Forestry	85%
Wabash College	85%

Butler University	84%
Howard University	84%
Milwaukee School of Engineering	84%
St. Louis College of Pharmacy	84%
Spelman College	84%
Allegheny College	83%
Beloit College	83%
Oglethorpe University	83%
Samford University	83%
University of Illinois at Urbana-Champaign	83%
Austin College	82%
Hamline University	82%
Knox College (IL)	82%
Elizabethtown College	81%
Eugene Lang College, New School for Social Research	81%
University of Dallas	81%
Augustana College (IL)	80%
Birmingham-Southern College	80%
Concordia College (Moorhead, MN)	80%
Cornell College	80%
Eckerd College	80%
Harvey Mudd College	80%
Hiram College	80%
Illinois Institute of Technology	80%
Illinois Wesleyan University	80%
LeTourneau University	80%
Luther College	80%
North Central College	80%
Rice University	80%
Saint Joseph's University	80%
Saint Louis University	80%
Stetson University	80%
Stevens Institute of Technology	80%
University of Chicago	80%
University of Redlands	80%
University of Scranton	80%

Ten Largest Colleges

University of Texas at Austin	49,961
University of Wisconsin–Madison	43,196
Michigan State University	42,088
Texas A&M University (College Station)	40,997
University of Minnesota, Twin Cities Campus	39,315
Pennsylvania State University University Park Campus	38,989
University of California, Los Angeles	36,366
University of Michigan (Ann Arbor)	36,228
Purdue University (West Lafayette)	36,163
University of Illinois at Urbana-Champaign	36,139

Ten Smallest Colleges

Deep Springs College	26
Webb Institute of Naval Architecture	80
Thomas Aquinas College	201
Marlboro College	268
Simon's Rock College of Bard	286
Eugene Lang College, New School for Social Research	360
Wells College	400
St. John's College (NM)	450
St. John's College (MD)	481
Albert A. List College, Jewish Theological Seminary of America	490

Colleges Accepting Fewer than Half of Their Applicants

Amherst College
Bates College
Baylor University
Bowdoin College
Brown University
California Institute of Technology
Claremont McKenna College
Colby College
Colgate University
College of William and Mary
The Colorado College
Columbia College (NY)
Columbia University, School of Engineering and Applied Science
Cooper Union for the Advancement of Science and Art
Cornell University
Dartmouth College
Davidson College
Deep Springs College
Duke University
Georgetown University
Grove City College
Hamilton College
Harvard University
Harvey Mudd College
Haverford College
Illinois Wesleyan University
James Madison University
Johns Hopkins University
Lafayette College
Mary Washington College
Massachusetts Institute of Technology
Middlebury College
Morehouse College
New College of the University of South Florida
Northwestern University
Pomona College
Princeton University
Rice University
Rutgers, The State University of New Jersey, College of Pharmacy
Rutgers, The State University of New Jersey, Rutgers College
St. Mary's College of Maryland
Sarah Lawrence College
Shepherd College

Competitive Colleges Directories

Colleges Accepting Fewer than Half of Their Applicants (cont.)
Spelman College
Stanford University
State University of New York at Binghamton
State University of New York at Buffalo
State University of New York College at Geneseo
State University of New York College of Environmental Science and Forestry
Swarthmore College
Trenton State College
Tufts University
United States Air Force Academy
United States Coast Guard Academy
United States Merchant Marine Academy
United States Military Academy
United States Naval Academy
University of California at Berkeley
University of California, Davis
University of California, Irvine
University of California, Los Angeles
University of Chicago
University of Detroit Mercy
University of North Carolina at Chapel Hill
University of Notre Dame
University of Pennsylvania
University of Virginia
Vassar College
Wake Forest University
Washington and Lee University
Webb Institute of Naval Architecture
Wellesley College
Wesleyan University
Williams College
Yale University

Colleges Requiring All Students to Take a Computer Course

Augustana College (SD)
Babson College
Bradley University
Butler University
California Institute of Technology
Clarkson University
College of Insurance
Colorado School of Mines
Columbia University, School of Engineering and Applied Science
Florida Institute of Technology
GMI Engineering & Management Institute
Hamline University
Harding University
Harvard University
Harvey Mudd College
Illinois Institute of Technology
James Madison University
Juniata College
La Salle University

LeTourneau University
Michigan Technological University
Milwaukee School of Engineering
Nebraska Wesleyan University
New Jersey Institute of Technology
New Mexico Institute of Mining and Technology
Northeast Missouri State University
Ohio Northern University
Polytechnic University, Brooklyn Campus
Polytechnic University, Farmingdale Campus
Rose-Hulman Institute of Technology
Rutgers, The State University of New Jersey, College of Engineering
Scripps College
Shepherd College
Simon's Rock College of Bard
South Dakota School of Mines and Technology
Southwestern University
Spelman College
State University of New York Maritime College
Stevens Institute of Technology
Taylor University
Texas A&M University (College Station)
Trinity University
United States Air Force Academy
United States Coast Guard Academy
United States Merchant Marine Academy
United States Military Academy
United States Naval Academy
University of Connecticut (Storrs)
University of Denver
University of Detroit Mercy
University of Minnesota, Morris
University of Missouri-Rolla
University of Tulsa
Webb Institute of Naval Architecture

Single-Sex Colleges

Agnes Scott College	W
Barnard College	W
Deep Springs College	M
Hampden-Sydney College	M
Hobart College	M
Mills College	W
Morehouse College	M
Mount Holyoke College	W
Randolph-Macon Woman's College	W
Rose-Hulman Institute of Technology	M
Rutgers, The State University of New Jersey, Douglass College	W
Saint John's University (MN)	M
Scripps College	W
Smith College	W
Spelman College	W
Wabash College	M
Wellesley College	W
Wells College	W
William Smith College	W

Predominantly African-American Colleges

Fisk University
Howard University
Morehouse College
Spelman College

Colleges with Religious Affiliation

Baptist
Baylor University
Bethel College (MN)
Linfield College
Samford University
Stetson University
University of Richmond
William Jewell College

Brethren
Elizabethtown College
Messiah College

Christian Church (Disciples of Christ)
Hiram College
Texas Christian University
Transylvania University

Churches of Christ
Harding University
Pepperdine University (Malibu)

Episcopal
Hobart College
University of the South

Friends
Earlham College
Guilford College

Jewish
Albert A. List College, Jewish Theological Seminary of America

Latter-day Saints (Mormon)
Brigham Young University

Lutheran
Augustana College (IL)
Augustana College (SD)
Concordia College (Moorhead, MN)
Gettysburg College
Gustavus Adolphus College
Luther College
Muhlenberg College
Pacific Lutheran University
St. Olaf College
Valparaiso University
Wartburg College
Wittenberg University

Mennonite
Goshen College

Methodist
Albion College
Albright College
Allegheny College
American University
Birmingham-Southern College
Centenary College of Louisiana
Cornell College
DePauw University
Drew University
Duke University
Emory University
Hamline University
Hendrix College
Illinois Wesleyan University
Kentucky Wesleyan College
Millsaps College
Nebraska Wesleyan University
North Central College
Ohio Northern University
Ohio Wesleyan University
Randolph-Macon Woman's College
Simpson College (IA)
Southern Methodist University
Southwestern University
University of Puget Sound
Willamette University
Wofford College

Nondenominational
LeTourneau University
Wheaton College (IL)

Presbyterian
Agnes Scott College
Alma College
Austin College
Buena Vista College
Carroll College (WI)
Centre College
Coe College
The College of Wooster
Davidson College
Eckerd College
Grove City College
Hampden-Sydney College
Lafayette College
Macalester College
Millikin University
Monmouth College (IL)
Presbyterian College
Rhodes College
Trinity University
University of Tulsa

Reformed Churches
Calvin College
Central University of Iowa
Hope College

Roman Catholic
Bellarmine College
Boston College
Catholic University of America

Colleges with Religious Affiliation (cont.)
Christian Brothers University
College of the Holy Cross
Creighton University
DePaul University
Fairfield University
Fordham University
Georgetown University
John Carroll University
La Salle University
Le Moyne College
Loyola College
Marquette University
Mount St. Mary's College (CA)
Providence College
Quincy College
Rockhurst College
Saint John's University (MN)
Saint Joseph's University
Saint Louis University
St. Norbert College
Santa Clara University
Siena College
Thomas Aquinas College
University of Dallas
University of Detroit Mercy
University of Notre Dame
University of Scranton
Villanova University

United Church of Christ
Fisk University
Ursinus College

Wesleyan
Houghton College

Public Colleges

Auburn University
College of William and Mary
Colorado School of Mines
Colorado State University
Florida State University
Georgia Institute of Technology
Iowa State University of Science and Technology
James Madison University
Mary Washington College
Miami University
Michigan State University
Michigan Technological University
New College of the University of South Florida
New Jersey Institute of Technology
New Mexico Institute of Mining and Technology
North Carolina State University
Northeast Missouri State University
Pennsylvania State University University Park Campus
Purdue University (West Lafayette)
Rutgers, The State University of New Jersey, College of Engineering
Rutgers, The State University of New Jersey, College of Pharmacy
Rutgers, The State University of New Jersey, Cook College
Rutgers, The State University of New Jersey, Douglass College
Rutgers, The State University of New Jersey, Rutgers College
St. Mary's College of Maryland
Shepherd College
South Dakota School of Mines and Technology
State University of New York at Binghamton
State University of New York at Buffalo
State University of New York College at Geneseo
State University of New York College of Environmental Science and Forestry
State University of New York Maritime College
Texas A&M University (College Station)
Trenton State College
United States Air Force Academy
United States Coast Guard Academy
United States Merchant Marine Academy
United States Military Academy
United States Naval Academy
University at Albany, State University of New York
University of Alabama in Huntsville
University of Arizona
University of California at Berkeley
University of California, Davis
University of California, Irvine
University of California, Los Angeles
University of California, Riverside
University of California, San Diego
University of California, Santa Barbara
University of California, Santa Cruz
University of Colorado at Boulder
University of Connecticut (Storrs)
University of Delaware
University of Florida
University of Georgia
University of Illinois at Urbana-Champaign
University of Iowa
University of Kansas
University of Maryland College Park
University of Massachusetts at Amherst
University of Michigan (Ann Arbor)
University of Michigan-Dearborn
University of Minnesota, Morris
University of Minnesota, Twin Cities Campus
University of Missouri-Columbia
University of Missouri-Kansas City
University of Missouri-Rolla
University of New Hampshire (Durham)
University of North Carolina at Chapel Hill
University of Pittsburgh

University of Pittsburgh at Johnstown
University of Tennessee, Knoxville
University of Texas at Austin
University of Vermont
University of Virginia
University of Washington
University of Wisconsin–Madison
Virginia Polytechnic Institute and State University

Colleges with the Most Students Completing a Degree

College	%
Albert A. List College, Jewish Theological Seminary of America	98%
Amherst College	97%
Harvard University	96%
Dartmouth College	94%
Duke University	94%
Princeton University	94%
University of Notre Dame	94%
Williams College	94%
Yale University	93%
College of the Holy Cross	92%
Pomona College	92%
Brown University	91%
Connecticut College	91%
University of Texas at Austin	91%
Bates College	90%
Bowdoin College	90%
Columbia College (NY)	90%
Davidson College	90%
Hamilton College	90%
Haverford College	90%
Massachusetts Institute of Technology	90%
Middlebury College	90%
Shepherd College	90%
Tufts University	90%
University of Virginia	90%
Georgetown University	89%
Lafayette College	89%
La Salle University	89%
Wesleyan University	89%
Bucknell University	88%
Carleton College	88%
Cornell University	88%
Lehigh University	88%
Northwestern University	88%
Rice University	88%
Swarthmore College	88%
University of Pennsylvania	88%
Babson College	87%
Colby College	87%
Colgate University	87%
Providence College	87%
St. Louis College of Pharmacy	87%
Smith College	87%
Johns Hopkins University	86%
Kenyon College	86%
Wellesley College	86%
Bryn Mawr College	85%
Fairfield University	85%
Franklin and Marshall College	85%
Taylor University	85%
University of Scranton	85%
Boston College	84%
College of William and Mary	84%
Dickinson College	84%
Fordham University	84%
Oberlin College	84%
State University of New York at Binghamton	84%
Union College (NY)	84%
Villanova University	84%
Wake Forest University	84%
Washington and Jefferson College	84%
Grinnell College	83%
University of Michigan (Ann Arbor)	83%
University of Richmond	83%
Barnard College	82%
Claremont McKenna College	82%
Illinois Wesleyan University	82%
Monmouth College (IL)	82%
St. Olaf College	82%
University of Chicago	82%
Washington University	82%
William Smith College	82%
Cooper Union for the Advancement of Science and Art	80%
Emory University	80%
Furman University	80%
Gettysburg College	80%
Hobart College	80%
Mount Holyoke College	80%
Muhlenberg College	80%
Rollins College	80%
St. Lawrence University	80%
Sarah Lawrence College	80%
Siena College	80%
Skidmore College	80%

Profiles of Competitive Arts Colleges and Conservatories

The listings below show the autonomous colleges specializing in art and/or music that have highly selective application/acceptance ratios.

Art Center College of Design
Pasadena, California 91103

Founded 1930; suburban setting; independent; coed; awards B, M.

Enrollment 1,289 total; 1,259 undergraduates (223 freshmen).

Faculty 306 total; 56 full-time; student-faculty ratio is 5:1.

Expenses (1992–93) Tuition: $11,660.

Majors Advertising, art/fine arts, commercial art, environmental design, film studies, graphic arts, illustration, industrial design, painting/drawing, photography.

Applying Required: high school transcript, essay, portfolio. Recommended: 3 years of high school math, some foreign language, interview.

Application deadlines: rolling, 3/1 priority date for financial aid.

Contact: Mr. Gregory Price, Director of Admissions, 818-584-5035.

Boston Conservatory
Boston, Massachusetts 02215

Founded 1867; urban setting; independent; coed; awards B, M.

Enrollment 306 total; 265 undergraduates (61 freshmen).

Faculty 95 total; 35 full-time.

Expenses (1991–92) Comprehensive fee of $15,650 includes tuition ($9900), mandatory fees ($450), and room and board ($5300).

Majors Dance, music, music education, opera, piano/organ, stringed instruments, theater arts/drama, voice, wind and percussion instruments.

Applying Required: essay, high school transcript, 3 recommendations, audition. Recommended: 3 years of high school math and science, some high school foreign language, SAT or ACT. Interview required for some.

Application deadlines: rolling, 3/15 priority date for financial aid.

Contact: Ms. Allison T. Ball, Director of Admissions, 617-536-6340 Ext. 16.

California Institute of the Arts
Valencia, California 91355

Founded 1961; small-town setting; independent; coed; awards B, M.

Enrollment 955 total; 661 undergraduates (226 freshmen).

Faculty 232 total; student-faculty ratio is 8:1.

Expenses (1992–93) Comprehensive fee of $17,950 includes tuition ($12,875), mandatory fees ($75), and room and board ($5000).

Majors Animation, art/fine arts, commercial art, computer graphics, dance, film studies, graphic arts, jazz, music, photography, sculpture, stringed instruments, studio art, theater arts/drama, voice.

Applying Required: essay, high school transcript, portfolio or audition. Interview, recommendations, test scores required for some.

Application deadlines: 2/1, 3/1 priority date for financial aid.

Contact: Mr. Kenneth Young, Director of Admissions, 805-253-7863.

Cleveland Institute of Music
Cleveland, Ohio 44106

Founded 1920; urban setting; independent; coed; awards B, M, D.

Enrollment 318 total; 176 undergraduates (41 freshmen).

Faculty 119 total; 39 full-time.

Expenses (1991–92) Comprehensive fee of $17,115 includes tuition ($11,500), mandatory fees ($770), and room and board ($4845).

Majors Audio engineering, music, music education, piano/organ, stringed instruments, voice, wind and percussion instruments.

Applying Required: essay, high school transcript, 2 recommendations, audition or tape, SAT or ACT. Recommended: 3 years of high school math and science, some high school foreign language, interview.

Application deadlines: 2/1, 3/1 priority date for financial aid.

Contact: Mr. William Fay, Director of Admission, 216-795-3107.

Corcoran School of Art
Washington, District of Columbia 20006

Founded 1890; urban setting; independent; coed; awards B.

Enrollment 285 total—all undergraduates (63 freshmen).

Faculty 81 total; 45 full-time; student-faculty ratio is 10:1.

Expenses (1991–92) Tuition: $9500. Room only: $3500.

Majors Applied art, art/fine arts, ceramic art and design, commercial art, drafting and design, graphic arts, painting/drawing, photography, sculpture, studio art.

Applying Required: high school transcript, portfolio. Recommended: campus interview, SAT or ACT.

Application deadlines: rolling, 3/15 priority date for financial aid.

Contact: Mr. Mark Sistek, Director of Admissions, 202-628-9484 Ext. 700.

Curtis Institute of Music
Philadelphia, Pennsylvania 19103

Founded 1924; urban setting; independent; coed; awards B, M.

Enrollment 161 total; 132 undergraduates (32 freshmen).

Faculty 84 total; 2 full-time.

Expenses (1992–93 estimated) Tuition: $0. Mandatory fees: $550.

Majors Music, stringed instruments, voice, wind and percussion instruments.

Applying Required: high school transcript, recommendations, audition, SAT. Recommended: 3 years of high school math and science, some high school foreign language.

Application deadlines: 1/15, 6/1 priority date for financial aid.

Contact: Ms. Judi L. Gattone, Admissions and Financial Aid Officer, 215-893-5262.

Fashion Institute of Technology
New York, New York 10001

Founded 1944; urban setting; state and locally supported; coed; awards A, B, M.

Enrollment 12,085 total; 12,007 undergraduates (1,657 freshmen).

Faculty 820 total; 225 full-time; student-faculty ratio is 15:1.

Expenses (1992–93) State resident tuition: $1860. Nonresident tuition: $4260. Mandatory fees: $210. Room and board: $4655.

Majors Advertising, applied art, art/fine arts, commercial art, communications, fashion design and technology, fashion merchandising, illustration, industrial administration, interior design, jewelry and metalsmithing, management engineering, marketing/retailing/merchandising, photography, textile arts, textiles and clothing.

Applying Required: essay, high school transcript, portfolio for art and design majors, SAT or ACT. Interview required for some.

Application deadlines: 1/15, 3/15 priority date for financial aid.

Contact: Mr. Jim Pidgeon, Director of Admissions, 212-760-7675.

Juilliard School
New York, New York 10023

Founded 1905; urban setting; independent; coed; awards B, M, D.

Enrollment 849 total; 487 undergraduates (92 freshmen).

Faculty 220 total—all full-time; student-faculty ratio is 4:1.

Expenses (1991–92) Comprehensive fee of $16,680 includes tuition ($9800), mandatory fees ($550), and room and board ($6330).

Majors Dance, music, opera, piano/organ, stringed instruments, theater arts/drama, voice, wind and percussion instruments.

Applying Required: high school transcript, audition. Essay required for some.

Application deadlines: 1/8, 2/15 priority date for financial aid.

Contact: Mrs. Carole J. Everett, Director of Admissions, 212-799-5000 Ext. 223.

Manhattan School of Music
New York, New York 10027

Founded 1917; urban setting; independent; coed; awards B, M, D.

Enrollment 818 total; 398 undergraduates (67 freshmen).

Manhattan School of Music (cont.)

Faculty 249 total; 12 full-time.

Expenses (1991–92) Tuition: $9950. Mandatory fees: $300. Room only: $3800.

Majors Jazz, music, piano/organ, stringed instruments, voice, wind and percussion instruments.

Applying Required: high school transcript, essay, audition. Recommended: SAT or ACT, 3 years of high school math and science, some high school foreign language, recommendations.
Application deadlines: 7/1, 3/1 priority date for financial aid.
Contact: Mr. James Gandre, Director of Admissions, 212-749-3025.

Mannes College of Music
New York, New York 10024

Founded 1916; urban setting; independent; coed; awards B, M.

Enrollment 6,250 university (New School for Social Research) total; 237 unit total; 107 undergraduates (42 freshmen).

Faculty 216 total; 15 full-time; student-faculty ratio is 5:1.

Expenses (1991–92) Comprehensive fee of $16,273 includes tuition ($10,100), mandatory fees ($150), and room and board ($6023).

Majors Music, opera, piano/organ, stringed instruments, voice, wind and percussion instruments.

Applying Required: high school transcript, 1 recommendation, audition. Recommended: 3 years of high school math and science, campus interview.
Application deadlines: 7/15, 7/15 priority date for financial aid.
Contact: Ms. Marilyn Groves, Director of Admissions and Registration, 212-580-0210 Ext. 46.

Maryland Institute, College of Art
Baltimore, Maryland 21217

Founded 1826; urban setting; independent; coed; awards B, M.

Enrollment 970 total; 886 undergraduates (187 freshmen).

Faculty 133 total; 59 full-time; student-faculty ratio is 11:1.

Expenses (1991–92) Comprehensive fee of $14,560 includes tuition ($10,600) and room and board ($3960).

Majors Applied art, art education, art/fine arts, ceramic art and design, commercial art, graphic arts, illustration, interior design, painting/drawing, photography, sculpture, studio art, textile arts.

Applying Required: high school transcript, essay, portfolio, SAT or ACT. Recommended: campus interview, 2 recommendations.
Application deadlines: 6/1, 3/1 priority date for financial aid.
Contact: Ms. Theresa M. Lynch, Director of Admissions, 410-225-2222.

Massachusetts College of Art
Boston, Massachusetts 02115

Founded 1873; urban setting; state-supported; coed; awards B, M.

Enrollment 1,176 total; 1,080 undergraduates (259 freshmen).

Faculty 89 total; 58 full-time; student-faculty ratio is 14:1.

Expenses (1991–92) State resident tuition: $1374. Nonresident tuition: $5934. Mandatory fees: $2170. Room and board: $5247.

Majors Applied art, architecture, art education, art/fine arts, art history, ceramic art and design, commercial art, computer graphics, fashion design and technology, film and video, graphic arts, illustration, industrial design, jewelry and metalsmithing, painting/drawing, photography, sculpture, studio art, textile arts.

Applying Required: essay, high school transcript, 3 years of high school math and science, 2 years of high school foreign language, portfolio, SAT. Recommended: recommendations, campus interview.
Application deadlines: 4/1, 5/1 priority date for financial aid.
Contact: Ms. Kay Ransdell, Director of Admissions, 617-232-1555 Ext. 235.

New England Conservatory of Music
Boston, Massachusetts 02115

Founded 1867; urban setting; independent; coed; awards B, M, D.

Enrollment 736 total; 358 undergraduates (120 freshmen).

Faculty 191 total; 55 full-time.

Expenses (1991–92) Comprehensive fee of $18,950 includes tuition ($12,800) and room and board ($6150).

Majors Jazz, music, music education, music history, opera, piano/organ, stringed instruments, voice, wind and percussion instruments.

Applying Required: essay, high school transcript, 1 recommendation, audition, SAT or ACT.
Application deadlines: 1/15, 3/1 priority date for financial aid.
Contact: Ms. Jacqueline Evans, Admissions Counselor, 617-262-1120 Ext. 430.

New York School of Interior Design
New York, New York 10022

Founded 1916; urban setting; independent; coed; awards A, B.

Enrollment 600 total—all undergraduates (12 freshmen).

Faculty 71 total; 4 full-time; student-faculty ratio is 18:1.

Expenses (1991–92) Tuition: $7560. Mandatory fees: $50.

Major Interior design.

Applying Required: essay, high school transcript, 2 recommendations, portfolio or visual test (for BFA applicants), SAT or ACT. Recommended: interview. Interview required for some.
Application deadlines: rolling, 3/1 priority date for financial aid.
Contact: Ms. June Soyka, Director of Admissions, 212-753-5365 or toll-free 800-69N-YSID (in-state), 800-33N-YSID (out-of-state).

From the College NYSID (FIDER-accredited) is a unique college that offers programs that focus exclusively on interior design. Because of NYSID's reputation in the design industry, many graduates find work in the best design and architectural firms in New York City. Approximately 10 percent of the interior designers profiled in the August 1990 (AD 100) edition of *Architectural Digest* were former students and graduates.

North Carolina School of the Arts
Winston-Salem, North Carolina 27117

Founded 1963; suburban setting; state-supported; coed; awards B, M.

Enrollment 730 total; 466 undergraduates (107 freshmen).

Faculty 115 total; 91 full-time; student-faculty ratio is 7:1.

Expenses (1991–92) State resident tuition: $1178. Nonresident tuition: $7617. Mandatory fees: $622. Room and board: $3163.

Majors Dance, music, theater arts/drama.

Applying Required: high school transcript, 3 years of high school math and science, 2 recommendations, audition, SAT or ACT. Recommended: 2 years of high school foreign language. Essay required for some.
Application deadlines: rolling, 4/1 priority date for financial aid.
Contact: Ms. Carol Palm, Acting Director of Admissions, 919-770-3290 or toll-free 800-282-2787.

Otis/Parsons School of Art and Design
Los Angeles, California 90057

Founded 1918; urban setting; independent; coed; awards A, B, M.

Enrollment 704 total; 693 undergraduates (204 freshmen).

Faculty 225 total; 20 full-time; student-faculty ratio is 4:1.

Expenses (1991–92) Comprehensive fee of $15,799 includes tuition ($10,714), mandatory fees ($380), and room and board ($4705).

Majors Applied art, art/fine arts, ceramic art and design, commercial art, environmental design, fashion design and technology, graphic arts, illustration, interior design, painting/drawing, photography, sculpture, studio art.

Applying Required: high school transcript, portfolio, 4 assigned art exercises. Recommended: recommendations. Essay, interview, SAT or ACT required for some.
Application deadlines: rolling, 3/1 priority date for financial aid.
Contact: Mr. Joseph Suszynski, Director of Admissions, 213-251-0504.

Parsons School of Design, New School for Social Research
New York, New York 10011

Founded 1896; urban setting; independent; coed; awards A, B, M.

Enrollment 6,250 university total; 1,770 unit total; 1,646 undergraduates (294 freshmen).

Faculty 332 total; 22 full-time; student-faculty ratio is 14:1.

Expenses (1991–92) Comprehensive fee of $18,650 includes tuition ($12,500), mandatory fees ($150), and room and board ($6000).

Majors Architecture, art education, art/fine arts, business administration/commerce/management, ceramic art and design, commercial

Parsons School of Design (cont.)

art, environmental design, fashion design and technology, fashion merchandising, graphic arts, illustration, industrial design, interior design, jewelry and metalsmithing, marketing/retailing/merchandising, painting/drawing, photography, sculpture, textile arts.

Applying Required: high school transcript, campus interview, portfolio, SAT or ACT. Recommended: essay, recommendations, English Composition Test (with essay). Essay, recommendations required for some.

Application deadlines: rolling, 3/1 priority date for financial aid.

Contact: Mr. Timothy Gunn, Director of Admissions, 212-741-8910 or toll-free 800-252-0852.

Rhode Island School of Design
Providence, Rhode Island 02903

Founded 1877; suburban setting; independent; coed; awards B, M.

Enrollment 1,912 total; 1,809 undergraduates (366 freshmen).

Faculty 279 total; 104 full-time; student-faculty ratio is 12:1.

Expenses (1991–92) Comprehensive fee of $20,013 includes tuition ($14,036), mandatory fees ($85), and room and board ($5892).

Majors Architecture, art/fine arts, ceramic art and design, fashion design and technology, film studies, graphic arts, illustration, industrial design, interior design, jewelry and metalsmithing, landscape architecture/design, painting/drawing, photography, sculpture, textile arts, textiles and clothing.

Applying Required: essay, high school transcript, portfolio, drawing assignments, SAT or ACT. Recommended: 3 recommendations. 3 years of high school math required for some.

Application deadlines: 1/21, 12/15 for early action, 2/15 priority date for financial aid.

Contact: Mr. Edward Newhall, Director of Admissions, 401-454-6300.

Rutgers, The State University of New Jersey, Mason Gross School of the Arts
New Brunswick, New Jersey 08903

Founded 1976; small-town setting; state-supported; coed; awards B, M.

Enrollment 48,693 university total; 625 unit total; 421 undergraduates (97 freshmen).

Faculty 81 full-time; student-faculty ratio is 12:1.

Expenses (1991–92) State resident tuition: $3114. Nonresident tuition: $6338. Mandatory fees: range from $668 to $734, according to college affiliation. Room and board: $4018.

Majors Art/fine arts, ceramic art and design, dance, film studies, graphic arts, jazz, music, painting/drawing, photography, sculpture, theater arts/drama.

Applying Required: high school transcript, 3 years of high school math, audition or portfolio or interview, SAT or ACT. Recommended: 2 years of high school foreign language. 3 Achievements required for some.

Application deadlines: 1/15, continuous to 3/1 for financial aid.

Contact: Dr. Elizabeth Mitchell, Assistant Vice President for University Undergraduate Admissions, 908-932-3770.

San Francisco Conservatory of Music
San Francisco, California 94122

Founded 1917; urban setting; independent; coed; awards B, M.

Enrollment 270 total; 169 undergraduates (18 freshmen).

Faculty 68 total; 23 full-time; student-faculty ratio is 7:1.

Expenses (1991–92) Tuition: $9200. Mandatory fees: $200.

Majors Music, opera, piano/organ, stringed instruments, voice, wind and percussion instruments.

Applying Required: high school transcript, 2 recommendations, audition, SAT or ACT. Recommended: some high school foreign language.

Application deadlines: 4/1, 4/1 priority date for financial aid.

Contact: Mr. David Moebs, Admissions Officer, 415-759-3431.

Savannah College of Art and Design
Savannah, Georgia 31401

Founded 1978; urban setting; independent; coed; awards B, M.

Enrollment 2,209 total; 1,999 undergraduates (733 freshmen).

Faculty 121 total; 110 full-time; student-faculty ratio is 19:1.

Expenses (1992–93) Tuition: $8325. Mandatory fees: $150. Room only: $3050.

Majors Applied art, architecture, art/fine arts, art history, commercial art, computer graphics, drafting and design, fashion design and technology, film studies, graphic arts, historic preservation, illustration, interior design, painting/drawing, photography, studio art, textile arts.

Applying Required: high school transcript, 3 recommendations, SAT or ACT. Recommended: interview. 3 years high school math required for some.

Application deadlines: rolling, 4/1 priority date for financial aid.

Contact: Ms. May Poetter, Dean of Admissions, 912-238-2424.

Westminster Choir College
Princeton, New Jersey 08540

Founded 1926; small-town setting; independent; coed; awards B, M.

Enrollment 314 total; 220 undergraduates (46 freshmen).

Faculty 64 total; 38 full-time; student-faculty ratio is 7:1.

Expenses (1991–92) Comprehensive fee of $15,880 includes tuition ($11,100) and room and board ($4780).

Majors Liberal arts/general studies, music, music education, piano/organ, sacred music, voice.

Applying Required: essay, high school transcript, 3 years high school math and science, 3 recommendations, audition, music test, SAT or ACT. Recommended: some high school foreign language, interview.

Application deadlines: rolling, 4/1 priority date for financial aid.

Contact: Ms. Deborah J. Erie, Director of Admissions, 609-921-7144 or toll-free 800-96-CHOIR.

Geographical Index of Colleges

Alabama
Auburn University	23
Birmingham-Southern College	37
Samford University	222
University of Alabama in Huntsville	263

Arizona
University of Arizona	264

Arkansas
Harding University	118
Hendrix College	122

California
Art Center College of Design	352
California Institute of Technology	49
California Institute of the Arts	352
Claremont McKenna College	60
Deep Springs College	83
Harvey Mudd College	120
Mills College	164
Mount St. Mary's College	169
Occidental College	181
Otis/Parsons School of Art and Design	355
Pepperdine University (Malibu)	187
Pitzer College	188
Pomona College	191
San Francisco Conservatory of Music	356
Santa Clara University	223
Scripps College	225
Stanford University	236
Thomas Aquinas College	249
University of California at Berkeley	265
University of California, Davis	266
University of California, Irvine	267
University of California, Los Angeles	268
University of California, Riverside	269
University of California, San Diego	270
University of California, Santa Barbara	271
University of California, Santa Cruz	272
University of Redlands	302
University of Southern California	306
Whittier College	335

Colorado
The Colorado College	70
Colorado School of Mines	71
Colorado State University	72
United States Air Force Academy	257
University of Colorado at Boulder	274
University of Denver	278

Connecticut
Connecticut College	76
Fairfield University	97
Trinity College	252
United States Coast Guard Academy	258
University of Connecticut (Storrs)	275
Wesleyan University	332
Yale University	343

Delaware
University of Delaware	277

District of Columbia
American University	21
Catholic University of America	55
Corcoran School of Art	353
Georgetown University	104
George Washington University	105
Howard University	128

Florida
Eckerd College	93
Florida Institute of Technology	99
Florida State University	100
New College of the University of South Florida	172
Rollins College	205
Stetson University	242
University of Florida	280
University of Miami	287

Georgia
Agnes Scott College	14
Berry College	35
Emory University	95
Georgia Institute of Technology	106
Morehouse College	167
Oglethorpe University	182
Savannah College of Art and Design	356
Spelman College	235
University of Georgia	281

Illinois
Augustana College	24

Geographical Index of Colleges

Bradley University	41
DePaul University	85
Illinois Institute of Technology	129
Illinois Wesleyan University	130
Knox College	139
Lake Forest College	141
Millikin University	162
Monmouth College	166
North Central College	177
Northwestern University	179
Quincy College	196
University of Chicago	273
University of Illinois at Urbana-Champaign	282
Wheaton College	333

Indiana

Butler University	48
DePauw University	86
Earlham College	92
Goshen College	109
Purdue University (West Lafayette)	195
Rose-Hulman Institute of Technology	206
Taylor University	246
University of Notre Dame	297
Valparaiso University	317
Wabash College	322

Iowa

Buena Vista College	47
Central University of Iowa	57
Coe College	63
Cornell College	78
Drake University	88
Grinnell College	110
Iowa State University of Science and Technology	131
Luther College	150
Simpson College	229
University of Iowa	283
Wartburg College	324

Kansas

University of Kansas	284

Kentucky

Bellarmine College	32
Centre College	58
Kentucky Wesleyan College	137
Transylvania University	250

Louisiana

Centenary College of Louisiana	56
Tulane University	255

Maine

Bates College	30
Bowdoin College	40
Colby College	64

Maryland

Johns Hopkins University	134
Loyola College	149
Maryland Institute, College of Art	354
St. John's College	212
St. Mary's College of Maryland	219
United States Naval Academy	261
University of Maryland College Park	285
Washington College	327

Massachusetts

Amherst College	22
Babson College	27
Boston College	38
Boston Conservatory	352
Boston University	39
Brandeis University	42
Clark University	62
College of the Holy Cross	67
Hampshire College	117
Harvard University	119
Massachusetts College of Art	354
Massachusetts Institute of Technology	156
Mount Holyoke College	168
New England Conservatory of Music	354
Simon's Rock College of Bard	228
Smith College	231
Tufts University	254
University of Massachusetts at Amherst	286
Wellesley College	330
Williams College	338
Worcester Polytechnic Institute	342

Michigan

Albion College	16
Alma College	20
Calvin College	50
GMI Engineering & Management Institute	108
Hillsdale College	123
Hope College	126
Kalamazoo College	136
Michigan State University	159
Michigan Technological University	160
University of Detroit Mercy	279
University of Michigan (Ann Arbor)	288
University of Michigan–Dearborn	289

Minnesota

Bethel College	36
Carleton College	51
Concordia College (Moorhead)	75
Gustavus Adolphus College	113
Hamline University	115
Macalester College	151
Saint John's University	214
St. Olaf College	221
University of Minnesota, Morris	290
University of Minnesota, Twin Cities Campus	291

Geographical Index of Colleges

Mississippi
Millsaps College ... 163

Missouri
Drury College ... 90
Maryville University of St. Louis ... 154
Northeast Missouri State University ... 178
Rockhurst College ... 204
St. Louis College of Pharmacy ... 217
Saint Louis University ... 218
University of Missouri–Columbia ... 292
University of Missouri–Kansas City ... 293
University of Missouri–Rolla ... 294
Washington University ... 328
William Jewell College ... 337

Nebraska
Creighton University ... 80
Nebraska Wesleyan University ... 171

New Hampshire
Dartmouth College ... 81
University of New Hampshire (Durham) ... 295

New Jersey
Drew University ... 89
New Jersey Institute of Technology ... 173
Princeton University ... 193
Rutgers, The State University of New Jersey, College of Engineering ... 207
Rutgers, The State University of New Jersey, College of Pharmacy ... 208
Rutgers, The State University of New Jersey, Cook College ... 209
Rutgers, The State University of New Jersey, Douglass College ... 210
Rutgers, The State University of New Jersey, Mason Gross School of the Arts ... 356
Rutgers, The State University of New Jersey, Rutgers College ... 211
Stevens Institute of Technology ... 243
Trenton State College ... 251
Westminster Choir College ... 357

New Mexico
New Mexico Institute of Mining and Technology ... 174
St. John's College ... 213

New York
Albert A. List College, Jewish Theological Seminary of America ... 15
Alfred University ... 18
Bard College ... 28
Barnard College ... 29
Clarkson University ... 61
Colgate University ... 65
College of Insurance ... 66
Columbia College ... 73
Columbia University, School of Engineering and Applied Science ... 74
Cooper Union for the Advancement of Science and Art ... 77
Cornell University ... 79
Eugene Lang College, New School for Social Research ... 96
Fashion Institute of Technology ... 353
Fordham University ... 101
Hamilton College ... 114
Hobart College ... 125
Houghton College ... 127
Juilliard School ... 353
Le Moyne College ... 145
Manhattan School of Music ... 353
Mannes College of Music, New School for Social Research ... 354
New York School of Interior Design ... 355
New York University ... 175
Parsons School of Design, New School for Social Research ... 355
Polytechnic University, Brooklyn Campus ... 189
Polytechnic University, Farmingdale Campus ... 190
Rensselaer Polytechnic Institute ... 199
Rochester Institute of Technology ... 203
St. Lawrence University ... 216
Sarah Lawrence College ... 224
Siena College ... 227
Skidmore College ... 230
State University of New York at Binghamton ... 237
State University of New York at Buffalo ... 238
State University of New York College at Geneseo ... 239
State University of New York College of Environmental Science and Forestry ... 240
State University of New York Maritime College ... 241
Syracuse University ... 245
Union College ... 256
United States Merchant Marine Academy ... 259
United States Military Academy ... 260
University at Albany, State University of New York ... 262
University of Rochester ... 304
Utica College of Syracuse University ... 316
Vassar College ... 319
Webb Institute of Naval Architecture ... 329
Wells College ... 331
William Smith College ... 339
Yeshiva University ... 344

North Carolina
Davidson College ... 82
Duke University ... 91
Guilford College ... 112
North Carolina School of the Arts ... 355
North Carolina State University ... 176

University of North Carolina at Chapel
  Hill   296
Wake Forest University   323

Ohio

Case Western Reserve University   54
Cleveland Institute of Music   352
The College of Wooster   69
Denison University   84
Hiram College   124
John Carroll University   133
Kenyon College   138
Miami University   158
Oberlin College   180
Ohio Northern University   183
Ohio Wesleyan University   184
Wittenberg University   340

Oklahoma

University of Tulsa   310

Oregon

Lewis and Clark College   147
Linfield College   148
Reed College   198
Willamette University   336

Pennsylvania

Albright College   17
Allegheny College   19
Bryn Mawr College   45
Bucknell University   46
Carnegie Mellon University   52
The Curtis Institute of Music   353
Dickinson College   87
Elizabethtown College   94
Franklin and Marshall College   102
Gettysburg College   107
Grove City College   111
Haverford College   121
Juniata College   135
Lafayette College   140
La Salle University   142
Lehigh University   144
Messiah College   157
Muhlenberg College   170
Pennsylvania State University University
  Park Campus   186
Saint Joseph's University   215
Swarthmore College   244
University of Pennsylvania   298
University of Pittsburgh   299
University of Pittsburgh at Johnstown   300
University of Scranton   305
Ursinus College   315
Villanova University   320
Washington and Jefferson College   325

Rhode Island

Brown University   44
Providence College   194
Rhode Island School of Design   356

South Carolina

Furman University   103
Presbyterian College   192
Wofford College   341

South Dakota

Augustana College   25
South Dakota School of Mines and
  Technology   232

Tennessee

Christian Brothers University   59
Fisk University   98
Rhodes College   200
University of Tennessee, Knoxville   307
University of the South   309
Vanderbilt University   318

Texas

Austin College   26
Baylor University   31
LeTourneau University   146
Rice University   201
Southern Methodist University   233
Southwestern University   234
Texas A&M University (College Station)   247
Texas Christian University   248
Trinity University   253
University of Dallas   276
University of Texas at Austin   308

Utah

Brigham Young University   43

Vermont

Bennington College   34
Marlboro College   152
Middlebury College   161
University of Vermont   311

Virginia

College of William and Mary   68
Hampden-Sydney College   116
James Madison University   132
Mary Washington College   155
Randolph-Macon Woman's College   197
University of Richmond   303
University of Virginia   312
Virginia Polytechnic Institute and State
  University   321
Washington and Lee University   326

Washington
Pacific Lutheran University 185
University of Puget Sound 301
University of Washington 313
Whitman College 334

West Virginia
Shepherd College 226

Wisconsin
Beloit College 33
Carroll College 53
Lawrence University 143
Marquette University 153
Milwaukee School of Engineering 165
Ripon College 202
St. Norbert College 220
University of Wisconsin-Madison 314